Endangered Animals of Thailand

Stephen R. Humphrey and James R. Bain

Front Cover: **Greater Adjutant Stork,** *Leptoptilos dubius* (Ciconiidae), ranging from India to Vietnam.

Frontispiece. We dedicate this work to Boonsong Lekagul, here shown looking for birds in the mangroves at Bang Poo, in May 1980. Professionally a medical doctor, he also was a big game hunter when a young man. Later he became an active conservationist, museum curator, author, and patriot. Winner of the J. Paul Getty Prize for Conservation, he is best known for projecting a conservation ethic into the national conscience of Thailand. His life shows how much the good work of one person can influence his country and those around him.

Endangered Animals of Thailand

by

Stephen R. Humphrey and James R. Bain

SANDHILL CRANE PRESS, INC.
Gainesville, Florida
1990

ENDANGERED ANIMALS OF THAILAND
Acquisitions Editor: Ross H. Arnett, Jr.
Production Editor: Michael C. Thomas

Copyright 1990 by Sandhill Crane Press, Inc. All rights reserved. No part of this publication may be reproduced in any form or by any means, without permission in writing from the publisher.

ISBN 1-877743-05-4, cloth
ISBN 1-877743-07-0, paper

LIBRARY OF CONGRESS CATALOGING-IN-PUBLICATION DATA:

Humphrey, Stephen R.
    Endangered animals in Thailand / by Stephen R. Humphrey and James R. Bain.
        p.   cm.
    Includes bibliographical references
    ISBN 1-877743-05-4, cloth
    ISBN 1-877743-07-0, paper
    1. Rare animals--Thailand. 2. Endangered species--Thailand. 3. Wildlife conservation--Thailand. I. Bain, James R. II. Title
QL84.5.T5H86 1989
591.52'9'09593--dc20   89-48431
                        CIP

Flora & Fauna Handbook No. 6

THE SANDHILL CRANE PRESS, INC.
2406 N.W. 47th Terrace
Gainesville, FL 32606

Manufactured in the United States of America

Acknowledgments

This work was conducted for the United States Fish and Wildlife Service, Office of International Affairs, and was funded under the United States Agency for International Development/U.S. Man and the Biosphere Project. The Florida Museum of Natural History operated cooperatively with the many scientists of the Species Survival Commission of the International Union for the Conservation of Nature and Natural Resources.

We are grateful to F. Wayne King, who while Deputy Chairman of the Species Survival Commission facilitated communication with IUCN experts throughout the project; his efforts made that process operate smoothly. We thank the many scientists of the SSC specialist groups, and other scientists active in Thailand to whom they directed us, who were prompt and cooperative in responding to our inquiries and contributing recent and unpublished information. Their efforts added substantial quality to the data base of the report. Many natural resource professionals and interested citizens in Thailand were extremely helpful in providing information and perspectives on species' biology, problems, and possible solutions. We thank those who took time to show us Thai natural resources in the field--Boonsong Lekagul, Schwan Tanhikorn, Taweesak Trirawatpong, A.H.V. Sharma, Warren Y. Brockelman, Doyle Damman, and Warren Evans. Terry Grandstaff of the USAID mission staff in Bangkok helped us visualize the role of foreign aid in development projects and gave us specific information on the nature of the Mae Chaem Watershed project. Flawless administrative support and clear direction was provided by David A. Ferguson of the U.S. Fish and Wildlife Service, James W. Corson of the U.S. Man and the Biosphere Secretariat in Washington, D.C., and Molly Kux, Albert Prinz, and Jane Stanley of the U.S. Agency for International Development. Warren Y. Brockelman, Ardith A. Eudey, Joe T. Marshall, Jr., Jeffrey A. McNeely, David S. Melville, Edward O. Moll, Illar Muul, and Philip D. Round enabled us to improve the manuscript by reviewing its technical content.

Contents

Chapter 1. Introduction 1
Methods 4
Using this Document 6
Terrestrial Habitats 7
Designation of Survival Status 13
Species Accounts 17
Chapter 2. Summary 19
Listed Species and Their Habitats 19
Evaluating Potential Impacts of Development Projects 26
Chapter 3. Invertebrates 29
Emerita emeritus (Sea Grasshopper, Sand Crab) 29
Bhutanitis lidderdalei (Bhutan Glory Butterfly) 31
Sticopthalma godfreyi (Godfrey's junglequeen butterfly) 32
Chapter 4. Fishes 35
Scleropages formosus (Asian Bonytongue) 35
Notopterus blanci (Featherback) 38
Notopterus borneensis (a featherback) 40
Macrochirichthys macrochirus (a carp) 41
Chela caeruleostigmata (no common name) 43
Catlocarpio siamensis (Giant Carp) 44
Puntius sarana (Barb, Olive Carp) 47
Balantiocheilos melanopterus (Burnt-tail Carp) 48
Labeo behri (a carp) 50
Xenocheilichthys gudgeri (Backwater Fish) 51
Hemisilurus heterorhynchus (Catfish) 52
Prophagorus nieuhofi (a walking catfish) 54
Pangasius sanitwongsei (Sanitwongse's Catfish) 55
Pangasianodon gigas (Giant Catfish) 57
Datnioides microlepis (Triple Tails) 62
Chapter 5. Amphibians and Reptiles 65
Tylototriton verrucosus (crocodile salamander) 65
Rana fasciculispina (Spine-breasted Giant Frog) 68
Platysternon megacephalum (Chinese Big-headed Turtle) 69
Batagur baska (Saltwater or River Terrapin) 72
Heosemys (Geomyda) spinosa (Spiny Terrapin) 76
Testudo (Geochelone) emys (Six-legged Tortoise) 77
The Sea Turtles--Introductory Comments 80
Lepidochelys olivacea (Pacific Ridley's Turtle) 90

Eretochelys imbricata (Hawksbill Turtle)..................................92
Chelonia mydas (Green Turtle)..94
Caretta caretta (Loggerhead Turtle) 97
Dermochelys coriacea (Leatherback Turtle)................................99
Pelochelys bibroni (a giant soft-shelled turtle) 101
The Crocodiles--Introductory Comments......................................103
Crocodylus porosus (Saltwater Crocodile)................................105
Crocodylus siamensis (Siamese Freshwater Crocodile) 108
Tomistoma schlegelii (False Gavial) 111
Varanus bengalensis (Bengal Monitor).....................................114
Varanus rudicollis (Red-headed Monitor).................................115
Varanus dumerilii (Black Jungle Monitor) 117
Python molurus bivittatus (Burmese Python) 118
Python curtus (Blood or Short Python) 120
Chapter 6. Birds..123
Pelecanus philippensis (Spot-billed Pelican) 123
Anhinga melanogaster (Darter)...126
Fregata andrewsi (Christmas Island Frigate-bird) 127
Egretta eulophotes (Chinese Egret)...130
Ibis leucocephalus (Painted Stork) 132
Anastomus oscitans (Open-billed Stork) 136
Ciconia nigra (Black Stork) 140
Ciconia (Dissoura) episcopus (White-necked Stork) 141
Xenorhynchus asiaticus (Black-necked Stork) 143
Leptoptilos dubius (Greater Adjutant Stork) 144
Leptoptilos javanicus (Lesser Adjutant Stork)..........................146
Threskiornis melanocephala (White Ibis).................................148
Pseudibis papillosa davisoni (Black or White-shouldered Ibis) 149
Pseudibis (Thaumatibis) gigantea (Giant Ibis)..........................151
Cairina scutulata (White-winged Wood Duck) 153
Sarkidiornis melanotos (Comb Duck) 155
Torgos calvus (King vulture)..158
Gyps indicus (Long-billed vulture)...159
Gyps bengalensis (White-backed vulture) 160
Ictinaetus malayensis (Black eagle)..162
Spizaetus nanus (Wallace's hawk eagle)...................................163
Falco peregrinus (Peregrine Falcon, Duck Hawk).....................164
Rollulus roulroul (Roulroul) 166

vii

Lophura leucomelana (Kalij Pheasant)..........168
Lophura nycthemera (Silver Pheasant)..........171
Lophura ignita (Crested Fireback Pheasant)..........173
Lophura diardi (Siamese Fireback Pheasant)..........175
Syrmaticus humiae (Mrs. Hume's Pheasant)..........177
Polyplectron bicalcaratum (Burmese Gray Peacock Pheasant)..........179
Polyplectron malacense (Malay Brown Peacock Pheasant)..........181
Argusianus argus (Great Argus Pheasant)..........182
Pavo muticus (Green Peafowl)..........184
Grus antigone sharpii (Nok Karien, Eastern Sarus Crane)..........188
Heliopais personata (Masked finfoot)..........190
Tringa guttifer (Spotted Greenshank)..........192
Limnodromus semipalmatus (Asian Dowitcher, Snipebilled Godwit)..........194
Sterna zimmermanni (Chinese Crested Tern)..........196
Treron seimundi (Yellow-vented Green Pigeon)..........198
Ducula bicolor (Pied Imperial Pigeon)..........199
Columba pulchricollis (Ashy Wood Pigeon)..........200
Columba punicea (Pale-capped Pigeon)..........201
Caloenas nicobarica nicobarica (Nicobar Pigeon)..........203
The Hornbills--Introductory Comments..........205
Berenicornis comatus (White-crested Hornbill)..........206
Ptilolaemus tickelli (Brown or Tickell's Hornbill)..........208
Anorrhinus galeritus (Bushy-crested Hornbill)..........210
Aceros nipalensis (Rufous-necked Hornbill)..........212
Rhyticeros leucocephalus (Wrinkled hornbill)..........214
Buceros rhinoceros (Rhinoceros Hornbill)..........215
Buceros bicornis bicornis (Great Hornbill)..........217
Buceros bicornis homrai (Great Hornbill)..........217
Rhinoplax vigil (Helmeted Hornbill)..........219
Megalaima rafflesii (Many-colored barbet)..........221
Mulleripicus pulverulentus (Great Slaty Woodpecker)..........222
Dryocopus javensis (White-bellied Woodpecker)..........224
Pitta gurneyi (Gurney's Pitta)..........225
Pseudochelidon sirintarae (White-eyed River Martin)..........228
Eupetes macrocerus (Rail-babbler)..........231
Pachycephala cinerea (Mangrove Whistler)..........234
Graminicola bengalensis (Large Grass Warbler)..........232

Chapter 7. Mammals 237
   Craseonycteris thonglongyai (Kitti's Hog-nosed Bat)................237
   Macaca nemestrina (Pig-tailed Macaque) 239
   Macaca assamensis (Assamese Macaque) 242
   Macaca arctoides (Stump-tailed Macaque)...............................243
   Macaca mulatta (Rhesus Macaque) 246
   Macaca fascicularis (Long-tailed Macaque) 249
   Presbytis melalophos (Banded Langur)...................................252
   Presbytis obscura (Dusky or Spectacled Langur).....................255
   Presbytis cristata (Silvered Langur)..256
   Presbytis phayrei (Phayre's Langur) 258
   The Gibbons--Introductory Comments......................................259
   Hylobates lar (White-handed Gibbon) 260
   Hylobates pileatus (Pileated Gibbon) 262
   Hylobates agilis (Agile Gibbon)...264
   The Pangolins--Introductory Comments 266
   Manis javanica (Malayan Pangolin).......................................267
   Manis pentadactyla (Chinese Pangolin).................................269
The Squirrels--Introductory Comments...271
   Ratufa affinis (Cream-colored Giant Squirrel) 272
   Ratufa bicolor (Black Giant Squirrel)......................................274
   Petaurista elegans (Lesser Giant Flying Squirrel)..................278
   Aeromys tephromelas (Large Black Flying Squirrel) 281
   Petinomys setosus (White-bellied Flying Squirrel)..................282
   Belomys pearsoni (Hairy-footed Flying Squirrel) 284
   Pteromyscus pulverulentus (Smoky Flying Squirrel) 286
   Eothenomys melanogaster (Pere David's Vole).......................287
   Hapalomys longicaudatus (Marmoset Rat).............................288
   Rattus sikkimensis remotus (Island Rat)................................290
   Rattus neilli (Neill's Rat) 292
   Rattus hinpoon (Limestone Rat)...293
The Cetaceans--Introductory Comments...294
   Sotalia plumbea (Plumbeous Dolphin) 295
   Sotalia borneensis (Indonesian White Dolphin) 295
   Sotalia chinensis (Chinese White Dolphin) 295
   Steno bredanensis (Rough-toothed Dolphin) 296
   Stenella malayana (Malay Dolphin).......................................296
   Delphinus delphis (Common Dolphin) 297
   Tursiops aduncus (Eastern Bottle-nosed Dolphin)..................297

Orcaella brevirostris (Irrawaddy Dolphin) 298
Neophocaena phocaenoides (Black Finless Porpoise) 298
Physeter catodon (Sperm Whale) 299
Balaenoptera borealis (Sei Whale) 299
Balaenoptera acutirostrata (Lesser Rorqual) 300
Canis aureus (Golden Jackal)..301
Cuon alpinus (Dhole) 306
Selenarctos thibetanus (Asiatic Black Bear)..........................311
Helarctos malayanus (Malayan Sun Bear).............................313
Mustela strigidorsa (Back-striped Weasel)............................315
The Otters--Introductory Comments...316
Lutra lutra (Common Otter) 320
Lutra (Lutrogale) perspicillata (Smooth-coated Otter)...............325
Lutra sumatrana (Hairy-nosed Otter) 326
Amblonyx (Aonyx) cinerea (Small-clawed Otter)...................328
Prionodon pardicolor (Spotted Linsang) 330
Prionodon linsang (Banded Linsang)......................................331
Arctictis binturong (Binturong)...333
Hemigalus derbyanus (Banded Palm Civet) 335
Cynogale bennetti (Otter Civet) 337
Felis marmorata (Marbled Cat)...339
Felis viverrina (Fishing Cat)..340
Felis bengalensis (Leopard Cat) 342
Felis planiceps (Flat-headed Cat) 344
Felis chaus (Jungle Cat)...346
Felis temmincki (Asian Golden Cat) 347
Neofelis nebulosa (Clouded Leopard)......................................349
Panthera pardus (Leopard, Panther) 352
Panthera tigris corbetti (Tiger)..358
Elephas maximus (Asian Elephant)...365
Dugong dugon (Dugong)..372
Tapirus indicus (Malayan Tapir) 375
Rhinoceros sondaicus (Javan Rhino).......................................379
Dicerorhinus (Didermocerus) sumatrensis (Sumatran Rhino)..381
Muntiacus feae (Fea's Barking Deer)......................................384
Cervus (Axis) porcinus annamiticus (Indochina Hog Deer).......387
Cervus schomburgki (Schomburgk's Deer) 389
Cervus eldi (Eld's Brow-antlered Deer)..................................391
Bubalus bubalis (Wild Water Buffalo) 394
Bos javanicus (Banteng) 397

Bos gaurus (Gaur, Seledang) 401
Bos (Novibos) sauveli (Kouprey) 406
Capricornis sumatraensis (Serow) 410
Naemorhedus goral (Goral) 413
Literature Cited 417

Chapter 1

Introduction

This work presents the state of knowledge on the endangered and threatened species of Thailand. Its pragmatic purpose is to improve Thailand's future by providing access to technical guidance for planning development projects or other land-use changes. This information also should stimulate naturalists, professional biologists, or anyone who wishes to learn about the status of animals in Thailand. Which species are now on the brink of extinction from Thailand, and why? How can the Thai people reorganize themselves to reverse the course of destruction? Can ways be found for both the people and the rest of the fauna to prosper?

Another purpose is to present a case study of the effects of longterm development for human use on the biological diversity of a tropical country. Thailand has been subject to intensive agriculture for 1,000 years, with little regard for conservation of the nation's natural heritage until recently. Observers from other nations, especially from countries with a less complete history of destruction of native habitats or with more elaborate programs for conservation, pondering the futures of their own biota, may find object lessons in the Thai experience. What sorts of wildlife have become extinct, and from what causes? Why were development and conservation incompatible, and what alternate pathways are now available?

This study identifies cases of misuse or neglect of renewable resources. For almost every species here considered, enough is known to outline the problems it faces. For each, we propose conservation measures that represent opportunities to solve problems. These are management practices that need implementation or information gaps that need to be filled. In a few cases of rare, migratory animals, the problem is not entirely in Thai hands, and international solutions are required. More often, the resources needed by the endangered species occur in several political jurisdictions within Thailand, so actions need to be coordinated. Whatever the case,

Fig. 1. Relict teak trees in a slash-and-burn agricultural plot in the teak-bamboo forest of Kanchanaburi Province, near the Burma border. Though this national forest reserve is not supposed to be settled by people, its logging, hunting, and farming can and does support a low density of people.

both the information about problems and their proposed solutions provide guidance in land-use planning.

This document must not be construed as being critical of Thailand, her government agencies or officials, or her people. Like all countries, Thailand faces the realities of making available the limited resources of the earth to an ever-increasing number of people. Foremost among competing land uses are human economic enterprise and the non-monetary economies of plants and animals sharing our biological community (Fig. 1). The optimal solution to this problem is to identify renewable resources useful to man and base as much of the human economy as possible on harvesting these species at a level that will not exceed their limits of self-replacement; to convert a portion of the land to intensive agriculture and industry to drive the human economy, but keep that portion low enough that essential natural resources remain as abundant as possible; and to preserve special places for the survival of species that have no presently perceived resource value. This last step recognizes that all species may have uses in the future, as well as real though perhaps intangible value because of their embodied beauty, intrinsic complexity, or joy of humans in learning about them. Maintaining this balance is difficult, and in practice humans everywhere fall short of the ideal.

With passage of the National Parks Act in 1962, Thailand abruptly changed its course of land use and now is among the world's leaders in the amount of land reserved for conservation of vegetation and wildlife. Her national parks and wildlife sanctuaries encompass about 4.3 million hectares, or 8.5% of the country's area (Jintanugool et al. 1982). Her greatest shortfall is in the public will to follow government leadership. As explained by Srikosamatara and Doungkhae (1982), "The local farmers do not understand the value of establishing a national park and see no benefits in it for themselves. Consequently, relations with the park personnel are poor and enforcement of regulations is light for fear of upsetting the villagers too much and perhaps driving them over to . . ." insurgency. As articulated by Ali (1983), a philosophy of conservation divorced from economics is irrelevant in a country like Thailand, or perhaps anywhere. Instead, the task at hand is to teach the rural dweller the value of the resource and how it can serve him both immediately and on a sustained basis. This cannot be done for every species of wildlife, but for some we suggest ways to proceed. "The major challenge [of the contemporary extinction crisis is how] to incorporate the socioeconomic needs and utilitarian values of developing nations into the establishment of species preservation programs" (Kellert 1985). The World Resources Institute (1985) has called for an accelerated investment program by governments and international development agencies in tropical forestry, agriculture, and conservation, to provide farmers and landless people adjacent to threatened forests with an alternative to deforestation. For Thailand, this proposal is for investment of US $35 million in industrial forest management and US $27.7 million in ecosystem conservation.

Thailand has three special attributes that hold hope for the future of her wild animals. First, her fauna includes an extraordinary range of species that can become sustained-yield resources for human use: work animals; animals that can be farmed for meat and leather; wild genetic stocks for domestic producers of eggs, milk, and meat; and fish and game. Second, the high diversity and interesting nature of her fauna can be a source of great national pride. Third, the Buddhist philosophical principal of reverence for life can become a force behind a new national tradition of conservation and wise use of renewable natural resources.

Methods

Rather than conducting new research--which would require many years, the work of many scientists, and substantial funding--our intent was to compile the existing information from all sources to determine the state of knowledge and to identify information gaps, with a relatively modest investment of time and funding. We gathered information on listed species in three simultaneous phases--literature search, correspondence with experts associated with the International Union for the Conservation of Nature and Natural Resources (IUCN), and in-country interviews and site visits--all contributing substantially to the data from which the lists and species accounts were prepared. We began with information already compiled in the IUCN Red Data books. We gathered further information through the world-wide network of experts in the specialist groups of the IUCN Species Survival Commission and through first-hand contact with Thailand's knowledgeable government officials, university scholars, and private individuals. Additional information was gathered from the world's scientific journals and books.

Literature was sought using computer-based bibliographic services, by manual search for general and recent publications, and by library work in Thailand. The most useful bibliographic services were Biosis Previews (incorporating Biological Abstracts and formerly BioResearch Index), AGRICOLA (Agricultural On Line Access, incorporating mostly Bibliography of Agriculture, National Agricultural Library, U.S. Department of Agriculture), and CAB-ABS (Commonwealth Agricultural Bureau Abstracts). Computer literature searches were very efficient compared with manual work. Manual literature searches were done to include literature too old or too recent to be in the computer files or in general works that do not have names of species in the titles.

Library work was done in Thailand to obtain literature that was not readily available otherwise. The libraries of the Royal Forest Department, the National Inland Fisheries Institute, the Thailand Institute for Scientific and Technological Research, the Siam Society, and the personal library and museum of Dr. Boonsong Lekagul

Introduction

were especially useful. One new general work was discovered by visiting bookstores in Bangkok. Additional literature thus gathered in Thailand included regional journals--specifically the Natural History Bulletin of the Siam Society and Malayan Nature Journal--and general works including Mammals of Thailand (Lekagul and McNeely 1977a) and The Turtles of Thailand (Wirot 1979), plus numerous individual monographs and articles.

At the beginning of the project, correspondence was begun with scientists of the IUCN's Species Survival Commission, which has 31 Specialist Groups relevant to endangered and threatened species of Thailand. Experts in the Specialist Groups were very helpful in providing reprints, unpublished reports, evaluations of status based on their extensive experience, and information providing access to new work being done in their area of speciality. This information included many state-of-knowledge reports and led to wider follow-up correspondence through the duration of the project.

Prior to travel in Thailand, correspondence was sent to biologists in Thailand to introduce the project, request information, and ask whether any meetings or conferences on wildlife-related issues were scheduled there. This served as an introduction and gave government agencies an opportunity to delegate responsibility for interviews to the most appropriate people. The beginning of the interview trip coincided with a national workshop on wildlife management in national parks. Meeting most natural resource officials, university biologists, and private conservationists there facilitated subsequent individual meetings both socially and logistically. At these meetings we discussed the survival status and biology of listed species. The list was discussed also in terms of candidates for listing, possible delistings, and degree of threat. In association with interviews, opportunities were taken to use institutional and personal libraries.

Travel was done as a second priority to visit first-hand some examples of ecosystems, parks, and management areas in which endangered species exist. Assistance with this travel was requested in advance by correspondence with several government agencies and the private conservation community, so several local residents were available to arrange trips on short notice.

Development of a useful planning document depends heavily on an ability to map the distributions of listed species. Because enough field surveys and museum work are unlikely to have been done in most countries, animal distributions can only be inferred from knowledge of the distribution of habitats. To eliminate from range maps any land that can no longer be occupied by forest animals, availability of a current or recent map of deforested areas also is important. These kinds of data, although approximate and at a coarse scale, were available in Thailand because maps of vegetation and the extent of deforestation had already been prepared by the Royal Thai Survey Department and Royal Forestry Department. These were modified to prepare Figs. 2-8.

Using This Document

The bulk of this work lists endangered and threatened species and relates their biology and management needs. We anticipate that biologists and those with a concern about a particular species will consult the appropriate technical details. However, land-use planners and some biologists who are more interested in a specific tract of land or type of habitat would find that approach inefficient. For such purposes it will be more effective to use the maps of species' distributions to prepare a list of endangered and threatened species that may live in the area of interest. After compiling a list of species expected in a project area, general impacts on them can be anticipated from the details in the species accounts.

Users are cautioned, however, to avoid misuse of this document. It should be used only as a source of background information. The following limitations of this information must be recognized, and deficiencies should be remedied and specific impacts evaluated by conducting detailed field studies in the areas of interest. (1) The maps are of insufficient scale, and the data on which they are based are outdated and of insufficient accuracy, to be sure if a particular species or habitat is present in a project area. (2) Information on distribution and population status can become outdated quickly because of changes in land use and population levels. (3) Only the best-known species are covered, and ignorance of the status of many species has led to their omission, because no data are available or published to support the opinion that a problem exists. This uneven coverage extends to entire groups of organisms, particularly invertebrates and small fishes. (4) Development projects can have adverse effects unrelated to endangered species--loss of valuable services of ecosystems such as watershed protection by upland forest, floodwater retention and dispersal by wetlands, and soil accumulation and stabilization; loss of harvestable natural resources; and air or water pollution with detrimental effects downwind or downstream.

One more caveat is needed. Research on animals of Southeast Asia has been dominated by foreigners who lack the confident knowledge brought by long-term experience in place. We noted frequently that once an anecdote appeared in published literature, it recurred nearly verbatim in most subsequent accounts. We attempted to screen such observations by critically examining related information for concordance. No doubt we too have repeated inaccurate or misleading information. Worse, our own experience with Thailand's fauna has been brief, and perhaps we have generated new errors in attempting to articulate the management implications of scanty basic data. Academic biologists prefer to admit ignorance rather than reach poorly substantiated conclusions, but managers routinely must act with the knowledge at hand, or even without it. In the case of endangerment, the risk of inaction is extinction. We have chosen to err on the side of drawing inferences, perhaps incorrectly on occasion, from which an approach to management action can be prescribed. Where we have repeated or generated errors, we expect Thailand's able scholars to be stimulated by this compilation to upgrade the state of knowledge. The next generation of biologists in Thailand should have an exciting time.

Terrestrial Habitats

To understand the distribution and habitat of endangered species, it is helpful to know the existing types of terrestrial vegetation. Several useful publications on vegetation types are available (Robbins and Smitinand 1966, Smitinand 1966, 1968, 1977, Williams 1967, Smitinand et al. 1970, Whitmore 1975, Christiansen 1979, Bunavejchewin 1983). The major categories of forests recognized by Smitinand (1977) are listed below, along with their physical correlates of rainfall (millimeters per year), elevation (meters), and soil type. Where applicable, equivalent terms from the Holdridge Life Zone system (Holdridge 1967) are given in parentheses.
1. Tropical evergreen or rain forest. Precipitation 2,500 mm or more (Fig. 2).

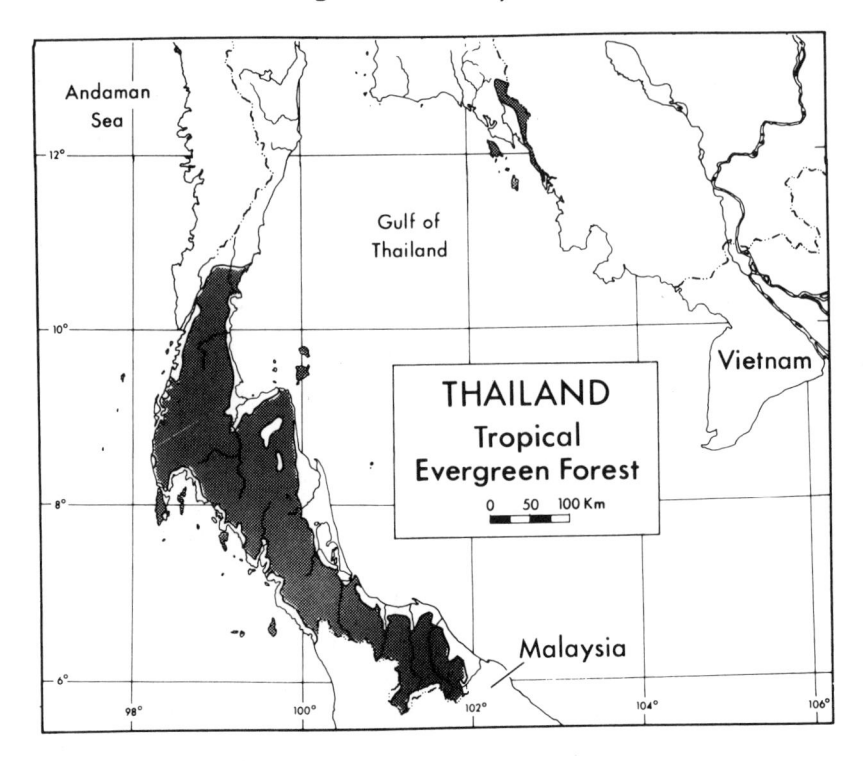

Fig. 2. Original distribution of tropical evergreen or rain forest in Thailand.

    a. Lower tropical rain forest (tropical lowland rain or wet forest). Elevation 0-600 m.
    b. Upper tropical rain forest (tropical premontane rain or wet forest). Elevation 600-900 m.
2. Dry or semi-evergreen forest (tropical lowland moist forest). Precipitation 1,000-2,000 mm, elevation 0-500 m (Fig. 3).
3. Hill evergreen forest (lower montane moist forest). Precipitation 1,500-2,000 mm, elevation 1,000 m or higher (Fig. 4).
4. Freshwater swamp forest. Periodically or permanently flooded lowlands.
5. Mangrove forest. Edge of seacoasts and estuaries tidally flooded with brackish or salt water (Fig. 5).
6. Deciduous forest (tropical very dry forest). Precipitation less than 1,000 mm.

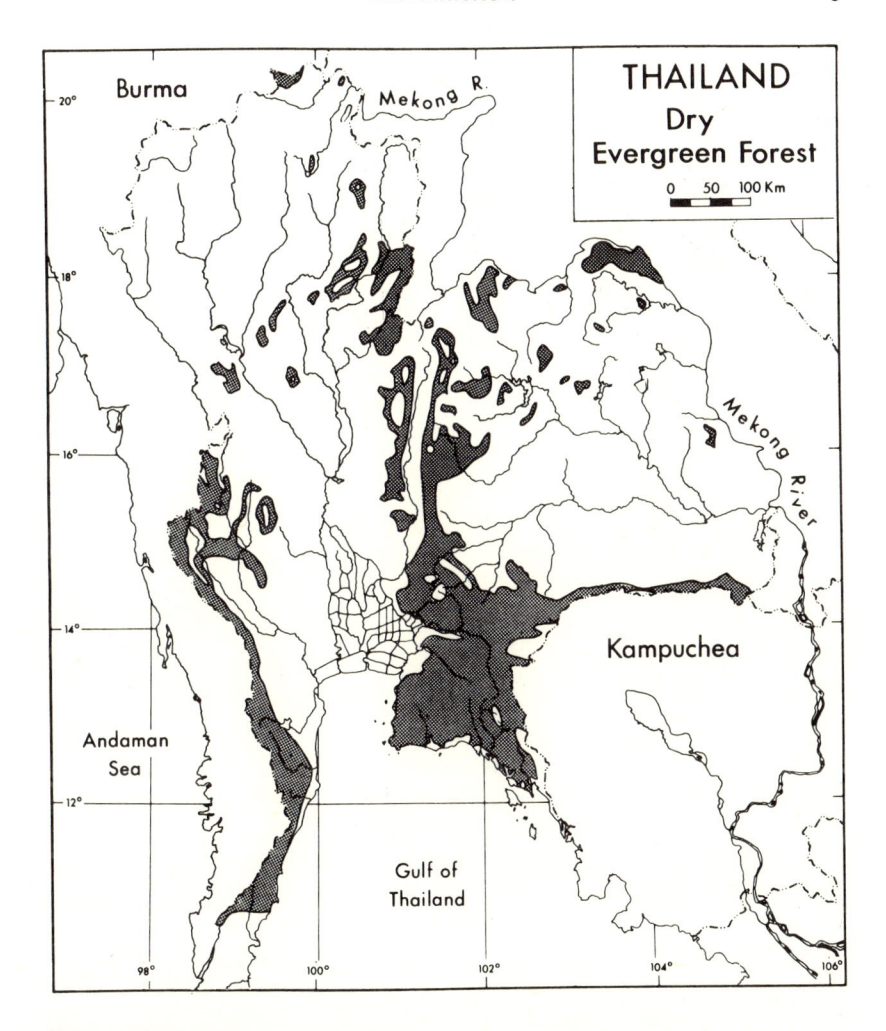

Fig. 3. Original distribution of dry evergreen forest in Thailand.

    a. Mixed deciduous forest. Elevation 50-600 m, loamy soil (Fig. 6).

    b. Dry deciduous dipterocarp forest. Lowlands, sandy or lateritic soil (Fig. 7).

7. Savanna forest (tropical thorn woodland). Precipitation 50-500 mm, sandy or lateritic soil.

    An additional association, pine forest, occurs as an edaphic or

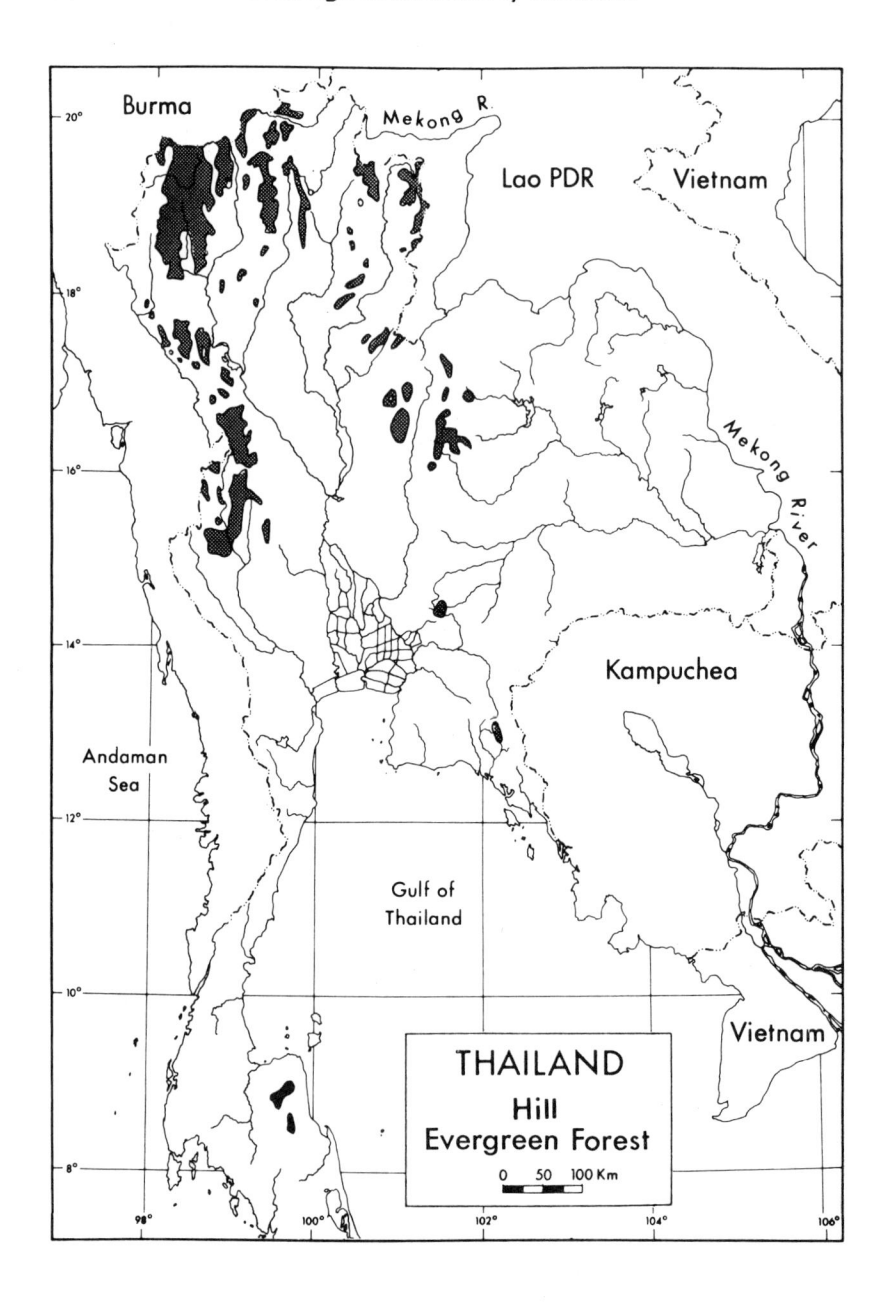

Fig. 4. Original distribution of hill evergreen forest in Thailand.

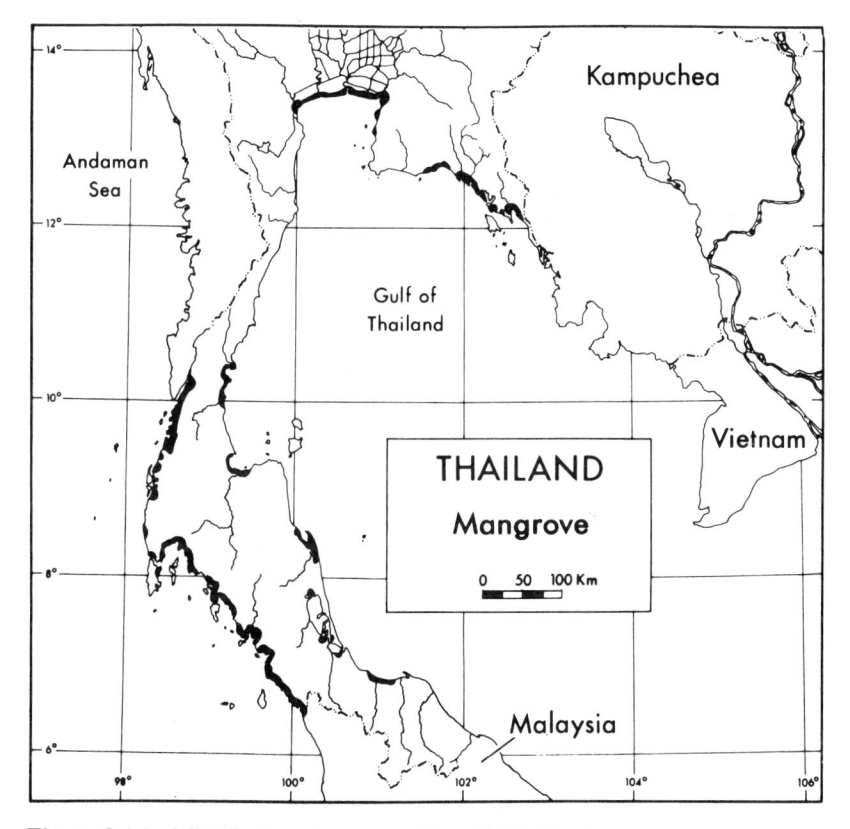

Fig. 5. Original distribution of mangrove forest in Thailand.

fire subclimax in small areas of montane eastern and northern Thailand (Fig. 8).

Most of the original vegetation of Thailand is shown in Figs. 2-8 in simplified form, from a map by the Royal Thai Survey Department in the Resource Atlas of Thailand, Applied Science and Technology Corporation of Thailand, 1977. These maps should be viewed with caution, because the available data are limited and botanical authorities are not in complete agreement about the original distribution of forest types. For example, the Royal Thai Survey Department shows more deciduous dipterocarp forest and less mixed deciduous forest than does the map of Williams (1967; map 4).

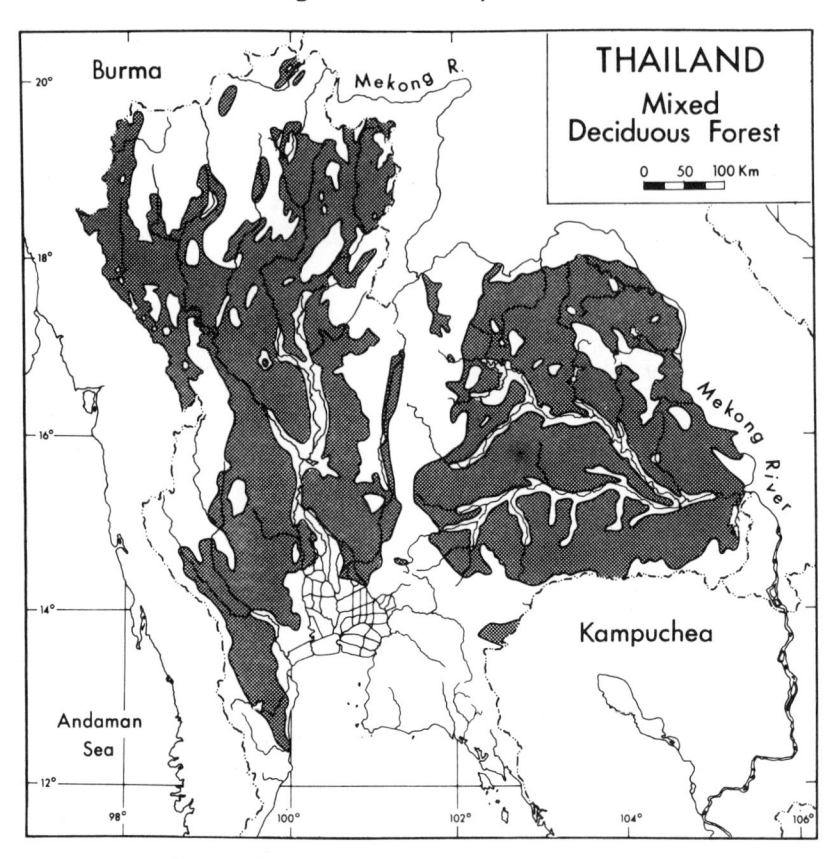

Fig. 6. Original distribution of mixed deciduous forest in Thailand.

Missing from these maps is swamp/savanna habitat that occurred on the floodplains of the Chao Phraya, Mun, Chi, and Mekong rivers and their tributaries, of smaller rivers of peninsular Thailand, and on the seasonally flooded land around Songkhla Lake. Of all these, only a severely cut-over remnant of *Melaleuca-Alstonia* forest remains around Thale Noi and a few other places bordering Songkhla Lake. The identity of these wetlands is problematic. Their original vegetation has never been described carefully, probably because little remained when recorded history began. As used by Whitmore (1975), the term "freshwater swampforest" encompasses a heterogeneous array of habitats, including forest that may include *Mallotus*, *Camnosperma*, *Metroxylon*, and *Alstonia*; fire-climax *Melaleuca* forest; open plains of sedge or grass; and even floating grass mats. This diversity of possibilities is concordant with early references and current opinions referring to forests, wet savannas, and plains, which differ in the ways they are controlled by various combinations of fire and flooding.

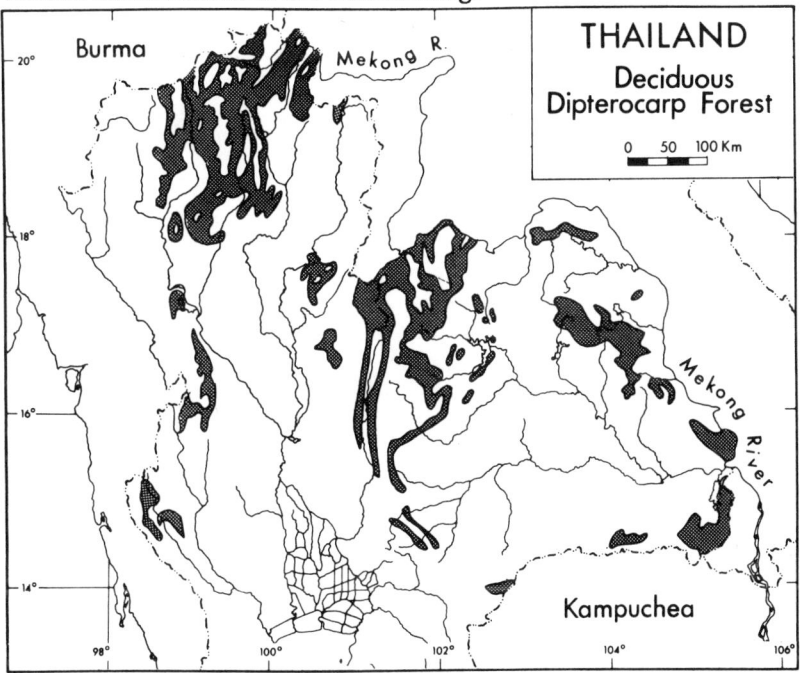

Fig. 7. Original distribution of deciduous dipterocarp forest in Thailand.

Deforested areas of Thailand were mapped in 1963 (Royal Forestry Department) and 1972 (Resource Atlas of Thailand and Royal Forestry Department). The 1972 map failed to show extensive tracts of rubber plantations in peninsular Thailand as deforested. The rate of deforestation was quantified regionally by Myers (1980), including 1978 figures provided by Thailand's National Research Council. From an original 80 percent, forest cover of Thailand had declined to 53 percent in 1961, 39 percent in 1973, and 25 percent in 1978 (Myers 1980).

Designation of Survival Status

The list on which this work is based originated as those species enumerated in lists of: the Thai Fisheries Act of 1947, Thailand's Wild Animals Reservation and Protection Act of 1961 (as amended in 1972 and 1980), the United States Fish and Wildlife Service (USFWS 1980a) relating to the Endangered Species Act of 1973, the Convention on International Trade in Endangered Species (CITES 1979), the IUCN Red Data books, and the IUCN report on Conservation for Thailand--Policy Guidelines (1979). Additionally, we prepared a new list reflecting our professional judgment of what species are endangered or threatened and of their current status, based on the information we obtained in Thailand in 1980. As expected from the progressive nature of the processes leading toward extinction, our evaluation compared with pre-existing lists includes more species and often indicates more precarious status.

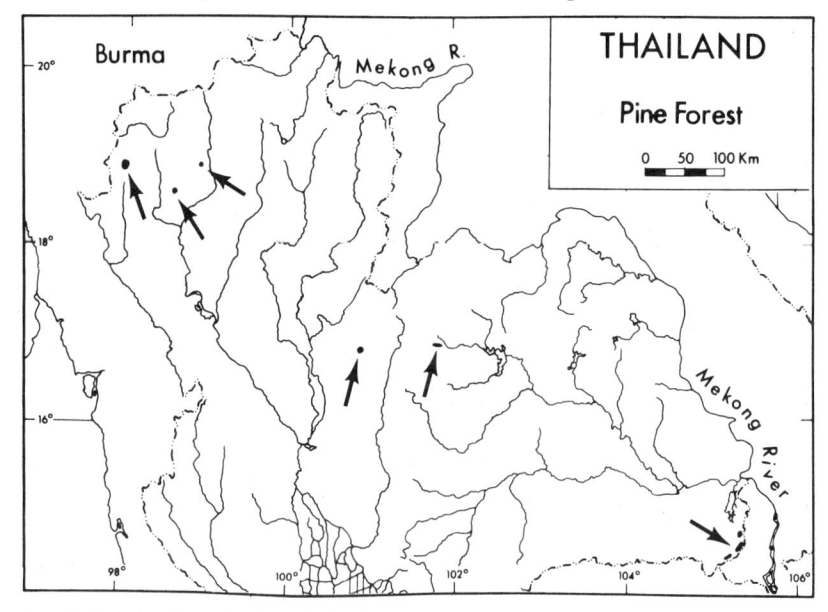

Fig. 8. Original distribution of pine forest in Thailand.

Unlike the status designations of lists developed from international perspectives, our status designations resemble those of WARPA (1980) in referring only to Thailand. A species could be endangered in Thailand but neither endangered nor threatened on a range-wide basis. The hog deer (*Cervus porcinus*) is an example. Likewise, some species are extirpated from Thailand but are not extinct, remaining elsewhere in their ranges.

Because we found lists of species legally designated as endangered and threatened to be conservative, we concurred with most official listings. In a few cases we were unable to find enough information to independently evaluate current status. These cases are blanket listings by CITES of all species of falcons (7 in Thailand), parrots (7), hornbills (9), owls (19), and accipiters (37). Presumably listing the accipiters is justifiable--probably all these forest hawks are threatened by deforestation. However, some other species may be common or favored by human activities, and they should not be listed. Hence these listings will remain awkwardly unjustified until data can be gathered to support species-by-species evaluations. We have attempted to accelerate this process by listing particular species for which data on status are available.

In one respect these lists are woefully inadequate. Of the thousands of species potentially endangered or threatened by deforestation, drainage, or pollution, many are not yet known to science. For most, whether they can survive in habitats modified by human activity is unknown, or not recorded. Therefore the basis for a listing decision is lacking. In several cases where a suite of closely related forms faces similar threats, and where information gaps prevented thorough coverage (as in the bird family Pittidae), we selected one or a few species to illustrate the problems of the whole group. In cases of extreme ignorance (as with Thailand's 17 genera of corals), we attempted no coverage.

Insufficiency of the species-by-species approach to conservation can be supplemented by focusing at the levels of the biotic community and the ecosystem to help set the agenda for conservation. When we began writing this volume in 1980-1, no research using a community approach to conservation of Thailand's animals had been done. Since then, a landmark study (Round 1984) compared the bird community in 1978-84 at Doi Suthep-Pui National Park, Chiang Mai Province, with the one present in 1928-37 (Deignan 1945). In the intervening 50 years, extensive human settlement of the mountain has resulted in greatly increased harvest of animals and modification of the vegetation due to hunting, shifting cultivation, grazing, forest burning, log-felling, and road-building. Fifty (37 residents) of the 265 species of birds listed by Deignan were not found in 1978-84. Of the resident species, Round suggested that 10 medium-to-large species were extirpated or threatened by hunting,

12 species were extirpated or diminished by loss of mixed deciduous forest from and urbanization of the surrounding plains, and 4 species were extirpated or made rare by modification of hill evergreen and pine forest.

Details of these changes are discussed in the species accounts. Equally illuminating is that 19 of the 26 species discerned by Round to be extirpated or made rare by overharvest and habitat conversion were not identified by us initially as endangered or threatened. This fact shows how severely our treatment of the subject underestimates the true magnitude of the problem.

The various listing authorities use overlapping categories to designate species' status. Following is a list of these and definitions of the status categories as we assigned them.

CITES (1979):
    Appendix I, threatened with extinction.
    Appendix II, may become threatened with extinction.
    Appendix III, species listed at the request of Convention nations.

IUCN Red Data Book (year varies):
    Endangered.
    Vulnerable.
    Rare.
    Indeterminate.

USFWS (1980a):
    Endangered.
    Threatened.

WARPA (1980):
    Reserved, completely protected.
    Protected, first category. Permits for personal possession may be requested, but hunting and trade are prohibited.
    Protected, second category. May be hunted under specific regulations.

TFA 1947:
    Capture forbidden.

This study:
    Extinct. No longer known to exist anywhere in the world.
    Possibly extinct.
    Extirpated from Thailand. No longer known to exist in Thailand but still survives somewhere else in its range.

Probably extirpated from Thailand.

Endangered. Populations or distribution have declined so much that the organism may become extinct or extirpated from Thailand in the near future unless corrective measures are taken.

Threatened. Populations or distribution are declining so rapidly that the organism will become endangered in Thailand in the near future unless corrective measures are taken.

Species Accounts

The accounts that follow are organized in phylogenetic sequence: invertebrates, fishes, amphibians, reptiles, birds, and mammals. Most stand alone, but in a few groups, such as the sea turtles and hornbills, the nature of the data made it desirable to include a section of introductory comments, followed by species accounts.

The technical data are organized into accounts of the status, biology, and management needs of the listed species. Each account is organized into data categories, in two groups. The first group is the more useful one for land use planners, for it permits evaluation of distribution and status, with the following categories of data: status, population size and trend, distribution and history of distribution, geographic status (peripheral, endemic, migratory, vagrant, etc.), habitat requirements and habitat trend, and vulnerability of species and habitat. The second group provides details on the biology of the species, for use by managers to solve conservation problems and by planners to find ways to avoid or mitigate undesirable impacts of development projects. Data categories in this group are causes of threat, responses to habitat modification, demographic characteristics, key behaviors, conservation measures taken, and conservation measures proposed.

Maps accompany the species accounts for which sufficient distribution or habitat data exist. Maps prepared with dots represent actual documented distributions. Those prepared with lines shading an area are approximations, representing the probable ranges of the species based on knowledge of habitat requirements or elevation limits. A few maps of this type are done with spots but have legends indicating maximum potential range. Question marks (?) indicate possible or uncertain localities. Whenever data permitted, we chose to show probable rather than documented range, because maps of probable range provide the more realistic picture of what is possible or necessary in planning for endangered species conservation.

Chapter 2

Summary

Listed Species and Their Habitats

The number of species listed and their status designations assigned in this study are given in Table 1. Analysis of essential habitats is restricted to the 174 individually listed species of animals, for which detailed biological characteristics are presented in the written accounts.

Examination of the species in most danger (Table 2)--ranging from "extinct" to "probably extirpated from Thailand"--highlights the most serious or long-standing habitat changes. Schomburgk's deer is extinct. It lived in the mosaic of swamp forest and marsh of the lower Chao Phraya River basin, as did the extirpated large grass warbler. Three species that probably are extirpated--black ibis, giant ibis, and eastern sarus crane--also depended on wetlands habitats. Other species lived in deciduous dipterocarp forest, mixed deciduous forest, and tropical rain forest--Eld's deer, kouprey, and Javan rhinoceros, respectively. Five additional species (fish and reptiles) reached their precarious status because of harvest rates unregulated by fish and wildlife management practices, a contributing factor in some of the other cases as well. The Chinese tern's habitat problem is not in Thailand.

The listed species can be categorized into a few groups based on the habitats essential to their survival. Given in order of importance based on the number of endangered or threatened species in them and the imminence of conversion plans, they are wetlands; the Mekong River basin; tropical rain forest; hill evergreen forest; dry evergreen, deciduous dipterocarp, and mixed deciduous forest; mangrove forest; and the coastal rivers of southeastern Thailand.

Wetlands.--At least 21 species of listed animals require freshwater marshes, swamp forests, and associated habitats. Once an extensive component of the Thai landscape (Fig. 9), nearly all

Table 1. Summary of survival status designations in this study, by group of organism.

	Invertebrates	Fishes	Amphibians and reptiles	Birds	Mammals	Total
Number of species						
Listed	>3	14	20	135	77	249
Individually listed	3	14	20	60	77	174
Status designation						
None given	0	0	0	75	12	87
Extinct	0	0	0	0	1	1
Possibly extinct	0	0	0	1	0	1
Probably extirpated	0	0	0	2	1	3
Extirpated	0	2	3	2	3	10
Endangered	0	7	8	21	21	57
Threatened	3	5	9	34	39	90

marsh and swamp in the country has been drained and converted to agricultural uses. The only sizable wetland known to remain is marshland and *Melaleuca-Alstonia* swamp around Songkhla Lake and Thale Noi in southern Thailand. Even this site is affected by government housing projects, widespread illegal residences intended to establish personal ownership of government land, a proposed road, and deforestation for charcoal and building materials. A national inventory of remaining wetlands is urgently needed, and existing remnants should be protected as wildlife refuges. Otherwise extinction or extirpation of these species will occur.

The Mekong River Basin.--Ten species of listed fishes occur in the Mekong River basin. Though overharvesting is responsible for the current plight of these fishes, a basin-wide plan for developing agriculture and hydroelectric power now threatens these and many other species. A series of navigation channels and five mainstream dams would replace river habitat with reservoir habitat, destroy shoalwater habitat, prevent spawning of migratory fishes, and prevent spawning of non-migratory fishes in the seasonally flooded land they require for breeding. A total of 23 fish species that are either migratory (Pantalu and Bardach 1969 in Mekong Committee 1976, Lagler 1976*a*) or else incapable of living in reservoir habitat (Lagler 1976*b*) are expected to be lost from the Mekong. The basin-wide economic loss of protein resources, taking into account the anticipated reservoir fishery, is estimated at US $4-6,000,000 per year (Lagler 1976*b*). Additionally, loss of the annual refertilization of existing agricultural land by the silt from annual floodwater will necessitate substitution of imported commercial fertilizer.

A preferable alternative would be to consider smaller hydroelectric development on tributary rivers while stabilizing the mainstream fishery with a research and management program aimed at long-term sustainable yield. Implementation of an effective effort would reestablish these species as an important food resource for humans. Before embarking on the Mekong development plan, it would be prudent to learn the ecological consequences of China's Gezhouba Project in which three hydroelectric dams were built across the Yangtse River, with construction begun in October 1980.

Tropical Rain Forest.--Of the 174 animals, 37 occur in this habitat, 20 of them exclusively there. Well more than half of the original extent of this habitat (Fig. 10) in Thailand has been defor-

Table 2. Habitat requirements of Thailand's extinct and extirpated animals.

Status Species	Habitat
Extinct	
Schomburgk's deer	Swamp/marsh of the lower Chao Phraya basin.
Possibly Extinct	
Chinese crested tern	Breeding habitat in China.
Extirpated	
large grass warbler	Swamp/marsh of the lower Chao Phraya basin.
Probably Extirpated	
Asian bonytongue	Coastal rivers of southeastern Thailand.
burnt-tail carp	Chao Phraya River and its tributary rivers.
saltwater crocodile	Estuaries and coastal waters.
freshwater crocodile	Freshwater lakes, swamps, and rivers.
false gavial	Unclear.
black ibis	Lowland wetlands.
giant ibis	Lowland wetlands.
eastern sarus crane	Swamp forest/marsh wetlands.
Javan rhino	Tropical rain forest up to 1,000 m.
Eld's brow-antlered deer	Dry deciduous forest, plains, marshes.
kouprey	Mixed deciduous forest in the dry season, evergreen forest in the rainy season.

Summary

Fig. 9. Whistling teal (*Dendrocygna javanica*) and fisherman at Thale Luang in Songkhla and Patthalung provinces show that lakes can provide stable resources for both wildlife and people. However, it is the forested wetland behind them that represents Thailand's single most important opportunity for conservation.

Fig. 10. All the originally forested lowlands of peninsular Thailand have been converted to rice paddies and other uses, as at this site in Songkhla Province. Second only to loss of wetlands, loss of habitat for tropical lowland animals has been disasterous for Thailand's wildlife. Many of the steep limestone hills and mountains at low elevations retain secondary forest occupied by wildlife.

ested, and the economic incentive for conversion to rubber plantation is growing because of the rising cost of petroleum.

Hill Evergreen Forest.--This habitat is required by 8 of the 174 animal species given status designations by this study, and it is used along with lower elevation forests by at least 25 others. This highland type has the smallest area of the three evergreen forest types, and it is under increasing deforestation pressure from mountain-dwelling people (Fig. 11). As practiced by high-density human populations, shifting agriculture has become extractive. After the forest is cut, the land is farmed for a few years until it is too infertile for agriculture, and then it is burned annually to maintain *Imperata* grassland for low-density cattle grazing.

Dry Evergreen (Fig. 12), *Dry Dipterocarp* (Fig. 13), *and Mixed Deciduous Forest* (Fig. 14).--Twenty-seven listed species occupy these xeric forests. Most prefer these habitats, but few are strictly limited to them. These forests once were widely distributed but now are mostly converted to agriculture, except for sizable tracts remaining in northern and western Thailand.

Mangrove Forest.--Six listed species occupy mangrove habitat but also occur elsewhere. Mangrove forest has been very heavily cut for charcoal, and it is doubtful if any primary mangrove forest exists in the country. To reverse the loss of this vegetation and stabilize use of this renewable resource, the Royal Forestry Department has begun to regulate mangrove harvest in units of 30 strips, with one cut per year in a 30-year rotational sequence. Effective enforcement of this regulation should provide both use of the wood on a sustainable basis and habitat for endangered and threatened species.

Coastal Rivers of Southeastern Thailand.--Two species of fish from this region are listed. Their problem is presumed to be overharvest, not habitat loss, but more information is needed.

Other Habitats.--Coral reefs contain an unknown number of species of corals. Sandy coastal beaches are nesting habitat for five species of sea turtles. Coastal mudflats are habitat for three listed species of birds, and coastal islands support three others. Sandy beaches of Songkhla Lake and river banks of the region are habitat for a listed turtle.

Fig. 11. Deforestation by people living on the flank of Doi Inthanon, Chiang Mai Province. A small settlement is visible at left center. Formerly montane evergreen forest, the dominant vegetation now is lalang or cogon grass (*Imperata*). It supports cattle grazing at very low density.

Fig. 12. Now in a rice paddy, four trees (*Dipterocarpus alatus*) remain from the dry evergreen forest in the Lam Huai Takrong valley approaching Khao Yai National Park, Nakhon Ratchasima Province.

Fig. 13. Intact dry dipterocarp forest in the foothills of Doi Inthanon, Chiang Mai Province.

Evaluating Potential Impacts of Development Projects

An example of how this information can be used to consider potential impacts on endangered and threatened species is provided by proposed development in the Mae Chaem Watershed. A cooperative land-use development program between the Royal Thai Government and the United States Agency for International Development is planned to convert land now under periodic slash-and-burn agriculture to permanent agricultural use. The proposal is to establish and operate an agricultural research and extension service to introduce cash crops and improved farming techniques in the 300 km^2 watershed of the Mae Chaem, a tributary of the Ping River in the western part of Chiang Mai Province. This plan has obvious advantages of strengthening the local economy of an area known best for production and smuggling of opium.

Use of the maps in this document gives the following indication of what endangered species may be expected in the project area. The project area includes mixed deciduous forest along the river and hill evergreen forest on the two flanking mountain ridges. As of 1972 the forest cover was nearly continuous, with little deforested area. Our data indicate that at least 49 endangered or threatened species of vertebrates were present (Table 3).

Once such a list is compiled, additional steps will be necessary to obtain the best possible evaluation of the impacts of land-use changes on endangered species. Wildlife experts and professional ecologists should conduct field surveys to determine the status, distributions, and habitats of species that may be affected. These experts should prepare a written report evaluating the impacts of the development project, suggesting modifications that would reduce undesirable effects, and recommending natural-resource-management initiatives in the vicinity of the project that would compensate for unavoidable losses of natural resources within the project area.

Fig. 14. Lalang grassland (*Imperata*) cleared in the mixed deciduous forest of Khao Yai National Park and maintained by annual burning. A game trail is visible in the grass. The dark patches are nutritious young grass maintained by regular grazing by sambar deer (*Cervus unicolor*).

Table 3. Provisional list of endangered or threatened species potentially present and vulnerable to impacts of development in the Mae Chaem Watershed.

Amphibians and Reptiles:
Tylototriton verrucosus
Platysternon megacephalum
Pelochelys bibroni
Varanus bengalensis
Python molurus bivittatus

Birds:
Sarkidiornis melanotos
Ictinaetus malayensis
accipiters
Lophura nycthemera
Syrmaticus humiae
Polyplectron bicalcaratum
Pavo muticus
Columba pulchricollis
parrots
owls
Ptilolaemus tickelli

Birds (continued):
Aceros nipalensis
Buceros bicornis
Mulleripicus pulverulentus
Dryocopus javensis

Mammals:
Macaca nemestrina
Macaca arctoides
Presbytis phayrei
Hylobates lar
Manis pentadactyla
Petaurista elegans
Ratufa bicolor
Petinomys setosus
Eothenomys melanogaster
Canis aureus
Cuon alpinus
Selenarctos thibetanus

Mammals (continued):
Helarctos malayanus
Lutra lutra
Amblonyx cinerea
Prionodon pardicolor
Arctictus binturong
Felis marmorata
Felis viverrina
Felis bengalensis
Felis chaus
Felis temmincki
Neofelis nebulosa
Panthera pardus
Panthera tigris
Cervus eldi
Bos javanicus
Bos gaurus
Capricornis sumatraensis

Chapter 3

Invertebrates

Jakajantalay, sea grasshopper, sand crab
Emerita emeritus (Linnaeus 1767)
Crustacea, Decapoda, Hippidae

Status: Threatened.

Population Size and Trend: *E. emeritus* was the most abundant of the anomuran sand crabs on the west coast of peninsular Thailand during an intensive survey from 1971 to 1973. The number of individuals per net haul (65 x 70 cm) per wave averaged from 0.1 to 8 over this geographic range (Boonruang and Phasuk 1975). However, by 1981 this species was virtually gone from the heavily harvested beaches of Phuket (Pensri Boonruang, personal communication).

Distribution and History of Distribution: This species occurs on 9 discontinuous beaches in Phuket and Phangnga provinces on the west coast of peninsular Thailand (Fig. 15). It is absent from similar sites along Ranong, Krabi, Trang, and Satun provinces. *E. emeritus* (= *E. asiatica* H. Milne-Edwards) also is known from the east coast of India (Boonruang and Phasuk 1975).

Geographic Status: Thailand is on the eastern edge of the documented Indian Ocean range.

Habitat Requirements and Habitat Trend: *E. emeritus* are found between the low and high tide lines on sandy beaches. Several features of the physical environment have been quantified by Boonruang and Phasuk (1975), who considered the organic mud content of the substrate to be the most obvious physical limit to suitable habitat. No habitat loss has been documented, but pollution (such as organic sewage or nearshore seabed mining) could destroy required substrate qualities.

Vulnerability of Species and Habitat: Restriction of the species to a narrow zone of habitat at clearly defined sites makes it highly vulnerable to harvesting. The populations are isolated by segments of nonsuitable habitat, and the ability of individuals to move among suitable sites is unknown.

Causes of Threat: This species formerly was used as bait for surf-fishing. Since about 1965, a commercial market has developed both locally and in Bangkok (Boonruang and Phasuk 1975), and harvesting intensified until the demise of populations occurred (Pensri Boonruang, personal communication).

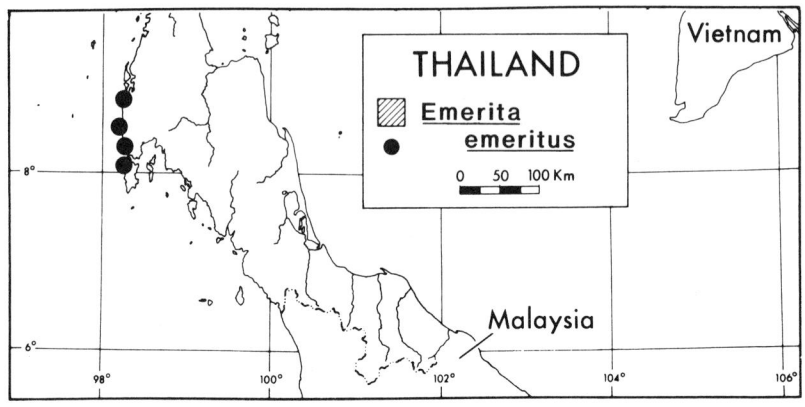

Fig. 15. Distribution of the Sand Crab (*Emerita emeritus*).

Responses to Habitat Modification: Unknown.
Demographic Characteristics: Females in the size range of 20-29 mm carapace length bear eggs, numbering 500-6,000 eggs per individual. Fecundity is directly proportional to body size, with eggs = 3,505(carapace length) - 3,618. The population consists of a single year-class of males and 3 year-classes of females. The males and the youngest cohort of females arrive on the beach from December to April. The males and the two younger cohorts of females occupy the upper part of the beach, whereas the largest, egg-bearing cohort of females occupies the lower beach. Males mate with the second year-class of females on the upper beach during the monsoon season (June to November), and the females move to the lower beach to form the large-sized cohort. This cohort of ovigerous females is most abundant in June and contains the most marketable individuals because of their size.
Key Behaviors: Unknown.
Conservation Measures Taken: None.
Conservation Measures Proposed: Beaches where populations have been depleted should be closed to fishing for 4-5 years to allow a complete reproductive cycle to occur. Population monitoring in year 4 and later should be done to justify reopening the harvest at

these beaches. Where populations are robust, sections of each beach should be closed to harvesting, with monitoring done to adjust the length of closed areas to a size that will sustain the harvestable populations at stable levels.

Bhutan glory butterfly
Bhutanitis lidderdalei
Insecta, Lepidoptera, Papilionidae

Status: Threatened.
Population Size and Trend: Unknown.
Distribution and History of Distribution: The only reported locality in Thailand is Chiang Mai (Igarashi 1979). However, this must be an approximate designation, for Chiang Mai is well below the elevations at which the Bhutan glory is known to occur. The subspecies in Thailand has been reported variously as *lidderdalei* (Pinratana 1974) and *ocellatomaculata* (Igarashi 1979). The species ranges from Sikkim in China, the Naga Hills of Bhutan, India (Assam and Manipur), the Chin Hills of Burma (Ackery 1975), to northern Thailand.
Geographic Status: The Thailand population is a relict.
Habitat Requirements and Habitat Trend: Unknown in Thailand. *B. lidderdalei* occurs at elevations from 1,550 to 2,750 m in Bhutan and 2,290 to 2,750 m in Manipur; it flies weakly in the forest canopy and seldom is seen near the ground (Elwes 1891). Tytler (1912) found the species at 1,675-2,130 m from late August to early October in the Napa Hills. The larvae of the related species *B. thaidina* in southern China feeds on *Aristolochia* (Ackery 1975).
Vulnerability of Species and Habitat: Unknown.
Causes of Threat: Hundreds of individuals are exported from Thailand annually to collectors (Jarujin Nabhitabhata, personal communication). Deforestation also may be a threat.
Responses to Habitat Modification: Unknown.
Demographic Characteristics: Unknown.
Key Behaviors: Unknown.
Conservation Measures Taken: None.
Conservation Measures Proposed: Entomologists at the Department of Agriculture and Thailand Institute of Scientific and Technological Research should undertake a search for this species

in the montane forests of northern Thailand and work with Wildlife Conservation officials to develop a management plan. It may be possible to both conserve these butterflies and harvest them for commerce (Pyle and Hughes 1978).

Godfrey's junglequeen butterfly
Sticopthalma godfreyi **Rothschild**
Insecta, Lepidoptera, Satyridae

Status: Threatened.

Population Size and Trend: Unknown. Godfrey's junglequeen was considered rare (p. 82) or possibly extirpated (p. XIX) from Thailand (Lekagul et al. 1977). The species had not been seen since soon after its discovery in 1914 until a new population was found very recently (Samruadkit and Nabhitabhata, manuscript in preparation).

Distribution and History of Distribution: S. *godfreyi* ranges from the Dawna Range, Tavoy, and the Mergui Islands in southern Burma, western Thailand, to the upper part of peninsular Malaysia. In Thailand the species has been reported at Thong Pha Phum in Kanchanaburi Province, and Khlong Nakha Wildlife Sanctuary in Ranong Province (Fig. 16; Samruadkit and Nabhitabhata, manuscript in preparation). (The Dawna Range is on the Thai-Burmese border.)

Geographic Status: Thailand is central in the range of this species; however, populations appear isolated and may be relictual.

Habitat Requirements and Habitat Trend: Unknown.

Vulnerability of Species and Habitat: Unknown.

Causes of Threat: Populations may be naturally ephemeral, but any commercial or scientific collecting could be a significant threat.

Responses to Habitat Modification: Unknown.

Demographic Characteristics: Unknown.

Key Behaviors: Unknown.

Conservation Measures Taken: The species occurs in Khlong Nakha Wildlife Sanctuary.

Conservation Measures Proposed: Wildlife officials at Khlong Nakha Wildlife Sanctuary should take measures to protect the population there from butterfly collectors, because the market value of specimens is inversely proportional to their rarity. Field research is needed to determine habitat requirements and to learn what food plants could be promoted for managing this species. The successes of Papua New Guinea in protective law, management, butterfly farming for commerce, and promotion of butterfly-oriented park tourism (Pyle and Hughes 1978) show a number of ways that Thai butterflies could be conserved while being harvested for profit.

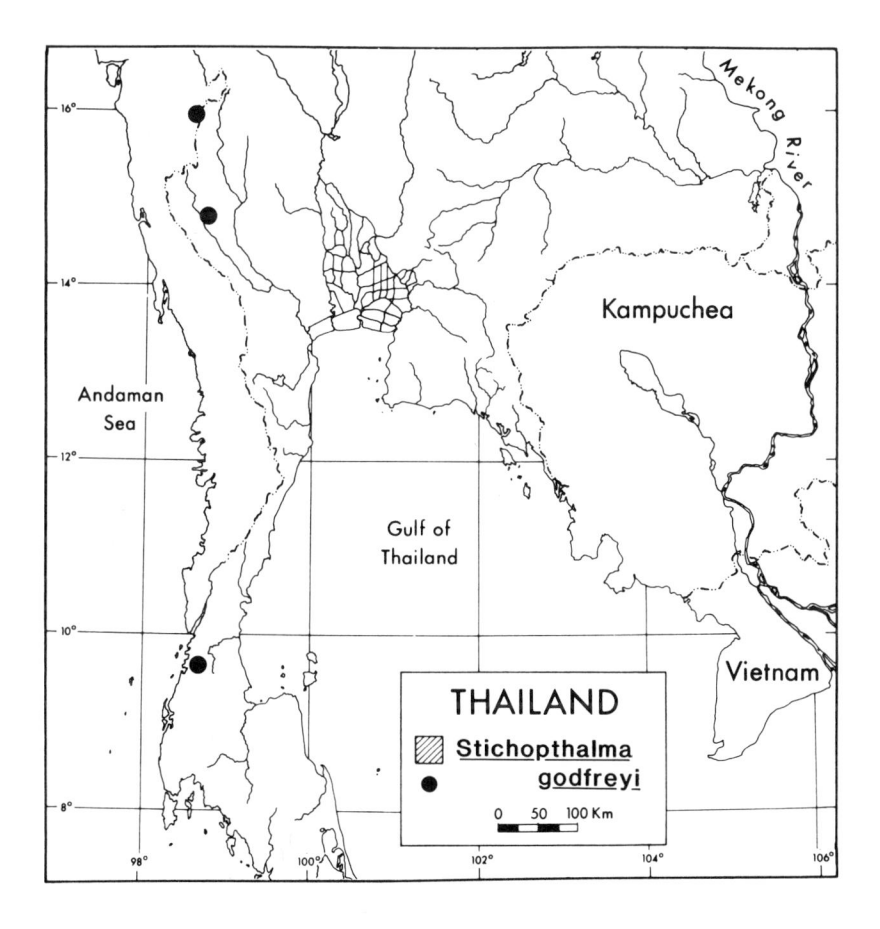

Fig. 16. Distribution of Godfrey's Junglequeen Butterfly (*Sticopthalma godfreyi*).

Chapter 4

Fishes

Pla tapad, ikan kelasa, Asian bonytongue
Scleropages formosus **(Muller and Schlegel 1844)**
Osteichthyes, Osteoglossiformes, Osteoglossidae

Status: Probably extirpated.
IUCN (1968): Threatened.
IUCN Red Data Book (1977): Vulnerable.
CITES (1979): Appendix I.
USFWS (1980a): Endangered.

Population Size and Trend: *S. formosus* is now thought to be extirpated from Thailand (Sompote Ukkatawewat, personal communication). It used to be common in Thailand (Smith 1945), but the rangewide population of the species was given as fewer than 2,000, based on a 1969 report (IUCN Red Data Book 1977). However, it was reported to remain common in Malaya in 1970 (Scott and Fuller 1976); in one swamp fishermen harvested 136 adults and 34 fry from July to October.

Distribution and History of Distribution: *S. formosus* is known from Vietnam, Kampuchea, Thailand, Malaya, Sumatra, the island of Bangka, Borneo, and the Phillipines (Smith 1945, Blanc and d'Aubenton 1965, Furtado and Scott 1971, Scott and Fuller 1976). No change in distribution is known other than apparent loss from Thai waters. Distribution includes the drainages of the Cardamon Mountains in Kampuchea and Thailand, with the Thai distribution (Fig. 17) confined to Trat and Chanthaburi provinces (Ukkatawewat 1979). An unconfirmed report of this species is from the Khlong Pattani, Yala Province, Thailand (Sompote Ukkatawewat, personal communication).

Geographic Status: This specialized form of primitive fish has a relict distribution, restricted to oriental, tropical, fresh water.

Habitat Requirements and Habitat Trend: *S. formosus* occupies

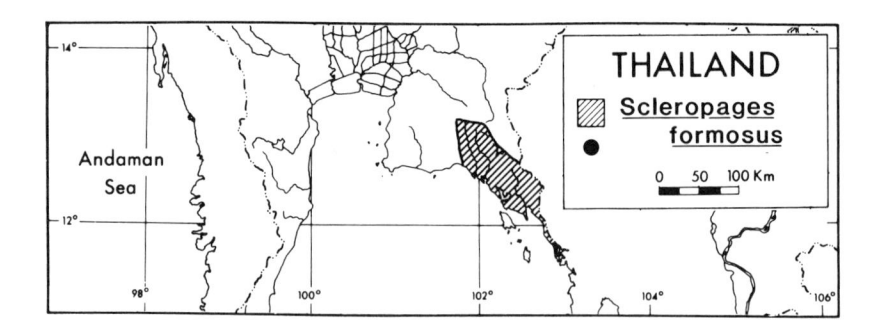

Fig. 17. Distribution of the Asian Bonytongue (*Scleropages formosus*).

rivers, streams, canals, swamps, and reservoirs (Smith 1945, Smedley 1931, Furtado and Scott 1971). Details are known only for the swamp at Tasek Bera, Pahang, Malaysia. That *Pandanus* swamp is surrounded by a *Eugenia* swamp forest. The small areas of open water are shallow, up to 12 m deep in a few places; water level varies up to 6 m seasonally. The water is peat-stained, acidic (average pH of 6), and has a temperature range of 25-30° C (Scott and Fuller 1976). Here the food in March consists of surface insects and arancids. In October the food is mostly non-woody roots and tubers, along with a few insects and araneids (Furtado and Scott 1971). Fish, frogs, and snakes also are included in the diet (Ukkatawewat 1979). No habitat trend is documented.

Vulnerability of Species and Habitat: The species is an important source of human food and is vulnerable to overfishing. Excessive harvest can easily deplete the breeding stock because of reproductive adaptations. The swamp habitat in Malaya is considered to be threatened (Scott and Fuller 1976). Habitat in southeastern Thailand is being destroyed by dredging for rubies.

Causes of Threat: Decline and extirpation in Thailand apparently resulted from overharvest and river dredging.

Responses to Habitat Modification: Unknown. Clearing of swamp forest fringing swamp habitat, by increasing nutrient flow into the swamp, could speed succession from swamp to more terrestrial habitat.

Demographic Characteristics: Reproduction of *S. formosus* is highly specialized, with late sexual maturity, low natality, and high survival of young, apparently in response to natural selection imposed by a diverse community of predators. Adults possess only one ovary or testis. Females produce a small number of large eggs, which measure 19 mm when mature in August to October (Scott and Fuller 1976), coinciding with a seasonal rise in water level. The number was 20 to 30 eggs in Malaya (Scott and Fuller 1976), with a case of 37 recorded in Thailand (Ukkatawewat 1979). After spawning, the male (contrary to earlier reports regarding females) incubates the eggs in his mouth until they hatch, and the fry remain near the parent until at least 80 mm long. Females are sexually mature when 3 years old; possibly the largest 2-year-olds also spawn (Scott and Fuller 1976). These authors documented population structure of year classes from fry to 3-year-olds and attributed the absence of older fish to possible emigration or heavy mortality, the latter possibly due to intensive fishing with poison 4 years before sampling. Distinct age structure indicates that spawning is highly seasonal. In Malaya, this fish reaches a maximum size of 7.4 k in weight and about 1 m in length (Alfred 1964).

Key Behaviors: In swamps, the fish retire to *Pandanus* stands during daytime and move into open water at night to feed at the surface. Here they are vulnerable to spearfishing. The fish are territorial. At spawning time, *S. formosus* become difficult to catch, and fishermen seek them in lagoons fringed by *Eugenia*. This suggests that the fish may move toward the shallow swamp edge to spawn (Scott and Fuller 1976).

Conservation Measures Taken: An early attempt at commercial pond culture apparently was unsuccessful, presumably because of low fecundity (Furtado and Scott 1971). The Thai Inland Fisheries Division procured 37 eggs from one of the last *S. formosus* captured in southeastern Thailand and succeeded in rearing 4 animals to large size. These siblings are housed (1980) in the National Inland Fisheries Institute at Kasetsart University, Bangkok.

Conservation Measures Proposed: A survey of the range of *S. formosus* should be made to confirm that a costly reintroduction program is needed. The availability of Malayan populations and a small native stock make a captive breeding and/or reintroduction program possible, though rapid action will be necessary to take advantage of the latter. A captive breeding program may have to accommodate the species' territorial behavior and use of swamp forest in spawning. Attention should be given to genetic differences between native and non-native stocks. Reintroduction should be accompanied by a closed season and research to determine what harvest level later will be compatible with maximum sustained yield. Such a well-managed fishery cannot be attained until prohibitions against fishing with explosives and poisons (Alfred 1969, Anonymous 1976) are enforced.

Pla tong lai, featherback
Notopterus blanci d'Aubenton 1965
Osteichthyes, Osteoglossiformes, Notopteridae

Status: Threatened.
IUCN Red Data Book (1977): Rare.
IUCN (1979): Threatened.

Population Size and Trend: Unknown. Apparently few now exist. When first described, *N. blanci* was abundant in the Mekong (d'Aubenton 1965).

Distribution and History of Distribution: The featherback has been found in the Mekong River in Kampuchea upstream of Kratie and along the border of northeastern Thailand, and in the Mun River (Fig. 18; d'Aubenton 1965, Sontirat and Monholrasit 1968, Rainboth et al. 1976).

Geographic Status: This is a freshwater, riverine fish. Congeneric species occur in rivers, canals, and swamps (Davidson 1975).

Habitat Requirements and Habitat Trend: Habitat is in the rocky zones of major rivers where the current is strong (d'Aubenton 1965) but was later reported as the backwaters and pools of large rivers (IUCN Red Data Book 1977). Trends are unknown, but major reduction of habitat may be expected to result from the several dams and navigation channels (Lagler 1976b) planned along the length of the Mekong.

Vulnerability of Species and Habitat: Unknown.

Causes of Threat: Reasons for the apparent rarity of *N. blanci* are unknown. Its meat is considered moderately good (Davidson 1975). Whether the planned reservoirs are a threat depends on whether the species can live in lentic habitat. Rocky shoalwater habitat is threatened by inundation and clearing for navigation.

Responses to Habitat Modification: Unknown. The species was not recorded in surveys of Lam Dom Noi, Lam Pao, and Nam Pong reservoirs (Lagler 1976a). However, the rivers flooded by these reservoirs were not known to be occupied by *N. blanci*.

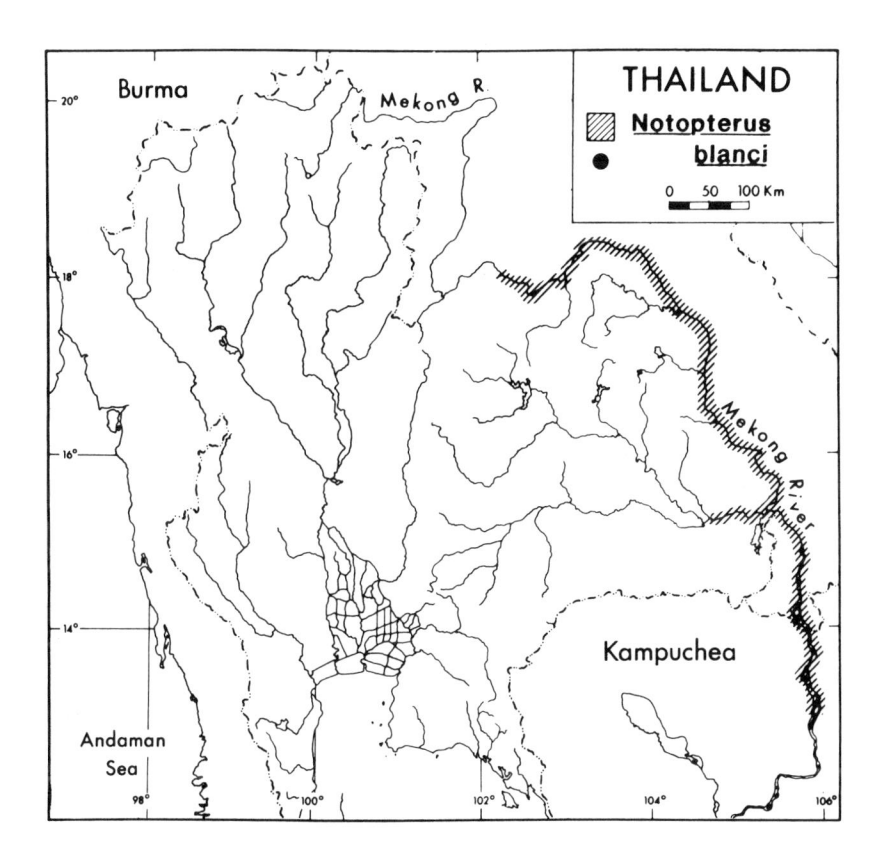

Fig. 18. Distribution of the Featherback (*Notopterus blanci*).

Demographic Characteristics: Unknown. In the congener *N. chitala*, breeding at Bung Boraphet occurs from February to August, when flooding begins. Several hundred to several thousand eggs are laid in a mass. Each female lays three batches of eggs per year at wide intervals. Incubation takes 5-6 days (Smith 1933).

Key Behaviors: Unknown. In the congener *N. chitala*, the parent fish clear a circular depression in the mud at the base of a stake or stump, and the eggs are attached to the wood above the mud. The male tends these, fanning them with his tail to keep them aerated and free of sediment, and guarding them against predatory catfish and minnows. Upon hatching, the fish drop into the depression and remain there until the yolk sac is absorbed. Then the young swim about and feed (Smith 1933).

Conservation Measures Taken: The Thai Inland Fisheries Division has captured 10-20 *N. blanci* in the Mekong. Two individuals are in an aquarium in the National Inland Fisheries Institute in Bangkok (1980). Attempts to breed the animals at the fisheries research station in Nong Khai have been unsuccessful so far (Sompote Ukkatawewat, personal communication).

Conservation Measures Proposed: A status survey in the field would provide information on distribution, abundance, and habitat. Monitoring of harvest and documentation of size and age classes would begin the process of evaluating whether the harvest is sustainable. If parental care is as in *N. chitala*, fishing around egg-laying sites will remove the male and doom the eggs; reproduction should be favored by eliminating this practice. Smith (1933) reported methods for hatchery rearing of *N. chitala*.

Pla satu, a featherback
Notopterus borneensis Bleeker 1851
Osteichthes, Osteoglossiformes, Notopteridae

Status: Endangered.

Population Size and Trend: Unknown. *N. borneensis* is apparently very rare in Thailand; attempts to collect them from fishermen have yielded 2 specimens (Sompote Ukkatawewat, personal communication).

Distribution and History of Distribution: Records are known (Fig. 19) from the Mae Klong, Kanchanaburi Province (Sompote Ukkatawewat, personal communication), and the Suret River in Surat Thani Province (Sontirat et al. 1971). Elsewhere the species is known from Borneo and Sumatra (Smith 1945).

Geographic Status: Unknown.
Habitat Requirements and Habitat Trend: Unknown.
Vulnerability of Species and Habitat: Unknown.
Causes of Threat: Unknown.
Responses to Habitat Modification: Unknown.
Demographic Characteristics: Unknown.
Key Behaviors: Unknown.
Conservation Measures Taken: None.
Conservation Measures Proposed: Information could be gathered by continued work in the field and correspondence with fish biologists elsewhere in the species' range.

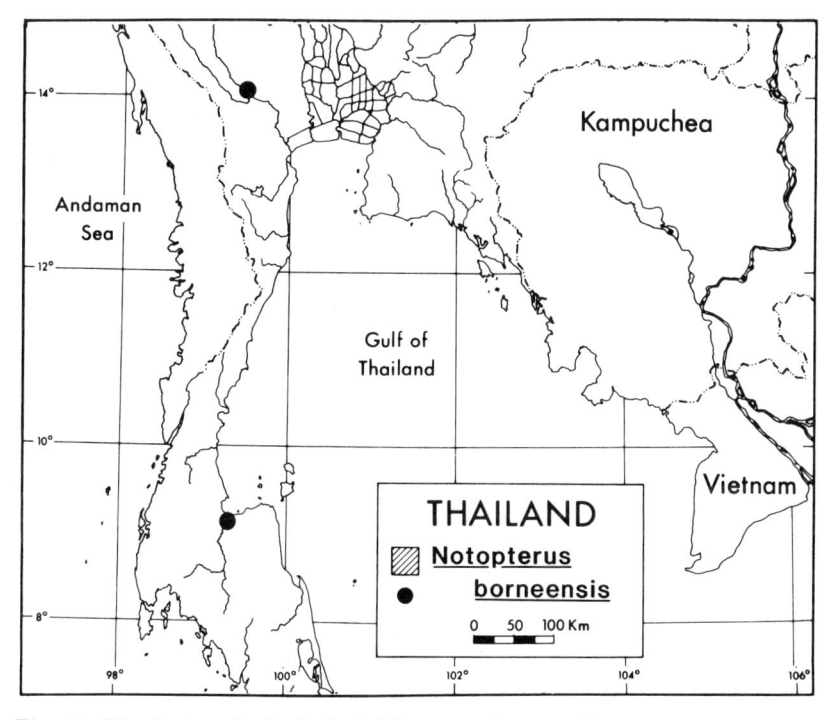

Fig. 19. Distribution of a featherback (*Notopterus borneensis*).

Pla dab lao, pla tong plu, pla pak pra, a carp
Macrochirichthys macrochirus
(Cuvier and Valenciennes 1844)
Osteichthyes, Cypriniformes, Cyprinidae

Status: Threatened.

Population Size and Trend: Population size is unknown. A decline is evident in the Chao Phraya River; the species has not been reported there in the last decade but was abundant prior to 1960 (Suebsin Sontirat, personal communication).

Distribution and History of Distribution: In Thailand *M. macrochirus* is known from the Chao Phraya River, the "Tapi" River (Khlong Thepha?), Thale Sap, Thale Noi (Smith 1945), and the Mun River (Fig. 20; Suebsin Sontirat, personal communication).

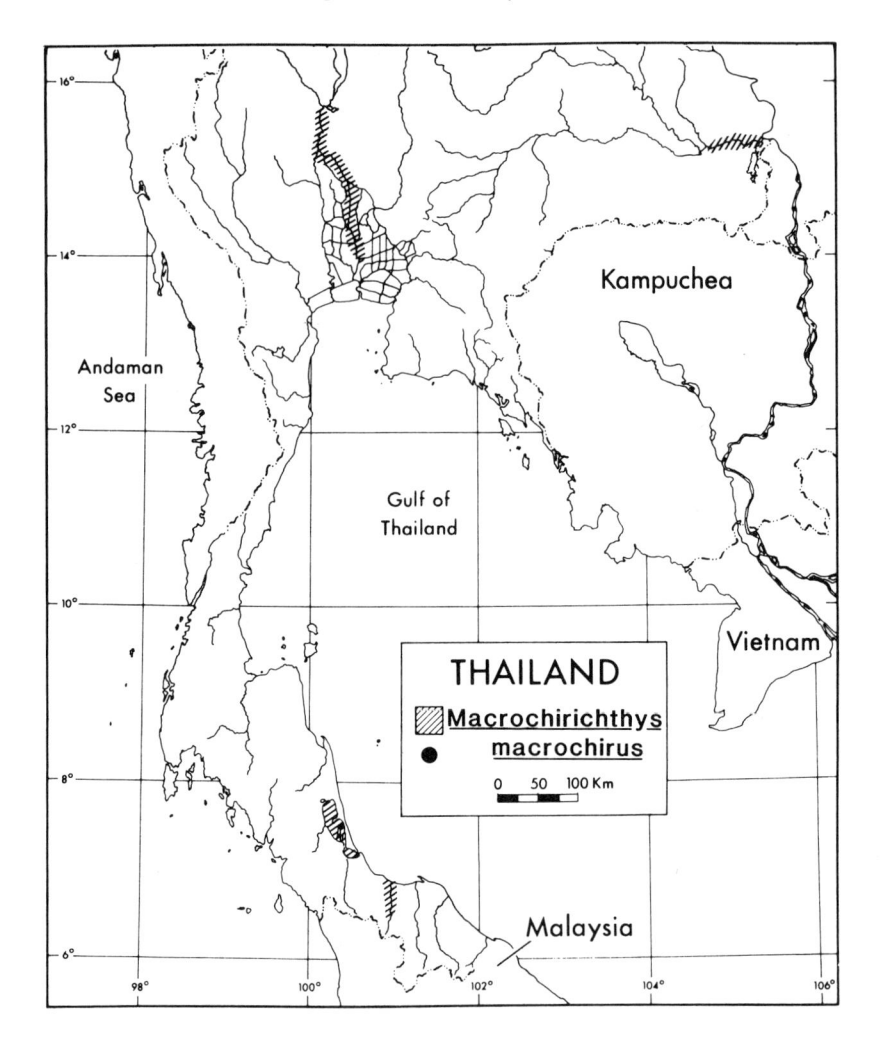

Fig. 20. Distribution of a carp (*Macrochirichthys macrochirus*).

Elsewhere it occurs in Kampuchea, Vietnam, Java, Sumatra, and Borneo (Smith 1945).

Geographic Status: Thailand is on the northeastern edge of the species' range.

Habitat Requirements and Habitat Trend: The species inhabits large rivers and lakes (Smith 1945).

Vulnerability of Species and Habitat: This is the largest local species of abramid carp, and it is highly sought as a game fish, by using a light rod (Smith 1945).

Causes of Threat: None are documented, but the population decline in the Chao Phraya may have resulted from excessive harvest.

Responses to Habitat Modification: Unknown.

Demographic Characteristics: Unknown. The species reaches more than half a meter in length (Smith 1945).

Key Behaviors: Unknown.

Conservation Measures Taken: None.

Conservation Measures Proposed: A field survey of the status of *M. macrochirus* should be conducted to determine the nature of the problem and the need for corrective management.

(no common name)
Chela caeruleostigmata (Smith 1931)
Osteichthyes, Cypriniformes, Cyprinidae

Status: Threatened.
IUCN Red Data Book (1977): Rare.
IUCN (1979): Threatened.

Population Size and Trend: Population size is unknown but very small. No trend data are available, though a decline is apparent (IUCN 1977).

Distribution and History of Distribution: The range of this species in Thailand (Fig. 21) is restricted to the upper Chao Phraya River, and all reported specimens are from 1923-25. Reported localities are a stream flowing out of Bung Boraphet near Paknampo, sites in the Chao Phraya below Nakhon Sawan and near Chainat (Smith 1931, 1945), and Khlong Nong Moh, Phra Nakhon Si Ayutthaya Province (Ukkatawewat and Ratanalhauee 1978). The species also occurs in the lower Mekong, downstream from the Thai border (Rainboth et al. 1976).

Geographic Status: *C. caeruleostimata* is endemic to the Chao Phraya River, Thailand, and the lower Mekong.

Habitat Requirements and Habitat Trend: Habitat consists of large, turbid rivers (IUCN 1977).

Vulnerability of Species and Habitat: Unknown.

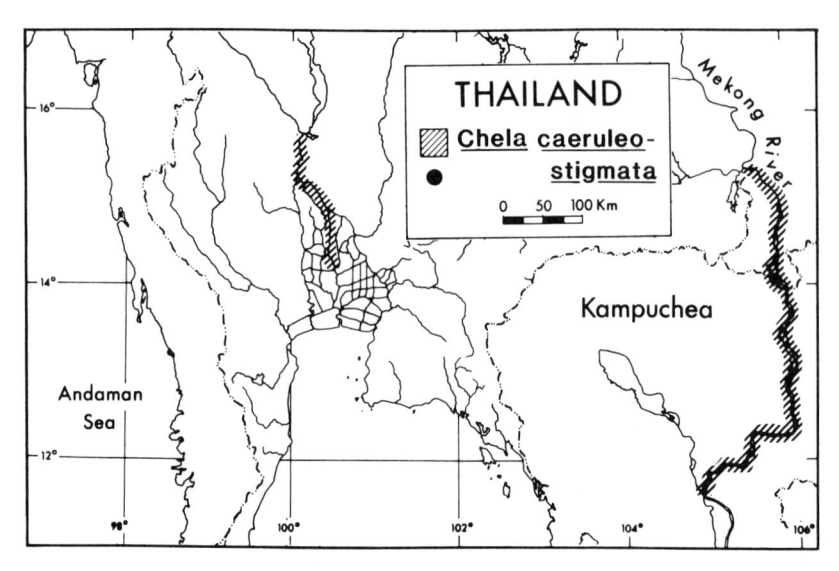

Fig. 21. Distribution of the fish *Chela caeruleostigmata*.

Causes of Threat: Exportation as an aquarium fish is the only reported threat (IUCN 1977).

Responses to Habitat Modification: Unknown. Impoundment of Bung Boraphet as a reservoir may have had significant impacts on this species.

Demographic Characteristics: Unknown.

Key Behaviors: Unknown.

Conservation Measures Taken: None.

Conservation Measures Proposed: A field survey of population status should be conducted to determine the current dimensions of the problem. The extent of aquarium trade should be monitored and halted if the threat is confirmed.

Pla kaho, giant carp
Catlocarpio siamensis Boulenger 1898
Osteichthyes, Cypriniformes, Cyprinidae

Status: Endangered.

Population Size and Trend: *C. siamensis* was once abundant and a major source of food, but now it is very rare and might be extirpated from Thailand. One of the largest cypriniform fishes in

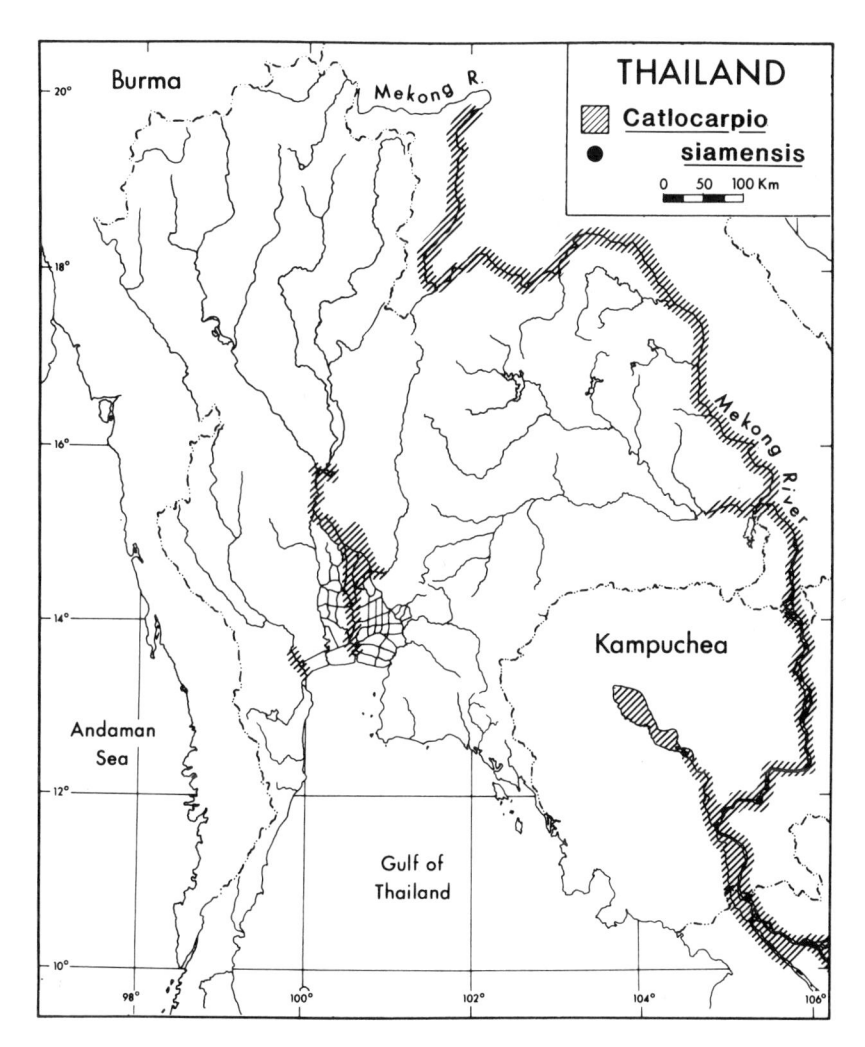

Fig. 22. Historical distribution of the Giant Carp (*Catlocarpio siamensis*).

the world, this species formerly reached 2.5-3 m in size (Smith 1945).

Distribution and History of Distribution: The giant carp occurred (Fig. 22) throughout the Chao Phraya River, from Pak Nam north, and up its tributaries at least as far as Ratchaburi on the Mae Klong River, Lop Buri on the Bang Kham River, and Dha Luang (possibly Nakhon Luang in Phra Nakhon Si Ayutthaya

Province) on the Pa Sak River. It bred in Bung Boraphet and other swamps that receive Chao Phraya floodwater (Smith 1945). The most recent specimen taken in the Chao Phraya, in 1969, was 1.45 m long and weighed 80.5 kg (Sompote Ukkatawewat, personal communication). Giant carp also occurred in the Mekong River from Luang Prabang, Lao PDR, downstream to southern Vietnam and Tonle Sap, Kampuchea; Thai localities include Ban Pak Som at the mouth of Huai Nam Som, Nong Khai, Mukdahan, Khemmarat, and above Tha Tum on the Mun River (Rainboth et al. 1976). However, no specimens of giant carp were reported from recent sampling of the Mekong by Lagler.

Geographic Status: This is a basin-wide, mainstream, riverine fish.

Habitat Requirements and Habitat Trend: Habitat is large rivers, but the fish enter ponds, canals, and swamps connected to the rivers. Smith (1945) indicates that breeding occurs in swamps. The diet consists of algae, plankton, and plant seeds (Ukkatawewat 1979).

Vulnerability of Species and Habitat: The species is considered fairly good to eat and is vulnerable to overfishing, which has caused its decline. Its riverine habitat is vulnerable to impoundment.

Causes of Threat: C. siamensis is endangered by excessive harvest. Loss of this species to impoundment of its habitat in the Mekong has been predicted by Lagler (1976a).

Responses to Habitat Modification: Unknown. The ability of giant carp to live in reservoirs has not been tested, but records of its presence in Tonle Sap, Kampuchea, suggest the possibility.

Demographic Characteristics: Natality depends on size of the female. One weighing 61 kg is reported with 11 million eggs, whereas one of 55 kg had about 5 million. Hatching time at 29.3° C is 12 hours (Ukkatawewat 1979).

Key Behaviors: Spawning occurs between July and September (Ukkatawewat 1979).

Conservation Measures Taken: Captive breeding methods have been developed by the Thai Inland Fisheries Division, but no propagation and restocking program has been implemented (Suebsin Sontirat, personal communication).

Conservation Measures Proposed: Fishing for giant carp should be closed while a survey is undertaken to determine what populations remain in the wild. A reintroduction program should be accompanied by a continued closed season, experimental restocking in reservoirs, and research to determine what harvest level will be compatible with maximum sustained yield.

Tapien, barb, olive carp
Puntius sarana (Hamilton 1822)
Osteichthyes, Cypriniformes, Cyprinidae

Status: Threatened.

Population Size and Trend: Unknown. Apparently this species is very rare in Thailand but is an important fishery resource farther west.

Distribution and History of Distribution: *P. sarana* is known from India, Bangladesh, Burma, and Thailand. Only two specimens are reported from Thailand (Fig. 23), one from the Wong River and one from the Mekong west of Vientiane (Smith 1945, Rainboth et al. 1976).

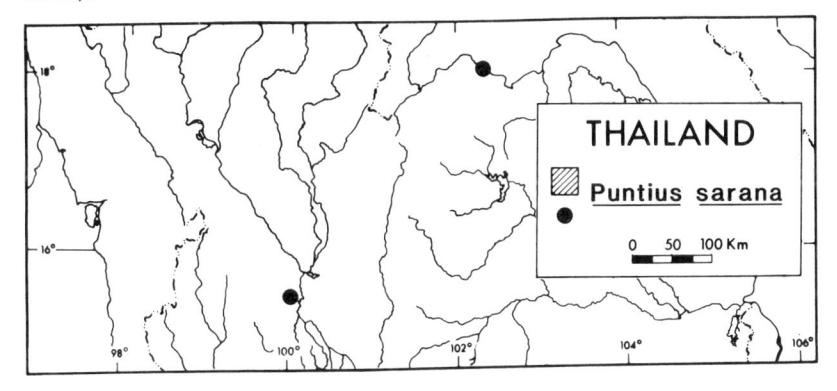

Fig. 23. Distribution of the Olive Carp (*Puntius sarana*).

Geographic Status: The Thai distribution of *P. sarana* is peripheral to the species' range.

Habitat Requirements and Habitat Trend: The species is known from rivers, backwaters (Sobhana and Nair 1977), and lakes (Murty 1976). The diet consists of aquatic plants (Murty 1976).

Vulnerability of Species and Habitat: Unknown.

Causes of Threat: *P. sarana* is considered incapable of living in reservoir habitat (Lagler 1976b), so its Mekong population is threatened by the proposed Pa Mong reservoir.

Responses to Habitat Modification: Unknown.

Demographic Characteristics: The average length of females at first maturity is 183 mm. The number of eggs ranges from about 15,000 to 140,000 per spawning period. The spawning season in different parts of India variously involves a single batch of eggs in July-August and two batches of eggs in May-November (Sinha 1975, Sobhana and Nair 1978). Growth checks occurring on the scales are not formed annually (Murty 1976).

Key Behaviors: Breeding in southwestern India occurs from May to November (Sobhana and Nair 1977).

Conservation Measures Taken: None.

Conservation Measures Proposed: The distribution of *P. sarana* in Thailand and its ability to live in lentic habitat need to be investigated.

Pla hang mai, burnt-tail carp
Balantiocheilos melanopterus (Bleeker 1851)
Osteichthyes, Cypriniformes, Cyprinidae

Status: Probably extirpated.

Population Size and Trend: Once common in Thai rivers (Smith 1945, Rainboth et al. 1976), *B. melanopterus* apparently has been extirpated from the country (Sompote Ukkatawewat, personal communication).

Distribution and History of Distribution: Original distribution of this species (Fig. 24) included the entire basin of the Chao Phraya River from Bangkok to Nakon Sawan, to Chiang Mai on the Ping River, the lower Nan River and Bung Boraphet, and the Pa Sak River to Dha Luang (possibly Nakhon Luang in Phra Nakhon Si Ayutthaya Province; Smith 1945)). Distribution also included the lower Mekong basin, from Tonle Sap and its drainage into the Mekong, up to Khemmarat, Thailand, and Vientiene, and in the lower Nam Ngum, Lao PDR (Rainboth et al. 1976). To the south, this species is known from Borneo, Sumatra, and Malaya.

Geographic Status: *B. melanopterus* is a basin-wide, mainstream, freshwater species.

Habitat Requirements and Habitat Trend: Unknown.

Vulnerability of Species and Habitat: The species is highly vulnerable to capture.

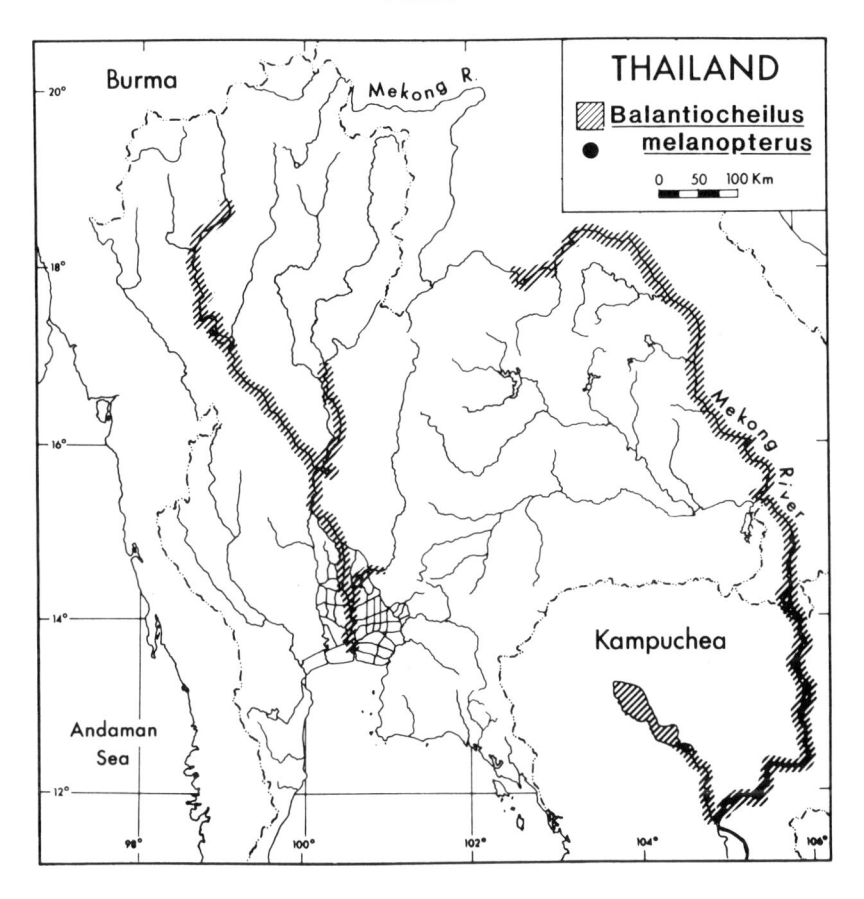

Fig. 24. Distribution of the Burnt-tail Carp (*Balantiocheilos melanopterus*).

Causes of Threat: The apparent extirpation of this species from Thailand was caused by excessive harvest for the aquarium trade. At present the demand within Thailand is being satisfied by importation of the species from Indonesia (Sompote Ukkatawewat, personal communication).
　Responses to Habitat Modification: Unknown.
　Demographic Characteristics: Unknown.
　Key Behaviors: Unknown.
　Conservation Measures Taken: None.
　Conservation Measures Proposed: The economic value of this renewable resource could be restored by research on captive propagation and habitat requirements, based on non-native stock. A

reintroduction program should be accompanied by a closed season and research to determine what harvest level would be compatible with maximum sustained yield.

Carp
Labeo behri **Fowler 1937**
Osteichthyes, Cypriniformes, Cyprinidae

Status: Endangered.

Population Size and Trend: Unknown.

Distribution and History of Distribution: Published information indicates that *L. behri* is restricted to the Mekong River, from its confluence with the Mun River, Thailand, upstream to Luang Prabang, Lao PDR (Rainboth et al. 1976). A single specimen is ascribed to Bangkok (Smith 1945). However, the species also is reported to occur in the Mae Klong and Salween rivers in Kanchanaburi, Tak, and Mae Hong Son provinces (Suebsin Sontirat, personal communication).

Geographic Status: Most of the range of this species occurs along the Thai border.

Habitat Requirements and Habitat Trend: Habitat is the mainstream of a large river. No other information is available.

Vulnerability of Species and Habitat: The entire species is vulnerable to the series of dams and navigation channels planned along the length of the Mekong, from Kampuchea to Luang Prabang.

Causes of Threat: *L. behri* is not expected to be able to establish itself in impoundments (Lagler 1976*b*) and hence may become extinct if the Mekong developments take place.

Responses to Habitat Modification: Unknown.

Demographic Characteristics: Unknown.

Key Behaviors: Unknown.

Conservation Measures Taken: None.

Conservation Measures Proposed: A survey is needed to determine the current status of *L. behri* populations, and the ability of the species to live in reservoirs should be investigated. Current information indicates that mainstream dams on the Mekong should be avoided in order to conserve this species.

Pla nam fai, backwater fish
Xenocheilichthys gudgeri Smith 1934
Osteichthyes, Cypriniformes, Cyprinidae

Status: Endangered.

Population Size and Trend: Though thought by Smith (1945) to be rare, *X. gudgeri* is common in the Mekong. It was among the most important species taken in trawl collections near Khemmerat-

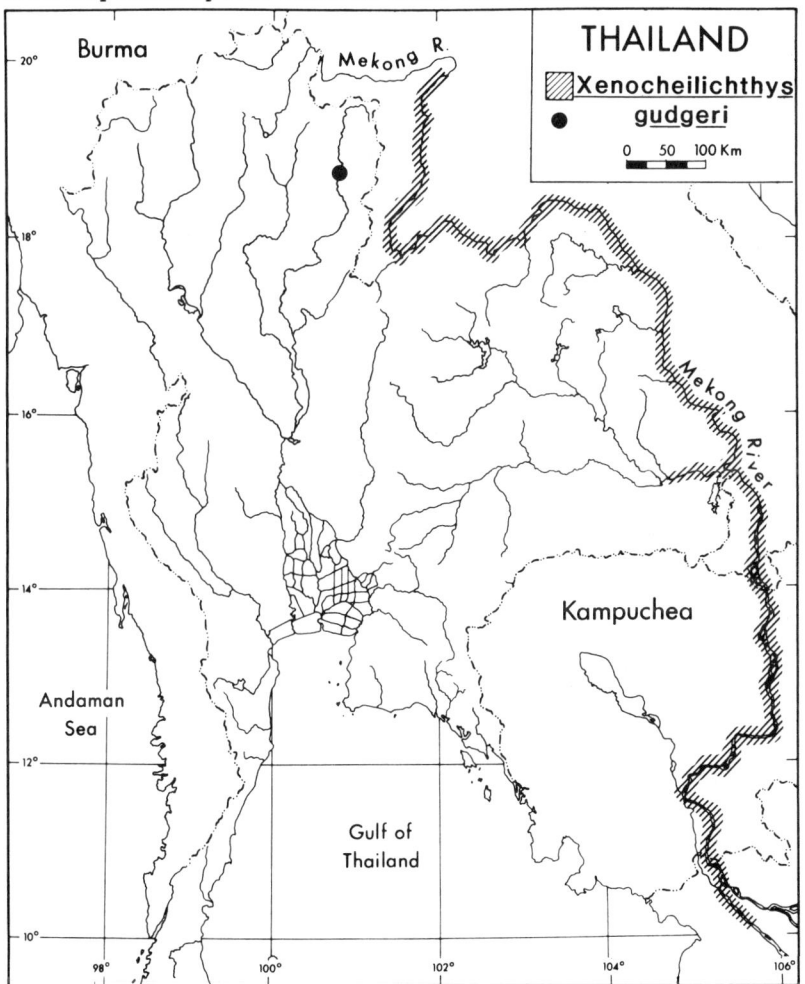

Fig. 25. Distribution of the Backwater Fish (*Xenocheilichthys gudgeri*).

Mukdahan-Nakhon Phanom and in beach seining near Vientiane-Nong Khai (Lagler 1976a).

Distribution and History of Distribution: *X. gudgeri* is known from the upper Nan River, near Nan, Thailand (Smith 1945), from the Mekong River from southern Vietnam upstream to Luang Prabang, Lao PDR, and from the lower Mun River to Ubon Ratchathani (Rainboth et al. 1976; Fig. 25). The species also has been recorded in the Lancang River, Yunnan Province, China (Li 1976).

Geographic Status: Nearly the entire species' range is in Thailand or along its borders.

Habitat Requirements and Habitat Trend: Habitat is the mainstream of large rivers. No other information is available.

Vulnerability of Species and Habitat: The species is vulnerable to the five mainstream dams and navigation channels planned along the Mekong from Sambor to Luang Prabang.

Causes of Threat: *X. gudgeri* is not expected to be able to establish itself in impoundments (Lagler 1976b) and hence may become extinct if the Mekong developments take place.

Responses to Habitat Modification: Unknown.

Demographic Characteristics: Unknown.

Key Behaviors: Unknown.

Conservation Measures Taken: None.

Conservation Measures Proposed: The ability of this species to live in reservoirs should be investigated. Current information indicates that mainstream dams on the Mekong should be avoided to conserve this species.

Catfish
Hemisilurus heterorhynchus **(Bleeker 1853)**
Osteichthyes, Siluriformes, Siluridae

Status: Endangered.

Population Size and Trend: Unknown.

Distribution and History of Distribution: *H. heterorhynchus* is known from Sumatra, Borneo, and the lower Mekong basin. Its continental distribution is in the Mekong River from Pakse, Lao PDR, upstream to Mukdahan, Thailand, and in the Mun River from

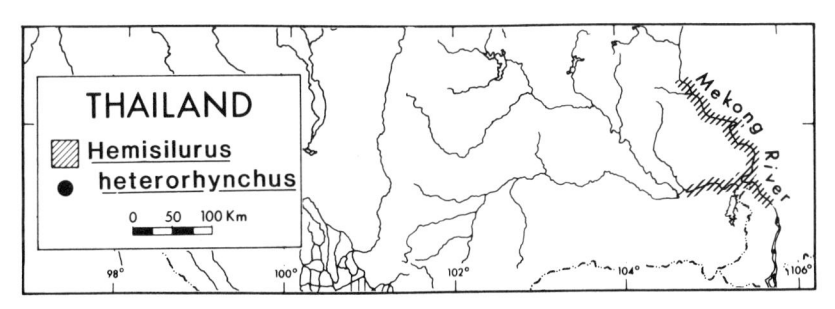

Fig. 26. Distribution of the Catfish (*Hemisilurus heterorhynchus*).

its confluence with the Mekong upstream to Ubon Ratchathani (Fig. 26; Weber and De Beaufort 1965, Rainboth et al. 1976).

Geographic Status: This continental population has a small range and appears to be relictual.

Habitat Requirements and Habitat Trend: Habitat is the mainstream of large rivers. No other information is available.

Vulnerability of Species and Habitat: The species is vulnerable to the series of dams and navigation channels planned along the Mekong.

Causes of Threat: *H. heterorhynchus* is not expected to be able to establish itself in impoundments (Lagler 1976*b*) and hence may become extirpated if the Mekong developments take place. Dams that block migration would halt reproduction.

Responses to Habitat Modification: Unknown.

Demographic Characteristics: Unknown.

Key Behaviors: Unknown. A high proportion of this species in samples during June high water was interpreted by Lagler (1976*a*) as evidence of a migration in progress.

Conservation Measures Taken: None.

Conservation Measures Proposed: A survey is needed to determine the current status of the *H. heterorhynchus* population, and the ability of the species to live in reservoirs should be investigated. Current information indicates that mainstream dams on the Mekong should be avoided to conserve this species.

Pla duk lampan, a walking catfish
Prophagorus nieuhofi (Cuvier and Valenciennes 1840)
Osteichthyes, Siluriformes, Clariidae

Status: Threatened.
Population Size and Trend: Unknown.

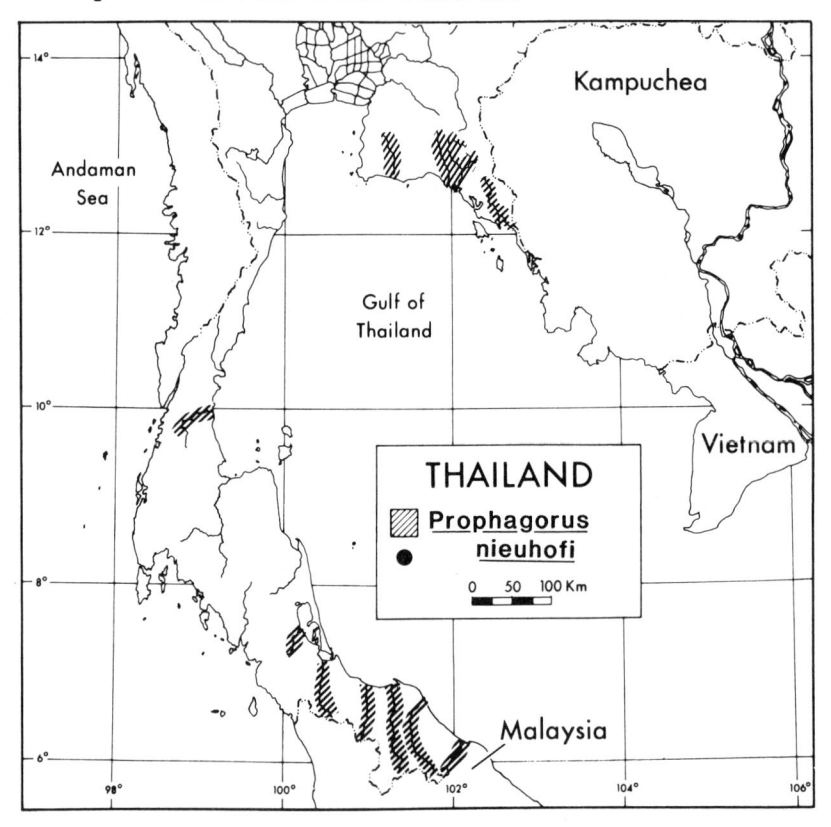

Fig. 27. Distribution of a walking catfish (*Prophagorus nieuhofi*).

Distribution and History of Distribution: *P. nieuhofi* in Thailand is known from very few specimens. The records are from southeastern Thailand, at Nong Khor, near Si Racha, Ban Hup Bon near Si Racha, and from the Trat River near Khao Saming (Smith 1945). Additional records are from Patthalung and from Lang Suan in Chumphon Province (Areeratana 1970). Elsewhere the species is known from the Philippines, Malacca, and many islands in the Indo-Australian Archipelago. Distribution in Thailand (Fig. 27) is in Satun, Narathiwat, Patthalung, and Pattani provinces (Suebsin Sontirat, personal communication).

Geographic Status: The species is peripheral in Thailand.
Habitat Requirements and Habitat Trend: Unknown.
Vulnerability of Species and Habitat: Unknown.
Causes of Threat: Unknown.
Responses to Habitat Modification: Unknown.
Demographic Characteristics: Unknown. Maximum length was reported to Smith (1934) as about 0.5 m.
Key Behaviors: Unknown.
Conservation Measures Taken: None.
Conservation Measures Proposed: A survey is needed to verify the status of *P. nieuhofi* and determine what conservation measures are appropriate. Fish farming methods developed for other Thai walking catfish (Sidthimunka 1972) might be useful in captive propagation of this species.

Pla thepa, Sanitwongse's catfish
Pangasius sanitwongsei **Smith 1931**
Osteichthyes, Siluriformes, Pangasiidae

Status: Endangered.
IUCN (1968, 1979): Threatened.
IUCN Red Data Book (1977): Rare.
USFWS (1980a): Endangered.

Population Size and Trend: Numbers in 1967 were estimated at fewer than 2,000 (IUCN 1977); no recent estimate is available. Based on the trend in the size of harvested fish, Smith (1945) stated that "its numbers appear to be decreasing yearly with the increase in the activity and efficiency of fishing operations."

Distribution and History of Distribution: *P. sanitwongsei* occurs (Fig. 28) in the Chao Phraya River and its tributaries, including the Ping River to above Raheng (Smith 1945). It also occupies the Mekong River from Luang Prabang, Lao PDR, along the Thai-Lao border, through Kampuchea to Vietnam, including the lowest portion of the Mun River, Thailand (Rainboth et al. 1976).

56   *Endangered Animals of Thailand*

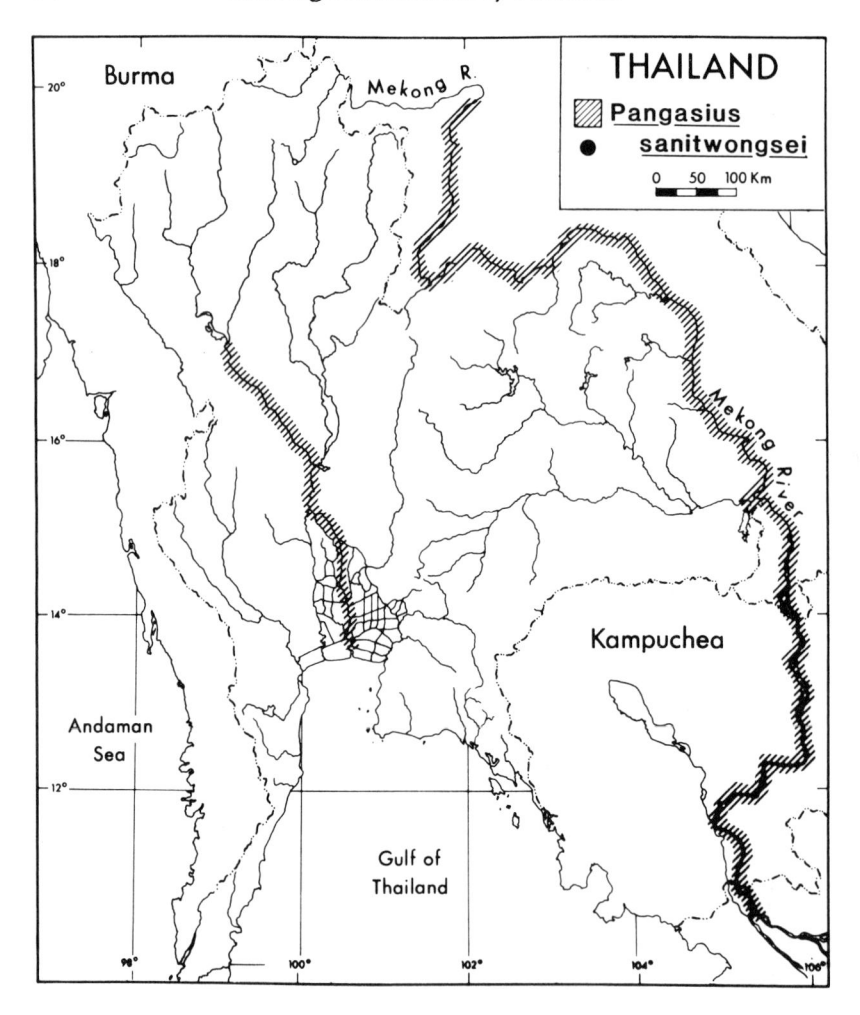

Fig. 28. Distribution of Sanitwongse's Catfish (*Pangasius sanitwongsei*).

Geographic Status: The species is a mainstream, freshwater, riverine fish.

Habitat Requirements and Habitat Trend: These fish prefer deep areas of rivers, with only young individuals occurring short distances up minor tributaries. Individuals in rivers confluent with Bung Boraphet do not enter the swamp during annual floods. During flood stage, the fish stay in deep holes in the rivers (Smith

1945). Spawning habitat has not been described. Diet is not documented but is reputed to include dogs (Smith 1945).

Vulnerability of Species and Habitat: *P. sanitwongsei* is vulnerable to overfishing despite its relatively low quality and excessive fat in its meat. Fishing for this species formerly was constrained by cultural rites, as for *P. gigas* (Davidson 1975). Large portions of riverine habitat would be converted into lentic habitat where reservoirs are constructed. If, as suspected, *P. sanitwongsei* undergoes a spawning migration, construction of dams would prevent reproduction.

Causes of Threat: Loss of this species to impoundment of its habitat has been predicted by Lagler (1976a). Excessive harvest is the primary threat and has been a continual problem since about 1920 (Smith 1931). Capture of individuals 3 m long was relatively common prior to that time, but the largest one seen by Smith was 2.5 m, and most of the fish reaching the Bangkok market were 0.4-0.6 m long (Smith 1945).

Responses to Habitat Modification: Unknown.

Demographic Characteristics: Unknown.

Key Behaviors: Migration to spawning grounds is suspected but not documented (Lagler 1976a).

Conservation Measures Taken: None.

Conservation Measures Proposed: The status of *P. sanitwongsei* appears to warrant prohibiting harvest while research is undertaken on habitat, movements, and population dynamics. This information should lead to a management strategy that would permit harvest on a long-term, sustainable basis. Habitat information would be helpful in determining where riverine fisheries should be avoided in planning reservoirs.

Pla buk, giant catfish
Pangasianodon gigas **Chevey 1930**
Osteichthyes, Siluriformes, Pangasiidae

Status: Endangered.
IUCN Red Data Book (1977): Vulnerable.
CITES (1979): Appendix I.
USFWS (1980a): Endangered.
Population Size and Trend: Population size is unknown, but

several authors indicate a declining trend. Seidenfaden (1923) reported the annual catch for 1890 as 6,000 individuals at Vienchan and 1,000 at Pak Lai, Lao PDR. According to Smith (1945), the annual catch was 40-50 *P. gigas* at a depression in the Mekong (Wang pla buk) at Ban Pha Tang, Nong Khai Province, during the 1930s, whereas in the October-December fishing season of 1967 only 11 individuals were captured there (average length 2.4 m, range 2.0-2.9 m; Pookaswan 1969). At Vientiane, Lao PDR, about 30 *P. gigas* are sold annually, with more at the end of the year than in the spring season (Davidson 1975). At Luang Prabang, Lao PDR, and Ban Xieng Mene, Thailand, the catch has declined from a norm of a dozen per year prior to 1965; three were caught in 1968, one in 1969, two in 1970, one in 1971, and none in 1972-1974 (Davidson 1975). At Ban Houei Sai, Khoueng Houa Khong, Lao PDR, the catch averages between 20-30 *P. gigas* in spring; the harvest was 34 fish in 1973 and 14 in 1974 (1974 average weight 160 kg, range 135-200 kg, Davidson 1975).

Distribution and History of Distribution: This fish occupies the Mekong River and its tributaries, and no changes in distribution are known (Fig. 29). Its range in the Mekong extends from the Vietnam-Kampuchea border through Kampuchea, along the borders of Thailand and Burma, and into Yunnan Province, China. Occupied tributaries include the Tonle River and Tonle Sap (Great Lake) of Kampuchea; the Mun, Songkhram, and Kok rivers of Thailand; the Yangpi River and Erh Hai ("Lake Tali") of China (Smith 1945, Pookaswan 1969, Rainboth et al. 1976). The distribution of young and half-grown fish has not been described, but small individuals have been reported in southern China (by Chinese biologists to Sompote Ukkatawewat, personal communication). The species has not been recorded in the mouth of the Mekong nor in the South China Sea.

Geographic Status: The species is a basin-wide, mainstream, freshwater, riverine fish.

Habitat Requirements and Habitat Trend: The habitat of adults is mainstream waters of large rivers, especially in basins and deep depressions with a gravel or rubble bottom (Smith 1945, Pookaswan 1969). Here the diet consists of algae grazed from stones in the river bed; frequently the digestive tract contains small stones swallowed during grazing (Smith 1945). Spawning habitat is in Erh Hai, China (Davie 1904, in Smith 1945), and in the Mae Nam

Songkhram about 60 km NW of Nakhon Phanom (Lagler 1976b), but has not been described, nor has habitat of young and half-grown *P. gigas*. Habitat trends appear to be minimal, but significant

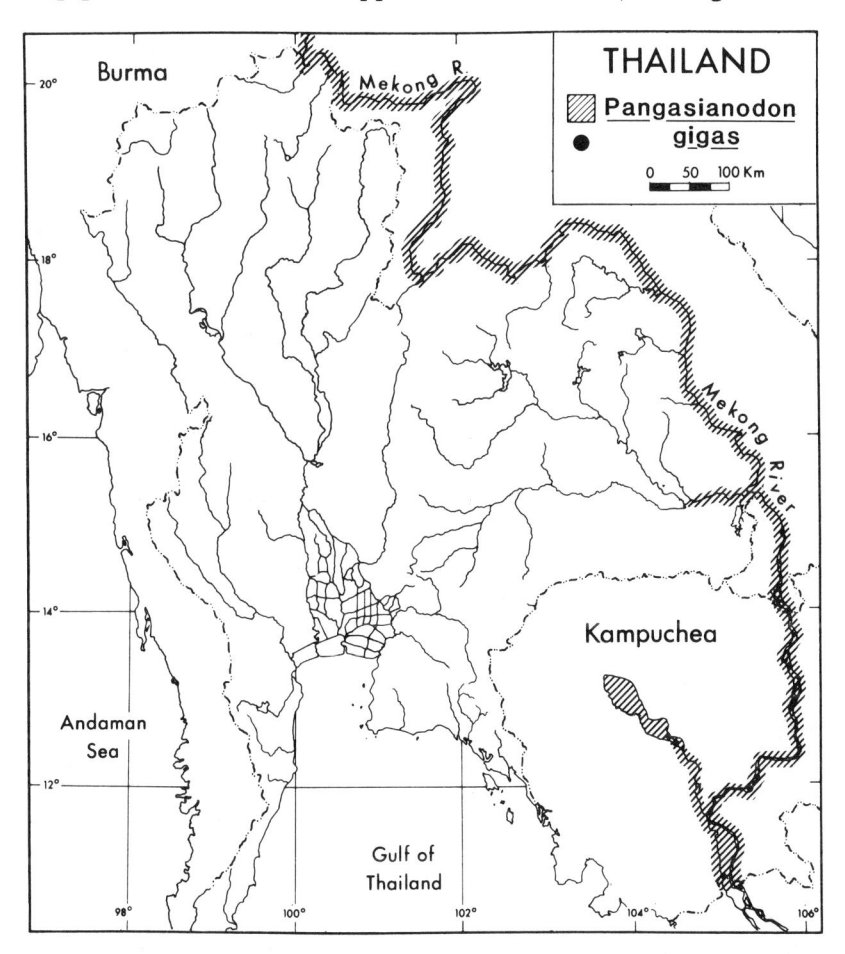

Fig. 29. Distribution of the Giant Catfish (*Pangasianodon gigas*).

reduction of habitat is imminent due to reservoirs planned along the Thai portion of the Mekong and several tributaries.

Vulnerability of Species and Habitat: The species is highly vulnerable to dams that would prevent upstream migration to spawning areas, preventing reproduction by downstream members of the population. *P. gigas* is prized because of its size and high-quality meat, so it also is vulnerable to overfishing, which may have resulted in the observed decline in catch rate. Excessive harvest may have been avoided prior to the mid-1900s by a cultural tradition that synchronized fishing to the post-spawning phase of the reproductive cycle and may have limited the harvest period to three days (Pookaswan 1969; Serene, in Davidson 1975). Now, no restraints on harvest remain in place. Large portions of riverine habitat would be converted into lentic habitat when reservoirs are filled.

Causes of Threat: Loss of this species to impoundment of its habitat has been predicted by Lagler (1976a). The most serious consequence would be inaccessibility of its traditional spawning grounds to some or all of the population. Overharvest is an equally serious though more gradual threat; if the current population trend continues, the species will become extinct. The economics of resource exploitation (Clark 1973) are expected to accelerate the trend.

Responses to Habitat Modification: Unknown.

Demographic Characteristics: Based on vertebral annuli, Pookaswan (1969) estimated the age of a male *P. gigas* (weight 135 kg, length 2.3 m) at 6 years old. He cited a report from a fisherman that a female of equal length contained ovaries weighing 16 kg and millions of eggs each about 5 mm in size. Formerly individuals reached 3 m in length (Smith 1945), making this one of the largest catfish species in the world.

Key Behaviors: Adult *P. gigas* undergo long-distance migration to spawn, reportedly moving from the lower Mekong Basin to spawning habitat in Erh Hai, China (Smith 1945). Presumably such migration also occurs to the reported spawning ground in the Songkhram River. Reports on the timing of migration are not consistent with a synchronous, range-wide migration, and probably the pattern is more complex. According to Smith (1945), the fish travel upstream as floodwater subsides after the rainy season (May-September), reaching Luang Prabang, Lao PDR, by February. Prior to this upstream movement, fish in Kampuchean waters are very fat and hence undesirable as food; by the time they reach Luang Prabang, little fat remains and the sex glands are enlarged. The downstream movement after spawning ceases by June at Luang Prabang (Pavie 1904, in Smith 1945). In contrast, Davidson

(1975) reported that at Ban Houei Sai, Khoueng Houa Khong, Lao PDR (about 275 km upstream from Luang Prabang), the upstream movement occurs during six weeks in late April and May, when the river is just beginning to rise. Females caught at this time are laden with eggs. Davidson also reported two periods of *P. gigas* catch at Vientiane, Lao PDR, one in spring and the other in the last few months of the year. Lagler (1976b) summarized fish migration in the middle Mekong as follows: a few species move upstream in February and March, as water level approaches the annual minimum; most species migrate upstream in late April, May, and June, as water level rises; and downstream migration occurs from September through November, as annual floodwater begins to recede.

Conservation Measures Taken: Efforts are underway in Thailand to breed this species aquaculturally (Lagler 1976b).

Conservation Measures Proposed: By proceeding with tributary reservoirs for necessary hydroelectric power while halting reservoirs on the Mekong, the central core of the adult habitat and migratory pathway of *P. gigas* (and of a suite of other endangered species) would be left intact. Fishing should be regulated with the objective of reversing the population decline by protecting the breeding stock. Appropriate limits would be to establish a legal minimum size of fish that can be removed from the water and to close the season during the period that fish are moving upstream to spawn. A major advantage of restoring this and other fishery stocks to their former level is that populations harvested at a sustainable level of yield will supply the greatest possible amount of food to humans over the long term. Because more information is needed to assure the success of a management program, harvests need to be documented on a regular, continuing basis. To monitor size and age classes, each fish harvested should be measured and a vertebra and pectoral spine from each should be collected and analyzed. Research on the Songkhram River breeding site and a cooperative research program with the Peoples' Republic of China at Erh Hai and confluent waters would produce information on reproductive biology and spawning habitat; tagging of young for recapture during harvest would yield data on survival and movements.

Pla soua taw, triple tails
Datnioides microlepis Bleeker 1853
Osteichthyes, Perciformes, Lobotidae

Status: Endangered.

Population Size and Trend: Apparently once abundant, *D. microlepis* has been overharvested for many decades (Smith 1945).

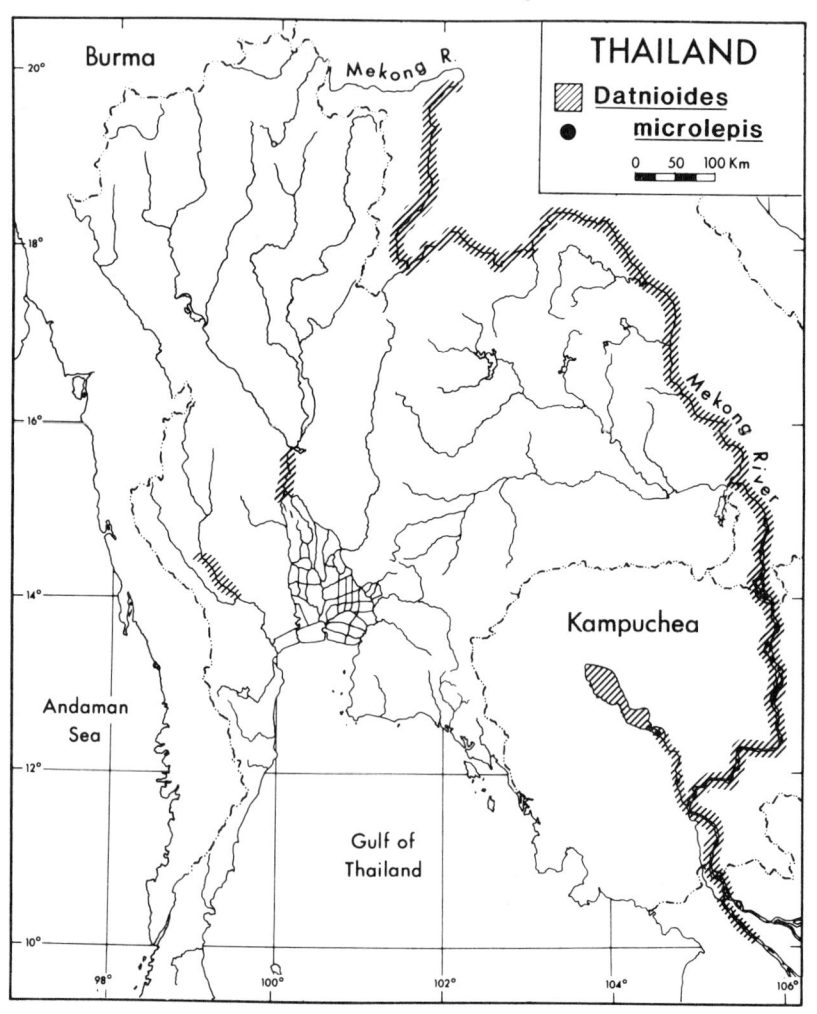

Fig. 30. Distribution of the Triple Tails (*Datnioides microlepis*).

The species is nearly extirpated from Thailand (Sompote Ukkatawewat, personal communication).

Distribution and History of Distribution: This species occurs in Thailand, Lao PDR, Kampuchea, northern Vietnam, Borneo, and Sumatra. Thai distribution is in the upper Chao Phraya and lower Mekong basins and the Mae Klong River. Historical range (Fig. 30) included the Chao Phraya, Pa Sak, and Nan rivers and Bung Boraphet. In the Mekong it occurred from southern Vietnam and Tonle Sap to Luang Prabang, Lao PDR, including lower reaches of the Nam Ngum, Lao PDR, and the Mun River, Thailand (Smith 1945, Rainboth et al. 1976, Ukkatawewat 1979). The last sizable populations were reported along the Mekong and Mun in Nakhon Phanom Province and Ubon Ratchathani (Ukkatawewat 1979). In 1975, Lagler (1976a) captured 33 juvenile individuals with a total weight of 6 g in 21 trawl collections in the Khemmarat-Mukdahan-Nakhon Phanom section of the Mekong.

Geographic Status: This is a basin-wide, freshwater, riverine and lake-dwelling fish.

Habitat Requirements and Habitat Trend: Unknown. Spawning has been reported in Bung Boraphet. The species is adaptable enough to tolerate aquarium life (Smith 1945). Young fish feed on zooplankton, and adult fish eat small shrimps, fish fry, and small fish (Ukkatawewat 1979).

Vulnerability of Species and Habitat: *D. microlepis* is highly vulnerable to overharvesting, because of very high demand for small fish for the aquarium trade and for large fish as food. In some areas, this is considered the best food fish available (Smith 1945, Ukkatawewat 1979). Prices are typically U.S. $5/kg (Sompote Ukkatawewat, personal communication).

Causes of Threat: The threat to this species is harvest above sustainable levels.

Responses to Habitat Modification: Mostly unknown. When Bung Boraphet was altered from a seasonal swamp to a permanent lake, the population of *D. microlepis* also became permanent instead of temporary. This suggests that the species could live in reservoirs.

Demographic Characteristics: Natality depends on the size of the female. Typical numbers of eggs are 30,000 for a 230 g fish and 720,000 for a 3.6 kg fish. The eggs are very small (1.0-1.2 mm) and float on the water surface in oily clumps. Hatching occurs in 17 hours at 29° C (Ukkatawewat 1979).

Key Behaviors: Spawning occurs from June to August (Ukkatawewat 1979).

Conservation Measures Taken: None.

Conservation Measures Proposed: Harvest of *D. microlepis* should be prohibited while a field survey is undertaken to locate any surviving populations. The high value of this renewable resource could be restored by research on captive propagation and habitat requirements. A reintroduction program should be accompanied by a closed season and research to determine what harvest level would provide the maximum sustained yield.

Chapter 5

Amphibians and Reptiles

Kra-taang nam, ma nam, crocodile salamander
Tylototriton verrucosus **Anderson 1871**
Amphibia, Caudata, Salamandridae

Status: Threatened.
IUCN (1968): Threatened.

Population Size and Trend: The total population size is unknown. This species is locally common around the town of Taunggyi in Burma (Gyi 1969) and is regularly found at two sites in northern Thailand.

Distribution and History of Distribution: In Thailand the crocodile salamander has been found on Doi Inthanon (2,000 m), Doi Chiang Dao (1,500-1,800 m), Doi Suthep (1,350 m), Doi Pui, Doi Ang-Khang, Doi Buang-ha, and Phu Luang in Chiang Mai and Loei provinces (Fig. 31). It is also known from the Kachin Hills (Northern Burma) and Taunggyi (1436 m, in the Southern Shan State) in Burma, western Yunnan in China, the Lao PDR, and west as far as Sikkim. *Tylototriton* was evidently a more widespread genus in the past. Fossils are known from the Miocene of Switzerland (Anderson 1871, Schmidt 1927, Liu 1950, Noble 1954, Taylor 1962, Soderburg 1967, Gyi 1969, Gressitt 1970, Cheke 1973, Wongratana 1984).

Geographic Status: The Thai population is peripheral, lying at the southern limits of the species' range.

Habitat Requirements and Habitat Trend: This animal is found from about 1,350-1,800 m. The adults are terrestrial, taking shelter during the day under moist, moss-covered rocks, logs, and debris. The aquatic larvae have been found in rocky pools, streams, inundated sand pits, quarries, ponds above and below dams, floodwater, and temporary ponds. The one requirement seems to be that the water be crystal clear. In Burma breeding ponds were noted to

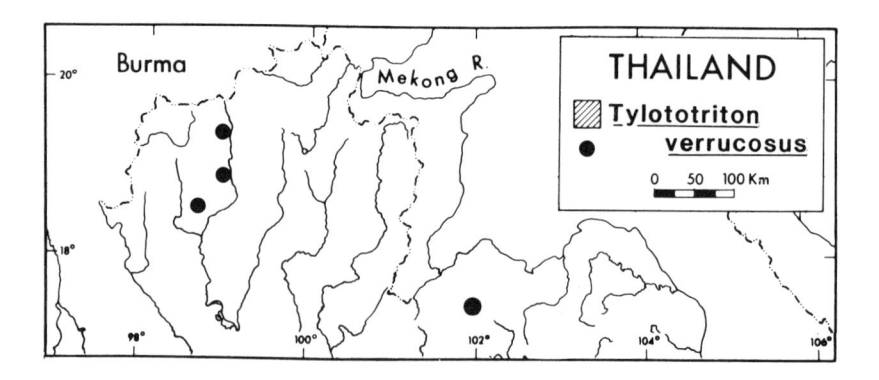

Fig. 31. Distribution of the Crocodile Salamander (*Tylototriton verrucosus*).

range in temperature from 15-21° C. These ponds were rich in aquatic plants, notably algae such as *Spirogyra* and *Chara*. Also breeding in the same ponds were molluscs, aquatic larvae of several insect orders (mayflies, dragonflies, and beetles), and the carnivorous serpent-head fishes *Ophiocephalus gachua* and *O. punctatus*. The latter two are known predators on *Tylototriton*. Adults are omnivorous and even cannibalistic at times. The diet includes algae, worms, and a wide array of insects. The aquatic larvae of mosquitoes are a preferred food item. Captives readily eat shrimp, rice, and dragonflies. Anglers in Burma frequently capture these newts on hooks baited with worms and pieces of *Tylototriton* (Taylor 1962, Gyi 1969).

Vulnerability of Species and Habitat: The clear waters this species needs for reproduction are easily polluted by human activities. During synchronous local migrations many adults in Burma are killed by automobiles and human trampling. Many people regard this animal as an omen of bad fortune and maliciously destroy it on sight (Gyi 1969). It is becoming increasingly attractive to collectors of biological specimens.

Causes of Threat: In Burma certain superstitious people believe that "the water lizard," as they call *T. verrucosus*, portends ill luck. They kill it at every opportunity. Of the more than 40 individuals Gyi (1969) tagged and released on the campus of Taunggyi College, 10 were found trampled. A new threat is developing in the form of trade in biological specimens. Gyi advocates the use of this species in zoological teaching laboratories in Southeast Asia to alleviate the expense of importing *Salamandra* and *Necturus* from Europe and the United States. Because of its abilities to regenerate lost limbs (Nakamura et al. 1978, for example), it is in growing demand among biomedical researchers. Students of salamander evolution have obtained viable intergeneric hybrids by crossing *T. verrucosus* and its relative, *Pleurodeles waltii* (Ferrier et al. 1971, Ferrier and Beetschen 1973), opening up new avenues of research and increasing the demand for the species. Additionally, the animal is coveted by the pet trade, zoos, and museums. During a study period of 31 March to 6 June 1975, 360 newts were declared for export at Bangkok's Don Muang Airport (Duplaix and King 1975). The total trade volume during that period was no doubt greater.

Responses to Habitat Modification: Unknown.

Demographic Characteristics: The eggs are some 6-10 mm in diameter when deposited. The young are about 11 mm long upon emerging and grow to 52 mm or more before they lose their gills and transform into the adult form at the end of the wet season. Adults grow to a snout-vent length of approximately 70 mm. A captive specimen in the Cincinnati Zoo lived over 5 years (Taylor 1962, Gyi 1969, Bowler 1977).

Key Behaviors: Early in the summer months adults make local migrations to breeding ponds, where they breed and spawn throughout the rainy season. The mating behavior has been observed in captivity and in the wild and is described by Noble (1954): "The male creeps up under the female and seizes her front legs from behind, with his front legs. The 'piggy-back ride' which follows finally results in the emission of the spermatophore by the male and its being secured by the female." Late in the wet season many young are lost because of drying of breeding ponds. Early in the dry season adults and young of the year make local migrations to more permanent bodies of water. Adults come to the surface for air, but they can remain motionless underwater for extended periods. Producing turbulence by stirring the water will bring the adults to the surface, dazed. People use this method to capture them. They are sluggish and easily captured when the water is cold (Noble 1954, Taylor 1962, Gyi 1969).

Conservation Measures Taken: In Thailand the known areas of occurrence of crocodile salamanders are protected in Doi Inthanon National Park, Doi Suthep-Pui National Park, Doi Chiang Dao Wildlife Sanctuary, and Phu Luang Wildlife Sanctuary. There are no specific Thai laws protecting this animal.

Conservation Measures Proposed: Biologists working in the mountains of northern Thailand should look for this species to determine its true range. Protection of *Tylototriton* in national parks and wildlife sanctuaries should be maintained. IUCN (1979) recommended that the habitat of this species in Thailand be identified and brought under protection. We applaud the efforts of Dr. Khin Mg Gyi to increase our knowledge of this species and to develop it as a dissection animal, removing the need to import expensive salamanders from Europe and the United States. However, we caution zoologists in Southeast Asia against overexploitation for scientific teaching purposes. Since this newt is known to occur only in a few, isolated places, harvest should not exceed sustainable yield, and population studies will be needed to determine acceptable harvest levels. Collection and export should be monitored and controlled. To the extent possible, educators should stress the natural role of these unique amphibians (as in eating mosquito larvae) and discourage their destruction because of superstitious beliefs.

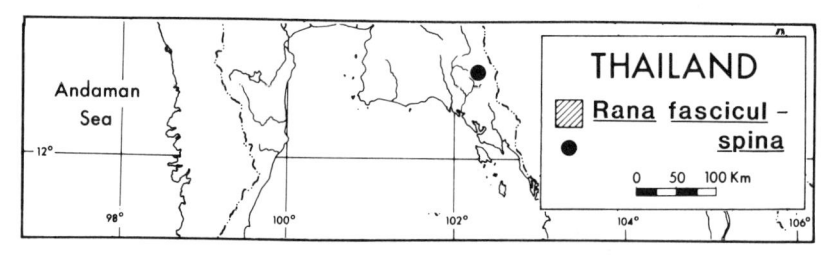

Fig. 32. Distribution of the Spine-breasted Giant Frog (*Rana fasciculispina*).

Spine-breasted giant frog
Rana fasciculispina **Inger 1970**
Amphibia, Anura, Ranidae

Status: Threatened.
IUCN (1979): Threatened.
Population Size and Trend: Unknown.
Distribution and History of Distribution: This species was discovered in 1961 by Mr. Boonak at Khao Soi Dao in Chanthaburi Province (Fig. 32). Additional populations may occur in Thailand and Lao PDR in mountain streams (Inger 1970) and in Kampuchea.

Although IUCN (1979) classified this animal as threatened, Inger (personal communication) writes that while it is rare in collections it "is apparently reasonably abundant . . . along forested mountain streams in southeastern Thailand . . . [and] not . . . threatened any more than a large array of forest species." This species is separated from its closest living relative, *R. verrucosina* at Bach Ma, Vietnam, by some 700 km (Inger 1970).

Geographic Status: *R. fasciculispina*, as far as is currently known, is endemic to Thailand.

Habitat Requirements and Habitat Trend: This species is found in swift, forested mountain streams (Inger 1970, personal communication). Montane forest is currently being lost at an alarming rate over much of Thailand.

Vulnerability of Species and Habitat: The large size of *R. fasciculispina* makes it quite conspicuous to man. The montane streams it requires are small, enabling people to decimate populations.

Causes of Threat: These giant frogs are actively sought as food at Khao Soi Dao, where villagers collect them by light at night (W. Brockelman, personal communication).

Responses to Habitat Modification: Unknown.

Demographic Characteristics: The paratype, an adult female collected in July, contained a few enlarged, unpigmented ova. Adults reach a snout-vent length of about 105 mm.

Key Behaviors: This frog apparently lays its eggs under large rocks in swift streams (Inger 1970).

Conservation Measures Taken: Khao Soi Dao Wildlife Sanctuary protects essential habitat for this species.

Conservation Measures Proposed: The protection of this animal in Khao Soi Dao should be enforced by patrolling the forest. Biologists studying montane streams in Thailand should look for this species to help determine its true range. In areas where harvest by man appears to threaten it, specific management plans should be instituted.

Tao pulu, tao pulu neua, Chinese big-headed turtle
Platysternon megacephalum **Gray 1831**
Reptilia, Testudines, Platysternidae

Status: Threatened.
IUCN (1968): Threatened.

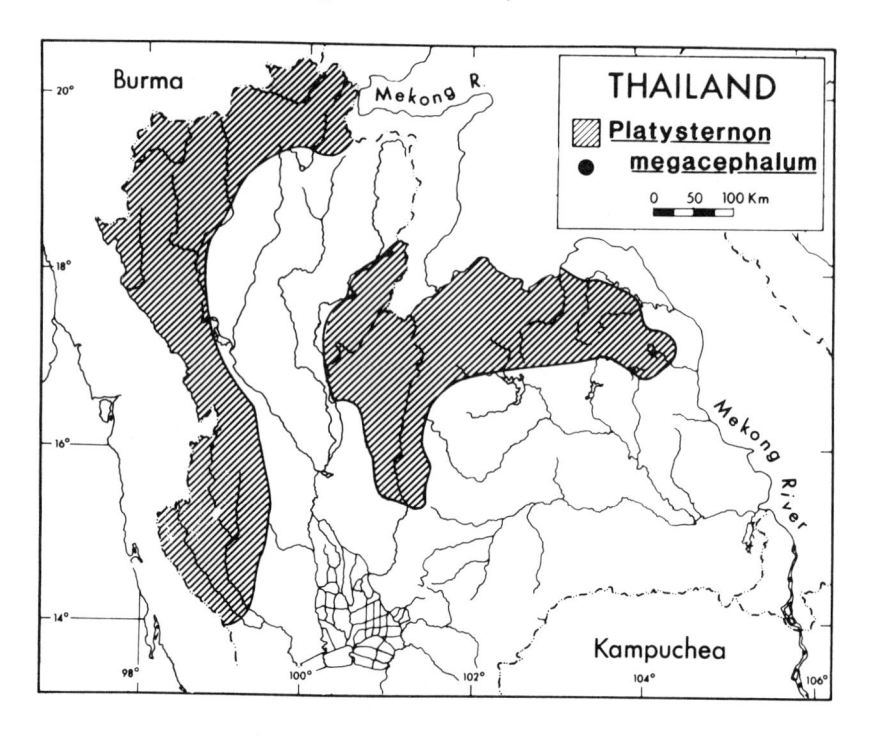

Fig. 33. Distribution of the Chinese Big-headed Turtle (*Platysternon megacephalum*).

WARPA (1980): Protected-1.

Population Size and Trend: The total population size of this widespread turtle is unknown. There has been a recent decline. The species is now believed to be threatened with extinction (IUCN 1968).

Distribution and History of Distribution: This species is widely distributed along streams in the mountains of northern Thailand (Fig. 33). Wirot (1979) believes that the population in Loei, Phetchabun, and Sakon Nakhon provinces is a separate subspecies (*P. m. peguense*) from the population in northwest Thailand (*P. m. megacephalum*). The species is also known from southern China, Lao PDR, Burma, Taiwan, Vietnam, Hong Kong, and Hainan (Smith 1931, Taylor and Elbel 1958, Taylor 1970, Wirot 1979).

Geographic Status: P. megacephalum is widespread in the mountains of Southeast Asia and southern China. The Thai population is peripheral, lying at the southern limits of the species' overall range.

Habitat Requirements and Habitat Trend: This carnivorous, semiaquatic turtle prefers remote mountain streams. It eats primarily small fish, molluscs, shrimp, and crabs, but is known to eat vegetation on occasion (Smith 1931, Wirot 1979). Unlike most turtles, it readily climbs trees, shrubs, and rocks near streams in search of food and basking sites.

Vulnerability of Species and Habitat: The unusual morphology of this species, with its large head, long neck, relatively flat carapace, and long, clawed, nonretractile limbs adapted for climbing make it an attractive acquisition for aquarists and scientific collectors. Moreover, among the people of Southeast Asia its flesh is thought to impart the same aphrodisiac properties as rhino horn, so it is collected for "medicine." Large *Platysternon* cost over US $30 on the Hong Kong market (H. W. Campbell, personal communication). The flesh is eaten in Thailand.

Causes of Threat: The observed decline is probably due primarily to collecting by humans. The destruction of montane forest habitat may have compounded the problem.

Responses to Habitat Modification: Unknown.

Demographic Characteristics: The breeding rate in the wild is unknown. The average clutch size is small, numbering two to four eggs (Wirot 1979). Adults grow to about 20 cm (carapace length) and weigh about 0.5 kg (Wirot 1979).

Key Behaviors: This species is very aggressive. With its long neck and large, powerful mouth it can inflict painful bites on man. It has well developed scent glands in the axillary and anal areas. These are probably used in social behavior, but their exact function is unknown. Its climbing behavior probably provides access to food and basking sites that otherwise would be unavailable to it. Captives at the zoo in Chiang Mai often escape by climbing out of high wire enclosures (Smith 1931, Taylor 1970, Wirot 1979).

Conservation Measures Taken: Many of the National Parks and Wildlife Sanctuaries in northern Thailand protect suitable habitat for *P. megacephalum*. Specimens are known from Phu Kradeung (1525 m) in Loei province, an area included in Phu Kradeung National Park. *P. megacephalum* is also known from Sai Yok in Kanchanaburi province, where the threatened bat *Craseonycteris thonglongyai* lives. Thai law (WARPA 1980) prohibits killing and regulates trade of this turtle.

Conservation Measures Proposed: All of the montane National Parks and Wildlife Sanctuaries within the species' range in Thailand should be surveyed to determine the status of *P. megacephalum* in each. In areas where it is found, conservation authorities should be aware of its presence and its protection should be maintained. Where the species occurs, stream habitats should be preserved with intact bank vegetation. Trade in this species should be monitored and controlled. The public should be educated that there is no scientific basis for the claim that *Platysternon* products are aphrodisiacs.

**Tao kra arn, tao charn, tuntong,
saltwater terrapin, river terrapin**
Batagur baska **(Gray 1831)**
Reptilia, Testudines, Emydidae

Status: Endangered.
IUCN (1968): Threatened.
IUCN Red Data Book (1978): Endangered.
CITES (1979): Appendix I.
IUCN (1979): Threatened.
USFWS (1980a): Endangered.
WARPA (1980): Protected-1.

Population Size and Trend: The species has declined throughout its range. The population in Burma was thought to be near extinction in 1911 (Maxwell 1911). The largest remaining population rangewide, along the Perak River, Malaysia, has declined from 5,700-8,100 to 400-1,200 nesting females from about 1940 to 1976 (E. O. Moll, personal communication). The pre-1940 egg production of 375,000-525,000 eggs has dropped to 20,000-30,000 (Khan 1964, Siow and Moll 1981). The species is in immediate danger of becoming extirpated from Thailand (Wirot 1979). A reward posted for live terrapins at Thale Luang in 1979 yielded only 8 small animals (our observations), showing that the population in that heavily fished lake is nearly gone.

Distribution and History of Distribution: *B. baska* ranges from Bengal in India through Burma, Thailand, and Malaysia to Sumatra. They were once quite abundant in India. The only large nesting colony that remains is in the Perak River of Malaysia. In Thailand *B. baska* is known from populations in Thale Sap and Thale Luang near Patthalung, from Ranote District in Songkhla Province, and from the mouths of rivers in Ranong Province (Fig. 34). Wirot (1979) considers the latter population to represent a discrete subspecies, *B. b. ranongensis* (Smith 1931, Balasingam and Khan 1969, Taylor 1970, IUCN Red Data Book 1978, Wirot 1979, E. O. Moll personal communication). The population at Thale Luang nests on three short beaches on the western shore, the largest being near Pak Payoon.

Geographic Status: The Thai population is centrally located in the species' overall range.

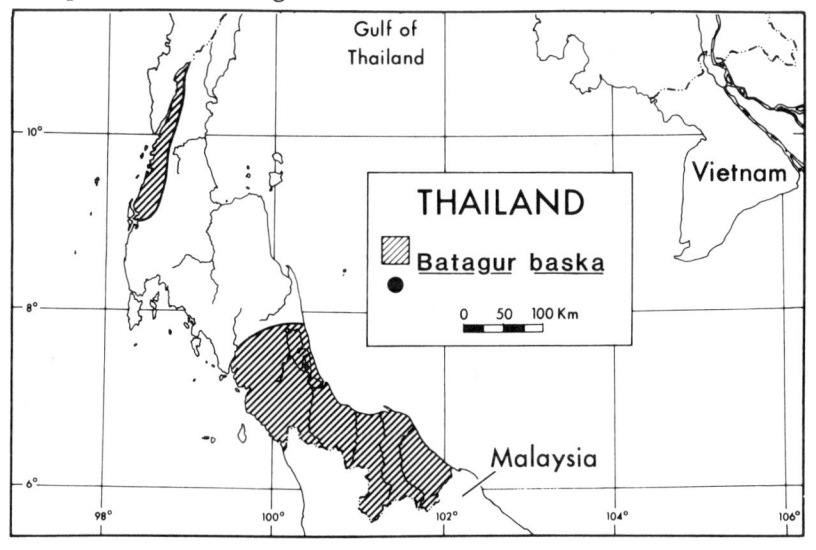

Fig. 34. Distribution of the Saltwater or River Terrapin (*Batagur baska*).

Habitat Requirements and Habitat Trend: Most *Batagur* populations live in the brackish water of estuaries and tidal rivers. A few occupy freshwater lakes or freshwater portions of rivers. For nesting, the species requires sand beaches or islands that remain above water after monsoon floods recede. In the Perak River, Malaysia, where no suitable nesting habitat occurs near the estuary, females migrate 80-100 km upstream to nest (E. O. Moll, personal communication). The major food is riverbank vegetation. Stems, leaves, and fruits are eaten, but the dominant item in the diet is fruit of *Sonneratia* mangroves; fish, molluscs, and crustaceans provide occasional dietary supplements (Moll 1978). However, young *Batagur* prefer fish as food (Sawat Boonthai). Adults move upriver as far as 13 km on the incoming tide to forage along the banks of tributaries, going back downstream with the ebb tide (Moll 1978). No clear habitat trend is evident, but E. O. Moll (personal communication) has noted habitat degradation from silt deposited from upstream mining and channel dredging, loss of mangrove vegetation, beach erosion, and dams and barrages that prevent use of essential terrapin habitat.

Vulnerability of Species and Habitat: Because *Batagur* congregate at a few traditional nesting sites and announce their arrival by sounds made while compacting the sand over the nests, females are vulnerable to harvest just when they should be protected. Their estuarine habitat is highly vulnerable to local and offsite impacts, such as clearing of mangroves and introduction of silt and pesticides upstream.

Cause of Threat: The precarious status of *Batagur* is a direct result of overharvest of eggs and meat without regard for the limits of this self-renewing resource. The eggs are considered to taste better than those of sea turtles and to have aphrodisiac properties. They sell for 2-3 times the price of poultry or sea turtle eggs (E. O. Moll, personal communication). *Batagur* populations on the verge of extirpation are still heavily exploited.

Responses to Habitat Modification: Unknown.

Demographic Characteristics: Females become sexually mature when they reach a carapace length of 430 mm. Clutches range from 5 to 38 eggs, averaging 26 (E. O. Moll, personal communication). In the Perak River and in Thailand breeding occurs from November to early March. Over a 6-week period a female is reputed to lay 3 clutches of eggs (Maxwell 1911), which would total 50-90 eggs. The young hatch in 71-84 days and emerge from the sand about 88 days after egg-laying (E. O. Moll, personal communication). Natural mortality from the time eggs are laid until hatchlings enter the water may be on the order of 90 percent. By contrast, hatching success in the Game Department hatchery in Malaysia has ranged from 13 to 76 percent (Balasingam and Khan 1969, E. O. Moll personal communication).

Key Behaviors: At the beginning of the nesting season, *Batagur* congregate in groups that originally numbered thousands of individuals. At night the females dig holes about 0.6 m deep in sand to lay their eggs. After the eggs are covered with sand, the terrapins repeatedly drop their 20-kg shells on the surface to compact the sand; the resulting drumming sound from a nesting group travels far along the coast. Females typically move a short distance from the nest and dig a false nest that may confuse nest predators. Terrapins on land are difficult to approach without alarming them (Moll 1978).

Conservation Measures Taken: Because of foresighted effort to preserve the last individuals of the *Batagur* population at Thale Luang, 12 adults and 6 young are in captivity at the Brackish Water Fisheries Research Station at Songkhla (1980, our observation). Facilities in which these could breed are not available. The Game Department and state governments in Malaysia conduct research and operate several hatcheries that ensure recruitment of hatchlings into several populations (E. O. Moll, personal communication). Thai law (WARPA 1980) prohibits killing and regulates trade of this species.

Conservation Measures Proposed: The habitat of the remaining Thai populations needs to be identified and portions of it should be protected (IUCN 1979). The entire turtle egg industry in Southeast Asia needs to be reorganized with due attention to sustained yield (IUCN Red Data Book 1978). If properly managed, *B. baska* could constitute a valuable renewable resource of very palatable animal food for Thailand. E. O. Moll (personal communication) estimated that commerce in eggs of the depleted *Batagur* population at the Perak River, Malaysia, now is US $2,500 per year and could reach 10-15 times that amount if the population could achieve its former abundance. The captive animals at Songkhla represent an immediate opportunity for the Thailand Fisheries Department to begin a hatchery program. Considering the extremely precarious status of the Thale Luang population, the first priority there should be to captive-rear most eggs laid in the wild and to release the hatchlings each year.

Tao chak, spiny terrapin
Heosemys (Geoemyda) spinosa Bell in Gray 1830
Reptilia, Testudines, Emydidae

Status: Threatened.

Population Size and Trend: Total numbers of *H. spinosa* are unknown. Wirot (1979) declared it to be in danger of becoming extinct.

Distribution and History of Distribution: The spiny terrapin is known definitely from Chumphon, Ranong, Surat Thani, and Nakhon Si Thammarat provinces, but probably occurs throughout the peninsula south of the Isthmus of Kra (Fig. 35). It is also known from Burma, Malaysia, Borneo, and Sumatra (Smith 1931, Taylor 1970, Wirot 1979).

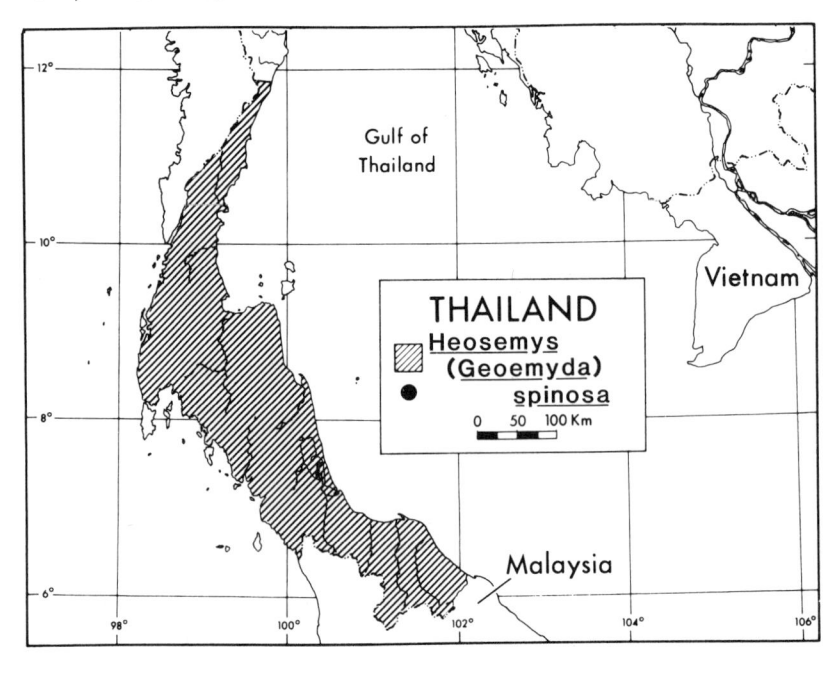

Fig. 35. Distribution of the Spiny Terrapin (*Heosemys spinosa*).

Geographic Status: The Thai population is peripheral, lying at the northern limits of the species' distribution.

Habitat Requirements and Habitat Trend: This species is

terrestrial. It feeds on primarily on plants, such as aquatic plants and bamboo, but will also consume crabs, small frogs, molluscs, shrimp, and worms. It prefers humid, shaded areas and takes cover in the leaf litter and grass clumps (Taylor 1970, Wirot 1979, E. O. Moll, personal communication).

Vulnerability of Species and Habitat: This is a sluggish species that forages in the daytime, making it conspicuous to man. The montane streams it requires are easily impacted by deforestation and erosion produced by agriculture and mining. Leaf litter and grasses, which *H. spinosa* uses for cover, are vulnerable to fire.

Causes of Threat: Unknown.

Responses to Habitat Modification: Unknown.

Demographic Characteristics: Unknown. This species reaches a size of about 225 mm and averages about 0.5 kg in mass (Taylor 1970, Wirot 1979).

Key Behaviors: With suitable shelter *H. sinosa* remains motionless for extended periods between foraging bouts. This probably alleviates some predation pressure.

Conservation Measures Taken: None.

Conservation Measures Proposed: The locations of spiny terrapin populations need to be identified so that forestry and watershed management plans can consider the needs of this species. The effects of different burning regimes on *H. spinosa* ground cover need to be considered, as do the effects of other habitat alterations. The unusual spiny shell of this terrapin could potentially make it vulnerable to the live animal trade, and it should be looked for in shipments of reptiles. If it is overexploited by hunting, measures should be instituted to conserve it on a sustained-yield basis.

Tao hok luang, six-legged tortoise, yellow giant tortoise, Chinese land tortoise
Testudo (Geochelone) emys
Schlegel and Muller in Temminck 1844
Reptilia, Testudines, Testudinidae

Status: Threatened.
IUCN (1968): Threatened.
CITES (1979): Appendix II.

Population Size and Trend: The total population size is

unknown. Once common and widely distributed in peninsular Thailand, these tortoises "are now becoming rare" (Taylor 1970).

Distribution and History of Distribution: In Thailand this form is known definitely from Nakhon Si Thammarat and Ranong provinces, but probably it occurs throughout the peninsula in montane habitat (Fig. 36). It is also known from India (Assam), Burma, Malaysia, Sumatra, and some smaller islands of the Indo-Australian Archipelago (Smith 1931, Taylor 1970, Wirot 1979). Smith (1931) believed that *T. emys* purchased in markets in Saigon and Canton and one captured at the mouth of the Yang-Tse Kiang were human imports.

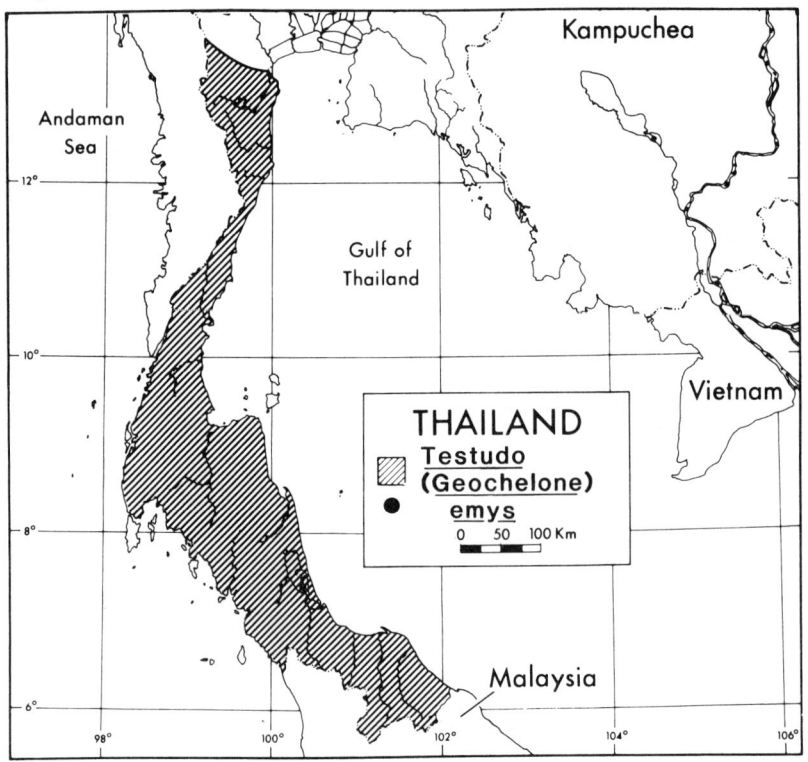

Fig. 36. Distribution of the Six-legged Tortoise (*Testudo emys*).

Geographic Status: The Thai population is centrally located in the species' overall range.

Habitat Requirements and Habitat Trend: This species prefers hill and mountain country. Unlike most members of the Testudinidae, it is fond of water. It is primarily herbivorous, eating aquatic vegetation and bamboo, but it also will eat worms, shrimp, crabs, molluscs, and small frogs (Smith 1931, Taylor 1970, Wirot 1979).

Vulnerability of Species and Habitat: *T. emys* is the largest Asiatic *Testudo*, averaging some 31 kg. Its flesh is eaten throughout its range in Thailand. The slow, plodding gait coupled with its large size makes *T. emys* quite visible and vulnerable to human hunters. Small individuals sell for US $6 in the Bangkok weekend market (our observation). Because the remote country it occupies is now being rapidly settled by humans, harvest rate and extent are increasing. Habitat disturbance brought on by human settlement also may be an important problem (Smith 1931, Taylor 1970, Wirot 1979).

Causes of Threat: Hunting for human food has apparently decimated this large tortoise. The effects of the extensive human settlement of upland areas in the past several decades are probably great but are unknown. Over 1,600 live *T. emys* were exported from Thailand to the United States in 1978 (Mack 1977). This number dropped to 27 in 1980 (TRAFFIC 1981).

Responses to Habitat Modification: Unknown.

Demographic Characteristics: The breeding rate of *T. emys* in the wild is apparently unknown. Wirot (1979) gave the average clutch size as 5-8 eggs. Adults of this large species are known to have reached a carapace length of 470 mm (Taylor 1970).

Key Behaviors: Unknown.

Conservation Measures Taken: Thai law (WARPA 1980) protects this species from killing and trade.

Conservation Measures Proposed: Effective regulation is needed to prevent extirpation by overexploitation (IUCN 1968). Relevant habitat must be identified and protected (IUCN 1979). Research on basic biology is needed to help conserve the Thai population of this species and to manage it as a renewable source of human food.

Families Cheloniidae and Dermochelyidae--The Sea Turtles
Introductory Comments

The Exploitation of Sea Turtles by Man

Five species of sea turtles are known from Thai waters--the leatherback, *Dermochelys coriacea*; the green turtle, *Chelonia mydas*; the olive or Pacific ridley, *Lepidochelys olivacea*; the hawksbill, *Eretmochelys imbricata*; and the loggerhead, *Caretta caretta*. Although widespread, all five are endangered by overexploitation and habitat modification by man. Each deserves the ongoing attention of conservation authorities. These turtles formed an important part of the subsistence of many indigenous peoples, including in Thailand the Sea Gypsies (in Thai, Chow Lay) of the tribes Moklen, Urak Lawoi', and Moken (Polunin 1975, Polunin and Sumertha Nuitja 1979). All five species are actively hunted for their eggs, meat, and shell in Thailand (Lekagul 1977). The current production of sea turtle products in Thailand is high (Polunin and Sumertha Nuitja 1979).

Though all five species considered here are strictly protected under Appendix I of CITES (1979), many Convention nations are still actively involved in their trade. The United States was once a leading importer of sea turtle products, but a 1978 law prohibited all imports of sea turtle products (Mack et al. 1979).

Thailand is among the world's leading exporters of raw tortoiseshell, mainly a product of the hawksbill. ("Tortoise-shell" is a misnomer, for sea turtles are not tortoises.) Shell production is certainly higher than it used to be (Polunin and Sumertha Nuitja 1979). Historically tortoise-shell was an important trade item in the region. The Chinese have traded in it for at least 2,000 years. It is made into jewelry and utensils. Whole shells are sometimes used as wall ornaments. Some importing countries pay more for hawksbill shell than for an equivalent weight of elephant ivory. Shell is available in the markets in Hat Yai, Phuket, and Bangkok (Polunin 1975). As shells get rarer they command higher prices. A hawksbill shell brings up to US $150-200, *Chelonia* up to US $100 or more, and *Caretta* and *Lepidochelys* fetch US $5-10 (Lekagul 1977). *Dermochelys* shell has little economic value in Thailand. For the period 1976-78, four of the five leading exporters of tortoise-shell were in the region: Indonesia, India, the Philippines, and Thailand itself. The total world export volume of raw shell increased from 250,000 kg in 1976 to over 390,000 kg in 1978. The latter figure probably represents between 100,000 and 500,000 hawksbills. Thailand's exports of raw tortoise-shell have increased dramatically since the early 1970s: 14,500 kg (1973), 14,522 kg (1974), 10,611 kg (1975), 23,859 kg (1976), 37,941 kg (1977), and 53,618 kg (1978). The major destinations of Thai shell are Hong Kong, Taiwan, and Singapore (Mack et al. 1979).

With increased tourism there has been an increased demand for the dried, stuffed, and varnished juvenile and adult sea turtles sold as curios. These are commonly seen for sale in markets. Juveniles are sometimes preserved whole in clear plastic paperweights (Ehrenfeld 1979). The leather, primarily from the flippers, is used to make handbags, shoes, and other items. There is a minor trade in live animals.

Sea turtles are an important, potentially renewable source of human food. The flesh of all five species is eaten in Thailand, especially the olive ridley and the green. The latter is well known for its use in soup. Taboos against eating turtles in the Islamic communities of southern Thailand are generally ignored, as are the sections of the Fisheries Act of B.E. 2490 (1947) that prohibit hunting of *C. mydas*, *E. imbricata*, and *C. caretta*. The meat of a single large turtle is worth about US $50 (Polunin 1975). Oil, primarily from the green, is used in the manufacture of cosmetics. In some areas the cartilage of the green ("calipee") is used to make a clear soup (Ehrenfeld 1979). The eggs of all five species are eaten (Polunin 1975, Lekagul 1977). The Thais call the eggs "Kai-ja-la-met" or "Kai-tao-thale" (Phasuk and Rongmuangsart 1973). They have a nutritional value similar to fowl eggs, but are higher in protein (IUCN 1971). The eggs of *Lepidochelys* cost US $0.075-0.09 (Lekagul 1977). Polunin (1975) estimated the total annual Thai egg yield to be about 400,000 eggs.

Nesting Beaches in Thailand

On the world level none of the Thai nesting beaches now can be considered to be of major significance. All five species have been reported from certain beaches in the region, but different species prefer different beaches. Data on population sizes and trends are

82   *Endangered Animals of Thailand*

scanty and often of questionable reliability (Polunin 1975, Polunin and Sumertha Nuitja 1979).

The known important sea turtle beaches in Thailand (Fig. 37) are:
- A. Ko Kut/Ko Chang Group, Trat Province.
- B. Ko Kram, Chon Buri Province.
- C. Ko Kra, Nakhon Si Thammarat Province.
- D. Pattani Province.
- E. Tarutao National Park (Ko Adang Group), Satun Province.
- F. Phuket Province.
- G. Phangnga Province.
- H. Ko Similan/Ko Surin (= Ko Sulin) Group, Phangnga and Ranong provinces.

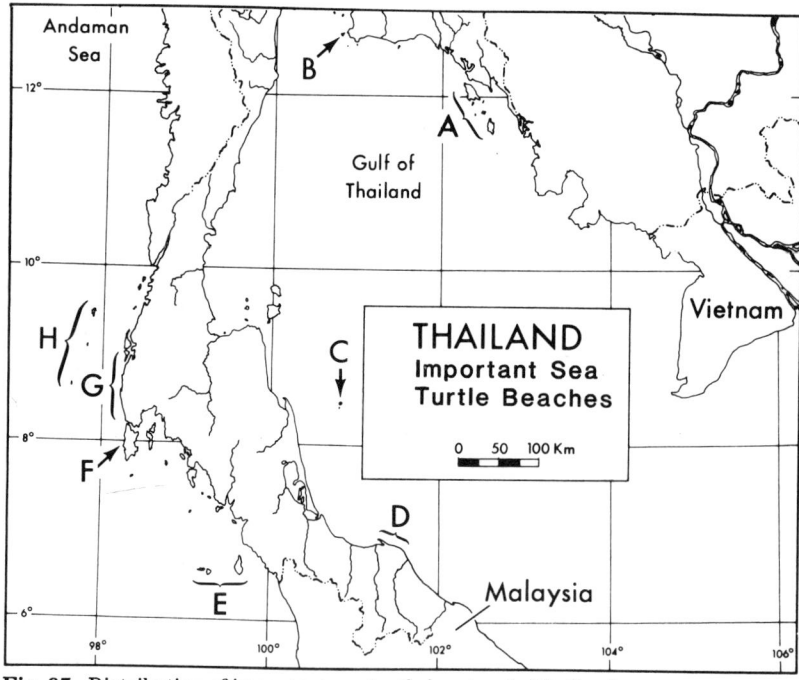

Fig. 37. Distribution of important sea turtle beaches in Thailand.

In the Gulf of Thailand the major nesting beaches are on Ko Kram in Chon Buri Province (Fig. 37), a continental island under the control of the Royal Thai Navy. Penyapol (1957) gave the ratio of 4 greens to 1 hawksbill for nesting turtles at Ko Kram and stated that nesting occurs all year in the Gulf, but most nesting takes place from March to September, with a peak in June. Polunin (1977) visited the island briefly in July of 1974 and gathered information on the status of nesting turtles. Egg yields at Ko Kram dropped from about 185,000 in 1963-1965 to 50,850 in 1972-1973 (average annual totals). Polunin saw intense nesting at Hat Kham and Hat Nuan on the southeast side of the island and was told that Hat Chek (southeast) and the southwest-facing beaches Hat Krathing and Hat Sadao were being used also. Beaches facing north and northeast were used less. The tiny, isolated island of Ko Kra east of Nakhon Si Thammarat Province is now a minor nesting area (Fig. 37). Penyapol (1957) gave a ratio of 5 greens to 3 hawksbills for that island. The present extent of nesting is unknown, but Polunin (1975) estimated the annual egg yield at 10,000 eggs. The Ko Kut/Ko Chang islands in Trat Province is a minor nesting area (Fig. 37). Polunin (1975) estimated the annual egg yield from this group to be 20,000 eggs. Suitable beaches in Pattani Province are still used as nesting areas. Polunin's estimate of annual egg yield (1975) there was 30,000.

The major nesting areas on the west coast were given by Polunin (1975) as Phangnga, Phuket, the Similan Islands, the Surin islands, and the Ko Adang group (Fig. 37). For the last of these, Polunin estimated annual egg yield at 80,000. The entire group, now protected in Tarutao Marine National Park, had only 2 or 3 turtles reported to come ashore in the 1979-1980 nesting season (November to March); in 1980-1, fewer than 100 nests were found. It has evidently experienced a dramatic and rapid decline (Boonruang Saisorn, personal communication; Ginsberg 1981). Polunin (1975) estimated that the beaches of Phuket Province yield 10,000 eggs annually. For the coasts of Phangnga Province he estimated 60,000 eggs annually, mainly from the districts of Churaburi, Thai Muang, and Takuatung. For the Surin Islands and the Similan Islands--lesser sea turtle areas--he estimated an annual yield of 20,000 eggs each. The most abundant sea turtles along the west coast are the green and olive ridley.

Sea Turtle Life History

Almost without exception male sea turtles do not come ashore. Females leave the water only to lay eggs. Marine turtles do not reach sexual maturity until about 10 years of age. If undisturbed by man, reproductive individuals may reach impressive ages, perhaps as old as 80 years. After mating, females can store viable sperm in their oviducts for up to a year. A female may come ashore to lay several times during a nesting season, but not necessarily every year. At high tide she crawls up onto the sandy beach with her front flippers and selects a spot up to 100 m beyond the high tide line. Contact with saltwater would kill the eggs. If the sand is too dry to support the walls of a hole she will seek moister sand. Proper nesting sand, then, must be above the level of liquid seawater but must not be completely dry. If disturbed before laying, the female will return to the water, but once oviposition commences sea turtles seem to be oblivious to disturbance. After spending about two hours excavating the hole, she lays the eggs (50-250) in about a half hour, covers them, and returns to the sea exhausted (Smith 1931, Phasuk and Rongmuangsart 1973, Ehrenfeld 1979, Wirot 1979).

The eggs are not sensitive to handling during the first few days, and that is the best time to move them if necessary for conservation efforts. Incubation takes about 2 months. Incubation temperature can affect the sex of the hatchlings. The young of a clutch hatch synchronously and require several days to dig out cooperatively. A single hatchling would be unable to reach the surface. When the topmost hatchlings are within a few inches of the surface they become quiescent until the surface temperature falls below a certain level (at night or on a cool, rainy day). Then they burst out explosively and run for the sea. Mortality at this phase is high--many avian, terrestrial, and fish predators capitalize on turtle emergences. The small hatchlings (30-60 g) and adult females are both thought to locate the water by heading for the brightest horizon. In settled areas many young are fatally attracted inland by electric lights. Hatchlings are inept at controlling their buoyancy and float around on the surface for a time, adding to their vulnerability. Fewer than 10 percent survive the first year (Smith 1931, Ehrenfeld 1979, Wirot 1979).

For their first several years of life, young loggerheads are pelagic, congregating where bouyant organisms and flotsam converge at downwellings generated by ocean currents, gyres, and wind-driven drift-lines (Carr 1986). This habitat may also be a key component of the life cycle of other species of sea turtle.

Adults feed on animals, especially invertebrates like sponges, marine worms, and molluscs. The green turtle also consumes sea grasses (angiosperms) and other plant matter. All sea turtles except leatherbacks (jellyfish specialists) prefer meat in captivity. All are air breathers, of course, and must stay near the surface when active. When quiescent they can remain under water for hours. Some wedge their bodies into cracks in the bottom to sleep submerged, but many prefer to sleep and bask afloat, where they are quite vulnerable to human predation. The only other significant enemies of adult sea turtles are large sharks. The adults are famous for their long-distance migrations between feeding grounds and nesting beaches, but the movements of the Thai populations are virtually unknown. It has been estimated that there are fewer than 1,000 adult female sea turtles of all species surviving in Thai waters (Smith 1931, Polunin 1975, Ehrenfeld 1979).

An entire issue of the American Zoologist (Volume 20 Number 3) has been published on behavioral and reproductive biology of sea turtles.

Causes of Threat

"In this century no major population of any species of sea turtle has been proved to increase its numbers significantly, either spontaneously or as the result of a conservation effort" (Ehrenfeld 1979). The single possible exception is the turtles nesting on the beaches near Tortuguero, Costa Rica. In Thailand all five species have declined in the last ten years and all are threatened with extirpation from Thai waters (Lekagul 1977, Lekagul and Damman 1977). Even though sea turtle populations have been seriously depleted, the levels of exploitation are at an all-time high and increasing. As the animals become rarer, their products command higher and higher prices, aggravating the situation (Lekagul and Damman 1977). The two major threats are direct human predation (Polunin 1975, Ginsberg 1981) and the accidental drowning of turtles in trawler nets (Boonruang Saisorn, personal communication; Ginsberg 1981).

Overexploitation of turtle egg resources directly reduces their numbers (Lekagul and Damman 1977). The existing Thai nesting beaches obviously once supported a far greater population of turtles than they do now. In Phangnga and Phuket provinces local government revenue from the rental of nesting beaches has fallen.

Supervision of nesting beaches, especially of hatchling release, is poor except in a few areas. Beach concessionaires do not consistently report egg yields and hatchling releases as they are required. Since 1965 probably fewer than 20,000 hatchlings per year have been released (Polunin 1975). The decline indicated by egg yield data from Phangnga and Ko Kram is statistically significant ($P < 0.05$, Spearman rank correlation, Polunin and Sumertha Nuitja 1979). In Thailand today the young and eggs are taken from virtually every nesting beach, and the minuscule number of young that join the adult population is insufficient to maintain sustained yields (Lekagul 1977, Polunin 1977).

The habitat of pelagic young loggerheads and perhaps other species--oceanic fronts of downwelling convergences--are increasingly polluted by human garbage (Carr 1986). van Nierop and den Hartog (1984) have reported tar, plastic scraps, and nylon in the stomachs of young loggerheads in the eastern Atlantic.

Adults are hunted on the beaches and in the water. The expansion of the human population and tourism has led to an increase in the killing of adult sea turtles. Curios, meat, eggs, and shell are still to be found regularly in Thai markets, especially the Sunday Market in Bangkok (Polunin 1975, 1977). The Sea Nomads of the Moken tribe have a special spear, the poleng-ba-penyui, that they use to kill sea turtles and crocodiles. They continue to hunt sea turtles. Such subsistence-level hunting by indigenous peoples did not threaten the animals historically, but its effects on reduced populations can be devastating (Polunin 1975, Ehrenfeld 1979).

In addition to intentional harvest, many sea turtles are killed incidentally by fishing activities. Purse seines and otter boards kill many (Lekagul 1977). Trawler activity in the Gulf of Thailand has increased dramatically in recent years. The catch of fish per unit of effort is falling. The verbal evidence indicates widespread killing of adult sea turtles around Thai coasts, with some trawlers reporting as many as 20 turtles killed per boat per year. Most trawler captures are in the Ko Kut/Ko Chang group, Ko Kram and vicinity, Ko Samui, and off Ranong Province. Also, the bamboo stake traps set inshore in the Gulf often kill turtles (Polunin 1975, 1977).

Indirect effects of habitat modification by man also threaten the turtles. At Ko Kra, the tiny islet off Nakhon Si Thammarat, much of the beach has been rendered unusable because coral rubble has been deposited on the beach as a result of fishing with dynamite in the reef offshore. Land development along beaches can lead to erosion and usually makes beaches unsuitable for nesting (Lekagul and Damman 1977, Polunin and Sumertha Nuitja 1979). The beach at Pattaya has suffered such a fate. The important nesting island of Ko Kram in Chon Buri Province may be affected by a new jetty constructed on the mainland nearby. In six turtle nesting attempts observed there, eggs were laid in only one (Polunin 1977). This may have been due to the new jetty. Its powerful floodlights illuminate several of the island's beaches. Large ships use the new facility. Loud noises and bright lights are known to interfere with turtle nesting (Lekagul and Damman 1977). Additionally, the effects of increased silt loads in coastal waters from mining and water pollution in general on sea turtles need to be studied.

Conservation Measures Taken

Historically the Buddhist monks in Thailand hatched and released sea turtles. This practice endured at Ko Kram until quite recently (Polunin 1975). The major modern Thai conservation efforts include the sections of the Fisheries Act of B.E. 2490 (1947) that give legal protection to adult *Caretta*, *Chelonia*, and *Eretmochelys*; the areas protected as reserves by the Royal Thai Navy, the National Park Act of B.E. 2504 (1961), and similar legislation; and the plans for nesting beach concessions and hatchling releases administered by certain provincial governments. Research on sea turtle biology has been conducted at the Phuket Marine Biological Center and elsewhere. Thailand's Queen Sirikit has taken a personal interest in sea turtle conservation and has donated an island (Mun Nai) for this purpose.

The availability of products made from the three species protected by the Fisheries Act attests to the fact that the law is generally ignored and is ineffective in conserving these reptiles. However, Thai law recently has been amended (WARPA 1980) to protect all five species of sea turtles from hunting and regulate trade by special permits from the Wildlife Advisory Committee of the Wildlife Conservation Division.

The Royal Thai Navy controls the important nesting beaches at Ko Kram, from the naval station at Sattahip in Chon Buri Province. With the cooperation of Admiral Jing Jullasukhum, the Navy has strictly reserved a beach on Ko Kram for turtle hatching (Lekagul

1977). A small amount of captive rearing has been carried out at Sattahip (Polunin 1975).

The reserves with significant potential as nesting areas are Ang Thong National Park, Ko Surin Wildlife Sanctuary, and Tarutao Marine National Park. The enforcement staff at the latter is spread thinly over 51 islands and cannot circumvent poaching (Boonruang Saisorn, personal communication). Though considered an important nesting area in the early 1970s, Tarutao, as has been mentioned, has suffered a serious decline in nesting turtles in recent years.

At the province level many, but not all, beaches are rented out to individuals under contract on a yearly basis. The contracts stipulate that a certain percentage (often 10 percent) of the eggs must be hatched and released. In some coastal provinces there are strict laws dealing with turtle releases. Polunin (1975) stated that "for failure to release the hatchlings the fines are: bht. 15,000 in northwest Phuket, bht. 5,000 in southwest Phuket, and bht. 45,000, bht. 33,000, and bht. 39,000 in the Takuatung, Thai Muang, and Churaburi districts of Phangnga Province, respectively. In Pattani each concessionaire pays a deposit of bht. 7,500, which is forfeited if the hatchlings are not released." (20 Baht = US $1.) Additionally, in Phuket and Phangnga provinces there are further fines for failing to protect rental beaches. These provincial beach concessions are sound in theory but need to be better enforced to be effective. Presently the tens of thousands of hatchlings meant to be released each year under these schemes (Polunin 1975) are simply not being hatched.

Under a program begun in 1974, 50 percent of the eggs from certain beaches are taken to fishery stations to be hatched, reared to a size large enough to reduce predation, and released. The turtles reared in this program are mainly olive ridleys, with some loggerheads and hawksbills, and a few greens. Releases under the new program have been 1,107 in 1977, 4,820 in 1978, 5,213 in 1979, and 3-4,000 (estimate) in 1980. Another new program requires the fishermen to fill out questionnaires reporting the number of nesting turtles in an area, but these data are often of questionable reliability because royalties on concessions depend on the presumed number of nesting turtles.

Two Thai researchers at Phuket, Boonlert Phasuk and Sayan Rongmuangsart, have studied the growth in captivity of *Lepidoche-*

lys and the feasibility of captive sea turtle farming in Thailand. They have also tagged wild animals in the hope of learning the movements of the Thai populations (Phasuk and Rongmuangsart 1973, Polunin 1975, Polunin and Sumertha Nuitja 1979). In addition to the aforementioned rearing efforts at Sattahip and Phuket there also has been small-scale turtle farming along the coast of Phangnga Province (Polunin 1975).

Conservation Measures Proposed

Drastic and immediate measures are needed if Thailand is going to leave viable sea turtle populations for its future generations. Improved enforcement of the relevant sections of the Fisheries Act, National Park Act, and Wild Animals Reservation and Protection Act is necessary. The most effective way to prevent harvest of the eggs is to erase tracks and other signs of nesting so local people cannot find the nests; however, pigs find these sites when the hatchlings are digging their way out (Ginsberg 1981). Several authorities have wisely suggested a total ban on the hunting of adults and the collection and sale of eggs for 6-10 years to allow populations a chance to recover (Polunin 1975, Polunin and Sumertha Nuitja 1979). More practical solutions would include the setting of size limits on adults, seasonal closures, and better supervision of commercial nesting beaches. In any case a thorough evaluation of the current beach concession system is in order. Since any conservation plans for these wide-ranging animals must of necessity be international in scope, it is unfortunate that different provincial governments (even different districts within a province) have differing laws on this issue. Management of this resource would be more effective if it was coordinated or controlled by the central Thai government. Perhaps the concession fees and any fines could be returned to the province so that this revenue would not be lost by local government. The Marine Fisheries Division should consider assuming control of sea turtle hatching and harvest. The feasibility of allowing the Sea Nomads to continue hunting turtles for their own use should be studied.

Improved legislation cannot be effective unless it is understood by the citizens as being in the long-term best interest of themselves and their countrymen. To promote this enlightened self-interest, it will be essential to educate the public about the problem and solutions that will sustain this renewable resource. Because the information must reach remote areas, perhaps the best approach would be a regular natural resource radio program prepared by the fishery, wildlife, and forestry experts at Kasetsart University and distributed widely to regional radio stations. Additionally it would be helpful in managing the beach concessions if the expertise of these scientists were made available through technology-transfer agents (agricultural extension agents) assigned to the areas having turtle nesting beaches.

Although sea turtles in Southeast Asia were mentioned in the European literature as early as Nieuhoff (1666) and there have been a plethora of observations published since (mostly anecdotal), today we remain ignorant of many basic facets of Southeast Asian sea turtle biology. Ongoing research on Thailand's sea turtles should be supported. Current data on population sizes and exploitation by man should be collected. The factors such as artificial lights, loud noises, coastal development, and the like, that affect nesting beaches should be studied and their impacts mitigated wherever possible. Ways of avoiding trawler/turtle conflicts deserve study. Basic data on the life history and movements of the Thai populations are needed before sound management plans can be formulated. Cooperative tagging studies between Thailand and other nations in the region would be desirable. With public education, research, improved controls on exploitation, and foresight it may be possible to save this dwindling resource.

Tao ya, tao sarai ta daeng, tao sung-asee, olive or Pacific Ridley turtle
Lepidochelys olivacea (Eschscholtz 1829)
Reptilia, Testudines, Cheloniidae

Status: Endangered.
IUCN Red Data Book (1975): Endangered.
CITES 1979): Appendix I.
IUCN (1979): Threatened.
USFWS (1980a): Threatened.
WARPA (1980): Protected-1.

Population Size and Trend: Most of the sea turtles along the west coast are olive ridleys, so this is Thailand's most common sea turtle. Worldwide there has been a precipitous drop in numbers of *L. olivacea* in recent years. There are now several hundred thousand females surviving in the species-wide range (Ehrenfeld 1979, A. H. V. Sharma personal communication).

Distribution and History of Distribution: In Thailand it is found all along the west coast and is still a locally common breeder in a few places, such as the Laem Phan Wa reserve at Phuket Marine Biological Center. It is widely distributed in the tropical and subtropical waters of the Indo-Pacific and parts of the Atlantic (Taylor 1970, Phasuk and Rongmuangsart 1973, IUCN Red Data Book 1975, Polunin 1975, Ehrenfeld 1979, Wirot 1979).

Geographic Status: The Thai populations are central to the species' overall range.

Habitat Requirements and Habitat Trend: This is one of the most tropical of sea turtles. It generally nests only on the beaches of continents and large islands such as Madagascar and Borneo (IUCN Red Data Book 1975). See the Introductory Comments.

Vulnerability of Species and Habitat: The flesh of this animal is considered by many to be second in flavor only to *Chelonia*. It is widely eaten in Southeast Asia. The flipper skin is prized as leather for shoes and handbags. Ridleys are also exploited for eggs, oil, and curios (Polunin 1975, Ehrenfeld 1979, Polunin and Sumertha Nuitja 1979).

Causes of Threat: See the Introductory Comments.

Responses to Habitat Modification: Unknown.

Demographic Characteristics: Individuals may breed every year. Nests in Sri Lanka have yielded from 90 to 135 eggs. Most breeding at Phuket takes place October to February. Eggs at Phuket hatch in 50-60 days. The growth of captive hatchlings in Thailand is very slow until after the first 6 months (Phasuk and Rongmuangsart 1973, IUCN Red Data Book 1975).

Key Behaviors: Wirot (1979) reported that olive ridleys sometimes lay eggs as far as 180 m from the water.

Conservation Measures Taken: Boonlert Phasuk and Sayan Rongmuangsart at Phuket Marine Biological Center studied the food preferences and growth of olive ridleys purchased as hatchlings from concessionaires and raised on differing diets. They found that all ages studied preferred meat, especially molluscs, and died if raised on a strict vegetarian diet. Although their captive hatchlings showed a high (33 percent) mortality in the first 6 months of life, this figure is undoubtedly far lower than the mortality of hatchlings in the wild. They thus demonstrated the feasibility of raising hatchlings in captivity through the dangerous first year and releasing the yearlings to supplement wild populations (Phasuk and Rongmuangsart 1973).

Conservation Measures Proposed: See the Introductory Comments.

Kra, hawksbill turtle
Eretmochelys imbricata (**Linnaeus 1766**)
Reptilia, Testudines, Cheloniidae

Status: Endangered.
Thai Fisheries Act of B.E. 2490 (1947): Capture forbidden.
IUCN Red Data Book 1975: Endangered.
IUCN 1979: Threatened.
CITES 1979: Appendix I.
USFWS 1980a: Endangered.
WARPA (1980): Protected-1.

Population Size and Trend: This animal was once common at certain localities in Thailand. It was especially abundant at Ko Klang in the Ko Adang Group in what is now Tarutao Marine National Park. In Thailand it has recently become rare. Because it usually does not nest in large aggregations its total numbers are hard to assess, but it is certainly endangered throughout the world (Polunin 1975, Ehrenfeld 1979, A. H. V. Sharma personal communication).

Distribution and History of Distribution: The hawksbill occurs in the tropical and subtropical waters of the world. It is known from both Thai coasts. In the Gulf of Thailand it nests at Ko Kram in Chon Buri Province, tiny Ko Kra off Nakhon Si Thammarat Province, and other areas. At two islands in the Ko Kut/Ko Chang Group in Trat, Ko Run, and Ko Kra provinces (not to be confused with the aforementioned islet off Nakhon Si Thammarat), this is the most common nesting sea turtle. On the west coast there are reports of nesting turtles from Phuket and the Ko Adang Group (Penyapol 1957, Polunin 1975, Lekagul and Damman 1977, Ehrenfeld 1979).

Geographic Status: Hawksbills are widespread in both oceans that touch Thailand.

Habitat Requirements and Habitat Trend: *Eretmochelys* nests both on islands and mainland shores and will use stretches of beach too short to be acceptable to other sea turtles. It prefers the reefs and inshore waters with hard bottoms. The young are carnivorous and prefer shrimp. Adults are mainly carnivorous, consuming fish, tunicates, coral, molluscs, crustaceans, and jellyfish, but they will take plant matter at times (Smith 1931, Deraniyagala 1939, Penyapol 1957, Phasuk and Rongmuangsart 1973, IUCN Red Data Book 1975, Ehrenfeld 1979, Wirot 1979). See the Introductory Comments.

Vulnerability of Species and Habitat: Although the meat is of an inferior grade and sometimes poisons (and rarely kills) people, these animals are relentlessly hunted for their shell, the main source of the tortoiseshell of commerce. The demand for shell is high, as is its price. The eggs are eaten widely. Stuffed *E. imbricata* curios sell for about US $8 per cm in markets in Bangkok and Phuket markets (Phasuk and Rongmuangsart 1973, Polunin 1975, Ehrenfeld 1979). See the Introductory Comments.

Causes of Threat: The overexploitation of this species by man is driving it to extinction.

Responses to Habitat Modification: Unknown.

Demographic Characteristics: In the Gulf of Thailand eggs are laid all year. At Ko Kram the nesting activity is concentrated from March to September. At Ko Kra (Nakhon Si Thammarat) most breeding takes place from December to February. At Phuket nesting occurs from October to February. Incubation takes 45-60 days in Thailand. An adult female lays about 200 eggs 2-3 times per season and may not breed in alternate years. Adults commonly weigh less than 50 kg, but specimens up to 140 kg are known (Penyapol 1957, Phasuk and Rongmuangsart 1973, IUCN Red Data Book 1975, Ehrenfeld 1979, Wirot 1979).

Key Behaviors: When approached on land this turtle will often defend itself by biting. Deraniyagala (1939) described the nesting behavior in detail. See the Introductory Comments.

Conservation Measures Taken: Hawksbills are legally protected under the Thai Fisheries Act, but this has not prevented their decline in Thai waters. Some have been kept in captivity at the naval station at Sattahip in Chon Buri Province. Rental turtle beaches have released thousands of hatchlings of this species since the early 1960s (Phasuk and Rongmuangsart 1973, Polunin 1975, IUCN Red Data Book 1975). See the Introductory Comments.

Conservation Measures Proposed: Although these animals are protected from capture, Thailand is among the world's leading exporters of tortoise-shell. Immediate action is needed to discourage this trade and to curtail hunting pressures on the already depopulated turtles. Hatchery programs raising young to supplement natural hatches should actively seek out hawksbill eggs and transport them to secure beaches for hatching. See the Introductory Comments.

Tao tu nu, tao saeng-atit, green turtle
Chelonia mydas (Linnaeus 1758)
Reptilia, Testudines, Cheloniidae

Status: Endangered.
Thai Fisheries Act of B.E. 2490 (1947): Capture forbidden.
IUCN Red Data Book (1975): Endangered.
IUCN (1979): Threatened.
CITES (1979): Appendix I.
USFWS (1980a): Threatened.
WARPA (1980): Protected-1.

Population Size and Trend: Although it has recently declined in Thai waters, this remains the most common sea turtle in the Gulf of Thailand and one of the most common on all Thai coasts. Before the recent decline at Tarutao Marine National Park it was an abundant turtle there. Within recorded history *Chelonia* numbered in the tens of millions in the world's warmer oceans. Overexploited for its flesh, eggs, and other products, it is drastically reduced throughout its range and missing altogether from areas where it was once abundant. It is unlikely that more than 500,000 survive worldwide (IUCN Red Data Book 1975, Polunin 1975, Ehrenfeld 1979, A. H. V. Sharma personal communication).

Distribution and History of Distribution: The major nesting site of Thai *Chelonia* is Ko Kram in the Gulf of Thailand. Tiny Ko Kra off Nakhon Si Thammarat and other beaches in the Gulf are still used by this species. It is known to breed at Tarutao Marine National Park in Satun Province, at the Laem Phan Wa marine reserve (Phuket Marine Biological Center) and elsewhere in Phuket

Province, along the beaches of Phangnga Province, and at other suitable sites on the west coast. Green turtles feed and breed in tropical and subtropical oceans around the world (Penyapol 1957, Phasuk and Rongmuangsart 1973, IUCN Red Data Book 1975, Polunin 1975, Ehrenfeld 1979, Polunin and Sumertha Nuitja 1979).

Geographic Status: *C. mydas* is widely distributed in both oceans that touch Thailand.

Habitat Requirements and Habitat Trend: Green turtles are found in oceans where the water temperature does not fall below 20° C in the coldest month. They do wander into colder seas at times, but breeding and feeding are restricted to low latitudes. Hatchlings and juveniles are carnivorous until about 6 months of age, preferring to dine on shrimp. Adults are primarily herbivorous, specializing on sea grasses (marine angiosperms), but seaweed (algae), crustaceans, molluscs, and fish are also taken. These turtles have recently been shown to have gut bacteria that aid them in digesting cellulose, an unusual adaptation for a "cold blooded" animal. No extensive beds of sea grass are known to exist in Thai waters, but Polunin (1975) reported some at Makam Bay and Chalong Bay in Phuket Province and possibly along the west coast of Ko Samui in the Gulf of Thailand. Greens are famous for their long-distance migrations between sea grass beds and nesting beaches. The grass beds occur in shallows and are thus sensitive to trawling, siltation, and other disruptive forces (Smith 1931, Penyapol 1957, IUCN Red Data Book 1975, Polunin 1975, Ehrenfeld 1979, Polunin and Sumertha Nuitja 1979).

Vulnerability of Species and Habitat: This species often has been called the most (economically) valuable reptile in the world. The key factor in its decline has been the delectable flavor of its flesh. In Thailand and around the world it is the preferred turtle for soup. Today adults range from 90 to 225 kg, and before the relentless overexploitation of recent times specimens over 360 kg were taken. The eggs are widely available in Thai markets and sell for US $0.01-0.015. Shells, dried curios, and other products also are available (Fisher et al. 1969, IUCN Red Data Book 1975, Polunin 1975, Lekagul and Damman 1977, Ehrenfeld 1979).

Causes of Threat: See the Introductory Comments.

Responses to Habitat Modification: Unknown.

Demographic Characteristics: In the wild, green turtles may take 8-15 years or longer to reach sexual maturity. In the Gulf of

Thailand nesting has been reported throughout the year, being concentrated in March-September (peak in June) at Ko Kram and December-February at Ko Kra. At Phuket on the west coast *Chelonia* nests from October to April, with a peak in December and January. The timing and location of sea turtle nesting in Thai waters may be affected by variations in the monsoons. A female might not nest every year (2-year, 3-year, and longer cycles are suspected), but over her lifetime she returns time and again to the same beach. Clutches range from 3 to 180 eggs. The mean of over 8,000 clutches studied by Hendrickson (1958) in Malaya and Sarawak was 105 eggs. Females often lay several clutches per season, with extremes of 7-8 clutches on record. At Ko Kra in the Gulf incubation lasts 45-50 days. At Phuket on the west coast it lasts 50-60 days. Hatching success at Ko Kram is high; about 90 percent of the eggs yield hatchlings (Penyapol 1957, Phasuk and Rongmuangsart 1973, IUCN Red Data Book 1975, Ehrenfeld 1979, Wirot 1979). For detailed accounts of the biology of this turtle in Sri Lanka and peninsular Malaysia and Sarawak see Deraniyagala (1939) and Hendrickson (1958). See the Introductory Comments, also.

Key Behaviors: Greens are better known than most sea turtles. Mating generally takes place in the shallow waters near nesting beaches. Hendrickson (1958) reported numerous observations of this behavior in the region. Copulation occurs both at night and during the daytime near the surface. When in coition the male is often exposed above the surface, and the pair is quite vulnerable to hunters. Many nesting sea turtles excavate only a pit for the eggs, but *Chelonia* digs a large body pit (as large as 2 m long and 1 m deep) and a second, smaller hole under the cloaca for the eggs. These turtles are gentle and will bite only rarely when provoked. In Thailand these are the turtles most frequently killed by trawlers. This may not be due merely to their abundance. Their habit of resting near the surface may make them especially vulnerable to this mortality (Polunin 1975, Ehrenfeld 1979).

Conservation Measures Taken: *Chelonia* is legally protected by the Thai Fisheries Act of B.E. 2490 (1947) and WARPA (1980). The beach concession system has released many hatchlings (21,350 in 1965, for example). In Thailand small-scale captive rearing has been conducted at Phuket and the naval station at Sattahip. The species can be propagated in captivity (Fisher et al. 1969, Phasuk and Rongmuangsart 1973, Polunin 1975).

Conservation Measures Proposed: Turtles nesting at Ko Kra and Ko Kram should be protected from capture, disturbance, and habitat alteration. It is hoped that the Royal Thai Navy will continue their worthy efforts to conserve the turtles at Ko Kram. A 6-10 year ban on all green turtle harvest should be considered. Efforts to acquire viable eggs for hatching at protected beaches should be pursued vigorously. The seasonal movements and foraging grounds of the Thai green turtles need to be identified and studied. The extent of sea grass beds in Thailand's coastal waters should be determined. Green turtles are the only edible creature capable of turning sea grass into human food on a large scale. Management of this turtle on a sustained-yield basis would have to include protection of the nesting beaches and foraging grounds. These animals help maintain the sea-grass system by cropping it and thus providing a continuous supply of young, relatively nutritious growth. The effects of trawling, increased siltation in coastal waters, and water pollution in general on sea grass habitat need to be investigated, as do the basic life history attributes of the green turtle in Thai waters.

Tao ta le, tao ya, tao charamed, loggerhead turtle
Caretta caretta **(Linnaeus 1758)**
Reptilia, Testudines, Cheloniidae

Status: Endangered.
Thai Fisheries Act of B.E. 2490 (1947): Capture forbidden.
IUCN (1968): Threatened.
IUCN Red Data Book (1975): Vulnerable.
IUCN (1979): Threatened.
CITES (1979): Appendix I.
USFWS (1980a): Threatened.
WARPA (1980): Protected-1.

Population Size and Trend: There are few reliable data on the status of this turtle in Southeast Asia. It has become the rarest of the five Thai sea turtles. It is known to have declined in many parts of its wide range. There are probably no more than 100,000 adult females remaining in the whole world (Ehrenfeld 1979, IUCN 1979, Polunin and Sumertha Nuitja 1979, Wirot 1979, A. H. V. Sharma personal communication).

Distribution and History of Distribution: The species occurs widely in the temperate and tropical oceans of the world. This is the only sea turtle that breeds outside the tropics to a significant degree. There are records of this animal from the Gulf of Thailand and the west coast (Deraniyagala 1939, Penyapol 1957, Phasuk and Rongmuangsart 1973, Polunin 1977, Ehrenfeld 1979).

Geographic Status: Thailand's tropical seacoasts are lower in latitude than the beaches this reptile normally prefers for nesting.

Habitat Requirements and Habitat Trend: For their first several years of life, young loggerheads are pelagic, congregating where bouyant organisms and flotsam converge at downwellings generated by ocean currents, gyres, and wind-driven drift-lines (Carr 1986). Adult *Caretta* prefers the marine littoral zone, especially rocky shallows and reefs. It breeds on surf-swept sandy beaches and feeds on molluscs, crustaceans, and other animals (Smith 1931, Deraniyagala 1939, IUCN Red Data Book 1975, Ehrenfeld 1979). See the Introductory Comments.

Vulnerability of Species and Habitat: The flesh of the loggerhead is inferior in quality. Oceanic fronts of downwelling convergences are increasingly polluted by human garbage, and van Nierop and den Hartog (1984) have reported tar, plastic scraps, and nylon in the stomachs of young loggerheads in the eastern Atlantic Ocean. See the Introductory Comments.

Causes of Threat: See the Introductory Comments.

Responses to Habitat Modification: Unknown.

Demographic Characteristics: Loggerheads are thought to breed in alternate years; a breeding female may lay three clutches in one season. Most breeding at Phuket occurs from October to February. The clutch size ranges from 60-200 eggs with an average of about 126. The sex ratio of hatchlings varies with incubation temperature; a higher temperature will produce a higher fraction of females. Incubation lasts about 55 days. Adults weigh 140-180 kg and have reached 230 kg (Phasuk and Rongmuangsart 1973, IUCN Red Data Book 1975, Ehrenfeld 1979).

Key Behaviors: These turtles are aggressive and will bite savagely, even when pulled into boats (Deraniyagala 1939).

Conservation Measures Taken: See the Introductory Comments.

Conservation Measures Proposed: The current status of the loggerhead in Southeast Asia needs to be ascertained. The IUCN

Red Data Book (1975) considers the potential for captive breeding to be "virtually nil". See the Introductory Comments.

Tao-ma-fuang, leatherback or leathery turtle
Dermochelys coriacea (Linnaeus 1766)
Reptilia, Testudines, Dermochelyidae

Status: Endangered.
IUCN (1968): Threatened.
IUCN Red Data Book (1975): Endangered.
IUCN (1979): Threatened.
CITES (1979): Appendix I.
USFWS (1980a): Endangered.
WARPA (1980): Protected-1.

Population Size and Trend: In the last century and the early part of the present one this turtle was quite abundant in some areas. The world's population of leatherbacks is now small, vulnerable, and declining. There are probably fewer than 50,000 adult females surviving. In Thailand this form has become rare (Deraniyagala 1939, Fisher et al. 1969, IUCN Red Data Book 1975, Polunin and Sumertha Nuitja 1979, A. H. V. Sharma personal communication).

Distribution and History of Distribution: The leatherback nests in the tropics but regularly feeds in colder waters when not breeding. It inhabits the Atlantic, Pacific, and Indian Oceans, and the Mediterranean Sea. The two major nesting areas that remain are at French Guiana in the New World and at Trengganu Beach in Malaysia in the Old World. It is found all along Thailand's west coast. The airport beach in Phuket Province is the most important Thai beach for this species. It also breeds regularly at the Laem Phan Wa marine reserve at Phuket Marine Biological Center. The coasts of Phangnga Province also are used by this species (Penyapol 1957, Bustard 1972, Phasuk and Rongmuangsart 1973, IUCN Red Data Book 1975, Polunin 1975, Lekagul and Damman 1977, Bhaskar 1979, Polunin and Sumertha Nuitja 1979, Wirot 1979).

Geographic Status: This turtle occurs in both oceans touching Thailand, but it is rare or absent over much of its former range.

Habitat Requirements and Habitat Trend: The airport beach in Phuket, like other beaches *Dermochelys* uses in Thailand, has a steep profile and coarse-grained sand seasonally exposed to rough seas. This turtle is thought to subsist almost entirely on jellyfish. This makes it very difficult to keep in captivity (IUCN Red Data Book 1975, Polunin 1975, Polunin and Sumertha Nuitja 1979).

Vulnerability of Species and Habitat: This is by far the world's largest living turtle. The flesh is rarely eaten but is sometimes used as bait. The shell has little or no commercial value. The primary exploitation of this species by man is for its eggs. They are the largest of sea turtle eggs, measuring 5-5.5 cm in diameter, about the size of a billiard ball. Although most sea turtle eggs collected in Thailand are sold and consumed locally, these are considered a specialty item and are shipped to distant markets, where they command premium prices. Polunin (1975) counted 500 *D. coriacea* eggs for sale at Bangkok's Sunday Market on 13 July and 800 on 27 July, 1974. The going price at that time was US $0.25. Because of their great value leatherback eggs seldom are handed over to fisheries stations (Bustard 1972, Phasuk and Rongmuangsart 1973, Polunin 1975, Lekagul 1977, Polunin and Sumertha Nuitja 1979).

Causes of Threat: The thorough removal of the eggs of this species from Thailand's beaches threatens to extirpate the species. See the Introductory Comments.

Responses to Habitat Modification: Unknown.

Demographic Characteristics: The main breeding season at Phuket is October-April. An adult female may nest 4-10 times a season at about 10-day intervals. The usual clutch is 80-110 eggs or more. The incubation at Phuket takes 65-70 days or longer, longer than for most sea turtles. From hatchlings 1-2 cm in length, leatherbacks grow to typical adult sizes of 300-360 kg. If left unmolested some grow to truly giant size: greater than 2 m in length and weights of over 680 kg (Smith 1931, Bustard 1972, Phasuk and Rongmuangsart 1973, IUCN Red Data Book 1975, Lekagul and Damman 1977, Ehrenfeld 1979, Wirot 1979).

Key Behaviors: The nesting behavior was described in detail in Deraniyagala's (1939) classic account. Leatherback turtles are rapid swimmers and apparently make long, poorly understood migrations (Smith 1931, IUCN Red Data Book 1975). See the Introductory Comments.

Conservation Measures Taken: Because of the poor success attained in captive rearing efforts (largely due to the animal's specialized diet), conservation of wild populations must be a major concern of all managing agencies. Although some leatherbacks have been hatched under Thailand's beach concessions program, the number is far outstripped by the eggs sent to market.

Conservation Measures Proposed: Thailand is fortunate to have a viable breeding population of *Dermochelys* in this decade. Hatching and release of young on rental beaches should be monitored carefully. The Thai government should consider giving this animal (eggs and adults) complete legal protection for the time being. The Malayan Nature Society has had good success with transporting eggs to special protected enclosures for hatching. The Malaysian Fisheries Department has assumed operation of the hatcheries (IUCN Red Data Book 1975). Thai Marine Fisheries Division officials should study the methods used in Malaysia and consider adopting them. Cooperative tagging studies with other nations in the region would be an important first step in attempting to learn more about the habits of Thailand's *Dermochelys*. See the Introductory Comments.

Man lai, ta pab hua gob, griu dao, grau kaew, giant soft-shelled turtle
Pelochelys bibroni **(Owen 1853)**
Reptilia, Testudines, Trionychidae

Status: Threatened.
IUCN (1968): Threatened.

Population Size and Trend: Unknown. Although this species is widely distributed, it is nowhere abundant.

Distribution and History of Distribution: *P. bibroni* is one of the most widely distributed of the freshwater turtles. In Thailand it is known definitely from the Chao Phraya in Bangkok, from Tak, Phra Nakhon Si Ayutthaya, Nakhon Si Thammarat, and Kanchanaburi provinces. It probably ranges over much of western and all of peninsular Thailand. It has also been recorded from "Indochina", Hainan, southern mainland China, Burma, India, Sumatra, Java, Borneo, the Philippines, and New Guinea. Taylor (1970) wrote that its wide distribution may be due to people carrying it from place to place as food items (Smith 1931, Taylor 1970, Radhakrishnan-Nair and Badrudeen 1975, Wirot 1979).

Geographic Status: This aquatic species is widespread and

occurs in a broad diversity of habitats. The Thai population is central to the species' overall range.

Habitat Requirements and Habitat Trend: In Thailand it is primarily an inhabitant of deep and slow-moving rivers upstream of salt intrusion (Smith 1931). A specimen was recently taken at sea off Mandapam in southern India (Radhakrishnan-Nair and Badrudeen 1975), proving Boulenger's (1912) early contention that *P. bibroni* is salt-tolerant and occasionally enters the sea. A captive in a Manila aquarium ignored the fishes *Cyprinus carpio* and *Megalops cyprinoides* but readily fed on the mud fish, *Ophiocephalus striatus* (Taylor 1970).

Vulnerability of Species and Habitat: This species is the second largest of the world's living soft-shelled turtles. Its large size makes it quite conspicuous to human hunters.

Causes of Threat: Throughout its range *P. bibroni* is extensively harvested as human food.

Responses to Habitat Modification: Unknown.

Demographic Characteristics: The female lays "a large number of eggs" (Wirot 1979). Adults reach a carapace length of almost 1 m and weigh as much as 85 kg (Wirot 1979).

Key Behaviors: This animal will bite when provoked. It often remains underwater for prolonged periods, apparently by absorbing oxygen from the water through its pharynx. The captive of Radhakrishnan-Nair and Barudeen (1975) was observed to bury all but its head in the sand substrate. In areas where *P. bibroni* routinely enters the sea its populations would tend to be spread over a much wider area than in areas where it stays only in fresh water.

Conservation Measures Taken: None. See Introductory Comments.

Conservation Measures Proposed: IUCN (1979) recommended that habitat for *P. bibroni* in Thailand should be identified and brought under protection. Research is needed to determine its role in fisheries and in the freshwater community in general. Basic research on its ecology in Thailand is needed to formulate management programs that would allow harvest on a sustained-yield basis. Laws should be considered to protect the species and its habitat and to regulate trade. Because it sometimes enters the sea, conservation measures need to be international in scope.

Family Crocodylidae--The Crocodiles
Introductory Comments

Thailand historically had three wild crocodilians, the saltwater crocodile (*Crocodylus porosus*), the Siamese freshwater crocodile (*C. siamensis*), and the false gavial (*Tomistoma schlegelii*). All are approaching extinction in the wild in Thai waters. A fourth species, the mugger crocodile (*C. palustris*), is known from Burma and the Malay peninsula and has long been expected to occur in Thailand, but its presence there has never been established (Taylor 1970).

The saltwater crocodile is one of the few animals alive today that regularly eats people. The Thais have long considered crocodiles to be enemies. "Crocodiles are often mentioned in classic Thai folk tales, in which they usually play the part of the villain" (IUCN 1971). Their former numbers are hard to assess, but the steady and dramatic decline of the Malaysian crocodile skin trade since 1953 (IUCN 1979, Whitaker 1979) attests to a depletion of natural populations. The world's trade in crocodile skins used to peak at over two million skins per year, but today most of the world's 22 species survive only in preserves and breeding stations. Most of this decline is directly attributable to hunting for skins, aggravated by habitat loss, trade in live specimens, and malicious killing (Whitaker and Daniel 1978).

Today the depletion of crocodilian stocks continues worldwide. A Sarawak National Parks and Wildlife officer summarized the factors contributing to the crocodile decline in his area: the pressures of a burgeoning human population, the proliferation of power boats and modern firearms, and increased logging activities, with attendant erosion of river banks and log rafting in rivers (Whitaker 1979). Laws protecting crocodiles in Southeast Asia are generally inadequate and poorly enforced. In Thailand they are lacking altogether (IUCN 1971, Whitaker 1979).

International trade in these animals is especially difficult to monitor and control. Live and dead specimens are obtained by raiding nests in Malaysia and are shipped to Singapore for sale elsewhere (Whitaker 1979). Such transshipment is common in the trade. King (1974) cited a case of a *T. schlegelii* imported to the United States from Sri Lanka, even though it occurs naturally only in southern Thailand, Indonesia, and Malaysia (Taylor 1970).

Fig. 38. Saltwater crocodiles (*Crocodylus porosus*) at the crocodile farm at Samut Prakan.

Crocodiles are a potentially renewable natural resource. Their role in controlling predatory fish, birds, and mammals is well established (Whitaker 1979). Less well-known in the scientific literature but common knowledge to fishermen in some parts of the world, fishing declines where crocodilians are extirpated. Though contrary to intuition, this stimulation of productivity of tropical waters is caused by the release of nutrients by crocodilian digestion (Fittkau 1973). Nonetheless, in Thailand today high-powered rifles are ubiquitous, and a crocodile skin can earn one a half-year's wages. Persistent, unregulated hunting, coupled with habitat destruction, makes it doubtful whether crocodilians can coexist with man in Thailand under the present circumstances (IUCN 1971).

The future of two Thai crocodilians, *C. siamensis* and *C. porosus*, rests in the hands of Mr. Utai Yangprapakorn. The crocodile farm he founded at Samut Prakan in 1950 with 20 wild crocodiles has grown to be one of the largest in the world (Fig. 38). It currently houses over 16,000 individuals and includes an active breeding population of over 400 sexually mature adults. There are far more *C. siamensis* at Samut Prakan than all the ones surviving in the wild and in the world's zoos combined. Although the farm has been hailed as a breakthrough in crocodile conservation and the Yangprapakorns have offered to donate stock for release in the wild when suitable preserves are developed, they allow the two species to hybridize (Whitaker 1979) because of the rapid growth of the hybrids. With the future of *C. siamensis* so much under their control, it is regrettable that they do not take measures to protect its genetic integrity. Hence, it would probably be preferable to base reintroductions on zoo populations whose genetic purity has been preserved.

Unlike the isolated and poorly documented case of crocodile farming in Thailand, similar experience in Papua New Guinea has been recorded and extended nationwide as a village industry that builds simultaneously a local economy and a constituency for conservation of wild crocodile stocks (National Research Council 1983a). That publication includes a section on practical crocodile farming, a history of the development and maturation of the crocodile farming effort in Papua New Guinea, and cautions about regulations, safeguards, and research that make exploitation and conservation compatible activities.

We know of no current research being carried on in Thailand on the few remaining wild crocodilians or on potential sites for reintroducing them. *Tomistoma* remains a mystery to modern science. Basic studies on the biology of wild populations are urgently needed to provide a basis for sound management plans. For the foreseeable future we concur with IUCN (1971) that, as members of the wild Thai herpetofauna, crocodilians "seem to be doomed."

Saltwater crocodile, buaya muara, charakee nam-khen
Crocodylus porosus **Schneider 1801**
Reptilia, Crocodilia, Crocodylidae

Status: Probably extirpated.
IUCN (1971): Almost extinct in the wild in Thailand.
CITES (1979): Appendix I.
IUCN (1979): Threatened.
IUCN Red Data Book (1979): Vulnerable, greatly reduced in numbers throughout its range.
USFWS (1980a): Endangered.

Population Size and Trend: "No more than ten adults are believed to remain in its range in southern Thailand" (King et al. 1979). There has been a dramatic decline in total world trade volume in *C. porosus* skins in the last decade, from 100,000 per year to 20,000 per year (King et al. 1979). Samut Prakan Crocodile Farm has extensive holdings of this species, but encourages them to hybridize with *C. siamensis* (Whitaker 1979). The last specimen from Thailand came from the area of Ko Tarutao in Satun Province in 1971, and no sightings or specimens have been confirmed since then (Boonruang Saisorn, personal communication). Numbers are greatly reduced over the species' range, except in Papua New Guinea (IUCN Red Data Book 1979): surviving populations are estimated at 300 on the mainland of India, 170-330 in the Andaman Islands, and 500-700 in Sri Lanka.

Distribution and History of Distribution: "Historically found from Cochin in southwest India, and Sri Lanka, east along the coast through Bangladesh, Burma, Thailand, Malaysia, Kampuchea, Vietnam, extreme southeast China, Philippines, Caroline Islands, Indonesia, Moluccas, Timor, Aru and Kei Islands, New Guinea, Bismarck Archipelago, Solomon Islands, New Hebrides, northern Australia. Scattered records [occur] from Fiji and Cocos Keeling Islands" (Neill 1971 in King et al. 1979). If this species remains in the wild in Thailand, it is in the vicinity of Ko Tarutao (Fig. 39).

Geographic Status: Saltwater crocodiles are widespread but restricted to isolated portions of their former range.

Habitat Requirements and Habitat Trend: These animals prefer salt water and are usually found in estuarine and coastal waters. Sometimes they are found in fresh water or at sea, far from the coasts (Schmidt 1928, Taylor 1970, IUCN Red Data Book 1979). Smith (1931) wrote that in Thailand they do not normally invade fresh water but are commonly found at the mouths of muddy rivers.

Vulnerability of Species and Habitat: *C. porosus* is most vulnerable because its hide is considered to be the finest of crocodile leathers. In areas where more than one crocodile species occur, *C. porosus* is preferred (IUCN Red Data Book 1979). This species does not tolerate much human disturbance, especially when nesting. The loss of suitable basking and nesting sites and human occupation of coastal areas are important factors in the demise of this animal (USFWS 1980b).

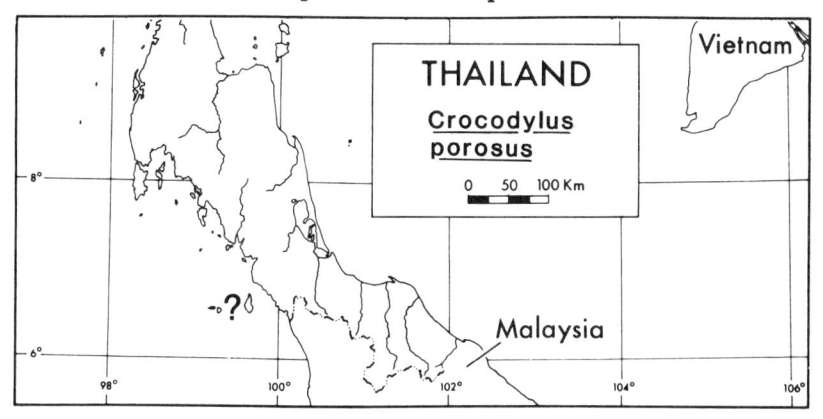

Fig. 39. Distribution of the Saltwater Crocodile (*Crocodylus porosus*).

Causes of Threat: In addition to intense hunting for hides, live specimens, and food, its occasional habit of feeding on humans has caused many *C. porosus* to be destroyed as "vermin." Prices of *porosus* hides continue to climb. In Thailand the animals and their eggs are eaten (King and Brazaitis 1971, IUCN 1971, Whitaker and Daniel 1978, Whitaker 1979, King et al. 1979, USFWS 1980b).

Responses to Habitat Modification: The effects of increased silt loads in estuaries, alteration of mangrove forests, and the destruction of coral reef habitats on *C. porosus* must be profound, but they are unknown.

Demographic Characteristics: In the wild *C. porosus* does not breed until it reaches a relatively large size (approximately 2.2 m), so many animals reach a size attractive to hunters before reaching sexual maturity. 25-90 eggs are deposited in a nest mound of decomposing organic debris. The young hatch in about 3 months (IUCN Red Data Book 1979). At Samut Prakan Crocodile Farm, demographic characteristics are similar to those for *C. siamensis*: Captive *porosus* are sexually mature at 12-15 years of age. Females lay 30-50 eggs, and 40-50 percent of them hatch in 78-80 days. In the first year of life 20-30 percent die; thereafter annual mortality is less than 5 percent. Samut Prakan's breeding stock ranges from 12-35 years of age. One captive at the National Zoological Park in Washington D. C. (U.S.A.) lived past 40 years of age (King and Dobbs 1975).

Key Behaviors: Female defense of the nest, as in other crocodilians, makes the species especially vulnerable to hunters. The infrequent but regular attacks on man produce an unforgiving attitude toward crocodiles. The ocean-going habit of this species tends to spread individuals over a wide area, magnifying the impact of reduced density and dictating that conservation measures be international in scope.

Conservation Measures Taken: Much habitat of the former population in the vicinity of Ko Tarutao is included in Tarutao Marine National Park. Hunting and export of skins are now prohibited in Sri Lanka, India, and Australia. India has established two sanctuaries for this species. In Papua New Guinea the species is carefully managed while the economic interest of subsistence hunters is protected, through a program of research, licensed harvesting, minimum size-limits on marketed skins, and public education (IUCN Red Data Book 1979, National Research Council 1983a). Research also is under way in Australia.

Conservation Measures Proposed: Thailand should enact and enforce laws to protect the few remaining crocodiles and any that might be reintroduced. This form is perhaps the largest of living reptiles, occasionally reaching lengths of 10 m (Taylor 1970), and it should not be allowed to go extinct because of human exploitation. Fewer than 50 live in the zoos of the United States and Europe (King and Dobbs 1975, Honegger 1975) and most of them are not reproductive. The conservation of wild populations, then, is of great importance to the continued existence of this species. The feasibility of restocking portions of Tarutao Marine National Park with saltwater crocodiles should be studied. However, reintroduction there would be fruitless without substantial support for personnel and equipment for enforced protection.

**Siamese freshwater crocodile,
buaya muara, chorakee nam-chued**
Crocodylus siamensis **Schneider 1801**
Reptilia, Crocodilia, Crocodylidae

Status: Probably extirpated.
IUCN (1971): Quite rare, approaching extinction in the wild.
IUCN Red Data Book (1975): Endangered.
CITES (1979): Appendix I.
IUCN (1979): Threatened.
MAB (1979): Endangered.

USFWS (1980a): Endangered.

Population Size and Trend: The Siamese crocodile became scarce in Thailand in the early 1940s (King and Brazaitis 1971). The wild population at Bung Boraphet in Nakhon Sawan Province is small (certainly fewer than 200 individuals) and declining. There have been no recent sightings of *C. siamensis* there. The commercial population at Samut Prakan numbers some 20,000 individuals, including *siamensis x porosus* hybrids (King and Brazaitis 1971, IUCN 1971, IUCN Red Data Book 1975, Whitaker and Daniel 1978, Whitaker 1979).

Distribution and History of Distribution: The only known surviving wild population is at Bung Boraphet (Fig. 40), and the status of that population is uncertain. Jeffrey McNeely believes that a few may survive in northern Thailand in Loei Province (IUCN 1979). The animal was formerly found in Java, Borneo, Kampuchea, Vietnam, and much of central and peninsular Thailand (King and Brazaitis 1971, IUCN 1971, IUCN Red Data Book 1975, Whitaker and Daniel 1978, IUCN 1979, Whitaker 1979). Distribution records in Thailand include the upper Yom River north of Phrae, the Kwae Noi River near Sai Yok, the lower Mekong near Khemmarat, swamps near Chumpon in the peninsula, the stream connecting Thale Sap Luang and Thale Sap Songkhla in Songkhla Province, and the upper Pattani River (Smith 1919).

Geographic Status: Extirpation over most of its former range has made this crocodile a confined Thai endemic.

Habitat Requirements and Habitat Trend: Siamese crocodiles

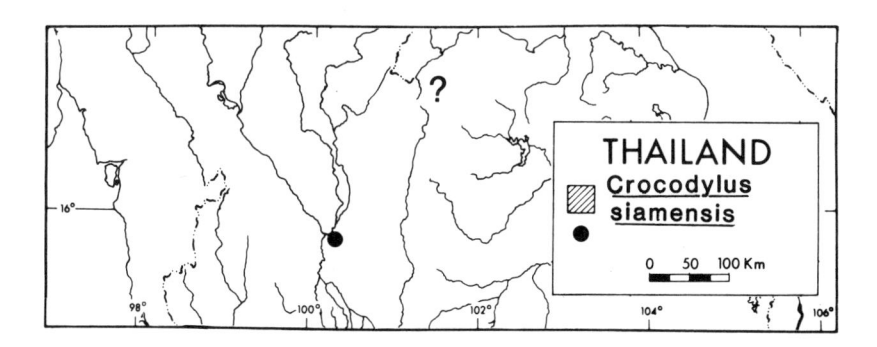

Fig. 40. Distribution of the Siamese Freshwater Crocodile (*Crocodylus siamensis*).

prefer freshwater lakes, rivers, and swamps, where they subsist on a varied diet. They were once abundant in the Kwae Noi River in western Thailand (Taylor 1970), in the stream connecting Thale Sap Luang and Thale Sap Songkhla in southern Thailand, and at Bung Boraphet (IUCN 1979).

Vulnerability of Species and Habitat: Maternal attachment to nesting sites and defense of the young make crocodiles especially vulnerable to hunters. The lowland freshwater habitat that this species requires is coveted by man for agriculture and other development activities.

Causes of Threat: Unrestricted hunting for hides and live specimens is the primary cause of the alarming decline of this species. This has been aggravated by habitat destruction and malicious killing. The eggs and meat are eaten in Thailand (King and Brazaitis 1971, Whitaker 1979).

Responses to Habitat Modification: Unknown.

Demographic Characteristics: The breeding rate in the wild is unknown (IUCN Red Data Book 1975). Wild adults average 3.15-3.8 m long and rarely may reach 4 m (Taylor 1970, IUCN 1971). The following information (IUCN 1971) describes the captive stock at Samut Prakan: Siamese crocodiles reach sexual maturity at 10-12 years. During the breeding season one male forms a relationship with only two females. Mating takes place mostly at night from December to March. The female builds a nest from the vegetation provided and lays some 20-40 eggs in late April through July. She actively defends the nest against other females. Human intervention helps maintain the nest temperature between 35 and 37° C by adjusting the amount of rotting vegetation. In 67 or 68 days 50-60 percent of the eggs hatch. Hatchlings are raised apart from adults. In the first year 20-30 percent of the young die. Thereafter annual mortality is less than 5 percent. Utai's breeding stock ranges from 12 to 35 years of age.

Key Behaviors: Female defense of the nest, although it enhances survivorship of the young in natural situations, makes the crocodiles quite susceptible to hunters. The use of exposed basking sites also makes them easily seen by humans.

Conservation Measures Taken: None.

Conservation Measures Proposed: Nocturnal surveys at Bung Boraphet, with boats and searchlights, should be conducted to determine if Siamese crocodiles survive there. Management plans for that wetland should include consideration of *C. siamensis*. The feasibility of restocking *C. siamensis* should be studied, though this may now be incompatible with the high intensity of human use of Bung Boraphet. If reintroduction in Thailand is accomplished, the population should be given complete protection until it reaches the carrying capacity of its environment. Thereafter a research and management program should be ir stituted to allow harvest of *C. siamensis* on a long-term sustainable basis. The management of Samut Prakan Crocodile Farm should be encouraged to maintain pure parental stock of the two *Crocodylus* species. Zoos and aquaria in the United States hold approximately 24 Siamese crocodiles, all sexually immature (King and Dobbs 1975). European zoos house some 11 individuals (Honegger 1975). In light of the cross-breeding allowed at Samut Prakan, these institutions should recognize their opportunity to help conserve the species by avoiding hybridization with other species and by pursuing cooperative breeding efforts.

**Tomistoma, false gavial,
false gharial, buaya sinyulong, ta-khong**
Tomistoma schlegelii **(S. Muller 1838)**
Reptilia, Crocodilia, Crocodylidae

Status: Probably extirpated.
IUCN (1968): Threatened.
IUCN (1971): Almost extinct in the wild in Thailand.
CITES (1979): Appendix I.
IUCN (1979): Threatened.
IUCN Red Data Book (1979): Endangered.
MAB (1979): Threatened.
USFWS (1980a): Endangered.
WARPA (1980): Protected-1.

Population Size and Trend: *Tomistoma* may have recently become extinct in the wild in Thailand. If it exists, probably fewer than 20 individuals remain. Throughout its range there has been a rapid decline in recent years. It is clearly one of the most endangered of the world's crocodilians (IUCN 1971, Whitaker and Daniel 1978, Whitaker 1979).

Distribution and History of Distribution: *T. schlegelii* formerly occurred in southern Thailand, Malaysia, Sumatra, Borneo, and

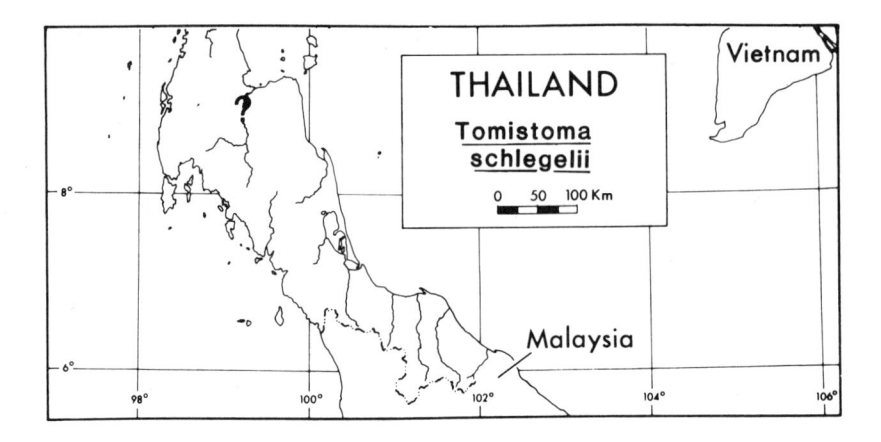

Fig. 41. Distribution of the False Gavial (*Tomistoma schlegelii*).

probably in other islands of the Indo-Australian Archipelago (Taylor 1970, King 1974). IUCN (1979) stated that a few individuals may still exist in Surat Thani Province (Fig. 41). Fossil species of *Tomistoma* are known worldwide.

Geographic Status: The Thai population, if it exists, is peripheral, lying at the northern limits of the species' distribution.

Habitat Requirements and Habitat Trend: *Tomistoma* presumably prefers freshwater lakes, rivers, canals, and swamps. Its diet is thought to be restricted to fish (Whitaker 1979).

Vulnerability of Species and Habitat: Unknown.

Causes of Threat: Hunting for hides has decimated this species. Although it is close to extinction, batches of young still appear on the Thai and Singapore markets from time to time. Depletion of freshwater fish stocks may have indirectly contributed to the decline (Taylor 1970, King and Brazaitis 1971, Whitaker 1979).

Responses to Habitat Modification: Unknown.

Demographic Characteristics: Unknown. Adults reach a maximum of 5.2 m (Taylor 1970). Captive specimens are known to have lived at least 11 years (King and Dobbs 1975).

Key Behaviors: Whitaker (1979) calls this animal one of the last mysterious crocodiles. Its habits in the wild are almost entirely unknown. The diet is reputed to consist entirely of fish. Whitaker (1979) believes that "it is likely to play a positive role in the fisheries of the waterways" as a top carnivore. It has never been known to attack man.

Conservation Measures Taken: Thai law (WARPA 1980) prohibits hunting and regulates trade of this species.

Conservation Measures Proposed: Surveys to determine the locations of existing populations are needed. American and European zoos hold about 50 individuals (King and Dobbs 1975, Honegger 1975). A few exist in the world's commercial crocodile farms, including about 170 at Samut Prakan Crocodile Farm south of Bangkok (IUCN Red Data Book 1979, our observation). Cooperative breeding efforts should be pursued, as most zoos that hold *Tomistoma* have only a single specimen. Romulus Whitaker (personal communication) is planning a study of *Tomistoma* in Malaysia and Indonesia. A wildlife reserve has been proposed in the upper Lalan River drainage, where the species survives in the river and at least four tributaries (Sudharma 1976).

Bengal monitor
Varanus bengalensis (Daudin 1802)
Reptilia, Squamata, Varanidae

Status: Threatened.
CITES (1979): Appendix I.
MAB (1979): Endangered.
USFWS (1980a): Endangered.

Population Size and Trend: Unknown at present. The Bengal monitor has been found to be common in Thailand in the past (Smith 1916, 1932) and more recently where good habitat remains (Seidensticker and McNeely 1974).

Distribution and History of Distribution: The Bengal monitor occurs in southern Iran, Nepal, India, Sri Lanka, Bangladesh, Burma, Thailand, Lao PDR, Kampuchea, Vietnam, and peninsular Malaysia (Boulenger 1885, Smith 1935, Taylor 1963, W. Auffenberg personal communication).

Geographic Status: Thailand is central in the species' range.

Habitat Requirements and Habitat Trend: This terrestrial species lives in many types of forest, but especially deciduous dipterocarp forest, from lowlands to at least 1,000 m elevation (M. A. Smith 1916, 1935, H. C. Smith 1931, Taylor 1963), but few details are known. If like most other monitors, this species is carnivorous and eats a wide variety of animals. From an original 80 percent, forest cover of Thailand has declined to 25 percent in 1978 (Myers 1980).

Vulnerability of Species and Habitat: This species is threatened by deforestation and by harvesting, both for food (H. C. Smith 1931, M. A. Smith 1932) and for export. From 1967 to 1971 the number of individuals exported from Thailand each year was 123, 96, 609, 1,049, and 1,664 (Royal Forestry Department 1972). The United States imported the following Bengal monitors: from all sources, 380 and 682 live animals in 1970 and 1971, and 6 and 4,207 pieces of skin products in 1970 and 1971; from Thailand, none in 1977 and 45 live animals in 1978 (USFWS 1974, CITES 1977, 1978). The United Kingdom reported importing a total of 52 Bengal monitors, all from Thailand, in 1977, but for the same year reported re-exporting 6,338 skins to 7 countries, under the antiquated name *V. nebulosus*, giving a CITES Appendix II listing (TRAFFIC 1978). In 1978, the United Kingdom reported no imports of Bengal monitors but reported re-exporting 6,362 "*V. nebulosus*" skins to 5 countries (TRAFFIC 1979).

Responses to Habitat Modification: Unknown.

Demographic Characteristics: Clutches include up to 25-30 eggs, which are laid early in the hot season (March and April) in Burma. Sexual maturity is attained at an age of 2-3 years, when total length is about 0.8 m (H. C. Smith 1931, Auffenberg 1981).

Key Behaviors: Individuals engage in pushing matches that may be territorial (R. Deraniyagala 1957). Though individuals of all ages and sexes fight, only females and subadults use their teeth and tails to damage their opponents. Male-male combat is a ritualistic test of strength. Males that win a ritual bout gain some advantage because females tend to engage in prolonged courtship with them soon after a bout, whereas courtship with losing males is delayed and abbreviated (Auffenberg 1981). Females bury their eggs in the soil and then dig several false nests nearby (P. Deraniyagala 1957). Males eat more than females, grow faster, and use the best basking sites, displacing other individuals from them if necessary (Auffenberg 1979).

Conservation Measures Taken: Bengal monitors occur in Huai Kha Khaeng Wildlife Sanctuary (Seidensticker and McNeely 1974) and Khao Yai National Park (W. Brockelman, personal communication).

Conservation Measures Proposed: The first step in planning for the management of this species is to conduct a detailed survey of its distribution and abundance. Trade should be regulated on a quota system, with the quota adjusted according to population trends determined by monitoring population size. If monitoring is not feasible, quotas should be set and maintained well below recent export levels. If export levels then were to fall below that quota figure, the cause probably would be a drastic population decline. In response, trade should be banned for perhaps 6 years, after which even lower quotas could be re-established.

Red-headed monitor
Varanus rudicollis (Gray 1845)
Reptilia, Squamata, Varanidae

Status: Threatened.
CITES (1979): Appendix II.
WARPA (1980): Protected-1.
Population Size and Trend: Unknown.
Distribution and History of Distribution: The red-headed monitor occurs in southern Burma and Thailand, peninsular Malaysia, Sumatra, Borneo, Banka, and the Philippines. In Thailand the species has been recorded in Ranong and Trang Provinces (Fig. 42; Boulenger 1885, Taylor 1963, 1966).
Geographic Status: Thailand is the northern limit of this species' range.
Habitat Requirements and Habitat Trend: The red-headed monitor lives in primary forest and has been recorded up to 610 m in elevation (de Rooij 1915), but no other details are known. Habitat loss has been extensive.
Vulnerability of Species and Habitat: This species is vulnerable to hunting and its habitat to deforestation.
Causes of Threat: The red-headed monitor is threatened by deforestation and by harvesting for food and export. The United States imported 51 and 43 live *V. rudicollis* from all sources in 1970 and 1971 (USFWS 1974). In 1977 the United States imported none of this species from Thailand, but in 1978, 66 live animals were

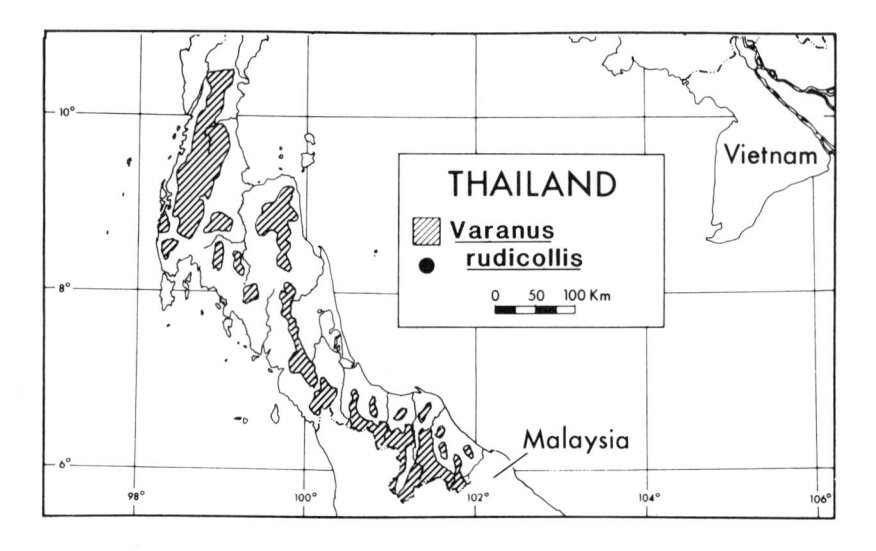

Fig. 42. Distribution of the Red-headed Monitor (*Varanus rudicollis*).

imported from Thailand (CITES 1977, 1978). The figure for 1980 was 37 animals (TRAFFIC 1981). The Federal Republic of Germany imported 5 *V. rudicollis* from Thailand in 1978 but none in 1979 (TRAFFIC 1980a). In 1978, 14 Thai *V. rudicollis* were imported into Switzerland, and 3 were imported into the United Kingdom (TRAFFIC 1978).

Responses to Habitat Modification: Unknown.
Demographic Characteristics: Unknown.
Key Behaviors: This species is arboreal.
Conservation Measures Taken: Thai law (WARPA 1980) protects this species from hunting and regulates trade.
Conservation Measures Proposed: The remaining forests in southern Thailand should be surveyed for this species.

Black jungle monitor
Varanus dumerilii **(Schlegel 1844)**
Reptilia, Squamata, Varanidae

Status: Threatened.
CITES (1979): Appendix II.

Population Size and Trend: Unknown. It was plentiful on Sir Charles Forbes Island, Burma (Smith 1931).

Distribution and History of Distribution: The black jungle monitor occurs in southern Burma and Thailand, peninsular Malaysia, Sumatra, Borneo, Batu Islands, Banka, Beliton, and Java. In Thailand the species is known from Trang Province (Boulenger 1885, de Rooij 1915, Taylor 1963).

Geographic Status: Thailand is the northern limit of the species' range.

Habitat Requirements and Habitat Trend: Unknown. Records exist from mangrove forest up to 1,200 m elevation (de Rooij 1915, H. C. Smith 1931).

Vulnerability of Species and Habitat: Unknown.

Causes of Threat: In 1980, 64 black jungle monitors were exported from Thailand into the United States (TRAFFIC 1981).

Responses to Habitat Modification: Unknown.

Demographic Characteristics: Unknown.

Key Behaviors: In captivity *V. dumerilii* swims and burrows well and is diurnal in its activity. Captive animals accepted raw meat, rodents, eggs, lizards, small fish, and crickets as food (Sprackland 1976).

Conservation Measures Taken: None.

Conservation Measures Proposed: The distribution and habitat of this poorly known species must be learned before anything more can be done.

Burmese python
Python molurus bivittatus (Schlegel 1837)
Reptilia, Squamata, Boidae

Status: Threatened.
IUCN Red Data Book (1975): Vulnerable.
CITES (1979): Appendix II.

Population Size and Trend: The Burmese python is rare (Boulenger 1912, Smith 1943) and declining over most of its range (IUCN Red Data Book 1975).

Distribution and History of Distribution: This subspecies is found in southern China, Hong Kong, Hainan, Vietnam, Thailand, Burma, Java, Sumbawa, Borneo, and Celebes. Specific records from Thailand are published for Raheng, Lopburi, and Chon Buri provinces (Schmidt 1927, Smith 1943, Taylor 1965). The other subspecies (*P. m. molurus*) occurs in India, Sri Lanka, Nepal, Bangladesh, and Pakistan.

Geographic Status: Thailand is central in the range of the Burmese python.

Habitat Requirements and Habitat Trend: Burmese pythons occur in a wide variety of habitats, from mangrove swamps to evergreen forest up to 2,000 m elevation. Requirements include a large undisturbed area in which to hunt and hiding places near a permanent water source. The diet consists of small to medium-sized birds and mammals, particularly rodents. Vast areas of habitat have been lost (IUCN Red Data Book 1975, Whitaker 1978).

Vulnerability of Species and Habitat: The Burmese python is vulnerable to deforestation and harvest for food and export. The skin is highly prized for its beauty.

Causes of Threat: Much habitat has been deforested. The meat and fat have been consumed traditionally for food and supposed medicinal purposes (Schmidt 1927, Whitaker 1978). Burmese pythons exported from Thailand in 1967-71 numbered 47, 49, 119, 174, and 496 (Royal Forestry Department 1972). In 1977, 993 live individuals and 1,000 skins were exported from Thailand to the United States (CITES 1977). In 1978, 6,681 live individuals and 1,000 m of skins were exported from Thailand to the United States (CITES 1977). In 1980, 5,106 Burmese pythons were exported from Thailand to the United States (TRAFFIC 1981). In 1979, 689 live Burmese pythons were exported from Thailand to the Federal Republic of Germany (TRAFFIC 1980b). In 1978, 298 Burmese pythons were exported from Thailand to the United Kingdom (TRAFFIC 1979).

Responses to Habitat Modification: Unknown.

Demographic Characteristics: This species is oviparous and reaches a length of up to 9 m. The clutch contains up to 107 eggs (Smith 1943), but the usual number is 30-50. The eggs are incubated by the mother, and they hatch after 2-3 months. Sexual maturity is reached at 3-5 years of age (IUCN Red Data Book 1975).

Key Behaviors: Mating occurs during hibernation in India, and eggs are laid in March-June (Whitaker 1978). The period from mating to egg-laying ranges from 60 to 120 days, varying with ambient temperature. Gravid females refuse to eat and begin to have elevated body temperature several weeks before the eggs are laid (Van Mierop and Barnard 1976). Spasmodic muscle contractions are used to generate heat, and the female coils around the eggs to incubate them for 55-66 days, losing 20 percent of her body weight in the process (Valenciennes 1841, Forbes 1881, Van Mierop and Barnard 1976, and many others). Males kept in captivity with a female established a stable, linear dominance hierarchy, and the subsequent frequency of matings was correlated with the hierarchical status of each male (Barker et al. 1979). Pythons sleep or bask in the day and travel at night, hunting. Large individuals have a regularly used home range (Whitaker 1978).

Conservation Measures Taken: None are known, but the species probably occurs in some of Thailand's national parks and wildlife sanctuaries.

Conservation Measures Proposed: This species is difficult to study in the field except by radiotelemetry, so population monitoring is not feasible. The best that can be done is to maintain tracts of native forest and regulate trade on a quota basis. Quotas should be set substantially below recent export levels and will have to be 7maintained arbitrarily, without scientific justification, unless a method is discovered for monitoring population trends. If export levels fall below such a quota figure, a drastic population decline probably would be the cause, and a complete ban on trade should be imposed for 7-10 years, after which lower quotas could be re-established. Burmese pythons breed well in captivity, so it has potential for captive breeding and rearing for market similar to Thailand's successful crocodile farming. Such endeavors should be stocked only from animals now in captivity, because supplementing them with wild-caught ones would aggravate the problem.

Blood or short python
Python curtus Schlegel 1872
Reptilia, Squamata, Boidae

Status: Threatened.
CITES (1979): Appendix II.

Population Size and Trend: Blood pythons are moderately common in good habitat (Ridley 1899). Populations probably are much reduced because of habitat loss.

120   *Endangered Animals of Thailand*

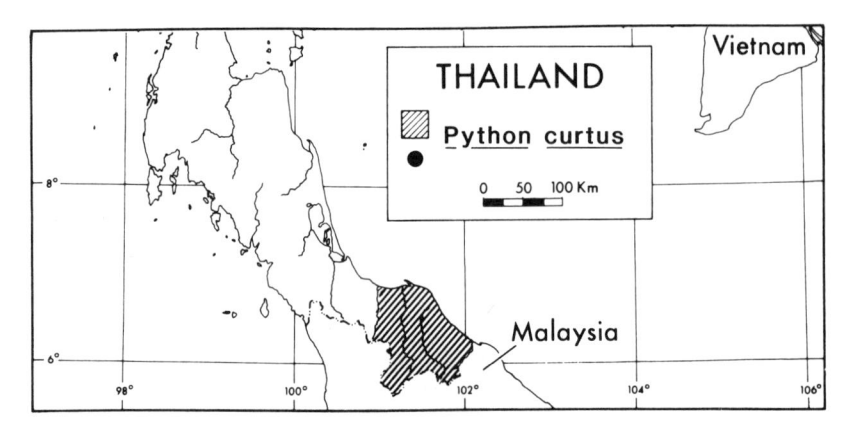

Fig. 43. Distribution of the Blood or Short Python (*Python curtus*).

Distribution and History of Distribution: This species occurs in southernmost Thailand, peninsular Malaysia, Singapore, Sumatra, and Borneo (Boulenger 1912, de Rooij 1917). In Thailand it is known only from Pattani Province (Fig. 43; Taylor 1965).

Geographic Status: Thailand is on the extreme northern edge of the species' range.

Habitat Requirements and Habitat Trend: The few published remarks indicate that blood pythons inhabit swamp forest (Boulenger 1912, de Rooij 1917, Tweedie 1954). If so, most of their habitat has been lost to cutting, draining, and use of mangroves for charcoal. In captivity, rats are accepted as food.

Vulnerability of Species and Habitat: The blood python is vulnerable to habitat loss and harvest for food and export.

Causes of Threat: Very little of this species' habitat may remain in Thailand. The following figures indicate the extent of recent trade. In 1977, 1978, and 1980, 62, 568, and 147 live blood pythons were exported from Thailand to the United States (CITES 1977, 1978, TRAFFIC 1981). In 1978, 49 were exported from Thailand to the United Kingdom (TRAFFIC 1979). In 1979, 55 were exported from Thailand to the Federal Republic of Germany (TRAFFIC 1980).

Responses to Habitat Modification: Unknown.

Demographic Characteristics: This species reaches a length of 2.5 m and an age of at least 28 years (Taylor 1965).

Key Behaviors: Blood pythons may be like other pythons in

exerting physiological control over body temperature (Vinegar et al. 1970).

Conservation Measures Taken: None, although the 30-year strip rotation system recently mandated for mangrove harvest may help this species.

Conservation Measures Proposed: The range and habitat of blood pythons in Thailand are restricted enough that field survey work may provide information on distribution and status, and population monitoring may be feasible. If this is not attempted or successful, a quota system as proposed for the Burmese python should be put into operation.

Chapter 6

Birds

Spot-billed pelican
Pelecanus philippensis **Gmelin 1789**
Aves, Pelicaniformes, Pelicanidae

Status: Endangered.
WARPA (1980): Protected-1.

Population Size and Trend: In 1877 Oates (1883) described a 260 km^2 Burmese swamp with millions of nesting pelicans and adjutant storks; by 1939 the trees and birds were gone. The spot-billed pelican occurred in large numbers in Thailand (Gyldenstolpe 1920). This species no longer breeds in Thailand, and only a few vagrant individuals have been seen in recent years.

Distribution and History of Distribution: The spot-billed pelican occurs in India, Pakistan, Bangladesh, Sri Lanka, Burma, Thailand, Kampuchea, Lao PDR, southern and eastern China, Hong Kong, Hainan, peninsular Malaysia, Sumatra, Java, and the Philippines. In Thailand the historical range includes the larger marshes of the Chiang Rai-Chiang Saen area and the central plains, the southeastern coast, and both coasts of the peninsula (Deignan 1963, Ali and Ripley 1969, King and Dickinson 1975, Medway and Wells 1976). Current distribution is poorly documented. Two individuals were seen at the Chiang Rak Dam, Pathum Thani, in 1977 (Pauley 1977). A single individual was present at Songkhla Lake in July-September 1979 but absent from December 1978 through June 1979 (Thailand Institute of Scientific and Technological Research 1979). One pelican (presumably this species) was seen flying south along the Khwae Noi River, near Sai Yok Noi, on 21 June 1981 (W. Brockelman, personal communication). Four birds occurred in Nakhon Sawan Province in January 1985 (Ogle 1986).

Geographic Status: Thailand is central in the species' range.

Habitat Requirements and Habitat Trend: Spot-billed pelicans feed in marshes, freshwater lakes, brackish lagoons, tidal creeks, and estuaries. Nesting is in large trees in swamp forest or swampy savanna (Smythies 1953, Deignan 1963, Ali and Ripley 1969). Vast areas of marsh and swamp have been drained, cleared, and converted to rice paddies. The diet consists of fish.

Vulnerability of Species and Habitat: Pelican nesting habitat is vulnerable to deforestation, and feeding habitat in marshes is vulnerable to draining. Pelicans are vulnerable to eggshell thinning and massive reproductive failure caused by chlorinated hydrocarbons like DDT, which is concentrated in the tissues of carnivorous species eaten by the pelicans. The result is region-wide population declines and extirpation (Schreiber 1980).

Causes of Threat: The species is threatened by shooting, use of persistent pesticides, and habitat loss.

Demographic Characteristics: The clutch contains 3-4 eggs. Incubation takes 30 days, and fledging occurs about 4 months after hatching (Ali and Ripley 1969). If similar to other pelicans, this species probably reaches sexual maturity in 3-5 years.

Key Behaviors: Nesting is colonial, with the season ranging from October to March in India. Both sexes incubate the eggs and feed the young (Ali and Ripley 1969). The species is only a seasonal visitor in northern Thailand (Deignan 1945) and a vagrant south of Songkhla and Trang (Medway and Wells 1976).

Conservation Measures Taken: Spot-billed pelicans are protected by Thai law (WARPA 1980).

Conservation Measures Proposed: All sight records of pelicans should be compiled, and evidence of possible breeding should be sought in the process of making an inventory of all existing waterbird rookeries in Thailand. Eggshells collected during the period from before 1945 to the present should be studied for evidence of thinning. High pesticide levels in the food chain threaten humans as well as wildlife, and evidence of a problem would mandate changing pest control practices nationwide to use of less dangerous pesticides.

Brown booby
Sula leucogaster
Aves, Procellariiformes, Sulidae

Status: Threatened.

Population Size and Trend: Unknown. This is the most common booby in most tropical seas (Ali and Ripley 1968), but it is rare in Thai waters. There are no recent sight records for Thailand (Philip D. Round, personal communication).

Distribution and History of Distribution: The brown booby breeds in the tropical Atlantic, Indian, and Pacific oceans. In Asia the species occurs from northern Australia north to the Bonin Islands and east to Laysan (Riley 1938, De Schauensee 1984). It was common on the west coast of Thailand (Robinson and Kloss 1921), and early specimens are from near the Aroa Islands and Pulo Perak, Straits of Malacca (Riley 1938), and from islets near Ko Rin and Ko Chuan in the Gulf of Thailand (Williamson 1916, 1918). Two specimens were collected on Ko Juang, Satthahip, Chonburi Province, by the Thailand Institute of Scientific and Technological Research in June 1973. No ornithologists have searched that area more recently.

Geographic Status: This is a cosmopolitan, tropical species with several described subspecies.

Habitat Requirements and Habitat Trend: Habitat of the brown booby is the oceans off both coasts of Thailand. It breeds on offshore islands.

Vulnerability of Species and Habitat: The concentration of nesting colonies on offshore islands make this species quite vulnerable to disturbance and hunting by humans.

Causes of Threat: Birds are shot, and fishermen take nestlings as food (Philip D. Round, personal communication).

Responses to Habitat Modification: Unknown.

Demographic Characteristics: This species takes 2-3 years to acquire adult plumage (Smythies 1953).

Key Behaviors: This species nests colonially on the ground (Smythies 1960, Ali and Ripley 1968) or occasionally in the lower branches of trees and bushes (Wildash 1968). It has a very characteristic behavior of flying in circles over a school of fish about 60-100 feet over the ocean surface and periodically diving into the water with half-closed wings to catch fish or pursue them underwater

(Smythies 1953, De Schauensee 1984). The diet consists mostly of flying fish and squid (Ali and Ripley 1968).

Conservation Measures Taken: It is possible that the brown booby still breeds on the islands off Satthahip, where the Navy restricts access to certain areas (Philip D. Round, personal communication).

Conservation Measures Proposed: Current information on status and threats is needed before conservation measures can be proposed.

Darter, anhinga, snakebird
Anhinga melanogaster
Aves, Procellariiformes, Anhingidae

Status: Threatened.
WARPA (1980): Protected-1.

Population Size and Trend: Darters once were common (Gyldenstolpe 1920) and now are seldom seen, but no details are available. Smythies (1960) reported that the darter populations of Borneo were declining rapidly in the 1950s. McClure and Lekagul (1961) saw only three while travelling down 150 km of the Mae Ping River on northern Thailand in 1957. More recent studies in which darters should have been encountered reported none (Holmes and Wells, 1975, Storer 1977, Thailand Institute of Scientific and Technological Research 1979).

Distribution and History of Distribution: This species occurs from the Middle East through Pakistan, India, and Southeast Asia to Java, Borneo, the Philippines, and Sulawesi (Riley 1938). Originally the darter occurred in suitable localities throughout Thailand (Gyldenstolpe 1920, Deignan 1945, Lekagul and Cronin 1974). A single, nonbreeding animal occurred at Khao Yai National Park from 1969-74 (McClure 1974a). The only recent sightings are one or two pair at Wat Tarn En (Philip D. Round, personal communication).

Geographic Status: The Thai populations are part of a much larger range.

Habitat Requirements and Habitat Trend: Darters inhabit freshwater ponds, lakes, reservoirs, swamps, and rivers; they do not occur on salt water. Though some marshes have been drained for agriculture, that is not a primary cause of threat.

Vulnerability of Species and Habitat: The darter is conspicuous and easily shot as it swims in the water or perches on a riverbank or low branches to dry its wings. Its colonial nests along the water's edge are vulnerable to people who take the eggs for food (Smythies 1953, 1960).

Causes of Threat: Unrestrained harvest by people apparently is the cause of threat to this species.

Responses to Habitat Modification: Largely unknown. This species will readily colonize reservoirs and ponds created by man.

Demographic Characteristics: The clutch contains 3 to 6 eggs (Smythies 1960, Ali and Ripley 1968). Both sexes incubate the eggs and feed the young.

Key Behaviors: The darter is highly specialized in body form and probably specific gravity for capturing freshwater fish and prawns by underwater pursuit. Propulsion while swimming under water is done with the feet, with the wings held half outstretched. Adaptations of the neck vertebrae allow the bill to be struck forward to spear prey (Ali and Ripley 1968). Some prey are eaten while the bird is underwater. A typical dive lasts 2 minutes. When resting on the water surface, the darter swims with just the head and part of the neck above water. Nesting is colonial.

Conservation Measures Taken: Thai law (WARPA 1980) prohibits killing and regulates trade of this species.

Conservation Measures Proposed: A survey is needed to determine if populations are available to reoccupy vacant range. If the birds were protected from hunting by humans, they should recover to substantial numbers.

Christmas Island frigatebird
Fregata andrewsi **Mathews**
Aves, Pelicaniformes, Fregatidae

Status: Endangered.
IUCN Red Data Book (1977): Vulnerable.
CITES (1979): Appendix I.
USFWS (1980a): Endangered.
Population Size and Trend: Population estimates were 1,000-

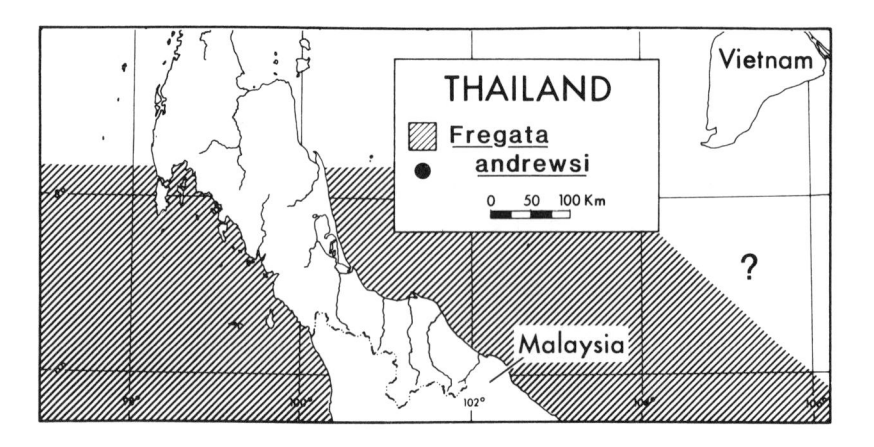

Fig. 44. Distribution of the Christmas Island Frigate-bird (*Fregata andrewsi*).

1,500 pairs in 1938-40, fewer than 2,000 pairs in 1967, and fewer than 1,000 pairs in 1965-74 (IUCN Red Data Book 1977). The most recent estimate is a population of fewer than 1,000 pairs, with a declining trend (Nelson 1976).

Distribution and History of Distribution: The Christmas Island frigatebird is known to breed only on Christmas Island, south of Java. Nonbreeding individuals range widely over the eastern Indian Ocean and South China Sea, with records from India, Java, Borneo, Malaya, peninsular Thailand, and Hong Kong. The species occurs on both coasts of Thailand south of the Isthmus of Kra (Fig. 44). Specimens have been collected on Ko Phuket (Gyldenstolpe 1920, Deignan 1963, Lekagul and Cronin 1974, King and Dickinson 1975, Medway and Wells 1976). A mixed-species flock of up to 400 frigatebirds, mostly of this species, were reported circling daily over Phi Phi Le Island, Krabi Province, from 20 November to 7 December 1977 (Boswall and Kanwanich 1978).

Geographic Status: The Thailand portion of the species' range is on the northern periphery of its distribution, presumably occupied seasonally by nonreproductive birds dispersed from the distant nesting site.

Habitat Requirements and Habitat Trend: Nesting habitat is tall trees behind the golf course and along 3.2 km of shore terrace on Christmas Island. The sea almond tree (*Terminalia catappa*) is preferred for nesting, and nests are always 10 m or more above the ground, either to avoid human nest predation or facilitate flight from the nest. Foraging habitat is the surface of the open sea, up to 1,500 km from land during nonbreeding dispersal. The diet is mainly flying fish and squid. A small portion of the diet includes fish stolen in flight from species of diving seabirds, and eggs and nestlings from seabird rookeries of their own and other species (Nelson 1976, IUCN Red Data Book 1977).

Vulnerability of Species and Habitat: Nesting frigatebirds have been taken by humans resident on Christmas Island for many years. The demographic adaptations of frigatebirds make them particularly vulnerable to any man-caused mortality. Nesting habitat is indirectly threatened by surface mining for phosphate, though the rookery is over low-grade deposits that may never be mined (IUCN Red Data Book 1977). However, the economics of phosphate resources are such that all available deposits are expected to become profitably extractable (H. T. Odum, personal communication), unless areas are defined for other reasons as too valuable to be mined.

Causes of Threat: Existing harvest and potential habitat loss threaten this species.

Responses to Habitat Modification: Unknown.

Demographic Characteristics: As in other frigatebirds, the population dynamics of this species are constrained by use of a limited food resource in impoverished seas. The result is low natality, high survival, and a poor ability to respond to population losses. The age at sexual maturity is unknown. Breeding females produce 1 egg every 2 years. The incubation period is about 54 days. The chick grows very slowly, and fledging occurs at about 6 months of age. The parents continue to feed the juvenile for another 9-10 months after fledging. Fledging success is about 30 percent (Nelson 1976). Nelson postulated that mortality during the first year of independence was 20-30 percent, and 4 percent annually thereafter, suggesting a mean life expectancy of 26 years and longevity extremes of 40-50 years; these figures are guesses.

Key Behaviors: The period of egg-laying is April to June. Both parents participate in nest-building and feeding of the young. Bouts of incubation are 2-3 days long, while the other parent forages. When the chick is about 45 days old, it is left unattended so both parents can feed at the same time (Nelson 1976).

Conservation Measures Taken: Frigatebirds are protected on Christmas Island, but the regulation is routinely ignored. A conservation officer was appointed there in 1975 (IUCN Red Data Book 1977).

Conservation Measures Proposed: The steps needed to conserve frigatebirds at the Christmas Island rookery are obvious. Thailand could help by ensuring that the individuals visiting Thai waters and coasts are not killed.

Chinese egret
Egretta eulophotes (Swinhoe 1860)
Aves, Ciconiiformes, Ardeidae

Status: Endangered.
IUCN Red Data Book (1977): Vulnerable.
IUCN (1979): Threatened.
USFWS (1980a): Endangered.
WARPA (1980): Protected-1.

Population Size and Trend: Population size has never been documented. Formerly a common species, the breeding population of Chinese egrets was decimated by hunting for the plume trade beginning in 1897-98, and by 1925 records of any species of egrets nesting in China were considered noteworthy. The Chinese egret has never recovered its former numbers and remains on the verge of extinction (Murton 1972, IUCN Red Data Book 1977). However, population size and trend on mainland China are unknown. In Hong Kong, 9 pair of Chinese egrets nested in 1959, but that number declined to 3 by 1969 (Murton 1972) and 2 in 1981 (David Melville, personal communication).

Distribution and History of Distribution: The following account of distribution is taken almost verbatim from the IUCN Red Data Book (1977): The Chinese egret formerly bred in the maritime provinces of Fukien and Kwangtung, China, North Korea, and possibly Cheju Do (Quelpart Island) in the Yellow Sea (La Touche 1931-34, Austin 1948). It was found breeding in Hong Kong in 1956 (Murton 1972). Its present breeding distribution is not well known, but recent specimens in Peking are from Kwangung, including Hainan, Chekiang, Fukien, Taiwan, Kiangsu, and Shantung (information from Tso-hsin Cheng). Whether the species still breeds in North Korea is unknown. Recent postbreeding records are from Amur-Ussuriland, USSR (regularly in the spring), Taiwan in

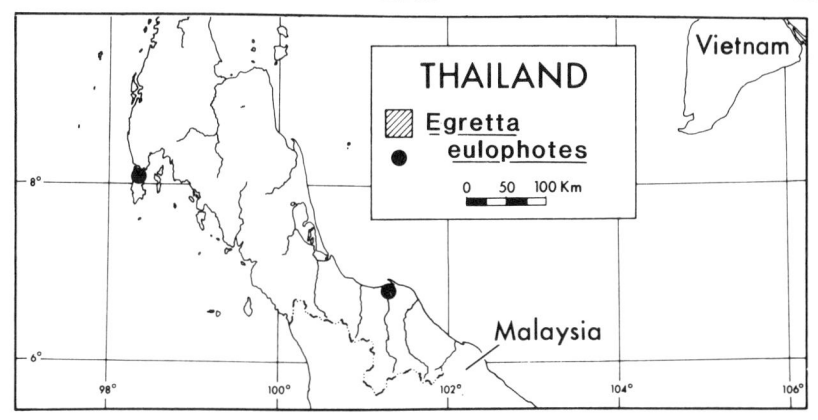

Fig. 45. Distribution of the Chinese Egret (*Egretta eulophotes*).

summer and winter, and other winter records from coastal South Korea, the Ryukyu Islands, Sabah, Malaya, and the Aleutian Islands. Former winter records, when the population was larger, included the Philippines, Sulawesi, peninsular Thailand, Malaysia, Sarawak, Honshu, Japan, and Natuna Island.

Geographic Status: The Thailand distribution constituted a small part of the Chinese egret's migratory and winter range. The species may no longer frequent Thailand coasts, as the last records (Fig. 45) occurred in 1901 (Deignan 1963).

Habitat Requirements and Habitat Trend: Foraging habitat in both summer and winter is tidal mudflats and the edge of estuaries (Swinhoe 1860, La Touche 1931-34, Murton 1972). Occasionally individuals are seen on salt pans, along the seashore, in rice paddies, or along rivers (Courtois 1927, La Touche 1931-34). The diet consists of fish, shrimp, and *Squilla* (Swinhoe 1860). In both foraging behavior and habitat the Chinese egret is specialized in the same ways as its North American ecological equivalent (Murton 1972), the reddish egret (*Dichromanassa rufescens*). Nesting habitat is in rookeries in trees, shared with many other species of herons and egrets. In Hong Kong, the number of nests is declining, from 9 in 1959 to 3 in 1969 (Murton 1972).

Vulnerability of Species and Habitat: Currently the species is not vulnerable to man-caused losses, but its nesting habitat is being impacted by human disturbance and land-use encroachment. In the past, the species was highly vulnerable to hunting for commerce in feathers, drastically reducing the total population. The Chinese egret is the central member of a 3-species guild, each weakly displaced in space, with marine habitat occupied by the reef egret (*Egretta sacra*) and freshwater habitat by the little egret (*Egretta garzetta*), each exhibiting some overlap in foraging habitat. Following the heavy harvest of egrets, the population of Chinese egrets became very small, and competition from its more abundant guild neighbors may explain the failure of this species to recover its former numbers (Murton 1972).

Causes of Threat: Disturbance and destruction of rookeries is a serious threat to the remaining Chinese egrets (Murton 1972). What threats may prevail on mainland China are unknown.

Demographic Characteristics: A clutch may contain 3 eggs (Rickett 1903). In Hong Kong, eggs are laid in late May, with incubation taking about 29 days (Murton 1972).

Key Behaviors: In the Malay Peninsula, migratory Chinese egrets have been observed between 14 August and 26 April (Medway and Wells 1976). This species hunts by "parasolling"--spreading and flicking its wings to frighten fishes from cover and running after them to attempt capture (Murton 1972).

Conservation Measures Taken: Mostly unknown. The remaining rookeries in Hong Kong are policed by game wardens (Murton 1972). Thai law (WARPA 1980) prohibits hunting and regulates trade of this species.

Conservation Measures Proposed: Nothing can be done in Thailand to enhance the survival of this species. Conservation steps should focus on the breeding range, once information on its extent and problems are known.

Painted stork
Ibis leucocephalus **(Pennant)**
Aves, Ciconiiformes, Ciconiidae

Status: Endangered.
IUCN (1968): Threatened.
WARPA (1980): Protected-1.

Population Size and Trend: In the past, painted storks were locally common in much of their range, including India, Burma, southern and eastern China, and peninsular Thailand (Gyldenstolpe 1920, Ali and Ripley 1968, Smythies 1953, La Touche 1931-

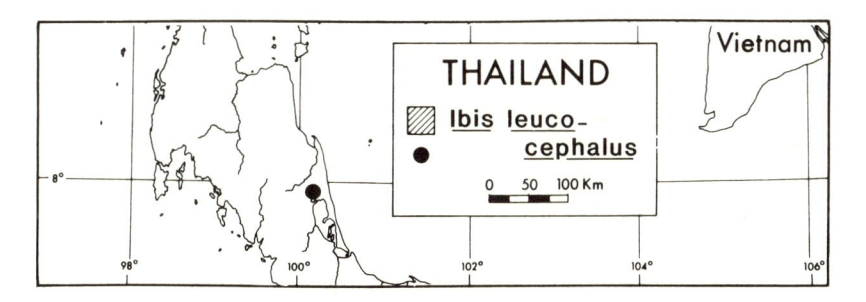

Fig. 46. Distribution of the Painted Stork (*Ibis leucocephalus*).

34, Glenister 1955, Robinson 1915 in Riley 1938). However, it was considered uncommon by Lekagul and Cronin (1974). At present, the only breeding population known in Thailand consists of 4 nesting pairs (Robert Dobias, personal communication) or 16 birds in 1979 (Thailand Institute of Scientific and Technological Research 1979), and this population has been declining in recent years (Thailand Institute of Scientific and Technological Research 1979). Several times this number occur in zoos in Bangkok and Samut Prakan (our observations).

Distribution and History of Distribution: Painted storks occur in lowlands from Sri Lanka and India east to Vietnam, eastern China, and Hainan, and from southern China to the island Pulau Langkawi just south of the Thai-Malaysian border (La Touche 1931-34, Riley 1938, Glenister 1955, Smythies 1953, Ali and Ripley 1968, King and Dickinson 1975, Wildash 1968). Whether the range has become smaller is uncertain. Only one rookery is known in Thailand (Fig. 46), deep in the *Melaleuca-Alstonia* swamp north of Thale Noi (Robert Dobias, personal communication), at Ao Moh, southeast of Kuan Kee Sian (Thailand Institute of Scientific and Technological Research 1979). About 30 painted storks stayed at Wat Phai Lom, Pathum Thani Province, for a few days in November 1980 (Pilai Poonswad, personal communication). A bird that may have been this species was reported to have been shot and eaten in 1978 at a village on the floodplain south of Khao Yai National Park, on Klong 31, Nakron Nayok Province (Virach Chantrasmi, personal communication). Other, more recent records include an individual reported by Dr. Boonsong Lekagul at Bor Muang beach, Krabi Province.

Geographic Status: The Thailand distribution is central within the species' range.

Habitat Requirements and Habitat Trend: Foraging habitat is in marshes, flooded rice paddies, wet savannas, and riverine and coastal mudflats (La Touche 1931-34, Smythies 1953, Ali and Ripley 1968, Wildash 1968). Nesting habitat is in large *Alstonia spathulata* trees that grow in or next to water (Ali and Ripley 1968, Thailand Institute of Scientific and Technological Research 1979). The diet consists mainly of fish, plus reptiles, frogs, crustaceans, and insects (Ali and Ripley 1968).

Vulnerability of Species and Habitat: The species is highly vulnerable to nest robbing and destruction of rookery habitat. Because the known population is so small, it also is vulnerable to chance occurrence of a series of drought years in which conditions fail to support reproduction. Drainage of marsh habitats around Thale Noi presumably would cause extirpation of the painted stork from Thailand.

Causes of Threat: All nesting painted storks that do not die of natural causes or are not taken into captivity by Wildlife Conservation officials are taken from the nests by people. The 1980 price for a nestling in Nakhan Si Thammarat was US $100 (Robert Dobias, personal communication). Painted storks exported from Thailand numbered 2 in 1967 and 8 in 1971 (Royal Forestry Department 1972). Hence the captive-rearing program of the Royal Forestry Department is the only force now slowing the imminent extirpation of this species from Thailand.

Responses to Habitat Modification: Unknown. Though painted storks use rice paddies when flooded, reproduction and seasonal distribution of the species are controlled by the temporal and spatial effects of flooding on food supply. Therefore it cannot be assumed that rice paddies developed in place of marsh habitat will continue to supply an adequate abundance and distribution of stork food. Any such negative effects would have disastrous impact if the habitat around the rookery were to be modified.

Demographic Characteristics: The clutch ranges from 2-5 eggs and is usually 3-4 (Ali and Ripley 1968). Nesting at Thale Noi begins in February to April, and both sexes incubate (Thailand Institute of Scientific and Technological Research 1979). Other features are undocumented.

Key Behaviors: The species is non-migratory but shifts its residence according to water conditions. Timing of the nesting season depends on the weather. Reproduction fails during drought years. Rookeries that are seldom disturbed and achieve a replacement rate of reproduction are used annually and hence are very important to the species (Ali and Ripley 1968). Reproduction at the Thale Noi rookery occurs in the hot season (Robert Dobias, personal communication).

Conservation Measures Taken: Several management practices favor the tenuous existence of Thailand's painted stork population. Thale Noi is designated as a No-hunting Area, and Wildlife Conservation officials are stationed there. Trees are protected from harvest to prevent deforestation of the Thale Noi swamp. The healthy fishing economy depends on the shallow lake, favoring current land use practices. Succession of the lake into marshland is slowed by protecting the fringing swamp forest, which serves as a nutrient trap that helps stabilize the present human economy. The practice of hand-rearing some of the painted stork nestlings at the Wildlife Conservation office has resulted in the only successful recruitment of subadults into the wild in recent years. Thai law (WARPA 1980) prohibits killing and regulates trade of this species.

Conservation Measures Proposed: Extension of the No-hunting Area provisions to the swamp forest around Thale Noi would give the small painted stork population the full benefit of its reproductive effort. Failing that, conservation officials should undertake a more intensive captive-rearing program, leaving one nestling in each nest to ensure that the rookery will not be abandoned. It probably is possible to greatly increase the amount of reproduction by designing the captive-rearing around a method of removing eggs for incubation rather than removing nestlings, if the adults respond by laying another clutch. Reproductive success and long-term survival of rookery birds should be studied annually, and emergency measures should be instigated at the first indication of any downward trend. It would be appropriate to investigate the potential for reintroduction of zoo-held painted storks to supplement the Thale Noi population.

Open-billed stork
Anastomus oscitans (Boddaert)
Aves, Ciconiiformes, Ciconiidae

Status: Threatened.
WARPA (1980): Protected-1.
Population Size and Trend: The Wat Phai Lom population of open-billed storks (Fig. 47) was estimated at 22,000 by Lauhachinda (1969). In 1980 the population was estimated at 30,000 based on a count of nests and assuming 3 fledged young per nest and an equal sex ratio of adults. Hence about 6,000 breeding females are indicated. Other Thai populations total 200-1,000 individuals (Taweesak Trirawatpong, personal communication). Annual nest counts in January by the Bangkok Bird Club, adding 20 percent to account for poor visibility in the thick bamboo groves, have shown a steady population increase from 1978 to 25,000 adults in 1980 but a reduction to 17,700 in 1981. Assuming 2 fledged young per nest and 1 nest for every 2 adults, the population in June 1981 was calculated to be 35,400 adults and fledged young (Virach Chantrasmi, personal communication).

Fig. 47. Immature open-billed storks (*Anastomus oscitans*) in the rookery at Wat Phai Lom, Pathum Thani Province, May 1980.

Distribution and History of Distribution: The open-billed stork occurs in Pakistan, India, Sri Lanka, Nepal, Bangladesh, Burma,

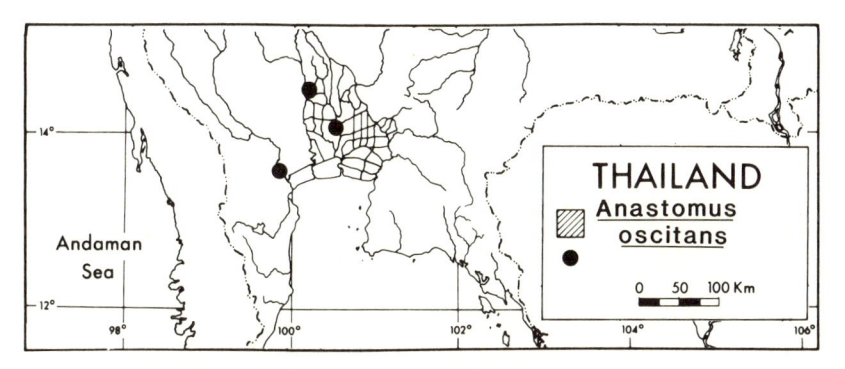

Fig. 48. Distribution of the Open-billed Stork (*Anastomus oscitans*).

Thailand, and Kampuchea (Ali and Ripley 1968, King and Dickinson 1975). In Thailand the species occurs in three rookeries (Fig. 48). The major one is at Wat Phai Lom, Pathum Thani Province, across the Chao Phraya River from Sam Khok. New rookeries, perhaps 2-3 years old, are occupied by 100-1,000 storks at Suphan Buri and 100 storks at Ban Po Rajaburi (Taweesak Trirawatpong, personal communication). Birds from the rookeries disperse widely to forage. During dispersal and migration they may be found in appropriate habitat throughout the country as far south in the peninsula as Krabi (Deignan 1963, Lekagul and Cronin 1974). In Nakhon Sawan Province, birds are seen occasionally from April to July and are fairly common in October and November; a colony of 100 occurs in Chumsaeng District in winter but apparently does not breed (Ogle 1986).

Geographic Status: The Thai portion of the range is a central part of the total distribution and is linked with other countries by seasonal habitat requirements.

Habitat Requirements and Habitat Trend: The original foraging habitat of open-billed storks in Thailand is presumed to have been marshland, most of which has been converted to agricultural uses. The storks now feed in wet rice fields and on the edge of canals and rivers. Nesting habitat is groves of large trees and bamboo where large arboreal predators are relatively few. The diet consists mainly of apple snails--*Pila globosa* in India, *P. pesmei* and *P. ampullacea* in Thailand--plus crabs, frogs, and other small marsh animals (Ali and Ripley 1968, McClure and Kwanyuen 1973, Poonswad 1979). Wet season habitat is in the Brahmaputra and Ganges deltas of Bangladesh.

Vulnerability of Species and Habitat: The species is highly vulnerable to vandalism and habitat destruction at the three rookeries that sustain the Thai population. In 1970, poachers used slingshots to kill several hundred storks at Wat Phai Lom, and the disruption nearly caused abandonment of the rookery (McClure and Kwanyuen 1973). The adult birds tolerate people walking through the rookery, but many young disturbed by such activity fall from the nests and subsequently die. Foraging habitat is vulnerable to drainage, but conversion of native marsh to artificial rice marsh is not a threat. Proper distribution and abundance of apple snails are essential to maintain the stork population.

Causes of Threat: Unknown, but the vulnerability of any species concentrated at one site is alarming. Marshes everywhere are disappearing. No information is available on the biology of the species or its habitat during the wet season. Birds soaring on thermals above the Wat Phai Lom rookery are a potential hazard to commercial aircraft, and a tragic accident could lead to destruction of the colony. The conflict involves jets originating in Europe and approaching the Don Muang Airport, Bangkok, via Burmese airspace from late February through early December, when the prevailing wind is from the south or southwest (Virach Chantrasmi, personal communication).

Response to Habitat Modification: Open-billed storks adapt to feeding in rice fields after marshes have been converted to agriculture. The biology of apple snails in rice paddies has not been studied, but snail distribution and abundance in paddies appear sufficient to support stork reproduction. When rookery trees die from excessive bird-dropping fertilizer, the storks shift to bamboo and any available support for nests. If winds more easily dislodge nests, eggs, and young from lesser vegetation, the recruitment rate of fledged young would decrease due to nest failure once the large trees die. When new trees are planted adjacent to the rookery, the storks soon use them for nesting. With nesting space apparently a limiting factor, the impact of reducing the rookery area for human development would presumably be negative.

Demographic Characteristics: The normal clutch consists of 4 eggs, but usually only 2 young survive to fledge, except in years without wind storms. Eggs are laid at about 2-day intervals, and hatching is at 27-29 days. Flight is possible after 40 days, but parental care can last for 2 months (Lauhachinda 1969 in McClure and Kwanyuen 1973).

Key Behaviors: Open-billed storks are annual migrants, arriving at Wat Phai Lom in October and November. The colony begins to disperse in April and May, and only a few hundred birds remain resident in the wet season (Lauhachinda 1969). Dispersal takes some birds to northern Thailand and a few to Kampuchea, but most migrate about 1,500 km to Bangladesh, living in the deltas of the Brahmaputra and Ganges rivers (McClure 1974). Birds disperse daily up to 80 km from Wat Phai Lom to forage (McClure and Kwanyuen 1973). The bill is specialized for holding and opening the shells of apple snails. Returning parents regurgitate snail meat into the nest for nestlings to eat, and much meat drops to the ground and is used by fledglings and adults. Nesting during the dry season, when food is concentrated in the remaining flooded areas, enables foraging at a level of efficiency that supports reproduction.

Conservation Measures Taken: Open-billed storks are protected by Thai law (WARPA 1980), which prohibits hunting and allows trade only with special permission from the Wildlife Advisory Committee of the Wildlife Conservation Division. Wat Phai Lom has been designated as a Non-hunting Area. A large portion of the Wat Phai Lom rookery on which the trees had died has been replanted by the Royal Thai Forestry Department, and the young trees are in use for nesting. Establishment of a new colony has been attempted by introducing 60 fledglings from Wat Phai Lom at a wildlife sanctuary in Surat Thani Province; in 1980, 10 adults remained (Virach Chantrasmi, personal communication).

Conservation Measures Proposed: The excellent protection of the stork rookery at Wat Phai Lom should be maintained and extended to the two new rookeries. The Wildlife Conservation Division may find it appropriate to work with the monks of Wat Phai Lom and neighbors to prevent human encroachment on nesting habitat. Signs and fences should be erected at the rookeries to prevent visitors from walking into the rookery areas, because such disturbance frightens the birds and leads to mortality of young (Pilai Poonswad, personal communication). Because an aircraft accident involving soaring storks from Wat Phai Lom might stimulate destruction of the colony, it would be helpful to conduct a study of horizontal and vertical distribution and timing of soaring birds, for the purpose of recommending altered aircraft approach times or routes to the Don Muang Airport. To establish a number of rookeries, introductions like that at Surat Thani should be made nationwide at wildlife sanctuaries and national parks that have suitable habitat (Virach Chantrasmi, personal communication). It is important to exchange information with wildlife officials in Bangladesh as a way of encouraging the well-being of this migratory species.

Black stork
Ciconia nigra (Linnaeus)
Aves, Ciconiiformes, Ciconiidae

Status: Threatened.
CITES (1979): Appendix II.
WARPA (1980): Protected-1.
Population Size and Trend: Unknown.

Distribution and History of Distribution: The black stork breeds from Sweden, Denmark, and Germany east through Russia and northern China, Korea, and Japan, in the Middle East including Turkey, Iran, Afganistan, and Pakistan, and in southern Africa. It winters in Africa and southern Asia, including the lower Yangtse River basin and southeastern Yunnan Province, China, India, Burma, and northern Thailand, northern Lao PDR, and northern Vietnam (La Touche 1931-34, Deignan 1945, Smythies 1953, Ali and Ripley 1968, Tarboton and Cardwell 1968, Gore and Pyong-Oh 1971, King and Dickinson 1975). In Thailand the black stork has been reported in winter from Chiang Rai and on the Mekong between Ban Nam Khuang and Huai Sai, Lao PDR (Fig. 49; Deignan 1945, 1963).

Geographic Status: The breeding range of this species is Palearctic, and in Thailand it occurs only as a vagrant. Whether the Chiang Rai marshes once were a regular wintering ground can never be known.

Habitat Requirements and Habitat Trend: This is a bird of marshes, rivers, and other freshwater wetlands. The species often feeds on the edges of small wooded streams or pools (Kahl 1972). It feeds on frogs, fish, insects, crustaceans, rodents, and small birds (Ali and Ripley 1968). Nests are built in tall trees or on high cliffs (La Touche 1931-34, Ali and Ripley 1968, Tarboton and Cardwell 1968).

Causes of Threat: Unknown.

Demographic Characteristics: A clutch contains 3-5 eggs (Ali and Ripley 1968), but usually only 1 or 2 chicks are raised because attacks among siblings result in early deaths (Tarboton and Cardwell 1968).

Key Behaviors: Migration occurs between breeding and winter range. The species often forages in association with the white-necked stork, *Ciconia (Dissoura) episcopus*, a fact probably important to the feeding ecology of both species.

Conservation Measures Taken: The black stork is protected by

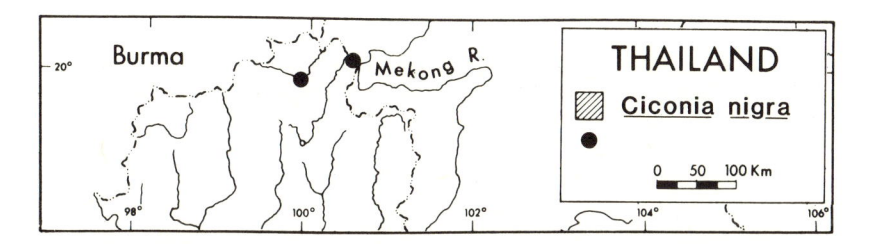

Fig. 49. Distribution of the Black Stork (*Ciconia nigra*).

Thai law (WARPA 1980), which prohibits hunting and allows trade only with special permission from the Wildlife Advisory Committee of the Wildlife Conservation Division.

Conservation Measures Proposed: Little done in Thailand can be relevant to the needs of this species. However, its history should be considered in evaluating wetlands that remain around Chiang Rai.

White-necked stork
Ciconia (Dissoura) episcopus **(Boddaert 1783)**
Aves, Ciconiiformes, Ciconiidae

Status: Endangered.
WARPA (1980): Protected-1.

Population Size and Trend: Unknown in Thailand; early reports show the species was widespread and perhaps common (Riley 1938, Deignan 1945), but now it is rare (Lekagul and Cronin 1974) and no longer may breed in the country. In Sri Lanka, white-necked storks have been greatly reduced in number (Henry 1971), and the subspecies occupying peninsular Malaysia, Sumatra, and Borneo has become rare (IUCN Red Data Book 1979).

Distribution and History of Distribution: This species occurs discontinuously throughout tropical Africa and Asia. Records in Thailand were numerous early in this century. Riley (1938) cited records from Trang Province (Prahmon, Tyching, Lay Long Hong), the Tenasserim area (Bok Pyin, Champang, Tanjong Badak), Patani, Trang, Surat Thani, Ko Samui, Nong Kok, Ghirbi, Ratchaburi, Phetburi, the Khorat Plateau (Sakerat and Muang Pai), Tha Law, Hat Sanuk, Koh Lak, on the Mae Ping River, and Chaing Saen. Deignan (1945) reported white-necked storks widely over the plains of Chaing Rai, at Fang, north of Wiang Pa Pao, on the plains between Thoeng and Chiang Rai, and on the marsh at Mae Chai.

Medway and Wells (1976) reported a breeding colony (no longer in existence) in northeastern Songkhla Province and a record at Phuket. Ogle (1974) reported birds 2 km northeast of Chanthaburi in December of 1971 and 1972.

Geographic Status: Thailand is central to the Asian part of the species' range.

Habitat Requirements and Habitat Trend: The white-necked stork forages in a wide variety of habitats, including streams in primary forest, edges of major rivers, swamps, wet or dry marshes, rice paddies, dry fields, plains, freshly burned lalang (*Imperata*) grassland, and exposed coral reefs. However, it most often uses dry sites (Deignan 1945, Smythies 1953, Hoogerwerf 1969, Kahl 1972). Nesting is in trees in deep forest, usually in single nests or small rookeries (Smythies 1953, Kahl 1972). The diet includes crabs, fish, frogs, molluscs, and many grasshoppers (Riley 1938, Henry 1971).

Vulnerability of Species and Habitat: Any large, conspicuous species like this is vulnerable to shooting, especially when nesting. Deforestation is considered to be a major threat to the subspecies *C. e. stormi* in Borneo (IUCN Red Data Book 1979).

Causes of Threat: Undocumented in Thailand.

Responses to Habitat Modification: Unknown.

Demographic Characteristics: The clutch contains 3-4 eggs (Smythies 1953).

Key Behaviors: The nesting season appears to be quite variable, ranging from September to June in Burma (Smythies 1953). Both members of the pair feed the young by regurgitating food onto the nest floor. Foraging is done at a slow walk, and prey are located visually (Kahl 1972). Most authors consider the species to be a permanent resident in Thailand, though Glenister (1955) termed it a winter visitor. Individuals have been seen in all months in peninsular Thailand (Medway and Wells 1976). Some populations in Africa are migratory or partly so (Elgood 1973).

Conservation Measures Taken: This species is legally protected in Thailand, Indonesia, and Sarawak (WARPA 1980, IUCN Red Data Book 1979).

Conservation Measures Proposed: A survey of the status of the white-necked stork in Thailand is needed to provide a basis for planning conservation measures.

Black-necked stork
Xenorhynchus asiaticus (Latham 1790)
Aves, Ciconiiformes, Ciconiidae

Status: Endangered.
WARPA (1980): Protected-1.

Population Size and Trend: The species is uncommon throughout its range (Deignan 1945, Ali and Ripley 1968, Henry 1971, Lekagul and Cronin 1974). It was seen relatively frequently early in this century, but it is seldom reported now, with the last published sighting in 1971 (Deignan 1945, Ogle 1974).

Distribution and History of Distribution: The range of the black-necked stork includes India, Pakistan, Bangladesh, Sri Lanka, Nepal, Burma, Thailand, Lao PDR, Kampuchea, southern Vietnam, peninsular Malaysia, New Guinea, and Australia (Gibson-Hill 1949, Ali and Ripley 1968, Wildash 1968, King and Dickinson 1975). Published records in Thailand are as follows: near Chiang Saen in August 1914, in May 1936 at Mae Chai and on the plains near the Nam Ing between Thoeng and Chiang Rai, and in January 1939 on the Mekong about 20 km below Ban Huai Sai (Deignan 1945); breeding on the north side of the Telibun Straits, Trang Province, and occurring widely in northern peninsular Thailand (Robinson and Chasen 1936); and flying about 2 km northeast of Chanthaburi in February 1972 (Ogle 1974).

Geographic Status: Thailand is central in the species' range.

Habitat Requirement and Habitat Trend: The black-necked stork inhabits marshes, swamps, lakes, large rivers and adjacent plains, and mangrove swamps. A pair builds an enormous nest of sticks 20-25 m high in a tree, which may be distant from foraging areas. Nesting in India is in September to December, depending on when the rains cease. The diet is mainly fish but also includes frogs, reptiles, and crabs (Ali and Ripley 1968, Lekagul and Cronin 1974, King and Dickinson 1975). The wetlands of Thailand have been reduced to small remnants.

Vulnerability of Species and Habitat: The species "is very wary, flying off . . . at the first sign of approach of its arch-enemy, man" (Henry 1971). Its habitat is vulnerable to deforestation, drainage, and conversion to agricultural uses.

Causes of Threat: Shooting and habitat loss threaten the black-necked stork.

Responses to Habitat Modification: Unknown. Unmolested birds will nest in trees left in cultivated areas (Ali and Ripley 1968).

Demographic Characteristics: The clutch contains 3-4 eggs, or rarely 5 (Ali and Ripley 1968).

Key Behaviors: This species occurs alone, in pairs, or in small groups of adults and their young. Pairs appear to have clearly defined activity ranges, and nesting is solitary. Both members of the pair build the nest and feed the young by regurgitating food onto the nest floor. Most food is located by slowly walking and probing in the water and submerged vegetation, but occasionally the birds run a few steps in pursuit of prey. Like other storks, this species soars and circles high in the sky during the heat of the day. The black and white pattern under the wings is used in pair-bonding displays (Ali and Ripley 1968, Kahl 1973).

Conservation Measures Taken: This species is protected under Thai law (WARPA 1980).

Conservation Measures Proposed: Surveys of wetland habitat and the status of black-necked stork populations are needed as first steps in planning a conservation program. Education is needed to teach the public that molesting these rare animals will lead to their extirpation.

Greater adjutant stork
Leptoptilos dubius **(Gmelin)**
Aves, Ciconiiformes, Ciconiidae

Status: Endangered.
IUCN (1968): Threatened.
WARPA (1980): Protected-1.

Population Size and Trend: Apparently once fairly common (Gyldenstolpe 1920), the greater adjutant stork is becoming rare in Thailand (Lekagul and Cronin 1974). No breeding colonies are known in the country and there are few recent records. The "vast armies" of greater adjutants that formerly congregated in southern Burma to breed (Hume and Oates 1890) no longer do so (Smythies 1953). "It has been suggested that the Indian adjutants probably all migrate to this area to nest" (Ali and Ripley 1968).

Distribution and History of Distribution: This species is known from India, Bangladesh, central and southern Assam, southern

Burma, Thailand except the Malayan Peninsula, southern Lao PDR, Kampuchea, and southern Vietnam (Ali and Ripley 1968, King and Dickinson 1975). The two rookeries and "incredible" numbers (Hume and Oates 1860) that arrived in southern Burma during October for the breeding season no longer occur (Smythies 1953). Ali and Ripley (1968) note an 1883 report by Baker that 40-50 pair of greater adjutants had nested for years at a spot in the Sundarbans of Bangladesh. No current sites of breeding are reported for the species. The range in Thailand was given as "The broader rivers and more extensive marshes of the northern plateau (Chiang Rai, Phayao), the southeastern provinces (Chon Buri), and of the central plains (Deignan 1963)." Three individuals were seen in Nakhon Sawan Province in July 1984 (Ogle 1986).

Geographic Status: Thailand is central in the species' original range, but whether it did or does support breeding is unknown.

Habitat Requirements and Habitat Trend: The greater adjutant stork occurs on open plains, wet savannas, marshes, lake edges, rice paddies, and open forest (Deignan 1963, King and Dickinson 1975), "particularly where the water is drying and concentrating the fish life in shallow puddles" (Ali and Ripley 1968). One nesting site in Burma was described as in trees on inaccessible cliffs along the Ataran River (Smythies 1953). The Sundarbans rookery was in "lofty trees in dense forest on the edge of a vast area of swamp and lake" (Ali and Ripley 1968). This carnivorous species eats carrion, fish, frogs, snakes, and crustaceans. The storks feed among kites and vultures on dead animals near villages. They regularly scavenged in Calcutta in the days when municipal sanitation was minimal (Ali and Ripley 1968).

Vulnerability of Species and Habitat: Native habitat is vulnerable to drainage and conversion to agricultural uses.

Causes of Threat: Unknown. Deignan (1945) reported the greater adjutant as so wary as to be unapproachable by hunters. This is likely to be untrue in rookeries. Annual exports from Thailand in 1969 and 1970 were 4 and 2 (Royal Forestry Department 1972). Clearly most marsh and wet savanna habitat has been lost.

Responses to Habitat Modification: Unknown.

Demographic Characteristics: The clutch contains 2-4 eggs, usually 3 or 4 (Ali and Ripley 1968).

Key Behaviors: Both sexes participate in nest building and incubation (Ali and Ripley 1968). The greater adjutant is widespread in southern Asia during the nonreproductive season from about April to November, when nomadic movements are determined by hot season and monsoon water levels. The birds migrate to breeding areas, which are occupied from about October to March. Breeding begins with the cessation of the rains, and young are reared as water levels diminish, concentrating marsh animals in pools (Smythies 1953, Ali and Ripley 1968).

Conservation Measures Taken: Thai law (WARPA 1980) protects this species from hunting and regulates trade.

Conservation Measures Proposed: An inventory of the wetlands remaining in Thailand is needed to determine what greater adjutant habitat is left in the country. A status survey and field study of this species are needed to determine population levels and to learn more of its basic biology. A search for rookeries should be undertaken cooperatively among southern Asian nations, perhaps to be begun by correspondence, with the ultimate goal being to develop international conservation measures to ensure the survival of the species.

Lesser adjutant stork
Leptotilos javanicus **(Horsfield)**
Aves, Ciconiiformes, Ciconiidae

Status: Endangered.
WARPA (1980): Protected-1.

Population Size and Trend: Unknown. The lesser adjutant stork once was common over most of its range, often referred to as the most abundant species of stork (Gyldenstolpe 1920, Glenister 1955, Wildash 1968, Hoogerwerf 1969, Medway and Wells 1976, Storer 1977). However, it has "declined in numbers during the present century" and is now scarce where it was common (Medway and Wells 1976). At Thale Noi, Thailand, where this species formerly was common, Storer (1977) saw one in 6 months, and eight individuals were present in 1979 (Thailand Institute of Scientific and Technological Research 1979) and 1980 (Robert Dobias, personal communication). Two were seen soaring over Khao Yai National Park in January 1979, and one was at Ban Muang beach, Krabi Province, on 28 December 1980 (Boonsong Lekagul, personal communication).

Distribution and History of Distribution: The species ranges from Sri Lanka, India, Nepal terai, Assam, Bangladesh, Burma, southern China, Indochina, Hainan, Thailand, Malaysia, Borneo, Sumatra, and Java (Riley 1938, Ali and Ripley 1968, Medway and Wells 1976). Lesser adjutants occurred throughout southwestern and peninsular Thailand, with specific records from south of Rat Buri, Ko Lak, Ko Naka Yai near Phuket, Chumphon, and Lay Song Hong and Prahmon in Trang Province (Riley 1938), plus Thale Noi.

Geographic Status: Thailand is north-central in the species' range.

Habitat Requirements and Habitat Trend: The lesser adjutant appears to be most common in mangrove and *Melaleuca* swamps, on coastal mudflats, and at the mouths of rivers, but it also occurs in rice paddies, dried-up swamps, recently burned plains, and pools in the forest. The birds at Thale Noi were seen irregularly around the *Melaleuca* forest east of Kuan Kee Sian (Thailand Institute of Scientific and Technological Research 1979). Breeding is in rookeries in very tall trees, but some nests are scattered singly in the forest. The diet consists of fish, frogs, reptiles, crustaceans, and insects, but not carrion (Glenister 1955, Ali and Ripley 1968, Hoogerwerf 1969, Medway and Wells 1976).

Vulnerability of Species and Habitat: The species is reputed to be very wary, but it is vulnerable to human nestling-stealers in rookeries. Annual exports from Thailand from 1969 to 1971 were 2, 4, and 23 (Royal Forestry Department 1972). Much of the mangrove swamp of Thailand has been cleared or reduced to young stands by cutting for charcoal, and much wetland habitat has been drained or converted to agricultural use.

Causes of Threat: Shooting and habitat destruction have been major threats to this species.

Responses to Habitat Modification: Unknown.

Demographic Characteristics: The clutch contains 3-4 eggs (Smythies 1953, Ali and Ripley 1968).

Key Behaviors: Nesting occurs in November to January in India (Ali and Ripley 1968) and August to October in Java (Hoogerwerf 1969). The species is considered nomadic and locally migratory (Ali and Ripley 1968).

Conservation Measures Taken: Thale Noi is a No-hunting area. Thai law (WARPA 1980) prohibits hunting and regulates trade of this species.

Conservation Measures Proposed: An inventory of the wetlands remaining in southwestern and peninsular Thailand is needed to determine what habitat for lesser adjutants is left in the country. A status survey and field studies of this species are needed to determine population levels and to learn more of its basic biology. That new information is needed for planning conservation measures.

White ibis, black-headed ibis
Threskiornis melanocephala **(Latham 1790)**
Aves, Ciconiiformes, Threskiornithidae

Status: Threatened.
WARPA (1980): Protected-1.

Population Size and Trend: The white ibis occurred "in large numbers on the great swampy plains of central" Thailand (Gyldenstolpe 1920), but it had not been seen in recent years (Lekagul and Cronin 1974) until two transitory populations were found in 1978 and 1979 (Virach Chantrasmi, personal communication). About 50 individuals were reported at Wat Tarn En in March 1982 (P. D. Round, personal communication). At the same time, others were reported at Thale Noi No-hunting Area by forestry officials. In the Malay Peninsula, numbers have declined in recent decades (Medway and Wells 1964). The species was considered abundant in portions of its range in Burma (Smythies 1953) and southern Vietnam (Wildash 1968).

Distribution and History of Distribution: The species is widespread in southern Asia: India, Pakistan, Bangladesh, Nepal, Sri Lanka, southeastern China, Japan, and lowland portions of Southeast Asia south to Sumatra, Java, and Borneo. In Thailand, the historical range of white ibis was the lowlands of the southeastern, central, and peninsular parts of the country (La Touche 1931-34, Medway and Wells 1976, Ali and Ripley 1968, Lekagul and Cronin 1974). Recent sightings are at Wat Tarn En, Bang Pa Han District, Ayutthaya Province, and at Thepparat, Chachoengsao Province (Virach Chantrasmi, personal communication). One was seen in Nakhon Sawan Province in October 1985 (Ogle 1986).

Geographic Status: Thailand is central in the range of the white ibis.

Habitat Requirements and Habitat Trend: White ibis inhabit river edges, marshes, flooded rice paddies, and tidal mudflats and lagoons. Nesting is colonial in shrubs or trees. The diet consists of wetland animals such as fish, frogs, molluscs, insects, and worms (Ali and Ripley 1968, Lekagul and Cronin 1974). Substantial drainage of wetland habitats has occurred.

Vulnerability of Species and Habitat: The habitat of white ibis is highly vulnerable to drainage and conversion to agriculture. Archibald et al. (1980) consider ibis to be vulnerable to hunting and pesticide poisoning.

Causes of Threat: Unknown.

Responses to Habitat Modification: White ibis make extensive use of rice paddies.

Demographic Characteristics: The clutch contains 2-4 eggs. Incubation is estimated to take 23-25 days (Ali and Ripley 1968).

Key Behaviors: Foraging is mainly tactile, as birds walk slowly while probing the substrate. In India, the nesting season is highly variable, from June to March, depending on flooding of marshland after the monsoon begins. Both foraging and nesting are done in groups, often in association with other species of wetland birds. Social interactions are important in pair bonding, sexual development of the individual, and stimulating breeding by other colony members (Ali and Ripley 1968, Archibald et al. 1980). The species is migratory in some areas but nomadic or resident in others (La Touche 1931-34, Medway and Wells 1961, Ali and Ripley 1968).

Conservation Measures Taken: Thai law (WARPA 1980) protects this species from hunting and regulates trade.

Conservation Measures Proposed: A survey of the status of this species is needed, with particular attention to the existence of breeding populations and sites.

Black ibis, white-shouldered ibis
Pseudibis papillosa davisoni **(Hume 1875)**
Aves, Ciconiiformes, Threskiornithidae

Status: Probably extirpated.
IUCN (1968): Threatened.
IUCN Red Data Book (1977): Indeterminate.
WARPA (1980): Protected-1.

Population Size and Trend: Details are lacking, but this bird was thought to be locally common in parts of southern Vietnam, northeastern Kampuchea, and Thailand in the early part of this century. It is now seriously reduced throughout its range in Southeast Asia. Except for one recent unconfirmed report from the Thale Noi wetland, there have been no Thai records for over two decades. There are no estimates of the total numbers of black ibis remaining in the region (IUCN 1968, IUCN Red Data Book 1977, G. Archibald personal communication, B. King personal communication).

Distribution and History of Distribution: The overall range of *P. papillosa* is Pakistan, India, southeastern China, Burma, Thailand, Lao PDR, Kampuchea, southern Vietnam, Malaya, and Borneo. In Thailand there are records from Chiang Rai Province in the northwest, from the central valley of the Chao Phraya, and from Phuket, Krabi, Trang, and Patthalung provinces in peninsular Thailand (Deignan 1945, Deignan 1963, Ali and Ripley 1968, King and Dickinson 1975, Medway and Wells 1976).

Geographic Status: Thailand is central in the distribution of this species.

Habitat Requirements and Habitat Trend: This ibis prefers the edges of large rivers and lakes, extensive marshes, grasslands, paddyfields, and other cultivation. The food is primarily insects, but seeds are taken (Wildash 1968). The diet of the nominate subspecies, *P. p. papillosa*, was given by Ali and Ripley (1968) as follows "Among the stomach contents of specimens, Mason and Lefroy (1912) identified frogs, small fish, earthworms, beetles, and other insects (including *Brachytrypes achatinus* adults, and larvae of *Cybister confuses, Agrotis* sp., and *Hydrophilus* sp.). In addition, lizards, small snakes, scorpions, crustaceans, and a quantity of grain have also been recorded."

Vulnerability of Species and Habitat: The large size of these birds makes them conspicuous to man. The lowland wetlands it prefers are being drained and turned into wet rice culture in much of Southeast Asia (Gibson-Hill 1949, King and Dickinson 1975, IUCN Red Data Book 1977).

Causes of Threat: Prolonged warfare in much of the species' range in former Indochina has probably contributed to its demise. The effects of the extensive conversion of wetlands to agriculture over the last century probably have been profound, but they are undocumented.

Responses to Habitat Modification: Unknown.

Demographic Characteristics: The demography of the subspecies *davisoni* is poorly known. In Burma nesting has been recorded in February and March (Smythies 1953). Ali and Ripley (1968) reported that in India the subspecies *papillosa* breeds from March to October in the north and later in the south. The normal clutch size was given as 2-4 eggs.

Key Behaviors: The black ibis in Thailand is shy and very difficult to approach (Deignan 1945). The subspecies *papillosa* nests individually, rarely in small colonies. The nest is a large stick platform 6-12 m up a large tree. Sometimes old kite and vulture nests are used. Both sexes incubate the eggs (Ali and Ripley 1968).

Conservation Measures Taken: In 1975 the Thai government designated Thale Noi as a No-hunting Area. It is the location of the only recent reputed sighting. Thai law (WARPA 1980) prohibits hunting and regulates trade of this species.

Conservation Measures Proposed: The systematic status of this bird is unclear. Some authors consider *davisoni* to be a full species, while others consider it a subspecies of *papillosa*. This problem requires further study. Wetlands should be inventoried to determine what original habitat of the black ibis remains in Thailand. The staff of such wetland reserves as Thale Noi should be on the alert for this species.

Giant ibis
Pseudibis (Thaumatibis) gigantea **(Oustalet 1877)**
Aves, Ciconiiformes, Threskiornithidae

Status: Probably extirpated.
IUCN (1968): Threatened.
IUCN Red Data Book (1977): Rare.
IUCN (1979): Threatened.
MAB (1979): Threatened.
WARPA (1980): Protected-1

Population Size and Trend: This bird has always been uncommon and local (Gyldenstolpe 1920) and is now rare throughout its range. The total world population may be fewer than 100 birds. Although they were sighted on the Kampuchean-Lao border in 1964, there have been no records for Thailand for many decades. It is likely that this bird has been extirpated in Thailand (IUCN 1968, Fisher et al. 1969, Medway and Wells 1976, IUCN Red Data Book

1977, G. Archibald personal communication, B. King personal communication).

Distribution and History of Distribution: The giant ibis is endemic to Southeast Asia. It is known from southern Vietnam, Kampuchea, central and southern Lao PDR, central Thailand including Rat Buri and Phet Buri provinces, and Trang and Satun provinces in peninsular Thailand (Williamson 1916*b*, 1921, Riley 1938, Gibson-Hill 1949, Deignan 1963, IUCN 1968, King and Dickinson 1975, Medway and Wells 1976, IUCN Red Data Book 1977). The populations in peninsular Thailand were apparently migrants or strays; there were no breeding records outside of central Thailand, Kampuchea, the Lao PDR, and southern Vietnam (Fisher et al. 1969).

Geographic Status: The Thai birds lived at the western and southern extremes of the species' known range.

Habitat Requirements and Habitat Trend: Primarily an inhabitant of the lowlands, this large ibis prefers lakes, swamps, marshes, wooded plains, open forest, and clearings and ponds in deep forest (Deignan 1963, Lekagul and Cronin 1974, King and Dickinson 1975, IUCN Red Data Book 1977).

Vulnerability of Species and Habitat: The large size of this bird makes it very conspicuous to man. In times of drought they are said to aggregate at permanent water holes. Moist lowland habitat in all of Southeast Asia is being drained and converted into wet rice culture.

Causes of Threat: War over most of its range undoubtedly has taken a toll of these magnificent birds. Overhunting and loss of wetland habitat threaten the remaining populations.

Responses to Habitat Modification: Conversion of the central valley of the Chao Phraya to agriculture was probably instrumental in the extirpation of *P. gigantea* from Thailand.

Demographic Characteristics: The clutch size and other demographic characteristics are unknown. Most ibises have 2-5 eggs per clutch (Archibald et al. 1980).

Key Behaviors: Very little is known of the habits of this bird. It is very shy and occurs in pairs and small groups.

Conservation Measures Taken: The giant ibis was once taken (Gibson-Hill 1949) in what is now Tarutao Marine National Park. Thai law (WARPA 1980) prohibits hunting and regulates trade of this species.

Conservation Measures Proposed: Whenever it becomes possible, an intensive survey of the area north of Tonle Sap in Kampuchea should be conducted to determine the current status of this species. Any surviving populations should be studied to determine the best methods for conserving them. In view of the fact that this bird once ranged far beyond its breeding range into suitable habitat in southern Thailand, biologists working at Thale Noi and other wetlands should watch for this species.

White-winged wood duck
Cairina scutulata (S. Muller)
Aves, Anseriformes, Anatidae

Status: Endangered.
IUCN Red Data Book (1977): Vulnerable.
CITES (1979): Appendix I.
IUCN (1979): Threatened.
MAB (1979): Threatened.
USFWS (1980a): Endangered.
WARPA (1980): Protected-1.

Population Size and Trend: Originally this species was fairly common in peninsular Thailand (Glenister 1955), but now only one population is thought to remain in the country (Lekagul and Cronin 1974, IUCN Red Data Book 1977, IUCN 1979). Modest numbers are reported from the Sweli River (Smythies 1953), the Pablakhali area of the Chittagong Hills (Husain 1977), and several other areas of Burma (Yin 1977), and in Lampung, Palembang, and Jambi provinces, Sumatra (Holmes 1977). The 1971 population of 1,000 ducks at the Moe-Yun-Gyi Waterfowl Sanctuary, Burma, has declined to 100 (Kear and Williams 1978).

Distribution and History of Distribution: The white-winged wood duck occurred discontinuously from India, Assam, Bangladesh, and Burma east to central and southern Lao PDR, Kampuchea, and Vietnam, and from northern Thailand south to Malaya, Sumatra, Siberut, and Java (Delacour 1959, Dickinson 1970, IUCN Red Data Book 1977). The species apparently has been extirpated from Malaya and Indochina, but isolated populations are still reported in Assam, Bangladesh, Burma, Thailand, Java, Sumatra, and Siberut (IUCN Red Data Book 1977, Kear and Williams 1978).

Geographic Status: Thailand is central in the species' range.

Habitat Requirements and Habitat Trend: The species lives in primary evergreen forest, from lowland swamps to forested intermontaine basins as high as 1,500 m (Deignan 1945, Husain 1977, IUCN Red Data Book 1977, Holmes 1977). Evidently low population densities are normal (Deignan 1945); a maximum of 1 pair per 100 ha of ideal habitat is estimated (MacKenzie and Kear 1976, Holmes 1977). The trees are used for roosting, and nesting is in tree hollows and on large branches. Foraging habitat is slow-moving streams and rivers, marshes, and sheltered wet depressions in the forest; foraging also may occur on the forest floor and nearby flooded rice fields. MacKenzie and Kear (1976) suggested that during the monsoon season all foraging may take place within the forest but during the dry season daily flights outside of the forest may be necessary. Hence populations need both primary forest with slow-moving waters and dry-season wetlands within a few km of the forest roost. In captivity the species is omnivorous, prefers animal food, and chases small fish (Ali and Ripley 1968). Discrepancies among various reports suggest seasonal changes in diet (MacKenzie and Kear 1976).

Vulnerability of Species and Habitat: Habitat of the white-winged wood duck is vulnerable to deforestation, which also increases the accessibility of the species to hunting.

Causes of Threat: From an original 80 percent, forest cover of Thailand has declined to 25 percent in 1978 (Myers 1980). Relictual areas of suitable habitat remain, but evidently all the wood ducks in them have been killed.

Responses to Habitat Modification: The species cannot survive loss of its forest habitat. Replacement of native forest with plantations of fast-growing species is an unsuitable substitution (MacKenzie and Kear 1976). The ducks can continue to occupy partially disturbed forest in which remnant patches of primary forest or dense, old, secondary forest are allowed to remain (Holmes 1977).

Demographic Characteristics: Clutch size ranges from 6-13 eggs, usually 10. A second clutch may be laid if the first is removed. The incubation period is 33-35 days. Females become sexually mature in 2-3 years.

Key Behaviors: Nesting is monsoonal in Assam, beginning in May, with molting occurring in September (MacKenzie and Kear 1976). However, breeding in Sumatra and Java has been reported in December and February, respectively (Hoogerwerf 1950), and was thought to span the Sumatran wet season from December to March or April by Holmes (1977). According to most authors (see Holmes 1977), when birds must commute to foraging areas, they do so just before dusk, remain on the feeding ground all night, and return to the roost in the morning.

Conservation Measures Taken: White-winged wood ducks are protected by WARPA (1980), but export of the birds is no longer a significant threat.

Conservation Measures Proposed: The report that the species occurs in Huai Kha Khaeng Wildlife Sanctuary (IUCN 1979) should be verified; if it is true, the population should be protected and managed as a top priority. It may be feasible to reestablish the white-winged wood duck in Thailand with a captive breeding program and reintroduction into the wild. Suitable habitat should be selected carefully, and a visit to become familiar with the habitat of the wood duck population in the Kassalong Reserve (Chittagong Hills, Bangladesh), the Way Kambas Wildlife Reserve (Sumatra), or the Reserve Forests of Assam would be useful in planning. Suitable habitat is reported to occur at Thung Thong Wildlife Sanctuary (IUCN 1979). MacKenzie and Kear (1976) recommend providing both wet and dry season feeding habitats within 4 km (Holmes 1977) of each other. Once chosen, the reintroduction area would need complete protection from logging and hunting. Captive breeding techniques have been developed by the Wildfowl Trust, Slimbridge, England. "By 1976, about 70 birds were held in captive wildfowl collections in Europe, North America, and Asia. All birds outside Asia are related to the Wildfowl Trust stock" (IUCN Red Data Book 1977), which came from Assam (Johnstone 1972). By 1978, over 100 wood ducks had been reared at Slimbridge, but the stock was becoming inbred (Kear and Williams 1978). MacKenzie and Kear (1976) listed research needs for sound conservation planning.

Pet hong, comb duck
Sarkidiornis melanotos **(Pennant 1769)**
Aves, Anseriformes, Anatidae

Status: Endangered.

CITES (1979): Appendix II.
WARPA (1980): Protected-1.

Population Size and Trend: There are no estimates of the total numbers of this widespread duck. There are numerous reports of it having once been locally common in Southeast Asia, though Gyldenstolpe (1920) considered it rather rare. Smythies (1953) noted that it was becoming scarce in Burma due to overhunting. Lekagul and Cronin (1974) considered it to be an uncommon resident in Thailand.

Distribution and History of Distribution: This tropical duck is known from Panama south to Peru and Argentina in the New World, throughout Africa south of the Sahara (including Madagascar), and in Asia from Pakistan, India, and Bangladesh east through Burma and southeastern China to Thailand, Kampuchea, central Lao PDR, and southern Vietnam. Its occurrence is patchy throughout its range and some populations (e.g., in Sri Lanka) are thought to have become extinct. In Thailand it is known from the northwest, the northeast, and the central valley of the Chao Phraya (Gyldenstolpe 1920, Deignan 1945, Smythies 1953, Delacour 1959, Deignan 1963, Ali and Ripley 1968, Henry 1971, Lekagul and Cronin 1974, McClure 1974*b*, King and Dickinson 1975, Kear and Williams, 1978). The only recent record is a single individual reported at Bung Boraphet in January 1985 (Ogle 1986).

Geographic Status: In Southeast Asia these birds are at the eastern extreme of the species' extensive range.

Habitat Requirements and Habitat Trend: In Thailand this tree duck prefers woodland ponds and streams in the dry season and marshes and flooded fields in the rainy season (Lekagul and Cronin 1974). It has been reported from a wide variety of habitats, from wet places in savannas to deep forest. It is thought to be primarily an herbivore, subsisting on the corms, shoots, and seeds of aquatic and marsh plants. Wild and domestic rice is also eaten, as are the aquatic larvae of insects, fish, and frogs (Delacour 1959, Ali and Ripley 1968, Wildash 1968, Henry 1971).

Vulnerability of Species and Habitat: This is the largest of the Thai ducks. Although its large size, relatively diurnal activity patterns, and habit of consuming rice would tend to bring it to the attention of hunters, it is usually silent and its flesh is reputed to be tough and coarse. It resembles domestic Muscovies and is taken alive for trade (Deignan 1945, Henry 1971).

Causes of Threat: Overhunting threatens this species. In addition to being killed as food, *S. melanotos* is captured alive in many parts of its range, including Thailand. Twelve were exported from Thailand in 1962, for example (Royal Forestry Department 1972, Kear and Williams 1978).

Responses to Habitat Modification: This species readily adapts to the conversion of wetlands to rice culture but may be excluded from an area by the lack of suitable nesting sites.

Demographic Characteristics: The breeding season varies over the species' range. Comb ducks have been reported to nest from July to September in India and from June to September in Burma. The usual clutch is 7-15 eggs. Incubation lasts a month. The average survival time of the birds banded by McClure (1974) was 11 months. The oldest recovery was 50 months (Smythies 1953, Delacour 1959, Ali and Ripley 1968, Henry 1971, McClure 1974*b*).

Key Behaviors: Comb ducks are less nocturnal than most ducks. It night-roosts in trees but walks well on the ground and often feeds there. It is a grazing duck. It does not normally dive to feed but readily dives to escape danger. Small groups of 4-10 are normal, but flocks of a hundred or more occur rarely. The flocks fly in loose association and do not form the orderly Vs characteristic of many waterfowl. Flight is strong and can be sustained for great distances. Band recoveries in Asian comb ducks averaged 320 km and movements as far as 960 km were recorded (McClure 1974*b*). The migratory habits of the Thai populations are unknown. These birds commonly make local migrations in search of water and breeding sites. The preferred nesting site is a large natural cavity in a large tree near water. Nests far removed from open water have been noted. When no suitable trees are available, comb ducks may nest in old vulture nests, earthen and rock cliffs, in ruins, or reeds. When nesting sites are scarce, comb ducks may share a cavity with another of their kind (up to 47 eggs have been taken from one nest) or other species of ducks. The mating behavior has been described by Delacour (1959). The female alone incubates the eggs and cares for the young (Smythies 1953, Delacour 1959, Ali and Ripley 1968, Henry 1971, Lekagul and McNeely 1974, McClure 1974*b*, King and Dickinson 1975).

Conservation Measures Taken: Thai law (WARPA 1980) protects this species. It will breed and live long in captivity. As late as 1937 Deignan (1945) saw captives in Chiang Mai descended from a group Gyldenstolpe (1916) had seen several decades earlier. Captives appeared in the West as early as 1876 at the London Zoo. The Wildfowl Trust now has a breeding population of about a dozen at Slimbridge. This bird will hybridize with the South American subspecies in captivity and therefore should be kept apart from it to maintain the genetic integrity of the captive stock (Delacour 1959, Lubbock 1979).

Conservation Measures Proposed: Sportsmen and conservation officials (especially those working at wetlands) should be trained to recognize this species and preserve it and its nesting trees. Cooperative banding studies with other Southeast Asian nations would help in elucidating the movements and life history of the Thai comb ducks. As a relative of our domestic fowl, it represents a valuable genetic resource and should be preserved.

King vulture, red-headed vulture, black vulture
Torgos calvus
Aves, Falconiformes, Accipitridae

Status: Endangered.
WARPA (1980): Protected-1.
Population Size and Trend: The king vulture used to be common (Gyldenstolpe 1920, Riley 1938, Deignan 1945, Lekagul and Cronin 1974), though perhaps never at high density, but it declined two decades or more ago (Philip D. Round, personal communication).

Distribution and History of Distribution: This species ranges from Pakistan, India, Nepal, and southernmost China throughout Indochina (excluding northern Vietnam) and south to northern Malaya. The only recent, confirmed sightings are from Huai Kha Khaeng Wildlife Sanctuary (Philip D. Round, personal communication).

Geographic Status: Thailand is central in the range of this species.

Habitat Requirements and Habitat Trend: Its habitat is open country, cultivated fields, and forests (Lekagul and Cronin 1974, De Schauensee 1984). Along the Mae Ping River in northern Thailand, McClure and Lekagul (1961) saw king vultures in the broad valleys associated with human habitation.

Vulnerability of Species and Habitat: This species' habitat is not vulnerable, but the birds are vulnerable to shooting.

Causes of Threat: Shooting is the probable cause of the disappearance of king vultures. Because this species reproduces slowly, the extra mortality of shooting is a very serious threat.

Responses to Habitat Modification: Unknown.

Demographic Characteristics: The breeding season is December to April. The same nest or site is used year after year. The clutch consists of a single egg (Riley 1938, Smythies 1953).

Key Behaviors: This species feeds on carrion. King vultures often feed on the same carcass with white-backed vultures, but even when the latter are numerous, at most two to three king vultures are present (Deignan 1945, Smythies 1953). Birds feeding daily in Chiang Mai flew to the lower slopes of nearby mountains to roost in trees, only rarely spending the night in trees in town (Deignan 1945). Records from Yunnan Province, China, are from summer only (Smythies 1953), so perhaps it is migratory there; elsewhere it is a year-round resident.

Conservation Measures Taken: Thai law (WARPA 1980) prohibits killing and regulates trade of this species. Huai Kha Khaeng Wildlife Sanctuary and perhaps other preserves still support remnant populations of this species.

Conservation Measures Proposed: This vulture must be protected from shooting if it is to recolonize vacant range.

Long-billed vulture
Gyps indicus
Aves, Falconiformes, Accipitridae

Status: Endangered.
WARPA (1980): Protected-1.

Population Size and Trend: Unknown. Based on the occurrence of up to 20 or 30 birds at carcasses in India (Ali and Ripley 1968), the long-billed vulture may be as common as the white-backed vulture. However, the long-billed vulture was never common in Thailand (Gyldenstolpe 1920, Lekagul and Cronin 1974); no recent sightings are known (Philip D. Round, personal communication).

Distribution and History of Distribution: The range is poorly known but includes Pakistan, India, Bangladesh, Nepal, Burma, Thailand, and northern Malaya. Gyldenstolpe (1920) reported records only from Bangkok and Sakerat but expected that it would be found elsewhere. The latest Thai record is one in Chanthaburi Province in the early 1970s (Ogle 1974).

Geographic Status: Thailand is central in the range of this species.

Habitat Requirements and Habitat Trend: No habitat preferences are known for this species.

Vulnerability of Species and Habitat: Cliff faces used for nesting are easily identified from a distance by the whitewash of the feces (Ali and Ripley 1968), so these sites are easily found by people inclined to disturb them. Birds feeding at carcasses also are vulnerable to shooting.

Causes of Threat: Shooting is the probable cause of the decline of this vulture.

Responses to Habitat Modification: Unknown.

Demographic Characteristics: The breeding season is November to March. Nesting is usually in small colonies, with the same sites used by tradition. The clutch is a single egg (Smythies 1953, Ali and Ripley 1968).

Key Behaviors: Surprizingly little is known about this species. The diet consists of carrion, usually around human habitations but sometimes at tiger or leopard kills in the forest. Nest sites of the western races are cliffs or hilltops, and nests are placed on the ground. The eastern race (the one in Thailand) nests in trees (Smythies 1953, Ali and Ripley 1968).

Conservation Measures Taken: Thai law (WARPA 1980) prohibits killing and regulates trade of this species.

Conservation Measures Proposed: Strict protection from shooting will be necessary before outlying populations of the long-billed vulture can recolonize Thailand.

White-backed vulture
Gyps bengalensis
Aves, Falconiformes, Accipitridae

Status: Endangered.
WARPA (1980): Protected-1.

Population Size and Trend: This formerly most common of Thailand's vultures (Gyldenstolpe 1920, Deignan 1945, Lekagul and Cronin 1974) has become very rare or extirpated (e.g., Round 1984), and only a few recent sightings are known (Philip D. Round, personal communication).

Distribution and History of Distribution: The white-backed vulture occurs in Pakistan, India, Nepal, southern China, southern Vietnam, and south in Malaya to Penang. The species was still widespread in southern Thailand in the early 1970s (Holmes and Wells 1975). Recent Thai records are from Thung Thong Waterfowl Reserve, Surat Thani Province, in October 1977 (Storer 1978), a few from Phetburi Province in the late 1970s by Virach Chantrasmi, and one at Doi Inthanon National Park in 1982 (Philip D. Round, personal communication).

Geographic Status: Thailand is central in the range of this species.

Habitat Requirements and Habitat Trend: White-backed vultures occupy a great range of habitats from open forest to desert, up to 2,500 m elevation. Despite widespread deforestation, habitat trends probably have had little effect on this species.

Vulnerability of Species and Habitat: Like other vultures, this one can be approached closely and hence is quite vulnerable to shooting while nesting or feeding at carcasses. The white-backed vulture sometimes becomes a local nuisance because its feces kill the trees under favorite roosts.

Causes of Threat: Shooting is the probable cause of the decline of this and other vultures in Thailand; this seems to be the last of the vultures so affected.

Responses to Habitat Modification: Unknown.

Demographic Characteristics: The breeding season is October to March. A single egg is laid, or rarely two. Incubation takes 45 days, and both sexes participate (Ali and Ripley 1968).

Key Behaviors: This is the best-known of Thailand's vultures. The species feeds exclusively on carrion, often with a large swarm of birds of several species gathering at a carcass. Such a flock can strip even a large carcass of all edible parts in 20 to 40 minutes (Ali and Ripley 1968). The nest is built high in a tree, often near a village (Deignan 1945). Sometimes nesting is in scattered colonies of 25 to 40 nests in a grove or patch of forest. Often several birds foraging from one colony return together to feed the young (Ali and Ripley

1968). This species is not migratory. Small mammals also are part of the diet (De Schauensee 1984).

Conservation Measures Taken: Thai law (WARPA 1980) prohibits killing and regulates trade of this species.

Conservation Measures Proposed: Complete protection from shooting will be necessary before the white-backed vulture can recolonize vacant range in Thailand.

Black eagle
Ictinaetus malayensis
Aves, Falconiformes, Accipitridae

Status: Threatened.
WARPA (1980): Protected-1.

Population Size and Trend: Unknown. The black eagle used to be a common bird (Lekagul and Cronin 1974). However, McClure (1974a) considered it rare at Khao Yai National Park, and Round (1984) considered it rare at Doi Suthep-Pui National Park.

Distribution and History of Distribution: The black eagle lives in Pakistan, India, Burma, southern China, all of Indochina except Kampuchea, Malaya, Borneo, Sulawesi, the Moluccas, and the Philippines. Populations persist in national parks and wildlife sanctuaries scattered across Thailand (Philip D. Round, personal communication).

Geographic Status: Thailand is a central portion of this wide distribution.

Habitat Requirements and Habitat Trend: Its habitat is montane evergreen and deciduous forest up to 2,700 m (Ali and Ripley 1968, Lekagul and Cronin 1974, Round 1984, De Schauensee 1984).

Vulnerability of Species and Habitat: The species is vulnerable to shooting and loss of habitat.

Causes of Threat: This species appears to be threatened by fragmentation of habitat and shooting (Philip D. Round, personal communication).

Responses to Habitat Modification: Unknown.

Demographic Characteristics: The clutch normally is a single egg, sometimes two. In India, the breeding season is November to April (Ali and Ripley 1968). Deignan (1945) reported a pair rearing two young at Doi Suthep.

Key Behaviors: The black eagle feeds mainly on birds' eggs and nestlings, which it obtains from nests; it also eats adult birds, rats, frogs, lizards, and large insects. The primary wing feathers are specially adapted for slow flight while flying through treetops looking for nests; they are widely splayed and upturned to generate extra lift. The feet also are specially adapted for grasping nests and their contents; the toes are short, the claws are only weakly curved and most are long, but the outer toe and claw are very short (Ali and Ripley 1968). The birds are always seen in pairs and presumably mate for life (Smythies 1960). The species appears not to migrate.

Conservation Measures Taken: Thai law (WARPA 1980) prohibits killing and regulates trade of this species. Black eagles are present in Om Koi and Phu Luang wildlife sanctuaries and Doi Inthanon, Doi Suthep-Pui, and Khao Yai national parks (Philip D. Round personal communication).

Conservation Measures Proposed: From the information available, it is unclear what conservation actions are needed. The primary need, therefore, is for better data on the status and threats to this species. Complete protection from shooting is one obvious safeguard.

Wallace's hawk eagle
Spizaetus nanus
Aves, Falconiformes, Accipitridae

Status: Endangered.
WARPA (1980): Protected-1.

Population Size and Trend: Unknown, but considered uncommon by Lekagul and Cronin (1974). The failure of Holmes (1973) and Holmes and Wells (1975) to record Wallace's hawk eagle from southern Thailand is ominous.

Distribution and History of Distribution: Wallace's hawk eagle ranges from peninsular Thailand and Burma to Malaya, Sumatra, and Borneo. A recent, unconfirmed sighting was reported at Ton Nga Chang Wildlife Sanctuary, Hat Yai Province, in 1982 (Philip D. Round, personal communication).

Geographic Status: Southern Thailand is the northern extremity of this species' range.

Habitat Requirements and Habitat Trend: This species prefers mature lowland forest (Smythies 1960, Lekagul and Cronin 1974), little of which remains in its range in peninsular Thailand.

Vulnerability of Species and Habitat: The preferred habitat in Thailand is virtually gone. Persistence of this species in the country is wholly dependent on lowland preserves and on non-preferred montane forest, which in peninsular Thailand is occupied by three other species of hawk eagles.

Causes of Threat: The major threat of habitat loss already is an accomplished fact. Any current threat would involve degradation of existing lowland preserves.

Responses to Habitat Modification: Unknown.

Demographic Characteristics: Unknown.

Key Behaviors: The diet includes birds, lizards, and bats (Smythies 1960).

Conservation Measures Taken: Thai law (WARPA 1980) prohibits killing and regulates trade of this species. Numerous national parks, wildlife sanctuaries, and no-hunting areas have been established in the range of Wallace's hawk eagle.

Conservation Measures Proposed: A survey of the forested preserves in southern Thailand is needed to define the nature of any remaining populations and the threats to which they are subject. The birds should be strictly protected from shooting.

Peregrine falcon, duck hawk
Falco peregrinus **Tunstall 1771**
Aves, Falconiformes, Falconidae

Status: Endangered.
CITES (1979): Appendix I.
WARPA (1980): Protected-1.

Population Size and Trend: Population size and trend in Asia are unknown (IUCN Red Data Book 1979). The species is rare to common (La Touche 1931-34, Smythies 1953, Deignan 1945, Cheng 1963, Lekagul and Cronin 1974) in the region.

Distribution and History of Distribution: The peregrine is widespread in open lowlands and along coasts in all of Thailand except the Khorat Plateau (Deignan 1945, Madoc 1961, McClure and Lekagul 1961, Dickinson 1966, Ogle 1974, Lekagul and Cronin 1974, Holmes and Wells 1975, Medway and Wells 1976).

Geographic Status: All records of this species in Thailand appear to be migrants and winter residents, occurring from July to February. A recent example is a pair seen at the limestone outcrops of Khao Kaeo, Nakhon Sawan Province, in July and August (Ogle 1986). These records have been assigned variously to subspecies *japonensis*, *calidus*, and *peregrinator*, but they are most likely to be *P. p. peregrinator*, which breeds in India, Bangladesh, Burma, and southern and eastern China. The hiatus between breeding populations of Chinese *peregrinator* and Malaysian *nesiotes* is peculiar. That peregrines do not breed in the humid tropical forest regions of the world (Brown and Amadon 1968) is disproved by the Malaysia-Indonesia breeding range of *nesiotes*.

Habitat Requirements and Habitat Trend: The peregrine frequents lowlands, river valleys, and coasts, particularly around marshes where waterfowl are abundant. It also occurs in large cities, where it roosts on tall buildings and eats mainly pigeons. Nesting is usually on a cliff ledge, sometimes on a tall building or in a tree. The diet is mostly birds, particularly ducks, gulls, shorebirds, pigeons, thrushes, and finches (Cheng 1963). In Burma, the favored foods are pigeons, parrots, bats, and ducks (Smythies 1953). The food requirement is about 11-12 percent of body weight, with 80-100 g of food consumed daily.

Vulnerability of Species and Habitat: As a top carnivore, the species ingests chlorinated hydrocarbon insecticides (such as DDT and its metabolite, DDE) that have been concentrated through the food chain in the tissues of its prey, causing reduced thickness of the egg shell, which breaks during incubation (see for example Hickey 1969, Peakall and Kiff 1979). Hence reproduction fails. Though these pesticides are not a problem in low-intensity agricultural land or native vegetation, they can be acquired in winter or breeding range, so a very large region without high-intensity agriculture is needed to maintain healthy populations. Reduction of waterfowl populations by excessive hunting can be a problem, and drainage of marshes causes loss of foraging habitat.

Causes of Threat: High-intensity agriculture is rapidly being adopted in Southeast Asia and is posing an increasing threat to reproduction of migratory peregrines from China. Most marshes in Thailand have been drained and converted to agricultural use.

Responses to Habitat Modification: The peregrine is tolerant of a wide array of habitat changes (IUCN Red Data Book 1979).

Demographic Characteristics: A normal clutch includes 3-4 eggs, with a range of 2-6. Incubation takes 28-29 days. The female tends the nestlings closely for their first 2 weeks of life, while they are provisioned by the male; thereafter she spends much time away from the nest (Brown and Amadon 1968). Young remain in the nest for 35-40 days (Cheng 1963). After the young are fledged, they may remain dependent on their parents for 2 months or more prior to migration. Peregrines live up to 12 years in the wild, but 2-3 years after reaching sexual maturity is the average longevity (Brown and Amadon 1968). Sharply declining populations in North America exhibit annual mortality rates of 70-74 percent in immatures and 25 percent in adults (Enderson 1969).

Key Behaviors: Peregrines mate for life, remating only when one of the pair dies. The nesting site is very important to peregrines, and a suitable cliff may be occupied over many successive generations. Migration usually occurs along river valleys and coasts (Brown and Amadon 1968).

Conservation Measures Taken: Thai law (WARPA 1980) protects this species from hunting and regulates trade.

Conservation Measures Proposed: An international shift from chlorinated hydrocarbons to less persistent pesticides will be necessary to conserve this long-distance migrant. Presumably at risk from any such environmental contamination in Thailand is a large portion of China's breeding population of peregrines. A positive step would be to inventory peregrines wintering at marshes in Thailand for the purpose of devising a conservation plan for these important habitats.

Roulroul, crested green wood-partridge
Rollulus roulroul (Scopoli 1786)
Aves, Galliformes, Phasianidae

Status: Threatened.
WARPA (1980): Protected-1.

Population Size and Trend: The total number of roulrouls in Thailand is unknown. It is considered to be an uncommon resident (Lekagul and Cronin 1974).

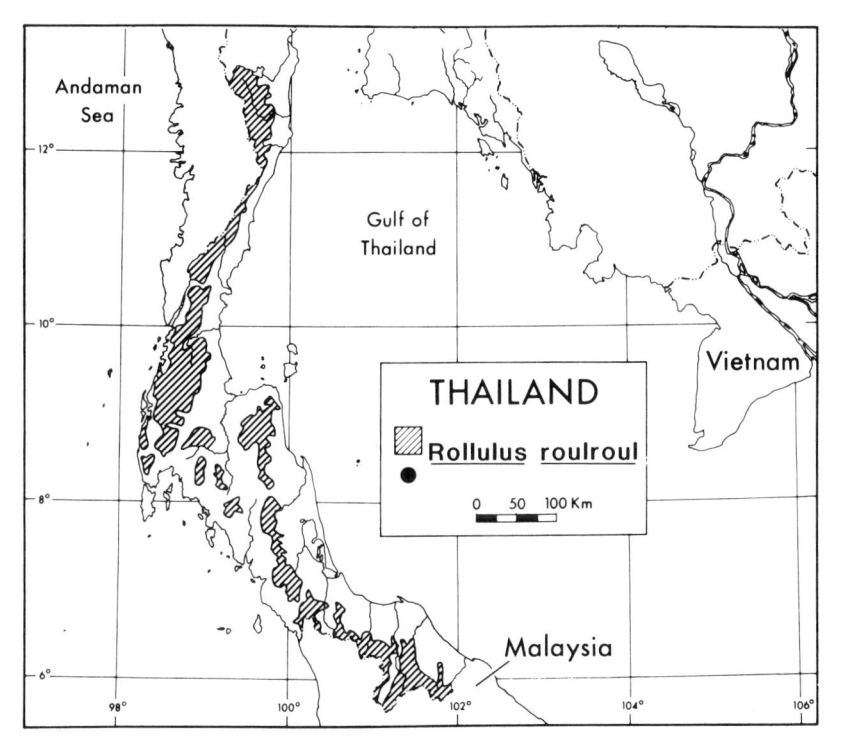

Fig. 50. Distribution of the Roulroul (*Rollulus roulroul*).

Distribution and History of Distribution: This animal is known from "peninsular Burma and from 13° N in peninsular Thailand to Sumatra, Banka, Belitung, and Borneo" (Fig. 50; Medway and Wells 1976).

Geographic Status: The Thai population is peripheral, lying at the northern limits of the species' distribution.

Habitat Requirement and Habitat Trend: Roulrouls are known from sea level to about 1,220 m. They inhabit dense undergrowth in drier primary and mature secondary forest and sometimes bamboo. They are said to subsist on berries and insects (Delacour 1947, Glenister 1955, Lekagul and Cronin 1974, King and Dickinson 1975, Medway and Wells 1976).

Vulnerability of Species and Habitat: The colorful plumage of this bird, including the male's copious red crest, makes it especially attractive to humans. Although quite shy and rarely seen, it is easily trapped (Riley 1938, Glenister 1955). The mature forests it requires are being cleared at an unprecedented rate.

Causes of Threat: Forest clearing and hunting threaten this species. Annual exports from Thailand from 1967 to 1971 were 94, 99, 104, 86, and 192 (Royal Forestry Department 1972).

Responses to Habitat Modification: Unknown.

Demographic Characteristics: Nests with eggs have been found during many parts of the year in Malaysia. Perhaps these birds breed throughout the year in Thailand. The usual clutch size is 5-6 eggs (Medway and Wells 1976).

Key Behaviors: The vocalization, a low whistle, is given most persistently at daybreak. Birds are seen singly, in pairs, and in small coveys (Delacour 1947, Glenister 1955, Holmes 1973, Medway and Wells 1976).

Conservation Measures Taken: Roulrouls are protected under Thai law (WARPA 1980), which prohibits hunting and allows export only with special permission from the Wildlife Advisory Committee of the Wildlife Conservation Division. They are said to occur in Ton Nga Chang Wildlife Sanctuary (IUCN 1979).

Conservation Measures Proposed: Field studies on the remaining roulrouls in southern Thailand would be most timely. Management of forest reserves should include provisions for the maintenance of dense undergrowth, which these animals require for cover. Methods for captive rearing have been demonstrated (Glenister 1955), and the species is bred commonly by private citizens in Thailand (Virach Chantrasmi, personal communication).

Kalij pheasant
Lophura leucomelana **(Latham)**
Aves, Galliformes, Phasianidae

Status: Threatened.
IUCN (1979): Threatened.
WARPA (1980): Protected-1.

Population Size and Trend: Unknown. Populations in suitable habitat can be common (Delacour 1951). In Burma the species was considered fairly common but becoming scarce in accessible areas because of hunting (Smythies 1953). Kalij pheasants were considered uncommon in Thailand (Lekagul and Cronin 1974).

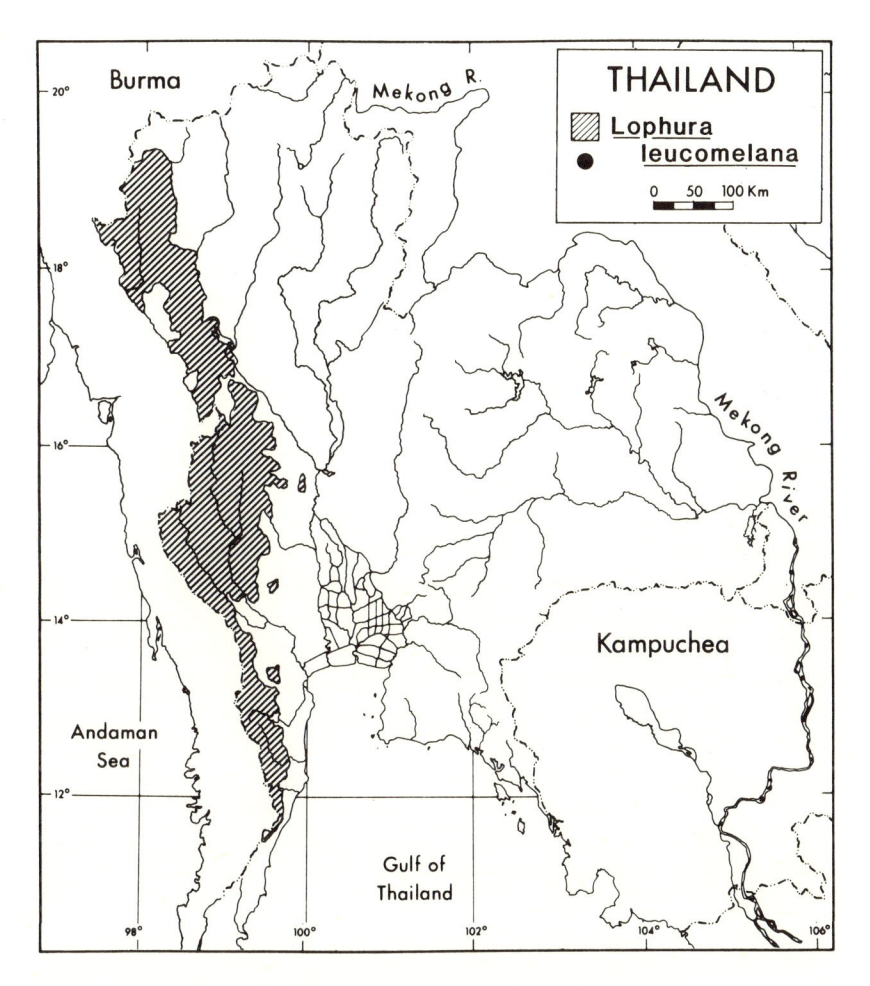

Fig. 51. Distribution of the Kalij Pheasant (*Lophura leucomelana*).

Distribution and History of Distribution: Kalij pheasants occur in the foothills and mountains (>100 m) of western Thailand, west of the Ping River and central plains, between latitudes 12° and 19° (Fig. 51). They do not remain where large expanses of forest are completely converted to agriculture (Delacour 1949, 1951). The reports of this species in Khao Yai National Park (McClure 1974) and Phu Luang Wildlife Sanctuary (IUCN 1979) presumably are erroneous. Elsewhere the species occurs in Burma, Bhutan, southwestern China, Nepal, and northern India.

Geographic Status: Thailand is the southeastern limit of the range of Kalij pheasants.

Habitat Requirements and Habitat Trend: This is a bird of the teak-bamboo forest, especially where undergrowth is thick, in rocky ravines, and near streams. It often occurs in association with junglefowl but prefers moister microhabitats than the latter species. Kalij pheasants move out onto roads, clearings, or edges of cultivated fields on moonlit nights and early in the morning. Nests are shallow scrapes on the ground. The diet includes grain, seeds, young leaves and grass, insects and their larvae, and small reptiles (Delacour 1951, Smythies 1953, Ali and Ripley 1969).

Vulnerability of Species and Habitat: The species is vulnerable to hunting--particularly the males, which readily come to decoys. However, the birds are difficult to see in the thick cover they prefer, and they run when disturbed (Smythies 1953). The habitat is vulnerable to deforestation.

Causes of Threat: Hunting is a cause of threat (Smythies 1953), and much habitat has been deforested.

Responses to Habitat Modification: Kalij pheasants use small areas of cultivation that are included in their activity ranges, but they cannot live where their forest habitat is removed.

Demographic Characteristics: The clutch contains 4-10 eggs. Incubation by the hen takes 25 days. Most birds breed from March to May, but in the south nesting may start as early as January. Second nests can occur until October (Smythies 1953, Delacour 1951). Birds are sexually mature when 1 year old (Delacour 1949).

Key Behaviors: Males display by making a drumming sound, from rapid wingbeats against the body.

Conservation Measures Taken: Hunting and trade of the species are controlled by Thai law (WARPA 1980). Kalij pheasants live in Huai Kha Khaeng Wildlife Sanctuary (McNeely and Seidensticker 1974), Salak Phra Wildlife Sanctuary (Wiles 1980), and probably in other parks or reserves in western Thailand. Many of these birds are in zoos and pheasantries around the world.

Conservation Measures Proposed: Parks, sanctuaries, and other forested tracts in western Thailand should be surveyed for this species. Research is needed to determine if legal control of harvest is adequate to maintain populations. If this species were shown to be polygamous, it may be possible to design a management strategy to harvest surplus males.

Silver pheasant
Lophura nycthemera (Linnaeus)
Aves, Galliformes, Phasianidae

Status: Threatened.
IUCN (1979): Threatened.
WARPA (1980): Protected-1.

Population Size and Trend: The silver pheasant is common in montane forest where hunting has not been excessive, though its range is inherently fragmentary. This species was common on Doi Pui 50 years ago (Deignan 1945), but now it is rare, apparently because of hunting (Round 1984).

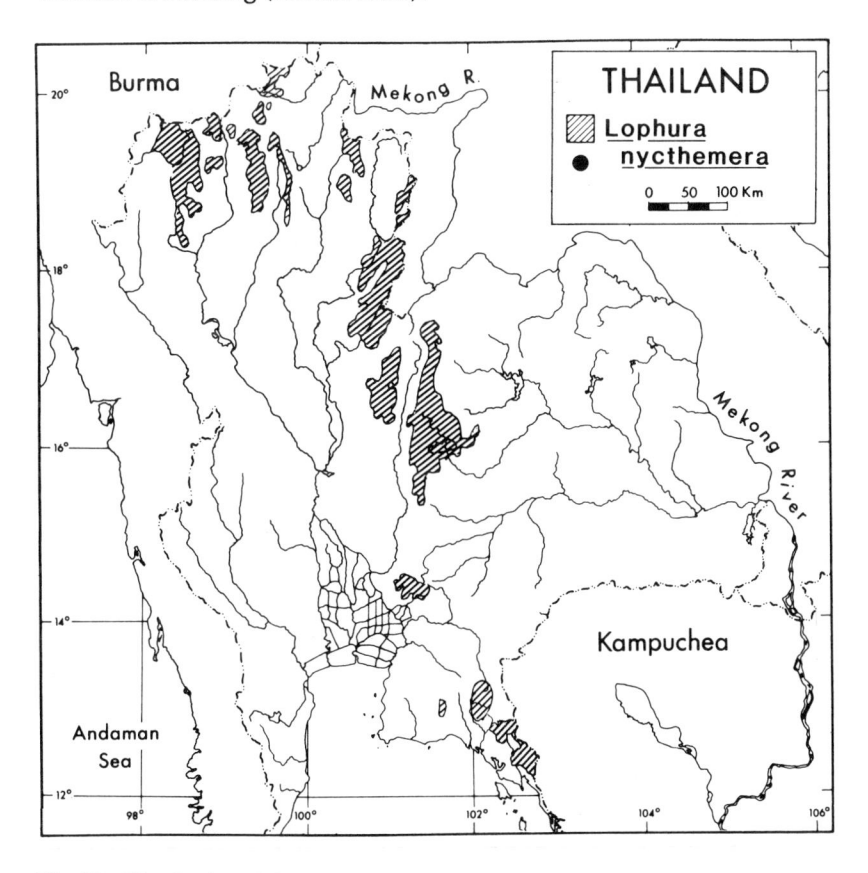

Fig. 52. Distribution of the Silver Pheasant (*Lophura nycthemera*).

Distribution and History of Distribution: This species occurs across southern China, on Hainan, in Vietnam, Lao PDR, western Kampuchea, Thailand, and Burma. In Thailand the species occurs discontinuously in mountain forest above 800 m in the north, the Petchabun Range, and the southeast (Fig. 52; Delacour 1949, 1951). Deforestation has increased the fragmentation of this range.

Geographic Status: Thailand is the southwestern limit of the range of silver pheasants.

Habitat Requirements and Habitat Trend: The silver pheasant lives in montane or premontane forest with dense undergrowth, from elevations of 800-2,750 m. Hence it occupies a variety of vegetation types, including mixed deciduous, pine, and hill evergreen forests. Foraging includes small clearings and roadways (Deignan 1945, Smythies 1953).

Vulnerability of Species and Habitat: The species is vulnerable to hunting. La Touche (1931-34) described how people in China shot from blinds at birds baited with grain, as well as at night roosts by torchlight. The habitat is vulnerable to deforestation.

Causes of Threat: Habitat loss threatens this species.

Responses to Habitat Modification: Unknown.

Demographic Characteristics: The clutch contains 2-4 eggs, and incubation takes 23 days (Delacour 1951). Birds are not sexually mature until 2 years old (Delacour 1949). The maximum life span of tame silver pheasants is 21 years (Cheng 1963).

Key Behaviors: Though usually monogamous in captivity, free-ranging silver pheasants are polygamous. Consequently, social groups in the breeding season typically consist of 1 male and several females (Delacour 1949).

Conservation Measures Taken: Hunting and export of silver pheasants are regulated in Thailand (WARPA 1980). The species occurs in several national parks (NP) and wildlife sanctuaries (WS): Khao Yai NP (Dickinson 1964); Phu Luang WS (IUCN 1979); Doi Inthanon NP, Doi Khuntan NP, and Doi Chiang Dao WS (Deignan 1945); Doi Pui, Nam Nao NP, and Om Koi WS (Boonsong Lekagul, personal communication); and Khao Chamao WS (Samaisuk Sophasan, personal communication). Many silver pheasants are in zoos and pheasantries around the world.

Conservation Measures Proposed: More detailed information is needed on the distribution of silver pheasants in Thailand, and the threat of deforestation needs better documentation. It may be possible to design a management plan of harvesting surplus males in this polygamous species, and research on population dynamics is needed to determine densities, the number of surplus birds, and the rate at which they are replaced. However, caution is appropriate, because the relatively long period this species takes to reach sexual maturity suggests that the reproductive ability to replace harvested individuals is limited.

Crested fireback pheasant
Lophura ignita (Shaw and Nodder 1797)
Aves, Galliformes, Phasianidae

Status: Threatened.
IUCN (1979): Threatened.
WARPA (1980): Protected-1.

Population Size and Trend: Unknown. Beebe (1926) found crested firebacks to be relatively common in peninsular Malaysia and Borneo but very patchy in local occurrence; similarly they are "sparingly distributed" in southern Burma (Smythies 1953). Glenister (1955) considered them rare, and Lekagul and Cronin (1974) termed them uncommon.

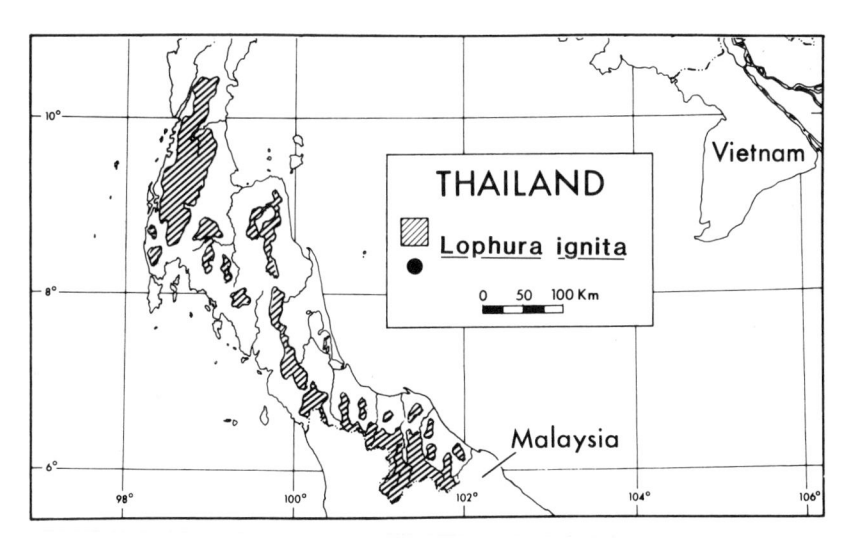

Fig. 53. Distribution of the Crested Fireback Pheasant (*Lophura ignita*).

Distribution and History of Distribution: Crested firebacks occur in the Mergui district of Burma, Thailand south of the Isthmus of Kra (including Ko Phuket), peninsular Malaysia, Sumatra, Bangka, and Borneo (Delacour 1949, Medway and Wells 1976). Actual distribution within this range is restricted to forest below 600-1,200 m. This range has been greatly reduced and fragmented by habitat loss (Fig. 53).

Geographic Status: Thailand is the northern limit of the species' range.

Habitat Requirements and Habitat Trend: The crested fireback occupies lowland tropical forest up to 600-1,200 m elevation (Delacour 1949). Beebe (1926) found flocks frequenting successional vine tangles on sites of previous swidden agriculture, and the birds foraged in the nearby primary forest. Such patches of dense cover also develop in light gaps made by fallen trees. The diet consists of seeds, leaves, berries, and small insects (Beebe 1926, Smythies 1953). Very little lowland forest remains in southern Thailand.

Vulnerability of Species and Habitat: The species is vulnerable to trapping, and its habitat is highly vulnerable to deforestation.

Causes of Threat: Habitat loss is an extremely serious threat to this species.

Responses to Habitat Modification: Crested firebacks never venture into forest clearings (Smythies 1953).

Demographic Characteristics: Birds are sexually mature when 2 years old. A clutch contains 5-8 eggs. Incubation takes 24-25 days (Delacour 1951).

Key Behaviors: Free-ranging birds occur in flocks containing one male and several females, indicating a polygamous mating system (Beebe 1926, Smythies 1953). Flocks can be found by stalking the location of calls or the whirring sound made with their wings (Smythies 1953).

Conservation Measures Taken: Thai law (WARPA 1980) prohibits hunting and regulates trade of this species. The species is reported to occur in Nong Thung No-hunting Area, Surat Province (W. Brockelman, personal communication) and in Thaleban National Park, Satun Province (Dobias 1982). Many crested firebacks are in zoos and pheasantries around the world.

Conservation Measures Proposed: Basic information on current status and distribution is needed. Loss of lowland forests in southern Thailand is so extreme that a search for surviving populations should focus on existing or proposed national parks, wildlife sanctuaries, and nonhunting areas.

Siamese fireback pheasant
Lophura diardi (Bonaparte 1856)
Aves, Galliformes, Phasianidae

Status: Threatened.
IUCN (1979): Threatened.
WARPA (1980): Protected-1.

Population Size and Trend: The Siamese fireback was common to abundant in suitable habitat (Delacour 1951) but now is considered uncommon (Lekagul and Cronin 1974). The species was rare in northern Thailand at the time of field work by Deignan (1945).

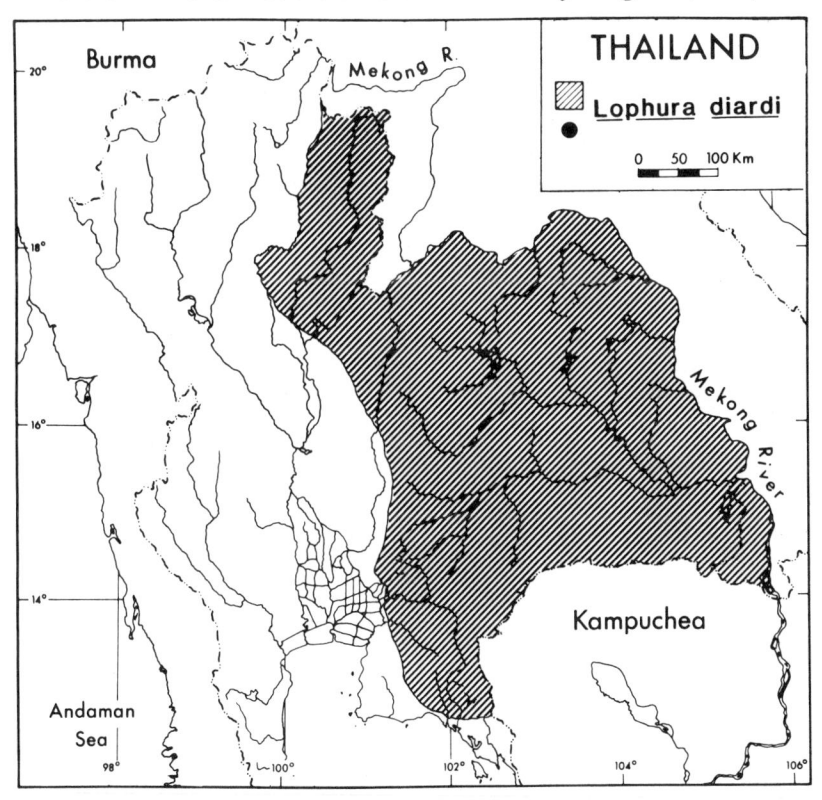

Fig. 54. Distribution of the Siamese Fireback Pheasant (*Lophura diardi*).

Distribution and History of Distribution: This species occurs in Vietnam, southern Lao PDR, northern Kampuchea, and eastern and north-central Thailand. Early reports of firebacks in eastern Burma have not been substantiated. In Thailand the species does not occur west of the Yom River or the Khuntan Mountains (Fig. 54; Delacour 1951). This distribution has become much reduced and fragmented by habitat conversion.

Geographic Status: Thailand provides the western half of the range of the species.

Habitat Requirements and Habitat Trend: The Siamese fireback occurs in lowlands up to 600 m, including forest, bamboo thickets, and abandoned, overgrown agricultural land (Deignan 1945, Delacour 1951). Because lowland forests are the first to be cleared, habitat loss has been great.

Vulnerability of Species and Habitat: The species is difficult to shoot in its dense cover, but it is very easy to trap. This fireback has been trapped for export for many decades (Beebe 1926). Very little lowland forest remains in Thailand, but early successional cover may support populations.

Causes of Threat: Deforestation and trapping threatens this species.

Responses to Habitat Modification: The species uses roads, clearings, and successional habitats (Deignan 1945, Delacour 1951).

Demographic Characteristics: Eggs are 5-8 to a clutch. Incubation takes 24-25 days. Females usually are not sexually mature until 3 years of age (Delacour 1951).

Conservation Measures Taken: Thailand regulates hunting and export of Siamese firebacks (WARPA 1980). The species is reported to occur in several national parks (NP) and wildlife sanctuaries (WS): Thung Salang Luang NP (Dickinson and Chaiyaphun 1970); Nam Nao NP, Khao Sabap NP, Sam Larn NP, Phu Luang WS, and Phu Miang-Phu Thong WS (IUCN 1979); and Khao Yai NP and Khao Soi Dao WS (W. Brockelman, personal communication). Many Siamese firebacks are in zoos and pheasantries around the world.

Conservation Measures Proposed: A detailed survey of distribution is needed. Studies of the dynamics of populations protected in parks and sanctuaries would show whether existing regulations provide adequate protection for populations not in reserve areas.

Mrs. Hume's pheasant, barred-back pheasant
Syrmaticus humiae (Hume 1881)
Aves, Galliformes, Phasianidae

Status: Endangered.
IUCN Red Data Book (1977): Rare.
CITES (1979): Appendix I.
IUCN (1979): Threatened.
USFWS (1980a): Endangered.
WARPA (1980): Protected-1.

Population Size and Trend: Unknown. Populations are discontinuous on mountains and range from locally rare to locally abundant. No clear view of population status emerges from existing information. Some populations may have declined because of overhunting. All authors have considered this pheasant rare in Thailand (Deignan 1945, Smythies 1953, Ali and Ripley 1969, Lekagul and Cronin 1974, IUCN Red Data Book 1977).

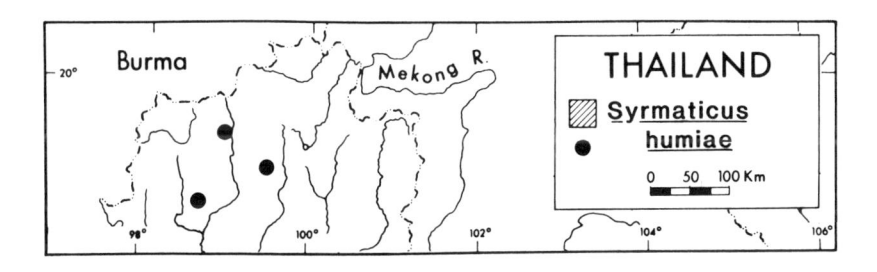

Fig. 55. Distribution of Mrs. Hume's Pheasant (*Syrmaticus humiae*).

Distribution and History of Distribution: Hume's pheasant "occurs from the hills of northern Burma west of the Irrawaddy River to Manipur, Naga, Patkai and the Lushai Hills of Assam, India, south through Burma's Chin Hills to Mt. Victoria, and north to the mountains of the border between Burma, and India and China including Tibet . . . and east of the Irrawaddy River in Burma, in the Shan highlands and into south-western Yunnan across the Salween River, south to northwestern Thailand" (IUCN Red Data Book 1977). In Thailand it is reported only from Doi Lang

Ka, Doi Suthep, and Doi Chiang Dao (Fig. 55), with the last published sighting in 1933 (Deignan 1945). In 1935-37, Deignan failed to find Hume's pheasants on Doi Suthep despite considerable effort. No change in distribution of the species is documented, but these reports suggest the possibility that it is extirpated from Thailand. On the other hand, a thorough survey of potential habitat might reveal other populations in northwestern Thailand.

Geographic Status: The Thailand populations are disjunct and on the periphery of the species' range.

Habitat Requirements and Habitat Trend: The habitat of Hume's pheasant is oak, oak-chestnut, and pine forests with interspersed patches of bracken fern and lalang (*Imperata* grassland) on hills and mountains from 900-3,355 m elevation. Nests are built on the ground. The trees are used for escape cover (Deignan 1945, Smythies 1953, Ali and Ripley 1969). Because this habitat mosaic is maintained naturally by local fires, Hume's pheasant should be considered a fire disclimax species.

Vulnerability of Species and Habitat: Hunting and trapping have the potential of extirpating localized populations (IUCN Red Data Book 1977). The species "frequents small clearings and open woodlands and may be especially vulnerable to hunters" (Round 1984). As human population densities increase, large-scale, permanent conversion of montane land to agriculture and grassland will cause increasing habitat loss.

Causes of Threat: Hunting is a major threat to this species. This species was already rare on Doi Pui 50 years ago (Deignan 1945), and now it is absent, apparently extirpated by hunting (Round 1984).

Responses to Habitat Modification: Though none are documented, presumably the former practices of slash-and-burn agriculture followed by fallow forest regeneration benefited Hume's pheasants by maintaining a mosaic of cover types, much as did local fires prior to man's presence. Now that high human population densities demand more intensive human land-use, reversion to forest is prevented and nutrient-poor former agricultural land is burned annually to maintain *Imperata* grassland for cattle grazing. This conversion of the habitat mosaic to large areas of pasture presumably destroys the habitat required by Hume's pheasant.

Demographic Characteristics: A clutch of eggs contains 6 to 10 eggs (Ali and Ripley 1969).

Key Behaviors: The species readily adapts to captivity (Delacour 1951), facilitating captive propagation.

Conservation Measures Taken: Doi Suthep-Pui is a National Park, and Doi Chiang Dao is a Wildlife Sanctuary. A captive breeding stock of the western subspecies of Hume's pheasant has been established at the Pheasant Trust (Norwich, England), the Rangoon Zoo (Burma), and other places. The captive population in Europe, Japan, and North America numbered 559 birds in 1976 (IUCN Red Data Book 1977). Thai law (WARPA 1980) prohibits hunting and trade in this species.

Conservation Measures Proposed: If the birds could be protected or harvest kept to sustainable levels, Hume's pheasant could be reintroduced in Doi Suthep-Pui National Park and other such areas from which it has been lost. Formal protected status also should be considered at Doi Lang Ka. Our observation of about 10 hunters combing the woodland 100 m from a manned guard station in the forest of Doi Pui shows that improved enforcement is needed to protect wildlife. In addition, people living in some national parks in northern Thailand are converting the pre-existing mosaic of habitats into extensive pasture; this practice must be controlled and the people given alternative means of support if wildlife is to be protected in national parks. A field survey is needed to determine if Hume's pheasants survive in their historical range or are present in other areas of montane habitat in northern Thailand. After the current status of the species is documented, specific management steps can be proposed.

Burmese gray peacock pheasant
Polyplectron bicalcaratum **(Linnaeus 1758)**
Aves, Galliformes, Phasianidae

Status: Threatened.
CITES (1979): Appendix II.
IUCN (1979): Threatened.
WARPA (1980): Protected-1.

Population Size and Trend: Unknown but surely declining. The species is common in suitable habitat (Gyldenstolpe 1920,

Beebe 1926, Smythies 1953). Though it is very secretive, Beebe once saw 13 during a walk of 6-8 km.

Distribution and History of Distribution: The gray peacock pheasant occurs in India (Sikki and Assam), Bhutan, Burma, northern and western Thailand, southern China, northern Lao PDR and Vietnam, and Hainan (Delacour 1951). In Thailand this species lives in the northern plateau, the northern part of the Petchabun plateau, and the western and peninsular provinces south to Prachuap Khiri Khan (Deignan 1963). Its distribution has been reduced and fragmented by deforestation.

Geographic Status: Thailand is on the southern edge of the species' range.

Habitat Requirements and Habitat Trend: The gray peacock pheasant lives in evergreen forest and bamboo jungle from near sea level to 1,800 m elevation. It uses very dense cover and rarely ventures into openings. Nests are on the ground in dense undergrowth. The diet consists of leaves, grain, seeds, berries, fruits, insects and their larvae, and snails (Beebe 1926, Smythies 1953, Ali and Ripley 1969). Much habitat has been lost.

Vulnerability of Species and Habitat: The birds are easily trapped, and their habitat is vulnerable to deforestation.

Causes of Threat: Deforestation is the major threat to this species.

Responses to Habitat Modification: Unknown.

Demographic Characteristics: The clutch usually contains 2 eggs but can have up to 5. Incubation takes 21 days (Ali and Ripley 1969).

Key Behaviors: Incubation is by the hen only. The mating system is apparently monogamy, at least within a breeding season, as the birds routinely are seen in pairs when not alone. The species escapes danger by running and is so wary that shooting is ineffective even with the aid of a dog (Ali and Ripley 1969). Breeding is from March to June in India and earlier in Burma (Smythies 1953, Ali and Ripley 1969).

Conservation Measures Taken: Hunting and export are regulated by Thai law (WARPA 1980). The species has been reported at Nam Nao National Park (IUCN 1979) and Doi Chiang Dao Wildlife Sanctuary (Deignan 1945). It is easy to keep in captivity.

Conservation Measures Proposed: The gray peacock pheasant probably occurs in other parks and sanctuaries; these should be surveyed by persons familiar with the species' call. Research is needed to determine whether populations persist where harvested.

Malay brown peacock pheasant
Polyplectron malacense **(Scopoli 1786)**
Aves, Galliformes, Phasianidae

Status: Endangered.
CITES (1979): Appendix II.
WARPA (1980): Protected-1.

Population Size and Trend: Unknown but surely declining. Though many authors consider the species rare or uncommon, this may be because of the birds' secretive habits and remote habitat. Beebe (1926) found this to be one of the most difficult-to-locate but not the rarest of the Malaysian pheasants.

Distribution and History of Distribution: The Malay Peacock pheasant occurs in southeastern Burma, peninsular Thailand and Malaysia, Sumatra, and Borneo (Delacour 1951). Its distribution has been greatly reduced and fragmented by deforestation (Fig. 56).

Geographic Status: Thailand is the northern part of the species' range.

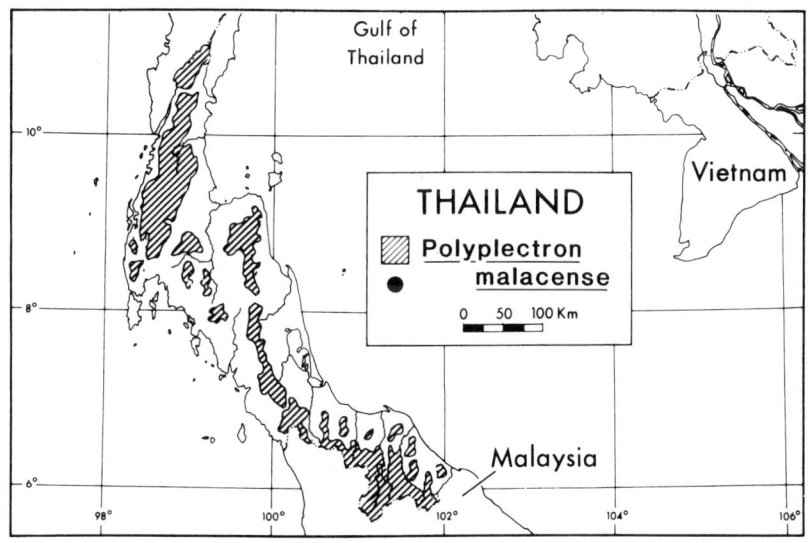

Fig. 56. Distribution of the Malay Brown Peacock Pheasant (*Polyplectron malacense*).

Habitat Requirements and Habitat Trend: This peacock pheasant lives in primary, lowland, tropical forest, up to 300-900 m (Beebe 1926, Medway and Wells 1976). Very little of this habitat remains in Thailand.

Vulnerability of Species and Habitat: The birds are shot and trapped. Their habitat is highly vulnerable to deforestation.

Causes of Threat: Deforestation.

Responses to Habitat Modification: Unknown.

Demographic Characteristics: Unknown.

Key Behaviors: Malay peacock pheasants usually are seen alone or in pairs, not in larger groups (Beebe 1926).

Conservation Measures Taken: Hunting and export are regulated by Thai law (WARPA 1980). This species is very difficult to keep in captivity (Delacour 1951).

Conservation Measures Proposed: The only hope for the survival of this species in Thailand is well-protected lowland forest. The national parks and wildlife sanctuaries in southern Thailand need to be examined for the presence of peacock pheasants.

Great argus pheasant
Argusianus argus (Linnaeus 1766)
Aves, Galliformes, Phasianidae

Status: Threatened.

CITES (1979): Appendix II.

WARPA (1980): Protected-1.

Population Size and Trend: The great argus is common in suitable habitat, though rarely seen (Beebe 1926, Delacour 1951, Smythies 1953, Holmes 1973). Populations are surely declining because of habitat loss.

Distribution and History of Distribution: The species occurs in Burma from Tavoy south, peninsular Thailand south of Prachuap Khiri Khan, peninsular Malaysia, Pangkor Besar, Sumatra, and Borneo (Delacour 1951, Smythies 1953, Deignan 1963). Its range is much reduced and fragmented by deforestation (Fig. 57).

Geographic Status: Thailand is most of the northern part of the species' range.

Habitat Requirements and Habitat Trend: The great argus lives in primary and secondary tropical forest up to 1,200 m. It frequents

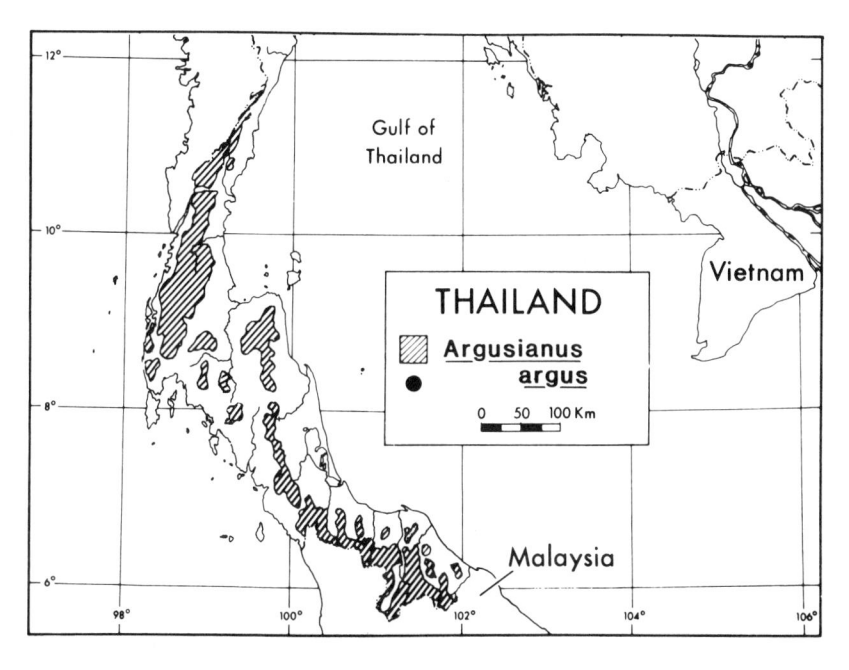

Fig. 57. Distribution of the Great Argus Pheasant (*Argusianus argus*).

dry hills and avoids swamp forest (Beebe 1926, Delacour 1951). In Malaysia, the density of individuals ranged from 0.5 to 3.5 per km^2, and the home range size of males ranged from 1.1 to 6.2 ha (Davison 1981). Very little of this habitat remains in Thailand. The diet consists mainly of fruit and large arthropods on the leaf litter of the forest (Beebe 1926, Davison 1981).

Vulnerability of Species and Habitat: Territorial birds are trapped easily (Beebe 1926). This is true for both sexes (Davison 1981). The habitat is highly vulnerable to deforestation.

Causes of Threat: Deforestation is the primary threat. Hunting and trapping also are serious threats because the low reproductive rate and strict territoriality of this species make it vulnerable to overharvest.

Responses to Habitat Modification: That argus pheasants can live in secondary forest is shown by their abundance in forest recovering from the eruption of Krakatoa on the tip of Sumatra (Beebe 1926).

Demographic Characteristics: The clutch contains 2 eggs, and incubation takes 24-25 days. The birds become sexually mature when 3 years old. The longevity record in captivity is 30 years (Delacour 1951). The breeding season continues over most of the year except for the 2-3 months of molting, and downy chicks have been found in February and August in peninsular Malaysia (Beebe 1926). However, because young do not reach full size until over a year old (Delacour 1951), probably a female can nest only once a year unless the clutch is lost. Population density appears to be regulated by food supply (Davison 1981).

Key Behaviors: Both sexes are solitary and territorial except during brief periods of courting and mating. Males maintain individual dancing grounds by clearing live and dead vegetation from an area about 4 m in diameter. The birds feed in the morning and evening and go to water in mid-morning. The rest of their time is spent resting, with the males on or near their display areas, where they call day and night to attract females. Males move to very dense forest when molting (Beebe 1926, Davison in Smythies 1953, Davison 1981).

Conservation Measures Taken: Thai law (WARPA 1980) prohibits hunting and regulates trade of the great argus. The species occurs in the following national parks (NP) and wildlife sanctuaries (WS): Khao Luang NP, Khlong Nakha WS, Khao Banthat WS, and Ton Nga Chang WS (IUCN 1979); Khlong Saeng WS (P. D. Round, personal communication); and Thaleban NP (Dobias 1982). Few individuals are bred in captivity (Delacour 1951).

Conservation Measures Proposed: The most effective conservation measures would be maintenance of existing protected areas. It would be valuable to census the calling birds in the parks and sanctuaries of southern Thailand in preparation for management planning. The impact of trapping males on their display grounds should be measured, perhaps by call-count density estimates of protected versus unprotected populations. Because of the biological characteristics of this species, harvest rates should be kept very low to sustain populations.

Green peafowl
Pavo muticus **Linnaeus 1766**
Aves, Galliformes, Phasianidae

Status: Threatened.

CITES (1979): Appendix II.
IUCN (1979): Threatened.
IUCN Red Data Book (1979): Vulnerable.
WARPA (1980): Protected-1.

Population Size and Trend: Once widespread and common, the peafowl has become rare or locally extirpated throughout its range in Southeast Asia. In Thailand it is now seen rarely and is considered to be in danger of extirpation (Deignan 1945, IUCN 1968, Lekagul and Cronin 1974, IUCN Red Data Book 1979, B. King personal communication).

Distribution and History of Distribution: Once found throughout Thailand below 900 m except in the central valley of the Chao Phraya and the southeastern provinces, *P. muticus* now probably is most abundant in the mountains of the northwest. It ranges from northeastern India east through Burma, Yunnan in southern China, Thailand, Lao PDR, Vietnam, Kampuchea, peninsular Malaya (where possibly extirpated), and Java. Curiously, it is not known from Sumatra or Borneo (Delacour 1951, Lekagul and Cronin 1974, King and Dickinson 1975, Medway and Wells 1976, IUCN Red Data Book 1979).

Geographic Status: Peafowl populations in Thailand are central in the species' overall range.

Habitat Requirements and Habitat Trend: In Thailand this bird is found primarily in lowland forest from sea level to 900 m. In southern China it is found as high as 1,400 m. It uses a wide variety of habitats, including open forest, which it prefers, and riverbanks, coastal scrub, teak, tea and coffee gardens, forest edges and clearings, dense secondary growth near shifting agriculture, and other areas. It tends to avoid dense, unbroken forest and the heavily settled river deltas of the Irrawaddy, the Chao Phraya, the Mekong, and the Red. The diet in China was described by Cheng (1963) as follows: "Its eating habits are omnivorous. It likes to eat berries, pears, and other fruit, also rice-grain and seedlings, grass seed, etc.; besides these, crickets, dragonflies, small moths, etc., and frogs and lizards, etc., are also eaten." There are also reports of green peafowl eating termites (Deignan 1945, Gibson-Hill 1949, Madoc 1950, Delacour 1951, Cheng 1963, Deignan 1963, Ali and Ripley 1969, Hoogerwerf 1969, Lekagul and Cronin 1974, King and Dickinson 1975, Medway and Wells 1976, IUCN Red Data Book 1979).

Vulnerability of Species and Habitat: Its habits of nesting on or near the ground and foraging on the ground in open areas probably make it conspicuous to human predators, as do its far-reaching vocalizations. In areas of India where the animals are held sacred and not molested, they become tame and frequent the haunts of man. In the rest of their range they are very shy. These giant pheasants are attractive, even more so than their more common Indian congener, *P. cristatus*, and are widely kept as pets. Their feathers alone are worth a good deal in local markets. There is an active trade in live birds (Delacour 1951, Cheng 1963, Ali and Ripley 1969, Hoogerwerf 1969, Medway and Wells 1976).

Causes of Threat: Overhunting threatens to eliminate this species from Thailand. Hunters intensively trap it for the feather and pet trade and villagers take it as food. McClure and Chaiyaphun (1971) noted 62 individuals for sale in Bangkok's Sunday Market between November 1966 and December 1968. In the past Thailand has exported live birds (178 in the period 1962-1971, for example), a practice now forbidden by Thai law (IUCN 1968, McClure and Chaiyaphun 1971, Royal Forestry Department 1972, WARPA 1980).

Responses to Habitat Modification: Green peafowl benefit from some forms of habitat alteration, such as the clearing of patches in forests, but conversion of native habitat to heavily settled agricultural areas is sufficient to exclude the species.

Demographic Characteristics: The breeding season in Thailand is unknown. The birds nest from July to October in Java, March to May (with some as late as September) in Burma, June to August in southern China, and January to April (and some July-September) in India. In Thailand, fledged young have been observed in June (P. D. Round, personal communication). The usual clutch size is 3-6 eggs. Incubation lasts about 28 days. The birds grow slowly. Females begin to mate and lay eggs at 22 months of age. The birds do not get their adult plumage until 3 years old and may live to be 20-25 if unmolested. Captives lay up to 40 eggs per year (Smythies 1953, Cheng 1963, Ali and Ripley 1969, Hoogerwerf 1969).

Key Behaviors: The specific epithet designated by Linnaeus, *muticus* ("mute"), is a misnomer or a joke. The birds' vocalizations, given most frequently at dawn and dusk, carry for a great distance. Foraging activity is terrestrial and crepuscular. Single birds, pairs, and small flocks (often harem/family groups) are seen. During the heat of the day the fowl rest in vegetative cover on the ground. At night they roost, often communally, in the tops of such trees as palms and pines, often as high as 25-30 m. They run rapidly and prefer to run downhill or hide in brushy cover when danger threatens, but they also fly into trees to escape. Green peafowl are less alert and shy than other pheasants. Males attract harems of 2-5 females. The mating behavior has been described in detail (Delacour 1951, Ali and Ripley 1969). Males of this species are famous for their strutting displays. The hen alone incubates the eggs and cares for the young (Deignan 1945, Smythies 1953, Cheng 1963, Hoogerwerf 1969, Lekagul and Cronin 1974).

Conservation Measures Taken: Thai law (WARPA 1980) controls hunting and export of this species. Green peafowl are reported to occur in the following national parks (NP) and wildlife sanctuaries (WS): Phue Khieo WS, Phu Wa WS, Phu Miang-Phu Thong WS, Salawin WS, and Khun Yuan WS (IUCN 1979); and Huai Kha Khaeng WS (W. Brockelman, personal communication). Recent reports of this bird in Tarutao Marine National Park (IUCN Red Data Book 1979) are unsubstantiated.

Conservation Measures Proposed: Management officials in areas where peafowl are known to survive should consider their requirements for secluded nightroosts, open forest, and escape cover when planning burning regimes, logging operations, and other forestry procedures. These birds breed well in captivity but require shelter on cold nights in temperate regions. The different races of *P. muticus* readily crossbreed in captivity and will outbreed with *P. cristatus* and many other phasianids if allowed. Though there are at least 500 captive *P. muticus* in the world, indiscriminate crossing between the distinct subspecies (Delacour et al. 1928, Delacour 1949) has made the captive stock undesirable as a source for any future restocking efforts. Therefore, efforts should be undertaken in Thailand to procure wild breeding stock of the two Thai subspecies for captive propagation before they are extirpated altogether. Thailand should strictly enforce its laws on hunting and export and initiate surveys to identify the surviving wild populations (Delacour 1951, Cheng 1963, Hoogerwerf 1969, IUCN Red Data Book 1979).

Nok karien, eastern sarus crane
Grus antigone sharpii (Linnaeus)
Aves, Gruiiformes, Gruidae

Status: Extirpated from Thailand. The eastern subspecies (*sharpii*) is endangered.
IUCN (1968): Rare.
WARPA (1980): Protected-1.

Population Status and Trend: The sarus crane was limited in numbers but widespread throughout Thailand (Gyldenstolpe 1920). The decline of this species has culminated in its extirpation from Thailand, where the last records were in 1965 (Boonsong Lekagul in Walkinshaw 1973). A single pair of sarus cranes was reported to persist on Luzon, Philippines, in 1979, but a field survey failed to confirm its presence, indicating extirpation from the Philippines (Madsen 1980a). The eastern subspecies "is definitely gone from Malaysia and the Philippines, it has not been confirmed in Thailand in the last decade, [is] reported gone from Burma . . . , and no information [is available] from Laos, Cambodia, or Vietnam, although the human turmoil in such areas undoubtedly claimed large birds of open land habitats. The subspecies is established in northern Australia as of 1964 and now numbers in the hundreds" (George Archibald, personal communication).

Distribution and History of Distribution: The western subspecies is reported from Pakistan, Kashmir, India, Nepal, Assam, Bangladesh, and Burma. The eastern subspecies is known from Assam, Burma, Thailand, southern Lao PDR, Kampuchea, southern Vietnam, and Luzon; vagrants have occurred in the Malay Peninsula, and a free-ranging population has been established in Queensland, Australia (Walkinshaw 1973). Records in Thailand are as follows: Northern--the open plains and savannas near Chiang Rai, Chiang Saen, Chiang Mai, Fang, and 10 km north of Ban Chong; Central--near Phu Kradeung in Loei Province, at Thung Salaeng Luang National Park near Phitsanilok, Sara Buri, Pathum Thani, the Ping River valley from Nakhan Sawan to Kamphaeng Phet, and Rat Buri and Phet Buri provinces; Eastern--the open plains near Surin; Southern--the open plains near Bandon, several places in Trang Province, near Sawi Bay south of Chumphon, and north of Songkhla Lake (Riley 1938, Deignan 1945, Madoc 1950, Boonsong Lekagul in Walkinshaw 1973, Lekagul and Cronin 1974).

Geographic Status: Thailand was in the center of the range of the eastern subspecies.

Habitat Requirements and Habitat Trend: The habitat of the sarus crane is the marshes and wet savannas that are maintained by annual flooding and drought, and by periodic fire. Tall grass and other herbaceous vegetation, scattered trees in some areas, minor topographic features, and the seasonally shifting availability of wet and dry sites provide a diverse habitat for cover and foraging. High visibility across this habitat facilitates escape from predators, as does roosting in shallow water at night. Nests are large piles of dead vegetation made from locally available materials. They usually are placed directly on the marsh soil or on dry land, but they float well enough to support the weight of a crane as floodwaters rise. This species is omnivorous to carnivorous, taking a great variety of insects, reptiles, amphibians, snails, fish, crustaceans, tubers and corms of marsh plants, grain from ripe rice plants or from harvested fields, and green shoots of grasses, including young rice plants (Riley 1938, Deignan 1945, Ali and Ripley 1969, Walkinshaw 1973, Madsen 1980a).

Vulnerability of Species and Habitat: The habitat of the sarus crane is ideal for conversion to rice agriculture by draining the marshland and/or artificially regulating water levels. Consequently most good habitat has been destroyed. This species can use rice paddies as alternative habitat if not hunted, and this is widely the case in India, where the cranes are informally protected--people there like cranes and consider it bad luck to kill them. Lacking threats from humans, sarus cranes in India become remarkably tame. Likewise, young cranes in Thailand formerly were sold as garden pets. The last crane known to be exported from Thailand was in 1962 (Royal Forestry Department 1972). When one member of a mated pair is killed or wounded, the mate refuses to escape and is added to the hunter's bag. Following nesting, the cranes lose their flight feathers in August, and at this time cranes in the Philippines were captured with ropes (McGreggor 1909, Deignan 1945, Madoc 1950, Ali and Ripley 1969, Walkinshaw 1973, Madsen 1980a).

Causes of Threat: Conversion of marshes to rice paddies and intensive hunting caused the extirpation of sarus cranes from Thailand.

Responses to Habitat Modification: Sarus cranes use rice

paddies and feed and nest in close proximity to roads, railroads, and human activities if not threatened by people or other predators.

Demographic Characteristics: Clutches contain 1-3 eggs (normally 2). However, the parents seldom raise more than 1 young. The young receives parental care for at least 10 months. When the adult pair begins breeding again, the subadults flock together. Birds become sexually mature at 34 months of age and thereafter nest annually (Walkinshaw 1973, Madsen 1980a).

Key Behaviors: Sarus cranes pair and remain together for life. Nesting begins at the onset of the monsoon season (June-September in India), so young are hatched at a time when marsh habitat is extensive. Reproduction may be curtailed in years of extreme drought. Local migrations occur in some regions or in drought years (Deignan 1945, Walkinshaw 1973).

Conservation Measures Taken: The species, though extirpated, remains protected by the Wild Animals Reservation and Protection Act of 1980, which prohibits hunting and allows export only with special permission from the Wildlife Advisory Committee of the Wildlife Conservation Division. The individual in the Dusit Zoo, Bangkok (1980, our observation), is of the nonendangered subspecies *antigone* (Virach Chantrasmi, personal communication). A captive population of this subspecies is kept by the International Crane Foundation, Baraboo, Wisconsin, USA.

Conservation Measures Proposed: The sarus crane could be reintroduced into Thailand, perhaps from Australian stock, if all necessary steps could be fully implemented. Much expertise has been developed in connection with the whooping crane recovery work of the International Crane Foundation and the United States Fish and Wildlife Service. General needs for a reintroduction program in the Philippines were given by Madsen (1980b). The remaining wetlands in Thailand could be inventoried to determine if sufficient crane habitat is available. Managing large areas as refuges would be essential for reintroduction to succeed.

Masked finfoot
Heliopais personata
Aves, Ralliformes, Heliornithidae

Status: Threatened.

Population Size and Trend: Unknown. The masked finfoot has always been considered rare (Gyldenstolpe 1920, Riley 1938, Smythies 1953, Lekagul and Cronin 1974), though in a few places it can be locally common (Hopwood 1921). The species was reported in Tarutao National Park in 1979-80 (Congdon, in litt. to Philip D. Round personal communication), but there are no other recent records.

Distribution and History of Distribution: The range of this species includes India, Burma, Thailand, Kampuchea, Malaya, and Sumatra.

Geographic Status: Thailand is central in the range of this species.

Habitat Requirements and Habitat Trend: This species breeds in forested wetlands (swamp forests); at other times of year it can be found more widely along water bodies in forests, such as mountain streams and tidal creeks lined with mangroves (Smythies 1953).

Vulnerability of Species and Habitat: Both meat and eggs of this species are relished as human food (Davison in Ali and Ripley 1969). Its forested wetlands are highly valued for conversion to rice paddies, and most of them have been.

Causes of Threat: Deforestation and hunting.

Responses to Habitat Modification: Unknown.

Demographic Characteristics: Nesting occurs during the monsoon, especially in July and August, and the clutch consists of 5 to 7 eggs (Hopwood 1921).

Key Behaviors: The species is secretive and seldom seen. It runs, swims, and dives well, and it commonly perches in trees over water. The diet consists of insects, molluscs, crabs, and vegetation (Deignan 1945, Davison in Smythies 1953). The nest is built in vines above the floodwater. Both sexes incubate the eggs.

Conservation Measures Taken: Numerous national parks, wildlife sanctuaries, and no-hunting areas have been established in the range of the masked finfoot.

Conservation Measures Proposed: A survey is needed to clarify the status of this species. It should be sought in Aw Phang-nga National Park (Philip D. Round, personal communication).

Spotted greenshank
Tringa guttifer (von Nordmann 1835)
Aves, Charadriiformes, Scolopacidae

Status: Endangered.
IUCN Red Data Book (1977): Indeterminate.
CITES (1979): Appendix I.
IUCN (1979): Threatened.
MAB (1979): Endangered.
USFWS (1980a): Endangered.

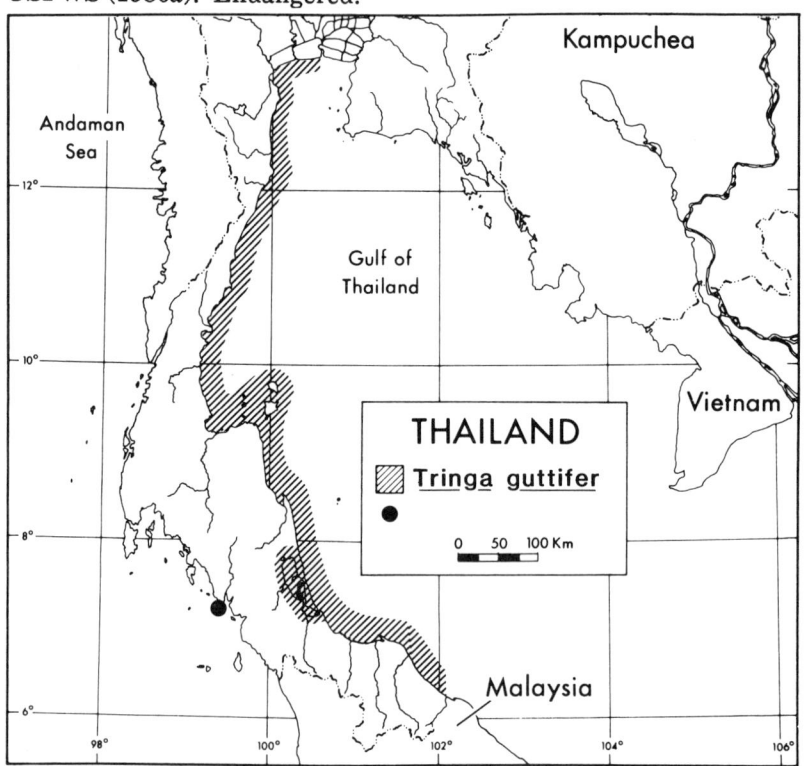

Fig. 58. Distribution of the Spotted Greenshank (*Tringa guttifer*).

Population Size and Trend: All authors consider the spotted greenshank to be uncommon or rare. The species is apparently disappearing (Red Data Books of USSR and Japan, in Nechaev 1978). 50-60 birds were seen on the breeding ground at Sakhalin

Island (Austin and Kuroda 1953). Migrant flocks of 39 were recorded in Korea (Fennell and King 1964) and up to 90 in Malaya (Medway and Nisbet 1966), but most reports are of one or a few individuals.

Distribution and History of Distribution: The spotted greenshank breeds on Sakhalin Island, USSR (Kuroda 1936), apparently at the mouth of the Okhota River near Okhotsk, Khabarovsk Territory, USSR (von Nordmann 1835, and possibly elsewhere in northeastern Siberia (IUCN Red Data Book 1977). Migration and overwintering occur over a wide area of eastern and southeastern Asia, including the Amur and Ussuri basins of eastern Siberia, Japan, Korea, China, Taiwan, Hong Kong, Hainan, Thailand, Malaya, Singapore, Borneo, Philippines, Burma, Tibet, Assam, and Bangladesh (Smythies 1953, Ali and Ripley 1969, King and Dickinson 1975, IUCN Red Data Book 1977). Thailand records are from the western shore of the Gulf of Thailand (Fig. 58; Deignan 1963, Lekagul and Cronin 1974). Recent sightings (1979-1981) have been made at Bangpoo, Samut Prakan, Krabi, Khao Sam Roi Yot, and Ko Libong No-hunting Area (Boonsong Lekagul, personal communication). The species probably is scattered along both coasts of Thailand during winter.

Geographic Status: Thailand provides a small portion of the migratory or winter range of the species.

Habitat Requirements and Habitat Trend: During migration and winter, spotted greenshanks occur on mudflats along seacoasts, at river mouths, and in grassy meadows near streams (Vaurie 1965, Ali and Ripley 1969). Nesting habitat on Sakhalin Island is in sparse larch forest, and nests are built on the tree crotches from 2.3-4.5 m above the ground. The young are reared in the nearby marshes along the coast (Nechaev 1978). No habitat trends are known. Specimens from Bangladesh ate small mudfish, crustaceans, molluscs, and insect larvae (Ali and Ripley 1969).

Vulnerability of Species and Habitat: The small breeding area and use of two adjacent habitats for rearing young suggest high vulnerability of breeding habitat.

Causes of Threat: Many authors have commented that reasons for the rarity of the species are unknown. Likewise, reasons for the reputed decline are unknown.

Responses to Habitat Modification: Unknown.

Demographic Characteristics: Clutches each contain 4 eggs, which are incubated by both female and male (Nechaev 1978).

Key Behaviors: Nesting and incubation occur during June. Within a day or two of hatching, the young are moved from the larch forest to coastal marshes (Nechaev 1978). During migration and winter, spotted greenshanks occur in mixed flocks with similar-looking common greenshanks and redshanks, so they are easily overlooked.

Conservation Measures Taken: Legal protection in Japan (IUCN Red Data Book 1977) may prevent birds there from being eaten. The species also is legally protected in Hong Kong (David Melville, personal communication).

Conservation Measures Proposed: Protection of the breeding birds and their habitats would be the most effective steps. In view of the species' rarity in Thailand and the difficulty of identifying this bird, no Thailand-oriented conservation measures are proposed.

Asian dowitcher, snipebilled godwit
Limnodromus semipalmatus **(Blyth 1848)**
Aves, Charadriiformes, Scolopacidae

Status: Threatened.
IUCN Red Data Book (1977): Rare.
IUCN (1979): Threatened.

Population Size and Trend: This dowitcher is nowhere numerous in its wide range. It occurs in Thailand only as a rare migrant. A recent increase in sightings in Hong Kong suggests that numbers may be increasing, but there has been no supporting evidence elsewhere (Lekagul and Cronin 1974, Webster 1976).

Distribution and History of Distribution: This large wader breeds in several small, widely separated localities in northern Asia and migrates south in winter. The breeding range includes the Argun River valley in Transbaikalia, northeastern and Central Mongolia (especially the shores of Lake Oroknor), an area near Tsitsihar in Manchuria, and the valley of the Irtysh River near Tara and the valley of the Ob in the Barnual region of Siberia. In the non-breeding season it has been recorded as a migrant or winter visitor in China, eastern India, Japan, the Philippines, central Annam, Hong Kong, central and peninsular Thailand (Fig. 59), Malaya, Burma, the Greater Sundas, Papua New Guinea, northern

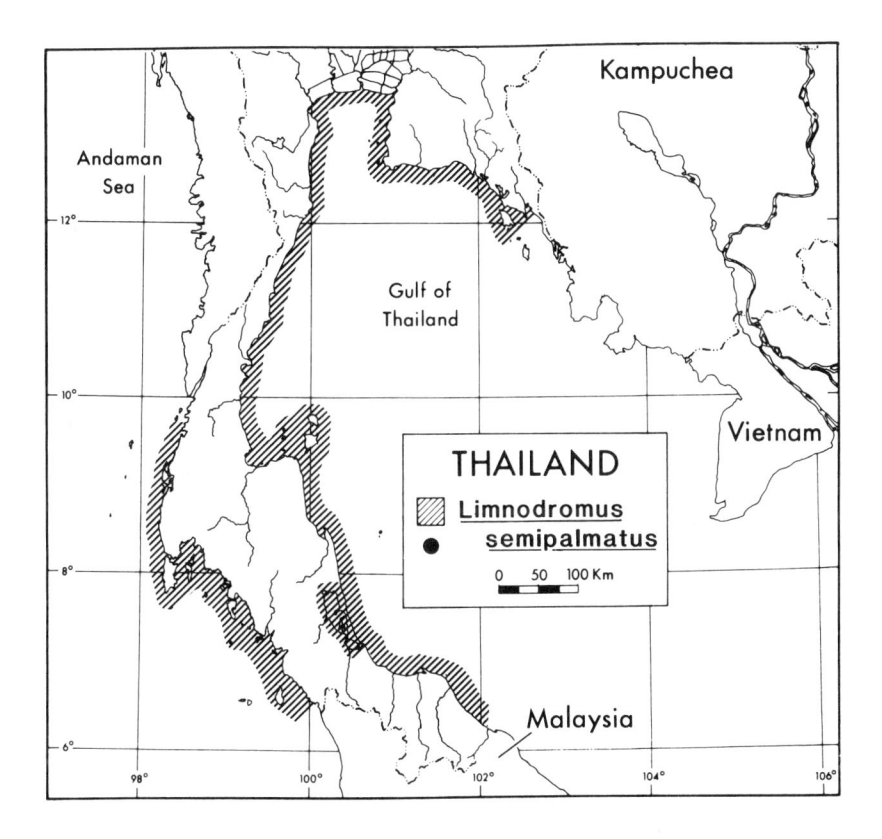

Fig. 59. Distribution of the Asian Dowitcher or Snipebilled Godwit (*Limnodromus semipalmatus*).

Australia, Indonesia, and even as far west as Aden (Jorgensen 1949, Paige 1964, Ali and Ripley 1969, Crawford 1972, Lekagul and Cronin 1974, King and Dickinson 1974, White 1974, Medway and Wells 1976, IUCN Red Data Book 1977). Eight individuals were seen at Samut Sakhon in 1981 (Boonsong Lekagul, personal communication). Additional records for Thailand are given in Melville and Round (1982).

Geographic Status: The Asian dowitchers seen in Thailand are winter migrants from the north.

Habitat Requirements and Habitat Trend: In north-central Asia the species breeds in wetlands, meadows, and grassy floodplains below 800 m elevation. Over its winter range in southern Asia it has been seen inland at elevations as high as 1,500 m, but most records are from prawn ponds or mudflats along seacoasts, the muddy banks of estuaries and large rivers, and coastal marshlands. It feeds on worms and other invertebrates from the mud (Paige 1965, Ali and Ripley 1969, Lekagul and Cronin 1974, King and Dickinson 1975, Medway and Wells 1976).

Vulnerability of Species and Habitat: The coastal areas this species prefers are heavily used by humans. Its large size makes it conspicuous to hunters.

Causes of Threat: Unknown.

Responses to Habitat Modification: Unknown.

Demographic Characteristics: The typical clutch size is 2 eggs (La Touche 1931-34).

Key Behaviors: This species seldom calls, and its vocalization is very quiet. When breeding it aggregates in colonies of 10-20 pairs, and birds often occur in flocks during the non-breeding season. The timing of migration is poorly understood. Its earliest arrival in Malaysia is 4 August. Specimens have been seen as late as April or May at the mouth of the Mai Nam River in Surat Thani Province and the coast of Nakhon Si Thammarat Province (La Touche 1931-34, Riley 1938, King and Dickinson 1975, Medway and Wells 1976, IUCN Red Data Book 1977).

Conservation Measures Taken: The species is protected in Japan and Hong Kong.

Conservation Measures Proposed: As with other wide-ranging species, any conservation measures considered need to be international in scope. Cooperative banding studies among nations this bird visits are needed to elucidate its migration patterns. Although this is the only *Limnodromus* reported from Thailand, biologists should learn to distinguish it from other scolopacids so it is not overlooked. If any regular wintering localities are discovered in Thailand, the coastal habitat and wetlands in that area should be preserved.

Chinese crested tern
Sterna zimmermanni **Reichenow 1903**
Aves, Charadriiformes, Laridae

Status: Endangered, possibly extinct.

IUCN Red Data Book (1977): Indeterminate.
IUCN (1979): Threatened.
WARPA (1980): Protected-1.

Population Size and Trend: This bird was noted in Thailand when three males in active wing molt were taken on 22 November 1923 (Hall 1956). There have been no published records of it anywhere since 1937 (Medway and Wells 1976, IUCN Red Data Book 1977). However, Atsuo Tsuji and Pilai Poonswad (personal communication) report seeing 10 individuals at Libong Wildlife Sanctuary, Trang Province, on 22 July 1980. A review of all published records is given by Mees (1975).

Distribution and History of Distribution: The Chinese crested tern bred in summer along China's east coast and wandered south in winter to southeastern China, the Philippines, the Moluccas, Borneo, and the east coast of peninsular Thailand. The three Thai specimens referred to above were taken in coastal waters off Nakhon Si Thammarat Province (Deignan 1963, King and Dickinson 1975, Medway and Wells 1976, IUCN Red Data Book 1977).

Geographic Status: The Thai records were evidently winter migrants from the north.

Habitat Requirements and Habitat Trend: This bird inhabited coastal shores (Lekagul and Cronin 1974).

Vulnerability of Species and Habitat: Unknown.

Causes of Threat: Unknown.

Responses to Habitat Modification: Unknown.

Demographic Characteristics: Unknown.

Key Behaviors: *S. zimmermanni* was evidently a long-distance migrant.

Conservation Measures Taken: Hunting and trade are regulated by Thai law (WARPA 1980).

Conservation Measures Proposed: Thailand should consider passing laws to protect any that might visit the country in the future. China should conduct surveys of the appropriate areas to determine the status of this bird.

Yellow-vented green pigeon
Treron seimundi (Robinson 1910)
Aves, Columbiformes, Columbidae

Status: Threatened.
IUCN (1979): Drastically reduced.
WARPA (1980): Protected-1.

Population Size and Trend: Very little is known about this species. It is said to be drastically reduced (IUCN 1979), but the species has never been noted as common and may have been rare for a long time. The species is known from 2 specimens taken in Thailand (Deignan 1963) and has not been seen recently in peninsular Malaysia (Medway and Wells 1976). King and Dickinson (1975) term the species an uncommon endemic resident.

Distribution and History of Distribution: The yellow-vented green pigeon is known from Vietnam, Annam, and Thailand, but most authors consider it primarily a Malaysian species (King and Dickinson 1975). Though some records have been thought to represent wanderers, the population centers are not clearly identified. Gibson-Hill (1949) noted that the montane records in Perak and Selangor, Malaysia, are of small series of specimens. The 2 reports from Thailand are from Nan and Bangkok provinces.

Geographic Status: Uncertain.

Habitat Requirements and Habitat Trend: The species has been recorded in mountains, lowlands, mangroves, and on offshore islands (Medway and Wells 1976). It feeds in high trees (Robinson 1928).

Vulnerability of Species and Habitat: Unknown.
Causes of Threat: Unknown.
Responses to Habitat Modification: Unknown.
Demographic Characteristics: Unknown.
Key Behaviors: In Annam it is reported to move from the mountains to the plains, where it nests in winter (Goodwin 1977).

Conservation Measures Taken: Hunting and trade are regulated by Thai law (WARPA 1980).

Conservation Measures Proposed: Observers should be alert for this species in montane forest. Too little is known to propose conservation action.

Pied imperial pigeon
Ducula bicolor (Scopoli 1786)
Aves, Columbiformes, Columbidae

Status: Threatened.

WARPA (1980): Protected-1.

Population Size and Trend: Populations of this species have not been counted. It ranges from locally common (Brockelman and Nadee 1977) to scarce (Hoogerwerf 1969).

Distribution and History of Distribution: The pied imperial pigeon occurs on coasts and small islands from the Bay of Bengal to New Guinea. Its range includes all of Thailand's coast and offshore islands (Goodwin 1977). Specific distribution records in Thailand are at Chumpon Bay and on Ko Phai (Gyldenstolpe 1920), on Ko Huyong, Phangnga Province (Dickinson 1966); Ko Surin Nua, Ranong Province (Brockelman and Nadee 1977); and Ko Samui, Surat Thani Province, and Ko Tarutao, Satun Province (W. Brockelman, personal communication).

Geographic Status: Thailand is a substantial portion of the northern part of the species' range.

Habitat Requirements and Habitat Trend: This species breeds only on small islands but forages more widely to include mangroves on the mainland and coastal woods and plantations. Nests are built on tree or shrub branches. The diet consists of fruits, including mangroves, figs, and nutmegs (Medway and Wells 1976, Goodwin 1977). Substantial areas of coastal mangroves and upland woods have been cleared.

Vulnerability of Species and Habitat: The habitat of this species is vulnerable to deforestation.

Causes of Threat: Cutting mangroves for charcoal and coastal deforestation threaten this species.

Responses to Habitat Modification: Unknown.

Demographic Characteristics: The clutch consists of a single egg (Goodwin 1977).

Key Behavior: The pied imperial pigeon is highly gregarious, nesting in loose colonies (Goodwin 1977) and at times roosting in the thousands (Smythies 1953). Nesting occurs from December to March in the Andaman and Nicobar Islands, with records in May and July on islands off peninsular Malaysia (Medway and Wells 1976, Goodwin 1977). Fruit-pigeons play a key role as seed dispersers for numerous species of forest trees, which thereby maintain their status in the forest community. The birds have very short digestive tracts through which small or large seeds pass intact. The kinds of fruits eaten by these birds have no structural protection from consumers and can be picked without complex reaching or handling procedures.

Conservation Measures Taken: The Royal Forestry Department now regulates the cutting of mangroves in sets of 30 strips, with 1 cut per year on a 30-year rotation. This should assure the maintenance of reproducing mangroves as a food source. The species occurs in Ko Surin Wildlife Sanctuary.

Conservation Measures Proposed: Breeding areas on other offshore islands should be protected. This fruit-eating species should not be captured for the pet trade, because it is difficult to keep alive in captivity.

Ashy wood pigeon
Columba pulchricollis **Blyth 1846**
Aves, Columbiformes, Columbidae

Status: Threatened.
IUCN (1979): Drastically reduced.

Population Size and Trend: The ashy wood pigeon is rare throughout its range, though its secretive habits contribute to that impression (Smythies 1953, Ali and Ripley 1969, Goodwin 1977). Only 2 records have been reported from Thailand (Deignan 1945), so the term "drastically reduced" (IUCN 1979) is inappropriate.

Distribution and History of Distribution: This is a bird of mountain forests. It occurs in Tibet, Nepal, Bhutan, India (Sikkim and Assam), northern Burma, northwestern Thailand, and Taiwan (Ali and Ripley 1969, Goodwin 1977). The 2 published records from Thailand are from the summit of Doi Lang Ka (Fig. 60; Deignan 1945). The species was recently reported from Doi Inthanon National Park (H. Flotow, personal communication).

Geographic Status: The Thailand population of ashy wood pigeons is on the margin of the range or perhaps disjunct from other populations.

Habitat Requirements and Habitat Trend: This species occupies premontane deciduous and montane evergreen forest, usually at elevations of 1,200-3,200 m. However it occasionally has been seen in lowlands (Smythies 1953, Ali and Ripley 1969, Goodwin 1977). Nests are in small forest trees, fairly low. The diet is mainly fruits but also includes acorns, seeds, grain, and snails (Ali and Ripley 1969). Much habitat suitable for this species has been destroyed.

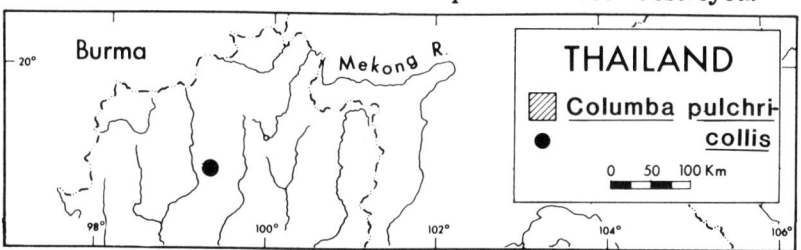

Fig. 60. Distribution of the Ashy Wood Pigeon (*Columba pulchricollis*).

Vulnerability of Species and Habitat: The habitat of this species is vulnerable to deforestation.
Causes of Threat: Deforestation is a threat to this species.
Response to Habitat Modification: Unknown.
Demographic Characteristics: The clutch consists of a single egg (Baker 1913, Ali and Ripley 1969).
Key Behaviors: Ashy wood pigeons forage and rest high in trees, and their flight is silent. As a result, they are seldom observed (Ali and Ripley 1969).
Conservation Measures Taken: None.
Conservation Measures Proposed: Observers need to listen for this species' call, a deep sonorous coo, in the mountains of northern Thailand. More information is needed before specific conservation action can be proposed.

Pale-capped pigeon
Columba punicea Blyth 1842
Aves, Columbiformes, Columbidae

Status: Threatened.
IUCN (1979): Drastically reduced.
WARPA (1980): Protected-2.
Population Size and Trend: Populations are poorly documented, but Gyldenstolpe (1920) thought it to be rather rare. Most

records are from several decades ago (Riley 1938, Medway and Wells 1976), so populations may indeed be drastically reduced (IUCN 1979).

Distribution and History of Distribution: The pale-capped pigeon occurs in eastern India, Bangladesh, Burma, Lao PDR, central Vietnam, Thailand, and peninsular Malaysia. In Thailand its distribution is in the southeast (Sara Buri and Chon Buri provinces, and the peninsula from Phet Buri to Satun provinces). Most of the peninsular records are from islands off the west coast. Specific island records are from Ko Muk, Ko Lak, Ko Phuket, and Ko Phra (Gyldenstolpe 1920, Riley 1938, Ali and Ripley 1969, King and Dickinson 1975).

Geographic Status: Thailand is near the southern edge of the species' range. Birds appear to be resident in the southeast, but in the peninsula they appear only as winter (January-March) migrants (Ripley 1938, Medway and Wells 1976).

Habitat Requirements and Habitat Trend: Pale-capped pigeons live in forest and second growth, including forests interspersed with farmland, from lowlands up to 1,600 m elevation. On islands they occur in mangrove as well as upland forest. The diet is fruit and seeds (including grains).

Vulnerability of Species and Habitat: The habitat of this species is vulnerable to deforestation.

Causes of Threat: Deforestation threatens this species.

Responses to Habitat Modification: Pale-capped pigeons use agricultural land adjacent to forest, but extensive deforestation removes their basic habitat.

Demographic Characteristics: A clutch contains 1 egg (Ali and Ripley 1969).

Key Behaviors: The breeding season is from May to July-August (Ali and Ripley 1969). In peninsular Thailand the species is present from January to March (Medway and Wells 1976). Hence pale-capped pigeons appear to be latitudinal migrants.

Conservation Measures Taken: This species may be hunted under permit from the Thailand Forestry Department (WARPA 1980). The pale-capped pigeon was recorded early in this century from what now is Ko Tarutao Marine National Park (Ripley 1938). The species also has been reported from Khao Yai National Park (Boonsong Lekagul, personal communication).

Conservation Measures Proposed: Research is needed to identify breeding and wintering populations and migration routes. Preserves should be established to support a network of sites that will provide year-round habitat for the species.

Nicobar pigeon
Caloenas nicobarica (Linnaeus 1758)
Aves, Columbiformes, Columbidae

Status: Threatened.
CITES (1979): Appendix I.
WARPA (1980): Protected-1.

Population Size and Trend: The total numbers of this bird are unknown. In Thailand it is a locally common resident on some offshore islands (Lekagul and Cronin 1974).

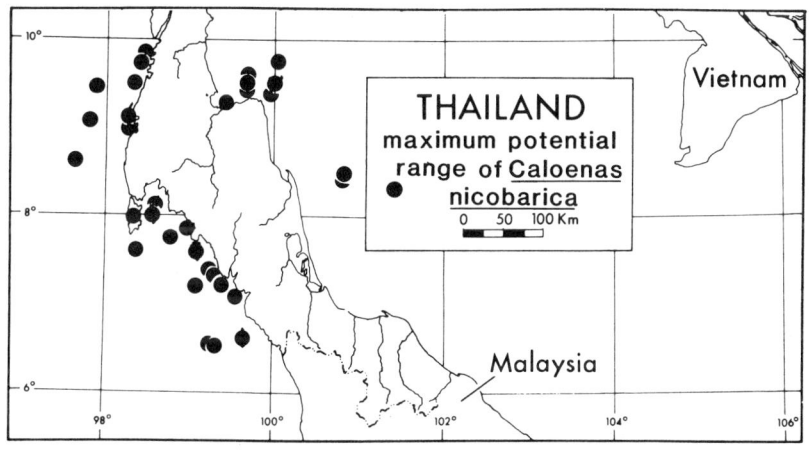

Fig. 61. Maximum potential distribution of the Nicobar Pigeon (*Caloenas nicobarica nicobarica*).

Distribution and History of Distribution: This island dweller is found from the Nicobar Islands, the Andaman Islands, and the Mergui Archipelago to the Philippine and the Solomon Islands. In Southeast Asia it is found in the islands off Tennaserim in Burma, on Con Son Island off Vietnam, off the coast of Kampuchea, and off both coasts of Thailand, primarily south of the Isthmus of Kra (Fig. 61). It migrates or wanders between island groups and sometimes strays to the mainland (Gibson-Hill 1949, Deignan 1963, King and Dickinson 1975, Goodwin 1977).

Geographic Status: The Thai populations are situated near the western limit of the species' range.

Habitat Requirements and Habitat Trend: The Nicobar pigeon is a ground forager in the forests of small islands adjacent to the mainland. These are usually uninhabited by people. It prefers heavy evergreen growth. Brockelman and Nadee (1977) saw it in most of the ravines on the Surin Islands in April of 1976. These large pigeons have impressive abilities to ingest and digest large, whole seeds. They forage in the undergrowth for fleshy fruits, grains, berries, and invertebrates, and for quartz particles to aid in grinding food (Delacour 1947, Gibson-Hill 1949, Wildash 1968, Ali and Ripley 1969, Lekagul and Cronin 1974, King and Dickinson 1975, Goodwin 1977).

Vulnerability of Species and Habitat: Its large size and habit of sometimes forming large breeding aggregations makes this bird vulnerable to hunters. Its reputation for preferring places unsettled by man suggest that it survives best in such places. Its preference for islands in itself adds to the species' vulnerability--a sizable fraction of the world's endangered and recently extinct birds are insular forms.

Causes of Threat: *C. nicobarica* is eaten and taken alive by man. Extensive human settlement and deforestation on accessible islands is also a problem. Annual exports from Thailand from 1967 to 1971 were 106, 106, 738, 54, and 249 (Royal Forestry Department 1972). McClure and Chaiyaphun (1974) recorded 352 of these birds for sale at the Bangkok weekend market.

Responses to Habitat Modification: Unknown.

Demographic Characteristics: The usual clutch size is 1 egg. Nesting in Malaysia has been reported in April, May, and September. In India the birds nest primarily in January through April (Ali and Ripley 1969, Medway and Wells 1976, Goodwin 1977).

Key Behaviors: These ground feeders are shy, quiet, and alert. They are seen singly, or sometimes in flocks up to 20-30. Captives perch during the day and forage nocturnally, but wild individuals are thought to forage diurnally on the dim forest floor. While foraging the bird walks about, kicking at leaves to expose food. *C. nicobarica* is a swift, powerful flier and is capable of flying long distances without rest. It usually nests in trees or bushes 3-10 m up. There may be several nests in one tree. In the older literature nesting aggregations of thousands of pairs were reported. In captivity both sexes incubate the egg and care for the young (Delacour 1947, Ali and Ripley 1969, Lekagul and Cronin 1974, King and Dickinson 1975, Goodwin 1977).

Conservation Measures Taken: Much island habitat is protected in such areas as Tarutao National Park, where *C. nicobarica* is known to occur (IUCN 1979). It also occurs in Ko Surin Wildlife Sanctuary (Brockelman and Nadee 1977). Thai law (WARPA 1980) prohibits hunting and regulates trade of this species.

Conservation Measures Proposed: The significant breeding populations on Thai islands need to be identified and protected. Hunting and trade should be monitored and controlled. Forest habitat on islands should be preserved.

Family Bucerotidae - The Hornbills
Introductory Comments

With 13 species of hornbills, Thailand has almost a third of the world's 45 known species. Except where they have been extirpated locally by hunting for food or sale, hornbill populations survive in all of Thailand's remaining forests. These large, long-lived forest birds range widely in their daily searches of food. Many flock and night-roost gregariously, sometimes by the hundreds. They are highly arboreal, feeding in the tree crowns. Hornbills are notoriously omnivorous, eating even bats and fish, but they subsist mainly on small fruits. Their breeding behavior is unique. The female seals herself inside a hollow in a large tree far above the forest floor, using mud, fruit pulp, and feces. The male feeds her through a narrow slit in the wall. She stays inside until the young are partially grown. The young will inflate their air sacks to keep from being pulled from the nest (McClure 1970, Lekagul and Cronin 1974, King and Dickinson 1975, Frith and Douglas 1978).

This family is known for the large bills of its species. With them the birds can deliver a formidable blow. The bills often have accessory casques, larger in males and adults. Unlike other hornbills, the helmeted hornbill, *Rhinoplax vigil*, has a very hard, solid casque that is carved into jewelry and many other items. This "ivory" was an important minor item of commerce in Southeast Asia for many centuries. During and since the Ming dynasty, Borneo has supplied China with hornbill "ivory." The tail feathers of several species are used ceremonially in the region. In Borneo certain peoples have learned to preserve the bills and feathers with the secretions of the bird's own uropygial gland. The birds are sometimes taken alive as pets, but they consume prodigious quantities of food and cannot be "house-broken." Much more often they are taken as food. Their habit of roosting in large groups make them especially vulnerable to overhunting. Over the centuries hornbills have become prominent in the mythologies of many indigenous peoples (Harrisson 1951).

All hornbills are protected under the Thai Wildlife Animals Reservation and Protection Act of 1980. The primary threats to the birds are hunting and deforestation. Round (1984) reported that all five species of hornbill formerly occurring on Doi Pui have been extirpated; "Hornbills are widely shot for food by rural people and appear to have been extirpated in all the more accessible parts of the Northwest." From an original 80 percent, forest cover of Thailand has declined to 25 percent in 1978 (Myers 1980). Large dead trees with cavities are necessary components of the environment for these and many other species. In forest management and reforestation efforts, the value of tree snags to wildlife always should be borne in mind. As with many other cavity nesters, their breeding biology is difficult to study and generally poorly understood. Before sound management practices can be formulated, more research needs to be done on their ecology. Preservation of forest habitat is of the utmost importance to hornbill conservation.

White-crested hornbill
Berenicornis comatus (Raffles 1822)
Aves, Coraciiformes, Bucerotidae

Status: Threatened.
WARPA (1980): Protected-1.

Population Size and Trend: This animal apparently never has been common in Thailand. Lekagul and Cronin (1974) classify it as an uncommon resident.

Distribution and History of Distribution: The white-crested hornbill is known discontinuously from southern Burma, central Annam, southern Vietnam, peninsular Thailand, Malaya, Sumatra, and Borneo. Most published records from Thailand are from Nakhon Si Thammarat and Trang Provinces (Fig. 62; Riley 1938, Deignan 1963, Lekagul and Cronin 1974, King and Dickinson 1975).

Geographic Status: The Thai populations are centrally located in the species' distribution.

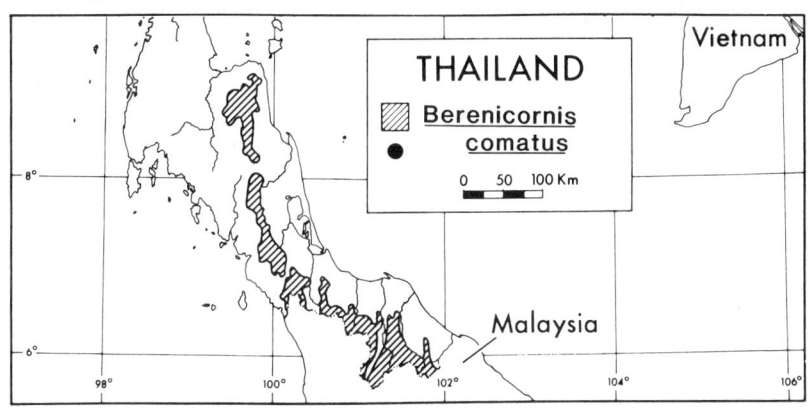

Fig. 62. Distribution of the White-crested Hornbill (*Berenicornis comatus*).

Habitat Requirements and Habitat Trena: *B. comatus* inhabits forest habitat from the lowlands to 1,677 m, typically from 120-820 m. Frith and Douglas (1978) recently saw it in "good primary hill forest just inland of Nakhon Si Thammarat." It supplements its fruit diet with lizards, small birds, and other animals (Delacour 1947, Smythies 1953, Glenister 1955, Lekagul and Cronin 1974, King and Dickinson 1975, Frith and Douglas 1978).

Vulnerability of Species and Habitat: Although their wings do not make as much noise in flight as in other hornbills, their raucous vocalizations make them quite noticeable to man.

Causes of Threat: Overhunting and deforestation threaten this bird.

Responses to Habitat Modification: Unknown.

Demographic Characteristics: The breeding habits of this bird in the wild are unknown. Frith and Douglas (1978) purchased 2 fledged young in Bangkok on 19 May 1975 (they died within 4 months). It is possible that they came from the same nest.

Key Behaviors: These hornbills have been reported to feed both in the canopy and among dense undergrowth near the ground. They forage in small groups. The group of at least three seen by

Frith and Douglas (1978) were flying and perching at the edge of a large, swift mountain river. The nesting behavior has not been described (Smythies 1953, Glenister 1955, Medway and Wells 1976).

Conservation Measures Taken: WARPA (1980) protects the species from hunting and export. A population occurs in Khao Banthat Wildlife Sanctuary (P. D. Round, personal communication).

Conservation Measures Proposed: A survey of the forested areas of southern Thailand is needed to determine the status of this species. Special attention should be given to the national parks, wildlife sanctuaries, and no-hunting areas with intact forest. Hunting should be controlled and forest cover preserved. The basic biology of this bird needs to be described.

Brown hornbill, Tickell's hornbill
Ptilolaemus tickelli (Blyth 1855)
Aves, Coraciiformes, Bucerotidae

Status: Threatened.
WARPA (1980): Protected-1.

Population Size and Trend: The total numbers of this bird are unknown. Lekagul and Cronin (1974) consider it to be an uncommon resident in Thailand.

Distribution and History of Distribution: Tickell's hornbill is known from the mountains of northwestern and southwestern Thailand (Fig. 63), the Tenasserim range in southern Burma, Lao PDR, northern and central Annam, northwestern Vietnam, Assam, and southwestern China (King and Dickinson 1975).

Geographic Status: The Thai populations are peripheral, lying near the southern limits of the species' distribution.

Habitat Requirements and Habitat Trend: This bird inhabits the tops of tall trees in mature evergreen forest up to 1,800 m. It is omnivorous, like other hornbills, eating wild figs, drupes, berries, insects, and other small animals (Deignan 1945, Smythies 1953, Deignan 1963, Ali and Ripley 1970, Pfanner 1974, Lekagul and Cronin 1974, King and Dickinson 1975).

Vulnerability of Species and Habitat: Their gregariousness and continual vocalizations make these birds conspicuous to hunters. Montane evergreen forest habitat is being depleted at an alarming rate.

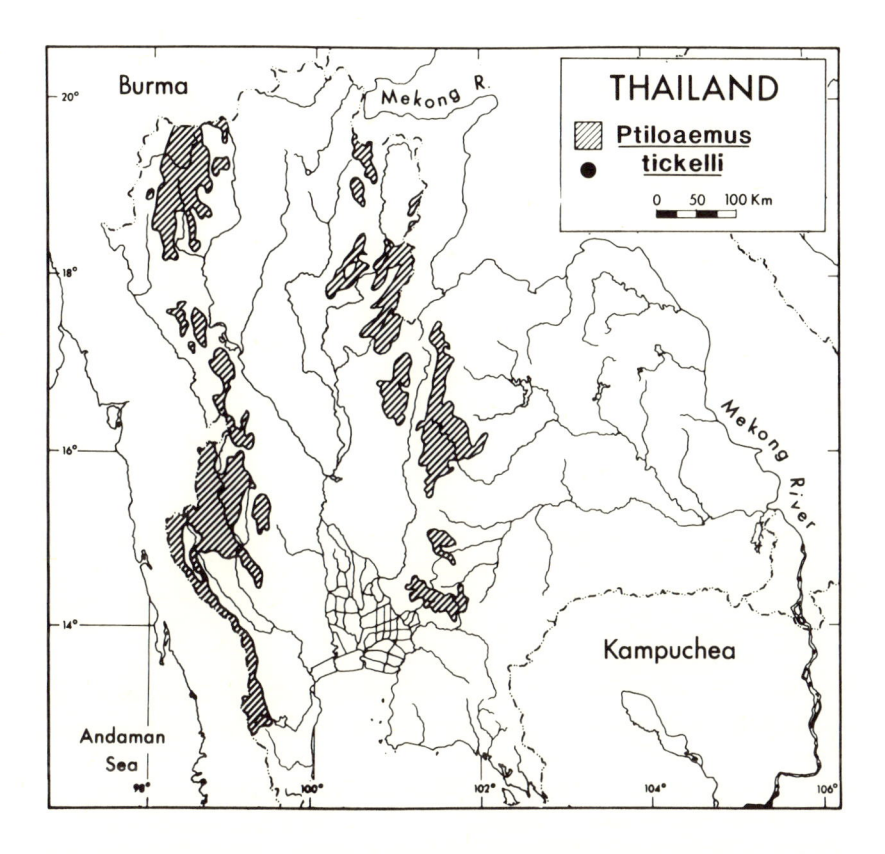

Fig. 63. Distribution of the Brown or Tickell's Hornbill (*Ptilolaemus tickelli*).

Causes of Threat: Overhunting and deforestation threaten this species. This species was considered rare on Doi Pui by Deignan (1945) but 50 years later was absent, apparently extirpated by hunting (Round 1984).

Responses to Habitat Modification: Unknown.

Demographic Characteristics: Breeding has been reported in February and March in Burma and April to June in India. The clutch is 3 or 4 eggs. The incubation period is unknown but is thought to be about 24 days (Smythies 1953, Ali and Ripley 1970).

Key Behaviors: These animals feed among the tree crowns in flocks of 8-20 or more. They are very active, constantly moving within and between trees. They fly in long lines. The wingbeat is relatively noiseless for a hornbill, but not nearly as silent as in *Berenicornis comatus*. However, they continually vocalize while perching or on the wing. They frequently form mixed-species flocks with other frugivorous birds. They are shy and difficult to approach. Their nest hollows are relatively close to the ground (4-9 m or higher). They sunbathe in typical hornbill fashion (Smythies 1953, Ali and Ripley 1970, Frith and Douglas 1978).

Conservation Measures Taken: Thai Law (WARPA 1980) protects the species. The brown hornbill is present in Khao Yai National Park (Pfanner 1974). A specimen was taken in Phu Kradueng National Park in Loei Province in the late 1960s (Dickinson and Chaiyaphun 1973). Deignan (1945) recorded it from what is now Doi Chiang Dao Wildlife Sanctuary and the Doi Suthep-Pui National Park; however, the species has since been extirpated from the latter area. Brown hornbills also occur in Nam Nao National Park (Boonsong Lekagul, personal communication), Huai Kha Khaeng Wildlife Sanctuary (P. D. Round, personal communication), and Thung Salaeng Luang National Park (W. Brockelman, personal communication).

Conservation Measures Proposed: The staff of forest reserves should assess the current status of this species in their jurisdictions. Hunting should be controlled and forest habitat with proper nesting trees should be preserved.

Bushy-crested hornbill
Anorrhinus galeritus **(Temminck)**
Aves, Coraciiformes, Bucerotidae

Status: Threatened.
WARPA (1980): Protected-1.

Population Size and Trend: This species apparently never has been very abundant in Thailand in recent times (Lekagul and Cronin 1974).

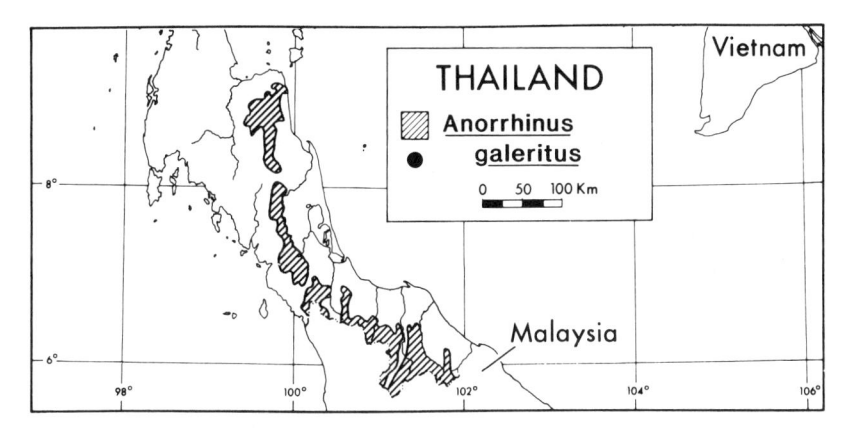

Fig. 64. Distribution of the Bushy-crested Hornbill (*Anorrhinus galeritus*).

Distribution and History of Distribution: Bushy-crested hornbills have been found from the Tenasserim range in southern Burma south through peninsular Thailand to Malaya, Sumatra, and Borneo. Published records from peninsular Thailand includes birds from Nakhon Si Thammarat, Trang, and Phangnga provinces (Fig. 64; Riley 1938, Smythies 1953, Deignan 1963, King and Dickinson 1975, Frith and Douglas 1978).

Geographic Status: *Anorrhinus* in Thailand exists near the northern limits of the species' distribution.

Habitat Requirements and Habitat Trend: This species has been recorded from sea level to 1,220 m in the canopy of evergreen forests and in old rubber plantations. An imprisoned nesting female observed in Selangor was fed "Rutaceae (?Evodia); Leguminosae (incl. ?Entada); Fagaceae (Lithocarpus cyclophorus); Sterculiaceae (Sterculia foetida); Sapindaceae (Sapindus rarak); Connaraceae (?Connarus); Palmae" (Medway and Wells 1976). They take a variety of small fruits and berries and readily catch fish. A captive was seen with a magpie robin, *Copsychus saularis*, which it had killed (Delacour 1974, Smythies 1985, Glenister 1955, Holmes 1973, Lekagul and Cronin 1974, King and Dickinson 1975, Medway and Wells 1976, Frith and Douglas 1978).

Vulnerability of Species and Habitat: Its ability to live in secondary growth, such as in old rubber plantations, may make this species less vulnerable than other hornbills.

Causes of Threat: Overhunting and habitat loss threaten this species.

Responses to Habitat Modifications: These hornbills are capable of surviving in at least some disturbed habitats.

Demographic Characteristics: In Selangor a nest in a hollow tree with two young was active from 21 July to 27 August (Medway and Wells 1976). Frith and Douglas (1978) purchased a fledgling on 19 April 1975 that was still alive as their report went to press. Reproduction in this species was studied by Madge (1969).

Key Behaviors: These birds are usually gregarious, feeding in the tree-tops in groups of 5-15. Though shy and seldom seen by man, they are more frequently heard. Unlike the other captive hornbills Firth and Douglas (1978) kept, this species would bathe in water. At a nest observed in Ampang Forest Reserve in Selangor, Malaysia, all flock members, including immatures, were seen to feed the nesting female and her young. This social behavior probably enhances the bird's reproductive success (Delacour 1947, Smythies 1953, Holmes 1973, Frith and Douglas 1978).

Conservation Measures Taken: This bird is protected from hunting and export by Thai law (WARPA 1980). It is present in Taleban National Park and Kao Banthat and Khlong Saeng wildlife sanctuaries (Boonsong Lekagul and P. D. Round, personal communication).

Conservation Measures Proposed: Hunting and trade in this species should be controlled. Where it is found to inhabit protected areas, the forests should be managed with hornbill requirements in mind. The extent to which it is able to thrive in disturbed habitats requires further study.

Rufous-necked hornbill
Aceros nipalensis (Hodgson 1829)
Aves, Coraciiformes, Bucerotidae

Status: Threatened.
WARPA (1980): Protected-1.

Population Size and Trend: The total numbers of this bird are unknown. Lekagul and Cronin (1974) consider it to be an uncommon resident in Thailand.

Distribution and History of Distribution: This hornbill is known from Nepal, Sikkim, Bhutan, India, Bangladesh, southwestern China, Burma, northwestern Thailand (Fig. 65), northern Lao

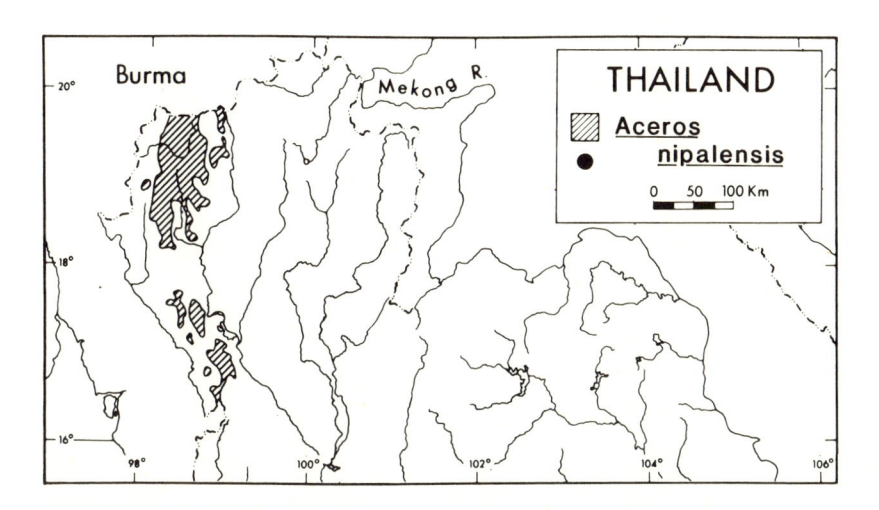

Fig. 65. Distribution of the Rufous-necked Hornbill (*Aceros nipalensis*).

PDR, and northwestern Vietnam, (Ali and Ripley 1970, Lekagul and Cronin 1974, King and Dickinson 1975).

Geographic Status: The Thai populations are peripheral, lying near the southern limits of the species' distribution.

Habitat Requirements and Habitat Trend: *A. nipalensis* prefers the tall evergreen forest of the higher hills and mountains, to an elevation of about 1,800 m (Smythies 1953, Ali and Ripley 1970, Lekagul and Cronin 1974). These arboreal animals are primarily frugivorous. Ali and Ripley (1970) described the diet as "large drupes and berries swallowed entire; *Dysoxylon* sp. and nutmegs (*Myristica*) are especially favoured."

Vulnerability of Species and Habitat: Their preference for mature evergreen forest makes them vulnerable to deforestation.

Causes of Threat: Overhunting and deforestation threaten this species. This species was considered uncommon on Doi Pui by Deignan (1945) but 50 years later was absent, apparently extirpated by hunting (Round 1984).

Responses to Habitat Modification: Unknown.

Demographic Characteristics: The normal clutch is 1-2 eggs. Deignan (1945) recorded a male with enlarged gonads taken on Doi Suthep in Chiang Mai Province on 22 January. In India breeding occurs primarily in April and May (Ali and Ripley 1970).

Key Behaviors: These birds are normally seen in pairs or small groups up to 4-5 individuals. Although most foraging is in the tree crowns, the birds descend to the forest floor to feed on fallen fruit. The male has a bizarre and dramatic nuptial display. The nest hollow, usually 10-30 m up the tree, is apparently used year after year (Deignan 1945, Ali and Ripley 1970).

Conservation Measures Taken: Thai law regulates hunting and export (WARPA 1980). The animals have been taken several times in what is now Doi Inthanon and Doi Suthep-Pui national parks (Ripley 1938, Deignan 1945), but now they are extirpated from both areas. Their presence elsewhere in the northwestern mountains is unconfirmed.

Conservation Measures Proposed: As with other hornbills, hunting should be controlled and forest habitat, including suitable nest trees, should be preserved. Studies on nesting of these and other hornbills are badly needed. Om Koi and Mae Tuen wildlife sanctuaries should be searched for this species.

Wrinkled hornbill
Rhyticeros leucocephalus
Aves, Coraciiformes, Bucerotidae

Status: Endangered.
WARPA (1980): Protected-1.

Population Size and Trend: Unknown, but there are no recent records of the wrinkled hornbill from Thailand (Philip D. Round, personal communication). Holmes (1973) recorded only a single pair in southern Thailand, in hilly forest at 500 m elevation in Yala Province. This species always has been considered uncommon (Lekagul and Cronin 1974).

Distribution and History of Distribution: This species ranges from peninsular Thailand south and east to the Philippines, Sulawesi, and New Guinea.

Geographic Status: Thailand is on the northern periphery of the range of this species.

Habitat Requirements and Habitat Trend: This species inhabits primary forest in the lowlands and coasts of Thailand (Smythies 1960, Lekagul and Cronin 1974).

Vulnerability of Species and Habitat: The habitat of this species is highly vulnerable to deforestation, and most of it is gone.

Causes of Threat: Deforestation, and perhaps hunting.
Responses to Habitat Modification: Unknown.
Demographic Characteristics: Unknown.
Key Behaviors: Unknown.
Conservation Measures Taken: Thai law (WARPA 1980) prohibits killing and regulates trade of this species. Several national parks, wildlife sanctuaries, and no-hunting areas have been established in the range of the wrinkled hornbill.
Conservation Measures Proposed: A status survey must be done before a conservation strategy can be proposed. This survey should include existing preserves and the precipitous, uninhabited offshore islands of peninsular Thailand.

Rhinoceros hornbill
Buceros rhinoceros **Linnaeus 1758**
Aves, Coraciiformes, Bucerotidae

Status: Threatened.
CITES (1979): Appendix II.
WARPA (1980): Protected-1.
Population Size and Trend: Lekagul and Cronin (1974) classified it as an uncommon resident. B. King (personal communication) considers it to be "probably rare at best."

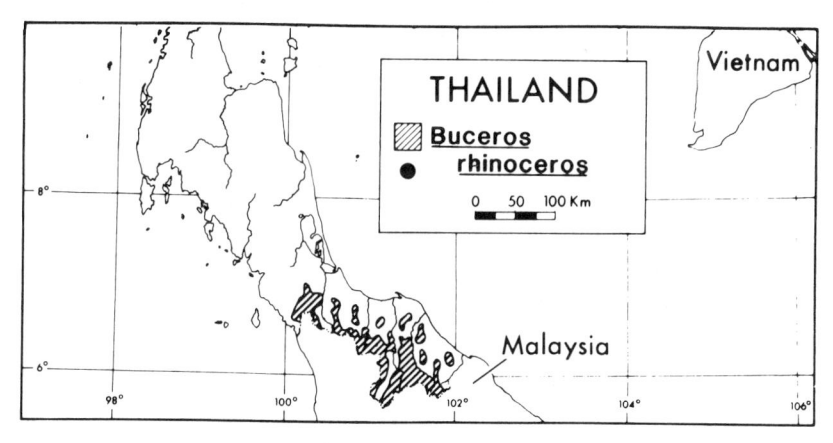

Fig. 66. Distribution of the Rhinoceros Hornbill (*Buceros rhinoceros*).

Distribution and History of Distribution: Rhinoceros hornbills are found from southern peninsular Thailand south through Malaya to the Greater Sunda Islands. It has been extirpated from Singapore. In Thailand it is known from Songkhla Province south (Fig. 66; Riley 1938, Deignan 1963, Lekagul and Cronin 1974, King and Dickinson 1975, Medway and Wells 1976).

Geographic Status: The rhinoceros hornbills in Thailand are at the northern limits of the species' distribution.

Habitat Requirements and Habitat Trend: This bird inhabits the canopy level of forests from the lowlands through the hills to 1,220 m. It is omnivorous, feeding mainly on fruits (Gibson-Hill 1949, Lekagul and Cronin 1974, King and Dickinson 1975, Medway and Wells 1976). Forests are, of course, being cleared at an unprecedented rate in southern Thailand.

Vulnerability of Species and Habitat: The flight of this species is loud and reminds many people of the sound of a steam engine. The birds also vocalize while perching and flying. They are moderately gregarious. All of these features make them conspicuous to man. In parts of the Greater Sundas the tail feathers and other parts have ornamental, ceremonial, and economic value (Harrisson 1951).

Causes of Threat: Overhunting and deforestation threaten this species. The nearly complete forest cover of southern Thailand has declined to 42 percent in 1961, 39 percent in 1965, 26 percent in 1972, and 24 percent in 1978 (Myers 1980).

Responses to Habitat Modification: Unknown.

Demographic Characteristics: The breeding biology of this bird in the wild is poorly understood. A nest was seen in early February and a flock containing mostly immatures was seen in late September in Malaya (Medway and Wells 1976). Frith and Douglas (1978) obtained a juvenile, estimated to be 4 months old on 4 November, from an animal dealer who said the bird was from Yala Province.

Key Behaviors: Pairs, small family groups, and flocks up to several dozen are seen in the wild. Within the flocks, many animals fly two by two and may be paired. Groups appear to cooperate in feeding the nesting females and young. One captive juvenile had to ingest feces in order to fully digest some foodstuffs (Medway and Wells 1976, Frith and Douglas 1978).

Conservation Measures Taken: Thai law (WARPA 1980) prohibits hunting and regulates trade.

Conservation Measures Proposed: A survey of Khao Banthat

Wildlife Sanctuary, Ton Nga Chang Wildlife Sanctuary, and other areas in the far south should be made to determine the status of *B. rhinoceros* in each. Hunting should be controlled and forested areas with suitable nest trees should be preserved.

Great hornbill
Buceros bicornis **Linnaeus 1758**
Aves, Coraciiformes, Bucerotidae

Status: Threatened.
CITES (1979): Appendix I (subspecies *homrai*; south of the Isthmus of Kra).
CITES (1979): Appendix II (subspecies *bicornis*; north of the Isthmus of Kra).
WARPA (1980): Protected-1.

Population Size and Trend: Where suitable habitat remains, this is a year-round common resident in Thailand. In some areas, such as Khao Yai National Park, it is commonly encountered during most of the year, though less conspicuous in the mating season (Lekagul and Cronin 1974, McClure 1974a).

Distribution and History of Distribution: This bird is known from several disjunct places in India, southwestern China, Bangladesh, Burma, throughout mainland Southeast Asia, Malaya, and Sumatra. It has been found throughout Thailand except in the central valley of the Chao Phraya and much of the northeastern Khorat Plateau (Deignan 1945, Wildash 1968, Ali and Ripley 1970, Lekagul and Cronin 1974, Holmes and Wells 1975, King and Dickinson 1975, Medway and Wells 1976). The species is very rare or extirpated from most of northwestern Thailand, including Doi Inthanon and Doi Suthep-Pui national parks, where it formerly occurred.

Geographic Status: The Thai populations of the great hornbill are central in the species' overall range.

Habitat Requirements and Habitat Trend: *B. bicornis* is primarily an inhabitant of tall evergreen forest from the lowlands to 2,000 m. They are mainly arboreal but have been known to descend to the ground to feed. They are omnivorous. Figs (*Ficus*) are the favored food. Nutmegs (*Myristica*) and many other fruits are eaten, as are insects, reptiles, birds, and mammals. They probably function more as raptors in avian communities than has been thought.

They will not drink water except falling rain (Deignan 1945, Gibson-Hill 1949, Deignan 1963, Ali and Ripley 1970, Lekagul and Cronin 1974, McClure 1974a, King and Dickinson 1975).

Vulnerability of Species and Habitat: The flight of these large birds makes a sound which can be heard over great distances. Their vocalizations are also loud. They are especially vociferous at the beginning of the mating season. Some weigh over 3 kg and make an attractive meal for people. The flesh has an excellent flavor. Traditionally the people in Thailand and Burma have hunted them for food and feathers. Today they are commonly sold in Bangkok's Sunday Market (Deignan 1945, Smythies 1953, Glenister 1955, Ali and Ripley 1970, McClure 1974a). Annual exports of great hornbills from Thailand from 1967 to 1971 were 78, 99, 128, 126, and 176 (Royal Forestry Department 1972).

Causes of Threat: Overhunting and deforestation threaten this species. This species was considered common on Doi Pui by Deignan (1945) but 50 years later was absent, apparently extirpated by hunting (Round 1984).

Responses to Habitat Modification: Unknown.

Demographic Characteristics: The clutch is usually 2 eggs, sometimes 1, and rarely 3. Incubation lasts about 31 days. Breeding is from January to April in Burma. Juveniles were found on 18 July at Doi Mon Khawm Long in Thailand. McClure (1974a) saw breeding behavior in January and July in Khao Yai National Park, and he inferred from the animals he observed for sale in the Sunday Market that the breeding season is primarily from January to May. Frith and Douglas (1978) obtained a nestling at the Sunday Market on 10 April (Deignan 1945, Smythies 1953, Ali and Ripley 1970).

Key Behaviors: This species has been reported to mate for life. In the nesting season the birds are much quieter than usual. They select nest trees far from the paths of man and often use the same tree year after year if unmolested. In a variation from the usual hornbill pattern, the female escapes from the nest about two weeks after hatching, recloses the nest, and forages for the young with the help of other birds. From August to January the family groups coalesce into larger flocks that roost communally at night. The roosts are in the tops of several tall, adjacent trees with scanty foliage. Within these communal roosts individuals apparently have territories. These groups range in size from a few pairs up to 16 birds. Rarely groups of several hundred have been reported. In the morning, before leaving to forage, there is much vocalization and intraspecific interaction. Although the home ranges of these flocks are unknown, they are thought to cover great distances in their daily searches for food and may use regular foraging beats (Deignan 1945, Wildash 1968, Ali and Ripley 1970, McClure 1970, Holmes 1973, McClure 1974a, Medway and Wells 1976).

Conservation Measures Taken: Thai law (WARPA 1980) prohibits hunting and regulates export. The presence of healthy populations in Khao Yai National Park demonstrates the value of such reserves to forest-dwelling species (Riley 1938, Deignan 1945, Dickinson 1964, McClure 1974a, Pauley 1977b). Other protected areas supporting this species include Khao Luang, Tarutao, Nam Nao and Teleban national parks and Doi Chang Dao, Ton Nga Chang, Kao Khieo, Khao Banthat, Khlong Saeng, Huai Kha Khaeng, Khlong Nakha, and Khao Soi Dao wildlife sanctuaries (Boonsong Lekagul and P. D. Round, personal communication). This species has been kept in captivity in Thailand and in many of the world's zoos, and it has bred in captivity (Choy 1980).

Conservation Measures Proposed: Great hornbill populations in protected areas should be censused and managed with their requirements for forest cover, nesting trees, and communal night roosts borne in mind. Hunting, sale, and export regulations should be enforced.

Helmeted hornbill
Rhinoplax vigil (Forster 1781)
Aves, Coraciiformes, Bucerotidae

Status: Endangered.
CITES (1979): Appendix I.
IUCN (1979): Threatened.
IUCN Red Data Book (1979): Indeterminate.
MAB (1979): Endangered.
USFWS (1980a): Endangered.
WARPA (1980): Protected-1.

Population Size and Trend: Although it may have been common in appropriate habitat in southern Thailand as late as the 1960s, it is now rare in Thailand. There are no estimates of total numbers (Lekagul and Cronin 1974, B. King personal communication).

Distribution and History of Distribution: This striking bird is known from Tenasserim in extreme southern Burma, from southern Thailand (Fig. 67), Malaya, Sumatra, and Borneo (King and Dickinson 1975). In February 1974, Holmes and Wells (1975) heard this species at Khlong Nakha Reserve in Ranong Province. Ben King (personal communication) saw one or two in Nakhon Si Thammarat Province.

Geographic Status: The Thai population is peripheral, lying near the northern limits of the species' distribution.

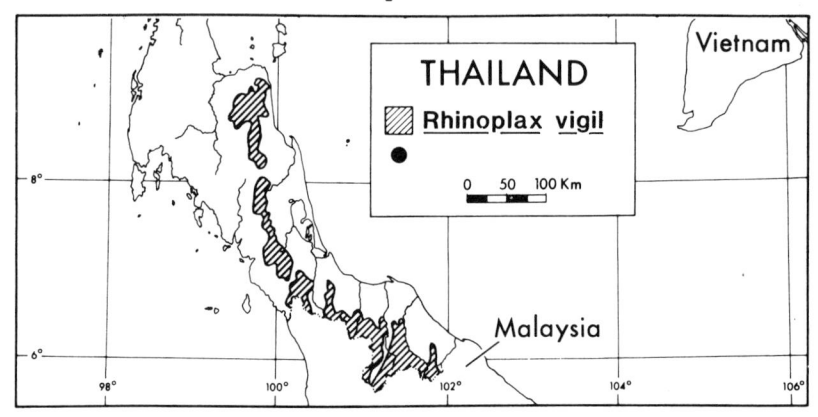

Fig. 67. Distribution of the Helmeted Hornbill (*Rhinoplax vigil*).

Habitat Requirements and Habitat Trend: *Rhinoplax* prefers the dense, tall, mature evergreen forests from the lowlands to about 1,500 m. Such forests are being destroyed at an accelerating rate in Southeast Asia (Gibson-Hill 1949), Harrisson 1951, Lekagul and Cronin 1974, King and Dickinson 1975, Medway and Wells 1976, IUCN Red Data Book 1979).

Vulnerability of Species and Habitat: The tail feathers and casque "ivory" of this bird are actively sought. Its raucous vocalizations and large size attract human predators. The flesh has a superior flavor (Harrisson 1951, King and Dickinson 1975, Medway and Wells 1976).

Causes of Threat: Hunting and deforestation threaten this bird. In Borneo the male is blowgunned outside the nest and the tree is cut down to capture the female and young (Harrison 1951). The once nearly complete forest cover of southern Thailand has declined to 42 percent in 1961, 39 percent in 1965, 26 percent in 1972, and 24 percent in 1978 (Myers 1980).

Response to Habitat Modification: Unknown.

Demographic Parameters: Unknown.

Key Behaviors: Unlike most hornbills this form is not gregarious. Single animals, pairs, and small groups are seen. Its habit of foraging high in the canopy undoubtedly relieves some human predation. Its specific epithet, *vigil*, is well deserved--it is very shy and avoids man (Harrisson 1951, Smythies 1953, Glenister 1955, Medway and Wells 1976).

Conservation Measures Taken: Some essential habitat is protected in preserves in the far south. The species occurs in Khlong Nakha Wildlife Sanctuary (Holmes and Wells 1975) and Khlong Saeng Wildlife Sanctuary (Round et al. 1982). Thai law (WARPA 1980) prohibits the hunting and export of helmeted hornbills without special permission.

Conservation Measures Proposed: A total ban on hunting this hornbill should be considered to allow populations to recover. Protection of the birds inhabiting reserved areas should be maintained. In areas where breeding populations still exist, deforestation should be halted and dead standing timber should not be removed.

Many-colored barbet
Megalaima rafflesii
Aves, Piciformes, Capitonidae

Status: Endangered.

WARPA (1980): Protected-1.

Population Size and Trend: Unknown. Lekagul and Cronin (1974) considered the many-colored barbet to be uncommon, and Holmes (1973) found it to be quite rare, based on a single record. However, it is common farther south in Malaya (Holmes 1973) and Borneo (Smythies 1960).

Distribution and History of Distribution: The distribution of this species includes peninsular Burma and Thailand, Malaya, Banka, Sumatra, Borneo, and Billiton.

Geographic Status: Thailand is on the northern periphery of the range of this species.

Habitat Requirements and Habitat Trend: This species lives in lowland forests (Delacour 1947, Lekagul and Cronin 1974). Though mainly in primary forest, it also occurs in secondary forest and rubber plantations (Smythies 1960).

Vulnerability of Species and Habitat: Its best habitat is vulnerable to conversion to other uses, and almost all of it has been cleared.

Causes of Threat: Deforestation.

Responses to Habitat Modification: Unknown.

Demographic Characteristics: Unknown.

Key Behaviors: Unknown.

Conservation Measures Taken: Thai law (WARPA 1980) prohibits killing and regulates trade of this species. Several national parks, wildlife sanctuaries, and no-hunting areas have been established in the range of the many-colored barbet.

Conservation Measures Proposed: A survey must be conducted before a way to conserve this species can be devised. The survey should include existing reserves of lowland forest in southern Thailand. Data also are needed on the degree to which it can survive in secondary forests and plantations.

Great slaty woodpecker
Mulleripicus pulverulentus (Temminck 1826)
Aves, Piciformes, Picidae

Status: Threatened.

WARPA (1980): Protected-1.

Population Size and Trend: Although reported as being common by some writers in this century (Glenister 1955, for example) Lekagul and Cronin (1974) classified this form as an uncommon resident. In some parts of its range it is still locally common (Smith 1977).

Distribution and History of Distribution: This large woodpecker is known from northern India, Nepal, Sikkim, Bhutan, southwestern China, Bangladesh, Burma, throughout Southeast Asia (except northern Annam, Tonkin, Hong Kong, and, in Thailand, the central valley of the Chao Phraya and much of the northeastern

Khorat Plateau), south through Malaya to Singapore, the Greater Sunda Islands, and Palawan (Ali and Ripley 1970, Lekagul and Cronin 1974, King and Dickinson 1975, Medway and Wells 1976).

Geographic Status: The Thai populations are central to the species' overall range.

Habitat Requirements and Habitat Trend: Great slaty woodpeckers have been reported from a wide variety of habitats from sea level through the hills to 2,000 m. Among the habitats reported are tall mangrove forest, swamp forest, teak, moist deciduous, semi-evergreen, and mature evergreen forest. It is frequently seen along forest edges and overgrown clearings. It feeds on insects. The preferred foods are the larvae and pupae of woodboring beetles, such as *Haplocerambyx*, but other insects, including ants and termites, are also eaten (Deignan 1945, Smythies 1953, Ali and Ripley 1970, Lekagul and Cronin 1974, Medway and Wells 1976).

Vulnerability of Species and Habitat: This is the largest woodpecker in Thailand. It is not particularly shy. Its large size, noisy flight, continual vocalizations, and gregarious habits make it quite noticeable to man (Deignan 1945, Smythies 1953, Lekagul and Cronin 1974, McClure 1974a).

Causes of Threat: Overhunting and deforestation threaten this species.

Responses to Habitat Modification: This species tolerates and may even benefit from disruption of continuous forest habitat. This "edge effect" is a well-known phenomenon in many species of wildlife. However, extensive deforestation leaves no habitat for woodpeckers. This species was considered rare on Doi Pui by Deignan (1945) but 50 years later was absent, apparently due to loss of mixed deciduous woodland and urbanization around the base of the mountain (Round 1984).

Demographic Characteristics: The normal clutch is 2-4 eggs. Nesting has been reported in March-May in India, April in Burma, and July-August in the Malay Peninsula (Smythies 1953, Ali and Ripley 1970, Medway and Wells 1976).

Key Behaviors: This bird is usually seen in pairs, family groups, and flocks of up to about 10 birds. Flocks fly in a sprawling, follow-the-leader fashion and can cover great distances over open ground. While foraging, the flock spreads out over several neighboring trees but maintains vocal communication. There have been reports of birds occupying territories in Khao Yai National Park. Nest holes are 25 m or more up large, often dead or dying trees. Dipterocarps are frequently used. Both sexes help to excavate the hole, incubate the eggs, and feed the young (Ali and Ripley 1970, Lekagul and Cronin 1974, McClure 1974*a*, Pfanner 1974, King and Dickinson 1975).

Conservation Measures Taken: Thai law (WARPA 1980) prohibits hunting and regulates trade in this species. Because of its wide range in Thailand and its use of many habitats, many populations undoubtedly occur in protected areas. It has been recorded in the literature to occur in what are now Khao Luang, Doi Suthep-Pui, and Tarutao Marine national parks (Ripley 1938, Deignan 1945, Medway and Wells 1976). More recently, the bird has been studied in Khao Yai National Park (McClure 1974*a*, Pfanner 1974). Additionally, the species occurs in Doi Inthanon National Park and Huai Kha Khaeng Wildlife Sanctuary (P. D. Round, personal communication).

Conservation Measures Proposed: The giant, senescent trees these birds require for nesting should not be removed. In educational and conservation programs the value of these animals in controlling forest pest insects should be stressed. The degree to which human modification of native habitats affects these large woodpeckers needs to be studied. Hunting should be controlled.

White-bellied woodpecker
Dryocopus javensis **(Horsfield 1821)**
Aves, Piciformes, Picidae

Status: Threatened.

Population Size and Trend: This woodpecker varies locally from common to rare, depending on the availability of suitable habitat (Ripley 1938, Smythies 1953, Glenister 1955, Ali and Ripley 1970). Habitat loss probably causes a declining trend.

Distribution and History of Distribution: The white-bellied woodpecker occurs from India, China, Korea, and Japan, south through Southeast Asia to Sumatra, Java, Borneo, Bali, and the Philippines. It occurs all over Thailand in suitable habitat (Medway and Wells 1976, Deignan 1963). Its range has been reduced and fragmented by deforestation in India (Ali and Ripley 1970) and elsewhere.

Geographic Status: Thailand is central in the species' range.

Habitat Requirements and Habitat Trend: This species is most common in mature deciduous and evergreen forest up to 600-1,400 m elevation. It also uses forest edge, secondary forest, and mature plantations. Nests are excavated in dead tree trunks about 8-16 m above the ground. Much habitat has been destroyed by deforestation (Deignan 1945, Ali and Ripley 1970, Medway and Wells 1976).

Vulnerability of Species and Habitat: The habitat of this species is highly vulnerable to deforestation.

Causes of Threat: Deforestation threatens this species.

Responses to Habitat Modification: This species is "very sensitive to deforestation and disturbance by humans, soon forsaking localities where lumbering is in progress or the forest has been felled" (Ali and Ripley 1970). This species was considered uncommon on Doi Pui by Deignan (1945) but 50 years later was absent, apparently due to loss of mixed deciduous woodland and urbanization around the base of the mountain (Round 1984).

Demographic Characteristics: The clutch usually contains 2 or sometimes 3-4 eggs. Reproduction occurs in January to March in India (Ali and Ripley 1970).

Key Behaviors: Both sexes participate in nest excavation and feeding the young. Foraging usually is done in pairs or family groups, in which the individuals maintain contact by calling (Ali and Ripley 1970).

Conservation Measures Taken: Thai law (WARPA 1980) prohibits killing and trade of this species. Many populations undoubtedly occur in protected areas in Thailand. Records exist for Doi Suthep-Pui (Deignan 1945) and Khao Yai national parks (McClure 1974a). The species also occurs in Doi Inthanon National Park and Huai Kha Khaeng Wildlife Sanctuary (P. D. Round, personal communication).

Conservation Measures Proposed: Preserving tracts of mature forest is the key to conservation of this species. Dead trees should be left standing, because their removal destroys nesting and foraging habitat for woodpeckers.

Gurney's pitta
Pitta gurneyi Hume 1875
Aves, Passeriformes, Pittidae

Status: Threatened.
IUCN Red Data Book (1979): Indeterminate.
WARPA (1980): Protected-1.

Population Size and Trend: This bird was considered to be common over its range in Thailand 40-50 years ago (Ripley 1938, Chasen 1939). It is now scarce over much of its range in Thailand. Its current status in Burma is unknown (IUCN Red Data Book 1979). There are no estimates of its total numbers.

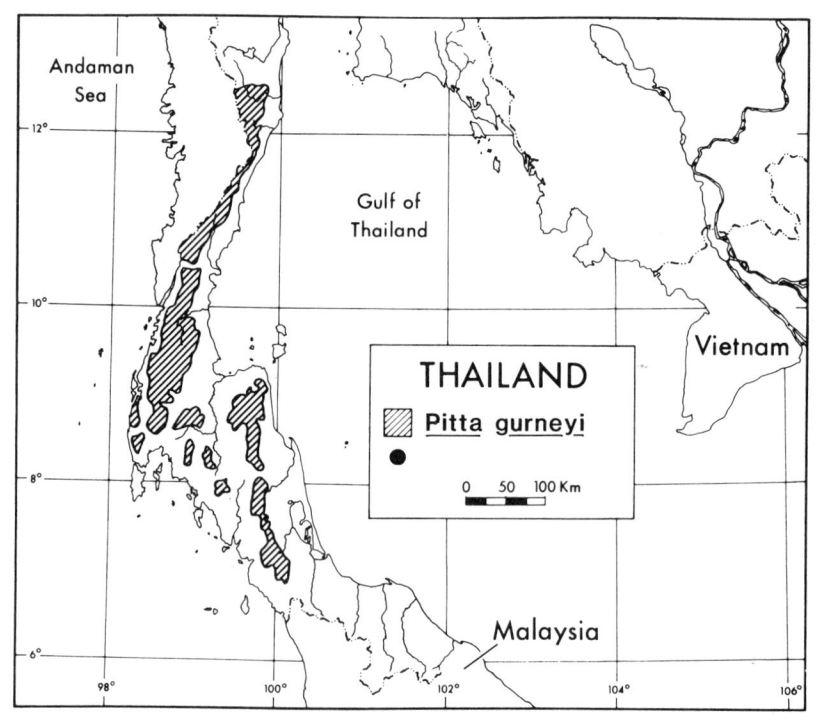

Fig. 68. Distribution of Gurney's Pitta (*Pitta gurneyi*).

Distribution and History of Distribution: Gurney's pitta is endemic to southern Tenasserim in Burma and parts of adjacent peninsular Thailand. In Thailand it ranges from Prachuap Khiri

Khan Province south to Trang (Fig. 68; Deignan 1963, King and Dickinson 1975).

Geographic Status: It has been suggested that the Burmese population is migratory and breeds in Thailand, but this has not been established. The Thai population is believed to be sedentary (Gibson-Hill 1949, Smythies 1953).

Habitat Requirements and Habitat Trend: This pitta dwells on the ground in dense primary evergreen forest in the lowlands below 900 m, especially in areas where there is little or no undergrowth. The lowland forest over much of its range has been cleared (Rutgers 1968, Smythies 1953, Lekagul and Cronin 1974, King and Dickinson 1975, IUCN Red Data Book 1979).

Vulnerability of Species and Habitat: Pittas are colorful birds and people find them attractive. There is an active trade in live animals. The lowland forests they require are among the first to be cleared.

Causes of Threat: Overhunting and deforestation threaten this species. During a study period of 31 March to 6 June 1975, almost 80 *Pitta* (all species combined) were known to have been exported through Bangkok's Don Muang Airport (Duplaix and King 1975). Annual exports of pittas from Thailand from 1967 to 1971 were 75, 71, 327, 542, and 74 (Royal Forestry Department 1972). This species still occurs in trade, as two captives were reported in 1982.

Responses to Habitat Modification: The disappearance of this bird over much of its Thai range is probably due to its intolerance of deforestation.

Demographic Characteristics: The normal clutch size is 4 eggs. A nest with eggs was found in Nakhon Si Thammarat Province on 9 October. A nestling was found in Krabi Province in August. Specimens dissected in Burma from April, May, and June were nonreproductive (Herbert 1924, Ripley 1938, Smythies 1953, Medway and Wells 1976).

Key Behaviors: These shy birds are notoriously difficult to find and study. They are usually found singly or in pairs and vocalize to each other in the morning and evening. Gurney's pittas hop along the ground in search of food. Although they prefer areas with little undergrowth, when danger threatens the birds run for the nearest canebrake or other dense cover (Smythies 1953, Rutgers 1968, B. King personal communication).

Conservation Measures Taken: This bird may occur in some of the wildlife sanctuaries and national parks in the south. Thai law (WARPA 1980) prohibits hunting and regulates trade of this species.

Conservation Measures Proposed: This species should be sought in biological surveys of Khao Luang National Park and Khlong Saeng, Khlong Nakha, and Khlong Phraya wildlife sanctuaries. In areas where populations survive, forest management officials should consider the needs of this forest-floor dweller. Where harvest occurs, tracts of uncut evergreen forest should be left interspersed among harvested areas, to retain local populations of these birds. The life history and habits of this and other pittas need to be studied more thoroughly. Cooperative banding studies with the Union of Burma should be considered to learn the true movements of the species to aid in formulating sound management plans. Hunting and export should be monitored and controlled.

Nok ta pong, white-eyed river martin, Princess bird
Pseudochelidon sirintarae **Kitti 1968**
Aves, Passeriformes, Hirundinidae

Status: Endangered.
CITES (1979): Appendix II.
IUCN (1979): Threatened.
IUCN Red Data Book (1979): Indeterminate.
WARPA (1980): Protected-1.

Population Size and Trend: Population size is unknown but small (Lekagul and Cronin 1974, King and Kanwanich 1978, IUCN Red Data Book 1979). Ogle (1986) considers the species close to extinction.

Distribution and History of Distribution: The species is known only from Bung Boraphet in Nakhon Sawan Province in central Thailand (Fig. 69; Kitti 1968, 1969; King and Kanwanich 1978). All records are from November to March. The summer range and breeding grounds are unknown.

This distinctive species was first captured in January 1968 by professional bird hunters hired to net swallows (*Hirundo rustica*) for the Migratory Animals Pathological Survey (MAPS). In January and February of 1968, nine specimens were procured from hunters. These included subadult males and adult females, but mostly juveniles. Kitti (1968) subsequently described the species and named it in honor of H. R. H. Princess Sirindhorn Thepratanasuda in recognition of her keen interest in natural history (Lekagul and Cronin 1974). Kitti searched unsuccessfully for river martins during the first two weeks of March of that year. He secured one specimen in November (Kitti 1968, 1969; King and Kanwanich 1978).

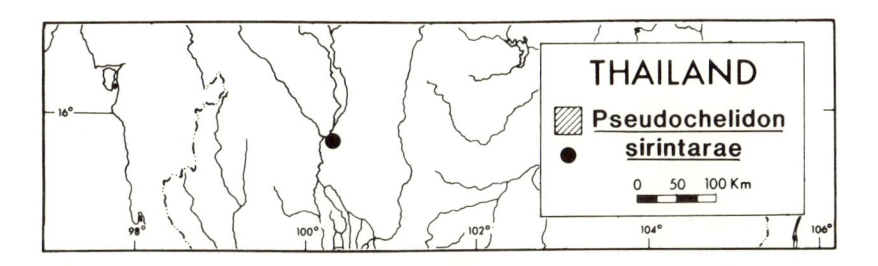

Fig. 69. Distribution of the White-eyed River Martin (*Pseudochelidon sirintarae*).

Between 1968 and 1977, several white-eyed river martins showed up in local markets in January and February (King and Kanwanich 1978). Two were found in 1972 (IUCN Red Data Book 1979). One individual was reported in 1978 (IUCN 1979).

The only close living relative of *P. sirintarae* is *P. eurystomina* of the Zaire (Congo) River in west-central Africa. Together the two compose the martin subfamily Pseudochelidoninae. The habit of the latter species of breeding on sand flats, sand islands, and sandbars (Chapin 1954) led Kitti to search the rivers north of Bung Boraphet for breeding river martins in the summer of 1969. Kitti searched from 21 May to 27 June along the Wang, Yom, and Nan rivers but found no *Pseudochelidon* (Kitti 1969).

From 31 January to 4 February 1977, King and Kanwanich (1978) made the first observations by professional ornithologists of wild *P. sirintarae*. Six sightings and two suspected sightings were made. All were thought to be adults. The birds were seen flying low and skimming the water in late afternoon and early evening. David Ogle of LaSalle Chotiravi College reported sighting four immature *P. sirintarae* on 4 January 1980, but no martins were captured by netting former roosting areas in winter 1980-81, and no sightings have occurred during observations since then (Dobias 1981, Sophasan and Dobias 1984, Ogle 1986).

Geographic Status: Existing data indicate that the white-eyed river martin is an endemic winter resident (King and Dickinson 1975), migrating to an unknown breeding locality, possibly in the north. Its separation from its African congener by 10,000 km suggests that the Thai population is relictual in nature.

Habitat Requirements and Habitat Trend: The birds roost among the extensive reed beds of the large, shallow, freshwater Bung Boraphet. This is the largest freshwater marsh in Thailand. It is an important wetland for waterfowl and historically supported the endangered Siamese crocodile (*Crocodylus siamensis*). During the time the river martins are present, thousands of barn swallows (*H. rustica*) and weavers (*Ploceus* sp.) and hundreds of yellow-breasted buntings (*Emberiza aureola*) also roost in the reeds (King and Kanwanich 1978). Observations suggest that the winter foraging habitat is over or near the lake. The summer habitat is unknown, and diet has not been documented.

Vulnerability of Species and Habitat: This species uses wetland habitat, which is vulnerable to changes in both the reservoir and the connected upland watershed. However, the only actual threat is due to the birds' vulnerability to capture at night.

Causes of Threat: When the Siamese crocodile population at Bung Boraphet was hunted to commercial extinction, local people switched their effort to netting birds roosting in the reed beds at night. Bird hunters usually take their catch to local markets where they are sold for food or for the religious practice of releasing captive birds to acquire merit (King and Kanwanich 1978). These authors believed that continued netting by bird hunters could extirpate the species. That may now have happened (Sophasan and Dobias 1984). The only available estimates suggest that the number of swallows (all species) roosting in the area has decreased from hundreds of thousands to fewer than 10,000 (Sophasan and Dobias (1984).

Responses to Habitat Modification: Unknown.

Demographic Characteristics: Unknown.

Key Behaviors: The river martin apparently migrates between summer and winter ranges.

Conservation Measures Taken: Within the 25,600-ha reservoir and marsh, 10,600 ha has been designated as the Bung Boraphet

No-hunting Area. Thai law (WARPA 1980) prohibits hunting and regulates trade of this species.

Conservation Measures Proposed: The available information suggests that the survival status of this species is an emergency, and it may already be too late for conservation action. Bird trapping at Bung Boraphet should be reduced or, ideally, eliminated altogether (King and Kanwanich 1978). Designation of Bung Boraphet as a No-hunting Area has been ineffective in preventing collecting of river martins, and more rigorous protection is needed. As suggested by Sophasan and Dobias (1984) and Ogle (1986), forceful protection should be combined with an effort to create alternative employment for the local people, such as accommodating recreational tourism at Bung Boraphet. Perhaps Thailand's Tourism Office could attract international tourists to see one of the rarest and newest birds known to science. Identification of the summer range and breeding grounds are of paramount importance to the conservation of the species. The initiation of cooperative banding studies with Burma, Lao PDR, China, and other countries should be considered, if this species still survives in Thailand.

Rail-babbler
Eupetes macrocerus **Temminck 1831**
Aves, Passeriformes, Muscicapidae

Status: Threatened.
WARPA (1980): Protected-1.

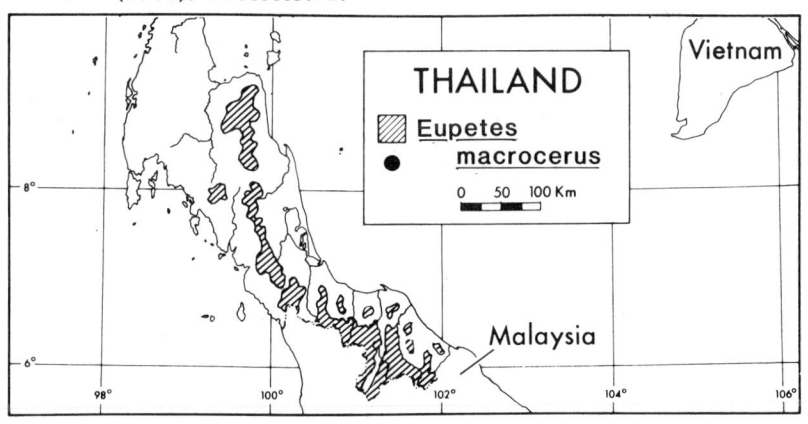

Fig. 70. Distribution of the Rail-babbler (*Eupetes macrocerus*).

Population Size and Trend: Unknown, but surely declining. Holmes (1973) found only two birds in southern Thailand.

Distribution and History of Distribution: The rail-babbler occurs in peninsular Thailand from Surat Thani and Trang south (Fig. 70) to peninsular Malaysia, Sumatra, the North Natunas, and Borneo (Riley 1938, Delacour 1947, Deignan 1963). Its range has been greatly reduced and fragmented by deforestation.

Geographic Status: The rail-babbler reaches its northern limit in southern Thailand.

Habitat Requirements and Habitat Trend: This species inhabits lowland forests up to 800 m elevation. Only primary or recovering secondary forest are known to be occupied (Riley 1938, Delacour 1947, Holmes 1973). Very little of this habitat remains in southern Thailand. The diet is insects found on the forest floor.

Vulnerability of Species and Habitat: Its habitat is highly vulnerable to deforestation.

Causes of Threat: Deforestation threatens this species.

Responses to Habitat Modification: Unknown. One of the birds observed by Holmes (1973) was in secondary forest that contained a few original trees.

Demographic Characteristics: Unknown.

Key Behaviors: Unknown.

Conservation Measures Taken: Thai law (WARPA 1980) prohibits killing and regulates trade of this species. Rail-babblers occur in Khao Banthat Wildlife Sanctuary (P. D. Round, personal communication).

Conservation Measures Proposed: Existing national parks and wildlife sanctuaries should be surveyed by listening for the distinctive call (Holmes 1973) to learn if protected habitat is occupied by this species. Proposed sanctuaries also should be examined to see if the number of protected populations can be increased.

Large grass warbler
Graminicola bengalensis **Jerdon 1863**
Aves, Passeriformes, Muscicapidae

Status: Extirpated from Thailand.

Population Size and Trend: The large grass warbler has not been recorded from Thailand since 1923 (Deignan 1963). Elsewhere it persists and is locally common (Ali and Ripley 1973).

Distribution and History of Distribution: In Thailand this species occupied the southern portion of the central plains (Fig. 71; Deignan 1963). Records also exist from Kwangtung Province, China, and Hainan (La Touche 1931-34, Ali and Ripley 1973). The best documented range is from the western Nepal terai, east through northern Bengal and the floodplains of Bangladesh to the Ganges (Ali and Ripley 1973). Other populations are known at low elevations in Tenasserim Province, Burma, and Tonkin (presumably the Hong or Red River basin of northern Vietnam, King and Dickinson 1975).

Geographic Status: The Thailand portion of the species' range presumably was a disjunct but sizable population occupying the lower floodplain of the Chao Phraya River and it tributaries.

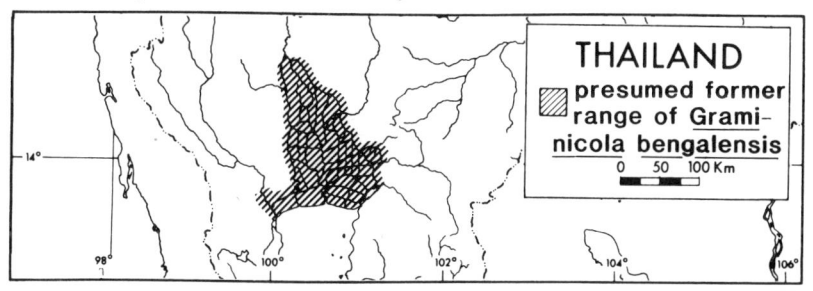

Fig. 71. Presumed former distribution of the Large Grass Warbler (*Graminicola bengalensis*).

Habitat Requirements and Habitat Trend: The large grass warbler lives in tall grass and reeds. Nests are placed in dense grass or reeds over deep water during the monsoon. This suggests an expanse of marsh, everglades, or wet savanna as the original vegetation of the lower Chao Phraya basin.

Vulnerability of Species and Habitat: The entire habitat in Thailand has been drained by canals and converted to rice paddies, orchards, and centers of human population.

Causes of Threat: Habitat loss may threaten the large grass warbler elsewhere in its range.

Responses to Habitat Modification: Unknown.

Demographic Characteristics: The number of eggs per clutch is "apparently 4" (Ali and Ripley 1973).

Key Behaviors: Breeding occurs in July and August. Observing this species is facilitated by their territorial display of soaring above the marsh vegetation to sing (Ali and Ripley 1973).

Conservation Measures Taken: None.

Conservation Measures Proposed: None for Thailand. Habitat requirements and effective management of the large grass warbler parallel those of the dusky and Cape Sable seaside sparrows in the United States, for which drainage of regional marshland is disastrous.

Mangrove Whistler
Pachycephala cinerea
Aves, Passeriformes, Muscicapidae

Status: Threatened.

Population Status and Trend: Common but probably declining.

Distribution and History Distribution: The mangrove whistler occurs along the coasts of eastern India, Bangladesh, Burma, Thailand (Fig. 72), southern Vietnam, the mainland and islands of Malaysia south to Singapore, the Philippines, and the Lesser Sunda Islands (Ali and Ripley 1972, Medway and Wells 1976). Nests are built in small trees 1-4 m above the ground. The diet is insects captured in the air and on vegetation (Ali and Ripley 1972). Mangrove and *Casuarina* forest are heavily harvested for charcoal, and few or no primary stands remain in Thailand.

Vulnerability of Species and Habitat: Coastal forest is highly vulnerable to deforestation for charcoal production and coastal development including housing, mines, and shrimp farms.

Causes of Threat: The mangrove whistler is threatened by habitat loss.

Responses to Habitat Modification: Unknown.

Demographic Characteristics: The clutch contains 2 eggs. The breeding season extends from April to July in India and March to June in peninsular Malaysia (Ali and Ripley 1972, Medway and Wells 1976). Banded individuals have been recaptured up to 68 months later (McClure 1974b).

Key Behaviors: This species is not migratory (McClure 1974b).

Conservation Measures Taken: To counter the unsustainable, high rate of harvest of mangroves for charcoal, the Royal Forestry Department has instituted a 30-year strip harvest regulation, de-

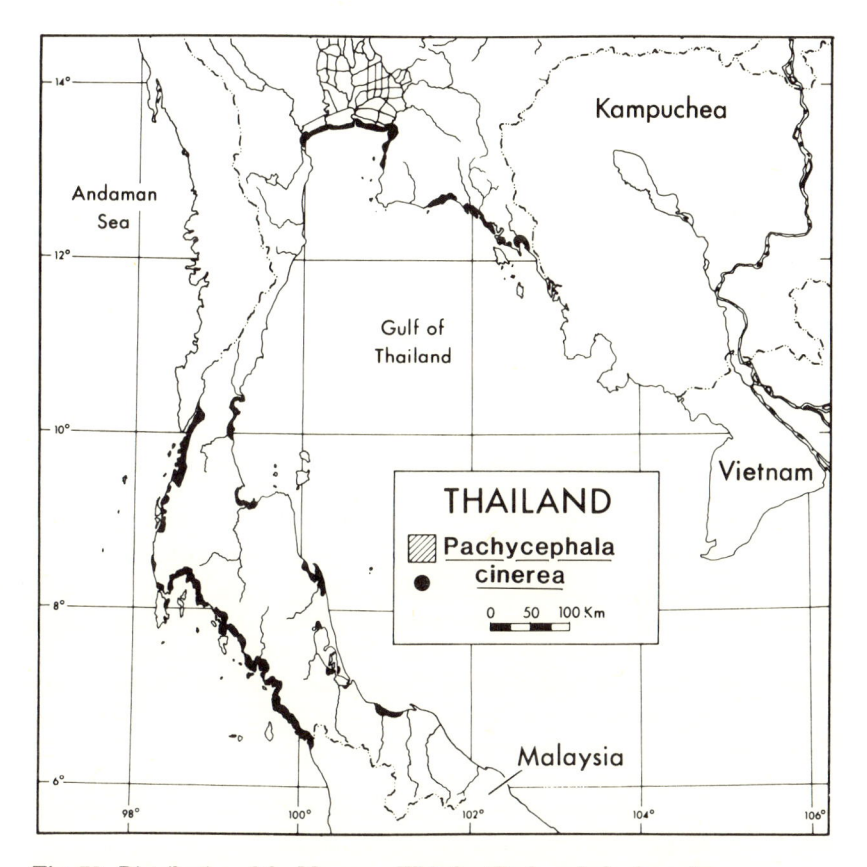

Fig. 72. Distribution of the Mangrove Whistler (*Pachycephala cinerea*).

signed to maintain a sustained yield of charcoal and retain the valuable ecosystem functions of coastal forests. The species occurs in Ko Libong No-hunting Area.

Conservation Measures Proposed: The strip rotation regulation should be enforced rigorously. Mangrove habitat is economically important because it provides protection from storms to inland developments and biological productivity that supports the young of many commercially valuable marine species of fish. The response of mangrove whistlers to habitat modification should be determined.

Chapter 7

Mammals

Kitti's hog-nosed bat
Craseonycteris thonglonyai **Hill 1974**
Mammalia, Chiroptera, Craseonycteridae

Status: Threatened.
WARPA (1980): Protected-1.

Population Size and Trend: Unknown. The population in the vicinity of Sai Yok National Park is approximately 160 animals (Halls 1982).

Distribution and History of Distribution: *C. thonglongyai* is known from five caves near Sai Yok waterfall (Hill 1974, Lekagul and McNeely 1977, Halls 1982) and one cave near Huai Bong Ti, Kanchanaburi Province (our observation, 1980; Fig. 73). Actual distribution may be much more extensive than documented. The species has been found resident from October through March and in May; data from the rainy season are lacking.

Geographic Status: The species is endemic to karst areas of the Bilauktaung mountain range of western Thailand and may extend to adjoining portions of Burma.

Habitat Requirements and Habitat Trend: Roosting habitat consists of the hot upper chambers of caves in limestone hills. Foraging habitat is teak-bamboo forest, where the bats feed around the tops of the co-dominant plants (Lekagul and McNeely 1977). Adaptations of the nose, wings, and tail were considered specializations for a gleaning mode of foraging (Hill 1974, McNeely 1979), but careful observation in the field of bats judged to be this species demonstrated only aerial feeding (Halls 1982). The diet consists of insects, but the preferred kinds and sizes of prey are unknown.

Vulnerability of Species and Habitat: Disturbance of the roost-

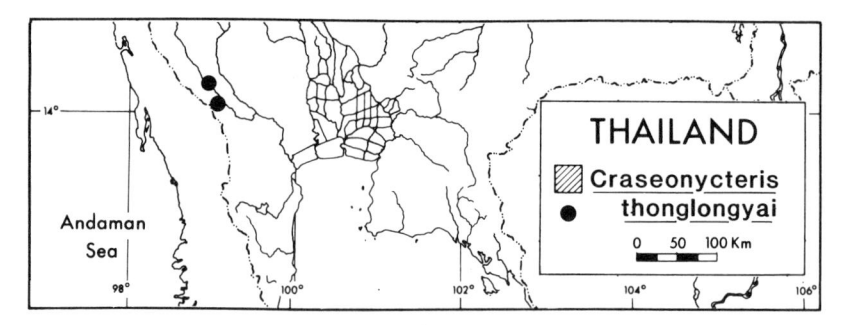

Fig. 73. Distribution of Kitti's Hog-nosed Bat (*Craseonycteris thonglongyai*).

ing caves apparently causes populations to abandon affected sites (Halls 1982), though they may simply move to nearby alternative sites, if available. This species' habitat is being deforested by teak logging above the sustainable rate. Vast areas of potential habitat have been affected.

Causes of Threat: Two caves frequently visited by people in Sai Yok National Park no longer are occupied by Kitti's bat (Halls 1982). Loss of foraging habitat may be a threat, but no impact is documented.

Responses to Habitat Modification: Unknown.

Demographic Characteristics: Populations are small, consisting of 5-100 individuals (Lekagul and McNeely 1977, Halls 1982, our observation). Birth of the young occurs in May, and litters appear to contain a single young (our observation, Fig. 74). Though touted as the world's smallest mammal, this species actually is equal in size to four other very small species of mammal.

Key Behaviors: Adult females roost individually in the nursery cave (Lekagul and McNeely 1977a); the significance of this behavior is unknown.

Conservation Measures Taken: Thai law (WARPA 1980) prohibits killing and regulates export of this species. Roosting habitat of three populations or former populations are included in Sai Yok National Park.

Conservation Measures Proposed: A survey of the distribution and status of this bat should be conducted, and reforestation should be accomplished in its range. A program is needed at Sai Yok National Park to prevent the high level of human activity from driving bats away from all the caves. This could be accomplished by directing recreational visits only to certain caves, installing indus-

Fig. 74. A pregnant female Kitti's hog-nosed bat (*Craseonycteris thonglongyai*) from a cave near Huai Bong Ti, Kanchanaburi Province, in May 1980.

trial-type fences or specially designed gates that prevent human entry without hindering bat flight at the entrances of caves, and educating park visitors about the reasons for this conservation action (Halls 1982).

Pig-tailed macaque
Macaca nemestrina **(Linnaeus 1766)**
Mammalia, Primata, Cercopithecidae

Status: Threatened.
CITES (1979): Appendix II.
WARPA (1980): Protected-1.

Population Size and Trend: Roonwal and Mohnot (1977) refer to a range-wide population decline.

Distribution and History of Distribution: The pig-tailed macaque occurs in India (Assam), Burma, Thailand, peninsular Malaysia, Sumatra, Borneo, and a few small offshore islands. The historical distribution in Thailand was widespread but discontinuous in suitable habitat, excluding the central lowlands and eastern plateau, but current range is undocumented (Lekagul and McNeely 1977a, Medway 1978, Fooden 1980). Crockett and Wilson (1980) cite a general range reduction caused by habitat loss.

Geographic Status: Thailand is central in the species' range. Eudey (1980) suggested that one subspecies of the pig-tailed macaque survived the arid late Pleistocene in refugia of montane evergreen forest and has experienced a great expansion of suitable habitat since then, until recent deforestation began.

Habitat Requirements and Habitat Trend: In the Dawna Range, pig-tailed macaques occur with other species of macaques in mixed deciduous and dry evergreen forest (Eudey 1979). In Malaysia, pig-tailed macaques have their highest densities in lowland and hill primary evergreen forest. To a lesser extent they use deciduous and swamp forest. The species is rare in secondary forest (Southwick and Cadigan 1972). They also raid cropland adjacent to primary forest. Pig-tails locally co-occur with crab-eating macaques (*M. fascicularis*) but differ in habitat, using upland forest instead of riparian or swamp forest, at higher elevations (an average of 366 m vs. 203 m for *fascicularis*), and on hillier terrain. Though social groups of the 2 species are the same size, averaging 19 individuals, the density of pig-tailed macaques (18-19/km^2) is much less than for *fascicularis* (48-54/km^2). As these densities suggest, pig-tailed macaques have larger home ranges (100-300 ha), compared with 25-100 ha for *fascicularis*. This pattern is attributable to a lower density of fruits in upland forest compared with riparian forest. The diet of *M. nemestrina* is mostly fruit, supplemented with leaves, seeds, fungi, and insects (Bernstein 1967, Chivers 1973, Rijksen 1978, Rodman 1978, Crockett and Wilson 1980).

Vulnerability of Species and Habitat: Pig-tailed macaques behave with deliberation and patience in captivity and are desired as research animals for these special qualities. For example, a Thai *nemestrina* was sent into earth orbit during early space research (Lekagul and McNeely 1977a). Primary evergreen forest is vulnerable to deforestation, and little of it remains in the lowlands of Thailand.

Causes of Threat: Both trapping for export and deforestation threaten this species. Exports of pig-tailed macaques from Thailand in 1974 and 1975 numbered 1,566 and 632 individuals (Eudey 1978). Between 1968 and 1970, 1,713 *M. nemestrina* were imported into the United States from all source countries (USFWS 1970,

1971, 1972). From an original 80 percent, forest cover of Thailand has declined to 25 percent in 1978 (Myers 1980).

Responses to Habitat Modification: See Key Behaviors.

Demographic Characteristics: Usually a single young is born. Gestation takes about 170 days, and young are weaned after 3 months. Females become sexually mature when 4 years old. The estrous cycle of 32-40 days includes a swelling of the hairless area of the buttocks that signals the female's period of receptivity. The maximum lifespan in captivity is 26 years (Medway 1978). Only half the females are pregnant simultaneously, so births probably occur every 2 years (Bernstein 1967). The mortality pattern is as in *M. mulatta* (Taub 1980).

Key Behaviors: Pig-tailed macaques in the wild move widely over the group's home range in search of their low-density food. They normally travel on the ground rather than in trees, and if disturbed while feeding in trees, they quickly drop to the ground to run away (Medway 1978, Crockett and Wilson 1980). "Although they occasionally range into secondary forest and scrub far from primary forest, their more common pattern is to sleep in primary forest and enter secondary habitats to raid croplands." Raids are carried out stealthily, often with an individual high in a tree to look for danger, and frequently they occur during rainstorms from which farmers have taken shelter (Crockett and Wilson 1980). Behavior of this species in the Sunda Shelf has been monographed (Caldecott 1985).

Conservation Measures Taken: In 1976 the Royal Forestry Department banned the export of all primates from Thailand. Now exportation is possible with case-by-case permission from the Wildlife Advisory Commission. Pig-tailed macaques occur in Huai Kha Khaeng Wildlife Sanctuary (Eudey 1980), Khao Chamao National Park, Khao Soi Dao Wildlife Sanctuary (W. Brockelman, personal communication), Nam Nao National Park, Phu Kheo Wildlife Sanctuary (J. McNeely, personal communication), Khao Yai National Park (our observations), and probably in other parks and preserves.

Conservation Measures Proposed: The many parks and sanctuaries known to be inhabited by some species of macaque (Prakobboon 1979) should be resurveyed to determine which species live where. Then the status of pig-tailed macaques should be monitored annually to document long-term population trends. Local threats should be evaluated so suitable responses can be implemented.

Assamese macaque
Macaca assamensis (McClelland 1840)
Mammalia, Primata, Cercopithecidae

Status: Threatened.
CITES (1979): Appendix II.
WARPA (1980): Protected-1.

Population Size and Trend: Little is known about the number of Assamese macaques in Thailand. The species is "not particularly abundant" there (IUCN 1979).

Distribution and History of Distribution: Assamese macaques occur at lower and middle elevations in the Himalayas from Uttar Pradesh and Nepal through Sikkim, and Bhutan to Yunnan province of China, northern Burma, northern and western Thailand, and northern Lao PDR and Vietnam (Lekagul and McNeely 1977a, Roonwal and Mohnot 1977, Fooden 1980). A widely disjunct but valid record is from the Sundarbans of Bangladesh (Fooden 1982).

Geographic Status: Thailand is in the southernmost portion of the species' range. Eudey (1980) suggested that this species is one of four species in the *M. sinica* group that became isolated during the late-Pleistocene glaciation.

Habitat Requirements and Habitat Trend: This species typically occupies evergreen and mixed deciduous forest, or nearby teak-bamboo forest. It usually occurs at elevations of 150-1,900 m, occasionally up to 2,750 m. In the Himalayas animals descend to 1,220 m or lower in the winter. Though this species co-occurs with *M. mulatta* and *M. arctoides*, the three differ in habitat or niche; *assamemsis* is more arboreal and occurs much less often in secondary and deciduous forests than *mulatta*, and it occupies the same forests but is much more arboreal than the terrestrial *arctoides* (Fooden 1971, 1982, 1986; Prater 1971; Lekagul and McNeely 1977a; Eudey 1980). The diet consists mostly of fruit, plus buds, insects, and lizards (Lekagul and McNeely 1977a, Fooden 1986). *M. assamensis* and gibbons have similar diets in the same forests, but they differ in their techniques and efficiency of harvesting arboreal fruit (Fooden 1986). Much habitat has been deforested.

Vulnerability of Species and Habitat: The species is killed for food and as a pest when settlers convert the forest to agricultural use. Its habitat is vulnerable to deforestation.

Causes of Threat: Deforestation and hunting threaten this species. No records of its export from Thailand are known to us.

Responses to Habitat Modification: Like other macaques, this species raids agricultural crops (Pocock 1939) adjacent to its forest habitat. However, the animals are so quickly extirpated that no stable response to the situation develops.

Demographic Characteristics: Similar to those of *M. mulatta*. Most sexually mature females probably bear one young each year, mating in the dry season and giving birth in the rainy season (Fooden 1982).

Key Behaviors: Assamese macaques occur in troops of 10-70 individuals (Fooden 1986). Typically they feed with a sentinel watching for danger. When it calls a warning, the animals escape to dense cover either through the trees or on the ground (Fooden 1982).

Conservation Measures Taken: In 1976 the Royal Forestry Department banned the export of all primates from Thailand. Now exportation is possible with the permission of the Wildlife Advisory Commission. Assamese macaques occupy Huai Kha Khaeng Wildlife Sanctuary (Eudey 1980) and probably other parks and sanctuaries.

Conservation Measures Proposed: The many parks and sanctuaries known to be inhabited by some species of macaque (Prakobboon 1979) should be resurveyed to determine which species live where. Then local threats should be evaluated so suitable responses can be implemented.

Stump-tailed macaque
Macaca arctoides Geoffroy 1831
Mammalia, Primates, Cercopithecidae

Status: Threatened.
CITES (1979): Appendix II.
USFWS (1980a): Threatened.
WARPA (1980): Protected-1.

Population Size and Trend: This monkey is now uncommon

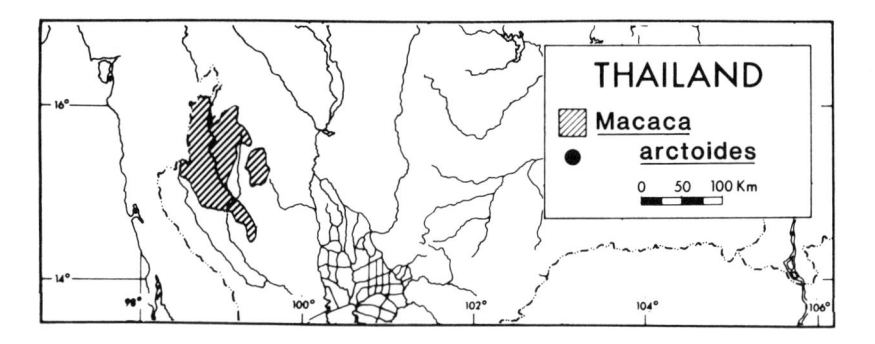

Fig. 75. Distribution of the Stump-tailed Macaque (*Macaca arctoides*).

throughout its range and occurs in isolated populations. It is nearing extirpation from peninsular Thailand, where it was once abundant (Southwick and Siddiqi 1970, Roonwal and Mohnot 1977, A. Eudey personal communication).

Distribution and History of Distribution: Stump-tailed macaques range from eastern India (Assam), southern China, Burma, Thailand, Lao PDR, Vietnam, Kampuchea, and possibly extreme northern Malaya. Some authorities consider the Malayan records to represent introduced populations (Medway 1969, van Peenen et al. 1969, Lekagul and McNeely 1977a, Roonwal and Mohnot 1977, A. Eudey personal communication). In Thailand the species is known only from the Dawna Range and a smaller range in peninsular Thailand adjacent to 100° E longitude (Fig. 75; Eudey 1980).

Geographic Status: Thailand is the southwestern portion of the species' range (Fooden 1980). Populations are disjunct, montane relicts of a presumably wider former range (Eudey 1980).

Habitat Requirements and Habitat Trend: In Thailand this primate is primarily an upland species, inhabiting primary and secondary forest from about 150 m to over 2,000 m. The sightings made by Eudey (1979) in Huai Kha Kaeng Wildlife Sanctuary in Uthai Thani Province in west-central Thailand were in dry evergreen forest. The food is fruits (especially *Ficus* species), berries, nuts, shoots, buds, leaves, stems, tubers, roots, insects, and other small animals (Medway 1969, Lekagul and McNeely 1977a, Roonwal and Mohnot 1977, Eudey 1979, 1980, personal communication).

Vulnerability of Species and Habitat: These terrestrial monkeys are not overly shy and will sometimes attack people when confronted. Their gregariousness and occasional habit of raiding crops make them vulnerable to hunters. They emit a fetid smell which may repel some predators and people, but they are eaten at times in Southeast Asia. Until recently, perhaps their physiological similarity to man was their most vulnerable feature--biomedical research consumed many.

Causes of Threat: Until 1976, the primary threat was trapping for export, aggravated by habitat loss. In 1974 exports of stump-tailed macaques from Thailand numbered 1,816 animals; 1,042 were exported in 1975. During 1971-76, this species was used in at least 20 countries and in at least 113 laboratories in the United States (Eudey 1978). Between 1968 and 1972, the United States imported over 6,700 from all sources (USFWS 1970, 1971, 1972, 1974). In the study period 31 March-6 June 1975, 80 were exported through Bangkok's Don Muang Airport (Duplaix and King 1975). In 1976 the Thai government imposed strict controls on primate exports. Illicit capture and smuggling still remove an undetermined number from Thailand each year. On 12-16 August 1978, a few *M. arctoides* were transshipped to Belgium from Vientiane, Lao PDR, through the Bangkok Airport. In the same shipment were Malayan tapirs and gibbons that could not have possibly originated in Lao PDR, as was claimed (IUCN 1978). It is possible that all were originally from Thailand. Additionally, subsistence hunting by villagers and insurgents probably kills many, (A. Eudey, personal communication).

Responses to Habitat Modification: This primate can survive in secondary forest, but clear-cutting upland forests probably is intolerable. It does not exhibit the broad range of ecological tolerance that some of its congeners do.

Demographic Characteristics: Although reproductive biology in captivity is well known, little is known about the situation in the wild. One young is produced every 2 years. This macaque has lived as long as 30 years in captivity (Medway 1969, Roonwal and Mohnot 1977).

Key Behaviors: This species feeds, sleeps, and takes shelter in trees when danger threatens, but it is mainly terrestrial. It is generally slower and less agile than more arboreal *Macaca*. Groups over 100 have been reported in remote forest, but they are generally smaller in areas where the monkeys are hunted. In Thailand foraging behavior may take up half of the waking hours. When *Ficus* is in fruit, groups will stay near a few trees and may cover less than

0.4 km in the course of a day. If trees are scattered the animals may move 1-3 km. Migrations between mountain ranges are suspected at times. Migrating macaques in the 20th century are vulnerable to being shot while moving and raiding crops in settled areas. The details of their gregarious behavior and movements are poorly known. A group is thought to have one leader. In Thailand a group of this species lived near a group of *Presbytis obscura* and fed on the same *Ficus* tree. This activity was peaceful, but the latter avoided the former (Bertrand 1969, Medway 1969, Lekagul and McNeely 1977a, Roonwal and Mohnot 1977).

Conservation Measures Taken: Thai law (WARPA 1980) prohibits hunting and regulates trade in this species. It occurs in Huai Kha Khaeng Wildlife Sanctuary and probably in other protected areas. Four stump-tails were recently released at an old Chinese temple 11 km SW of Chon Buri. *M. arctoides* can be and is raised in captivity (Roonwal and Mohnot 1977, Eudey 1980 and personal communication, our observation).

Conservation Measures Proposed: A survey of Thailand's reserves to determine current status is the top priority for this primate. Basic field studies on its ecology are needed. The effects of habitat modification on *M. arctoides* populations require study.

Rhesus macaque
Macaca mulatta (Zimmerman 1780)
Mammalia, Primata, Cercopithecidae

Status: Threatened.
CITES (1979): Appendix II.
WARPA (1980): Protected-1.

Population Size and Trend: No specific information is available on population size and trend of rhesus macaques in Thailand. This species, once the most abundant monkey in Asia, has experienced ubiquitous population declines caused by habitat destruction and exports for medical research. Declines of forest-dwelling populations are most notable (Muckenhirn 1975, Lekagul and McNeely 1977a, Zhang et al. 1981).

Distribution and History of Distribution: Rhesus macaques occur in Afganistan north to $35°$ N, India, Bangladesh, Burma, northern Thailand, Lao PDR, northern Kampuchea and Vietnam,

Hainan, and much of China. In western Thailand the species occurs as far south as 15° 30' N in Uthai Thani Province (Lekagul and McNeely 1977a, Eudey 1980, Fooden 1980). Rhesus are discontinuous within this range, and fragmentation has been increased by the loss of some populations (Prater 1971).

Geographic Status: This northern species reaches its southern range limit in western Thailand, where it overlaps with the southern *Macaca fascicularis*.

Habitat Requirements and Habitat Trend: The following sentences refer to India and Bangladesh, not Thailand. Though the major original habitat of rhesus probably was open deciduous forest at 0-1,500 m (Lindburg 1977), now they occupy remnants of deciduous forest, occur widely in deforested countryside, and live in or near human villages and cities (Southwick et al. 1961a, b). A few populations live in pine forests, semidesert, and mangrove swamps (Roonwal and Mohnot 1977). Extensive tracts of deciduous forest are unoccupied during the dry season (Southwick et al. 1961b), because the availability of drinking water is a limiting factor (Lindburg 1977). The annual activity ranges of social groups in forest are 1-15 km in area. Population density ranges from $10/km^2$ in high-elevation pine forests to $753/km^2$ in cities (Neville 1968, Lindburg 1977). In a forest population, the diet is 65-70 percent fruit, with lesser proportions of leaves, seeds, shoots, flowers, and insects (Lindburg 1977). In rural agricultural land, much food is procured by crop-raiding. In cities most food is given by or stolen from people, and cooked food is preferred (Singh 1969). Though most original habitat has been lost, rhesus macaques have adapted to human land uses. Rhesus are more tolerant of cold stress than their southern congener, *M. fascicularis*, and they winter as high as 2,440 m in the Himalayas (Tokura et al. 1975, Prater 1971).

Vulnerability of Species and Habitat: In other countries, this species' adaptability prevents habitat conversion from being a problem. However, in Thailand populations seem to remain only in national parks, wildlife sanctuaries, and remote forested areas. Before exportation was stopped, harvest greatly exceeded sustainable levels in many places.

Causes of Threat: The current threat is killing and deforestation. Formerly, the species was threatened by trapping for export. Exports from Thailand (all species of macaques) from 1962-66 numbered 10, 854, 17, 807, 5,377, 6,200, and 5,561 (Royal Forestry

Department 1972). From 1972-75 they numbered 5,456, 4,783, 5,291, and 3,088, of which rhesus accounted for 1,427 and 345 in 1974 and 1975 (Eudey 1978). Between 1968 and 1970, 81,697 rhesus macaques were imported into the United States from all sources (USFWS 1970, 1971, 1972).

Responses to Habitat Modification: The history of rhesus populations in India shows that they can develop a strong commensal relationship with man, and harassment by villagers and plantation owners will not drive the monkeys away unless many are killed or trapped out (Southwick et al. 1965). Urbanized rhesus become very shrewd (Singh 1969). Providing supplemental food to free-ranging rhesus can increase population growth by 16 percent (Koford 1965). In Thailand, however, rhesus populations in the vicinity of man are eliminated rather than tolerated.

Demographic Characteristics: Usually a single young is born; twins are rare. From 73 to 91 percent of the adult females produce young annually (Koford 1965, Southwick and Siddiqi 1970, Lindburg 1971). Gestation takes 5-6 months, and young are weaned when about 6 months old. Sexual maturity is attained at approximately 4 years of age (Roonwal and Mohnot 1971). Starvation of subordinate individuals during annual food shortages results in higher mortality of infant and juvenile females than of males of the same age. Among adults, infrequent fighting of males in the mating season causes severe wounds, deaths, and dispersal of subordinates, leading to higher survival of adult females than males (Dittus 1980).

Key Behaviors: Most births in India occur from February to May, and in some places a second birth period occurs in September and October (Southwick et al. 1961b, Roonwal and Mohnot 1977). Estrous cycles and mating occur throughout the year, but for most of the year the cycles do not include ovulation. Likewise, ovulation does not occur during lactation. Rhesus macaque groups consist of several genealogical units, each headed by a founding female (Sade 1965) and maintained by the group fidelity of her female offspring (Koford 1966, Lindburg 1969, Boelkins and Wilson 1972). Males, by contrast, disperse from their natal groups to join others when 4-7 years old (Roonwal and Mohnot 1977). The dominance hierarchy of a group is determined by the males (Southwick 1969), and the dominant male does most of the mating, fighting, and defense of the group against predators (Dittus 1980).

Conservation Measures Taken: In 1976 the Royal Forestry

Department banned the export of all primates from Thailand. Now exportation requires permission from the Wildlife Advisory Commission. Rhesus macaques occur in Doi Chiang Dao and Huai Kha Khaeng wildlife sanctuaries (IUCN 1979, Eudey 1980) and probably many other parks and sanctuaries.

Conservation Measures Proposed: The many parks and sanctuaries known to be inhabited by some species of macaque (Prakobboon 1979) should be resurveyed to determine which species live where. Then local threats should be evaluated so suitable responses can be implemented.

Long-tailed macaque, crab-eating macaque
Macaca fascicularis (Raffles 1821)
Mammalia, Primates, Cercopithecidae

Status: Threatened.
CITES(1979): Appendix II.
WARPA (1980): Protected-1.

Population Size and Trend: Although there are no estimates of the total numbers of *M. fascicularis*, it is common over much of its wide range and is the most abundant monkey in Thailand (McNeely 1977, Roonwal and Mohnot 1977).

Distribution and History of Distribution: This macaque is known from peninsular Burma, Thailand, southern Kampuchea, southern Vietnam, the Philippines, Malaya, Sumatra, Java, Borneo, and many other islands of the Sunda Shelf, but not Sulawesi (Celebes). The Thai population's range (Fig. 76) is largely parapatric with that of *M. mulatta* to the north, but overlap and intergrades occur in Kamphaeng Phet and Uthai Thani provinces. Long-tailed macaques have colonized many islands, including the Nicobar Islands and, in Thailand's waters, Ko Kut, Ko Chang, Ko Kram, and Ko Tarutao. The population on Ko Kram deserves special attention, as it is recognized as a distinct subspecies, *M. f. atriceps*. The species has been introduced in Mauritius (Lekagul and McNeely 1977a, Roonwal and Mohnot 1977, USNM 1980).

Geographic Status: The Thai populations lie at the northern limits of the species' range in mainland Southeast Asia (Lekagul and McNeely 1977a).

Habitat Requirements and Habitat Trend: Long-tailed ma-

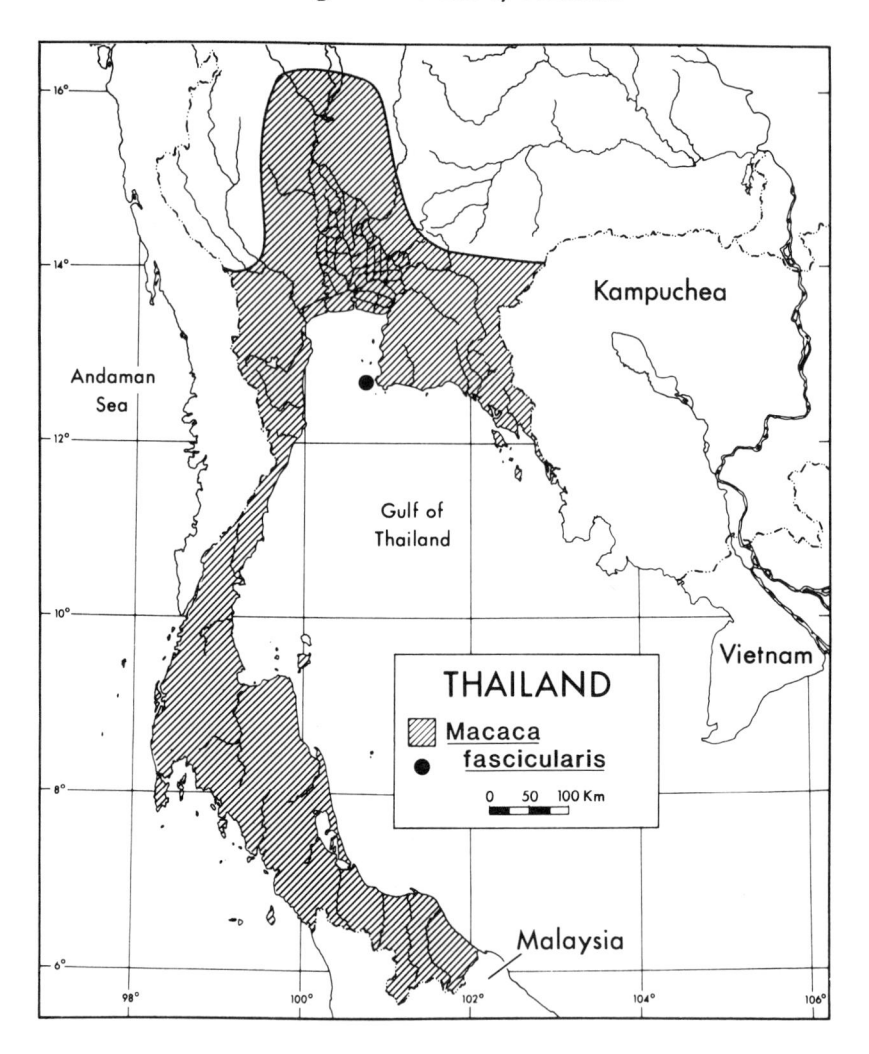

Fig. 76. Distribution of the Crab-eating Macaque (*Macaca fascicularis*).

caques use a wider variety of habitats than other *Macaca*. They have been reported from mangrove forest, tidal creeks, mudflats, beaches, throughout the lowlands in crops, isolated patches of woodland, orchards, nurseries, plantations, secondary forest, and primary forest. Mostly coastal and insular, the species ranges on the mainland to about 2,000 m. In forests they prefer riverine situations. The lability of this species' habitat usage makes it successful on large and small islands and in some urban situations. *M. fascicularis* is an omnivore, preferring fruits (especially figs), but also feeding on vegetative growth, flowers, cultivated varieties of rice, beans, potatoes and other crops, young rubber plants, crustaceans (especially crabs and prawns), molluscs, other small animals, and garbage (Medway 1969, Lekagul and McNeely 1977a, McNeely 1977, Roonwal and Mohnot 1977, Wheatley 1979, Eudey 1979 and 1980).

Vulnerability of Species and Habitat: These macaques can become serious crop pests, so they are often trapped or shot. Their habit of conspicuously sleeping in trees also attracts human attention.

Causes of Threat: This primate was seriously impacted by the trade in live animals. Many thousands were used in the development of polio vaccines. Imports to the United States in 1968-1970 were 2,137, 1,188, and 1,609, respectively (USFWS 1970, 1971, 1972). In Thailand this macaque is captured by villagers and often stars in local monkey shows (lakhon ling) (Lekagul and McNeely 1977a). It is less threatened than most Thai monkeys.

Responses to Habitat modification: This primate tolerates or benefits from habitat disturbance, even colonizing towns in some parts of its range. In Thailand this occurs mainly at religious shrines, where people do not molest them.

Demographic Characteristics: The menstrual cycle is 24-52 days. There are conflicting reports in the literature about the seasonality of breeding. In western Thailand, Fooden (1971) noted pregnant females (1-3 months preterm) in February and March and lactating females with infants in March and early April and concluded that parturition peaks in March-May. The gestation period is 160-170 days. Usually one young is born. Long-tailed macaques have lived 27 years in captivity (Asdell 1965, Medway 1969, Fooden 1971, Lekagul and McNeely 1977a, Roonwal and Mohnot 1977).

Key Behaviors: Although *M. fascicularis* swims well in fresh and saltwater, and although it walks well on the ground, it is highly arboreal, spending the majority of its time feeding and jumping from tree to tree. It is very gregarious. Groups number over a hundred. Linear dominance hierarchies are formed among the many males of the group. All males copulate, but the most dominant male does the most copulating. Females tend to form a more cohesive group than the males. This species is thought to be less wide-ranging than most *Macaca*. The home range has been estimated as 0.8 to 1.25 km² in Borneo. Groups typically use a habitual sleeping tree, preferably in riverine situations. The species often makes local movements in search of food. It prefers the edge of unbroken forests; deeper in the woods it is dominated by *M. nemestrina* where the two co-occur. It peacefully coexists with *Presbytis cristata, P. obscura, P. melalophos,* and *Hylobates lar*. Its biology in captivity is well known (Furuya 1965, Bernstein 1967, Medway 1969, Kurland 1973, Lekagul and McNeely 1977a, Roonwal and Mohnot 1977, Wheatley 1979, Eudey 1980).

Conservation Measures Taken: Thai law (WARPA 1980) prohibits hunting and regulates trade in this species. This monkey is common in many national parks and wildlife sanctuaries, but it does not persist elsewhere near human settlement, except at rural temples and religious shrines. At a temple in Lop Buri Province the monkeys are fed by monks, local people, and tourists (Lekagul and McNeely 1977a, Storer 1978, Eudey 1980).

Conservation Measures Proposed: Where they flourish in the recreation-oriented national parks and at shrines, long-tailed macaques provide visitors valuable opportunities for contact with wildlife. At the same time, new management problems arise because they become more dependent on humans and more aggressive in seeking handouts. Special attention needs to be given to protecting mangrove habitat and to re-establishing forests around temple populations.

Banded langur
Presbytis melalophos **(Raffles 1821)**
Mammalia, Primata, Cercopithecidae

Status: Threatened.
CITES (1979): Appendix II.
WARPA (1980): Protected-1.

Population Size and Trend: In parts of their range banded langurs are widespread and common (Lekagul and McNeely 1977a). Because of habitat loss, the overall trend must be downward.

Distribution and History of Distribution: This species occurs in southern Burma and Thailand, peninsular Malaysia, Sumatra, Borneo, and small offshore islands. It is now rare or extirpated from Singapore island (Lekagul and McNeely 1977a, Roonwal and Mohnot 1977, Medway 1978). This distribution has become fragmented by deforestation (Fig. 77).

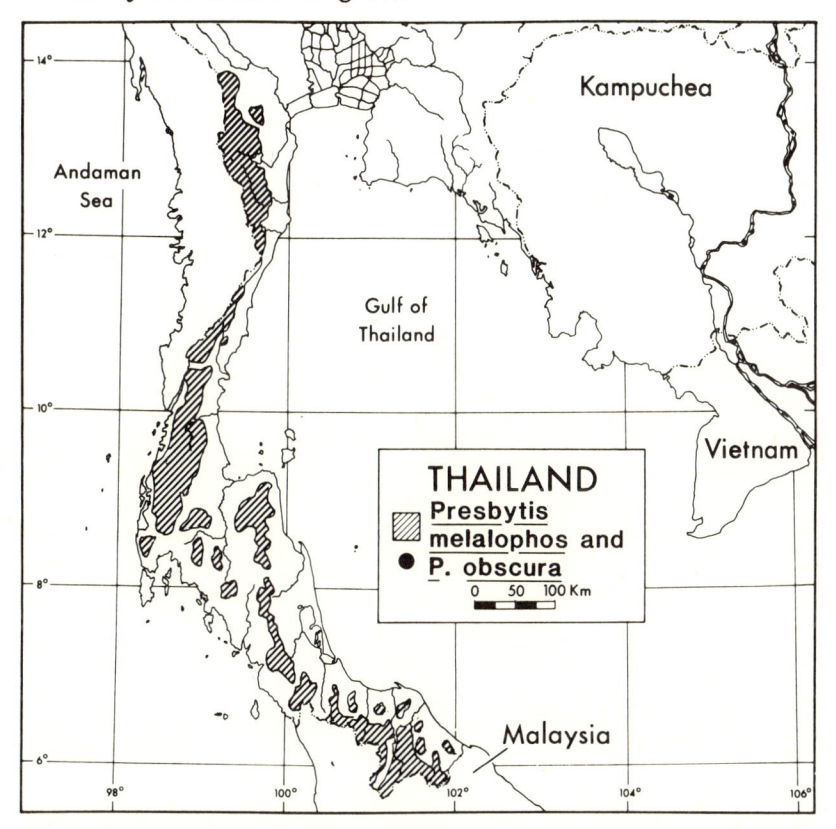

Fig. 77. Distribution of the Banded and Spectacled Langurs (*Presbytis melalophos* and *P. obscurua*).

Geographical Status: Thailand is the northern extent of the species' range.

Habitat Requirements and Habitat Trend: Banded langurs inhabit all types of forest from coastal mangroves to montane evergreen forest. They are most abundant below 610 m, but where congeneric species are absent they may be found in lesser numbers up to 2,100 m. They frequently enter rubber plantations and, occasionally, rice fields (McClure 1964, Lekagul and McNeely 1977a).

Banded langurs often co-occur with another langur species, but they use the forest resources differently. Their diet is dominated by fruit, disqualifying them from the common name "leaf monkey"; the sizable minority of leaves in the diet is restricted to new leaves, which contain relatively high amounts of protein and low amounts of cellulose and have not accumulated a full complement of toxic secondary compounds. Though they feed in all strata of the forest, banded langurs feed most often in the understory. Because the preferred microhabitat and diet are distributed discontinuously, banded langurs travel a great deal, by leaping and hopping (Fleagle 1978). However, the overall home range size is similar to that of groups of other langurs--16 ha (Curtin and Chivers 1978). Density is 0.8-1.2 groups per square kilometer (Southwick and Cadigan 1972). Groups contain 13 individuals on average (Curtin and Chivers 1978). Much habitat, especially lowland forest, has been deforested.

Vulnerability of Species and Habitat: The banded langur is vulnerable to hunting for food or as a pest. Its habitat, especially lowland forest, is vulnerable to deforestation.

Causes of Threat: The main threat to this species is loss of lowland forest; most has been converted to other land uses.

Responses to Habitat Modification: Banded langurs raid rubber plantations and other types of agriculture adjacent to forest. During selective logging in Malaysia, animals shifted their home ranges to avoid centers of logging activity. Afterwards, their home ranges were different than before, and the animals rested more and fed and travelled less than before (Johns 1986). The population persisted, however, because it was not hunted.

Demographic Characteristics: Normally a single young is born. The maximum life span recorded is 8.5 years (Medway 1978).

Key Behaviors: This and other langurs have large, semiruminant stomachs and intestinal tracts in which symbiotic bacteria make possible the digestion of large volumes of food with a high cellulose content (Freeland and Janzen 1974).

Conservation Measures Taken: Thai law (WARPA 1980) prohibits hunting and regulates trade in this species.

Conservation Measures Proposed: A detailed status survey of this species is needed before specific conservation measures can be proposed. Any improvement in the conservation of lowland forest in peninsular Thailand would help this species.

Dusky or spectacled langur
Presbytis obscura (Reid 1837)
Mammalia, Primata, Cercopithecidae

Status: Threatened.
CITES (1979): Appendix II.
WARPA (1980): Protected-1.
Population Size and Trend: Unknown in Thailand. The species was abundant in peninsular Malaysia (McClure 1964).

Distribution and History of Distribution: The dusky langur occurs in peninsular Thailand and southern Burma to 14° N, peninsular Malaysia, and the islands of Langkawi, Penang, and Perhentian Besar (Lekagul and McNeely 1977a, Medway 1978). This range has been fragmented by deforestation.

Geographic Status: Thailand is the northern extent of the species' range.

Habitat Requirements and Habitat Trend: Dusky langurs prefer mature forest, from coasts to mountains. Because this encompasses several types of forest, the species may occur together with *P. melalophos* or *P. cristata* in the lowlands. However, *P. obscura* is most common above 610 m elevation (McClure 1964, Lekagul and McNeely 1977a, Medway 1978). The diet consists of leaves, fruit, and flowers. Dusky langurs differ from *P. melalophos* in conducting most of their feeding in the forest canopy, eating only small amounts of fruit (35 percent of the diet), and including a significant share of mature leaves (39 percent) in the leafy component of the diet (Fleagle 1978, Curtin and Chivers 1978). The species also eats the leaves of rubber plants. Home range sizes of groups average 17 ha (Curtin and Chivers 1978). Density is 0.25-0.29 groups per square kilometer (Southwick and Cadigan 1972). Groups contain 14 individuals on average (Curtin and Chivers 1978). Much habitat has been deforested.

Vulnerability of Species and Habitat: The dusky langur is vulnerable to hunting for food or as a pest. Its habitat is vulnerable to deforestation.

Causes of Threat: The main threat to this species is the cutting of primary upland forest.

Responses to Habitat Modification: Dusky langurs raid rubber plantations adjacent to forest.

Demographic Characteristics: A single young is born. In captivity estrus occurs at intervals of 3 weeks, and gestation takes 20 weeks. A maximum life span of 10 years has been recorded (Medway 1978).

Key Behaviors: The consumption of mature leaves enables dusky langurs to reduce travel in search of newly flushed leaves (Fleagle 1978). Even so, feeding on tree species with the most highly toxic secondary compounds is restricted to young leaves that have not accumulated all their defensive chemicals. When feeding on mature leaves of somewhat less toxic species, dusky langurs eat only leaf tips or petioles 55 percent of the time, usually rejecting the leaf blades. They eat leaves from a striking diversity of tree and vine species, which probably prevents consumption of high concentrations of any particular toxic compound (Curtin and Chivers 1978). This ability to avoid plant toxicity allows the species to become a pest in rubber plantations.

Conservation Measures Taken: Thai law (WARPA 1980) prohibits hunting and regulates trade in this species.

Conservation Measures Proposed: Maintaining preserves of primary upland to montane forest is the key to conservation of this species. A detailed survey of the status of this species would make it possible to determine what conservation actions are appropriate. The species used to occur in the area set aside as Thung Thong Waterfowl Reserve and may remain on Khao Tok near the reserve (Storer 1978).

Silvered langur
Presbytis cristata **(Raffles 1821)**
Mammalia, Primata, Cercopithecidae

Status: Threatened.
CITES (1979): Appendix II.
WARPA (1980): Protected-1.

Population Size and Trend: Unknown.

Distribution and History of Distribution: The silvered langur has a discontinuous range in Bangladesh, southeastern Burma, western, southwestern, and possibly southern Thailand, Kampuchea, southern Vietnam, western peninsular Malaysia, Sumatra, Java, and Borneo (Lekagul and McNeely 1977*a*, Medway 1978, Roonwal and Mohnot 1980). Occupied range in western Thailand is in the mountains north of Ratburi, and in the south it includes the lowlands and Ko Chang. In southeastern Thailand, it occurs in Khao Khieo and Khao Soi Dao wildlife sanctuaries (W. Brockelman, personal communication). If in the peninsula, the species would be in Satun Province (Lekagul and McNeely 1977a).

Geographic Status: Two of the three populations in Thailand appear to be relictual.

Habitat Requirements and Habitat Trend: Habitat use by silvered langurs has not been studied in detail, but they appear capable of living in many, including mangrove and *Nypa* palm swamps, primary lowland forest, plantations, deciduous forest, and evergreen forest up to 1,700 m elevation (Fooden 1971, Lekagul and McNeely 1977a, Eudey 1979, Roonwal and Mohnot 1980). Habitat use can vary greatly from place to place. For example, Southwick and Cadigan (1972) found the species to be absent from primary forest and in secondary forest at a very low density. The diet is mostly new leaves and leaf buds but also includes fruits, flowers, and seeds (Roonwal and Mohnot 1980). Group home range can be up to 43 ha in size (Furuya 1962).

Vulnerability of Species and Habitat: The silvered langur is vulnerable to hunting for food or as a pest. Its habitat is vulnerable to deforestation.

Causes of Threat: Deforestation is this species' main threat.

Responses to Habitat Modification: Unclear.

Demographic Characteristics: Births are of single young. Births occur aseasonally in peninsular Malaysia (Medway 1970). A maximum life span of 12 years has been recorded (Jones 1968).

Key Behaviors: Groups of silvered langurs are territorial (Bernstein 1968).

Conservation Measures Taken: Thai law (WARPA 1980) prohibits hunting and regulates trade in this species. Silvered langurs occur in Huai Kha Khaeng, Khao Khieo, and Khao Soi Dao wildlife sanctuaries (Eudey 1979, 1980, W. Brockelman personal communication).

Conservation Measures Proposed: More information is needed on this species before conservation actions can be planned. Steps should be taken to be sure that protection of the known populations is adequate.

Phayre's langur
Presbytis phayrei (Blyth 1847)
Mammalia, Primata, Cercopithecidae

Status: Threatened.
CITES (1979): Appendix II.
WARPA (1980): Protected-1.
Population Size and Trend: Unknown.
Distribution and History of Distribution: Phayre's langur occurs in Bangladesh, Burma, southwestern China, northern Lao PDR and Vietnam, and northern and western Thailand as far south as 14° N (Lekagul and McNeely 1977a).
Geographic Status: This is the northern counterpart of the dusky langur. Thailand is the southern limit of its range.
Habitat Requirements and Habitat Trend: Habitat use by Phayre's langur is not known in detail, but it occurs in primary evergreen forest, deciduous forest, and bamboo thickets, usually in uplands sparsely populated by man. The diet consists of leaves and some fruit (Fooden 1971, Lekagul and McNeely 1977a, Eudey 1979, Roonwal and Mohnot 1980).
Vulnerability of Species and Habitat: The species is hunted for food and supposed medicinal value in Burma (Lekagul and McNeely 1977a, Roonwal and Mohnot 1980) and western Thailand (A. Eudey, personal communication).
Causes of Threat: The impact of hunting may be substantial (A. Eudey, personal communication).
Responses to Habitat Modification: Unknown.
Demographic Characteristics: Unknown.
Key Behaviors: Unknown.
Conservation Measures Taken: Thai law (WARPA 1980) prohibits hunting and regulates trade in this species. Phayre's langur is reported to occur at Huai Kha Khaeng Wildlife Sanctuary (McNeely and Seidensticker 1974, IUCN 1979, Eudey 1980), Doi Khuntan National Park (IUCN 1979), and Doi Inthanon National Park (P. D. Round, personal communication).
Conservation Measures Proposed: Too little is known about this species to plan conservation action, other than to ensure protection of the two populations known to be under the jurisdiction of the Royal Forestry Department. To begin learning more, a status

survey should be undertaken. Then habitat requirements, ecology, and management issues should be evaluated.

Family Hylobatidae--The Gibbons
Introductory Comments

Gibbons are among the first animals to disappear from a forest when its exploitation by man begins (W. Brockelman, personal communication). Gibbons are shot for food by loggers and are easy to hunt. Any young that survive the fall from the tree are sold as pets. Gibbon habitat is destroyed by deforestation.

The response of gibbons to habitat modification is not clear. Gibbons in Thailand do not use patches of selectively logged forest adjacent to occupied primary forest (W. Brockelman, personal communication), probably because the animals are shot for food or for sale.

Gibbons are monogamous and evidently pair for life. They are territorial at the family level, with a minimum of about 25 ha required for a family in optimal primary forest. This leads to maximum densities of about 4 families or 16 individuals per km^2. Territories are maintained by singing and by chasing intruders (W. Brockelman, personal communication, Srikosamatara 1980).

Gibbons are protected by WARPA (1980), which prohibits hunting and allows trade only with special permission from the Wildlife Advisory Committee of the Wildlife Conservation Division.

The key to conservation of gibbons is protection of large tracts of primary forest, preferably each larger than 1,000 km^2 (Brockelman 1975). Hunting and deforestation remain a problem even in national parks; in Khao Yai National Park, the most secure park in Thailand, illegal deforestation is estimated at 0.5 percent per year (Myers 1980). Detailed recommendations have been made for improving protection by adding staff, radios, weapons, vehicles, roads, and buildings (IUCN 1979). Perimeter security and frequent patrols by large groups of armed guards on foot and in appropriate vehicles are needed to ensure the integrity of parks and the wildlife in sanctuaries (Brockelman 1979). Research is needed to determine the response of gibbons to different forestry practices, to determine if it is possible to maintain viable gibbon populations in forests managed for multiple uses.

White-handed gibbon
Hylobates lar (Linnaeus 1771)
Mammalia, Primata, Hylobatidae

Status: Endangered.
CITES 1979): Appendix I.
MAB (1980): Endangered.
USFWS 1980a): Endangered.
WARPA (1980): Protected-1.

Population Size and Trend: The estimated carrying capacity in Thai forest existing in 1973 was 55,000 families or 220,000 individuals, perhaps 2 to 5 percent of the original population (Brockelman 1975). Now the population must be much smaller.

Distribution and History of Distribution: *H. lar* occurs east of the Salween River and west of the Mekong River south from southwestern Yunnan Province (China) through Burma, Thailand (Fig. 78), and western Lao PDR, to central Malaya. A disjunct population occupies northwestern Sumatra. The species is absent from eastern and southeastern Thailand (Marshall and Marshall 1976, Lekagul and McNeely 1977a, Srikosamatara and Doungkhae 1982). *H. lar* has small areas of overlapping distribution with *H. pileatus* in Khao Yai National Park, Thailand, and with *H. agilis* and in the vicinity of Lake Toba, Sumatra (Marshall et al. 1972, Brockelman 1975, Marshall and Marshall 1976, Gittins 1977). Local distributions of *H. lar* and *H. agilis* adjoin but do not overlap along the Thai-Malaysian border at Ulu Mudah, Kedah (Marshall 1981).

Geographic Status: Most of the range of *H. lar* is in Thailand.

Habitat Requirements and Habitat Trend: This species is exclusively arboreal. It occupies primary forest of various types, including rainforest, evergreen, and mixed deciduous-evergreen forest (Lekagul and McNeely 1977a, Brockelman 1975, 1978). *H. lar* has not been found in dry deciduous dipterocarp forest in Thailand (Marshall et al. 1972), and this habitat apparently is a barrier to dispersal of *H. lar* among islands of suitable habitat in the Khorat Plateau (Srikosamatara and Doungkhae 1982). From an original 80 percent, forest cover of Thailand has declined to 25 percent in 1978 (Myers 1980). Berkson et al. 1968) reported *H. lar* in secondary forest, but these were animals introduced onto an island without better habitat. Density of *H. lar* ranges up to about 3.5 families per km^2 (Brockelman 1975). The diet is about 75 percent fruit, 20 .lh8

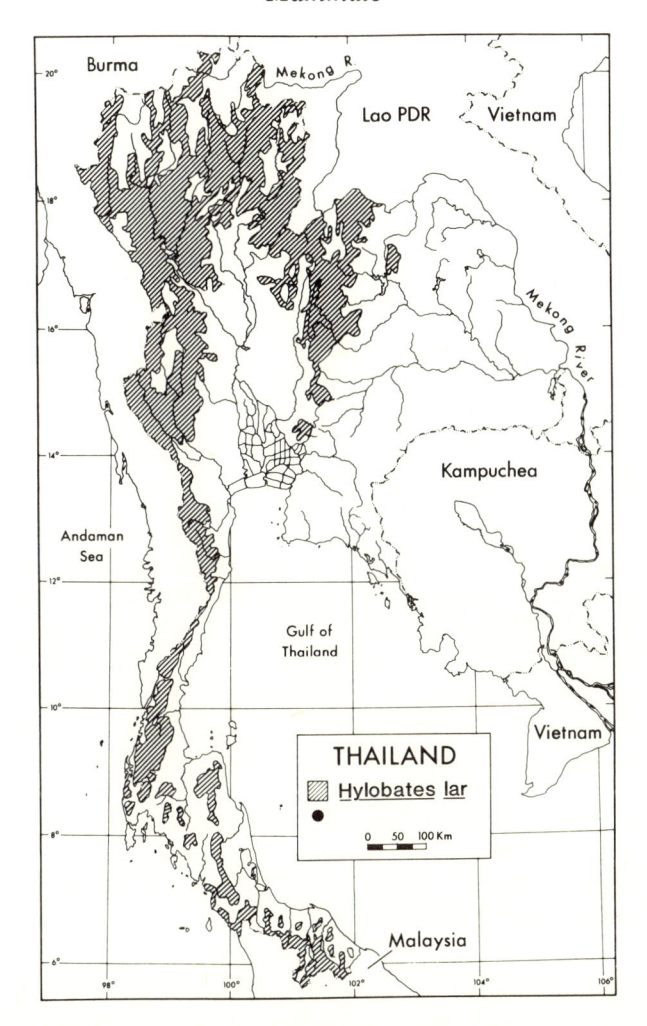

Fig. 78. Distribution of the White-handed Gibbon (*Hylobates lar*).

percent leaves and buds, and 5 percent small animals (Lekagul and McNeely 1977a). In the dry season, open water is a necessity.

Vulnerability of Species and Habitat: See the Introductory Comments. The 1980 price in the weekend market of Bangkok was US $90 (our observation).

Causes of Threat: See the Introductory Comments.

Responses to Habitat Modification: See the Introductory Comments. During selective logging in Malaysia, animals shifted their home ranges to avoid centers of logging activity. Afterwards, their home ranges were somewhat different than before, and the animals rested more and fed, sang, and travelled less (Johns 1986). The population persisted, however, because it was not hunted.

Demographic Characteristics: Population biology of *H. lar* appears similar to that of *H. pileatus*, which is better known.

Key Behaviors: See the Introductory Comments. Solo calls of adult males advertise their willingness to defend a territory, whereas subadult males engage in vocal duels, apparently enabling females to compare the vigor of potential mates and territory-holders (Raemaekers and Raemaekers 1984).

Conservation Measures Taken: See the Introductory Comments. *H. lar* occurs in Khao Yai, Doi Inthanon, Ramkhamhaeng, Tham Than Rot, and Nam Nao national parks and in Huai Kha Khaeng, Thung Yai, Khlong Saeng, Khao Banthat, Doi Chiang Dao, and possibly Khun Yuam, Phu Miang-Phu Thong, Salawin, Pachi River, and Mae Tun wildlife sanctuaries (IUCN 1979); and possibly Thaleban National Park (Dobias 1982).

Conservation Measures Proposed: See the Introductory Comments.

Pileated gibbon
Hylobates pileatus Gray 1842
Mammalia, Primata, Hylobatidae

Status: Endangered.
IUCN Red Data Book (1978): Endangered.
CITES (1979): Appendix I.
IUCN (1979): Threatened.
MAB (1979): Endangered.
USFWS (1980a): Endangered.
WARPA (1980): Protected-1.

Population Size and Trend: Populations are estimated to total 6,000 to 12,000 in Khao Soi Dao Wildlife Sanctuary and Khao Yai and Khao Chamao national parks (Brockelman 1979). Extrapolation from known densities yields estimates of 13,600 in Thailand, 28,800 in Kampuchea, and 800 in Lao PDR, a total of 43,200 (Brockelman 1975). Numbers everywhere are thought to be declining (IUCN Red Data Book 1978). An 80-90 percent reduction in the

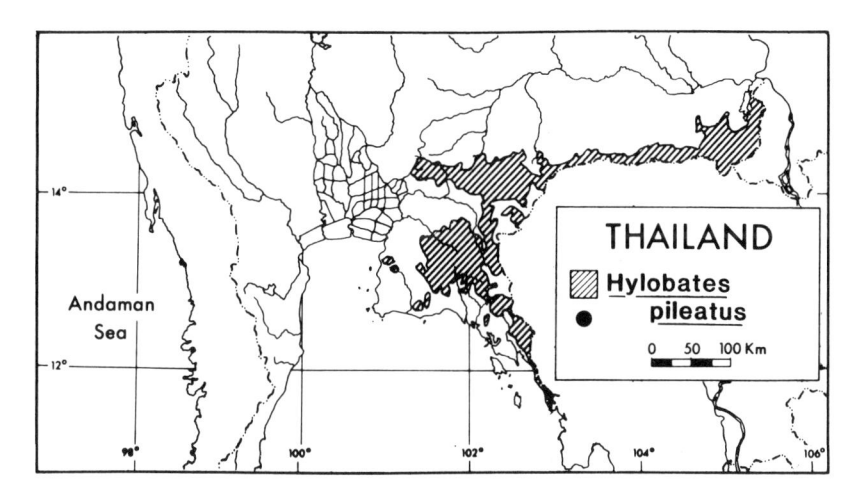

Fig. 79. Distribution of the Pileated Gibbon (*Hylobates pileatus*).

Thai population is predicted by the year 2000 at the present rate of deforestation, with *H. pileatus* likely to survive only in the best-protected preserves. Possibly 2 to 3 million lived in Thailand before deforestation began (Brockelman 1975).

Distribution and History of Distribution: This species occurs from Khao Yai National Park south and east in Thailand (Fig. 79) to the uplands of Kampuchea, and to extreme southern Lao PDR, and southwestern Vietnam west of the Mekong River (Marshall et al. 1972, Brockelman 1975, Marshall and Marshall 1976). Originally this range was continuous over large units of habitat, but now the distribution of *H. pileatus* is fragmented and rapidly shrinking (Brockelman 1975).

Geographic Status: Distribution in Thailand is roughly the northwestern one-third of the species' range.

Habitat Requirements and Habitat Trend: This species is exclusively arboreal. It occupies primary forest of several types, including rainforest, evergreen, and mixed deciduous-evergreen forests (Brockelman 1975, 1978; Lekagul and McNeely 1977a). From an original 80 percent, forest cover of Thailand has declined to 25 percent in 1978 (Myers 1980). All suitable habitat outside of protected areas is expected to be lost before the year 2,000 (IUCN 1978). Density of *H. pileatus* reaches 6.5 families per km^2 in part of Khao Soi Dao--perhaps the densest gibbon population in Asia (Brockelman 1979). At Khao Yai National Park, where both *H.*

pileatus and *H. lar* occupy the forest in non-overlapping territories, each has similar density of 1-2 families per km² (Brockelman 1975). The diet appears similar to that of *H. lar*, mostly fruit, plus leaves, buds, and small animals. In the dry season, open water is essential.

Vulnerability of Species and Habitat: See the Introductory Comments. Gibbons are shot for food by loggers and are easy to hunt. Any young that survive the fall are sold as pets, even though they may become dangerous to man when they mature. Gibbons are among the first animals to disappear from a forest when its exploitation by man begins (W. Brockelman, personal communication).

Causes of Threat: See the Introductory Comments.

Responses to Habitat Modification: See the Introductory Comments.

Demographic Characteristics: Age at sexual maturity is about 7.5 years, and one young is born every 2.5 years thereafter, though gestation takes only 7.5 months. Hence the time required for a female to produce sexually mature replacements for herself and her mate would be at least 17.5 years. The longevity record in captivity is 31 years, but survival rate in the wild is unknown. In stable, dense population of gibbons, 1.6 offspring are produced per km² per year, so if hunters kill only one per km² per year, the population will decline (W. Brockelman, personal communication).

Key Behaviors: See the Introductory Comments.

Conservation Measures Taken: See the Introductory Comments. *H. pileatus* occurs in Khao Soi Dao Wildlife Sanctuary and Khao Yai and Khao Chamao national parks.

Conservation Measures Proposed: See the Introductory Comments.

Agile gibbon
Hylobates agilis **Cuvier 1821**
Mammalia, Primata, Hylobatidae

Status: Endangered
CITES (1979): Appendix I.
MAB (1979): Endangered.
USFWS (1980a): Endangered.
WARPA (1980): Protected-1.

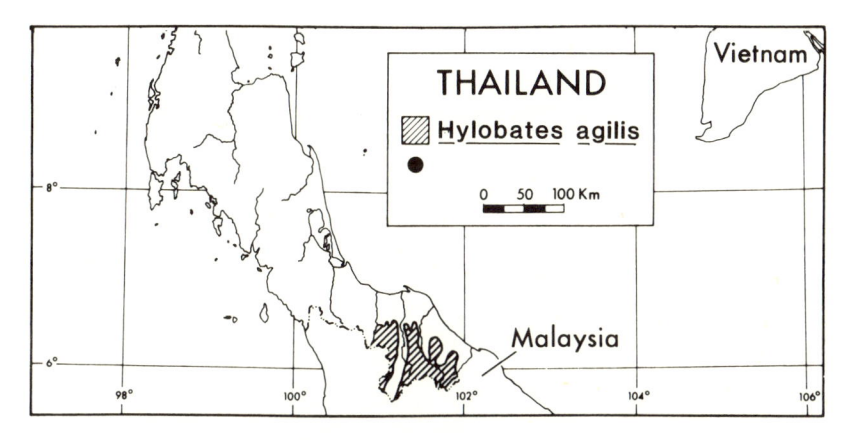

Fig. 80. Distribution of the Agile Gibbon (*Hylobates agilis*).

Population Size and Trend: Unknown. The population in Thailand is certain to be small.

Distribution and History of Distribution: *H. agilis* occurs in three isolated populations in Sumatra and Borneo, in Malaya between the Perak and Mudah Rivers, and in Yala Province, Thailand (Fig. 80; Medway 1969, Brockelman 1975, Marshall and Marshall 1976, Lekagul and McNeely 1977a, Marshall 1981). In Thailand, *H. agilis* occurs from the east side of Khlong Thepha eastward to Waeng, near Sungei Golok. *H. agilis* has small areas of overlapping distribution with *H. lar* in the vicinity of Lake Toba, Sumatra (Gittins 1977, Marshall and Marshall 1976), but along the Thai-Malaysian border at Ulu Mudah, Kedah, they adjoin without overlapping (Marshall 1981).

Geographic Status: The Thai populations are on the northern periphery of the species' range. *H. agilis* appears to have a relictual distribution, being surrounded by its congener, *H. lar* (Chivers 1978).

Habitat Requirements and Habitat Trend: This species is exclusively arboreal and occupies primary forest at all elevations (Chivers 1978). Essentially all lowland forest in the Thai portion of *agilis* range has been cleared, and the only remaining habitat is on high mountain ridges. Agile gibbons appear to occupy smaller territories than do lar gibbons (Chivers 1978), and density of agile gibbons is about one-third that of siamangs (Carpenter 1940). The diet may be similar to that of other gibbons, but Lekagul and McNeely (1977a) noted dental specializations that suggest otherwise. Observations of agile gibbons and siamangs feeding in the same tree (Carpenter 1940) indicate that these different-sized species do not compete for food.

Vulnerability of Species and Habitat: See the Introductory Comments.

Causes of Threat: See the Introductory Comments.

Responses to Habitat Modification: See the Introductory Comments.

Demographic Characteristics: Population biology of *H. agilis* is like that of *H. pileatus*.

Key Behaviors: See the Introductory Comments.

Conservation Measures Taken: See the Introductory Comments.

Conservation Measures Proposed: See the Introductory Comments. One or more preserves should be established based on the recent survey of *H. agilis* by J. T. Marshall, Jr.

Family Manidae--The Pangolins
Introductory Comments

Both of the pangolins, genus *Manis*, that occur in Southeast Asia are known from Thailand. The Malayan pangolin, *M. javanica*, is widespread in Thailand. The Chinese pangolin, *M. pentadactyla*, is known from two specimens taken on Doi Inthanon in Chiang Mai Province in the 1930s.

For many centuries and throughout the region, both have been eaten and their epidermal scales have been an important item of trade. Pharmacological tradition in Thailand, China, and elsewhere ascribes many medicinal properties to scales and other pangolin tissues. While this exploitation probably did little harm to pangolin populations in the past, at modern, high human densities it threatens many local populations with extirpation.

A new threat has arisen in recent years. Triangular marks appear on pangolin hides when the scales are removed. In the late 1970s these skins began to be used extensively in the manufacture of cowboy boots in Western nations. The trade is briskly escalating, as evidenced by the following U.S. import figures: none (1977), 5,000 (1978), 15,000 (1979), 31,000 (1980). Most of these were imported from Japan with lesser amounts from Taiwan, Spain,

Singapore, and Thailand. In over 50 percent of the cases, the declaration of country of origin was outside the biological range of the species being imported (TRAFFIC 1981). The effects of this exploitation on pangolin populations in Southeast Asia are undocumented.

Malayan pangolin
Manis javanica Desmarest 1822
Mammalia, Pholidota, Manidae

Status: Threatened.
CITES (1979): Appendix II.
WARPA (1980): Protected-1.

Population Size and Trend: There is scant information in the literature on the status of pangolin populations in Southeast Asia, but there is a concern that *Manis* are becoming increasingly rare (TRAFFIC 1981). Medway (1969) considered *M. javanica* to be "widespread and not uncommon" throughout peninsular Malaysia. Although over 900 skins imported into the United States between October 1979 and December 1980 from Japan and Singapore were claimed to have come originally from Singapore (TRAFFIC 1980), *M. javanica* is rare or extirpated there (Medway 1969).

Distribution and History of Distribution: This *Manis* is found in Burma, all of Thailand, southern Lao PDR, Vietnam, Kampuchea, peninsular Malaysia (including Penang Island), Singapore, Sumatra (including the Lingga and Rhio archipelagoes, Bangka, Belitung, Pagai, and Nias), Java, Bali, the North Natuna Islands in the South China Sea, Borneo (including Karimata), and the Philippine island of Palawan (Flower 1900, Chasen 1940, Lekagul and McNeely 1977*a*). A similar, but larger, pangolin is known from the Pleistocene of Java (Hooijer 1974).

Geographic Status: In northern Thailand, *M. javanica* occurs near the northern limit of its range.

Habitat Requirements and Habitat Trend: Malayan pangolins occur in a wide variety of habitats. Thai *M. javanica* prefer forest but are found in rubber plantations, gardens, and elsewhere around human settlement. They have been found at over 1,300 m in Borneo. Teeth are lacking. Ants, termites, and their larvae are gathered with the long, protrusible, sticky tongue. The stomach secretes powerful gastric juices and has chitinous "teeth" in the pyloric region to help digest the insects. Malayan pangolins may at times ingest small stones to help grind insects (Allen and Coolidge 1940, Harrison 1961, Davis 1962, Medway 1969, Krause and Leeson 1974, Lekagul and McNeely 1977a).

Vulnerability of Species and Habitat: The meat of this pangolin tastes good. Some individuals weigh over 7 kg. They are easily caught and killed. They are sometimes kept as semiwild pets. The Chinese pharmacological tradition attributes antiseptic and curative properties to the scales (Flower 1900, Davis 1962, Harrison and Yin 1965).

Causes of Threat: Overhunting is the major threat to these pangolins. Over 60 tons of dried scales were exported from Sarawak between 1958 and 1964, probably representing the deaths of over 50,000 pangolins. Most of these were probably captured in Kalimantan and smuggled over the border into Sarawak. In Sarawak the scales were removed from the skins and shipped to Hong Kong and Singapore, where they were cleaned, sorted, and reshipped to China (Harrison and Yin 1965). Over 24,000 skins were imported into the United States in 1979 and 1980 (TRAFFIC 1981). In 1982, the United States imported 4,147 skins and 875 manufactured products of this species with the country of origin declared as Thailand (TRAFFIC 1984). In famine-stricken areas, such as Kampuchea, these easily-killed animals are probably hunted heavily for meat. There is a minor trade in live animals, but the species is difficult to feed in captivity.

Responses to Habitat Modification: Malayan pangolins can survive and reproduce in cultivated areas and near villages.

Demographic Characteristics: The female has a single pair of mammae and gives birth to a single young, but rarely does so in captivity. Gestation is probably short (2-3 months?). Young are probably weaned by about 3 months (Davis 1962, Medway 1969, Lekagul and McNeely 1977a).

Key Behaviors: When approached by man or other predators, *M. javanica* rolls up into a ball to protect its soft underbelly. The female carries the young on her back and curls up around it when assuming the defensive posture. Pangolins are essentially asocial, but several adults are sometimes found in the same burrow. They are primarily terrestrial, making burrows in soil, but they can climb well (with the aid of the prehensile tail) when pursued by dogs or in search of termite nests. During the day they remain in the burrow, sealing off the entrance with dirt or vegetation. At night they feed on termites and ants by digging into the nests with their powerful, clawed forefeet. (Flower 1900, Davis 1962, Harrison and Yin 1965, Medway 1969, Lekagul and McNeely 1977a).

Conservation Measures Taken: Thai law (WARPA 1980) prohibits hunting and regulates trade in *M. javanica*. The species undoubtedly occurs in many Thai reserves. It is totally protected by law in peninsular Malaysia (Medway 1969).

Conservation Measures Proposed: Considering the large volume of world trade in *M. javanica* products, very little is known of its ecology. A better knowledge of its reproductive biology is needed. If harvested on a sustained yield basis, this species can continue to be a source of food and income for villagers. Because the meat is used as human food, the skin is sold to hide dealers, and the scales are sold to the Thai and Chinese apothecary trade, there is little waste. Few vertebrates can turn ants and termites into human food and items of commerce on such a large scale as *Manis* can. It is also probably an important food source to large predators in some areas.

Chinese pangolin
Manis pentadactyla Linnaeus 1768
Mammalia, Pholidota, Manidae

Status: Threatened.
CITES (1979): Appendix II.
WARPA (1980): Protected-1.

Population Size and Trend: This species has declined in parts of southeastern China because of overhunting (Allen 1940). It has been drastically reduced in Hong Kong (Wong 1975). The large number of trade skins said to be from Taiwan originally may not be congruent with the number that actually occur there (TRAFFIC 1981). It may be becoming rare in northern Southeast Asia (TRAFFIC 1981). It is not known if *M. pentadactyla* still survives in Thailand. The last (and only) Thai specimens were taken in the 1930s (Allen and Coolidge 1940).

Distribution and History of Distribution: Chinese pangolins occur in Nepal, Sikkim, Assam, Burma, China north to the Yangtze

River, Taiwan, Hainan, Vietnam, and Lao PDR (Allen 1940, Ellerman and Morrison-Scott 1951, Van Peenen et al. 1969). Wharton (1966:54) believed that they occur in northern Kampuchea. Allen and Coolidge (1940) reported taking two on Doi Inthanon in Chiang Mai Province, Thailand.

Geographic Status: If Chinese pangolins occur in Thailand today they do so near the southern limits of the species' range. If restricted to Thailand's highest mountain, Doi Inthanon, *M. pentadactyla* is probably a relict in Thailand.

Habitat Requirements and Habitat Trend: This species is found in both primary and secondary forest from near sea level to over 2,500 m in the Himalayas. Teeth are lacking. Ants and termites and their larvae (and possibly the larvae of bees and wasps) are gathered with the long, protrusible, sticky tongue. The stomach secretes powerful acids and has chitinous "teeth" in the pyloric region to help digest insects (Blanford 1888-1891, Allen 1940, Krause and Leeson 1974, Lekagul and McNeely 1977a)

Vulnerability of Species and Habitat: Chinese pangolins are easily caught and killed. The Chinese, who relish the flesh and use the scales for "medicine", build pitfalls near *Manis* burrows and hunt them with dogs (Allen 1940).

Causes of Threat: Overhunting for food, hides, and scales threatens many populations of *M. pentadactyla*. The United States imported over 12,500 skins of this species in 1979 and 1980 (TRAFFIC 1981). In 1982, the United States imported 152 skins and 100 manufactured products of this species with the country of origin declared as Thailand (TRAFFIC 1984). There is a minor trade in live animals.

Responses to Habitat Modification: Chinese pangolins thrive in secondary forest.

Demographic Characteristics: Captives sometimes give birth, but typically these are females that were captured while pregnant. One or rarely two young are born in spring in southern China. The scales begin to harden on the second day and the eyes open in 9-10 days (Blanford 1888-1891, Allen 1940, Allen and Coolidge 1940, Masui 1967, Lekagul and McNeely 1977a).

Key Behaviors: These nocturnal insectivores are excellent, rapid diggers. Their burrows may be 4 m deep and have a large chamber at the end. They block off the entrance when they are inside. They may take shelter in rock crevices, and they can climb (Blanford 1888-1891, Allen 1940).

Conservation Measures Taken: Thai law (WARPA 1980) prohibits hunting and regulates trade in this species. The single known Thai locality for *M. pentadactyla* is Doi Inthanon, now a national park.

Conservation Measures Proposed: Doi Inthanon and other high mountains of northern Thailand should be searched for *M. pentadactyla*. Any populations found would require special protection to prevent them from being hunted to extinction.

Family Sciuridae--The Squirrels
Introductory Comments

Twenty-seven species of squirrels of 13 genera are known to occur in Thailand, and several more may be found near the Malaysian border by future researchers (Askins 1977). Most require forest habitats and some are quite intolerant of habitat disturbance. Deforestation is a major threat to many of the Thai sciurids. Muul and Lim (1978) proposed that the depauperate flying squirrel fauna of Java resulted partly from the long history of deforestation on that island and that Borneo's rich flying squirrel fauna endures because of its large, intact forest tracts. Many Thai sciurids are colorful and attractive as pets. Almost 9,000 live *Callosciurus* were legally exported from Thailand between 1967 and 1971 (Royal Forestry Department 1972). Many of the flying squirrels are easily tamed, but they are delicate and do not survive for long in captivity without professional care (Prater 1971). Some Southeast Asian sciurids, such as the *Ratufa* species, are often exhibited (but rarely bred) in zoos. Many are large enough to eat, and some of the more colorful forms are stuffed and sold in curio shops (e.g., Jones 1975, Askins 1977:381).

Thailand has many endemic subspecies of squirrels. Some, especially the island races, have very restricted distributions, making them vulnerable to local habitat disturbance. Overall squirrel density is surprisingly low in the tropical forests of Southeast Asia. This may be due to the irregular, dispersed nature of the food resources, competition for food with other arboreal animals (notably primates--MacKinnon 1978), and diverse and abundant predators.

Inherently low population densities, coupled with the low reproductive rates and intolerance of disturbance by some species, make squirrels good indicators of habitat disruption. The flying squirrels are especially useful in this regard (I. Muul, personal communication). Muul and Lim (1978:368) summarized the differing responses of Malaysian flying squirrels to habitat changes.

Many arboreal kinds (especially the nocturnal flying squirrels) are seldom seen, poorly understood, and notoriously difficult to study (Muul and Lim 1974, Medway 1978). Most are reluctant to enter traps. Concentrating research activity on nests may be the best way to study these rodents (Muul and Lim 1974).

Controlling the direct commercial exploitation of some species is desirable, but the best way to preserve the arboreal Thai squirrels is to preserve intact stands of representative forest types. The selective extraction of relatively few tall trees can have profound deleterious effects on some species. Other species thrive in secondary forest and even in poorly-tended rubber plantations. Squirrel densities are much greater in mixed fruit-rubber plantations than in pure stands of rubber (Muul and Lim 1978).

We have chosen seven Thai sciurids to illustrate the problems facing the fauna. These include, but are not restricted to, species that fare best in unbroken primary forest.

Cream-colored giant squirrel
Ratufa affinis **(Raffles 1822)**
Mammalia, Rodentia, Sciuridae

Status: Threatened.
CITES (1979): Appendix II.
WARPA (1980): Protected-1.

Population Size and Trend: Askins (1977) gave no information on the status of this squirrel in Thailand, but it is quite abundant in the mature forests of northern Borneo (Davis 1962). In peninsular Malaysia it is definitely less common than *Ratufa bicolor* (Harrison and Traub 1950). In some areas, such as Singapore (Medway 1978), it is now rare or extinct.

Distribution and History of Distribution: *Ratufa affinis* is known from the southern part of the Tenasserim of Burma, Thailand south of the Isthmus of Kra (Fig. 81), peninsular Malaysia,

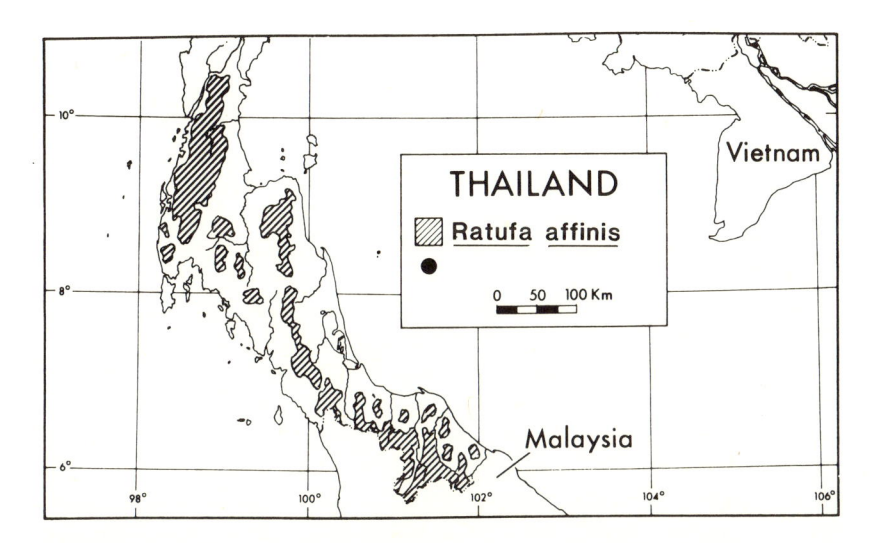

Fig. 81. Distribution of the Cream-colored Giant Squirrel (*Ratufa affinis*).

Singapore, Sumatra (including the Riau Archipelago, the Lingga Archipelago, Banjak, Mansala Island in Tapanuli Bay, and the Batu Islands), Bangka, Belitung, the Natuna Islands in the South China Sea, and Borneo (including the coastal islands of Panembangam, Banggi, Sandakan, Laut, and Sebuku). Except for its possible disappearance from Singapore, the historical range is not known to differ (Chasen and Kloss 1927, Kloss 1932, Chasen 1940, Askins 1977, Medway 1978).

Geographic Status: This squirrel reaches the northern limit of its range in southern Thailand.

Habitat Requirements and Habitat Trend: The cream-colored giant squirrel inhabits the canopy of tall, mature forests from the lowlands to over 1,600 m (in Borneo). It is also found in continuous stands of secondary forest (Allen and Coolidge 1940, Harrison 1961, Davis 1962, Askins 1977, Ide and Kethley 1977, Medway 1978, I. Muul personal communication). In peninsular Malaysia this species forages mainly at the mid-canopy level and spends less time in the upper canopy than *Ratufa bicolor* (Payne 1980). The diet consists mostly of seeds (Payne 1980) but also includes fruit pulp, leaves and shoots, flowers, and bark (Harrison 1954, 1961, 1962, Davis 1962, Walker 1975, MacKinnon 1978).

Vulnerability of Species and Habitat: *Ratufa* is coveted by zoos (Dobroruka 1975). The cream-colored giant squirrel is noisy and not afraid of man. The species weighs over 1 kg (Medway 1978). Its preference for tall forest makes it vulnerable to timber extraction.

Causes of Threat: Deforestation is the primary threat.

Responses to Habitat Modification: This species can survive in unbroken secondary forest, but if the forest is reduced to patches, *R. affinis* is lost (I. Muul, personal communication).

Demographic Characteristics: The female has six mammae (Medway 1978). Litters of three young are known, but most are probably smaller (Davis 1962).

Key Behaviors: These diurnal squirrels are rarely seen on the ground. Their greatest activity in the canopy of peninsular Malaysian rainforest was reported to be between 23 and 30 m above the ground. They build nests of leaves and twigs. They are less sedentary than the larger *R. bicolor* and use the lower canopy more (Harrison 1961, MacKinnon 1978, Medway 1978). Animals usually occur singly; pairs are rarely seen (Davis 1962). *Ratufa* does not cache seeds where they would be likely to germinate (Payne 1980).

Conservation Measures Taken: Thai law (WARPA 1980) prohibits hunting and regulates trade in this species.

Conservation Measures Proposed: Cream-colored giant squirrels are large, attractive, noisy, and diurnal, all of which make them highly visible to tourists. They thus enrich the experience of the visitor to national parks and other reserves. The conservation of intact stands of mature forest in southern Thailand would benefit *R. affinis* and a multitude of other forest species.

Black giant squirrel
Ratufa bicolor (Sparrman 1778)
Mammalia, Rodentia, Sciuridae

Status: Threatened.
CITES (1979): Appendix II.
WARPA (1980): Protected-1.

Population Size and Trend: Askins (1977) gave no information on the status of this squirrel in Thailand. In some areas, such as

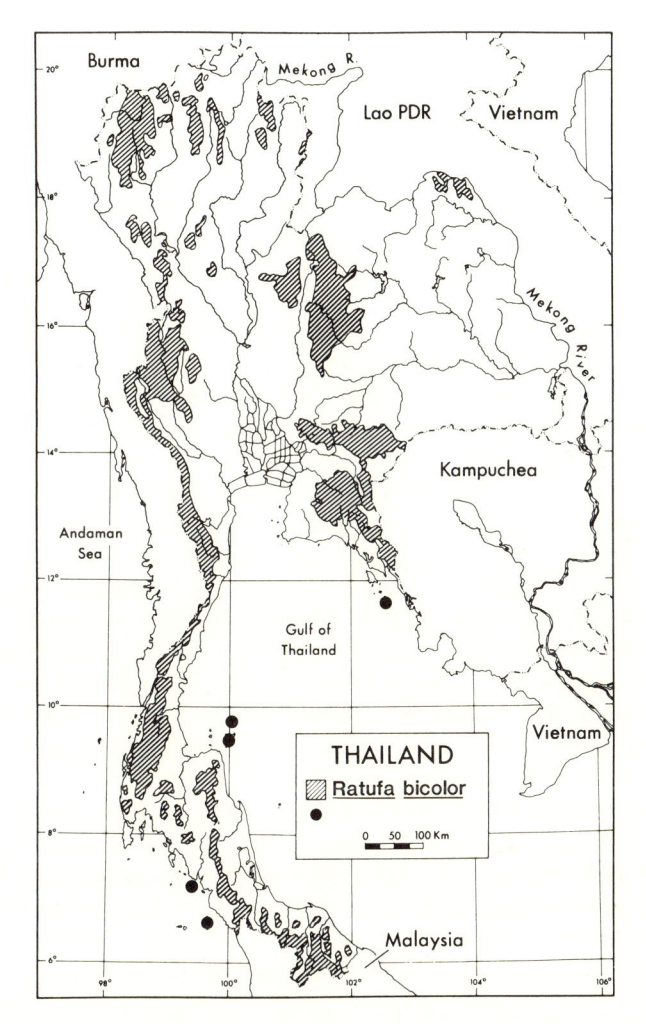

Fig. 82. Distribution of the Black Giant Squirrel (*Ratufa bicolor*).

Hainan (Allen 1940), it is rare and local. Wiles (1981) found it to be the least common of the diurnal tree squirrels at Salak Phra Wildlife Sanctuary, Kanchanaburi Province, because of restrictive habitat requirements.

Distribution and History of Distribution: This squirrel is known from Nepal, Sikkim, Bhutan, India (west Bengal, Assam, Nagaland), Burma (including many islands of the Mergui Archipelago), Yunnan, Hainan, Vietnam (including Con Son Island), Lao

PDR, Kampuchea, Thailand (except most of the northeastern Khorat Plateau), peninsular Malaysia (including the islands of Langkawi, Penang, and Tioman), Sumatra (including the Banjak and Batu Islands), Java, Bali, and the Anambas Islands and the Natuna Islands in the South China Sea. Four Thai subspecies are of special interest because of their restricted, insular distributions (Fig. 82): *R. b. sinus* of Ko Kut in the Gulf of Thailand; *R. b. decolorata* of Ko Samui and Ko Phangnga in the Gulf of Thailand; *R. b. melanopepla* of Telibon Island, Trang Province, in the Andaman Sea; and *R. b. fretensis* of Ko Tarutao and the Malaysian Langkawi Islands in the Straits of Malacca (Chasen and Kloss 1927, Allen 1940, Chasen 1940, Ellerman and Morrison-Scott 1951, Medway 1966, 1978, Van Peenen et al. 1969, Prater 1971, Askins 1977, Agrawal and Chakraborty 1979). Dobroruka's (1975) references to *R. b. bicolor* in Borneo were probably misidentified *R. affinis*.

Geographic Status: Thailand is central in the range of *bicolor*.

Habitat Requirements and Habitat Trend: This *Ratufa* is a canopy specialist, inhabiting the upper story of tall, mature forest from sea level to over 1,800 m. In peninsular Malaysia this species forages both in the middle and upper canopy, and it spends more time in the upper canopy than *Ratufa affinis* (Payne 1980). Most *R. bicolor* are found in the lowlands. At Salak Phra Wildlife Sanctuary, *R. bicolor* occurs only in the scattered portions of lowland bamboo forest that include large deciduous trees and is absent from upland bamboo forest and dry dipterocarp forest, which lack tall trees (Wiles 1981). Some inhabit continuous stands of secondary forest. The diet consists mostly of seeds (Payne 1980) but also includes fruit pulp (especially the figs, *Ficus*), leaves and shoots, flowers, bark, and possibly insects and the eggs of birds (Blanford 1888-1891, Allen 1940, Chasen 1940, Harrison and Traub 1950, Harrison 1961, 1962, Medway 1966, 1978, Prater 1971, Dobroruka 1975, Walker 1975, Askins 1977, MacKinnon 1978, I. Muul personal communication).

Vulnerability of Species and Habitat: *Ratufa* is coveted by zoos (Dobroruka 1975). The black giant squirrel is noisy and not afraid of man. Some individuals scold people. In certain areas they raid orchards and harm young coconut trees. Some weigh over 1.5 kg (Harrison and Traub 1950, Medway 1966, 1978). A preference for nesting in the highest trees in mature forests makes *R. bicolor* vulnerable to timber extraction. The four insular subspecies of

Thailand are particularly vulnerable to habitat disruption because of their restricted ranges.

Causes of Threat: Deforestation threatens all forms but is especially serious in the case of *R. b. decolorata* of Ko Samui. As early as 1915, Robinson and Kloss expressed concern that Ko Samui's 8,000 people were relentlessly destroying habitat and the native mammals. The population has grown to over 30,000 people, and all of the native primary forest is gone (Marshall and Nongngork 1970). There is a minor trade in live *R. bicolor*.

Responses to Habitat Modification: This species requires primary or mature secondary forest (I. Muul, personal communication).

Demographic Characteristics: Mating has not been observed and the gestation period is unknown. The female has six mammae (Medway 1978), but all reported litters have been single births. Young first leave the nest when about 33 days old. Females are apparently capable of producing several litters per year (Willis 1980), but the reproductive rate in the wild is unknown. Captives have lived 11 years (Medway 1978).

Key Behaviors: The black giant squirrel builds large, globular nests on thin, outer branches in the tops of tall trees. The nest is of twigs and leaves. In captivity, a male helped a female build the nest, but she was intolerant of him when she had young, and no paternal care of juveniles was seen (Harrison and Traub 1950, Askins 1977, Medway 1978, Willis 1980). *R. bicolor* is not a social rodent; most sightings are of solitary animals. Pairs and family groups of 3-4 are sometimes seen. Both sexes scent-mark with urine and by rubbing exudates from their cheek glands. Visible marks are made by gnawing the bark from sections of branches. These squirrels express alarm and agitation by arcing the tail and erecting the tail fur. They do not employ the upright bipedal alarm stance seen in most squirrels (Blanford 1888-1891, Dobroruka 1975, MacKinnon 1978, Medway 1978). A variey of vocalizations have been described for *R. bicolor* (reviewed by Dobroruka 1975), but the loudest sound Dobroruka's captives made was a chattering of the teeth. His animals lived together peacefully with no hierarchy. An animal to first reach a point on a branch treated later arrivals as subordinates. There was no consistent pattern of dominance. A few ritualized chases were seen, but no fights.

Black giant squirrels are diurnal or crepuscular and locate food visually. They are agile and can leap distances up to 6 m. Most of their activity in a peninsular Malaysian rainforest was reported to be between 23 and 30 m above the ground. Sometimes they ventured into the tall, emergent crowns. Captives cache food, but in the wild animals do not cache seeds where they would be likely to germinate (Allen 1940, Harrison 1961, Prater 1971, Dobroruka 1975, MacKinnon 1978, Medway 1978, Payne 1980, Willis 1980).

Conservation Measures Taken: Thai law (WARPA 1980) prohibits hunting and regulates trade in this species. *Ratufa bicolor fretensis* occurs in Tarutao Marine National Park. The species also is present at Salak Phra Wildlife Sanctuary (Wiles 1981). The black giant squirrel has bred in captivity (e.g., Acharjyo and Misra 1973, Olney 1980, Willis 1980).

Conservation Measures Proposed: Like *R. affinis*, *R. bicolor* has enhanced the tourism value of parks and reserves. Intact tracts of tall, mature forest should be preserved for the benefit of this and many other forest species. A survey is needed to document the presence or absence of this species on public lands.

Lesser giant flying squirrel
Petaurista elegans **(Muller 1839)**
Mammalia, Rodentia, Sciuridae

Status: Threatened.
WARPA (1980): Protected-1.

Population Size and Trend: The lesser giant flying squirrel apparently is scarce over much of its range. In some parts of the eastern Himalayas (Askins 1977) it is quite common.

Distribution and History of Distribution: This squirrel is found in the Himalayas (Nepal, Sikkim, Assam, Tibet), Burma, Yunnan, northern Vietnam, northern Lao PDR, Thailand (Fig. 83), peninsular Malaysia, Sumatra, Java, Borneo, and possibly in the Natuna Islands in the South China Sea (Allen 1940, Chasen 1940, Ellerman and Morrison-Scott 1951, Muul and Lim 1971, Askins 1977, Feng et al. 1980).

Geographic Status: Thailand is central to the Southeast Asian range of *P. elegans*.

Habitat Requirements and Habitat Trend: *Petaurista elegans* prefers mature upland forests. It has been reported from rhodo-

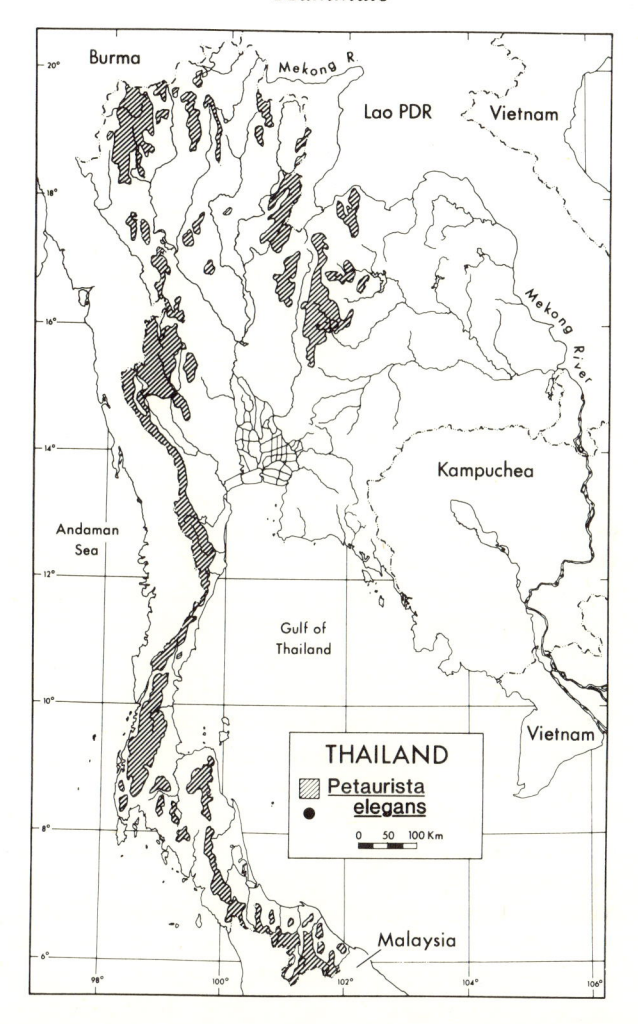

Fig. 83. Distribution of the Lesser Giant Flying Squirrel (*Petaurista elegans*).

dendron scrub and rocky cliffs in the Himalayas and pine forest in China. In tropical Southeast Asia, *P. elegans* is restricted to the tall primary forests of the hills and mountains. In peninsular Malaysia it ranges from about 225 m to above 1,500 m. It has been found at over 1,400 m in Borneo and as high as 4,000 m in the Himalayas (Allen 1940, Chasen 1940, Medway 1969, Muul and Lim 1971, Askins 1977). The digestive tract of *Petaurista* is highly modified for leaf eating, and squirrels of this genus probably are the most folivorous of the Malaysian flying squirrels (Muul and Lim 1978). They also are reported to eat shoots, twigs, nuts, fruits, and possibly insects and their larvae (Walker 1975, Askins 1977).

Vulnerability of Species and Habitat: Its preference for the primary forests of the hills and mountains makes this rodent highly vulnerable to logging operations.

Causes of Threat: Deforestation is the major threat. Even the selective extraction of the taller trees, required by *P. elegans* for nest sites, can harm populations (Muul and Lim 1978). The skins of *P. e. clarkei* have been reported to be used as trade items in China (Allen 1940).

Responses to Habitat Modification: These squirrels survive in reduced densities in primary forests that have been partially cut for timber. They do not occur in secondary forest or fruit-rubber plantations. In selectively logged forests and at lower elevations this species is replaced by *P. petaurista*. In Malaysia, it is replaced by *P. petaurista* and *Aeromys tephromelas* near human villages (Muul and Lim 1971, 1978).

Demographic Characteristics: Although the female has six mammae (Walker 1975), all of the recorded litters had only one young. The young takes 3-4 months postpartum to develop fully, and generation length in Malaysia is reported to be longer than in other squirrels, and very long compared with rats (*Rattus*). Hence, response to population loss is slow. In Malaysia, they "breed infrequently" (Muul and Lim 1978). Breeding is seasonal in the Himalayas (Askins 1977).

Key Behaviors: These nocturnal rodents prefer to make their nests in tall, hollow trees. They are quite solitary, occurring singly, in pairs, or in small family groups. With their long fingers and strong grasp they are able to reach out and pull branches toward themselves while feeding on leaves (Walker 1975, Askins 1977, Muul and Lim 1978).

Conservation Measures Taken: Thai law (WARPA 1980) prohibits hunting and regulates trade in this species. It occurs in Salak Phra Wildlife Sanctuary and Lum Nam Pai Wildlife Sanctuary (Prakobboon 1979).

Conservation Measures Proposed: The preservation of the primary forests of the hills and mountains would benefit *P. elegans* and a great variety of other forest species.

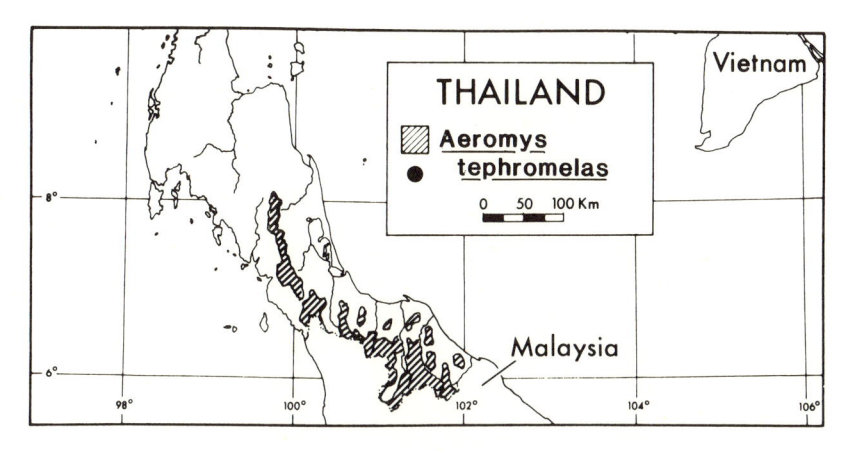

Fig. 84. Distribution of the Large Black Flying Squirrel (*Aeromys tephromelas*).

Large black flying squirrel
Aeromys tephromelas (Gunther 1873)
Mammalia, Rodentia, Sciuridae

Status: Threatened.

Population Size and Trend: This species is rare throughout its range (Muul and Lim 1978, I. Muul personal communication). It seems to have been rare since the time of its discovery.

Distribution and History of Distribution: The large black flying squirrel occurs in Thailand from Nakhon Si Thammarat Province south (Fig. 84), peninsular Malaysia (including Penang Island), Sumatra, and Borneo (Chasen 1940, Askins 1977, Medway 1978, I. Muul personal communication).

Geographic Status: *Aeromys tephromelas* reaches the northern limit of its range in southern Thailand.

Habitat Requirements and Habitat Trend: This squirrel is a denizen of the unbroken and partially cut mature forests of the lowlands and hills. It can subsist on leaves but also takes shoots, fruits, nuts, and possibly some insects (Harrison 1954, 1961, Walker 1975, Askins 1977, Medway 1978, Muul and Lim 1978).

Vulnerability of Species and Habitat: The lowland forests this rodent occupies are among the first to be cut.

Causes of Threat: Deforestation is its chief threat. Boonsong Lekagul has seen these squirrels being sold in curio stores in

Chiang Mai (Askins 1977), far removed from their natural range, indicating that there is a trade in taxidermic mounts of *Aeromys*.

Responses to Habitat Modification: This *Aeromys* is rare in undisturbed and partially cut primary forest. It is not found at all in secondary forest or plantations of fruit and rubber. In mixed secondary and primary forest in peninsular Malaysia it is able to live near human villages (Muul and Lim 1971, 1978).

Demographic Characteristics: The litter is always one young. The young needs 3-4 months postpartum to develop fully. The population turnover is slow and adults "breed infrequently" (Muul and Lim 1978).

Key Behaviors: These nocturnal, canopy-dwelling rodents spend the day in tree hollows (Harrison 1961, Walker 1975, Medway 1978). Their activity at night begins later than that of *Petaurista* (that is, about 10:00 pm; I. Muul, personal communication).

Conservation Measures Taken: None.

Conservation Measures Proposed: Conservation of the lowland forests of Thailand's far south would benefit this and many other species.

White-bellied flying squirrel
Petinomys setosus (**Temminck and Schlegel 1845**)
Mammalia, Rodentia, Sciuridae

Status: Threatened.

Population Size and Trend: No information is available on the status of *P. setosus* in Thailand. In some areas, such as northern Borneo, it is quite rare (Davis 1962).

Distribution and History of Distribution: As the species is currently defined, *P. setosus* occurs in Burma, Thailand, peninsular Malaysia, Sumatra, and Borneo. Two disjunct populations occur in Thailand (Fig. 85): *P. s. morrisi* in Chiang Mai Province (and possibly Mae Hong Song Province and elsewhere in the northwest); and *P. s. setosus* from Nakhon Si Thammarat Province south into Malaysia (Muul and Thonglongya 1971, Askins 1977, Medway 1978).

Geographic Status: The disjunct range of this species in Thailand suggests a relictual situation.

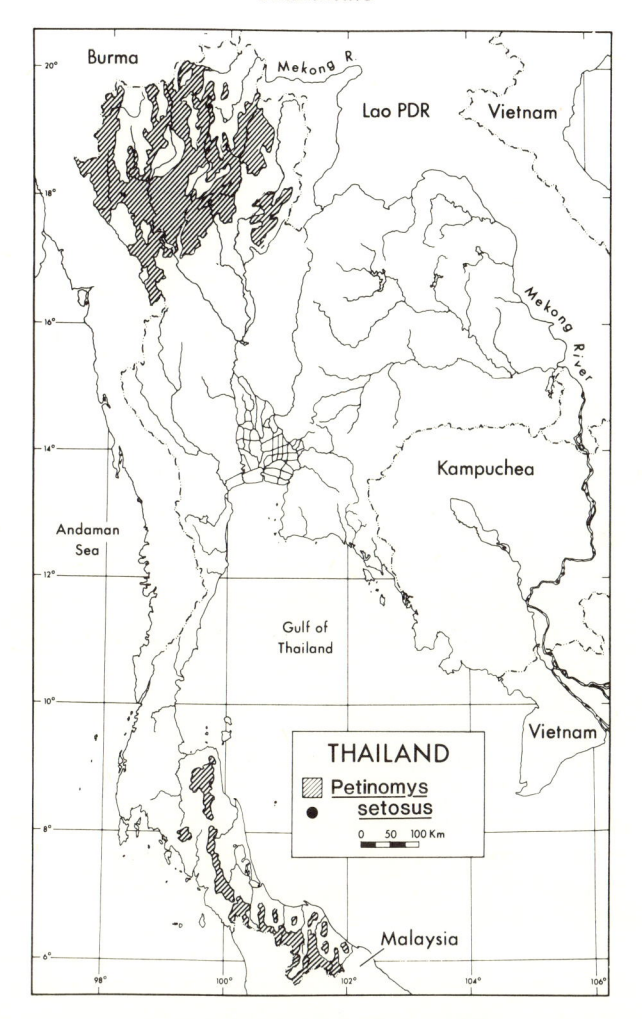

Fig. 85. Distribution of the White-bellied Flying Squirrel (*Petinomys setosus*).

Habitat Requirements and Habitat Trend: The two subspecies considered here differ somewhat in the type of forest they prefer. *P. s. morrisi* inhabits deciduous dipterocarp forest. It has been taken at 1,350 m on Doi Suthep-Pui and at 1,700 m on Doi Inthanon. *P. s. setosus* inhabits tropical evergreen forest and is most abundant in unbroken forest. The species feeds on fruits, nuts and other seeds, shoots, flowers, leaves, and possibly on bark and insects (Muul and Lim 1971, 1978, Muul and Thonglongya 1971, Walker 1975).

Vulnerability of Species and Habitat: The lowland rainforests exploited by the nominate race are coveted for timber, and most have been cut.

Causes of Threat: Deforestation is the major threat. Although this species is less sensitive to forestry than most of the squirrels considered here, it reaches its maximum densities in undisturbed forests. Some species of *Petinomys* raid fruit crops and are killed as pests by villagers (Muul and Lim 1978).

Responses to Habitat Modification: This rodent is less abundant in partially cut primary forest, in secondary forest, and in fruit-rubber plantations than in uncut primary forest, but it is able to survive in all of these habitats (Muul and Lim 1971, 1978).

Demographic Characteristics: The litter size ranges from one to two. The norm is two (Muul and Lim 1978).

Key Behaviors: These nocturnal squirrels are cryptic and difficult to observe (Medway 1978, I. Muul personal communication), and their habits in the wild are poorly known. Captives place hardshelled seeds in water for a few days before attempting to open them (Muul and Lim 1978).

Conservation Measures Taken: In the north, *P. s. morrisi* occurs in Doi Inthanon and Doi Suthep-Pui national parks. *P. s. setosus* probably occurs in some of the reserved forests in southern Thailand.

Conservation Measures Proposed: Biological surveys of reserves in the northwest and the far south should include searches for *P. setosus*. The mountains of northwestern Thailand may harbor undiscovered populations of *P. s. morrisi*.

Hairy-footed flying squirrel
Belomys pearsoni **(Gray 1842)**
Mammalia, Rodentia, Sciuridae

Status: Threatened.

Population Size and Trend: This squirrel is poorly represented in the world's museums and probably is rare over most of its range. It is known to be rare in Taiwan (Jones 1975).

Distribution and History of Distribution: There are apparently six disjunct populations of this species: one in Nepal, Sikkim, Assam, and northern Burma; one in the Phetchabun Range in

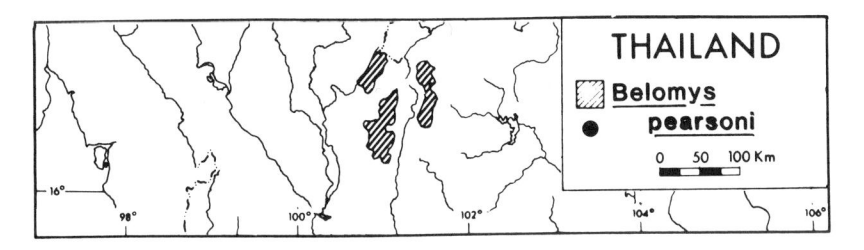

Fig. 86. Distribution of the Hairy-footed Flying Squirrel (*Belomys pearsoni*).

Thailand (Fig. 86; Phetchabun and Nakhon Ratchasima provinces); one in northern Lao PDR and adjacent northern Vietnam; one in southern Vietnam; one in Yunnan; and one in Taiwan (Allen 1940, Ellerman and Morrison-Scott 1951, Van Peenen et al. 1969, Jones 1975, Askins 1977).

Geographic Status: The disjunct nature of its range suggests that all populations of this squirrel are relicts.

Habitat Requirements and Habitat Trend: This monotypic genus prefers dense montane forests (Jones 1975, Askins 1977), but it also occurs in broken patches of forest and in fruit and coconut plantations around villages (I. Muul, personal communication). Montane forest is being lost at an alarming rate all across southern Asia (Myers 1980).

Vulnerability of Species and Habitat: Its preference for upland forests makes *B. pearsoni* vulnerable to timber extraction.

Causes of Threat: Deforestation threatens this species. In Taiwan, dried specimens are sold in curio shops and bounties are still paid on *Belomys* and other flying squirrels (Jones 1975).

Responses to Habitat Modification: The species can survive in secondary forest and plantations.

Demographic Characteristics: Unknown.

Key Behaviors: This species builds nests of bark fibers and leaves in crowns of coconut palms. Activity begins about 1 hour after sunset (I. Muul, personal communication).

Conservation Measures Taken: None.

Conservation Measures Proposed: A survey to determine the local distribution of *Belomys* in Thailand's Phetchabun Range, with special emphasis on the area's many reserves (from Phu Luang Wildlife Sanctuary south to Khao Yai National Park), would be a first step in assessing its conservation needs.

Smoky flying squirrel
Pteromyscus pulverulentus (Gunther 1873)
Mammalia, Rodentia, Sciuridae

Status: Threatened.
WARPA (1980): Protected-1.
Population Size and Trend: The monotypic genus *Pteromyscus* appears to be rare throughout its range. The degree to which this is an artifact of inadequate sampling is unknown (Walker 1975).

Distribution and History of Distribution: This squirrel is known from peninsular Malaysia (including Penang Island), Sumatra, and Borneo. It is quite possible that it will eventually be found in Thailand's far south (Chasen 1940, Hill 1961, Muul and Lim 1971, Askins 1977, Medway 1978, I. Muul personal communication).

Geographic Status: If *P. pulverulentus* occurs in Thailand, it would be at the northern extreme of its range.

Habitat Requirements and Habitat Trend: Most records of this animal are from lowland primary forests. It is less common in the uplands and has been taken only as high as 915 m. It can subsist on leaves, but also takes fruit and seeds (Harrison 1961, Hill 1961, Muul and Lim 1971, 1978, I. Muul, personal communication).

Vulnerability of Species and Habitat: The primary forests of the lowlands are among the first to be cut, and in Thailand most already have been.

Causes of Threat: Deforestation.

Responses to Habitat Modification: This rodent is very dependent on primary forest. It is far more abundant in unbroken than partially cut forest and has not been found in secondary forest or in fruit-rubber plantations (Muul and Lim 1978, Lim personal communication).

Demographic Characteristics: Data from Selangor and Johore indicate that this squirrel is an aseasonal breeder. Only a small fraction (about 9%) of the potentially reproductive females are pregnant at any one time. Litters range from one to two with a norm of two. The rate of population turnover is low (Muul and Lim 1974, 1977, Lim et al. 1977).

Key Behaviors: Like other flying squirrels, *Pteromyscus* is nocturnal. It forages in the canopy. It prefers to nest in undisturbed forest (Harrison 1961, Muul and Lim 1971, Medway 1978).

Conservation Measures Taken: Thai law (WARPA 1980) prohibits hunting and regulates trade in this species.

Conservation Measures Proposed: This is one of several Malaysian mammals that naturalists working in Thailand's far south should look for. Preservation of lowland primary forest is the best way to preserve *Pteromyscus*.

Pere David's vole
Eothenomys melanogaster (Milne-Edwards 1871)
Mammalia, Rodentia, Muridae

Status: Threatened.

Population Size and Trend: The total numbers of this rodent are unknown but probably are small because of the restricted nature of the habitat.

Distribution and History of Distribution: This murid ranges from central and southern China, Taiwan, extreme eastern India (Assam), south through northern Burma, northern Vietnam, to northern Thailand, where it is known only from the summit of Doi Inthanon in Chiang Mai Province (Fig. 87; Marshall 1977).

Geographic Status: The isolated Thai population exists at the extreme southern limits of the species range. It is probably relictual in nature.

Habitat Requirements and Habitat Trend: This temperate-zone vole lives at 2,500 m in the summit moss/rhododendron forest described by Robbins and Smitinand (1966). It has been recorded at elevations as high as 3,400 m in China (Allen 1940).

Vulnerability of Species and Habitat: The extremely restricted nature of its habitat makes *E. melanogaster* in Thailand vulnerable to local habitat disruption.

Causes of Threat: Without the ongoing protection now given its habitat, this rodent would probably lose its forest home to deforestation.

Responses to Habitat Modification: Unknown.

Demographic Characteristics: Unknown.

Key Behaviors: This mammal makes burrows in soft earthen banks (Marshall 1977).

Conservation Measures Taken: The essential habitat of this

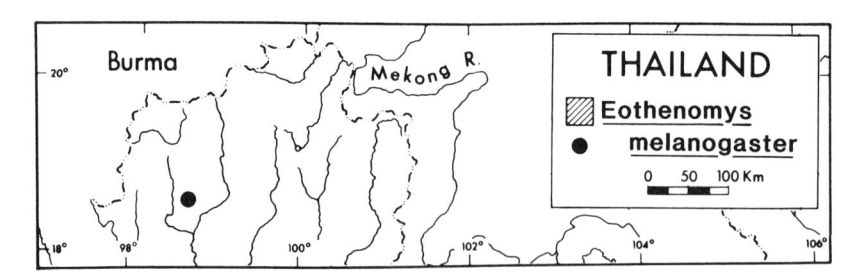

Fig. 87. Distribution of Pere David's Vole (*Eothenomys melanogaster*).

species is protected in Doi Inthanon National Park. There are no Thai laws that specifically protect the species.

Conservation Measures Proposed: The habitat protection in Doi Inthanon National Park should be maintained. The population on the summit offers biologists an opportunity to study the ecology of a rodent unlike most found in Thailand. The basics of its life history and such management questions as the effects of park visitation and the impact of roads and other watershed alterations on its habitat deserve study. Other mountains in northern Thailand should be searched for this species.

Marmoset rat
Hapalomys longicaudatus Blyth 1859
Mammalia, Rodentia, Muridae

Status: Threatened.

Population Size and Trend: This species is known only from a handful of specimens (Musser 1972) and appears to be rare.

Distribution and History of Distribution: *H. longicaudatus* is known from three locations in peninsular Malaysia (Selangor, Pahang, Kelantan), three in Burma (Victoria Point, Tavoy, Schwegyn), and three in Thailand (Fig. 88; Musser 1972). Gairdner (1914, 1915) took two on the Kwae Noi River in Kanchanaburi Province. One, or possibly both, are now in the British Museum. Flower (1900) reported one taken at Pattani in peninsular Thailand, but the specimen apparently has been lost. One was taken in Nakhon Sawan Province in 1924 and is preserved in the American Museum of Natural History. The only other species of *Hapalomys*, *H. dela-*

Mammals 289

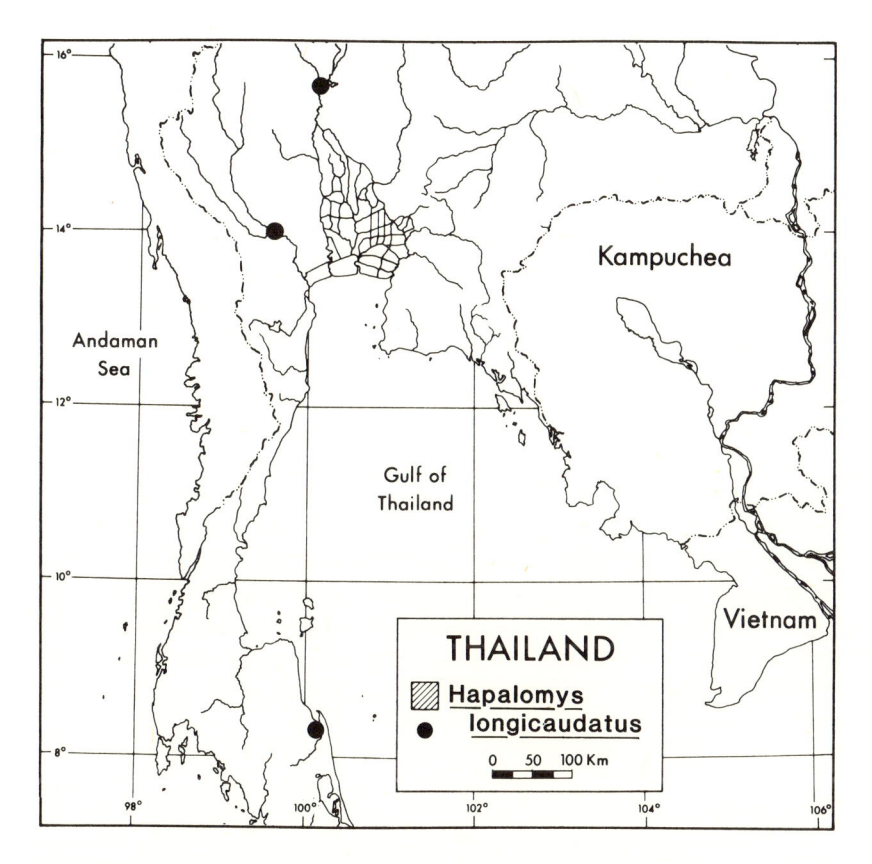

Fig. 88. Distribution of the Marmoset Rat (*Hapalomys longicaudatus*).

couri, occurs in Lao PDR, Vietnam, and Hainan. The latter should be sought in northeastern Thailand (Marshall 1977).

Geographic Status: Thailand is central to the range of this rare rodent.

Habitat Requirements and Habitat Trend: This climbing murid appears to be a bamboo specialist (Medway 1978). The specimens from Victoria Point and Kelantan were collected in bamboo (Musser 1972). Gairdner (1914) found the first Kanchanaburi specimen in "uninhabited bamboo and teak jungle." The recorded elevations are 250 m (Nakhon Sawan) and 500 m (Kelantan). Medway (1964 in Musser 1972) found marmoset rats only in association with the bamboo, *Gigantochloa scortechinii*, nesting in the internodes of large stems and feeding on their shoots, flowers, and fruits.

Vulnerability of Species and Habitat: Its dependence on one or a small set of plant species and its rare, local distribution make this rodent vulnerable to local habitat disruption.

Causes of Threat: Conversion of bamboo forests to agriculture threatens this species.

Responses to Habitat Modification: Unknown.

Demographic Characteristics: "Females have eight mammae (?)" Walker (1975). Breeding appears to be seasonal. A juvenile female was taken on 23 February in Nakhon Sawan. A young adult male was taken on 22 December at Victoria Point. Several young adult males and females were taken in Kelantan in late January (Musser 1972).

Key Behaviors: We were not able to obtain a copy of Medway's (1964) report on the habits of *H. longicaudatus*, but Musser (1972) and Marshall (1977) wrote favorably of it, and it should be consulted by persons with access to it. In Kelantan marmoset rats rest by day in nests in the internodes of standing green or dead stems. The spaces used are lined exclusively with bamboo leaflets. The marmoset rat chews a distinctive circular hole to gain access to the internodes of intact stems. It is a skillful climber and subsists entirely on bamboo (Medway 1978).

Conservation Measures Taken: None.

Conservation Measures Proposed: Elucidation of current local distributions and the bamboo species required by the Thai populations are necessary before any specific recommendations can be made.

Island Rat
Rattus sikkimensis remotus **(Robinson and Kloss 1914)**
Mammalia, Rodentia, Muridae

Status: Threatened.

Population Size and Trend: Total numbers of *R. s. remotus* are unknown but are certainly small.

Distribution and History of Distribution: This rat is known only from Ko Samui, Ko Phangnga, and Ko Tao in the Gulf of Thailand in Surat Thani Province (Fig. 89; Marshall and Nongngork 1970, Marshall 1977, IUCN 1979). It is a giant insular subspe-

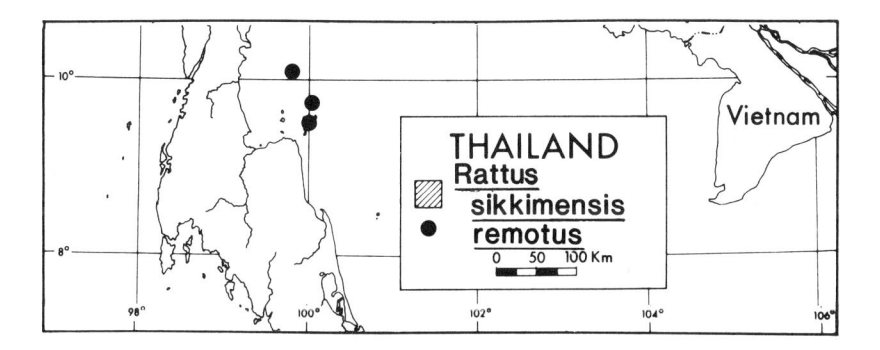

Fig. 89. Distribution of the Island Rat (*Rattus sikkimensis remotus*).

cies of the wide-ranging forest rat, *Rattus sikkimensis* (called *Rattus boratensis* in Marshall 1977).

Geographic Status: The island rat is endemic to several islands in the Gulf of Thailand. It is one of the few mammals known only from Thailand (Marshall 1977, IUCN 1979).

Habitat Requirements and Habitat Trend: "The habitat is the wildest approach to a forest remnant left on Ko Samui--orchards with secondary woods encroaching, and a patch of secondary forest at Hinlad Waterfall. *Rattus* [*sikkimensis*] *remotus* shares this with the equally wild *R. r*[*attus*] *robinsoni* and *R. bukit*" (Marshall 1977).

Vulnerability of Species and Habitat: The restricted insular distribution of the rat and the pressures of the growing human populations on the islands make *R. s. remotus* vulnerable to extirpation by habitat destruction.

Causes of Threat: As early as 1915 Robinson and Kloss expressed concern that Ko Samui's 8,000 people were relentlessly destroying habitat and the native mammals. The population has grown to over 30,000 people, and all of the native primary forest is gone (Marshall and Nongngork 1970).

Responses to Habitat Modification: Originally a dweller of the forest, *R. s. remotus* has moved into orchards and secondary growth with the loss of its ancestral habitat (Marshall 1977)

Demographic Characteristics: Unknown.

Key Behaviors: Unknown.

Conservation Measures Taken: The potential for captive rearing has been demonstrated. A female taken to Bangkok with her young successfully raised them (Marshall 1977).

Conservation Measures Proposed: The feasibility of creating a small forest reserve on Ko Samui with planted native trees should be considered. Studies on life history and reproduction of this species are needed. This rat is in the same species group as *R. rattus*. It and the other two *Rattus* considered in this report should be conserved because they represent valuable genetic resources for future studies on *R. rattus*, so vital to modern biomedical research.

Neill's rat
Rattus neilli Marshall 1977
Mammalia, Rodentia, Muridae

Status: Threatened.
MAB (1979): Threatened.
Population Size and Trend: Unknown.
Distribution and History of Distribution: The type specimen was collected by William Neill in July 1973, halfway up a wooded limestone cliff at 200 m elevation near Phu Namtok, Kaengkhoi District, Sara Buri Province (Fig. 90). It also has been taken in shaded crevices of limestone cliffs at Sai Yok in Kanchanaburi Province (Lekagul and McNeely 1977). A third capture site is Salak Phra Wildlife Sanctuary, in lowland bamboo forest on the Huai Salak Phra valley floor, 170 m elevation, about 115 m from the base of a limestone mountain (Wiles 1981).
Geographic Status: Neill's rat is one of the few mammals endemic to Thailand.
Habitat Requirements and Habitat Trend: *R. neilli* is a denizen of limestone cliffs. The Kaengkhoi population "shares the upper parts of the limestone cliffs with *Rattus hinpoon, Rattus rattus*, and the limestone babbler, *Napothera brevicauda calcicola*" [a passerine bird of the family Muscicapidae] (Marshall 1977). It lives in the crevices of the scrub-covered cliffs and has not been noted to enter the cave at Kaengkhoi as the roof rat, *R. rattus*, does.
Vulnerability of Species and Habitat: Unknown.
Causes of Threat: Its restricted range makes the species vulnerable to extirpation by local habitat disruption.
Responses to Habitat Modification: Unknown.
Demographic Characteristics: Unknown.
Key Behaviors: Unknown.

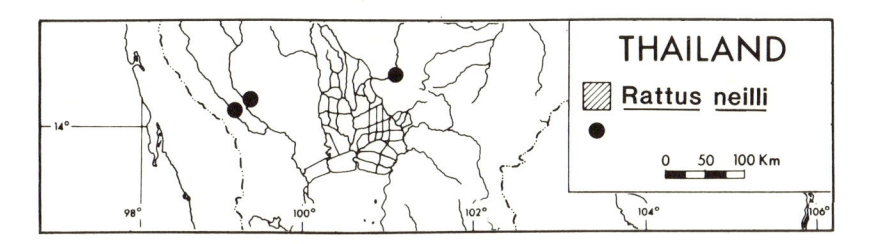

Fig. 90. Distribution of Neill's Rat (*Rattus neilli*).

Conservation Measures Taken: None.
Conservation Measures Proposed: IUCN (1979) proposed that the habitat of this species should be elucidated and preserved. However, the distribution of limestone outcrops is well known. This species should be sought in surveys of limestone areas. The cliff habitats at Kaengkhoi, Sai Yok, and other occupied areas should be protected from quarrying and cutting and burning for hill agriculture.

Limestone rat
Rattus hinpoon Marshall 1977
Mammalia, Rodentia, Muridae

Status: Threatened.
MAB (1979): Threatened
Population Size and Trend: Unknown.
Distribution and History of Distribution: The type specimen was collected by William Neill in July 1973 halfway up a wooded limestone cliff at 200 m elevation near Phu Namtok, Kaengkhoi District, Sara Buri Province (Fig. 91). It has also been taken in a limestone cave at Lopburi in Lop Buri Province (Marshall 1977).
Geographic Status: The limestone rat is one of the few mammals found only in Thailand. It is endemic to the Khorat Plateau.
Habitat Requirements and Habitat Trend: The limestone rat is a habitat specialist, inhabiting the scrubby vegetation high in limestone cliffs. "The new rat has a remarkably narrow ecologic range, shared with a very distinct endemic subspecies of bird, the limestone babbler, *Napothera crispifrons calcicola*, . . . *Rattus neilli*,

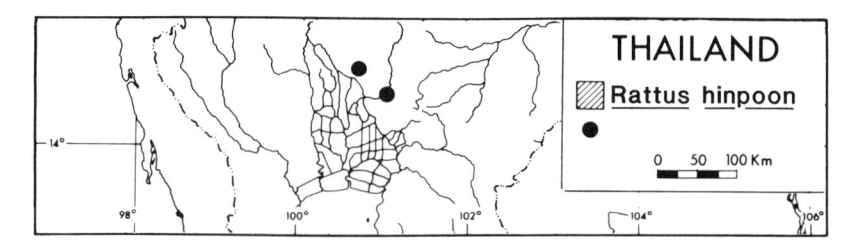

Fig. 91. Distribution of the Limestone Rat (*Rattus hinpoon*).

another new species" (Marshall 1977), and the roof rat, *Rattus rattus*.

Vulnerability of Species and Habitat: Unknown.

Causes of Threat: Its restricted range makes the species vulnerable to extirpation by local habitat disruption.

Responses to Habitat Modification: Unknown.

Demographic Characteristics: Unknown.

Key Behaviors: Unknown.

Conservation Measures Taken: None.

Conservation Measures Proposed: IUCN (1979) proposed that the habitat of this species should be elucidated and preserved, but only the latter is needed because the distribution of limestone outcrops is well known. An inventory and survey of Thailand's distinct association of plants and animals on limestone would help focus attention on its conservation needs. The cliff habitats at Kaengkhoi and Lopburi should be protected from mining and fire.

The Cetaceans
Whales, porpoises, and their allies
Introductory Comments

Very little is known about the biology of cetaceans in Thai waters. Current knowledge was thoroughly reviewed by Lekagul and McNeely (1977a). The accounts that follow are based primarily on their information. In spite of Thailand's extensive coastline (about 2,000 km) few observations have been made by qualified researchers and very few museum specimens have been taken (Bonhote 1903, Kloss 1916, Gyldenstolpe 1919, Jinda 1968). "There is no active hunting of cetaceans in Thai waters and the larger whales are very poorly known; it is likely that most wide-ranging species pass through Thai waters from time to time, especially travelling via the Straits of Malacca and the deep waters of the Andaman Sea" (Lekagul and McNeely 1977a). The twelve species whose presence is well established are considered below. All cetaceans are covered under Appendix II of CITES (1979) and many receive special consideration under Appendix I. Several cetaceans known from Thai waters are considered to be endangered by the U.S. Fish and Wildlife Service (USFWS 1980a).

Plumbeous dolphin
Sotalia plumbea

This dolphin is distributed from "Sarawak to the Suez Canal (Hershkovitz 1966); Ceylon [Sri Lanka] and the Malabar Coast of India to Burma and the Straits of Malacca (records from Perak and Penang). A stuffed specimen seen in Bangkok was said to have come from Chonburi" (Lekagul and McNeely 1977a). It also is known in Thailand from a early sight record. It reaches a length of 1.9-2.2 m. It is protected under Appendix I of CITES (1979).

Indonesian white dolphin
Sotalia borneensis

S. borneensis is known from the South China Sea from Sarawak to the Gulf of Thailand and the Straits of Malacca (Harrison 1966; Hershkovitz 1966). It is known in Thailand from an early sight record in the estuary of the Trang River and from a specimen of unknown origin in the Bang Saen Marine Museum. It inhabits shallow seas, coming close inshore to breed. It is often seen in small groups. Adults reach a length of 1.9-2.0 m. They are protected under Appendix I of CITES (1979).

Chinese white dolphin
Sotalia chinensis

This form may be conspecific with *S. borneensis*; taxonomic study is needed to resolve the question. It is distributed from the "coast of southern China, south to Thailand and Sarawak; Kloss (1916) reports seeing a large group near Chantaburi, close to shore . . . This little known species inhabits the coasts and estuaries of the South China Sea, often in harbors. They may form large groups" (Lekagul and McNeely 1977a). They reach a length of 2.0-2.2 m. This species is covered under Appendix I of CITES (1979).

Rough-toothed dolphin
Steno bredanensis

The rough-toothed dolphin ranges from the "Netherlands to Ivory Coast; Virginia to Argentina; Japan to Galapagos; Gulf of Aden to Bay of Bengal and Java (Hershkovitz 1966); recorded from Nicobar Islands by Blanford (1888) and from Thailand by Jinda (1968) . . . Little is known of this offshore dolphin; it is probably concentrated in warm currents (Nishiwaki 1966)" (Lekagul and McNeely 1977a). This primitive form reaches a length of 2.2-2.4 m and a mass of approximately 100 kg. It is protected under Appendix II of CITES (1979).

Malayan dolphin
Stenella malayana

If *S. malayana* is considered to be a species distinct from *S. longirostris*, a form widespread in temperate and tropical waters, then its distribution can be described as "from the Sundarbans to Singapore and Java, including the west coast of Thailand and the Gulf of Thailand" (Lekagul and McNeely 1977a). These animals occur in pairs and small groups. Their habits are poorly understood, but other *Stenella* are deep-ocean fish specialists. Their habit of accompanying schools of tuna is exploited by tuna seiners, who kill many in their nets. The Malayan dolphin reaches 1.5-1.8 m in length. It is protected under Appendix II of CITES (1979).

Common dolphin
Delphinus delphis

This widely distributed cetacean is found in "temperate and warm seas throughout the world, including the Straits of Malacca and the Gulf of Thailand, where they are plentiful; the Boonsong Collection contains a specimen from Ranong. Gibson-Hill (1949) calls *D. delphis* "the most common cetacean in Malay waters"... These are active, agile dolphins, found in clear ocean waters; the species is gregarious, often occurring in groups exceeding 100 individuals. They have been seen aiding wounded members of the group by supporting them in the water, pushing them to the surface to breathe. They are among the swiftest of cetaceans, travelling as fast as 35-40 km per hour, feeding on fish and cephalopods, generally close to the surface. A single young is born after a gestation of about nine months" (Lekagul and McNeely 1977a). Adults are 2.3-2.7 m long and weigh 60-75 kg. They are protected under Appendix II of CITES (1979).

Eastern bottle-nosed dolphin
Tursiops aduncus

If *T. aduncus* is considered to be a full species and not a subspecies of *T. truncatus*, its range can be described as the "South China Sea to Australia, Indonesia, and South Africa; in Thailand bottle-nosed dolphins are frequently seen off Pattaya, Sonkhla, and other shoal-water localities... [They] prefer water between 24° and 29° C and are generally confined to shallow tropical and subtropical waters, including bays, estuaries, shoal waters, and the mouths of large rivers. The diet consists mainly of fish... A single young about a meter long and weighing 12 kg is born after a gestation of 11-12 months... The age at weaning is variable, from 6 to 18 months" (Lekagul and McNeely 1977a). Adults are 1.75-2.6 m in length and weigh 80-180 kg. They are protected under Appendix II of CITES (1979).

Irrawaddy dolphin
Orcaella brevirostris

This small dolphin is found in the "Bay of Bengal, Irrawaddy River to above Bhamo (1440 km from the sea), Straits of Malacca, Gulf of Thailand, Java, Borneo; a specimen has been collected in the Mekong River and Gressitt (1970) considers this the only cetacean to occur in Laos. In Thailand, specimens have been reported from Pattani (Bonhote 1903) and Chantaburi (Kloss 1916); the species probably occurs in all Thai waters and may even enter the Chao Phya River. Kloss (1916) considered the species 'very common along the Chantabun coast' . . . Irrawaddy dolphins occur in small schools, often in heavily silted waters . . . Their diet consists of crayfish, shrimp, and small crustaceans, often found on the bottom. They are thought by fishermen to guide fish into their nets and for this reason are not hunted. The single young is born after a gestation of perhaps 9 months; the new-born young is about 40% of the length of its mother (Norman and Fraser 1937)" (Lekagul and McNeely 1977a) Adults are 1.8-2.75 m long. They are protected under Appendix II of CITES (1979).

Black finless porpoise
Neophocaena phocaenoides

N. phocaenoides is found in "Korea, Japan, China (including certain rivers; found as far as 1,600 km from the mouth of the Yangtze), Java, Sumatra, Borneo, Straits of Malacca, west to South Africa . . . The black finless porpoise is a rather sluggish cetacean found in shallow waters along the coasts of southern Asia, inhabiting estuaries, rivers, and lakes; it often occurs around reefs and islands . . . It is usually found alone or in pairs, feeding on prawns, squid, crustaceans, and small fish. Most births seem to take place in October (Blanford 1888), and the young mature rapidly" (Lekagul and McNeely 1977a). Adults reach 1.2-1.6 m and weigh 25-40 kg. They are protected under Appendix I of CITES (1979).

Sperm whale
Physeter catodon

This animal is the largest of the toothed whales. It is found in "all oceans, but generally avoids the polar regions, females and young staying in tropical seas throughout the year. Although reported from the South China Sea, sperm whales seldom enter the shallow Gulf of Thailand; they have been often reported from the Straits of Malacca and therefore are certain to occur in the deep waters off the west coast. Sperm whales feed largely on squid, which they hunt in deep oceans; they also take giant squid, sharks, barracuda, and other fish. They can dive as deep as 1 km (experiencing a pressure of 10 atmospheres), staying submerged as long as 90 minutes. They can swim at a speed of about 20 knots . . . These are the only known polygamous large whales, with males fighting for harems (a factor selecting for large size in males). The females are found in schools, called "pods" by whalers, of 15-20 to several hundred; non-harem males migrate widely, even entering polar oceans. A single young, 4-5 meters long, is born after a gestation of 12-16 months. The female lactates for about 16 months, and the young reaches sexual maturity at 4-5 years (for females) to 8-10 years (for males). Life span is at least 30 years, and may be as long as 60 years (at least under non-whaling conditions). One calf is born every 3 years, a rather slow rate of reproduction in a heavily-hunted species" (Lekagul and McNeely 1977a). Males are about twice the size of females and grow to 12-20 m in length and to 53,000 kg in mass. The U.S. Fish and Wildlife Service considers them endangered (USFWS 1980a) and they are protected under Appendix I of CITES (1981).

Sei whale
Balaenoptera borealis

This large baleen whale is known from "Norway and Alaska to the Antarctic but breeds in tropical and subtropical waters; reported from Java, Borneo, and Thailand (Harrison 1966); Gibson-Hill (1949) reports one that was beached in Thailand at Kandhuli. The Boonsong Collection contains jaw fragments thought to be of this species, from Chonburi . . . Sei whales are often considered the swiftest of the baleen whales, capable of speeds in excess of 35 knots (about 60 km per hour). They are highly migratory and are noted for their erratic appearances; they often enter shallow waters. They occur singly or in small groups, very rarely as many as 50. They feed near the surface, often with the muzzle and part of the back above the surface; diet consists mostly of copepods, very small zooplankton. A single young (twins have been reported) is born after a gestation of about 12 months, with one young born about every three years. Not systematically hunted until 1882, this is now the most heavily hunted of the larger whales, with up to 20,000 taken each year (combined with *B. endeni*). McVay (1966) suggests that the total Sei population never exceeded 60,000; even if this is an underestimate, it is clear that these whales are seriously threatened by overhunting" (Lekagul and McNeely 1977a). Adults reach lengths of 13 to 18 m and masses of up to 50,000 kg. This whale is considered endangered (USFWS 1980a) and is protected under Appendix I of CITES (1979).

Lesser rorqual or Minke whale
Balaenoptera acutirostrata

This small baleen whale is "found from Iceland to the Antarctic, with records from Malacca, Penang, and Thailand (specimens from Chumphon, Sam Roi Yod, Koh Chang, Koh Tao, and Nakhon Si Thammarat) . . . This is the smallest of the Balaenoptera, and it was seldom hunted until other species became seriously depleted; it is now one of the most heavily harvested baleen whales, hunted primarily for meat, mostly eaten by Japanese. The diet consists of krill. The highly migratory habits of Minke's whales often bring them to Thai waters, including close inshore. They are usually seen singly or in small groups up to 20 . . . A single calf is born every other year, after a gestation of about 10 months; the calf is 3 m long at birth" (Lekagul and McNeely 1977a). Adults reach a length of 8-9 m and weigh approximately 8,000 kg. They are protected under Appendix II of CITES (1979).

Golden jackal
Canis aureus Linnaeus 1758
Mammalia, Carnivora, Canidae

Status: Threatened.
IUCN (1979): Threatened.

Population Size and Trend: *C. aureus* is common in parts of Africa (e.g., Lamprecht 1978). In the Mideast its status is variable--it has declined in Lebanon since the early 1950s but has made a great comeback in Israel (Lewis et al. 1965). The golden jackal is increasing in numbers and extending its range in the Caucasus, probably because of a reduction in the area's wolf population (Bakeev 1978). In his studies in Pakistan, India, and Nepal from the late 1960s to the mid-1970s, Schaller (1977) found *C. aureus* to be uncommon everywhere except in the small (80 km^2) High Range plateau in India. In the Shan States of Burma near Thailand's Mae Hong Song Province, Grimwood (personal communication to J. Thornback) wrote that in the late 1970s the local people considered the jackal to be more common than the wild dog (*Cuon*), but rarer than the leopard or tiger. Glydenstolpe (1919) stated that the jackal was rare in Thailand. Lekagul and McNeely (1977a) gave no information on the current status of Thai jackals. IUCN (1979) wrote that there are now "small populations in most areas of Thailand" and that they are definitely rare in the northern highlands.

Distribution and History of Distribution: This jackal occurs across northern Africa from Morocco to Egypt and in eastern Africa as far south as Kenya and Tanzania. It occurs in southern Europe and throughout the Mideast. It is currently extending its range northward in the Caucasus. In southern Asia, it is found in Pakistan, Afghanistan, India, Sri Lanka, Nepal, Bhutan, Burma, and Thailand. *C. aureus* is widespread in Thailand north of the Isthmus of Kra, except possibly in the northeastern Khorat Plateau and the central valley of the Chao Phraya (Ellerman and Morrison-Scott 1951, Novikov 1965, Eisenberg and Lockhart 1972, Golani and Keller 1975, Lekagul and McNeely 1977a, Bakeev 1978, IUCN 1979).

Geographic Status: The golden jackal reaches the eastern extreme of its wide range in Thailand.

Habitat Requirements and Habitat Trend: In Africa (the Serengeti Plain and Ngorongoro Crater) *C. aureus* is primarily an animal of the shortgrass plains, with some individuals moving into the edge of woodlands in the dry season (Van Lawick and Van Lawick-Goodall 1970, Kruuk 1972, Schaller 1972, Lamprecht 1978). Schaller (1972) found that pairs defended an area about 3 km in diameter from conspecifics in the Serengeti, and he stated that territoriality may break down in times of food abundance. In the Serengeti, Van Lawick and Van Lawick-Goodall (1970) found hunting ranges of pairs to be 10-23 km^2. In the richer habitat of the floor of Ngorongoro Crater, they found hunting ranges of 2.5-5 km^2. They wrote that animals defended a much smaller breeding territory within the hunting range.

In Israel, Golani and Keller (1975) studied jackals in coastal sand dunes. Dens were made in patches of thick vegetation. In the Soviet Union, this canid is primarily an animal of the lowland forests, scrub, and reed beds. It is relatively uncommon in Soviet deserts (Ognev 1931, Novikov 1956, Reimov and Nuratdinov 1970). Reimov and Nuratdinov (1970) wrote that in reed and shrubs jackals reach average densities as high as 9-10 individuals per km^2. In Sri Lanka, Eisenberg and Lockhart (1972) found jackals localized around permanent water sources. Home range of a pair extended for a linear distance of about 4 km, an area the male could traverse in 24 hours. In India, this species is primarily an animal of the lowlands but has been recorded as high as 3,660 m in the Himalayas (Prater 1971). In many areas *C. aureus* is an animal of cultivated areas near human habitation (e.g., Lewis et al. 1968).

Golden jackals are opportunistic omnivores and scavengers. The degree to which they kill their own food varies with the activity of larger predators and the availability of small animals and fruit. In many areas they subsist mainly on small mammals (especially rodents) and birds. Mammalian prey ranges in size from smaller rodents, such as gerbils and springhares, to medium-sized langurs, hares, and coypu, to the young of deer and gazelles. Adult gazelles are taken on rare occasions. Birds (especially ground-nesting species and their eggs) are sought, and concentrations of migrating birds are readily exploited. Jackals also take snakes, lizards, amphibians, fishes, molluscs, crustaceans, grasshoppers, crickets, cockroaches, termites, moths, and other insects. Dung beetles and their larvae are crucial foods in some areas when other food is scarce. Like many other canids, *C. aureus* is fond of ripe fruit.

Melons, fallen figs (*Ficus*), *Balanites*, *Zizyphus*, grapes, grass, seeds, and mushrooms have all been reported as jackal food. Garbage is an important staple in many inhabited areas. Carrion is heavily used. During the calving peak of wildebeest at Ngorongoro Crater, wildebeest placentae are an important food item (Blanford 1888-1891, Ognev 1931, Novikov 1956, Schaller 1967, 1972, 1977, Lewis et al. 1968, Reimov and Nuratdinov 1970, Van Lawick and Van Lawick-Goodall 1970, Prater 1971, Eisenberg and Lockhart 1972, Kruuk 1972, Volozheninov 1972, Tarianniov 1974, Golini and Keller 1975, Nasher and Nader 1975, Lamprecht 1978).

Vulnerability of Species and Habitat: In other countries, golden jackals raid chicken houses, vineyards, orchards, and crops such as melons, sugarcane, and maize. They are destructive to the Russian rodent fur industry (coypu and muskrat) and they are alleged to sometimes attack young and sick goats and sheep (Blanford 1888-1891, Ognev 1931, Schaller 1967, Reimov and Nuratdinov 1970, Prater 1971). They are more easily trapped and attracted to bait than other wild Asian canids, and it is possible to attract them with recorded sounds. Jackals of some populations are not very wary of man, and in reserves they become unafraid of automobiles (Ognev 1931, Kruuk 1972, Lamprecht 1978). There are allegations in the older literature (e.g., Blanford 1888-1891), that *C. aureus* bites have caused rabies in man.

Causes of Threat: Novikov (1956) epitomized the attitude toward jackals that has for so long prevailed in Asian game management when he wrote, "It should be exterminated together with other noxious predators." Indiscriminate killing of jackals in the name of livestock protection has caused their extirpation in many areas. Farmers in northern Thailand kill many jackals on this ill-founded premise (IUCN 1979), and unrestrained shooting probably is the major threat in Thailand today. Domestic dogs (*C. familiaris*) often kill *C. aureus* (e.g., Ognev 1931, Schaller 1967), and in areas of low jackal densities and high dog densities (as in modern Thailand) this may also be a major threat. Golden jackals hybridize freely with dogs in captivity (e.g., Olney 1979), and in reduced, fragmented jackal populations, hybridization with dogs and inbreeding among themselves may threaten their genetic integrity. There is a minor trade in live jackals. The pelt is of little economic value at the present time.

Responses to Habitat Modification: In much of their range

(including Thailand), golden jackals are most frequently seen near human habitation and they may, in fact, be commensal with man (e.g., Schaller 1967, Lewis et al. 1968, Prater 1971, Lekagul and McNeely 1977a). The clearing of forests and settlement of the Thai hinterlands probably benefited the jackal at first, but the recent proliferation of modern firearms probably has negated this advantage.

Demographic Characteristics: In most areas there is a definite seasonality to mating and parturition. Captive and wild *C. aureus* copulate from November to March in Israel (Golani and Mendelssohn 1971, Golani 1973, Golani and Keller 1975). Females come into heat in January and February in the USSR (Ognev 1931). Wild *C. aureus* in the Serengeti give birth between December and April, a time when migratory prey are in the jackal's plains habitat (Schaller 1972). In European zoos, young are born from March to May (Ewer 1973, Wandrey 1975). Several litters were delivered at an Afghani zoo in April (Wandrey 1975). Prater (1971) and Lekagul and McNeely (1977a) stated that parturition is aseasonal in India. Schaller (1967) wrote that the young are born in India's Kanha National Park from February to April or May. Eisenberg and Lockhart (1972) observed a lactating female in Sri Lanka in March and assumed that copulation took place in December or January.

Gestation takes 60-63 days. Litters range from 1 to 9 and are usually 4-5. The female has ten mammae. The eyes open on about the tenth day. Young first take solid food in 28-35 days and weaning begins at just over two months (Ognev 1931, Van Lawick and Van Lawick-Goodall 1970, Ewer 1973, Golani and Keller 1975, Lekagul and McNeely 1977a). Birds of prey probably are the major cause of juvenile mortality in some areas. Young are sexually mature in the second year of life, and females are known to have first given birth at 24 months of age. Females can give birth within 6 months of weaning a litter, but most females probably deliver only one litter per year (Van Lawick and Van Lawick-Goodall 1970, Golani and Mendelssohn 1971, Eisenberg and Lockhart 1972). Some *C. aureus* may live over 12 years (Lekagul and McNeely 1977a).

Key Behaviors: Asian, Mideastern, and European populations of *C. aureus* have not been studied as much as the East African ones. Much of the following is based on studies of jackals in the Serengeti, Ngorongoro Crater, and captive groups. The basic social unit is the male-female pair. Most reports of larger groups probably refer to pairs with nearly grown offspring. Some pairs last only a breeding season while others have been observed together for years. Mates hunt and rest together. There is extensive mutual grooming. Courting pairs extensively scent-mark their home range with urine, both marking the same spots (Schaller 1967, Van Lawick and Van Lawick-Goodall 1970, Eisenberg and Lockhart 1972, Golani and Keller 1975, Wandrey 1975, Lamprecht 1978). Pups are born in burrows dug by the jackals or appropriated from other mammals, in rock crevices, in small caves, in ruins, in hollow trees, or in washed-out places under roots. The female stays with the young for the first few days postpartum and is fed by the male. In the first few months the young may be repeatedly moved to new dens. The area immediately surrounding the den is defended against conspecifics and other scavengers. Once weaning begins, both parents feed the young by regurgitation. Even in captivity adults watch the sky attentively, a response to airborne predators of young (Ognev 1931, Van Lawick and Van Lawick-Goodall 1970, Kruuk 1972, Wandrey 1975). In some populations the young are independent as early as autumn of their first year (Novikov 1956, Nikolskii and Poyarkov 1976), but in most the young stay with their parents at least a year, whereafter the males disperse and females often help raise the next litter (Van Lawick and Van Lawick-Goodall 1970, Eisenberg and Lockhart 1972, Wandrey 1975).

Most hunting is done at night, but in areas where there is little human disturbance they may be more diurnal. Golden jackals clean up after kills made by larger predators and will steal prey from similar-sized predators, such as African wild dogs and side-striped jackals. Sometimes up to 14 *C. aureus* may share a kill, and they have been seen sharing kills with hyaenas, sidestriped jackals, and black-backed jackals. Excess meat is cached in small quantities in several places. *C. aureus* is an agile, rapid, and enduring runner and in some areas it kills most of its own food. Even when grown young are present, adult pairs usually hunt without their aid. Only rarely are more than two jackals seen pursuing prey. When hunting young gazelles, the capture success of pairs is much greater than that of lone animals. Typically, one distracts the mother gazelle while the other kills the young. Jackals kill large prey by disembowlment. Ognev 1931, Novikov 1956, Estes and Goddard 1967,

Van Lawick and Van Lawick-Goodall 1970, Eisenberg and Lockhart 1972, Kruuk 1972, Schaller 1972, Ewer 1973, Lamprecht 1978).

In contrast to pack hunters such as dholes, African wild dogs, and wolves, golden jackals are less social canids. Visual, olfactory, and vocal signals all help to maintain the spacing between and dominance hierarchies within groups of jackals. Actual fights are rare (Kleiman 1967, Van Lawick and Van Lawick-Goodall 1970, Ewer 1973). Many sounds are important in parent-offspring communication, and communal howling by family groups within the defended territory probably helps to maintain territoriality (Kleiman 1967, Van Lawick and Van Lawick-Goodall 1970, Eisenberg and Lockhart 1972, Wandrey 1975, Nikolskii and Poyarkov 1976, 1979, Herre 1979).

Conservation Measures Taken: In Thailand, *C. aureus* occurs in the Salawin and Khun Yuam wildlife sanctuaries (IUCN 1979). It is not protected by Thai law. Many golden jackals are kept in the world's zoos, and captive breeding is underway (Olney 1979).

Conservation Measures Proposed: Indiscriminate shooting of jackals as pests in Thailand must stop if the animal is to survive. Animals that become habitual poultry thieves should be removed on an individual basis. Cover and permanent water sources are important to jackals. In reserves where jackals occur, feral dogs should be eradicated to prevent hybridization, predation on jackals, and transmission of canid diseases. Basic surveys and ecological studies are needed to determine the local distribution and conservation needs of Thai *C. aureus*. Villagers should be educated on the natural role of these carnivores in removing carcasses and helping to keep rodent populations in check and on the plight of the jackal in modern Thailand.

Dhole, Asiatic wild dog, red dog
Cuon alpinus (Pallas 1911)
Mammalia, Carnivora, Canidae

Status: Endangered.
IUCN Red data Book (1976): Vulnerable.
CITES (1979): Appendix II.
IUCN (1979): Threatened.
USFWS (1980a): Endangered.

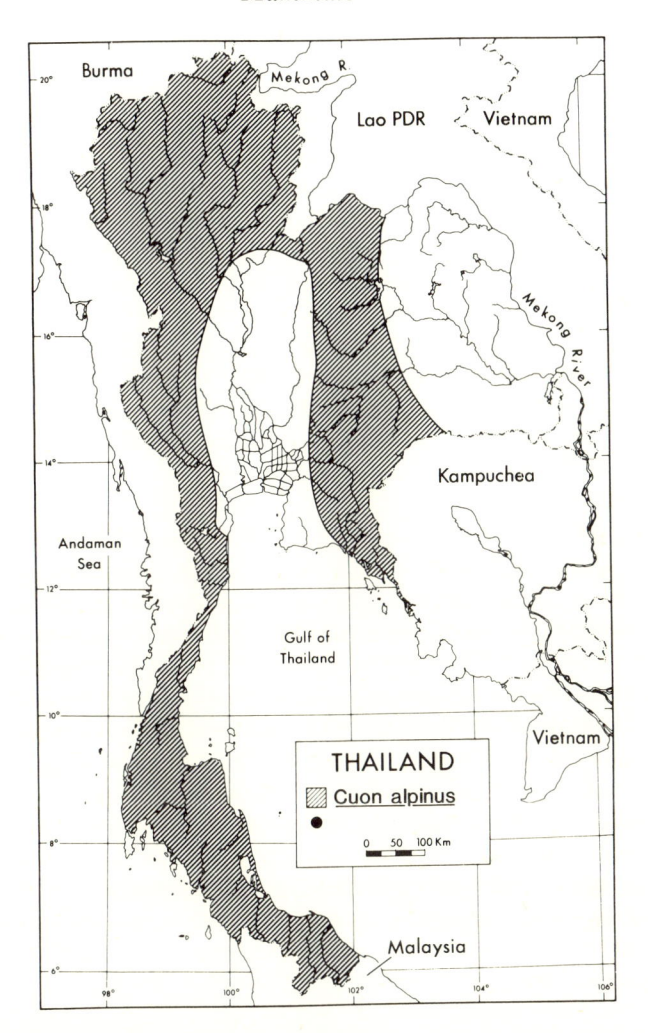

Fig. 92. Distribution of the Dhole (*Cuon alpinus*).

Population Size and Trend: The total population size is unknown, but it is certainly reduced and declining. The dhole is threatened with extinction over its entire wide range. It is quite rare in Thailand (Cohen 1977, Lekagul and McNeely 1977a).

Distribution and History of Distribution: *Cuon* was formerly found "from the Tyan-Shan and Altai mountains, and Maritime Province of the Soviet Union southward through Mongolia, Korea, China, Tibet, Nepal, India, and Southeast Asia, including the

Malayan Peninsula, Sumatra, and Java. [Its] present range remains unstudied, but remnant populations are known to exist in India, Malaysia, Thailand, and Java" (Cohen 1978). There are also relict populations in the Soviet Union. Fossil *Cuon* are known from the mid-Pleistocene of Austria. It occurs today in pockets over much of Thailand (Fig. 92), most commonly along the Tenasserim. Two subspecies are recognized in Thailand, *C. a. adustus* to the north of the Isthmus of Kra and *C. a. sumatrensis* to the south. It apparently does not occur in the central valley of the Chao Phraya nor in most of the northeastern Khorat Plateau (Lekagul and McNeely 1977a, Cohen 1978, Cohen et al. 1978, IUCN 1979).

Geographic Status: The remnant Thai populations occur in the south-central part of the species' overall range.

Habitat Requirements and Habitat Trend: The dhole is primarily a forest-dwelling species but is known from almost every type of habitat, from sea level to 3,000 m. It eats mainly large mammals, including the mouse deer (*Tragulus memmina*), reindeer (*Rangifer tarandus*), musk deer (*Moschus moschiferus*), chital (*Axis axis*), swamp deer (*Cervus duvauceli*), sambar deer (*Cervus unicolor*), brow-antlered deer (*Cervus eldi*), muntjak (*Muntiacus muntjak*), tahr (*Hemitragus hylocrius*), water buffalo (*Bubalus bubalis*), nilgai (*Boselaphus tragocamelus*), gaur (*Bos gaurus*), banteng (*Bos banteng*), wild sheep (*Ovis* spp.), markhor (*Capra falconeri*), domestic goat (*Capra hircus*), goral (*Naemorhedus goral*), and wild pig (*Sus scrofa*). Rarely it takes domestic cattle (*Bos taurus*). It also preys on smaller animals, such as badgers (*Meles meles*), hares (*Lepus nigricollis* and other *Lepus* spp.), field rats (*Millardia meltada*), other rodents, jungle fowl, and lizards. It is not clear whether Nilgiri langur (*Presbytis johni*) remains found in dhole scats represent kills or merely carrion feeding. Plants, such as grass and *Zizyphus* berries, are sometimes eaten, as is carrion. In times of extreme hardship *Cuon* has been known to eat its own young. Throughout its range forests are being cleared, reducing or modifying the preferred habitat (Davidar 1975, Lekagul and McNeely 1977a, Cohen 1977, 1978, Cohen et al. 1978).

Vulnerability of Species and Habitat: The dhole is very intolerant of human presence and flees at the sight of man unless defending a kill. Superstitious beliefs cause a negative view of this canid, and over most of its range it is shot on sight as vermin. A bounty is still paid for *Cuon* heads in India. The peculiar whistling call this species uses when hunting can be imitated by blowing across the top of an empty shotgun shell. This attracts dholes and is used by hunters to call them in to be shot (Cohen 1977). Dholes are also called by imitating the distress call of a fawn by blowing through leaves held between the thumbs (Davidar 1975).

Causes of Threat: Davidar (1975), invoking an old maxim about tigers, stated that until recently the only studies on the dhole were done along the sights of rifles. Dholes are endangered by relentless hunting, aggravated by reduced prey densities and wholesale habitat loss. They only rarely attack cattle (Cohen 1977). Burton (1940) reported one human death due to the bite of a rabid *C. alpinus*.

Responses to Habitat Modification: Unknown.

Demographic Characteristics: In India dholes mate from September to January. Captives in the Moscow Zoo typically mate in February. Gestation in both places is 60-63 days. The average litter size is 8 pups, with a maximum of about 11. Adults weigh some 10-20 kg. Captives in Moscow have lived 15-16 years (Lekagul and McNeely 1977a, Cohen 1978, Johnsingh 1979).

Key Behaviors: The mating behavior has been described by Davidar (1975). Dens range from rocky caverns to earthen burrows. The latter are enlarged diggings of other animals (such as the hyena, *Hyena hyena*, or the porcupine, *Hystrix indica*) or, rarely, are dug by the canids themselves. More than one breeding female may share a den and care for the young. A den may have multiple entrances, and several dens may be connected by underground passages. Females have up to 16 teats, although the average litter is 4-6 pups; this is possibly an adaptation for cooperative care of the young. After birth the female stays with the young until the second day postpartum. In the wild, other pack members feed the female and the pups with regurgitated meat. The strong mother-pup attachment lasts about a year. The social groups average about 5-12 members, with a maximum of about 40 in India, and appear to be extended family units. The evidence indicates that they form separate male and female hierarchies, and acts of overt aggression or competition are very rare. Much agonistic behavior between the young is noted, but this ceases at an age of about 7-8 months, when they enter the adult social structure. Size of the home range of *C. alpinus* packs is unknown. Packs do not appear to be territorial in the strictest sense of the word. They usually deposit feces in communal piles, especially at the points where trails cross. The factors that limit their numbers are unknown. It has been suggested that at high population densities they become especially susceptible to distemper (Davidar 1975). Although domestic dogs have been known to kill dholes they also have been seen foraging with them. Mixed groups of *C. alpinus* and Asiatic jackals (*Canis aureus*) have been noted infrequently. Hyenas are apparently ignored. Dhole packs sometimes have violent encounters with tigers (*Panthera tigris*) or leopards (*Panthera pardus*), which they drive off. They also have been known to attack Himalayan black bears (*Selenarctos thibetanus*) and sloth bears (*Melursus ursinus*).

During the heat of the day, dholes take shelter in dark shade or holes in the ground. Most hunting activity is concentrated in the early morning and early evening, but dholes also may feed during the day and on moonlit nights. Among the larger deer--staple food items in many areas--the fawns and does are preferred, especially gravid does. The pursuit and capture of large prey is similar to that described in the African wild dog (*Lycaon pictus*). The prey is tracked by scent and pursued by sight. Packs may stampede herds to separate a prey individual and then run it to exhaustion. Pack members bite at the prey and some hold on. Death is usually by disembowlment and feeding sometimes commences while the prey is still alive. Kills are often made in or near water. Smaller prey are stalked alone or in pairs and captured with a sudden burst of speed. The efficiency of their social killing led Davidar (1975) to label them "the most effective predators in the jungle." Dhole packs seek better hunting areas in times of prey scarcity. There is no evidence for claims that dholes wipe out entire deer populations; the two have coexisted for thousands of years (Davidar 1975, Lekagul and McNeely 1977a, Cohen 1977, 1978, Cohen et al. 1978).

Conservation Measures Taken: Many areas where dholes are known to occur in Thailand are protected, such as Khao Yai National Park and Khao Soi Dao Wildlife Sanctuary (IUCN 1979).

Conservation Measures Proposed: Basic data on life history, home range, movements, and reproduction are needed for sound conservation plans to be formulated (Cohen 1977). Surviving dhole populations in Thailand should be identified and studied. Game wardens and the general public should be encouraged not to shoot them. Forest cover in areas where healthy dhole populations are known to occur should be preserved. The Thai government should consider enacting laws to protect the species.

Asiatic black bear
Selenarctos thibetanus Cuvier 1823
Mammalia, Carnivora, Ursidae

Status: Threatened.
CITES (1979): Appendix I.
WARPA (1980): Protected-2.

Population Size and Trend: This bear's numbers have been greatly reduced over most of its wide range. The Baluchistan bear, *S. t. gedrosianus* is nearly extinct in Iran and Pakistan (IUCN Red Data Book 1972, Firouz 1976). The typical race, *S. t. thibetanus*, is rather rare in Thailand, and most individuals occur in the north and west (Gyldenstolpe 1919, Lekagul and McNeely 1977a). The black bear is in very great danger of extirpation in many parts of Japan (Nozaki et al. 1979).

Distribution and History of Distribution: Asiatic black bears were once found in the Soviet far east, most of China, Korea, the major islands of Japan, Taiwan, Hainan, Vietnam, Kampuchea, Lao PDR, Thailand north of Kra, Burma, Assam and Kashmir in northern India, Nepal, Afghanistan, Pakistan, and Iran. The total extent of their contemporary range is much the same, but they have been extirpated in many areas and they survive in disjunct populations (Ellerman and Morrison-Scott 1951, Prater 1971, IUCN Red Data Book 1972, Walker 1975, Lekagul and McNeely 1977a).

Geographic Status: Black bears in Thailand are peripheral, occurring at the southern limit of the species' distribution.

Habitat Requirements and Habitat Trend: In most of their range (including Southeast Asia), black bears prefer the forests of the hills and mountains but sometimes are found at lower elevations. They have been recorded at 3,660 m in the Himalayas. When food is abundant, their home range may be as small as 500-600 ha, but probably it more commonly covers a much more extensive area. Territorial behavior has not been reported. *Selenarctos* is an opportunist and an omnivore, but it is quite capable of killing large hooved mammals, including adult water buffalo (*Bubalus bubalis*). Honey is a favorite food. Carrion sometimes is taken. The following food items have been recorded: young growth of trees, grass, fruit, nuts, bulbs, berries, insects (especially bees, ants, termites, and beetles), and many vertebrates, large and small (Gyldenstolpe 1919, Ognev 1931, Novikov 1956, Prater 1971, Ewer 1973, Lekagul and McNeely 1977a, Keulen-Kromhout 1978, Takada 1979). The montane forests they prefer in Southeast Asia are rapidly being cleared.

Vulnerability of Species and Habitat: Black bears are very destructive of cultivated fruits, nuts, berries, and field crops. They also damage beehives and steal livestock feed. In Japan, where the remaining *Selenarctos* are confined to small patches of native forest and re-forested areas, their impact on trees is severe. They often kill sheep and goats and sometimes even horses, cattle, and buffalo. Many people have been mauled or killed by black bears in recent times, usually without apparent provocation. The widespread destruction of black bears has been prompted by fears of these bear-human conflicts. Furthermore, the Chinese apothecary tradition attributes medicinal values to certain tissues of *Selenarctos* (Prater 1971, IUCN Red Data Book 1973, Watanabe et al. 1973, Walker 1975, Watanabe and Komiyama 1976, Nozaki et al. 1979).

Causes of Threat: Deforestation, destruction of bears as pests, overhunting for food and sport, and capture for the live animal trade are all threats to *Selenarctos*. Thailand exported 237 live Asiatic black bears between 1967 and 1971 (RFD 1972). In a price list dated 12 June 1979, a Bangkok-based animal exporter offered eight young *Selenarctos* for sale at US $350 each. We have seen these animals for sale in Bangkok's Sunday Market. South Korean businesses are purchasing bear gall bladders for US $200 each (J. McNeely, personal communication).

Responses to Habitat Modification: Unknown, but deforestation is certainly detrimental to *Selenarctos*.

Demographic Characteristics: In India these bears mate in late autumn. Gestation is 7-8 months. Litters range from 1-3 and are usually two. The eyes open in about a week and the cubs are weaned in 3-3.5 months. Young bears attain sexual maturity in their third year. Females may not give birth annually in the wild. Captives may live as long as 33 years (Novikov 1956, Prater 1971, Walker 1975, Lekagul and McNeely 1977a). *Selenarctos* hybridize with *Ursus arctos* in captivity, and because of this Van Gelder (1977) proposed that *S. thibetanus* be included in the genus *Ursus*.

Key Behaviors: Cubs are kept in a den in a tree hollow, a cave, or thick underbrush. They do not leave their mother until the end of their second summer, and females are sometimes seen accompanied by the young of two successive litters. Adults are solitary except when breeding. They generally feed at night and spend the day in rock crevices, caves, tree hollows, or in nests of sticks in the crowns of trees. They are adept climbers and also swim well. Northern populations deposit fat in autumn and hibernate in tree hollows, caves, or rock crevices during winter (Novikov 1956, Prater 1971, Walker 1975, Lekagul and McNeely 1977a).

Conservation Measures Taken: Asiatic black bears may be hunted under permit from the Thailand Forestry Department (WARPA 1980). The coverage of the race that occurs in Thailand, *S. t. thibetanus*, by the CITES (1979) convention is unclear, because Appendix I lists "*S. thibetanus*" as being covered but gives "Baluchistan bear" (*S. t. gedrosianus*) as the common name. IUCN (1979) reported that Asiatic black bears occur in the following Thai national parks (NP) and wildlife sanctuaries (WS): Khao Yai NP, Thung Salang Luang NP, Nam Nao NP, Phu Phan NP, Salak Phra WS, Phu Khieo WS, Lum Nam Pai WS, Khao Khieo-Khao Chomphu WS, Phu Miang-Phu Thong WS, Salawin WS, Phachi River WS, Nam Mae Khong WS, and Khun Yuam WS. The zoos of the world hold many *Selenarctos*. In some collections, second generation captive births have occurred and the survival of cubs to maturity is quite high (Keulen-Kromhout 1978, Olney 1979).

Conservation Measures Proposed: The best way to preserve bears is to preserve forests (Takada 1979) and to control hunting and capture of the animals. The maintenance of suitable wild food plants and prey populations would help to reduce the destruction of crops and livestock by bears. If overhunting is shown to be causing bear declines, the Thai government should consider amending WARPA (1980) to Protected-1 status. Very little is known of the biology of *Selenarctos* in Southeast Asia. Research on any aspect of its life history in Thailand would be worthwhile.

Malayan sun bear
Helarctos malayanus **Raffles 1822**
Mammalia, Carnivora, Ursidae

Status: Threatened.
CITES (1979): Appendix I.
WARPA (1980): Protected-2.
Population Size and Trend: No estimates of the total numbers

of *H. malayanus* have been made. It is uncommon in India (Prater 1971). No recent status information is available from Burma, Lao PDR, Kampuchea, or Vietnam. Sun bears are widespread in Thai forests and are most common in the south (Lekagul and McNeely 1977a). They are widespread in peninsular Malaysia but not abundant (Medway 1978).

Distribution and History of Distribution: Sun bears are found in northeastern India south of the Brahmaputra River, Burma, Lao PDR, Vietnam, Kampuchea, Thailand, peninsular Malaysia, Sumatra, Borneo, and possibly southern China (Chasen 1940, Davis 1962, Prater 1971, Lekagul and McNeely 1977a, Medway 1978).

Geographic Status: Thailand is central to the sun bear's range.

Habitat Requirements and Habitat Trend: These small arboreal bears occur in forests at all elevations in Southeast Asia. They are omnivorous, eating fruits, vegetables, earthworms, termites, other invertebrates, and any small vertebrates they can catch. They eat carrion and may scavenge at tiger kills. They are very fond of honey and bee larvae (Davis 1962, Ewer 1973, Walker 1975, Lekagul and McNeely 1977a, Medway 1978). The forests they depend upon are being lost at an alarming rate throughout Southeast Asia.

Causes of Threat: Deforestation and capture for the live animal trade threaten this bear. At least 131 were exported from Thailand between 1967 and 1971 (RFD 1972). A Bangkok-based animal exporter, in a price list dated 12 June 1979, offered three young *Helarctos* for sale at US $350 each.

Responses to Habitat Modification: Unknown, but clear-cutting forests is certainly detrimental to sun bears.

Demographic Characteristics: There is no evidence of seasonality of breeding in sun bears (Ewer 1973). The gestation period has variously been give as 95, 96, 174, 228, and 240 days. These reports were of animals born in temperate-zone zoos, and the vagaries in gestation periods are probably the result of varying lengths of delayed fertilization or delayed implantation--phenomena well known in ursids. One or two cubs are born, and a female can produce two litters a year in captivity. Sun bears have lived over 20 years in captivity (Dathe 1961, Ewer 1973, McCusker 1974, Medway 1978). *H. malayanus* hybridizes with the sloth bear, *Melursus ursinus*, in captivity (Asakura 1969). Because of this, Van Gelder (1977) proposed that *H. malayanus* be included in the genus *Melursus*.

Key Behaviors: Sun bears are cautious, wary, and very intelligent (Walker 1975). They are the smallest, most lightly built, and most arboreal of the living bears (Ewer 1973). They are excellent climbers and sleep in nests in trees. They forage primarily at night but have been seen walking about in the daytime. Most reports have been of single animals, but pairs are seen, and Walker (1975) stated that they are monogamous. In the wild, young are kept on the ground, typically at the buttressed bases of tall trees, until they are old enough to climb safely (Davis 1962, Lekagul and McNeely 1977a, Medway 1978).

Conservation Measures Taken: This species may be hunted under permit from the Thailand Forestry Department. It probably occurs in many of Thailand's wildlife sanctuaries and national parks, especially in the south, but local distribution is poorly known. The species is present in Thaleban National Park (Dobias 1982) and Khao Yai National Park (J. McNeely, personal communication). There are many sun bears in the zoos of the world, and second-generation captive births have been reported (Dathe 1961, 1970, Keulen-Kromhout 1978, Olney 1979).

Conservation Measures Proposed: Preservation of tracts of mature forest, especially in the south, benefits a multitude of forest species including the sun bear. Surveys are needed to determine the distribution and abundance of this carnivore in Thailand. The effects of hunting, capture for the live animal trade, and different forestry practices on sun bear populations need to be studied. If overhunting is shown to be causing bear declines, the Thai government should consider amending WARPA (1980) to Protected-1 status.

Back-striped weasel
Mustela strigidorsa **Gray 1853**
Mammalia, Carnivora, Mustelidae

Status: Threatened
WARPA (1980): Protected-1.

Population Size and Trend: If this weasel survives in Thailand its numbers are certainly small.

Distribution and History of Distribution: This animal may be rare, but it is widespread, having been collected in Sikkim, Nepal, India (Assam), Lao PDR, Burma, "Tenaserim", and Thailand. It also

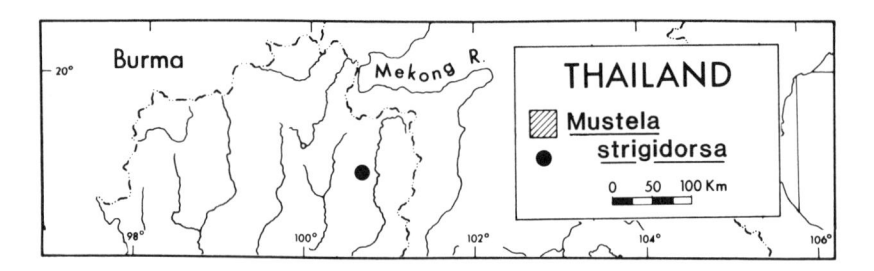

Fig. 93. Distribution of the Back-striped Weasel (*Mustela strigidorsa*).

occurs in western and southern Yunnan and southern Guangxi in China (Schrieber et al. 1987). The one Thai specimen was collected in a village in Ban Na Kha Subdistrict of Nan Province by Kitti Thonglongya (Fig. 93; Lekagul and McNeely 1977a).

Geographic Status: Back-striped weasels in Burma and Thailand lie at the southern limits of the species' distribution.

Habitat Requirements and Habitat Trend: *M. strigidorsa* is reported to inhabit temperate forest between 900 and 2,135 m (Prater 1971, Schrieber et al. 1987).

Vulnerability of Species and Habitat: Unknown.
Causes of Threat: Unknown.
Responses to Habitat Modification: Unknown.
Demographic Characteristics: The female has two pairs of mammae, suggesting that the usual litter is about four.

Key Behaviors: This mustelid has been reported to attack prey several times it own size (Hutton 1922 in Lekagul and McNeely 1977a).

Conservation Measures Taken: Thai law (WARPA 1980) prohibits hunting and regulates trade in this species.

Conservation Measures Proposed: Because better information is needed on the status of this animal, hunters, biology students, and local conservation officials should learn to distinguish this form from other small carnivores and report its presence to the proper authorities.

Family Mustelidae--Subfamily Lutrinae--The Otters
Introductory Comments

Four otters occur in Thailand; the common otter, *Lutra lutra*, the smooth-coated otter, *L. (Lutrogale) perspicillata*, the hairy-nosed otter, *L. sumatrana*, and the small-clawed otter, *Amblonyx (Aonyx) cinerea*. Very little is known of their biology in Southeast Asia. The recent books on the mammals of Thailand (Lekagul and McNeely 1977a) and peninsular Malaysia (Medway 1978) contain almost no original or recent information on wild otters. However, apparently all have declined in Thailand and are threatened with extirpation in at least parts of their Thai range (Anonymous 1976, Leng-Ee 1979, B. Lekagul and D. Damman personal communication). The biology of most of the world's tropical otter populations has not been well studied. There is a clear and urgent need for field studies on the ecology of otters in Thailand.

Vulnerability and Causes of Threat: Direct economic exploitation of otters for the fur trade and the live animal trade have been implicated as causes of otter declines in many areas. Hunting probably did not harm otter populations in most areas until the 20th century, but its effects on modern low-density populations can be devastating (MacDonald and Mason 1976). Overhunting was a primary cause of the great decline in Thai otters since the mid-1960s (Anonymous 1976, Leng-Ee 1979). Over 1,100 live otters were legally exported from Thailand between 1967 and 1971 (RFD 1972), and Thailand was a major source of the live otters imported into the United States in the same period (USFWS 1970, 1971, 1972). Otters are intelligent and have considerable appeal as pets. They are kept as pets by villagers in Southeast Asia (Wayre 1976), and we have seen them for sale in Bangkok's Sunday Market. If taken while young they rapidly become tame (e.g., Novikov 1956). Wild young are not as wary as adults (Hewson 1973) and are relatively easy to catch. "They [*L. lutra*] make engaging pets, following one about like a dog" (Prater 1971), but they are notoriously hard to breed in captivity without technical knowledge.

Fishermen have long killed otters as pests, not recognizing their beneficial role in fisheries (discussed below). Many are shot or poisoned in Thailand each year (Anonymous 1976, B. Lekagul and D. Damman personal communication). Destructive and illegal fishing methods used by some Thai fishermen, including the use of explosives, electrical shocks, and poisons (typically pesticides), are widespread, serious threats to otters (Anonymous 1976). In some areas, bounties were paid on otters until quite recently to encourage their destruction as pests (Fairley and Wilson 1972b). Many are inadvertently killed each year by being drowned in such devices as fish traps, fish nets, crab and lobster traps, and by being run over by cars (Southern 1964, Erlinge 1968a, Fairley and Wilson 1972b, Jenkins 1980).

The widespread alteration and outright destruction of freshwater and coastal habitats is probably the major threat to most otter populations, including those in Thailand, where most wetlands have been converted to rice cultivation and many rivers are being dammed (Anonymous 1976). The draining of marshes and other wetlands, the impoundment and channelization of rivers, and the clearing of bankside vegetation are threats to otters throughout Eurasia (MacDonald and Mason 1976, IUCN Red Data Book 1978, MacDonald et al. 1978, Jenkins 1980, Wayre 1980). Most otters are naturally shy of man, and seclusion from human disturbance is critical to successful reproduction. Females with young cubs are highly sensitive to disturbance (IUCN Red Data Book 1978, Wayre 1979, 1980, Jenkins 1981). Otters avoid houses, towns, highways, crops, and heavily grazed areas along rivers (Jenkins and Burrows 1980). Human settlement is typically concentrated along rivers, lakes, and seacoasts. Waterways have been the highways of the Thai people since their earliest days, and the inadvertent impairment of otter reproduction by human disturbance is probably an important problem in Thailand today.

The effects of water pollution are difficult to assess, but there is a growing concern that otters are highly vulnerable to certain pollutants. DDT, dieldrin, other pesticides, herbicides, and their metabolites have been implicated as causes of otter declines in Europe (e.g., IUCN Red Data Book 1978, Wayre 1980). Mercury concentrations thought to be capable of impairing reproduction have been found in the tissues of otters in some areas (e.g., Halbrook et al. 1980). There are now indications that mercury pollution of industrial origin is severe in some Thai waters (Suckcharoen 1978, 1979, Suckcharoen et al. 1978). Many otter species have relatively low reproductive rates (for small carnivores), and even a minor reduction can have severe consequences. Additionally, oil spills are known to cause death of coastal otters (Wayre 1980). Because they are sensitive to pollution, otters are useful as indicators of environmental degradation.

Conservation Measures Taken and Proposed: Thai law

(WARPA 1980) prohibits hunting and regulates trade in otters. Additionally, the capture of otters should be banned, and selected otter habitats in Thailand should be preserved. Otter populations in several areas, such as the Netherlands and Israel, have increased since the Second World War because the animals and selected habitats are strictly protected (e.g., Lewis et al. 1968, MacDonald and Mason 1976). The local distribution of otters in Thailand is unknown, but outside of the Mekong and Chao Phraya rivers (IUCN 1979, II:45) they are said to be largely restricted to reserves. Wayre (1976) reported that otters are abundant in the area that is now Tarutao Marine National Park. Anonymous (1976) proposed that Thung Thong Non-hunting Area be declared an otter sanctuary. Eudey (1979) reported that otters occur in Huai Kha Khaeng Wildlife Reserve.

In areas where total protection is not feasible, Wayre (1979), Jenkins and Burrows (1980), and Jenkins (1981) have developed the concept of small "otter havens" in Britain, which, if modified to meet Thai conditions and established at intervals along selected rivers, could do much to relieve the pressures facing the Thai Lutrinae without unduly infringing on human interests. An area with side streams entering the river is chosen where forest with good undergrowth or other suitable plant cover is available on both banks. Havens need to include not only both banks, but some inland forest along secluded streams as well, for use by breeding females. Freedom from human disturbance is essential, especially during the rearing of the young. If the area is open to human foot traffic, pedestrians should be restricted to one bank and (ideally) to the daytime hours only. Paths should be constructed well back from the bank.

The ecology of otters in Thai coastal waters is not known well enough to indicate conservation measures at this time. Research on many aspects of the ecology of Thai otters is needed to allow the formulation of sound management plans. The local distribution, habitat requirements, and reproductive biology of each species are high-priority topics for research. Because of the important role the three *Lutra* species play in freshwater fisheries, they are worthy subjects of research by graduate students and professional researchers in fisheries and wildlife. Methods now exist for estimating otter distributions by studying their feces (e.g., Jenkins and Burrows 1980, Robson and Humphrey 1985). Northcott and Slade

(1976) developed an effective live-trapping method for river otters that causes very little inadvertent mortality. By injecting an individual otter with small quantities of radioactive zinc, Jenkins (1980) was able to identify the animal's feces and study its movements. Melquist and Hornocker (1980) have developed telemetry technology for radiotracking river otters. The biology of otters along seacoasts is poorly known, so the coastal Thai *Amblonyx* offer a promising subject for research.

The continual monitoring and control of levels of such contaminants as mercury and pesticides in water, fish, and otters would benefit not only otters but the Thai people as well, since they consume aquatic plants and derive so much of their animal protein from freshwater fish.

There is a great need to educate the public (especially students and villagers) about the plight of otters in Thailand, the need to conserve them, and their natural role in the ecosystem. Fish-eating otters (*Lutra* species) do not select certain species of fish. Instead, they capture those that are the easiest to catch, often the diseased and injured ones (e.g., Erlinge 1968*b*). They thus help maintain the health of the fish population and are beneficial to man. In Thailand, *Amblonyx* is thought to benefit rice farmers by consuming destructive freshwater crabs (Lekagul and McNeely 1977*a*).

These small carnivores are now threatened in Thailand by habitat degradation and human disturbance, but with foresight, research, sound conservation measures, and public education there is hope for their recovery and future in the Thai fauna.

Common otter
Lutra lutra **(Linnaeus 1758)**
Mammalia, Carnivora, Mustelidae

Status: Threatened.
IUCN Red Data Book (1978): Vulnerable (*L. l. lutra* only).
CITES (1979): Appendix 1.
WARPA (1980): Protected-1.

Population Size and Trend: The vernacular name of *L. lutra*, "the common otter," is rapidly becoming a misnomer throughout most of its wide range in Eurasia and northern Africa. This otter has experienced a great decline in the 20th century and is now uncommon, endangered, or extirpated in many areas where it was once abundant (e.g., Novikov 1956, Lewis et al. 1968, Erlinge 1972, MacDonald and Mason 1976, IUCN Red Data Book 1978, Kruuk and Hewson 1978, Wayre 1980). The Southeast Asian race, *L. l. barang* has been uncommon in Thailand throughout recorded history (Gyldenstolpe 1919) and has suffered a recent decline in Thailand and elsewhere (IUCN Red Data Book 1978, B. Lekagul and D. Damman personal communication). There are no estimates of the total population size.

Distribution and History of Distribution: *L. lutra* is known from Europe (including Ireland and Great Britain), Africa north of the Sahara, Asia Minor, most of the Soviet Union (including many offshore islands), most of China (including Hainan), Japan, and Taiwan; across southern Asia from Iran to northern India, Nepal, Sikkim, Burma, northern Thailand, possibly northern Lao PDR, and Vietnam. There is also an isolated population in Singapore, Sumatra, and Java, and one in southern India and Sri Lanka. The only record from peninsular Malaysia is one specimen from the Langkawi Islands (Flower 1900, Miller 1900, Chasen 1940, Ellerman and Morrison-Scott 1951, Novikov 1956, Van Peenen et al. 1969, Prater 1971, Lekagul and McNeely 1977a, IUCN Red Data Book 1978, Medway 1978).

Geographic Status: Thailand is peripheral to the mainland range of *L. lutra* in eastern Asia.

Habitat Requirements and Habitat Trend: Very little is known of the biology of tropical populations. Most of the information in this account was gleaned from European studies. *L. lutra* ranges from seacoasts to 3,660 m in the Himalayas (Prater 1971). In Thailand it is found in the streams and lakes of the mountains of the north (Lekagul and McNeely 1977a, Leng-Ee 1979). In some places *L. lutra* lives along coasts and feeds in the sea (e.g., Southern 1964, Kruuk and Hewson 1978), but in most areas their favorite habitat is the cold streams and lakes of the hills and mountains. Otters have well-defined home ranges and may remain in the same area for years (Erlinge 1967). In Sweden, Erlinge (1967, 1968a) found the following situation. The density in optimal habitats is one otter per 2-3 km of lakeshore or 5 km of stream. An adult male otter uses a home range 15-25 km in diameter, the size varying with the topography, access to water, the food supply, and the density and distribution of den sites. A male's range may include the smaller ranges of several females and their young. Females use a range about 7 km in diameter. The female's range may be greatly restricted when the young are small. The habitat in which the nursery den is made often differs from the habitat where the young are weaned and reared (Jenkins 1980). Densities in France and Britain are about one otter per 10 km of river (MacDonald and Mason 1976).

These otters subsist mainly on fish. They readily exploit (and may even follow) fish spawning migrations. Instead of selecting certain species of fish, they take the ones that are the easiest to catch, and injured and diseased fish are thus culled from the population. Crayfish and frogs are seasonally important in some areas. The following minor food items have been recorded: earthworms; terrestrial, freshwater, and marine crustaceans; terrestrial and aquatic insects (notably beetles); slugs, snails, and bivalves; newts, toads, and the tadpoles of frogs; small reptiles; waterfowl and shorebirds (especially the young); shrews, voles, muskrats, hares, rabbits, and other small mammals. Berries and other plant food are rarely taken. *L. lutra* will eat dead fish, but only if very hungry and unable to find other food (Ognev 1931, Novikov 1956, Southern 1964, Erlinge 1968a, 1968b, 1969, Hewson 1969, 1973, Prater 1971, Fairley and Wilson 1972a, 1972b, Webb 1975, Kucherenko 1976, Kruuk and Hewson 1978, Jenkins et al. 1979, Jenkins and Burrow 1980, Jenkins and Harper 1980).

Vulnerability of Species and Habitat: See the Introductory Comments.

Causes of Threat: See the Introductory Comments.

Responses to Habitat Modification: Human disturbance and the clearing of vegetation along riverbanks are known to be detrimental to this otter. A certain degree of eutrophication may be beneficial, as it tends to increase the availability of easily-caught species of fish (IUCN Red Data Book 1978).

Demographic Characteristics: In some warm and cold temperate areas mating is seasonal (e.g., Novikov 1956, Erlinge 1968b), but in others it is not (e.g., Southern 1964, Jenkins 1980). There is no evidence of seasonality of births in tropical populations. Females are capable of producing a litter each year, but most do not (Erlinge 1968a, IUCN Red Data Book 1978). In captives, estrus is monthly (Duplaix-Hall 1975). Gestation lasts 60-63 days (Ewer 1973, Duplaix-Hall 1975, Medway 1978). Litters of 1-5 have been reported.

Most are 1-3 (Novikov 1956, Erlinge 1968a, Ewer 1973). The eyes open in 9-10 days (Novikov 1956). In temperate zones, winter mortality is heavy in otters less than 1 year old (Jenkins 1980). Sexual maturity is attained in 2-3 years (Erlinge 1968a). Captives may live to be 20 years old (Southern 1964).

Key Behaviors: *L. lutra* is an essentially asocial carnivore. The male does not help rear the young. Adult males continually check the receptivity of females within their range (Erlinge 1968a). A brief male-female pair bond is formed during mating. Copulation occurs in the water (Cocks 1881, Erlinge 1967, Duplaix-Hall 1975). A female with young is very aggressive toward adult males. Young leave their mothers after 7-12 months (Erlinge 1967, Duplaix-Hall 1975, Jenkins 1980, 1981).

Common otters use two types of shelters: dens and more exposed resting places. Dens are made in hollow trees, in burrows excavated by other animals, beneath roots, among rocks, in small caves, or in dense vegetation such as sedges or reeds. Dens often have more than one entrance. Entrances are typically near water, but there is no evidence to support the often-repeated notion that dens have underwater entrances like the lodges constructed by beavers. Entrances are typically above the level of flood risk. Other resting places are made in a variety of sheltered locations, including tree cavities, under bank overhangs, in sandbanks, in hollows under boulders, and in dense vegetation (Erlinge 1967, Hewson 1969, Lekagul and McNeely 1977a, Kruuk and Hewson 1978, Jenkins 1981).

Varying degrees of territoriality have been described in otter populations in different areas. In Sweden, Erlinge (1967, 1968a) found otters maintaining well-defined territories, defended against members of the same sex. Some subadults ranged widely and had no territories. Adult male ranges adjoined and overlapped, and there were continual territorial conflicts in the zones of overlap. Males were primarily solitary but travelled for short periods with female-young family groups within their ranges. Adult males controlled the most favorable habitats. Subadult males were relegated to marginal habitats. When a male's range became vacant by mortality or emigration it was quickly appropriated by neighboring males. Territorial conflicts between females are rare once territories have been established, and there is typically an unoccupied zone between the ranges of female-young family groups. These ranges continually expand as the young grow up. Erlinge proposed that territories were maintained by avoidance, facilitated by visual and olfactory signals (primarily fecal piles), and not by aggression. Pursuits were rare and actual fights very rare. Marking behavior was intense at high otter densities.

In a coastal British population, Kruuk and Hewson (1978) found dens to be quite evenly spaced. In freshwater habitats in Scotland, Jenkins (1980) observed that otter families tended to avoid each other but sometimes came together to play, and that at high densities temporal displacement was the rule, rather than strict spatial territoriality.

Otters forage mostly at night, but at high densities and in some areas where there is little human disturbance many individuals are diurnal (Novikov 1956, Jenkins 1980). Prey (especially large fish) are often taken to shore to be consumed. In the ocean, *L. lutra* rarely ventures more than 100 m offshore. Birds are attacked from underwater or stalked on shore. In some situations, several mother-young family groups may cooperatively fish. Food caching has been described. *L. lutra* are known to move locally in response to changes in food availability (Novikov 1956, Prater 1971, Kruuk and Hewson 1978, Jenkins 1980). Otters spend most of their time near the center of their home ranges. They use runways and work regular routes while hunting, stopping at traditional resting and rolling places, slides, feeding sites, and fecal piles (Erlinge 1967).

Conservation Measures Taken: Until quite recently there has been very little success at breeding otters in captivity (Cocks 1881, Duplaix-Hall 1975). Animals believed to be *L. l. barang* have been bred in captivity (Wayre 1976), and the Otter Trust is having such great success with breeding *L. l. lutra* that careful plans for reintroducing them in selected European habitats are being considered (Wayre 1980). Eudey (1980) reported that *L. lutra* occurs in Thailand's Huay Kha Khaeng Wildlife Sanctuary. See the Introductory Comments.

Conservation Measures Proposed: See the Introductory Comments.

Smooth-coated otter
Lutra (Lutrogale) perspicillata **Geoffroy 1826**
Mammalia, Carnivora, Mustelidae

Status: Threatened.
CITES (1979): Appendix II.
WARPA (1980): Protected-1.

Population Size and Trend: The smooth-coated otter is now uncommon in Thailand (B. Lekagul and D. Damman, personal communication). There are no estimates of its total numbers.

Distribution and History of Distribution: This otter is found in most of India, Nepal, Sikkim, Bhutan, Bangladesh, Burma, possibly southern China, Thailand, Lao PDR, Kampuchea, possibly southern Vietnam, peninsular Malaysia (including Penang and the Langkawi Islands), and Sumatra. It ranges throughout Thailand (Chasen 1940, Ellerman and Morrison-Scott 1951, Van Peenen et al. 1969, Wayre 1976, Lekagul and McNeely 1977a, Medway 1978, Leng-Ee 1979). There is a small, isolated, relict population of the smooth-coated otter in the marshes of the Tigris River in Iraq (Hatt 1959).

Geographic Status: Thailand is central to the Southeast Asian range of *L. perspicillata*.

Habitat Requirements and Habitat Trend: This *Lutra* is an animal of low elevations. It ranges from seacoasts up into low hills. It hunts in fresh water, estuaries, and coastal waters. In India it is even found in some arid regions. It prefers fish but also takes frogs, turtles, aquatic invertebrates, and other small animals. A family group needs 7-12 km of river or a greater length of seacoast (Prater 1971, Desai 1974, Lekagul and McNeely 1977a, Medway 1978).

Vulnerability of Species and Habitat: *L. perspicillata* are kept by fishermen in India to drive fish into nets and to attract river dolphins (Prater 1971), but this limited exploitation probably does little harm to otter populations. See the Introductory Comments.

Causes of Threat: See the Introductory Comments.

Responses to Habitat Modification: Unknown.

Demographic Characteristics: Females come into estrus every month. There is no evidence of seasonality of reproduction in captive or wild smooth-coated otters. Gestation lasts 61-63 days. Litters of 1-6 have been reported. Postpartum estrus is known. The eyes open at 10 days. Weaning begins at 3 months and is completed by about 18-20 weeks. Captives attain adult size at 1 year, first mate as early as 22 months, and females first give birth as early as 24 months. Captives have lived over 15 years (Yadav 1967, Ewer 1973, Desai 1974, Duplaix-Hall 1975, Medway 1978).

Key Behaviors: Copulation and parental care have been observed in captive *L. perspicillata*. Estrous females are friendly toward males and solicit copulation. There is a prolonged period of playful precopulatory behavior. Mating usually occurs in the water. This species is a powerful digger. Both sexes build an extensive burrow leading to a den. The den is lined with dry vegetation and kept clean. For the first few days postpartum the female may drive off the male, but afterward he helps to feed and rear the young. Captive groups are dominated by one female and defended from intruders by a dominant male. The typical wild family group in peninsular Malaysia is reported to include an adult male, an adult female, and up to four young. Cooperative fishing between several family groups has been reported. *L. perspicillata* is very dexterous and shows great skill in capturing and handling aquatic prey. It is reported to carry objects tucked under its forearm while swimming, a behavior that was once thought to be unique to the sea otter, *Enhydra lutris* (Prater 1971, Badham 1973, Ewer 1973, Desai 1974, Duplaix-Hall 1975, Lekagul and McNeely 1977a, Medway 1978).

Conservation Measures Taken: Since the mid-1960s many zoos have bred this otter in captivity (e.g., Yadav 1967, Badham 1973, Desai 1974, Duplaix-Hall 1975, Olney 1979). See the Introductory Comments.

Conservation Measures Proposed: See the Introductory Comments.

Hairy-nosed otter
Lutra sumatrana **(Gray 1865)**
Mammalia, Carnivora, Mustelidae

Status: Threatened.
CITES (1979): Appendix II.
WARPA (1980): Protected-1.

Population Size and Trend: The hairy-nosed otter is now uncommon and threatened in Thailand (B. Lekagul and D. Damman, personal communication). There are no estimates of its total numbers.

Distribution and History of Distribution: *L. sumatrana* is found in Thailand south of the Isthmus of Kra, peninsular Malaysia (including Penang), Singapore, Sumatra, Bangka, Java, and Borneo. Apparently there also is a population in southern Vietnam that may extend into southern Kampuchea and southeastern Thailand. Except for its possible extirpation in Singapore, its historical range has not changed (Flower 1900, Gyldenstolpe 1919, Chasen 1940, Ellerman and Morrison-Scott 1951, Davis 1962, Van Peenen et al. 1969, Hoogerwerf 1970, Lekagul and McNeely 1977a, McNeely 1977, Medway 1978, Leng-Ee 1979).

Geographic Status: The major population of *L. sumatrana* reaches the northern limits of its distribution in southern Thailand. This *Lutra* may be a tropical derivative of *L. lutra*.

Habitat Requirements and Habitat Trend: Hairy-nosed otters forage in freshwater habitats, but more often they occur on beaches, in brackish waters, and in shallow coastal waters. Mangroves and estuaries may be important habitats for *L. sumatrana*. They are thought to rely more on fish than on crustaceans and other invertebrates (Hoogerwerf 1970, Lekagul and McNeely 1977a, McNeely 1977, Medway 1978, Leng-Ee 1979).

Vulnerability of Species and Habitat: Like most other *Lutra*, *L. sumatrana* is easily tamed (Medway 1978). See the Introductory Comments.

Causes of Threat: See the Introductory Comments.

Responses to Habitat Modification: Unknown.

Demographic Characteristics: Unknown.

Key Behaviors: Very little is known of the status and habits of this otter (Lekagul and McNeely 1977a). Hunting groups of 3-4 individuals have been reported (McNeely 1977). Copulation probably takes place exclusively in the water (Duplaix-Hall 1975).

Conservation Measures Taken: We found no indications that *L. sumatrana* is currently being bred or kept at all by zoos. See the Introductory Comments.

Conservation Measures Proposed: See the Introductory Comments.

Small-clawed otter
Amblonyx (*Aonyx*) *cinerea* (Illiger 1815)
Mammalia, Carnivora, Mustelidae

Status: Threatened.
CITES (1979): Appendix II.
WARPA (1980): Protected-1.

Population Size and Trend: Although it is the most common of the four Thai otters, it has been reduced in numbers and is now threatened in Thailand (Anonymous 1976, B. Lekagul and D. Damman personal communication).

Distribution and History of Distribution: There is an isolated population of *Amblonyx* in southern India in the Nilgiri Hills and Coorg. This otter is also found across northern India from eastern Punjab to Assam, in Nepal, Sikkim, possibly Bhutan, northern Burma, southern China (Yunnan, Fukien, Tibet, Hainan), Thailand (except the northeastern Khorat Plateau and the central valley of the Chao Phraya), possibly Lao PDR, southern Vietnam, southern Kampuchea, peninsular Malaysia, Singapore, Sumatra (including the Riau and Ligga archipelagoes), Java, Borneo, and the Philippine island of Palawan. Its absence from central India may be due to ecological displacement by *Lutra perspicillata*. The historical range is not known to differ from the above (Flower 1900, Chasen 1940, Ellerman and Morrison-Scott 1951, Davis 1962, Van Peenen et al. 1969, Hoogerwerf 1970, Furuya 1976, Lekagul and McNeely 1977*a*, Medway 1978, Leng-Ee 1979, Feng et al. 1980).

Geographic Status: Thailand is central to the Southeast Asian range of *A. cinerea*.

Habitat Requirements and Habitat Trend: In India *A. cinerea* is a hill otter, but in Southeast Asia it is found from the sea to over 1,000 meters (Borneo). It is generally more common in fresh water than salt- or brackish water, and it prefers the streams and lakes of the hills, but it is quite common in mangroves and there are numerous reports of *A. cinerea* foraging in the sea. It is sometimes seen far away from water. It subsists more on crustaceans and molluscs and less on fish than other Thai otters, but captives will eat fish and Malay fishermen have long trained *Amblonyx* capture fish for them (Davis 1962, Hoogerwerf 1970, Prater 1971, Duplaix-Hall 1972, Walker 1975, Furuya 1976, Lekagul and McNeely 1977*a*, Medway 1978).

Vulnerability of Species and Habitat: Their gregarious behavior probably makes them very noticeable to humans. See the Introductory Comments.

Causes of Threat: *Amblonyx* suffers more from being shot as a pest by fishermen than any of the other Thai otters (B. Lekagul and D. Damman, personal communication). See the Introductory Comments.

Responses to Habitat Modification: Unknown.

Demographic Characteristics: Mating is aseasonal, even in zoos in temperate regions. Estrus occurs every 24-30 days and lasts about 3 days. Gestation lasts 60-64 days and females are thought to be capable of producing two litters per year. Litters range from one to seven and are usually two to four. The eyes open in 5 weeks. Young swim as early as 9-12 weeks. Captives have lived over 10 years (Hoogerwerf 1970, Ewer 1973, Duplaix-Hall 1975, Lancaster 1975, Lekagul and McNeely 1977a, Medway 1978, Carson 1981).

Key Behaviors: Copulation is initiated by the female chasing the male. *Amblonyx* typically mates in water, but captives have been observed mating on land. A den is excavated and lined with dry vegetation. In the wild, dens are made in holes in riverbanks and similar situations. A captive male was seen to assist in the delivery of a litter, and many authors report adult males helping to feed and rear young. These otters are gregarious. Wild family groups comprising up to 15 members have been seen. In captivity one female dominates a group and a dominant male drives away intruders. *A. cinerea* swim and dive with great agility. The forepaws are very sensitive and are used to explore for and manipulate prey. Food and young are carried by pressing them against a cheek or the chest and employing a tripedal walk. Bipedal walks are seen when *A. cinerea* carry older young or armloads of bedding. Manual dexterity is obviously of great importance to them in locating and handling prey. Shellfish are sometimes collected and placed in the sun, whereafter they open by themselves. Many otters are relatively silent, but this species has an impressive vocal repertoire (Hoogerwerf 1970, Timmins 1971, Duplaix-Hall 1972, 1975, Ewer 1973, Lancaster 1975, Lekagul and McNeely 1977a, McNeely 1977, Medway 1978, Carson 1981).

Conservation Measures Taken: Small-clawed otters breed well in captivity when properly cared for. Some zoos have recorded as many as 70 captive births in recent times (e.g., Timmins 1971,

Duplaix-Hall 1975, Lancaster 1975, Carson 1981). Their occurrence in Thai preserves has not been surveyed, but they are known to be present in Thung Thong Waterfowl Reserve in Surat Thani Province (Storer 1978). See the Introductory Comments.

Conservation Measures Proposed: See the Introductory Comments.

Spotted linsang
Prionodon pardicolor **Hodgson 1842**
Mammalia, Carnivora, Viverridae

Status: Endangered.
CITES (1979): Appendix I.
IUCN (1979): Confined to a few habitats in Thailand.
USFWS (1980a): Endangered.
WARPA (1980): Protected-1.

Population Size and Trend: Though widespread, *P. pardicolor* has been uncommon throughout its range since its discovery. It is very rare in Thailand (e.g., Prater 1971, Lekagul and McNeely 1977a, B. Lekagul and D. Damman personal communication).

Distribution and History of Distribution: The spotted linsang is known from Nepal, Sikkim, Bhutan, India (Assam), southern China, northern Burma, northern Thailand, most of Lao PDR, and northern Vietnam. It is rare and local in northern Thailand (Ellerman and Morrison-Scott 1951, Van Peenen et al. 1969, Prater 1971, Walker 1975, Lekagul and McNeely 1977a, IUCN 1979).

Geographic Status: The spotted linsang occurs in Thailand near the southern limit of its distribution.

Habitat Requirements and Habitat Trend: These largely arboreal civets are confined to the thick forests of the mountains and hills from 150 m to at least 2,000 m. They are quite carnivorous, subsisting mainly on birds, but they also take insects and small mammals (Prater 1971, Walker 1975, Lekagul and McNeely 1977a, Wemmer 1977).

Vulnerability of Species and Habitat: Their need for forested habitat makes spotted linsang vulnerable to deforestation. Their confinement to a few isolated habitats in northern Thailand makes them very susceptible to localized habitat disruptions.

Causes of Threat: Deforestation of upland habitats by logging and high density slash-and-burn agriculture threatens this rare carnivore in Thailand. *P. pardicolor* is an attractive animal and becomes tame in captivity. It sometimes is kept as a pet (Prater 1971).

Responses to Habitat Modification: Unknown.

Demographic Characteristics: Little is known of the demography of these elusive civets. Litters of two and three young are known. *P. pardicolor* bears two litters per year--one in February and one in October (Prater 1971, Walker 1975).

Key Behaviors: The habits of wild spotted linsang are poorly known. They are said to nest and bear their young in hollow trees. They forage at night in the trees and on the ground. They are excellent climbers and descend head first like many other viverrids. (Prater 1971, Walker 1975, Lekagul and McNeely 1977a, Wemmer 1977).

Conservation Measures Taken: Thai law (WARPA 1980) prohibits hunting and regulates trade in this species. IUCN (1979) and Prakobboon (1979) did not report the occurrence of *P. pardicolor* in any of Thailand's reserved areas, and few established reserves exist in the parts of northern Thailand where the spotted linsang occurs. It is rarely kept in captivity and few, if any, are now held in the world's zoos.

Conservation Measures Proposed: The forest cover of the hills and mountains of northern Thailand must be preserved if the spotted linsang is to survive in that area. Basic studies on the distribution and ecology of this animal are urgently needed.

Banded linsang
Prionodon linsang **(Hardwicke 1821)**
Mammalia, Carnivora, Viverridae

Status: Endangered.
CITES (1979): Appendix II.
IUCN (1979): Confined to a few habitats in Thailand.
WARPA (1980): Protected-1.

Population Size and Trend: Though widespread, *P. linsang* has been uncommon throughout its range since its discovery. It is rare in Thailand (Lim 1973, Medway 1978, B. Lekagul and D. Damman personal communication).

Distribution and History of Distribution: Banded linsang are known from the Tenasserim and peninsular Burma and Thailand, peninsular Malaysia, Sumatra (possibly including Bangka Island), Java, and Borneo. It is rare and local in Thailand (Chasen 1940, Ellerman and Morrison-Scott 1951, Davis 1962, Walker 1975, Lekagul and McNeely 1977a, Medway 1978, IUCN 1979).

Geographic Status: This linsang reaches the northern limit of its distribution in the Thai Tenasserim.

Habitat Requirements: *P. linsang* is largely restricted to dense lowland forests, although it sometimes is found next to settled areas. Unlike other Thai viverrids it is strictly carnivorous. The following food items have been reported: large insects, fish, frogs, lizards, snakes, birds and their eggs, arboreal and terrestrial rodents, and probably any other small animals they can catch. Captives refuse crabs and fruits (Harrison 1961, Lim 1973, Walker 1975, Lekagul and McNeely 1977a, Lim and Betterton 1977, Medway 1978).

Vulnerability of Species and Habitat: Lowland forests in Southeast Asia are among the first habitats to be cleared, and most already have been.

Causes of Threat: Deforestation is detrimental to banded linsang. There is also a minor trade in live animals (e.g., USFWS 1970, 1971, 1972).

Responses to Habitat Modification: In some areas, *P. linsang* may respond favorably to secondary growth and ecotonal habitats (Lim 1973).

Demographic Characteristics: Pregnant females (including ones near term) have been taken in May in peninsular Malaysia, and lactating females have been taken there in April and October. *P. linsang* is believed to give birth twice a year in the wild. Captives have lived over 9 years (Lim 1973, Walker 1975).

Key Behaviors: The habits of wild banded linsang are poorly known because they are rare and nocturnal. They are excellent climbers and descend head first, like most viverrids. They are largely arboreal but also forage on the forest floor. They make nests of sticks and leaves in tree cavities, in fallen logs, under roots, and sometimes in burrows in the ground (Lim 1973, Walker 1975, Lekagul and McNeely 1977a, Wemmer 1977, Medway 1978).

Conservation Measures Taken: Thai law (WARPA 1980) prohibits hunting and regulates trade in this species. Prakobboon

(1979) stated that banded linsang occur in the Phu Miang-Phu Thong Wildlife Sanctuary; there is no evidence of their occurrence elsewhere in Thailand. Although captives have given birth (Louwman 1970), they do not do well in captivity (Lekagul and McNeely 1977a), and few, if any, are now held in the world's zoos.

Conservation Measures Proposed: Basic studies on the distribution and ecology of Thai banded linsang are needed to determine the locations of viable populations and their conservation needs. The true degree to which they tolerate (or even benefit from) habitat disturbance requires elucidation.

Binturong
Arctictis binturong **(Raffles 1821)**
Mammalia, Carnivora, Viverridae

Status: Threatened.
IUCN (1968): Threatened.
IUCN (1979): Rare.
WARPA (1980): Protected-1.

Population Size and Trend: Though widespread, the binturong is rare throughout its range. No estimates of its total numbers have been made. It has long been considered rare in Thailand (Gyldenstolpe 1919, Harper 1945, Hoogerwerf 1970, Lekagul and McNeely 1977a, Medway 1978).

Distribution and History of Distribution: Wild binturong occur in Burma, Thailand, Lao PDR, Vietnam, Kampuchea, peninsular Malaysia, Sumatra (including Nias, Bangka, Bintan, Kundur, and other offshore islands), Java, Borneo, and the Philippine island of Palawan. Suggestions that binturong occur in India (Assam), Bhutan, Sikkim, and Nepal probably are based on imported live animals purchased in markets--there is no hard evidence to support their occurrence in the wild in that region (Chasen 1940, Harper 1945, Ellerman and Morrison-Scott 1951, Davis 1962, IUCN 1968, Van Peenen et al. 1969, Prater 1971, Walker 1975, Lekagul and McNeely 1977a, Medway 1978).

Geographic Status: Binturong in northern Thailand occur near the northern limit of the species' range.

Habitat Requirements and Habitat Trend: These arboreal civets are confined to tall forests. They occur from sea level to over 1,000

m. Although thy have been reported to take a wide variety of plant and animal foods, wild binturong are primarily frugivores, and they may be the most frugivorous of the Paradoxurinae. Binturong also feed on tree shoots and leaves, insects, fish, roosting birds, small mammals, garbage, and carrion. Captives eat almost anything but show marked individual variation in food preference (Ogilvie 1958, Harrison 1961, Davis 1962, IUCN 1968, Hoogerwerf 1970, Prater 1971, Ewer 1973, Walker 1975, Lekagul and McNeely 1977a, Medway 1978).

Causes of Threat: Deforestation and capture for the live animal trade threaten this rare, large viverrid. At least 161 live *A. binturong* were exported from Thailand between 1962 and 1971 (RFD 1972). A Bangkok-based animal exporter, in a price list dated 12 June 1979, offered binturong for sale at US $250 each. We have seen binturong on sale in Bangkok's Sunday market.

Response to Habitat Modification: Binturong can survive in secondary forest if mature food trees are available (B. Lekagul and D. Damman, personal communication).

Demographic Characteristics: Binturong have long lives and a relatively low reproductive potential. They are aseasonally polyestrous. Gestation averages 91 days (range 84-99). Litters range from one to six young but average two. One litter per year is typical for pairs in captivity. Young begin taking solid food at 6-8 weeks. Age at sexual maturity averages 30 months for females. Captives have lived 25 years, but the maximum known reproductive life is 14 years (Bulir 1972, Kuschinski 1974, Xanten et al. 1976, Lekagul and McNeely 1977a, Medway 1978, Aquilina and Beyer 1979, Wemmer and Murtaugh 1981).

Key Behaviors: These civets are primarily nocturnal and arboreal, but diurnal foraging and terrestrial activity are known. Some captives become crepuscular or diurnal. Binturong can swim and fish-catching is suspected. The only social groups that have been reported are females with young. Wild young are reared in tree hollows. Adults sleep by day in tree hollows or on high branches. Most foraging is done in the canopy. Binturong climb slowly but skillfully. The distal portion of the tail is prehensile and is used as an aid in climbing. Captives descend head first. In trees, wild *A. binturong* approach roosting birds silently and slowly. They have not been seen to leap. Scent marking is accompanied by a quadrupedal squat, an upright stance, and a perianal drag; the last method is seen in juveniles as young as 102 days. Captive binturong practice site-specific defecation (Ogilvie 1958, Davis 1962, Prater 1971, Kleiman 1974, Walker 1975, Xanten et al. 1976, Lekagul and McNeely 1977a, Wemmer 1977, Medway 1978). Lekagul and McNeely (1977a) suggested that wild binturong are territorial.

Conservation Measures Taken: Thai law WARPA (1980) prohibits hunting and regulates trade in this species. IUCN (1979) reported that binturong occur in Khao Luang National Park and Khlong Nakha, Khlong Saeng, and Khao Banthat wildlife sanctuaries. They also occur in Khao Yai National Park (W. Brockelman, personal communication). Binturong breed successfully in captivity and many are held in the world's zoos (e.g., Gensch 1963, Bulir 1972, Kuschinsk 1974, Xanten et al. 1976, Aquilina and Byer 1979, Olney 1979).

Conservation Measures Proposed: Field studies on the ecology and behavior of these arboreal civets would allow a better understanding of their conservation needs. Radiotracking would permit investigations of activity patterns and home ranges. The effects of different forestry practices on binturong populations require elucidation.

Banded palm civet
Hemigalus derbyanus **(Gray 1837)**
Mammalia, Carnivora, Viverridae

Status: Threatened.
CITES (1979): Appendix II.
WARPA (1980): Protected-1.

Population Size and Trend: Banded palm civets are common in parts of northern Borneo (Davis 1962), but on the mainland they are rare, though widespread. Few museum specimens with good locality data are known from Thailand (Lim 1973, Lekagul and McNeely 1977a, Medway 1978).

Distribution and History of Distribution: This *Hemigalus* is found in the Tenasserim of Burma and Thailand south of the Isthmus of Kra (Fig. 94), peninsular Malaysia, Sumatra (including Sipora, South Pagi, and other offshore islands), and Borneo (Gyldenstolpe 1919, Chasen 1940, Ellerman and Morrison-Scott 1951, Davis 1962, Lekagul and McNeely 1977a, Medway 1978).

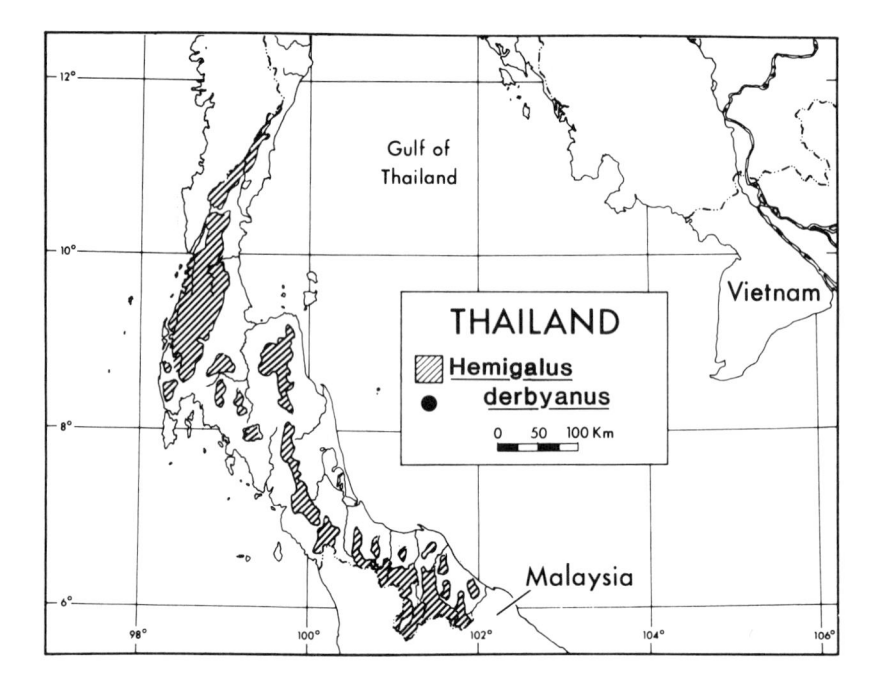

Fig. 94. Distribution of the Banded Palm Civet (*Hemigalus derbyanus*).

Geographic Status: *H. derbyanus* occurs in Thailand at the northern extreme of its range.

Habitat Requirements and Habitat Trend: Banded palm civets are apparently confined to tall primary forests, where they occupy ground level. They may prefer streams and streambanks. Their diet is mainly invertebrates. In Borneo they have been found to subsist primarily on orthopterans and earthworms. They are also known to eat spiders, scorpions, centipedes, millipedes, crabs, beetles, larval lepidopterans, hemipterans, ants, wasps, termites, aquatic and terrestrial molluscs, frogs, caecilians, lizards, and rodents (Davis 1962, Lim 1973, Medway 1978).

Vulnerability of Species and Habitat: Their preference for primary forest renders them vulnerable to deforestation. They are sought by zoos.

Causes of Threat: Deforestation and the degradation of forest streams threaten *H. derbyanus*. There is a minor trade in live animals (e.g., USFWS 1971, 1972).

Responses to Habitat Modification: Unknown.

Demographic Characteristics: Few banded palm civets have been bred in captivity and next to nothing is known of their reproduction in the wild. A pregnant female examined by Medway (1978) had one embryo. Females have six mammae (Liat 1973). In captivity the eyes open in 8-12 days and young take solids at about 70 days (Ewer 1973).

Key Behaviors: The habits of wild banded palm civets are almost completely unknown. Davis (1962) reported that these civets forage primarily on the forest floor and do not dig into the ground or rotten logs. The climbing abilities of captives led Lekagul and McNeely (1977a) to speculate that wild individuals may be at least partially arboreal. Wild *Hemigalus* have been found in nests in tree hollows (Lim 1973). Captives are nocturnal. Females carry their young by the middle of the back (Ewer 1973). These civets have scent glands (Lekagul and McNeely 1977a), and captive *Hemigalus* have been seen wiping objects with their hindquarters (Wemmer 1977)--presumably scent-marking.

Conservation Measures Taken: Thai law (WARPA 1980) prohibits hunting and regulates trade in this species. The potential for captive breeding has been demonstrated (Louwman 1970), but few are now held in the world's zoos.

Conservation Measures Proposed: Studies on the ecology and distribution of the *H. derbyanus* in southern Thailand are needed to allow an assessment of their conservation needs. Burning, grazing, and disruptive forestry practices should be avoided in the primary forest where this species survives. If it is indeed dependent on streams, then the preservation of forest streams also is essential.

Otter civet
Cynogale bennetti **Gray 1837**
Mammalia, Carnivora, Viverridae

Status: Threatened.
CITES (1979): Appendix II.
IUCN (1979): Threatened.
WARPA (1980): Protected-1.

Population Size and Trend: Judging from the few literature records, this aquatic civet has always been uncommon in Southeast

Asia. It is rare but widespread in peninsular Malaysia (Flower 1900, Medway 1978).

Distribution and History of Distribution: Otter civets are known from southern Thailand, peninsular Malaysia, Sumatra, and Borneo (Chasen 1940, Lekagul and McNeely 1977*a*, Medway 1978). The single record from northern Vietnam (Pocock 1933) is questionable.

Geographic Status: The otter civet reaches the northern extreme of its range in southern Thailand.

Habitat Requirements and Habitat Trend: This viverrid is aquatic, keeping to streams, rivers, and swamps. It lives on fish, frogs, crustaceans, freshwater molluscs, and, to a lesser extent, small mammals, birds, and fruit (Ewer 1973, Walker 1975, Lekagul and McNeely 1977*a*, Medway 1978). Wetlands in Thailand have been converted almost completely to permanent wet rice culture.

Vulnerability of Species and Habitat: Its dependence on aquatic habitats makes *Cynogale* vulnerable to many development activities that degrade aquatic habitats.

Causes of Threat: The loss of wetlands threatens this specialized civet. Siltation from mines, persistent pesticides in the food chain, and other kinds of water pollution pose serious threats.

Responses to Habitat Modification: Unknown.

Demographic Characteristics: Otter civets have not been bred in captivity and little is known of their reproduction. Medway (1978) noted cases of females with two to three embryos. The female has four mammae (Lekagul and McNeely 1977*a*).

Key Behaviors: *Cynogale* can close its ears to exclude water (Ewer 1973), and its nostrils open upward. It is said to lie in ambush in the water with only its eyes and nostrils exposed, much like crocodilians (Lekagul and McNeely 1977*a*). These civets have scent glands. They can climb and do so when pursued by dogs (Walker 1975).

Conservation Measures Taken: Thai law (WARPA 1980) prohibits hunting and regulates trade in this species. Olney (1979) reported that only one otter civet, a male, is held in the world's zoos.

Conservation Measures Proposed: The protection of wetland habitats in southern Thailand is of paramount importance to the survival of this animal. Basic studies on its distribution and ecology are needed.

Marbled cat
Felis marmorata Martin 1837
Mammalia, Carnivora, Felidae

Status: Endangered.
IUCN Red Data Book (1978): Indeterminate.
CITES (1979): Appendix I.
USFWS (1980a): Endangered.
WARPA (1980): Protected-1.

Population Size and Trend: The marbled cat is thought to be rare and endangered over most of its range, but this may be due in part to its highly secretive habits and preference for inaccessible areas. Viable populations still exist in the hill states of eastern India. It is now quite uncommon in Thailand (IUCN Red Data Book 1978, B. Lekagul personal communication).

Distribution and History of Distribution: This felid is found in Nepal, Sikkim, Assam, Burma, Thailand, Lao PDR, Kampuchea, Vietnam, peninsular Malaysia, Sumatra, and Borneo. In Thailand there have been few reports in the north in the past three decades. Marbled cats are least rare along the Tenasserim (Chasen 1940, Ellerman and Morrison-Scott 1951, Medway 1969, Van Peenen et al. 1969, Cheke 1973, Lekagul and McNeely 1977a, IUCN Red Data Book 1978).

Geographic Status: Thailand is central to the range of *F. marmorata*.

Habitat Requirement and Habitat Trend: Marbled cats are arboreal and restricted to tropical forests. The diet probably consists of insects, lizards, snakes, birds, and a wide variety of small mammals (Pocock 1932, Lekagul and McNeely 1977a, P. Leyhausen personal communication).

Vulnerability of Species and Habitat: Its dependence on forests makes *F. marmorata* vulnerable to deforestation. It has been reported to kill domestic fowl on rare occasions.

Causes of Threat: There is a minor trade in live animals for zoos and private collections. The major threat is habitat destruction (P. Leyhausen personal communication).

Responses to Habitat Modification: Although it does occur to some extent in secondary forest (B. Lekagul, personal communication), it does not tolerate human presence (IUCN Red Data Book 1978).

Demographic Characteristics: All available data deal with captive animals. In zoos there is no confined breeding season. Gestation is 66-82 days. The eyes of young begin to open at 12 days, the kittens first try to walk at 15 days, and they begin accepting meat at 121 days. Captives have lived over 12 years (Medway 1969, Barnes 1976).

Key Behaviors: Because it is nocturnal, arboreal, and very secretive, nothing is known of its habits in the wild. Captives are said to have a vocal repertoire very similar to that of a domestic cat (Barnes 1976).

Conservation Measures Taken: Thai law (WARPA 1980) prohibits hunting and regulates trade in marbled cats. They have been reported to occur in Khao Soi Dao Wildlife Sanctuary, Phu Luang Wildlife Sanctuary, and Khao Kitchakut National Park (IUCN 1979, Prakobboon 1979), and in Khao Yai National Park (W. Brockelman, personal communication). They have been bred in captivity, and there are at least seven held in the world's zoos (Olney 1979).

Conservation Measures Proposed: Basic studies on the distribution, status, ecology, and effects of human disturbance on these cats are needed (IUCN Red Data Book 1978). The extent to which they can thrive in secondary forest requires elucidation.

Fishing cat
Felis viverrina **Bennett 1833**
Mammalia, Carnivora, Felidae

Status: Threatened.
CITES (1979): Appendix II.

Population Size and Trend: This cat is still fairly common in many areas in Thailand. It is one of the least threatened of the Thai felids (B. Lekagul, personal communication).

Distribution and History of Distribution: *F. viverrina* has a disjunct distribution, occurring in three areas. One population is found in southern India and Sri Lanka. Another ranges from Nepal, east through eastern India, Bangladesh, Burma, and Thailand north of the peninsula, to Kampuchea, Lao PDR, and Vietnam. A third group occupies Sumatra and Java. It is not known from peninsular Malaysia (Ellerman and Morrison-Scott 1951, Medway 1969, Lekagul and McNeely 1977a).

Geographic Distribution: Thailand is central to the range of the population that occurs from Nepal to Vietnam. Its disjunct range suggests a relictual situation (Lekagul and McNeely 1977a).

Habitat Requirements and Habitat Trend: Fishing cats prefer brush or scrub near water. They also frequent mangroves, marshy meadows, and forest edges and tall grass near water. Most sightings are of animals sitting next to moving water. Fish are their staple food item, but molluscs, crustaceans, birds, rodents, and other small animals are taken. Captives readily feed on milk, beef, and chicken (Hoogerwerf 1970, de Alwis 1973, Ewer 1973, Jayewardene 1975, Lekagul and McNeely 1977a, McNeely 1977).

Vulnerability of Species and Habitat: These cats do kill chickens and other domestic animals and there are records in the older literature of *F. viverrina* carrying off small children in India. In Thailand, mangrove and freshwater swamp forests are threatened by excessive harvest and by various development activities. Fortunately, the pelt of this cat has little economic value.

Causes of Threat: Hunting, live capture, and habitat destruction place all the wild Thai felids in a precarious situation (Lekagul and McNeely 1977a:604). Between 1967 and 1971, 448 *F. viverrina* were declared for export from Thailand (RFD 1972). In many parts of Southeast Asia, development is opening up inaccessible habitats that were once strongholds of the fishing cat. In Sri Lanka there has been a recent increase in the capture of live young and hunting for food and pelts (de Alwis 1973).

Responses to Habitat Modification: The loss of concealing vegetation near water is probably detrimental to fishing cats. Siltation from tin mining and upstream deforestation may allow the expansion of mangrove habitats (McNeely 1977), to the benefit of the fishing cat.

Demographic Characteristics: A mating season has not been described in Thailand. In Sri Lanka, wild kittens are found in April and October, indicating two mating periods per year (Jayewardene 1975). The length of gestation is variously given as 63 days (Ulmer 1968, Hemmer 1976) or 90-95 days (Lekagul and McNeely 1977a). The usual litter is two. Captive kittens first leave the nest in 3-4 weeks and first take meat at about 53 days of age. In 6-7 months they are completely weaned. Adult size is attained in 8-9 months. The life span is unknown (Ulmer 1968, Lekagul and McNeely 1977a).

Key Behaviors: Wild animals are believed to rear their young in tree hollows. Fishing cats take fish by crouching near the water and swatting the fish out onto dry ground. The feet are partially webbed. They do not enter water to feed as readily as the flat-headed cat, *F. planiceps*. Captive kittens are seen batting at water when less than 2 months old. These cats tend to hold struggling prey rather than dropping it and attacking again. *F. viverrina* is very aggressive and does not tame easily. There are records of fishing cats killing leopards much larger than themselves (Ulmer 1968, de Alwis 1973, Ewer 1973, Jayewardene 1975, Lekagul and McNeely 1977a, McNeely 1977).

Conservation Measures Taken: Thai law prohibits hunting and regulates trade in this species. Fishing cats occur in many protected areas in Thailand, including Khao Sam Roi Yot National Park, Doi Chiang Dao Wildlife Sanctuary, Salawin Wildlife Sanctuary, Khun Yuan Wildlife Sanctuary, and Bung Boraphet No-hunting Area (IUCN 1979). Suggestions that these cats occur in the south at Thale Noi No-hunting Area (IUCN 1979:113) and Thung Thong waterfowl Reserve Area (Storer 1978) are probably erroneous. Fishing cats are successfully bred in captivity, and many zoos keep them (Olney 1979).

Conservation Measures Proposed: Suitable vegetation for cover near water should be preserved in areas where fishing cats occur. Basic studies on the distribution and ecology of fishing cats are needed to allow a more precise determination of their status and conservation needs.

Leopard cat
Felis bengalensis bengalensis **Kerr 1792**
Mammalia, Carnivora, Felidae

Status: Threatened.
CITES (1979): Appendix I.
USFWS (1980a): Endangered.
WARPA (1980): Protected-1.

Population Size and Trend: This is the commonest wild cat in Thailand and most of Southeast Asia. It is certainly the least threatened of the Thai felids (Paradiso 1972, Lekagul and McNeely 1977a, B. Lekagul, personal communication).

Distribution and History of Distribution: The leopard cat is one of the most widespread of the Asian cats. It is found in the Amur Valley in the eastern Soviet Union, throughout eastern China and Korea, on the South Korean island of Cheju (Quelpart) and the Japanese island of Tsuchima off the Korean coast, Hainan, Vietnam, Lao PDR, Kampuchea, Thailand, peninsular Malaysia, Singapore, Sumatra, Nias Island, Java, Bali, Borneo, the Philippine island of Palawan, Burma, Assam, Bangladesh, and across northern India, Bhutan, Sikkim, and Nepal to Jammu and Kashmir. It ranges throughout Thailand and occurs on many offshore islands (Chasen 1940, Ellerman and Morrison-Scott 1951, Medway 1969, Kowalski 1976, Lekagul and McNeely 1977a). Geptner (1971) proposed that the Soviet population and part of the Chinese one are a distinct species, *F. euptilura*.

Geographic Status: Thailand is central to the range of the leopard cat.

Habitat Requirements and Habitat Trend: *F. bengalensis* occurs in a wide variety of habitats, from undisturbed primary forest to early seral stages. It is known to eat insects, fish, amphibians, lizards, snakes, birds, rodents, civet cats, small deer, and sometimes leaves. Leopard cats have been seen in caves, feeding on fallen bats and swifts (Lim and Omar 1961, Medway 1969, Hoogerwerf 1970, Muul and Lim 1970, Ewer 1973, Lekagul and McNeely 1977a, Lim and Betterton 1977).

Vulnerability of Species and Habitat: Chicken raiding has been widely reported. This brings leopard cats into direct conflict with local human interests.

Causes of Threat: There is a major trade in live animals for zoos, safari parks, and pets. Thailand exported at least 1,128 between 1967 and 1971. The United States imported 748 live leopard cats between 1968 and 1970; over 97% of the 1970 imports were from Thailand. In recent times, leopard cats have been captured in Thailand, smuggled into Lao PDR, given Lao certificates of origin, and re-exported through the Bangkok airport (USFWS 1970, 1971, 1972; Paradiso 1972, RFD 1972, Harrisson 1974, IPPL 1979).

Responses to Habitat Modification: Leopard cats thrive in secondary growth, even near villages, and have been reported from plantations and suburbs (Lim and Omar 1961, Medway 1969, Lekagul and McNeely 1977a).

Demographic Characteristics: Most data indicate aseasonal

mating in the wild, but Lim and Omar (1961) suggest that in peninsular Malayasia *F. bengalensis* may breed twice a year--once in February and March and again in August and September. Gestation averages about 66 days. Litters range from one to four and are usually two to three. The eyes open at 10 days. If a litter is lost, a female may give birth to another in 4-5 months (Dathe 1968, Hemmer 1976, Lekagul and McNeely 1977a). The age at sexual maturity has been variously given as 18 months (Lekagul and McNeely 1977a) and 32 months (Hemmer 1976). Captives may live 13 years (Medway 1979).

Key Behaviors: Leopard cats climb trees readily and may leap from trees onto their prey. They tend to hold struggling prey rather than drop it and reattack. Pairs and small family groups have been seen. Dens are found in tree hollows. The male plays a tolerant, active role in raising the young. Leopard cats are excellent swimmers and have colonized many islands. Indeed, the type specimen was captured while swimming in the Bay of Bengal. They do not tame easily (Liat and Omar 1961, Denis 1965, Medway 1969, Ewer 1973, Lekagul and McNeely 1977a).

Conservation Measures Taken: Thai law (WARPA 1980) prohibits hunting and regulates trade in this species. These cats occur in many protected areas in Thailand. They are easily kept and bred in captivity, and there are many in the world's zoos (Dathe 1968, Olney 1979).

Conservation Measures Proposed: Leopard cats are easily crossed with domestic cats to produce fertile, viable hybrids. They are thus a valuable genetic resource to biomedical research (e.g., Benveniste and Todaro 1975) and the pet industry.

Flat-headed cat
Felis planiceps **Vigors and Horsfield 1827**
Mammalia, Carnivora, Felidae

Status: Endangered.
IUCN Red Data Book (1978): Indeterminate.
CITES (1979): Appendix I.
IUCN (1979): Threatened.
USFWS (1980a): Endangered.
WARPA (1980): Protected-1.

Population Size and Trend: No estimates have been made of the total numbers of this cat. It is thought to be rare and endangered throughout its range (Lim and Omar 1961, Medway 1969, Muul and Lim 1970, Lekagul and McNeely 1977a, IUCN Red Data Book 1978).

Distribution and History of Distribution: Flat-headed cats are found in the extreme southern province in Thailand, through peninsular Malaysia, to Sumatra and Borneo. Records from Singapore are thought to represent captive animals that have escaped. The local distribution in southern Thailand is unknown (Chasen 1940, Ellerman and Morrison-Scott 951, Medway 1969, Lekagul and McNeely 1977a, IUCN Red Data Book 1978, P. Leyhausen personal communication).

Geographic Status: *F. planiceps* reaches the northern limit of its mainland distribution in southern Thailand.

Habitat Requirements and Habitat Trend: This cat is essentially a strict carnivore, eating fish, frogs, and lizards, but frugivory has occasionally been reported. It lives in marshes, riverbanks, and other mesic lowland habitats. It has nonretractile claws and other morphological features that are probably related to its fishing habits. It is more aquatic than *F. viverrina* (Lim and Omar 1961, Muul and Lim 1970, Ewer 1973, Lekagul and McNeely 1977a, Lim and Betterton 1977, IUCN Red Data Book 1978, P. Leyhausen personal communication). Muul and Lim (1970) believe that this cat may be the ecological equivalent of a semiaquatic mustelid.

Vulnerability of Species and Habitat: Unknown.

Causes of Threat: The major threat to *F. planiceps* is habitat destruction (P. Leyhausen, personal communication). There is a minor trade in live animals. The species is eaten in Southeast Asia (Hill 1964).

Responses to Habitat Modification: Unknown.

Demographic Characteristics: The demography of this carnivore is almost completely unknown. Young animals have been taken in Borneo in January and peninsular Malaysia in March. The female has four pairs of teats (Lim and Omar 1961, Denis 1965, Ewer 1973).

Key Behaviors: *F. planiceps* is very elusive. It is probably the least known of the Thai felids. It shows no reluctance to submerge its face--unusual behavior for a felid. It enters water freely, dives well, and frequently captures prey by snapping it up with the mouth. Prey are carried at least 2 m away from the water before being eaten, preventing slippery prey from easily reentering the water (Muul and Lim 1972, Ewer 1973, Lekagul and McNeely 1977a, McNeely 1977).

Conservation Measures Taken: Thai law (WARPA 1980) prohibits hunting and regulates trade in this species. It is not known to occur in any of the Thai wildlife sanctuaries or national parks. It does breed in captivity, and at least 10 are now held in the world's zoos (Olney 1979).

Conservation Measures Proposed: Surveys are needed to determine the distribution and status of *F. planiceps* in southern Thailand. Before meaningful conservation measures can be proposed, basic ecological studies are needed. Thale Ban National Park and Sakayo Kuwing Labu Wildlife Sanctuary, both on the Malaysian border, fall within the presumed range of this cat. If viable populations are discovered in southern Thailand, strict protection of the animals and their habitat at the local level will be needed to ensure their continued survival.

Jungle cat
Felis chaus Guldenstaedt 1776
Mammalia, Carnivora, Felidae

Status: Threatened.
CITES (1979): Appendix II.
WARPA (1980): Protected-1.

Population Size and Trend: This cat is still fairly common in many parts of India and Southeast Asia (e.g., Schaller 1967). It is one of the least threatened Thai felids.

Distribution and History of Distribution: The jungle cat is found from Egypt north to the Caucasus, east through Iran, Afghanistan, Pakistan, India (except Kashmir) and Sri Lanka, Nepal, and Bangladesh, to Burma, southern Yunnan, Lao PDR, Vietnam, Kampuchea, and Thailand north of the Isthmus of Kra (Ellerman and Morrison-Scott 1951, Lekagul and McNeely 1977a).

Geographic Status: Thailand is central to the Southeast Asian part of the jungle cat's range.

Habitat Requirements and Habitat Trend: The common name is a misnomer. These cats are found in tall grass, deciduous forest, thick bush, and the banks of canals and streams (Lekagul and McNeely 1977a). They feed on insects, frogs, lizards, birds up to the size of peafowl, rodents, hares, small deer, and the young of larger ungulates. They eat carrion, too, and are said often to clean up after tigers. Grass sometimes is eaten (Schaller 1967, Ewer 1973, Lekagul and McNeely 1977a).

Vulnerability of Species and Habitat: The pelt is of little commercial value (Paradiso 1972). This species is less shy of man than most cats, and it readily takes domestic fowl.

Causes of Threat: Hunting, live capture, and habitat destruction place all the wild Thai felids in a precarious situation (Lekagul and McNeely 1977a:604). There is a minor trade in live jungle cats.

Responses to Habitat Modification: Jungle cats are the most common wild cat near villages in certain parts of northern Thailand (Lekagul and McNeely 1977a).

Demographic Characteristics: Although this cat is widespread and abundant in the wild and commonly kept in zoos, very little has been written about its demography. Gestation takes about 66 days (Hemmer 1979).

Key Behaviors: This cat is terrestrial and runs down its prey. It is less nocturnal than most felids. Mating congregations have been reported. Captives tame easily and groom each other (Denis 1965, Schaller 1967, Jayewardene 1975, Lekagul and McNeely 1977a).

Conservation Measures Taken: Thai law (WARPA 1980) prohibits hunting and regulates trade in this species. Jungle cats undoubtedly occur in many protected areas in Thailand north of the Isthmus of Kra. They breed successfully in captivity and are widely kept in the world's zoos (Olney 1979).

Conservation Measures Proposed: Wildlife conservation officials should include the jungle cat in their surveys of small mammal populations in game reserves and continue to monitor the trade in this species.

Asian golden cat
Felis temmincki **Vigors and Horsfield 1827**
Mammalia, Carnivora, Felidae

Status: Threatened.
IUCN Red Data Book (1978): Indeterminate.

CITES (1979): Appendix I.
IUCN (1979): Threatened.
USFWS (1980a): Endangered.
WARPA (1980): Protected-1.

Population Size and Trend: There are no estimates of the total population of *F. temmincki*. It is rare in Sumatra and peninsular Malaysia and thought to be declining in India, Sumatra, and peninsular Malaysia. There is no recent information on its status in Burma, southern China, Lao PDR, Kampuchea, or Vietnam. In Thailand it is still locally common in some places (IUCN Red Data Book 1978, B. Lekagul personal communication).

Distribution and History of Distribution: The Asian golden cat ranges from Nepal and Sikkim, east through Assam and Burma, to southern China, Thailand, Lao PDR, Kampuchea, Vietnam, peninsular Malaysia, and Sumatra. In Thailand it is found in suitable habitat throughout the country, except the cultivated central valley of the Chao Phraya, and is most abundant along the Tenasserim (Ellerman and Morrison-Scott 1951, Lekagul and McNeely 1977a, IUCN Red Data Book 1978).

Geographic Status: Thailand is central to the range of *F. temmincki*.

Habitat Requirements and Habitat Trend: *F. temmincki* is a ground-dwelling cat of forest and dense bushland. It is strictly carnivorous, consuming rodents, hares, small deer, birds (especially pheasants), lizards, and other small animals (Lekagul and McNeely 1977a).

Vulnerability of Species and Habitat: These cats do kill chickens, sheep, goats, and young cattle and water buffalo. They are the largest of the Thai *Felis*, and their terrestrial habits may make them especially noticeable to man (Medway 1969, Lekagul and McNeely 1977a).

Causes of Threat: Deforestation is the major threat. There is a minor trade in live animals.

Responses to Habitat Modification: *F. temmincki* does not adjust well to human settlement and cultivation (IUCN Red Data Book 1978, P. Leyhausen personal communication).

Demographic Characteristics: There is apparently no special breeding season. Gestation lasts about 95 days. One or two young are born. The eyes open at about 9 days of age. If a litter is lost a female may produce another within 4 months. Captives have lived as long as 18 years (Louwman and van Oyen 1968, Hemmer 1976, Lekagul and McNeely 1977a).

Key Behaviors: This cat is secretive and little is known of its habits. It raises its young in hollow trees, in rock hollows, and in holes in the ground. Hunting pairs have been reported. In captivity the male takes a tolerant and active role in rearing the young (Louwman and van Oyen 1968, Lekagul and McNeely 1977a).

Conservation Measures Taken: Thai law (WARPA 1980) prohibits hunting and regulates trade in this species. IUCN (1979) reported that golden cats occur in the following national parks (NP), wildlife sanctuaries (WS), and no-hunting areas (NHA): Khao Kitchakut NP, Doi Suthep-Pui NP, Khao Soi Dao WS, Phu Luang WS, Doi Chiang Dao WS, Salawin WS, Khun Yuan WS (prop), and Nong Thung Thong NHA. This cat breeds successfully in captivity, and many are kept in the world's zoos.

Conservation Measures Proposed: Basic studies on the distribution, status, and ecology of this cat are needed (IUCN Red Data Book 1978). In areas where they occur, suitable forest habitat should be protected.

Clouded leopard
Neofelis nebulosa **(Griffith 1821)**
Mammalia, Carnivora, Felidae

Status: Endangered.
IUCN (1968): Threatened.
IUCN Red Data Book (1978): Vulnerable.
CITES (1979): Appendix I.
IUCN (1979): Endangered.
MAB (1979): Endangered.
USFWS (1980a): Endangered.
WARPA (1980): Protected-1.

Population Size and Trend: This cat has become quite rare throughout its range. There are no estimates of its total numbers. It may be extinct in Hainan, and the endemic Taiwanese race, *N. n. brachyurus*, is precariously close to extinction. In India, hides were commonly seen on the market in the 1950s and 1960s but are now rarely available. Clouded leopards were fairly common in the montane forests of northern Thailand in the early part of this century, but now they are rare, local, and seriously endangered (Gyldenstolpe 1919, IUCN 1968, Paradiso 1972, Lekagul and McNeely 1977a, IUCN Red Data Book 1978, B. Lekagul personal communication).

Distribution and History of Distribution: Clouded leopards are found in eastern Nepal, Sikkim, Bhutan, northeastern India, Burma, southern China (including Hainan), Taiwan, Vietnam, Lao PDR, Kampuchea, Thailand, peninsular Malaysia, Sumatra, and Borneo. Whether *F. nebulosa* survives in Hainan is uncertain (Ellerman and Morrison-Scott 1951, Lekagul and McNeely 1977a, IUCN Red Data Book 1978).

Geographic Status: Thailand is central to the Southeast Asian part of the clouded leopard's range.

Habitat Requirement and Habitat Trend: Clouded leopards are more confined to unbroken primary forest than the other large cats of Asia. Their prime habitat is undisturbed evergreen forest. They have also been seen in mangroves and other remote areas. They are largely arboreal. From an original 80 percent, forest cover of Thailand has declined to 25 percent in 1978 (Myers 1980). Clouded leopards eat a variety of animals, including birds, rodents (even porcupines), monkeys, orangutans, and the young of ungulates (Gibson-Hill 1950, Medway 1969, Paradiso 1972, Lekagul and McNeely 1977a, B. Lekagul personal communication, P. Leyhausen personal communication).

Vulnerability of Species and Habitat: The pelt of this species is among the most attractive of all cats and is in great demand. Since clouded leopards tame remarkably well if taken while young, the demand for kittens is high. The purported habit of rearing young in tree hollows makes the young vulnerable to capture. Captives are quite susceptible to feline infectious enteritis. Wild clouded leopards habitually return to fresh kills so they are easily hunted at bait. The species has been reported to kill domestic chickens and goats (Denis 1965, Medway 1969, Paradiso 1972, Geidel and Gensch 1976, IUCN Red Data Book 1978, B. Lekagul personal communication).

Causes of Threat: Deforestation, hunting for pelts, and capture for the live animal trade are all serious threats to the clouded leopard in Thailand. Despite Thai law, a price list dated 12 June 1979 issued by a Bangkok-based animal exporter offered a male *N. nebulosa* for US $3,000 and a female (blind in one eye) for US $2,000. The magnitude of the current trade in live animals and skins is hard to assess because, with the exception of authorized exchanges and acquisitions by legitimate zoos, trade in clouded leopards is illegal in most of the world (IUCN 1968, WARPA 1980, Harrisson 1974, Lekagul and McNeely 1977a, IUCN Red Data Book 1978, CITES 1979, P. Leyhausen personal communication).

Responses to Habitat Modification: Deforestation is detrimental to *N. nebulosa*.

Demographic Characteristics: There is no evidence of a confined breeding season in the wild. Gestation ranges from 85 to 109 days and is usually 88 to 93 days. Litters of up to four young have been reported, but most are twins. The eyes open in 2 to 11 days and the kittens first walk at 19-20 days. Captive young begin to climb and show an interest in solid food by 6 weeks and begin killing their own prey at 11 weeks. They are weaned by about 80-100 days and exhibit adult pelage by 6 months. Despite the many cases of captive breeding, the age at sexual maturity is not documented in the literature. Captives may live 17 years (Fellner 1965, Fontaine 1965, Geidel and Gensch 1976, Hemmer 1976, Murphy 1976, Lekagul and McNeely 1977a).

Key Behaviors: These nocturnal cats are arboreal, secretive, and little-known. Hunting pairs have been seen. Clouded leopards often hunt by leaping on prey from an overhanging branch. Prey are stunned with a blow from a forepaw and killed with a bite from the long canines; this is the world's only living saber-toothed cat. Feathers or fur are thoroughly removed before the prey is eaten. Large kills are revisited until the food is gone. Individuals communicate by calling from elevated sites, which are used habitually (Gibson-Hill 1950, Paradiso 1972, Lekagul and McNeely 1977a, P. Leyhausen personal communication).

Conservation Measures Taken: Thai law (WARPA 1980) prohibits hunting and regulates trade in this species. Effective enforcement of international law has reduced the trade in pelts and live animals (IUCN Red Data Book 1978). *N. nebulosa* is reported to occur in the following national parks (NP) and wildlife sanctuaries (WS): Nam Nao NP, Khao Kitchakut NP, Khao Soi Dao WS, Phu Luang WS, Khlong Phraya WS, (IUCN 1979). Over 100 are held in captivity in the world's zoos, including many that were captive-born. A studbook is maintained (Olney 1979).

Conservation Measures Proposed: As long as wild *Neofelis* exist in Thailand and as long as their pelts and live young are coveted, the vigorous investigation and prosecution of animal smugglers will be necessary. Basic surveys should be undertaken to elucidate the local distribution and ecology of these secretive predators. The technology now exists for radiotracking such animals at moderate expense. Areas found to harbor *N. nebulosa* populations should be protected from poaching and deforestation.

Leopard, panther
Panthera pardus (**Linnaeus 1758**)
Mammalia, Carnivora, Felidae

Status: Endangered.
IUCN (1968): Threatened.
IUCN Red Data Book (1976): Vulnerable.
CITES (1979): Appendix I.
MAB (1979): Endangered.
USFWS (1980a): Endangered (Asian populations).
WARPA (1980): Protected-2.

Population Size and Trend: All Asian populations of this widespread cat are now endangered. Many populations are extirpated or nearly so. Range-wide, numbers are estimated at 1,155,000 animals (or an absolute minimum of 233,050) as of the 1970s (USFWS 1980c). The leopard is still found from Iran to Vietnam in isolated populations, mostly in reserves and inaccessible areas. It is now rare in peninsular Malaysia and Java. Although it is thought to be common in parts of southern China, it has been seriously depleted in northeastern China, Korea, and the Soviet far east. There are no more than 400-500 widely scattered leopards left in Thailand (Hoogerwerf 1970, IUCN Red Data Book 1972, 1976, Paradiso 1972, Myers 1973, 1975, 1976, Lekagul and McNeely 1977a, Medway 1978, Prynn 1980).

Distribution and History of Distribution: The leopard is the most widespread cat of the Old World. In recent times it ranged throughout most of sub-Saharan Africa, across northern Africa, and in isolated populations in certain mountain massifs in the Sahara itself. It ranged across southern Asia from Asia Minor through Pakistan, Afghanistan, all of India, Sri Lanka, Nepal, Bhutan, Bangladesh, Burma, Thailand, all of former Indochina, peninsular Malaysia, Singapore, and Java. Leopards were once found in Tibet,

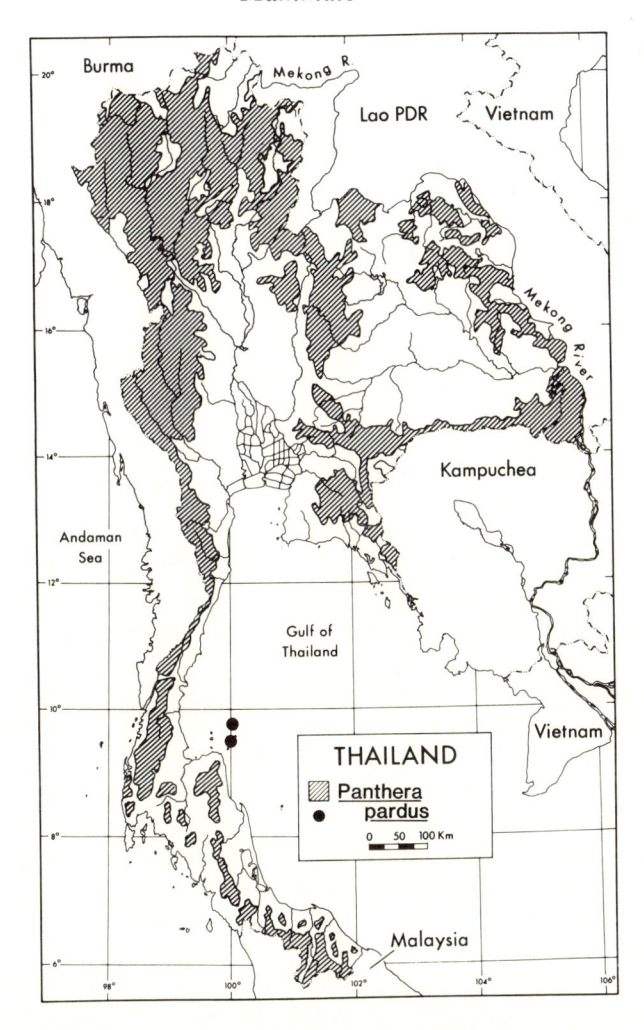

Fig. 95. Distribution of the Leopard or Panther (*Panthera pardus*).

most of China, Korea, and the Soviet far east. There are no specimens to substantiate its reputed occurrence in Japan, Sumatra, the Kangean Islands north of Bali, Borneo, or Timor. The total extent of the leopard's range is much the same today, but it has been exterminated over vast areas, so its contemporary range is fragmented. Today most wild leopards in Thailand are found in the forests of the far south (Fig. 95; Chasen 1940, Ellerman and Morrison-Scott 1951, Hoogerwerf 1970, Myers 1976, Lekagul and McNeely 1977a, Medway 1978).

Geographic Status: Thailand is central to the Southeast Asian part of the leopard's range.

Habitat Requirements and Habitat Trend: Leopards occur in a wide array of habitats (Myers 1973), from high mountains to deserts and from rainforests to seacoasts. They are both terrestrial and arboreal (Myers 1976). The one major requirement is cover from which prey can be surprised (Kruuk and Turner 1967, Ewer 1973), so the dense vegetation of transitional habitats (ecotones) is particularly suitable. In ecotones and montane forests they may reach densities as high as one animal per 2.6 km^2 (Myers 1976). In Sri Lanka, Eisenberg and Lockhart 1972) and Muckenhirn and Eisenberg (1973) found home ranges of 8-10 km^2. The home ranges of breeding adults were centered around permanent waterholes. No overlap was seen in the ranges of animals of the same sex. Subadult males occupied peripheral, suboptimal habitats. Seidensticker (1976) found the home range of a reproductive female in Nepal to be 8.0 km^2. During the first few months after bearing young, the movements of the female were greatly restricted by the relative immobility of the kittens. Wilson (1976) gave the home range of a Zambian pair of leopards as 23 km^2. Schaller (1972) estimated the density of the Serengeti population at one leopard per 22 to 26.5 km^2. Home ranges overlapped, and female ranges averaged about 50 km^2. Although leopards are sympatric with lions or tigers over most of their African and Asian range, they are ecologically separated from the larger *Panthera* by differential habitat exploitation and by direct avoidance behavior (Schaller 1967, 1972, Seidensticker 1976). There are numerous literature records of lions and tigers killing leopards and some of leopards taking young tigers. The leopard is reputed to be more tolerant of heat than the tiger (e.g., Lekagul and McNeely 1977a).

Leopards are primarily predators of medium- to large-sized mammals (Seidensticker 1980), but they are quite opportunistic and have been reported to hunt insects, crabs, fish, amphibians, reptiles (including turtles, *Python*, and *Varanus*), birds of many sorts, bats, flying lemurs, primates (including man), pangolins, hares and rabbits, aardvarks, rodents, canids, young bears, viverrids, felids (including other leopards), hyraxes, and many ungulates--even the young of *Bubalus* (Schaller 1967, 1972, Kruuk and Turner 1968,

Hoogerwerf 1970, Prater 1971, Eisenberg and Lockhart 1972, Ewer 1973, Muckenhirn and Eisenberg 1973, Myers 1976, Wilson 1976, Lekagul and McNeely 1977a, Seidensticker 1980). Leopards will feed on carrion. Grass-eating has been reported infrequently. *P. pardus* exhibit great individual variation in food preference (Kruuk and Turner 1968).

Vulnerability of Species and Habitat: The leopard is vulnerable because of its valuable hide. The spotted form is coveted for the fur trade. Some leopards habitually use the same tree cache, and all make return visits to kills (Schaller 1967, Hoogerwerf 1970). They are easily attracted to live and dead bait, making them vulnerable to hunters using poison and guns (B. Lekagul, personal communication). Leopards kill domestic fish, fowl, and mammals. Dogs are a favored food item in many areas. The killing of man and his ancestors by leopards dates from Australopithecine times (Brain 1970). This unfortunate behavior continues today but is not nearly as widespread or common as man-killing by the larger *Panthera*.

Causes of Threat: Most Asian and African nations now have laws protecting leopards, but poaching for hides is still a serious threat. Before the enactment of contemporary laws, no less than 18,000 *P. pardus* skins were imported into the United States between 1968 and 1970 (Paradiso 1972). In those days the world trade in spotted cat skins approached US $30 million a year (Myers 1973). Even with the current international treaty prohibiting commercial trade (CITES 1979), leopard hides are still available in many markets. Thai leopards have been depopulated by illegal hunting for hides and live animals (IUCN 1968, Lekagul and McNeely 1977a). Commercial overexploitation has been aggravated by ranchers systematically shooting leopards as vermin. In South Africa this has caused the near-extinction of most leopard populations. Although leopards tolerate many forms of habitat disturbance, the reduction of prey densities by habitat disruption or by direct competition with human hunters can cause declines in their populations.

Responses to Habitat Modification: *P. pardus* adapts well to human habitat manipulation, as long as it finds suitable cover and prey and is not subjected to overhunting. It readily exploits burned areas if cover is available (Seidensticker 1976), but complete conversion to short grass habitat is detrimental (Myers 1976). Leopard populations occur in teak plantations and other permanent agriculture (Hoogerwerf 1970). In Africa, they sometimes hunt in and around smaller villages (Wilson 1976) and even occur in suburban Nairobi (IUCN Red Data Book 1976).

Demographic Characteristics: The available data do not indicate a definite seasonality of births in captivity or in the wild. Females are polyestrous. Heat occurs at intervals of 3-8 weeks and lasts for 4-12 days. Gestation normally ranges from 90-105 days and averages 96 days. However, healthy young have been born after pregnancies as long as 115 days. Litters of up to six are known, but most are two or three. The female has two pair of teats. The eyes open at 0-9 days and kittens first walk at about 2 weeks. Adult size is attained in 1.5-2 years and females are sexually mature at 30-36 months. Captive females can produce litters annually, when young are taken from them at weaning. Wild kittens remain with their mothers into their second year, so wild females probably give birth every 2 years, unless they lose a litter. Captives have lived as long as 21 years (Dobroruka 1968, Eisenberg and Lockhart 1972, Schaller 1972, Ewer 1973, Muckenhirn and Eisenberg 1973, Hemmer 1976, Wilson 1976, Lekagul and McNeely 1977a, Medway 1978).

Key Behaviors: Leopards are essentially solitary animals. Most records of groups are of mated pairs or mothers with young. Mated pairs associate for at least 3 days during an estrous period before resuming their solitary habits. Nursery dens are made in caves, cavities in cliffs, hollow trees, and other concealed places. Young do not accompany the female until 4-6 months of age. Young may move about the female's home range somewhat independent of her well into their second year.

Definite pathways are used while hunting within the home range. Daily movements vary with the quality of the habitat. An animal may travel from one end of its home range to the other in 24 hours. Individual spacing is maintained by a variety of communication signals rather than by direct aggression. The grunting call may serve to facilitate locating companions and discouraging the approach of strangers. The roar, likened to the sound of sawing wood, carries far and is given at midday by females in heat. Visual and olfactory signals include scratching trees, scraping the substrate, confident or conspicuous movements in the home range, tail posture, urination, and rubbing objects with exudates from the paws, ventrum, or face.

In most places leopards are primarily nocturnal, spending the day in caves, rockpiles, or vegetation, but in areas where there are no other large predators, such as Sri Lanka, they are more diurnal and less retiring. These cats use a variety of hunting techniques. Most prey are ambushed or stalked from cover. Prey not taken in the initial charge generally are not pursued for long. Cooperative killing by leopard pairs is rare. There is scant evidence to support the popular notion that leopards leap on their prey from trees. Leopards will spot prey from elevated vantages, but then the cats leap to the ground and stalk or ambush their quarry in the usual manner. *P. pardus* readily climbs trees in search of monkeys and other arboreal prey. Small prey, such as fish, turtles, and rodents, are actively hunted. Large prey are killed by grabbing with the forepaws and biting at the throat or the back of the neck.

Leopards are slow feeders. Prey not consumed in one sitting are dragged into trees or other cover or buried between visits. Leopards revisit kills until all the meat is gone. The literature is rife with records of canids, hyaenas, and other felids stealing kills from leopards. In areas such as Namibia, where there are few terrestrial scavengers, leopards do not try to drag prey into inaccessible places unless kills are made near human habitation (Kruuk and Turner 1967, Schaller 1967, 1972, Brain 1970, Hoogerwerf 1970, Eisenberg and Lockhart 1972, Ewer 1973, Muckenhirn and Eisenberg 1973, Wilson 1976).

Conservation Measures Taken: Leopards may be hunted under permit from the Thailand Forestry Department (WARPA 1980). They have been reported to occur in the following national parks (NP) and wildlife sanctuaries (WS): Khao Yai NP, Khao Luang NP, Khao Kitchakut NP, Khlong Nakha WS, Khao Soi Dao WS, Ituai Kha Khaeng WS, Thung Yai-Naresuan WS, Khlong Saeng WS, Khao Banthat WS, Phu Miang-Phu Thong WS, Salawin WS, Mae Tun WS, Khlong Phraya WS, Mae Taeng WS, Khun Yuam WS (IUCN 1979), and Ton Nga Chang WS (Prakobboon 1979). Many leopards are kept in the world's zoos, and they breed well in captivity. The wildlife department in India solves pest leopard problems on the settled periphery of sanctuaries and thereby prevents the habit of unauthorized killing of leopards, by tracking and live-trapping the individual, releasing it in the heart of the reserve, and informing the local villagers (Chavan 1980).

Conservation Measures Proposed: The Thai and international bans on unauthorized capture, killing, and trade should be continued in the foreseeable future. Basic surveys are needed to elucidate the true distribution and abundance of leopards in Thailand, with special emphasis on the forests of the far south. Areas with viable leopard populations should be managed with consideration for their requirements for dens, cover, prey, and permanent waterholes. Poaching and smuggling should be suppressed. Education of the public on the plight and the natural role of these predators would be helpful.

Tiger
Panthera tigris **(Linnaeus 1758)**
Mammalia, Carnivora, Felidae

Status: Endangered.
IUCN Red Data Book (1978): Endangered.
CITES (1979): Appendix I.
IUCN (1979): Threatened.
MAB (1979): Endangered.
USFWS (1980a): Endangered.
WARPA (1980): Protected-2.

Population Size and Trend: The tiger has experienced a sharp decline throughout its range in this century, and only 5,000-7,500 now occur in the wild (Paradiso 1972, IUCN Red Data Book 1978). *P. t. virgata*, the Caspian race of Turkey, Iran, and the southwestern USSR, and *P. t. balica* of Bali, are probably extinct (IUCN Red Data Book 1978). Fewer than ten individuals of the Javan race (*P. t. sondaica*) survive, and the decline continues (FPS 1980, Seidensticker 1980). As many as 500 Sumatran tigers, *P. t. sumatrae*, may survive in the wild (McNeely 1979). The Siberian tiger, *P. t. altaica* (the largest living felid), is extinct in South Korea. Its status in North Korea is unknown, but there were several reports from the Demilitarized Zone in 1974 (IUCN Red Data Book 1978). There may be as many as 150 Siberian tigers in northeastern China and as many as 200 in the Soviet far east (Jackson 1979, Zhu-Jin 1979, Prynn 1980). A few individuals of the Chinese race, *P. t. amoyensis*, are thought to remain in the Yangtse Valley (IUCN Red Data Book 1978). The nominate race, *P. t. tigris*, still occurs sparingly in most of the major forest tracts in India, and in Nepal, Bhutan, southern China, Bangladesh, and Western Burma. The total population may exceed 2,000, with most in India. The Sundarbans delta of India and Bangladesh harbors a thriving population (Schaller 1967, IUCN Red Data Book 1978, Srivastava 1979). *P. t. corbetti*, recently described by Mazak (1968), occurs in eastern Burma, Thailand, Lao PDR, southeastern China, Vietnam, Kampuchea, and peninsular Malaysia. It is thought by most authorities to be the least endangered race of *P. tigris*. Probably no more than several thousand survive (IUCN Red Data Book 1978). Reports of tigers during the Vietnam war were numerous (e.g., Van Peenen et al. 1969), but there is no recent status information from Burma, Lao PDR, Kampuchea, or Vietnam. In peninsular Malaysia 500-600 may remain, but the decline continues (IUCN Red Data Book 1978). The most recent estimates for Thailand (Lekagul and McNeely 1977a, Leng-Ee 1979) are 500-600, with a continuing decline.

Distribution and History of Distribution: Tigers were once found from Turkey across southern Asia (but not Sri Lanka), most of China (including Hong Kong), to the Soviet far east (including Sakhalin Island). The Southeast Asian range included peninsular Malaysia, Penang, Singapore, Sumatra, Java, and Bali. Tigers are extinct in Turkey, Iran, the southwestern USSR, Afghanistan, Pakistan, Sakhalin Island, Hong Kong, Singapore, Bali, and many other parts of their former range. The prognosis for the Javan population is grim. In Asia today, most *P. tigris* occur in limited numbers in small, widely separated preserves. Most tigers in Thailand are found along the Tenasserim and in the forests of the south. Viable populations are also found in the Phetchabun Range, Khao Yai National Park, and the forests of the southeast (Chasen 1940, Ellerman and Morrison-Scott 1951, Schaller 1967, Lekagul and McNeely 1977a, IUCN Red Data Book 1978, Medway 1978, Mishra and Smith 1979).

Geographic Status: Thailand is central to the range of *P. t. corbetti*.

Habitat Requirements and Habitat Trend: The tiger occupies a wide array of Asian habitats, from tropical beaches and mangroves to the Himalayan snows at 4,000 m. "The only requisites for its survival appear to be some form of vegetative cover, a water supply, and sufficient prey" (Schaller 1967:225). In Southeast Asia, riparian grasslands and lowland dipterocarp forest were rich habitats for tigers. The riparian grasslands and most dipterocarp forests are gone. Reproductive females need better cover and higher prey densities than adult males, and subadult males may be relegated to suboptimal habitats (Smith 1980). Tigers are fond of water and often swim to cool themselves (Lekagul and McNeely 1977a). Schaller (1967) reviewed the literature on the variable home range sizes and land tenure systems of tigers. Schaller conducted most of his studies in Kanha National Park in India, where 319 km^2 of reserve supported 10-15 *P. t. tigris* all or part of the time. The total area covered by a female in a year's time was 65 km^2. A male covered 78 km^2 in the same period. Schaller stated that males probably selectively defend their territories against other males. He found no evidence of territoriality in females. Tigers in Nepal maintain relatively small and exclusive home ranges. A male's territory typically includes the smaller home ranges of several females (Sunquist 1979). One female in Nepal had a home range of 9.3 km^2 and used 5.0-6.9 km^2 of it each month (Seidensticker 1976). Seidensticker (1976) discussed the ecological separation between tigers and leopards.

Tigers feed primarily on hooved mammals, but they are quite opportunistic. The following prey items have been recorded: large insects including termites and locusts), crabs, fish, amphibians, snakes, lizards, turtles, crocodiles, birds, primates (including man), pangolins, hares, rodents (especially porcupines), canids, felids (including other tigers), mustelids, bears, viverrids, elephants, and virtually all of the ungulates with which they are sympatric. In India, where natural prey have been so greatly depleted, they eat mainly cattle and buffalo. In Thailand, deer and wild pigs are staple food items. Carrion is readily taken. Infrequent consumption of grass and fruit has been reported (Schaller 1967, Ewer 1973, Lekagul and McNeely 1977a, McNeely 1977, IUCN Red Data Book 1978, Medway 1978, Seidensticker 1980). The tigers Schaller studied in India seasonally ingested a fine black, micaceous soil.

Vulnerability of Species and Habitat: Their habit of eating carrion and their sensitivity to common pesticides has led many villagers to poison tigers as vermin, using insecticides in animal carcasses (Schaller 1967, Srivastava 1979). They are easily hunted at live bait (B. Lekagul, personal communication). Predation on domestic fowl and mammals is common (Schaller 1967, Medway 1978). The Chinese attribute many medicinal properties to various tiger tissues and continue to consume many each year (Myers

1975). Tigers in reserved areas often develop an indifference toward automobiles, making them vulnerable to poaching.

Man-eating was once a relatively common occurrence in certain areas. Over a thousand people a year were once eaten in India. Attacks on man have tended to increase as wild prey have declined. Most contemporary cases are the result of chance meetings with tigers--not active hunting of man by *P. tigris* (Schaller 1967, Ewer 1973, Lekagul and McNeely 1977a, IUCN Red Data Book 1978). Schaller (1967) gave five possible ways *P. tigris* can acquire a man-eating habit: 1) the tiger turns to humans because some disability prevents it from hunting its usual prey; 2) other food is lacking in an area; 3) it learns the habit from its mother; 4) it kills a man inadvertently and finds the taste agreeable; 5) it starts out by scavenging unburied corpses and transfers its attention to live prey. Orians and Pfeiffer (1970) wrote that during the succession of wars in Vietnam tigers learned to associate the sounds of gunfire with food and consumed many casualties. Van Peenen et al. (1969) gave records of tigers near military activity in Vietnam. In Thailand, several children were eaten in Loei Province in 1971 (Lekagul and McNeely 1977a), and there have been two recent man-killings in Khao Yai National Park (Schwan Tanhikorn, personal communication). The latter cases possibly were associated with the frequent feeding of free-ranging sambar deer at the homes of local residents. The tragic incidents have led to widespread killing of tigers. Man-eatings, however, are few in modern times, and most tigers prefer to avoid or ignore man.

Causes of Threat: Indiscriminate hunting and loss of cover and prey populations or deforestation have decimated the tiger and fragmented its range. Hunting, both legal and illegal, for hides, live young, sport, and the Chinese apothecary trade, continues to strain the remaining populations. Most Asian nations give *P. tigris* legal protection, but poaching and smuggling are widespread. The trade in tiger products still flourishes in Thailand, Burma, and Singapore (Paradiso 1972, RFD 1972, IUCN Red Data Book 1978, our observations). In the Salawin Valley of eastern Burma, the tiger was once killed mainly in protection of livestock, but after 1976 the rebel army of the Shan States became actively involved in the hide trade. This trade declined in the late 1970s with improved enforcement on the Thai side of the border (I. R. Grimwood, personal communication to J. Thornback). Fears for the safety of man and his domestic animals have brought about widespread killing of tigers. Killing by man is the major cause of tiger mortality in India (Schaller 1967) and probably in most of Asia. Until the mid-1960s, the Chinese government encouraged the eradication of tigers (Myers 1975, IUCN Red Data Book 1978). Conversion of natural habitats of permanent agriculture has increased tiger-human conflicts (Roy 1979).

Responses to Habitat Modification: Secondary growth may harbor a greater density of tiger prey than the original forest (IUCN Red data Book 1978). The depletion of prey populations by habitat disruption or overhunting is thought to bring about an increase in tiger predation on domestic animals (IUCN Red Data Book 1978). Tigers are not as tolerant of open habitats as leopards are, and they are more reluctant to cross cultivated areas than *P. pardus* (Seidensticker 1976). Total deforestation is clearly detrimental (B. Lekagul, personal communication).

Demographic Characteristics: Both captive and wild females are polyestrous, with a tendency for a peak of mating behavior at certain times of the year in some areas. The interval between heat periods ranges from about 20-82 days and averages 49-54 days. The length of estrus shows great individual variation and averages 5-8 days. If cubs die or are taken from the tigress, estrus can return within 3 weeks. Gestation ranges from 93-114 days. Litters range from one to seven and are usually two to three. Tigresses rarely are accompanied by more than three cubs in the wild. The eyes open at 0-17 days. Variation in the age at which the eyes open may be due to subspecific differences or to variation in the types of dens used. Cubs first show a interest in solid food in 6-13 weeks and are weaned in 5-6 months. In 18-24 months the young are independent. Juvenile mortality is high and may be greater in males. Tigers may copulate when 2.5 years old, but females are not sexually mature until 3-3.5 years and males not until about 4 years. Tigers have a high reproductive potential. In captivity, where cubs are removed when weaned, females commonly have more than one litter in a calendar year. Captive individuals have produced as many as 15 litters. Females can be reproductively active for 10 years or more. When the young survive in the wild, a female produces a litter every 2-2.5 years or more. Captives have lived 20 years (Schaller 1967, Ewer 1973, Kleiman 1974, Lekagul and McNeely 1977a, Medway 1978, Smith 1980).

Key Behaviors: Tigers are essentially solitary, but they are not unsociable. Most groups that have been reported were mated pairs or tigresses with cubs, but groups of up to nine adults have been seen. The tigress hides the young in a den, in a cave, rock overhang, hollow tree, or dense vegetation. The young leave the den at 4-8 weeks. In the first 6 months they wait for her to bring them food or to lead them to larger kills. She teaches them to handle prey by bringing them disabled animals. Newly independent young move within the female's home range into their second year. Young are independent at 18-24 months (females generally later than males). Wild estrous females travel widely and advertise their condition with vocal, visual, and olfactory cues. They are sometimes followed by several males. Copulation is brief, but tigers may copulate many times over several days. Tigers have stable home ranges with definite centers of activity. Individuals have been known to frequent the same area for years. In some places (possibly where water is localized, cover is scant, or human disturbance is excessive), they return daily to the same cool lair. Some individuals in a given population do not have established territories. These are typically dispersing young animals reaching maturity. Territories are too large to be regularly surveyed by their owners, so tigers make extensive use of scent marking. The pungent exudate of the anal glands is noticeable to humans weeks after deposition, and it may allow individual recognition. Tigers sniffing these scent marks grimace with the nose wrinkled and the tongue protruding (flehmen). *P. tigris* does not bury its feces but makes them conspicuous by scratching the ground around them. Tree scraping also has been reported. Though normally silent, tigers have an impressive vocal repertoire and also communicate with postures and gestures (see Schaller 1967, for an in-depth account).

Hunting is usually concentrated at night, when most ungulates are active, but in some places tigers are active throughout the 24-hour cycle. They hunt alone. Tigers hunt by moving through the home range, and they may cover as much as 50 km in a night if hunting is unsuccessful. Roads and dry streambeds are commonly travelled. A tiger will sometimes wait in ambush along a trail or near a waterhole. Tigers can climb but have not been reported to hunt in trees. One or two kills are made each week. Prey are located by sight, aided with hearing. Carrion is sought by scent. Tigers are adept stalkers. They do not take great leaps at prey. Instead, the basic pattern is to sneak up to within 10-30 m of the target, charge the final distance, knock the prey off its feet, and bite the throat or the back of the neck. Death is by damage to the central nervous system, blood loss, or strangulation. Prey that escape the initial attack are not pursued at length.

Tigers typically begin eating large prey at the hindquarters. Adults sometimes associate amicably at kills. When this happens, the animal that made the kill may have priority rights, even if it is smaller. *P. tigris* can consume great quantities of food in a sitting. They often rest in cover near kills between feeding sessions. Prey, even when it weighs several times the tiger's own weight, is typically dragged into cover or buried. Vultures and other scavengers attracted to tiger kills are driven off or killed. Sometimes tigers steal kills made by other predators (Schaller 1967, Ewer 1973, Singh 1973, Kleiman 1974, Seidensticker 1976, Lekagul and McNeely 1977a, Medway 1978, Brahmachary 1979, Sunquist 1979).

Conservation Measures Taken: Tigers may be hunted under permit from the Thailand Forestry Department (WARPA 1980). "Operation Tiger", the conservation effort coordinated and funded by IUCN and the World Wildlife Fund, has done much to help preserve the tiger in southern Asia, especially in helping to establish and upgrade preserves (IUCN Red Data Book 1978, Jackson 1979). There are at least 13 *P. t. corbetti* in the world's zoos, about half in Rangoon, and they have been successfully bred in captivity in Japan (Olney 1979). IUCN (1979), Leng-Ee (1979), and Prakobboon (1979) list 14 national parks and 21 wildlife sanctuaries in Thailand as harboring tigers.

Conservation Measures Proposed: The suppression of poaching of tigers and their prey should continue, as should the efforts to halt smuggling of tiger products. The selective destruction of man-eaters should, of course, be continued. Most tiger reserves are too small and isolated and should be connected with dispersal corridors to enhance the survival of dispersing young and to alleviate the deleterious effects of inbreeding (Ranjitsinh 1980, Smith 1980). Buffer zones between reserves and permanent agriculture help to prevent tiger-human conflicts (Smith 1980). The effects of different burning and logging practices on prey populations should be studied to allow the formulation of sound management plans. The tiger's requirements for prey, cover, water, and dens should be considered by conservation officials in tiger areas. Radiotracking of tigers in

Nepal is producing promising results (e.g., Seidensticker 1976, Sunquist 1979). Such technology would be most useful in studying the ecology of tigers in Thai habitats. A logistics-oriented management plan emphasizing the integration of tiger conservation into a program of sustained-yield forestry has been designed by Seidensticker and Hai (1983) for the Sundarbans mangrove forests of Bangladesh.

Asian elephant
Elephas maximus **Linnaeus 1758**
Mammalia, Proboscidea, Elephantidae

Status: Endangered.
IUCN Red Data Book (1978): Endangered.
CITES (1979): Appendix I.
IUCN (1979): Threatened.
MAB (1979): Endangered.
USFWS (1980a): Endangered.
WARPA (1980): Protected-1.

Population Size and Trend: Total population of the species was estimated at 28,000 to 42,000 and declining rapidly (IUCN 1978). A more recent estimate is 25,000 to 36,000 (Olivier 1977, 1978a). In Thailand, elephants were formerly very abundant. In northern Thailand alone, an estimated 20,000 domestic elephants were in use in 1884; in 1900, 1,000 elephants were employed on a single trade route from Chiang Mai to Chiang Saen (Seidenfaden 1967). Only 13,397 domestic elephants remained in Thailand in 1950, and this number dropped to 11,022 in 1969 and 8,432 in 1972; elephant exports numbered 245 from 1967 to 1971 (McNeely 1975). As indicated by Olivier (1978b), these harvest data illustrate a population crash in which an important economic resource was destroyed because the living resource was not managed on a sustainable basis.

Lekagul and McNeely (1977b) thought that 2,600-4,450 wild elephants remained in Thailand, in isolated areas as follows: Petchabun Range 200-500, southeast Thailand 200-350, Kra Peninsula 900-1,500, North 400-600, and West 900-1,500. Storer (1979) estimated from questionnaire results and interviews that the elephants in all Thai national parks and wildlife sanctuaries total 650-925 individuals.

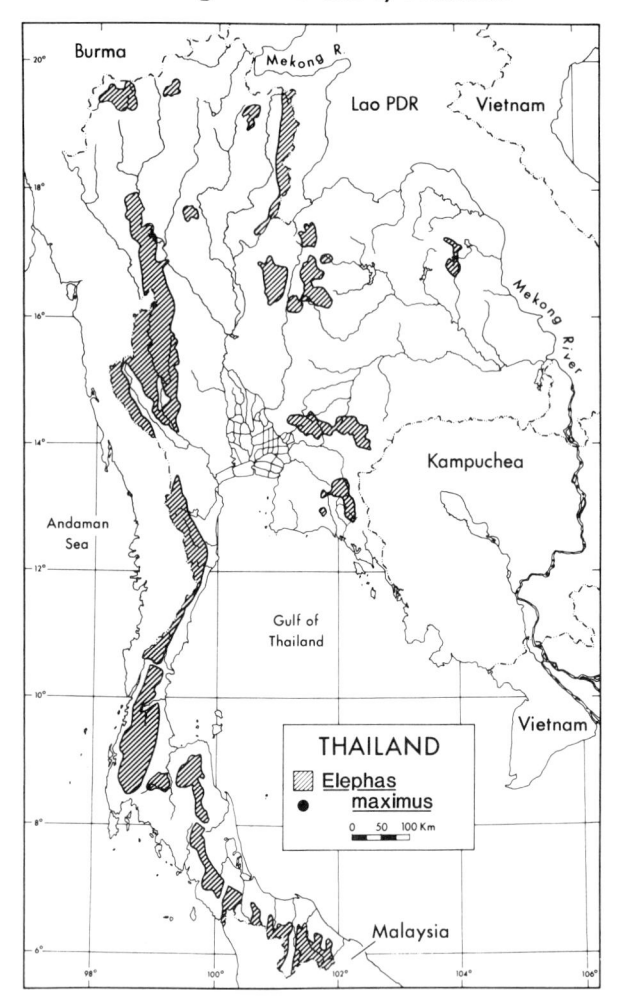

Fig. 96. Distribution of the Asian Elephant (*Elephas maximus*).

Distribution and History of Distribution: "The species once ranged from the Tigris and Euphrates (45° E) in the west, east through Asia south of the Himalayas, and north into China at least as far as the Yangtse Kiang (30° N) and probably farther. It may also have existed on Java. Elephants are still found in Bangladesh, Bhutan, Burma, China, India (including the Andaman Islands), Indonesia (Sumatra and Kalimantan), Kampuchea, Lao PDR, Malaysia (Malaya and Sabak), Nepal, Sri Lanka, Thailand, and

Vietnam" Olivier 1978b). Elephants were lost from the Middle East by the 5th century BC, the Yangtze Kiang by the 10th century AD, and southeastern China in the 11th century (IUCN 1978). Except for parts of Southeast Asia, elephants are extirpated from most of their original range and remnant populations are highly fragmented (Olivier 1978a). Elephants formerly occurred throughout Thailand (Mouhout 1864, Bradley 1876, Olivier 1978b). The population of about 300 in the grassland and around Thale Sap-Thale Noi (Havmoller 1924) was extirpated when the area was developed for rice cultivation around 1935 (Lekagul and McNeely 1977a). Distribution in Thailand now is fragmented (Fig. 96), with only two sizable ranges remaining in contact with elephant distribution in neighboring countries (one in Tak and Kanchanaburi provinces in the Bilauktaung Range adjoining Burma, and one in Nan and Uttaradit provinces next to Lao PDR). Other elephant populations are isolated in various areas of the country (Storer 1979). Distribution in the Kra Peninsula has not been assessed lately.

Geographic Status: Once widespread over the lowlands of southern Asia, the elephant remains in remnant populations in mountainous, subtropical habitat.

Habitat Requirements and Habitat Trend: Habitat consists of grasslands, savannas, and forests, ranging from lowland to mountain and from evergreen to deciduous forest. Optimal habitat is a combination of grassland maintained by seasonal flooding or fire and open woodlands resulting from human disturbance or from seasonal drought or fire. Most optimal habitat occurs on lowlands and floodplains. Suboptimal but usable habitat is primary forest, where elephant density is 18 percent of the density in secondary, successional forest (Olivier 1978c). In areas with a strong cycle of wet and dry seasons, like central and northern Thailand, elephants restrict their dry season activity to areas with streams and lush vegetation (Douglas Vincent, personal communication), whereas elephants move to grasslands for the wet season (Olivier 1978b). The result is a seasonal migration between habitats. In Sri Lanka, solitary males tend to use a specific home range for a prolonged period, shifting to another only when the water source dries out; by contrast, herds of females and young shift daily to weekly among a series of areas of activity, each focused around a water source. Hence the seasonal pattern there involves major changes in the intensity of use of local areas, with movements on the order of 5 km at the onset of the rainy and dry seasons (Eisenberg and Lockhart 1972). Nearly all elephant populations in lowlands and floodplains were eliminated during conversion to agriculture by high-density human populations. Low-density slash-and-burn agriculture in hilly regions has improved forest habitat for elephants by maintaining early seral stages, but as human populations grow and the slash-and-burn cycle is shortened, habitat quality for elephants degenerates. Most remaining elephant habitat is in remote mountains or in primary forest of preserves, so densities of remnant populations are low (IUCN 1978).

Diet is a combination of grass and the leaves and twigs of shrubs and small trees. Where abundant, bamboo leaves also are an important dietary component. In Sri Lanka, feeding preference is highest for short grasses, lower for woody plants, and lowest for tall grasses (McKay 1973). This preference rank illustrates why, in a fire-controlled habitat lacking short grasses, too-frequent fires promoting tall grass at the expense of browse reduce the quality of elephant habitat (Vancuylenberg 1977). Alternate feeding on grasses and woody plants during the day indicates the importance of having both kinds of plants in the same or adjacent habitats. Selection of twigs and branches up to 10 cm in diameter suggests that suitable food may be scarce in primary forest (Olivier 1978c). An elephant typically spends 70-80 percent of its time feeding, or 17-19 hours per day, and eats about 150 kg of food per day, wet weight (McKay 1973, Vancuylenberg 1977).

Vulnerability of Species and Habitat: The elephant is vulnerable to both habitat loss and excessive harvest, and both have contributed to the elephant's endangered status. Habitat loss typically has the first effect as settlers convert elephant habitat to human uses. As human settlements grow, the impact of hunting grows also, and finally remnant populations are shot or poisoned as crop-raiding pests.

Causes of Threat: Storer (1979) considered habitat loss to be the most serious threat to elephants, and he showed all their populations to be in various stages of range fragmentation. Habitat loss involves both seasonal range and migration routes. Irrigation projects that convert forest to agriculture and illegal settlement in forest reserves are major causes of habitat loss. Poaching also is a serious problem, with an estimated 30 elephants killed in Thailand's national parks and sanctuaries from 1974-1979. Annual exports of elephants from Thailand from 1967 to 1971 were 30, 34, 24, 69, and 66 (Royal Forestry Department 1972).

Responses to Habitat Modification: Elephants respond favorably to slash-and-burn agriculture, selective logging, and bamboo extraction, if these are done at a sustained-yield level, because early successional forest is maintained. Consequently, elephant management is compatible with long-term multiple use of forests (Olivier 1977, Lekagul and McNeely 1977b). Elephants will feed in rubber plantations, a strong incentive for killing them as pests (Olivier 1978b). When the native habitat through which elephants migrate is replaced by villages and farms, the migration is discontinued so the elephants can avoid human activity. This results in prolonged use of one segment of the annual range at seasons when carrying capacity is reduced, causing long-term damage to the plant community (Vancuylenberg 1977). Eventually elephants from isolated, deteriorating habitat begin to forage on crops and are shot or poisoned as pests. In Sri Lanka, annual burning of grassland by cattle herders effectively increases grass cover while reducing browse, reducing habitat quality for elephants (Vancuylenberg 1977). Naturally caused fires, perhaps every 10 years or so, probably would be helpful in maintaining good elephant habitat. The relation of fire and elephants in the extensive teak-bamboo forests of Thailand is unknown.

Demographic Characteristics: Female Asian elephants reach sexual maturity at the age of 10-12 years. Gestation takes 20 months, a single young is born, and the interval between births is about 5 years (Khan 1969, Lekagul and McNeely 1977a). The age at which reproduction ceases is unknown; a female would be expected to produce only 6 young by the time she is 40 years old. Khan (1969) estimated that 60-70 percent of the young survive to reach maturity. Though mortality rates must be low to maintain stable populations, elephants in good habitat and protected from predation by humans exhibit steady population growth that permits removal of excess individuals for work animals, introduction to vacant habitat, or commercial purposes.

Key Behaviors: Elephants have matriarchal social organization, with a herd consisting of an extended family of about 6 animals (range 1-20). In suboptimal habitat such as primary forest, where resources for elephants are limited, the family unit is reduced to its smallest possible size--the female and her smallest young (Olivier

1978c). Typically only one bull mates with the females in a herd, and most bulls are solitary in behavior. Hence several bulls can be removed without harming social structure or reproduction (Khan 1969). Khan also indicates that postreproductive females can be culled, but Lekagul and McNeely (1977a) state that the herd leader usually is a grandmother, with the greatest experience at finding resources in all parts of the activity range. Traditional use of the same range for generations makes the use of wildlife refuges as a management tool both feasible and necessary.

Seasonal movement is essential for obtaining food as the supply changes seasonally, and migration routes are the same year after year. To make wet and dry season ranges available to an elephant herd, it is essential that the native habitat remain on traditional migration routes as "elephant corridors" through developed areas.

Conservation Measures Taken: Elephants have been protected by Thai law since early in the Chakri Dynasty (about A.D. 1800), and currently are covered by the Wild Elephant Protection Act of 1960 and the Wild Animals Reservation and Protection Act (1980). Nonetheless, poaching for meat and ivory (the latter worth US $60/g) continues even in national parks and wildlife sanctuaries, and elephant habitat is disappearing rapidly both inside and outside protected areas. Many of the remaining elephant herds are on government land designated as national parks or wildlife sanctuaries, as follows (Storer 1979): parks with elephants are Khao Yai, Phu Kadeung, Thung Salaeng Luang, Phu Phan, Erawan, Khao Chamao-Khao Wong, Khao Kitchakut, Srisatchanalai, Thaleban, and Than Thom Rat; sanctuaries with elephants are Salak Phra, Khlong Nakha, Phu Kheo, Khao Soi Dao, Huai Kha Khaeng, Thung Yai, Khlong Saeng, Phu Luang, Phu Wua, Khao Banthat, Ton Nga Chang, Khao Ang Ru Nai, and Mae Nam Pha Chi. However, many of these parks and sanctuaries provide habitat for only part of the local elephant populations for only part of the year. Park and sanctuary guards are in place in these areas to enforce national resources laws and regulations.

Conservation Measures Proposed: Olivier (1977) proposed the concept of managed Elephant Ranges--multiple use buffer zones surrounding national parks or wildlife sanctuaries--as a way of providing the seasonally required elephant habitat and preventing further fragmentation of populations. This approach was applied to Thailand by Lekagul and McNeely 1977b), who proposed two

Fig. 97. Asian elephant (*Elaphas maximus*) feeding in teak-bamboo forest in Kanchanaburi Province after a day of logging. Both forest and elephant could serve the economy of Thailand forever, but exploitation rates that maximize short-term profit probably would destroy the biological basis of both resources.

Elephant Ranges, one in the Petchabun Range and one in the Bilauktaung Range. Based on his survey of population status, Storer (1979) concluded that the populations already are too fragmented for Elephant Ranges to work. Consequently he recommended that the government should acquire and consolidate its holdings of protected elephant habitat as much as possible, including migration corridors, and continue to strengthen its law enforcement capabilities. However, examination of Storer's map suggests that sufficient habitat may remain in the Bilauktaung

Range and the Luang Prabang Range for the Elephant Range approach to work there, though not in other areas.

Rather than a large interagency group, a small task force of Royal Forestry Department and university biologists should be formed to recommend research and management priorities to the Wildlife Conservation Division. This group should consider acquisition needs around fragmented populations, the use of professional trackers to study herd foraging range and migration routes where populations are fragmented and accessible, and the use of radio-tracking to study these subjects in large, remote areas. Guidance is available on preventing depredation by wild elephants on agricultural or forestry projects (Seidensticker 1984).

Education and government managerial assistance should be promoted to continue and encourage the availability of domesticated elephants as draft animals (Fig. 97). By maintaining the supply and use of elephants as appropriate technology in its forestry industry, government can justify strengthened conservation of this renewable resource as essential to the economic interests of the county and many individual citizens. At one time, timber-working elephants in Thailand involved employment of 36,000 people. A 5-6 year course to prepare elephants for work is available at the Young Elephant Training Center south of Chiang Mai, and the annual Elephant Roundup in Surin Province is a leading tourist attraction. Kahn (1976) considered the use of elephants in forestry to be uneconomical in lowland Malaysia but suggested their employment in promoting nature-oriented tourism in national parks. A wealth of technical literature is available on the husbandry of work elephants (Evans 1910, Benedict 1936, Deraniyagala 1955, Gale 1974).

Dugong, sea cow
Dugong dugon **(Muller 1776)**
Mammalia, Sirenia, Dugongidae

Status: Endangered.
Thai Fisheries Act (1947): Capture forbidden.
IUCN Red Data Book (1976): Vulnerable.
CITES (1979): Appendix I.
IUCN (1979): Threatened.
MAB (1979): Endangered

USFWS (1980a): Endangered
WARPA (1980): Protected-2.

Population Size and Trend: Unknown. Dugongs formerly occurred in herds of several hundreds, but now they are extirpated from large parts of their range, rare in most other areas, and common only in the waters in southern Australia and eastern Africa (IUCN Red Data Book 1976, Husar 1978). The decline and rarity of dugongs on the coast of India was reported nearly a century ago

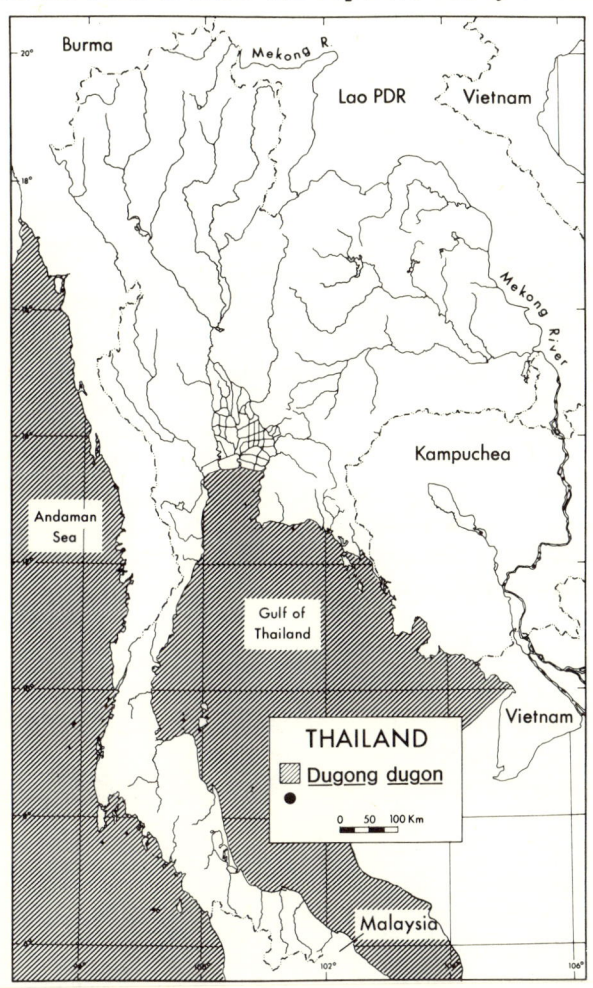

Fig. 98. Distribution of the Dugong (*Dugong dugon*).

(Blanford 1888-1891). No sizable populations are known to persist in Thai waters, though occasional individuals still are reported to be killed by fisherman (Urupun Boonprakob, personal communication).

Distribution and History of Distribution: The range of dugongs is the coastal waters in tropical and subtropical waters of the Pacific and Indian oceans, from Mozambique and the Red Sea to Queensland, the Palau Islands, Caroline Islands, and Ryukyu Archipelago. Animals survive in the waters of southern Burma, Thailand (Fig. 98), Kampuchea, Malaysia, and the Andaman Islands, but they are gone from waters of the Nicobar Islands, Philippines, and Indonesia (Husar 1978).

Geographic Status: Thailand is central in the range and is the core of the reduced distribution in Southeast Asia.

Habitat Requirements and Habitat Trend: Optimal dugong habitat is salt water 3-15 m deep, with shelter from rough winds and heavy waves, water temperatures of 21-38° C, and abundant sea grasses of the families Potomogetonaceae and Hydrocharitaceae (Husar 1978). *Zostera* is prominent among the sea grasses in Thai waters. Silt pollution from inland and nearshore mining in peninsular Thailand has damaged vast areas of seagrass beds (Lekagul and McNeely 1977a).

Vulnerability of Species and Habitat: Dugongs can be approached easily by boat, though individuals subjected to hunting efforts are somewhat wary. The long life and low rate of reproduction of dugongs is incompatible with heavy harvesting; the population will be extirpated if this pressure is not removed. The shallow marine habitat is vulnerable to water-borne sediment from human activities.

Causes of Threat: Despite legal protection by most nations, dugongs everywhere are threatened by hunting and incidental death from marine fisheries. The animal is prized for its meat, oil, hide for leather, and bones and teeth for charcoal, worked articles, and reputed aphrodisiac qualities. Seagrass habitat is threatened by mining practices that do not minimize pollution.

Responses to Habitat Modification: When a severe cyclone damaged seagrass beds, local dugongs switched their diet to brown algae (*Sargassum*; Spain and Heinsohn 1973).

Demographic Characteristics: The age at sexual maturity is 10-17 years for females, 9-16 years for males. Females over 40 years old no longer produce young. The longevity record is 51 years. Gestation takes 13 months. Mating and calving are seasonal in Australia, with the young born in spring. Only one young is born at a time. Lactation lasts 2 years, and the interval between litters is 3-6 years. A 40-year-old female had six placental scars, indicating her lifetime reproductive effort (Helen Marsh, personal communication).

Key Behavior: Males use their tusks for fighting (Helen Marsh, personal communication). Dugongs spend most of their time feeding or sleeping. Conspicuous feeding trails are made through seagrass beds. The rough mouth plate is used to uproot roots and tubers. Debris is washed from mouthfuls of food by vigorously shaking the head. In some areas dugongs undergo seasonal migration (IUCN Red Data Book 1976, Husar 1978).

Conservation Measures Taken: Dugongs in Thai waters have been protected since 1947 by the Fisheries Act of B.E. 2490. However, citizen support for such protection appears to be weak, and enforcement is inadequate. Additionally, dugongs may be hunted under permit from the Thailand Forestry Department (WARPA 1980). Active research programs are under way by James Cook University (Queensland, Australia), the government of Kenya, and the World Wildlife Fund.

Conservation Measures Proposed: An aerial survey of the coastal waters of Thailand should be conducted, at seasons when calm winds clear the water, to estimate the distribution and abundance of dugongs. The results should be used to decide if it is feasible to establish one or more marine sanctuaries for the animals. These should be areas in which other commercial activities could be continued, but where heavy patrolling and a highly visible education program would provide strong protection. Education all along both coasts is needed to warn fishermen and consumers of the vulnerability of dugongs to overharvest.

Malayan tapir
Tapirus indicus **Desmarest 1819**
Mammalia, Perissodactyla, Tapiridae

Status: Endangered.
IUCN (1968): Threatened.

IUCN Red Data Book (1973): Endangered.
CITES (1979): Appendix I.
IUCN (1979): Endangered.
MAB (1979): Endangered.
USFWS (1980a): Endangered.
WARPA (1980): Protected-1.

Population Size and Trend: Malayan tapir populations have been depleted throughout the species' range. Remnants survive in

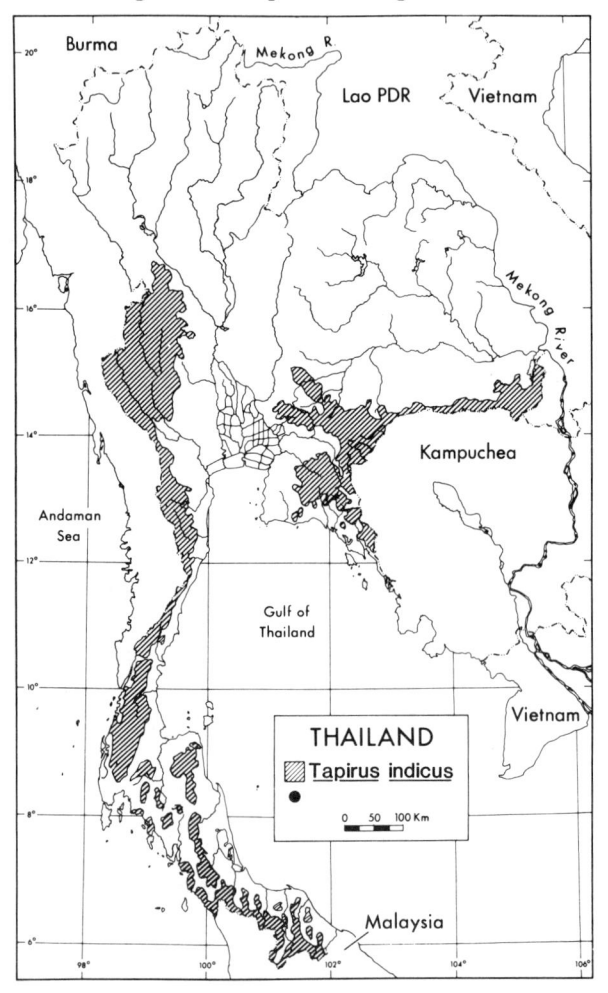

Fig. 99. Distribution of the Malayan Tapir (*Tapirus indicus*).

disjunct and isolated habitats. The species is almost extinct in Burma. It was once common in southern Thailand (Gyldenstolpe 1919), but it has suffered a great decline there. Leng-Ee (1978) reported that as many as 1,500 may survive in three wildlife sanctuaries in southern Thailand. No more than 50 remain in Sumatra (IUCN Red Data Book 1973).

Distribution and History of Distribution: In isolated populations, tapirs survive throughout the species' historical range, from Burma and Thailand south of 18° N (Fig. 99), south through the Malay Peninsula to Sumatra. Fossil *T. indicus* are known from Borneo. A form almost identical to this species is known from the Pliocene of India (Lekagul and McNeely 1977a, Williams and Petrides 1980).

Geographic Status: *T. indicus* in Thailand occurs at the northern limits of the species' range.

Habitat Requirements and Habitat Trend: This tapir is a denizen of mesic, dense primary rainforest. It browses on a variety of understory trees and shrubs (especially of the Euphorbiaceae and Rubiaceae), selecting young leaves and twigs. Some young herbaceous growth and fallen fruits are also taken. Radiotracking revealed the home range of one male to be 12.75 km^2. This area overlapped with the ranges of several other individuals. Where tapirs are sympatric with gaur and elephants, these species may compete for food (Lekagul and McNeely 1977a, Williams 1979, Williams and Petrides 1980). Primary rainforest is being lost at an alarming rate throughout Southeast Asia.

Vulnerability of Species and Habitat: Aborigines in some areas in Malaysia rarely kill tapirs. Tapirs are normally silent. They prefer pushing through vegetation to using trails. Although generally slow, they can be swift and agile when alarmed. Human disturbance is thought to be deleterious, but its effects on reproduction and survival are not known. Tapirs sometimes raid young rubber plantations. The primary forest they require is vulnerable to timber extraction and other development activities (Lekagul and McNeely 1977a, Williams and Petrides 1980).

Causes of Threat: Before the passage of WARPA (1972, 1980), Thailand exported dozens of *T. indicus* each year (Royal Forestry Department 1972). Although Thai law now strictly protects this animal, there have been several recent cases of tapirs included in shipments of mammals of probable Thai origin, given Lao certificates of origin, and trans-shipped through the Bangkok airport to Belgium and Japan (IPPL 1978, 1979). Capture for the live animal trade, overhunting, and massive habitat loss threaten the continued existence of this tapir. The nearly complete forest cover of southern Thailand has declined to 24 percent in 1978 (Myers 1980).

Responses to Habitat Modification: Tapirs apparently will feed in disturbed forest (Medway 1975), but not if primary forest is available (Williams and Petrides 1980). The exact nature of their responses to different forestry practices is unknown.

Demographic Characteristics: Breeding probably occurs in April or May. A single young, weighing 6-7 kg, is born after a gestation of 390-395 days. The young remains with the mother at least 6-8 months. Adults weigh 260-375 kg. A female may give birth as often as once every 2 years. Captives have lived 30 years (Medway 1969, Lekagul and McNeely 1977*a*).

Key Behaviors: Malayan tapirs are nocturnal and solitary. Groups of two or three are sometimes seen. Saplings and shrubs are commonly pushed or walked down, allowing browsing on the foliage and twigs from 6 m above the ground. Feeding is concentrated near water. Tapirs are excellent swimmers but do not normally wallow like rhinos (Medway 1969, Lekagul and McNeely 1977*a*, Williams and Petrides 1980).

Conservation Measures Taken: Thai law (WARPA 1980) prohibits hunting and regulates trade in this species. Tapirs are thought to survive in many protected areas in Thailand, some of which were established as tapir sanctuaries, including Khlong Nakha Wildlife Sanctuary (Ranong Province), Khlong Saeng Wildlife Sanctuary (Surat Thani), Khao Banthat Wildlife Sanctuary (Trang, Patthalung, Songkhla, and Satun), Huai Kha Khaeng Wildlife Sanctuary (Uthai Thani), Phu Kieo Wildlife Sanctuary (Chaiyaphum), Ton Nga Chang Wildlife Sanctuary (Songkhla, Satun), Khao Luang National Park (Nakhon Si Thammarat), and Thaleban National Park (Satun) (Seidensticker and McNeely 1975, Leng-Ee 1978, IUCN 1979, Prakobboon 1979).

Conservation Measures Proposed: Ratification of CITES by Thailand would ease the burdens placed on tapirs by the live animal trade. Survey work is needed to determine the population ranges of Thailand's remaining tapirs. Basic research on tapir biology is needed, with emphasis on the effects of different forestry practices.

Javan rhinoceros
Rhinoceros sondaicus Desmarest 1822
Mammalia, Perissodactyla, Rhinocerotidae

Status: Probably extirpated.
IUCN Red Data Book (1976): Endangered.
CITES (1979): Appendix I.
IUCN (1979): Endangered.
MAB (1979): Endangered.
USFWS (1980a): Endangered.
WARPA (1980): Reserved.

Population Size and Trend: At Ujung Kulon Nature Reserve in Java, the sole known remaining viable population of *R. sondaicus* increased from 20-30 individuals in the late 1960s to 50 in 1979 (Schenkel and Schenkel 1979). It is now generally believed to be extirpated from Thailand (McNeely 1977, K. Snidvongs personal communication).

Distribution and History of Distribution: This rhino formerly ranged from Bangladesh throughout Southeast Asia (including Burma, Thailand, Lao PDR, Kampuchea, Vietnam, and peninsular Malaysia) to Sumatra and Java. It may have also occurred in southern China. In Thailand it was once common in Trang, Krabi, Phangnga, and Ranong provinces. Tracks were reported in Khao Soi Dao Wildlife Sanctuary in Chanthaburi Province in February 1978, but there have been no confirmed sightings in recent years. There have been suggestions of surviving Javan rhinos along the Tenasserim on the Thai-Burmese border, on the Kampuchean-Lao border, and in extreme southern Thailand on the Malay border. Control by insurgents makes survey work dangerous in many of these areas, but it seems highly unlikely that viable populations of *R. sondaicus* have survived to this late date in Thailand and adjacent countries (Lekagul 1963, Milton and Estes 1963, IUCN 1968, Fisher et al. 1969, McNeely and Cronin 1972, IUCN Red Data Book 1976, Neese 1976a, b, Lekagul and McNeely 1977a, McNeely 1977, McNeely and Laurie 1977, Leng-Ee 1978).

Geographic Status: This animal is restricted to Ujung Kulon Nature Reserve (360 km^2) in Java.

Habitat Requirements and Habitat Trend: The Javan rhino is a forest-dwelling browser, consuming primarily low branches, saplings, and other young growth. "Compared with the Sumatran rhino, the Javan rhino is better adapted to lowland, flat terrain, soft and wet soil, to disturbed forest and to the vegetation transitional between forest and low growing vegetational cover. It not only wallows, but frequently lies in river basins, also in brackish water" (Schenkel and Schenkel 1979). Schenkel et al. (1978) showed that selectively cutting the dense palm understory in Ujung Kulon increased the availability of rhino food. In natural situations, their cropping activities acted to help maintain the young growth upon which they depend. Typical densities are 7-10 km^2 per individual under favorable conditions.

Vulnerability of Species and Habitat: In recent years, most killing of rhinos has resulted from a cultural belief in aphrodisiac qualities. Though the horn is most highly desired, all parts of the animal are valued. Sport hunting and damage to agriculture contributed to this rhino's decline. Rhino hunting methods are thought to be selective for females (Lekagul and McNeely 1977a, Schenkel and Schenkel 1979).

Causes of Threat: Clearing of nearly all the lowland forests, combined with relentless hunting, caused loss of this animal from Thailand. Poaching is still a threat in Java.

Responses to Habitat Modification: This species tolerates disturbed forest reasonably well, but the intense human settlement of lowlands in Southeast Asia drove the survivors into suboptimal upland habitats. The penetration of mangrove forests by man may have been important in extirpation of *R. sondaicus* in Thailand (Schenkel and Schenkel 1979).

Demographic Characteristics: Because few *R. sondaicus* have been kept in captivity or followed in the wild, much of what follows is extrapolated from our knowledge of the Indian rhino, *R. unicornis*. Mature females probably do not breed more frequently than once every 4-5 years. They probably are polyestrous, coming into heat every 46-48 days. The single young is born after a gestation of about 16 months. Young may nurse for several years. Females reach puberty in 3-4 years, males in 6. They may live as long as 40 years, but the greatest longevity of the few captive Javan rhinos was 21 years (Medway 1969, Lekagul and McNeely 1977a).

Key Behaviors: Javan rhinos are predominantly solitary, but mated pairs may form for short periods. Individual home ranges overlap. Vocalizations and scent marking with glands on the forefeet may help to maintain individual separation and communication

(Lekagul and McNeely 1977a, Schenkel and Schenkel 1979). For a detailed account of its behavior, see Hoogerwerf (1970).

Conservation Measures Taken: Thai law (WARPA 1980) prohibits hunting of this species. Suitable habitat is preserved in several of Thailand's national parks and wildlife sanctuaries, including Khao Soi Dao. Thai conservation officials promptly react to reported rhino sightings. Only six individuals are known to have been kept in captivity (Reynolds 1960) and none are known to exist today outside of Ujung Kulon.

Conservation Measures Proposed: Any individuals discovered in Burma, Thailand, Lao PDR, Kampuchea, or Vietnam should be captured and moved to areas where their protection is assured. Students and wildlife officials should learn to recognize the tracks of the Javan and Sumatran rhinos and to distinguish them from those of tapirs. The government of Indonesia, WWF, FAO, and IUCN should be encouraged to continue their worthy efforts to preserve the population in Ujung Kulon Nature Reserve. Improvements in the guard system and caution in the development of rhinos as a tourist attraction have been recommended. Because of the dangers inherent in maintaining a species near extinction in a single population (e.g., diseases, catastrophic storms), Schenkel and Schenkel's (1979) suggestion of the establishment of a second population should be considered seriously. At some future date, if the Indonesian herd overpopulates and the government makes animals available, Thailand should seize the opportunity to reintroduce the species to protected areas.

Sumatran rhinoceros
Dicerorhinus (Didermocerus) sumatrensis **(Fischer 1814)**
Mammalia, Perissodactyla, Rhinocerotidae

Status: Endangered.
IUCN Red Data Book (1976): Endangered.
CITES (1979): Appendix I.
IUCN (1979): Endangered.
MAB (1979): Endangered.
USFWS (1980a): Endangered.
WARPA (1980): Reserved.

Population Size and Trend: The total population was estimated in the low hundreds in the IUCN Red Data Book (1976), as follows: 17-24 in Burma, 10-20 in Thailand, 11-23 in Malaya, 6 in Sabah, and 45-85 in Sumatra. The population in peninsular Malaysia is 50-75 (Flynn and Abdullah 1984). These are very rough estimates, and the number is still declining. A few animals also remain in Borneo (van der Zon 1977). Whether any still occur in southern Vietnam (Groves 1967) is unknown.

Distribution and History of Distribution: The species formerly ranged widely from Assam and Bangladesh through Southeast Asia to Vietnam, south to Sumatra and Borneo. Now isolated and very small populations occur in Burma, Thailand, Malaya, Sabah, Sumatra, and Borneo. Possibly some remain in Lao PDR, Kampuchea, or Vietnam (IUCN Red Data Book 1976, McNeely and Laurie 1977). In Thailand, the four areas last reported to be occupied by Sumatran rhinos were Phu Kheo Wildlife Sanctuary and Nam Nao National Park in Chaiyaphum Province, Khao Soi Dao Wildlife Sanctuary in Chantaburi Province, Huai Kha Khaeng Wildlife Sanctuary in Uthai Thani Province, and Thung Nakha and Khlong Saeng wildlife sanctuaries in Surat Thani Province. Possibly some occur along the Thai-Malaysian border also (McNeely and Laurie 1977, Schenkel and Schenkel (1979).

Geographic Status: The present range represents fragments of the original range, with Thailand located in the north-central part of it.

Habitat Requirements and Habitat Trend: Originally a large variety of habitats was used, including lowland forests and swamps. Now Sumatran rhinos are restricted to the forests of steep mountains, particularly steep upper valleys with thick undergrowth (Lekagul and McNeely 1977a, McNeely and Laurie 1977). Loss of habitat has been extensive. Population density is typically low--1 animal per 10 km^2 (Strickland 1967). The diet consists of leaves, twigs, bark, and fruit, with a majority of the species being characteristic of disturbed forest or forest edge in some areas (Strickland 1967), and of primary forest in other areas (IUCN Red Data Book (1976).

Vulnerability of Species and Habitat: Though rhino habitat is vulnerable to conversion to agriculture and lalang grassland, much suitable, unoccupied habitat occurs in national parks and wildlife sanctuaries. The high demand for body products with supposed medicinal and religious properties maintains heavy hunting pressure on the species.

Causes of Threat: Legal protection offered the Sumatran rhino is inadequate to counteract the strong economic incentive for hunting. A rhino carcass is valued at more than US $2,000, or 10-20 years' income for a Thai farmer, and poaching of the last populations is rampant, even in protected areas (McNeely and Cronin 1972, McNeely and Laurie 1977). Poachers use superior numbers and weaponry in opposing law enforcement efforts.

Responses to Habitat Modification: This species avoids areas where the primary forest has been modified by logging. Therefore parks or sanctuaries designed for rhino conservation should include large tracts of primary forest (Flynn 1978).

Demographic Characteristics: The gestation period is about 7-8 months, much shorter than in other rhinos. The maximum longevity in captivity was 32.6 years (Lekagul and McNeely 1977a). In other rhinoceros species, the age at sexual maturity is about 3 years in females and 6 in males, and one young is born every 3 years.

Key Behaviors: These rhinos are solitary. Females have relatively stable home ranges, which are very large and partially overlapping. Males are nomadic and wander along stream beds, old game trails, or just cross-country. Communication is largely olfactory, by means of sexually distinct scent during the mating season (July to October). The same wallows and salt licks are used year after year (Lekagul and McNeely 1977a). The front horn is used to remove the bark from saplings.

Conservation Measures Taken: Hunting of the Sumatran rhinoceros is prohibited (WARPA 1980). Most recent reports in Thailand are from areas protected by the Royal Forestry Department in Khlong Nakha, Khlong Saeng, Thung Yai, Huai Kha Khaeng, Khao Soi Dao, and Phu Kheo wildlife sanctuaries and in Nam Nao National Park.

Conservation Measures Proposed: Emergency measures are needed to prevent the imminent extirpation of the Sumatran rhino from Thailand. As pointed out by McNeely and Cronin (1972), these steps will be unpopular. To effectively halt the market in rhino products, new legislation is needed prohibiting their possession and sale. Trade then should be eliminated at both ends by active monitoring of medicine shops and by adding large numbers of well-armed guards to undertake aggressive patrolling of sanctuaries and parks in which rhinos live. As a second priority, once the capability to protect these areas is in place, acquisition of the suggested addition to Phu Kheo Wildlife Sanctuary (McNeely and Laurie 1977) would protect more rhinoceros habitat. An up-to-date survey, research, and public education also have been called for by Schenkel and Schenkel (1979). Tracking is a very effective means of documenting rhino distribution (Flynn and Abdullah 1984).

Fea's muntjak
Muntiacus feae **(Thomas and Doria 1889)**
Mammalia, Artiodactyla, Cervidae

Status: Endangered.
IUCN Red Data Book (1972): Endangered.
IUCN (1976): Endangered.
IUCN (1978): Endangered.
IUCN (1979): Endangered.
USFWS (1980a): Endangered.
WARPA (1980): Protected-2.

Population Size and Trend: This small barking deer was apparently never very abundant. It is now quite rare. Its total numbers are unknown but are certainly small. There is no reliable information on population trends (Lekagul and McNeely 1977a, IUCN 1978).

Distribution and History of Distribution: Until recently, Fea's muntjak was considered restricted to the Tenasserim range, from Rat Buri to Tak provinces in Thailand (Fig. 100) and from the districts of Thaton, Amherst, Tavoy, and Mergui in Burma (IUCN Red Data Book 1972, Whitehead 1972, Lekagul and McNeely 1977a). However, in 1981 an individual was captured in Surat Thani Province. Local villagers were unfamiliar with the species, so it must be quite rare there (Conservation News Volume 3, Association for the Conservation of Wildlife, Bangkok).

Geographic Status: Uncertain. This muntjak may be endemic (possibly relictual) in the Tenasserim range along the Thai-Burmese border and in a few mountainous areas of southern Thailand.

Habitat Requirements and Habitat Trend: *M. feae* inhabits the evergreen forest of the hills and mountains (Gairdner 1914, Lekagul and McNeely 1977a, IUCN 1978).

Vulnerability of Species and Habitat: Its relatively diurnal activity patterns probably make it vulnerable to human predation. Its flesh is said to have a most delectable flavor.

Causes of Threat: Human settlement in the range of Fea's muntjak has increased in recent years. The flesh is relished in Thailand. Armed insurgents living off the land, especially in the Burmese part of its range, probably account for much mortality. In general, overhunting and the destruction of native habitats threaten this cervid with extinction (IUCN Red Data Book 1972, Lekagul 1980 and personal communication). Gairdner (1914) recorded a Fea's muntjak killed by a leopard.

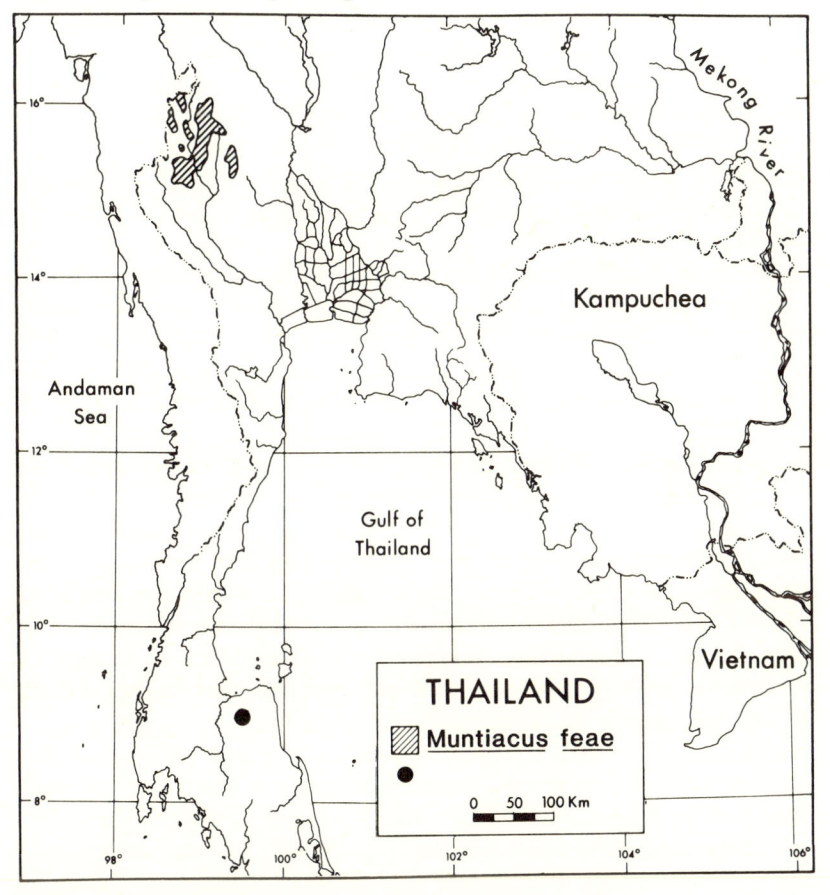

Fig. 100. Former distribution of Fea's Muntjak (*Muntiacus feae*).

Responses to Habitat Modification: Unknown.

Demographic Characteristics: A single young is born after a gestation of 6 months (Lekagul and McNeely 1977a, Lekagul 1980 and personal communication).

Key Behaviors: This deer is normally solitary. Pairs may form during the breeding season. "Its habits are said to closely resemble those of the common barking deer [*M. muntjak*]; they are less nocturnal than most other deer, visiting fields, fruiting trees, open clearings, salt licks, and pools of water at times when other wild animals are resting in heavy cover" (Lekagul and McNeely 1977a).

Conservation Measures Taken: The species may be hunted under permit form the Thailand Forestry Department (WARPA 1980). *M. feae* possibly occurs in the following wildlife sanctuaries: Huai Kha Khaeng, Salak Phra, and Thung Yai. One female is currently held at Dusit Zoo in Bangkok. The Association for the Conservation of Wildlife has recently donated funds to purchase a male for the establishment of a captive breeding program (Seidensticker and McNeely 1975, IUCN 1976, 1978, Lekagul 1980 and personal communication).

Conservation Measures Proposed: The aforementioned reserves and neighboring forests should be surveyed to ascertain the current status of this unique deer. Any viable populations found should be strictly protected and studied so management plans can be based on a sound understanding of the species' biology. Cooperation between Thai and Burmese conservation officials in such a endeavor would be crucial. Clearing of upland evergreen forest in the limited range of this animal should be prohibited. Biology students, wildlife officials, and the general public should be educated to distinguish this mammal from the common muntjak and to help in its conservation. For reasons not immediately apparent, Fea's muntjak is not listed by CITES. Appendix I protection under that Convention seems appropriate. International conservation organizations can support Thailand's worthy efforts to establish captive breeding populations of Fea's muntjak by supplying expertise, logistical support, and funds.

Indochinese hog deer
Cervus (Axis) porcinus annamiticus (Heude 1888)
Mammalia, Artiodactyla, Cervidae

Status: Probably extirpated.
CITES (1979): Appendix I.
MAB (1979): Endangered.
USFWS (1980a): Endangered.
WARPA (1980): Reserved.

Population Size and Trend: In India, the nominate race is still locally common in certain reserves. In Thailand *C. p. annamiticus* was common in the Chao Phraya Basin in the early part of this century but was completely extirpated by about 1965. Today the Forestry Department, zoos, and private collectors hold about 40 captive *C. p. annamiticus* of Burmese origin in Thailand. There is no reliable information on the status of populations in Vietnam, Burma, Lao PDR, or Kampuchea (Lekagul and McNeely 1977a, Leng-Ee 1978, B. Lekagul personal communication).

Distribution and History of Distribution: This species was found across northern India and Nepal, east through Burma and Thailand, to Lao PDR, Kampuchea, and Vietnam. It has been introduced in Sri Lanka. (If the Bawean deer *Axis [Hyelaphus] kuhli*, is considered a race of hog deer [USFWS 1980a], the range also includes the Bawean Islands between Borneo and Java.) *C. p. annamiticus* once ranged throughout Thailand north of the peninsula in suitable habitat. The hog deer is now restricted to disjunct fragments of its former range. Apparently the last reliable sighting of wild hog deer in Thailand was made by Pong Leng-Ee in Nong Khai Province in November 1963. IUCN (1979) suggested that a few may survive in Nam Nao National Park and in Huai Kha Khaeng Wildlife Sanctuary.

Geographic Status: Thailand is central to the historic range of *C. p. annamiticus*.

Habitat Requirements and Habitat Trend: Hog deer graze more than they browse. The captive herd at Khao Khieo Wildlife Sanctuary studied by Miller (1975) took 80% grass and 20% forbs and browse. Hog deer inhabit swampy meadows, low-lying marshes, open forest, reed beds, and grasslands bordering streams. They do not penetrate closed forest (Schaller 1967, Miller 1975, Lekagul and McNeely 1977a, Leng-Ee 1978, B. Lekagul personal communication). Most suitable habitat in Thailand has been converted to wet rice agriculture. Miller (1975) suggested that captive herds require at least 10 rai (1.6 ha) per hog deer at maximum capacity, including at least 4 rai (0.64 ha) of grassland per animal.

Vulnerability of Species and Habitat: Wet, low-lying grasslands were the first habitats to be converted to agriculture in Thailand.

Causes of Threat: Overhunting and habitat loss extirpated wild *C. porcinus* from Thailand.

Responses to Habitat Modification: Although their ancestral habitat has been lost, hog deer readily adapt to the bamboo-*Imperata* grass habitat that follows slash-and-burn agriculture on lowland soils in Thailand (Miller 1975). With protection of water resources and protection from poaching, the potential for reintroduction in the wild in Thailand is good.

Demographic Characteristics: Schaller (1967) reviewed the literature on hog deer reproduction. The rutting season in northern India had been reported as September and October, but his field observations suggested that rutting occurs from June to January in Uttar Pradesh, with a peak in September and October. September and October has been given as the time of the rut in Burma and Thailand. Captives rut all year. Gestation is generally agreed to be 8 months. One fawn is the rule, but twins have been reported (Schaller 1967, Miller 1975, Lekagul and McNeely 1977a). Miller (1975) saw fawns as old as 6 months allowed to nurse. The life span is unknown.

Key Behaviors: Hog deer are essentially solitary animals, although family groups and herds up to several dozen have been reported. During the rut, groups may congregate at certain feeding sites. Barking and stamping alarm signals have been described. In captives, the males soon establish a dominance hierarchy, with one buck clearly dominant. Aggression between males includes pawing, lateral displays, and pushing fights with interlocked antlers. Olfactory signals are important in these deer; social behavior often involves sniffing, and males scent-mark with the preorbital gland. Bucks aggressively follow close behind does and try to lick, smell, and mount them. The fawn hides during the first 2-3 weeks after birth and does not accompany the doe. Hog deer change their beds frequently during the day and night. They typically bed down with their backs to bamboo or small trees, facing the open. Their common name refers to their habit of running under brush or tall grass rather than jumping over it (Schaller 1967, Miller 1976, Lekagul and McNeely 1977a).

Conservation Measures Taken: Hunting of this species is prohibited (WARPA 1980). Suitable bamboo-*Imperata* habitat with streams is protected in many Thai reserves. A captive breeding program is underway at Khao Khieo under the auspices of the Royal Forestry Department. In early 1980 three nonpregnant females escaped from the enclosure. Boonsong Lekagul saw their tracks in suitable habitat near Bang Phra reservoir in April. Schwan Tanhikorn (personal communication) wants to obtain males for release in the area.

Conservation Measures Proposed: Because of the dangers inherent in keeping an endangered species in a single enclosure, Boonsong Lekagul recommends that the Forestry Department spread its breeding population to other reserves, where the deer will need strict protection from poaching. Miller (1975) recommended the following reserves as release sites: Khao Yai National Park, Khao Soi Dao Wildlife Sanctuary, Thung Yai Wildlife Sanctuary, Huai Kha Khaeng Wildlife Sanctuary, and Phu Khieo Wildlife Sanctuary. Feeding studies need to be done on the captive herd at Khao Khieo. Acquisition of fresh wild-caught stock would increase the size of the gene pool of the captive herd (Miller 1975).

Neua saman, Schomburgk's deer
Cervus schomburgki (Blyth 1863)
Mammalia, Artiodactyla, Cervidae

Status: Extinct.
WARPA (1980): Reserved.

Population Size and Trend: There are no surviving Schomburgk's deer. The last known individual, a semi-wild temple pet at Maha Chai in Samut Sakhon Province, died in 1938 (Lekagul and McNeely 1977a).

Distribution and History of Distribution: This unique cervid ranged throughout the central plains of the Chao Phraya from Samut Prakan to Sukothai (Fig. 101). There are no specimens to support suggestions (Gyldenstolpe 1914; Pocock 1943) that *C. schomburgki* once occurred around Chiangrai and in Lao PDR and Yunnan. The last reliable reports of wild individuals were from Sai

Yok on the Kwae Noi and the Kwae Yai in 1932. The last captive died in 1938. Of the 40 deer species currently recognized, *C. schomburgki* is the only one known to have become extinct in the past several hundred years (Guehler 1933, Lekagul and McNeely 1977a, Cowan and Holloway 1978).

Geographic Status: This deer was a Thai endemic.

Habitat Requirements and Habitat Trend: Schomburgk's deer was a habitat specialist, preferring the riverine plains "where there were long grasses, cane, and shrubs" (Lekagul and McNeely 1977a) and avoided the closed forest. The opening of Thailand in 1856 to trade with foreign countries prompted the conversion of virtually

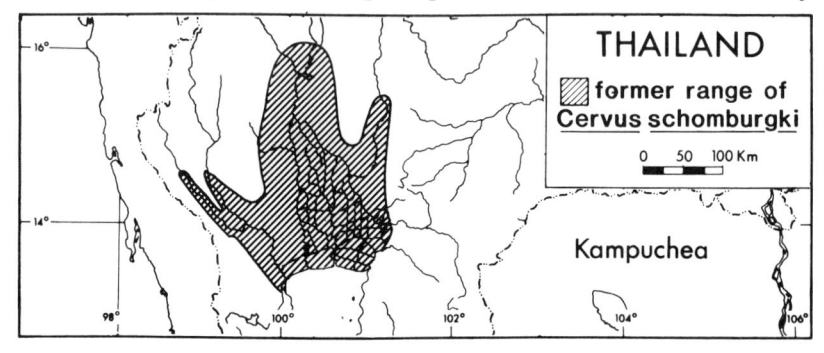

Fig. 101. Former distribution of Schomburgk's Deer (*Cervus schomburgki*).

the entire central valley to wet rice culture by the early 1900s. Conversion to agriculture was so complete that biologists today are somewhat uncertain about the exact nature of the original habitat. This wholesale destruction of deer habitat also affected other habitat specialists.

Vulnerability of Species and Habitat: Its preference for open areas and gregarious habits made *C. schomburgki* quite visible.

Causes of Threat: Hunting pressure and complete conversion of its required habitat to paddy fields doomed this species.

Responses to Habitat Modification: Habitat modification, aggravated by overexploitation, drove this animal to extinction.

Demographic Characteristics: Unknown.

Key Behaviors: This deer spent its days in the shade and foraged at night, apparently on young shoots. It occurred in family groups. When the central plain was inundated with flood water in the rainy season, the deer (and many other species) sought refuge on patches of raised ground. These "islands" were exploited by large hunting groups of men on water buffalos and in boats (Lekagul and McNeely 1977a).

Conservation Measures Taken: Although many efforts were made to establish captive breeding populations of Schomburgk's deer outside of Thailand, none met with success. When the Wild Animals Reservation and Protection Act of BE. 2503 (1961) was first drafted, *C. schomburgki* was classified as a "reserved species" to protect any undiscovered populations that may have survived to that late date.

Conservation Measures Proposed: None.

Eld's brow-antlered deer, thamin
Cervus eldi McClelland 1842
Mammalia, Artiodactyla, Cervidae

Status: Probably extirpated.
IUCN (1968): Seriously threatened.
IUCN Red Data Book (1972): Endangered (*C. e. siamensis*).
IUCN (1978): Endangered (*C. e. siamensis*).
CITES (1979): Appendix I.
IUCN (1979): In very great danger of extinction.
MAB (1979): Endangered.
USFWS (1980a): Endangered.
WARPA (1980): Reserved.

Population Size and Trend: More than four decades ago, Harper (1945) expressed concern for the future of all races of Eld's deer. In this century it has rapidly declined throughout its range. In India fewer than two dozen individuals of the nominate race, *C. e. eldi*, survive in the wild in a small sanctuary in the State of Manipur (IUCN 1978). Whitehead (1972) estimated the total numbers of the Burmese race, *C. e. thamin*, at 4,000, and it has certainly declined since then. Eld's deer was once common throughout Thailand north of the peninsula (Lekagul and McNeely 1977a), but by 1949 it was nearing extinction in the wild (Sanborn and Watkins 1950), and it is doubtful that any survive in the wild in Thailand today (M. K. Ranjitsinh, personal communication). A few *C. e. siamensis* survive in Hainan, China (IUCN 1978). There is no recent information on the status of *C. e. siamensis* in Kampuchea, Lao PDR, or Vietnam.

Distribution and History of Distribution: Eld's deer ranged from Manipur, west through Burma, Thailand, Lao PDR, Kampuchea, and Vietnam, to Hainan island. It is now confined to a few isolated fragments of its former range. In Thailand, Eld's deer still occurred in Lop Buri, Chiang Rai, and Uthai Thani provinces at the end of the second world war (B. Lekagul, personal communication). The last certain occurrence of wild individuals in Thailand was a *C. e. thamin* shot near Ban Rai in Uthai Thani in 1974 (Lekagul and McNeely 1977a). It has been suggested that a few wild individuals may survive in the Tanaosi Range in western Thailand and in the Dongrak Range along the Kampuchean border (Seidensticker and McNeely 1975, IUCN 1979, Prakobboon 1979, M. K. Ranjitsinh personal communication). A 1974 Chinese publication reported that *C. e. siamensis* is still found in 14 counties in Hainan in small scattered herds (IUCN 1978).

Geographic Status: Thailand is central to the overall historic range of Eld's deer. In Thailand *C. e. thamin* occurred at the eastern extreme of its range and *C. e. siamensis* at the western extreme of its range.

Habitat Requirements and Habitat Trend: Eld's deer is more of a grazer than a browser and is fond of wild fruit. In Thailand it inhabited deciduous dipterocarp forest and open plains, entering the edges of dense growth for shade (Lekagul and McNeely 1977a, B. Lekagul personal communication).

Vulnerability of Species and Habitat: Its flesh is good to eat, which probably caused it to be selectively hunted. Open grasslands were among the first habitats to be converted to agriculture in Thailand. As agriculture encroached on its habitats, Eld's deer began feeding in rice fields. This undoubtedly hastened its decline.

Causes of Threat: Habitat loss and overhunting have driven this deer close to extinction in the wild. The last major stronghold of *C. e. siamensis* was in northern Kampuchea, where political turmoil and human famine have probably taken a great toll on wildlife. Chemical defoliation during the Vietnam war probably aggravated the decline (IUCN Red Data Book 1972).

Responses to Habitat Modification: Past reports of the species using rice fields indicates some adaptability to land use changes.

Demographic Characteristics: In Thailand the rut is from February to April (Lekagul and McNeely 1977a). The captive herd of *C. e. thamin* held by the National Zoological Park (NZP), Smithsonian Institution, at Front Royal, Virginia, mates from November to early June. The gestation is 240-244 days (Blakeslee et al. 1979). Usually a single fawn is born. Both sexes are probably fertile at an age of 1 year, but males are probably not sociologically mature until at least 2 years of age (NYZS-NZP 1980). Ralls et al. (1979) documented the deleterious effects of inbreeding in captive *C. e. thamin*.

Key Behaviors: Wild *C. eldi* were once seen in herds of up to 50 animals (Lekagul and McNeely 1977a), but survivors in Southeast Asia are solitary or form small groups. Blakeslee et al. (1979) described the behavior of the captive herd at NZP. Scent marking with the preorbital gland occurs in several social contexts. Sparring and other aggressive behaviors between males were seen. Female aggression was limited to nipping. As in other cervids, males apparently assess the reproductive condition of females by sniffing their urine, feces, and anogenital areas, typically exhibiting flehmen afterward. Lekagul and McNeely (1977a) speculated that their fondness for mud wallows may indicate that man drove the Eld's deer from swampy areas into the dry habitats they used in Thailand in modern times.

Conservation Measures Taken: Hunting of this species is prohibited (WARPA 1980). The New York Zoological Society and NZP have a cooperative program for the captive breeding of *C. e. thamin* (NYZS-NZP 1980). In Thailand, the Wildlife Conservation Division of the Royal Forestry Department bought a female *C. e. siamensis* from an animal dealer who imported it from the Lao PDR. She is kept at Khao Khieo Wildlife Sanctuary (Miller 1975). Two male *C. e. thamin* were shipped to Khao Khieo from NZP. One died. The remaining pair bore a fawn at Khao Khieo in 1979, but it died accidentally. In May 1980 the female was pregnant again (Schwan Tanhikorn, personal communication). Before the male *C. eldi* were acquired, the female aborted dead fawns after being caged with sambar and hog deer bucks. Furthermore, sambar does were aggressive toward the doe Eld's deer. Since then the *C. eldi* has been kept in a separate pen to prevent wasted reproductive effort and premature death (Miller 1975).

The latest census (Olney 1979) indicates that there are 37 *C. e. eldi* in various Indian zoos (all captive-born), one male and two female *C. e. siamensis* in the Paris Zoo (all captive-born), and 89 *C. e. thamin* in various collections, notably the zoos in Rangoon, Bronx (NYZS), Front Royal (NZP), San Diego, and Leipzig.

Conservation Measures Proposed: NYZS-NZP (1980) hope to enlarge their *C. e. thamin* herd to 500 by the year 2000. Their long-term goal is the maintenance of a genetically diverse, self-sustaining population, as a viable source for reintroduction into the wild. Immediate efforts are necessary if *C. e. siamensis* is to survive; an attempt should be made to obtain some from Kampuchea (B. Lekagul, personal communication) to build a pure *siamensis* breeding stock. Chinese officials should be approached about the possibility of obtaining some from Hainan. The Wildlife Conservation Division hopes that someday it will be able to reintroduce Eld's deer in Thailand. Reforestation at Khao Khieo Wildlife Sanctuary is under way to provide shelter adjacent to marsh grassland, to prepare the area for reintroduction.

Wild water buffalo
Bubalus bubalis **Linnaeus 1758**
Mammalia, Artiodactyla, Bovidae

Status: Endangered.
IUCN (1968): Seriously threatened.
IUCN Red Data Book (1972): Vulnerable.
CITES (1979): Appendix III (Nepal).
WARPA (1980[2]): Reserved.

Population Size and Trend: Great herds of *Bubalus* were once found in southern Asia. In Nepal and India, fewer than 2,000 wild animals remain in scattered locations. The size of the Burmese population is unknown but is certainly small. About 40 individuals occur in two adjoining reserves in western Thailand. The current status in Kampuchea, Lao PDR, and Vietnam is unknown (Harper 1945, Schaller 1967, IUCN Red Data Book 1972, Lekagul and McNeely 1977*a*, IUCN 1979). In contrast, domesticated water buffalo number at least 130 million worldwide (National Research Council 1981).

Distribution and History of Distribution: Wild water buffalo once ranged from northern India to Vietnam. Remnant populations occur today in Nepal, in Assam and Orissa in India, and in Huai Kha Khaeng Wildlife Sanctuary and the adjacent Thung Yai-Naresuan Wildlife Sanctuary in Thailand (Fig. 102). Domestic and feral animals are now found in much of the tropical and warm-temperate world, including Australia, southern Asia, the Middle East, southern Europe, southwestern USSR, Egypt, and eastern Africa, Central and South America south to southern Brazil, and Florida (USA). The wild form is more robust and considerably larger than the domestic *Bubalus*. Thailand's wild buffalo is the largest water buffalo in the world (Osbourn 1965, Fisher et al. 1969, Maia 1970, Eisenberg and Lockhart 1972, IUCN Red Data Book 1972, Seidensticker and McNeely 1975, Walker 1975, Lekagul and McNeely 1977a, Tulloch 1978, 1979, IUCN 1979).

Geographic Status: Thailand is central to the historic range of wild *Bubalus*.

Habitat Requirements and Habitat Trend: Water buffalo are grazers. In Thailand they prefer open forests and elephant grass unless near swamps. The Huai Kha Khaeng population does not frequent salt licks. *Bubalus* are fond of mud wallows, and they

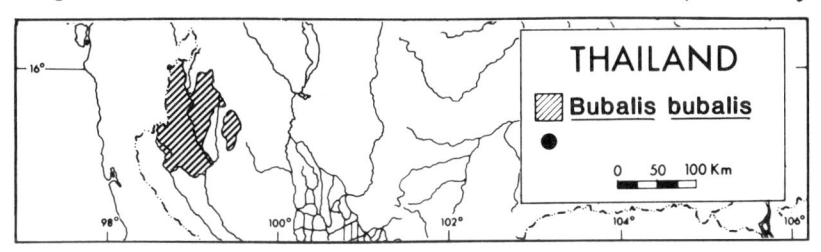

Fig. 102. Distribution of the Wild Water Buffalo (*Bubalus bubalis*).

immerse themselves in cool, clear streams to escape heat and insects. Habitat with ample grass and water can support dense populations of this bovid (Seidensticker and McNeely 1975, Lekagul and McNeely 1977a).

Vulnerability of Species and Habitat: The coastal areas and valleys of large rivers that once supported large buffalo populations were the first to be settled by man. The open habitat they prefer is easily traversed by hunters on elephants or in vehicles. Individuals habitually return to mud wallows and are thus easily hunted. In the past they raided paddy and other crops. *Bubalus* is very susceptible to rinderpest. Bulls do attack people, sometimes without apparent provocation (Fisher et al. 1969, IUCN Red Data Book 1972, Lekagul and McNeely 1977a, B. Lekagul personal communication).

Causes of Threat: Wild *Bubalus* are endangered by loss of habitat, poaching, diseases, competition from domestic cattle, and loss of their genetic integrity by breeding with domestic water buffalo.

Responses to Habitat Modification: Conversion of open habitats (especially those near water) to rice and cattle farming hastened the decline of wild water buffalo.

Demographic Characteristics: In Thailand most *Bubalus* mate in October and November, but the breeding season may last as long as 5 months. Gestation is 10-11 months (Lekagul and McNeely 1977a, Tulloch 1979). The maximum life span is approximately 18 years (Walker 1975). Much more detail is available for domestic water buffalo. Reproductive performance depends strongly on nutritional condition. Females routinely conceive at 16-18 months of age and calve at 22-30 months. Estrus usually lasts about 24 hours (range 11 to 72, and it occurs on an average 21-day cycle. Calving is seasonal in many areas where nutrition is seasonal. Gestation is about 310 days (range 300 to 334), and females can come into estrus as early as 40 days after calving. Typical calving rates are two every 3 years and three to four every 5 years (National Research Council 1981).

Key Behaviors: The behavior of wild water buffalo is poorly known. Before their decline, large herds formed. Bulls are very aggressive and group defense against tigers is known. A harem mating system has been reported (Walker 1975, Lekagul and McNeely 1977a). Tulloch (1978, 1979) described the behavior of feral domestic *Bubalus* in the Northern Territory of Australia.

Conservation Measures Taken: In 1931 the Siam Society recommended a year-round closed season on females (Harper 1945, Leng-Ee 1978). Thai law now prohibits killing of wild *Bubalus* (WARPA 1980). The habitat of the only remaining wild water buffalo in Thailand is protected in Huai Kha Khaeng Wildlife Sanctuary and Thung Yai-Naresuan Wildlife Sanctuary (IUCN 1979).

Conservation Measures Proposed: Basic studies on the behavioral ecology of the wild buffalo in Huai Kha Khaeng and Thung Yai-Naresuan are needed to aid in formulating sound management plans. Improved enforcement against poaching and illegal grazing in the two sanctuaries is desirable. Vigilance should be maintained to prevent any grazing of domestic *Bos* with *Bubalus* to guard against crossbreeding, competition, and disease. There are at least two chromosomal races of domestic buffalo, but the karyotype of the wild *Bubalus* is unknown. To take better advantage of the large wild Thai *Bubalus* as a genetic resource in animal husbandry, its genetic relationships to the domestic breeds should be elucidated (Lekagul and McNeely 1977a). An enormous amount of information is available on the domestic water buffalo, including basic science, economics, husbandry, and ideas for taking better advantage of the genetic resources of the wild population (Cockrill 1974, Chantalakhana 1975, National Research Council 1981).

Banteng
Bos javanicus D'Alton 1823
Mammalia, Artiodactyla, Bovidae

Status: Endangered.
IUCN (1968): Threatened.
IUCN Red Data Book (1978): Vulnerable.
IUCN (1979): Threatened.
MAB (1979): Endangered.
USFWS (1980a): Endangered.
WARPA (1980): Protected-2.

Population Size and Trend: The banteng is extinct in Manipur, India. Claims by the Burmese government that the banteng is widespread and plentiful have not been independently confirmed, and a continuation of the decline noted by Wharton (1968) is probable. In Thailand, *B. javanicus* was still abundant and widespread at the end of the second world war but since then has been decimated. Fewer than 500 wild banteng survive in Thailand. The majority of these are found in Huai Kha Khaeng Wildlife Sanctuary and the adjacent Thung Yai-Naresuan Wildlife Sanctuary. In peninsular Malaysia, a few may persist in Kedah, but recent reports are lacking. There is no information on the current status of the banteng in Kampuchea, Lao PDR, or Vietnam. The total population of the continental subspecies, *B. j. birmanicus*, probably does not exceed several thousand. The Bornean endemic subspecies, *B. j. lowi*, is extinct in Sarawak and Brunei, but small herds persist in Kalimantan and Sabah. The typical race, *B. j. javanicus*, survives in small herds in certain parts of Java and Bali, but the genetic integrity of many herds is questionable (IUCN 1968, Lekagul and McNeely

1977a, IUCN Red Data Book 1978, IUCN 1979, B. Lekagul personal communication).

Distribution and History of Distribution: Banteng once occurred in Manipur, Burma, Thailand, Lao PDR, Kampuchea, Vietnam, from Perlis to Perak in peninsular Malaysia, Borneo, Java, and Bali. In Thailand it occurred throughout the country (only sparingly in the far south), except in the swamps in the present location of Bangkok (Fig. 103; Ellerman and Morrison-Scott 1951, Wharton 1968, Medway 1969, Lekagul and McNeely 1977a, IUCN Red Data Book 1978).

Geographic Status: Thailand is central to the historical range of the mainland race.

Habitat Requirements and Habitat Trend: Banteng are primarily grazers, but leaves and fruit are also taken. Most of the food plants listed by Hoogerwerf (1970) are characteristic of young secondary growth--none are species confined to primary forest. In

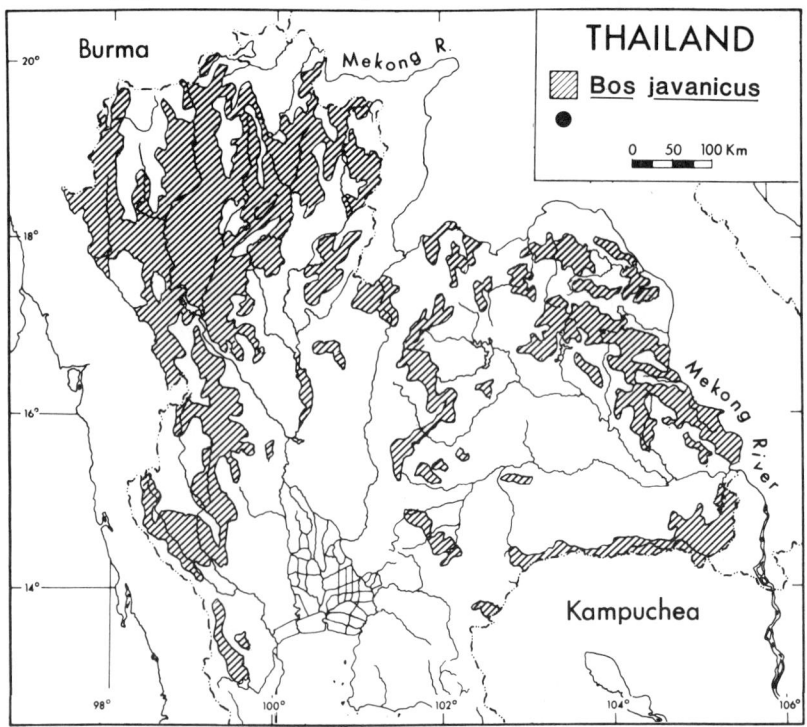

Fig. 103. Distribution of the Banteng (*Bos javanicus*).

Thailand today, banteng feed in the plains and deciduous forests by night and hide in thick forest by day. Evergreen rainforest is avoided. Each animal needs at least 0.5 ha of suitable grazing habitat. Banteng drink large quantities of water, so it is important that a permanent water source be near the feeding grounds. Salt licks are also required. Banteng have been reported to drink from the sea to fulfill their salt requirements (Wharton 1968, Hoogerwerf 1970, Halder 1976, Lekagul and McNeely 1977a).

Vulnerability of Species and Habitat: Banteng are susceptible to many diseases of domestic cattle. Domestic cattle and banteng readily crossbreed. Fortunately, banteng are not as aggressive toward man as water buffalo, and they generally shy away from permanent agriculture (Wharton 1968, Lekagul and McNeely 1977a).

Causes of Threat: Habitat loss and overhunting, aggravated by warfare and insurgency in many areas, greatly endanger the remaining wild banteng. Crossbreeding with domestic cattle and inbreeding, brought on by range fragmentation, threaten their genetic integrity. Competition and disease from domestic stock are real threats in many reserves where wild banteng survive.

Responses to Habitat Modification: It has been proposed that banteng followed human settlement into humid areas such as peninsular Malaysia. In many of the high-rainfall parts of its current range, it may be wholly dependent on the habitats that follow slash-and-burn agriculture. Because of the early-successional habitat requirement of banteng, Hoogerwerf (1970) advocates responsive management practices at Ujung Kulon Nature Reserve in Java.

Banteng readily exploit the young growth that follows burns. In most of Southeast Asia, development activities in the lowlands have driven the surviving banteng into upland forest. Before the second world war, *B. javanicus* in Thailand were diurnal denizens of the open plains. Modern habitat loss and hunting pressures have made them nocturnal grazers that take cover in dense vegetation by day (IUCN 1968, Wharton 1968, Lekagul and McNeely 1977a, B. Lekagul personal communication).

Demographic Characteristics: The time of the rut has been given as May and June in Thailand (Lekagul and McNeely 1977a) and all year, with a peak in September and October in Java (Hoogerwerf 1970). Captive Javan banteng rut for 2-3 days every 21-24 day period. Gestation is 9-10 months. One or two calves are born. Most calves are weaned by age 14-16 months, but some nurse until an age of 2 years. Cows come into heat 6-8 weeks after parturition and may be able to give birth every year. Young cows are mature at 2 years, young bulls somewhat later. Data from Ujung Kulon indicate a high mortality of females aged 2-5 years. Maximum longevity is thought to be 20-25 years (van Bemmel 1967, Medway 1969, Hoogerwerf 1970, Halder 1976, Lekagul and McNeely 1977a).

Key Behaviors: In Thailand, herds of 2-25 or more are known, usually containing only one mature bull. In their daily movements, they are typically led by an old cow. Other bulls are solitary or form small bachelor herds. Snorting and stamping alarm signals have been described, and banteng react to the warning cries of peafowl. Groups other than cows with calves are not stable through time. Young bulls leave their mothers at age 2-3 years; young cows may remain well after sexual maturity. Rutting bulls lick the hind quarters of cows, and often exhibit flehmen afterward. These occurrences are often followed by a mounting attempt. Nocturnal mating is suspected in Java (Hoogerwerf 1970, Halder 1976, Lekagul and McNeely 1977a).

Conservation Measures Taken: Banteng may be hunted under permit from the Thailand Forestry Department (WARPA 1980). Their major stronghold in Thailand, the Huai Kha Khaeng-Thung Yai-Naresuan wildlife sanctuaries, is under the protection of the Royal Forestry Department. There have also been recent banteng reports from the following national parks (NP) and wildlife sanctuaries (WS): Mae Taeng WS, Salawin WS, Khun Yuan WS, Mae Tun WS, Phu Phan NP, Phu Luang WS, Phu Kradung NP, Nam Nao NP, Phu Khieo WS, Phanom Dongrak WS, Yot Dom WS, Ram Khamhaeng NP, Lan Sang NP, Erawan NP, Tham Than Rot NP, Salak Phra WS, Mae Nam Phachi WS, Khao Soi Dao WS, Khao Kitchakut NP, and Khao Chamao NP (IUCN Red Data Book 1978, IUCN 1979, Prakobboon 1979). There are several hundred captive banteng around the world (IUCN Red Data Book 1978).

Conservation Measures Proposed: To prevent competition, crossbreeding, and transmission of disease, domestic cattle should be excluded from banteng reserves. Resources should be made available for improved enforcement and prosecution of poachers. Enough is known about the biology of this bovid in Thailand to allow the Division of Wildlife to conduct local surveys and prepare and implement banteng management plans on a preserve-by-preserve basis. The population of banteng in Thailand is an important stock of genetic material for domestic banteng. Most of the latter--nearly 2 million head--are in Indonesia, especially Bali, Lombok, Sulawesi, and Timor (National Research Council 1983*b*).

Gaur
Bos gaurus **Smith 1827**
Mammalia, Artiodactyla, Bovidae

Status: Endangered.
IUCN (1968): Threatened.
IUCN Red Data Book (1976): Vulnerable.
CITES (1979): Appendix I.
MAB (1979): Endangered.
IUCN (1979): Threatened
USFWS (1980a): Endangered.
WARPA (1980): Protected-2.

Population Size and Trend: Throughout this century the gaur has declined over its entire range. No estimates have been made of the total population in India, but in several reserves, such as Mudumalai Sanctuary, it is locally abundant. There is no reliable information on its current status in Burma, Lao PDR, Kampuchea, or Vietnam. Leng-Ee's (1978) suggestion of 2,500-3,000 in Thailand is almost certainly an overestimate. Lekagul and McNeely's (1977a) estimate of 500 in Thailand is probably more realistic. There are fewer than 500 remaining in peninsular Malaysia (Stevens 1968).

Distribution and History of Distribution: The once extensive populations have been restricted to isolated fragments over the historic range. In the Indian region the gaur persists in the Western Ghats, the central Indian highlands, and in the Himalayan foothills in Bhutan, Assam, and possibly Nepal (Schaller 1967). Uncertainty exists about the possible former occurrence of *B. gaurus* in Sri Lanka. The gayal or mithan (*B. frontalis*) of Burma and adjacent India is probably a domesticated gaur (Scheurmann 1975). The gaur once ranged throughout Burma, Lao PDR, Kampuchea, and Vietnam in suitable habitat. It may have inhabited extreme southern Yunnan in China. In Thailand, *B. g. readei* occurs north of the Isthmus of Kra and *B. g. hubbacki* (the seledang of Malaysia) occurs in the south (Fig. 104; Lekagul and McNeely

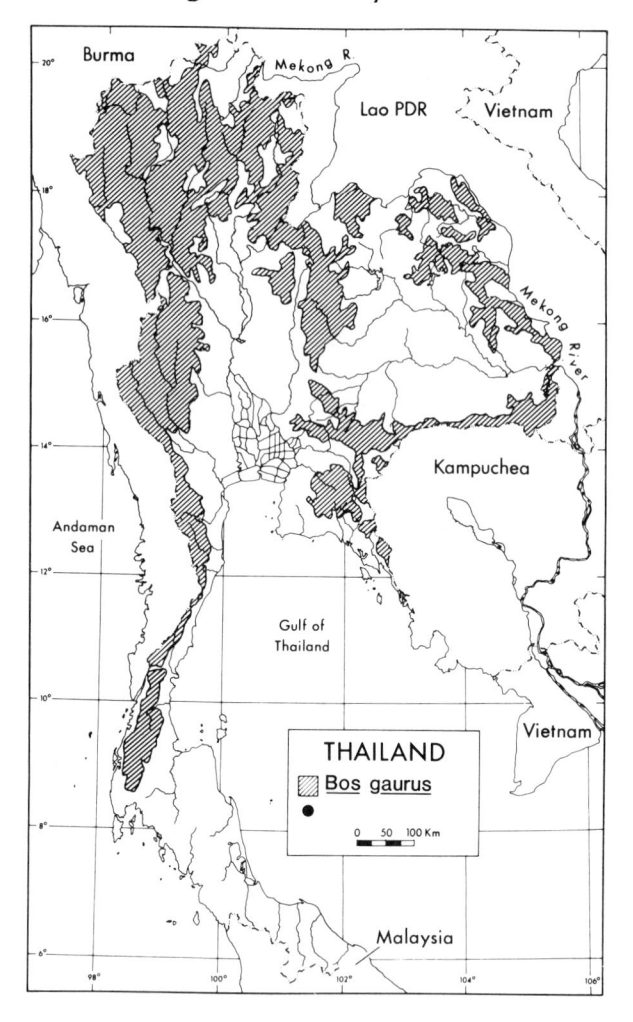

Fig. 104. Distribution of the Gaur or Seledang (*Bos gaurus*).

1977a). Gaur are found sparingly in peninsular Malaysia. Wharton (1968) suggested that the gaur followed shifting cultivation down the peninsula after the sea-level rise associated with the end of the last glaciation, explaining its absence from the rest of Sundaland.

Geographic Status: Thailand is central to the gaur's range.

Habitat Requirements and Habitat Trend: The gaur is both a grazer and browser. It prefers young grass but will eat a wide variety of coarse grasses (including bamboo), leaves of shrubs and trees, forbs, vines, fruits, seeds, and bark (see Schaller 1967 and Khan 1973 for detailed accounts of plant foods). In Thailand, gaur gather in bamboo forests in August and September to feed on shoots. They benefit from the destructive feeding activities of elephants (Lekagul and McNeely 1977a). Waterholes and salt licks are essential. Licks are visited nightly. If possible, a gaur will use several licks to get a variety of minerals. Gaur have been reported from many habitat types and in Thailand they are found at all elevations. The prime requirement seems to be forest with adjacent open areas for grazing. Gaur readily exploit the young growth that follows fire and clearly benefit from low-density shifting agriculture. In Kanha National Park, India, which supports many other ungulates (including a large population of domestic cattle), gaur densities have been reported to be 3.4-4.4 animals per km^2 (Wharton 1966, 1968, .pa Schaller 1967, Stevens 1968, Medway 1969, Khan 1973, Lekagul and McNeely 1977a).

Vulnerability of Species and Habitat: Their gregarious behavior, large size, and grazing activities expose them to human predators. They can be closely approached in automobiles (much more so than on foot) and will even make lateral threat displays to vehicles. Their copious and odiferous sweat allows experienced hunters to track them by scent. Their resemblance to the sacred cow confers some protection on the gaur in India. They are known to raid crops, especially when displaced by land-use changes (Schaller 1967, Khan 1973). Gaur do not attack people unless wounded (Lekagul and McNeely 1977a).

Causes of Threat: Diseases from domestic cattle (rinderpest, hoof-and-mouth disease, anthrax) sometimes cause gaur die-offs. Total deforestation removes the tree cover and affects water resources they need. Water impoundment projects have flooded areas of concentrated salt licks in Malaysia and elsewhere. The isolation of small herds by range fragmentation may bring about deleterious inbreeding. Fortunately, in areas where they co-occur with domestic cattle, gaur do not normally mate with them. Overhunting was a major cause of the present situation and poaching continues to be a problem, even in such protected areas as Khao Yai National Park. The continued existence of gaur populations is incompatible with high human populations and intensive modern agriculture (Wharton 1968, Schaller 1967, IUCN 1968, Lekagul and McNeely 1977a).

Responses to Habitat Modification: At low to moderate human densities, gaur benefit from shifting cultivation. Unlike many wild ungulates, they will consume the *Imperata* grass that follows fires. In Malaysia the recent decline of shifting agriculture may have been harmful to *B. gaurus*. At high human densities, hunting and general disturbance by man are detrimental to the gaur. In Southeast Asia it does not thrive in settled areas. This is in contrast to India, where it is seldom molested and hence frequents some developed areas (Pelandok 1938, Schaller 1967, Stevens 1968, Wharton 1968, Medway 1969, Khan 1973, Lekagul and McNeely 1977a). Gaur in Khao Yai National Park appear to avoid roads (W. Brockelman, personal communication).

Demographic Characteristics: Young gaur reach sexual maturity when 2-3 years old. Mating is concentrated in December-January in central India, but in Burma and Malaysia young are apparently born throughout the year (except October-December in Malaysia). Gestation is about 9 months. Single calves are born--no twins have been reported. The sex ratio at birth is equal. Young are able to walk within minutes of being delivered. The age at weaning is unknown. In Malaysia females breed again 2-3 months after giving birth. Predation by tigers is a major cause of death in juveniles. About half of the young may die in the first year of life. It has been suggested that differential mortality leads to a preponderance of females in older age classes. Gaur have lived 24 years in captivity and some may exceed 30 years of age in the wild. Progressive changes in size and pelage allow field workers to estimate the composition of herds under observation. In India, a calf to cow ratio of 39-45:100 was seen January-June and a ratio of 29:100 was seen in the latter half of the year. In a Malaysian herd 21.5 percent of the *B. gaurus* were breeding adult females and 12.9 percent were unweaned young (Hubback 1937, Schaller 1967, Medway 1969, Khan 1973).

Key Behaviors: Herds range in size from 2-40, averaging about 8-11. Composition is variable and changes are especially frequent during the rut. Mature black bulls associate with cows primarily at that time. Bull herds sometimes form. In Thailand, Boonsong Lekagul often has seen males fighting for the position of "lord of the herd" during the mating season. Schaller did not observe such definite leadership patterns in India. Schaller (1967) described posturing displays, sparring, and other agonistic behaviors, but proposed that size is the major criterion determining the rank of an individual in a herd. In Thailand, gaur once grazed in the open at dusk and dawn, but since vehicles and automatic weapons became widely available after World War II gaur have become more strictly nocturnal. Herds range widely and may cover several km daily. Schaller found no evidence of territoriality among herds in India. One member of the herd may act as a sentinel while the others forage. Saplings may be walked down or otherwise broken to obtain leaves from high above the ground. Dust baths and wallows are rarely used. When alarmed, gaur snort and thump the ground with the forelegs. Group defense against tigers is suspected. The flight distance of a herd from a man on foot is 60-90 m. When confronted by man, gaur prefer to run away but will attack if wounded or cornered. Some older bulls attack without apparent provocation (Schaller 1967, Stevens 1968, Wharton, 1968, Medway 1969, Khan 1973, Lekagul and McNeely 1977a). Scheurmann (1975) described the behavior of the domestic form (*B. frontalis*) and compared it with the behavior of the gaur and other bovids.

Conservation Measures Taken: As early as 1931, the Siam Society recommended a year-round closed season on female gaur (Harper 1945). At present, gaur may be hunted under permit from the Thailand Forestry Department (WARPA 1980). Gaur are now thought to occur in the following national parks (NP) and wildlife sanctuaries (WS): Khao Yai NP, Thung Salang Luang NP, Nam Nao NP, Khao Chamao-Khao Wong NP, Khao Kitchakut NP, Erawan NP, Lan Sang NP, Ram Khamhaeng NP, Tham Than Rot NP, Khlong Nakha WS, Phu Khieo WS, Khao Soi Dao WS, Huai Kha Khaeng WS, Thung Yai-Naresuan WS, Phu Luang WS, Phu Wua WS, Khao Ang Ru Nai WS, Phu Miang-Phu Thong WS, Salawin WS, Mae Tun WS, Mae Taeng WS, Khun Yuam WS, Phanom Dongrak WS, Mae Num Pachee WS, and Yot Dom WS (IUCN 1979, Prakobboon 1979). In many of these, gaur may be represented by only a few animals. Currently the Association for the Conservation of Wildlife, Bangkok, donates salt for use by ungulates in reserves.

Conservation Measures Proposed: Gaur are among the largest of cattle and are thought to be one of the ancestors of modern domestic cattle. Their value in increasing tropical beef production and as a basic bovine genetic resource needs further exploration. They are capable of turning *Imperata* grassland into human food. Because their diseases can have devastating effects on gaur, domestic cattle (at least unhealthy ones) should be excluded from gaur reserves. Resources should be made available for improved enforcement and prosecution of poachers. Further research is needed on the biology of this bovid in Thailand to allow the formulation of sound management practices.

Kouprey
Bos sauveli (Urbain 1937)
Mammalia, Artiodactyla, Bovidae

Status: Probably extirpated.
IUCN (1968): Threatened.
IUCN Red Data Book (1976): Endangered.
CITES (1979): Appendix I.
IUCN (1979): Highly endangered.
USFWS (1980a): Endangered.
WARPA (1980): Reserved.

Population Size and Trend: Political turmoil over most of its range has made surveys difficult, but there has clearly been a steady decline since the kouprey became known to science in the 1930s. In the early part of the 20th century it was said to be numerous in Thailand north of the Dongrak Mountains. Estimates of the maximum number surviving were 800 in 1938, 500 in 1951, 300 in 1964, 100 in 1969, and 50 in 1975. The remaining numbers are certainly small (Wharton 1955, Fisher et al. 1969, Lekagul and McNeely 1977a, WWF 1979).

Distribution and History of Distribution: Since its discovery, the range of this primitive bovid has been centered in northern and eastern Kampuchea. It also ranged into eastern Thailand, southern Lao PDR, southern Vietnam, and possibly even southern China. However, Hoffman (1986) noted that the ranges of numerous species of large mammals (Sumatran rhinoceros, elephant, gaur, and kouprey) have retreated southward in Southeast Asia in recent history. A herd was sighted in 1950 at Dong Eo-jan Forest southwest of Korat, Thailand. A hunter reported a herd on the Thai side of the Dongrak range in Sisaket Province in July 1975. A subsequent research expedition in April 1976 found what was believed to be an old track, but no kouprey were seen. A second expedition in August 1976 was also unsuccessful. Neese (1976b) received what he considered to be reliable reports of *B. sauveli* in the Lao-Kampuchean border area in 1974-75. While under house arrest in Kampuchea, Prince Norodom Sihanouk recently reported that he had a young male kouprey in his garden (Sauvel 1949, IUCN 1968, Enderlein 1976, Enderlein and Maxwell 1976, WWF 1979, Hoffmann 1986). An authoritative sighting of five animals was made in Sisaket Province, Thailand, in 1982 (Conservation News Volume 3, Association for the Conservation of Wildlife, Bangkok). A sighting has also been reported by veterinary department personnel of Kralanh Srok, Siem Reap Province, Kampuchea, in 1986 (Richard Spiegel, personal communication). The most recent sightings are in Vietnam (G. Schaller, personal communication).

Geographic Status: In this century kouprey in Thailand existed at the western extreme of the species' range. The total modern range may be relictual.

Habitat Requirements and Habitat Trend: Kouprey spend most of the year in low rolling hills in open areas affording good grazing and maximum visibility. These open areas are a fire climax mosaic of dry dipterocarp savannas and patches of dense forest. Fires are annual in the dry season, most of them set by man. Kouprey capitalize on the young growth in burned-over areas. They feed primarily on grasses (including *Arundinella* spp and *Chloris* spp), sedges, and tree leaves. Sufficient water in the dry season and salt licks are also required. Local residents in Sisaket Province in Thailand report that the kouprey migrates from Kampuchea up into evergreen forests of the Dongrak range during the monsoon, when the Kampuchean plains are overgrown with tall grass (Enderlein and Maxwell 1976). It has been estimated that 125 km^2 of good habitat can support 30-40 kouprey (Wharton 1955, 1957, Lekagul 1952, Lekagul and McNeely 1977a). Nearly all of the deciduous and dry dipterocarp forest of northeastern Thailand has been cleared, and this animal may now depend largely on slash-and-burn agriculture. Recent illegal deforestation on the Thai side in the Dongrak range has destroyed much wet season kouprey habitat (Enderlein 1976, B. Lekagul personal communication).

Vulnerability of Species and Habitat: Because of their large size, gregarious behavior, comparatively low reproductive rate, and preference for open areas, kouprey are vulnerable to hunting. The impressive horns and other tissues are valued as trophies and by the apothecary trade.

Causes of Threat: The succession of wars over most the

kouprey's range has left many hungry, well-armed, and displaced people who prey on all the larger vertebrates. The two remnant areas of kouprey range in northern Kampuchea have been the sites of recent military action. Human settlement of once sparsely populated areas of northern Kampuchea has threatened *B. sauveli* since its discovery. Diseases from domestic livestock may also be a problem. If kouprey can hybridize with other cattle (there is no evidence that they can, but it seems likely), then mating of any surviving kouprey with domestic cattle could administer the coup de grace by genetic swamping. On the Thai side of the Dongrak range, the remaining kouprey are threatened by land mines on roads and trails near the border, and by illegal timber extraction, hunting, slash-and-burn agriculture, and charcoal burning. New logging roads have improved access for hunters (Wharton 1955, Enderlein 1976, Enderlein and Maxwell 1976, Lekagul and McNeely 1977a, B. Lekagul personal communication).

Responses to Habitat Modification: Whether kouprey can survive the conversion of native habitat to permanent agriculture is unknown because the animals are simultaneously killed by hunters. Where the native habitat is intact in northern Kampuchea, the early historic land use pattern of shifting agriculture and spotty annual burning, associated with low-density human settlement, was beneficial in maintaining kouprey habitat (Wharton 1955, 1966, 1968). However, more intensive human use will destroy patches of dense forest (which have escaped fire) that the kouprey need for cover.

Demographic Characteristics: Kouprey are thought to breed in April and bear their young in December-February. Cows and young calves stay apart from the herd until the young are a month old. Longevity records do not exist (Lekagul and McNeely 1977a). Wharton (1955) reported seeing a 1:3 ratio of calves to cows.

Key Behaviors: Herds of 20 or more have been reported. These are of mixed composition, often with more than one adult male. Herds are usually led by an old female. Groups are not particularly cohesive. Adult bulls sometimes form bachelor herds. Kouprey also may form mixed-species herds with banteng and wild water buffalo. *B. sauveli* herds may cover 5-15 km daily. Digging with the horns and wallowing have been described (Edmond-Blanc 1947, Wharton 1955).

Conservation Measures Taken: Almost since the kouprey's

discovery, pleas have been made for hunting restrictions and other conservation measures (Coolidge 1940, Harper 1945). A captive taken to France in the 1930s died before it reached maturity. The fate of Prince Norodom Sihanouk's captive is unknown. Attempts to capture stock for the establishment of a captive breeding herd in the early 1960s failed. In 1964 it was declared the Cambodian national animal and several reserves were created for it, but later these were overrun by military operations. Thai law (WARPA 1980) prohibits the killing or unauthorized capture of this species. Suitable habitat for it is protected in Thailand in Yot Dom Wildlife Sanctuary, Phanom Dongrak Wildlife Sanctuary, and Loeng Li Wildlife Sanctuary (Edmond-Blanc 1947, Lekagul and McNeely 1977a, IUCN 1979, WWF 1979). The King of Thailand recently has decreed that a 32,000-ha wildlife sanctuary be set aside for kouprey in the Dongrak Mountains of Sisaket Province (FSP 1980).

Conservation Measures Proposed: Because of the kouprey's precarious status and apparent migratory habits, cooperation between governments is of paramount importance (Leng-Ee 1978). At the earliest possible date, Thai wildlife officials should meet with their Kampuchean, Lao, and Vietnamese counterparts to discuss ways to discover and conserve any remaining kouprey. If the extinction of any remaining herds is imminent, captive propagation may be the preferred conservation method. Wet-season habitat, dry-season habitat, and migration routes need to be identified and protected (Wharton 1955, Enderlein and Maxwell 1976, Lekagul and McNeely 1977a, WWF 1979). The protection of habitat in the Dongrak region should be maintained and strengthened by the Thai government. Possibly a population could be reintroduced there if the Vietnamese herd becomes secure and populous. An effort should be made to educate the citizenry about the plight of this animal and to enlist local help in its recovery, using radio programs and pamphlets in several languages.

Pfeffer and Kim-San (1967) presented convincing arguments that *B. sauveli* is a valid species and not merely a hybrid of other bovid forms. Although hybridization has not been documented, the kouprey is considered similar enough to domestic cattle to allow crossbreeding. It is potentially a valuable genetic resource to the cattle industry. If a purebred captive herd can be established, selective crossing with domestic stock might produce strains that are more productive in hot, dry climates. The suggestion has been made that kouprey are resistant to rinderpest. Additionally, the kouprey is a candidate for domestication, and it may have become domesticated temporarily during the Khmer culture, 400 to 800 years ago (National Research Council 1983*b*).

Serow
Capricornis sumatraensis **(Bechstein 1799)**
Mammalia, Artiodactyla, Bovidae

Status: Endangered.
IUCN (1968): Threatened.
IUCN Red Data Book (1972): Endangered (*C. s. sumatraensis* only).
CITES (1979): Appendix I.
USFWS (1980*a*): Endangered.
WARPA (1980): Reserved.

Population Size and Trend: This species has been extirpated from most of the more accessible parts of its range (Fisher et al. 1969). It is in danger of extinction in southeastern China and has disappeared from much of Vietnam. It is rare and poorly known in Lao PDR (Harper 1945). In Thailand its numbers have been greatly reduced and its range has become fragmented in recent times (IUCN 1968). Leng-Ee (1978) estimated that 3,000-4,000 survive in Thailand. It has suffered a great decline and range reduction in Sumatra (Harper 1945, IUCN Red Data Book 1972, West 1979). The closely allied form, *C. crispus*, has declined in numbers and is restricted in its distribution in the mountains of Taiwan and Japan (Fisher et al. 1969).

Distribution and History of Distribution: The serow occurs in the Himalayas from Punjab and Kashmir to Assam, Burma, southern China, Vietnam, Lao PDR, Thailand, peninsular Malaysia, and Sumatra (Harper 1945, Ellerman and Morrison-Scott 1951). It occurs throughout Thailand in suitable habitat, including many coastal islands (IUCN 1968, Lekagul and McNeely 1977*a*, Leng-Ee 1978). Lekagul and McNeely (1977*a*) recognized two subspecies in Thailand: *C. s. milneedwardsi* from Tenasserim north, and *C. s. sumatraensis* in the mountains of the south.

Geographic Status: Thailand is central to the Southeast Asian range of this bovid.

Habitat Requirements and Habitat Trend: Like the goral, the serow makes its home among thickly wooded cliffs and precipices. In Thailand and peninsular Malaysia it is restricted to limestone outcrops, hills, and mountains, including the limestone islands along both coasts of the peninsula. In Thailand it has been found from seashores to the upper slopes of the highest mountains (e.g., Doi Inthanon). Most Thai *Capricornis* survive in inaccessible uplands. They range from 200 to 2,450 m in the Burmese hills, from 1,850 to over 3,000 m in the Himalayas, and to over 4,000 m in southern China. The serow shows a strong tendency to remain in rocky and vegetative cover but will venture out into meadows to graze. The degree to which it depends on permanent water sources is uncertain. Where its range overlaps with that of the goral, the serow tends to occupy moister places. Wild and captive serow eat a great variety of plants, including leaves, shoots, grasses, twigs, and tubers. Mushrooms may be seasonally important in some areas (Irwin 1914, Allen 1940, Harper 1945, Medway 1969, Prater 1971, Lekagul and McNeely 1977a, Schaller 1977, Leng-Ee 1978, IUCN 1979, West 1979).

Vulnerability of Species and Habitat: Most authors consider the flesh of *Capricornis* to be superior to domestic goats and many species of game. They are widely eaten in Southeast Asia. The hide is valued and the horns are made into utensils. Serow are kept and sold as livestock and as pets. Villagers in many regions, including China and Thailand, attribute curative properties to many *Capricornis* tissues. They are difficult to hunt because of the rugged nature of their habitat, but they can be actively pursued with dogs. They are easy to catch with snares and pitfalls and can be killed easily when swimming or when driven into deep snow. They will attack men and dogs when cornered. Their habitat is one of the last to be cleared by man, and in Southeast Asia it is usually not frequented by the serow's only two significant predators, the tiger and (until recently) man (Allen 1940, Harper 1945, IUCN 1968, Lekagul and McNeely 1977a, Schaller 1977, Leng-Ee 1978, West 1979).

Causes of Threat: Overhunting has decimated or extirpated most populations of *C. sumatraensis*. In many areas habitat disturbance is an increasingly important problem. The surviving Thai serow may suffer from deleterious inbreeding brought on by range fragmentation and depopulation.

Responses to Habitat Modification: "This shy animal appears unable or unwilling to coexist in areas occupied by man" (Fisher et al. 1969:162). In Thailand, some steep limestone mountains remain covered with trees and dense vegetation and function as miniature reserves, even when the surrounding areas have been completely converted to agriculture (Lekagul and McNeely 1977a).

Demographic Characteristics: Serow in Thailand, the Himalayas, and Japan (*C. crispus*) mate in October and November (Prater 1971, Lekagul and McNeely 1977a, Schaller 1977). During the mating season, *C. crispus* comes into heat for about 3 days every 3 weeks. Gestation in both *Capricornis* species is about 7 months. One kid (rarely twins) is born. Captives have lived over 10 years (Ito 1971, Prater 1971, Lekagul and McNeely 1977a, Schaller 1977).

Key Behaviors: In the wild, young may have a brief hiding phase before beginning to follow the female (Schaller 1977). Kids may stay with their mother as long as a year (Lekagul and McNeely 1977a). Serow are essentially asocial beasts. Most reports of pairs and small groups probably refer to courting pairs or mother-kid family groups. Up to six adults may be seen feeding in the same meadow, but there have been no reports of true herds. Serow may be territorial. Wild *Capricornis* make visual signals by pawing earth and rubbing trees with their horns. Wild and captive Thai *C. sumatraensis* habitually defecate in the same spot. Captives mark trees and shrubs at the margins of their enclosure with exudates of the interdigital and large preorbital glands. Wild *Capricornis* probably remain in their chosen home ranges all year, except in parts of the Himalayas, where they move to lower elevations to escape severe winter conditions.

Serow are sure-footed, active animals. They use well-defined runways. By day they rest in caves, rock crevices, or dense vegetation, emerging to feed early in the morning and late in the evening. In some areas they are never seen out in the open. Serow are very shy in the presence of man. When approached, they tend to remain quietly hidden unless approached closely; then they bound away, loudly vocalizing (Irwin 1914, Allen 1940, Harper 1945, Prater 1971, Lekagul and McNeely 1977a, Schaller 1977, West 1979).

Conservation Measures Taken: *Capricornis* is protected by law in Sumatra, peninsular Malaysia, Thailand, and Japan (WARPA 1980, Hoi-Sen 1973, Hayashi and Mori 1979, West 1979). The strict protection of the animals and certain habitats in Japan has allowed a promising increase in some populations (Harper 1945, Hayashi and Mori 1979). About a dozen *C. sumatraensis* are held in the world's zoos (West 1979, Olney 1980). One was recently born in captivity in Peking (Olney 1980). *C. sumatraensis* occurs in the following Thai national parks (NP) and wildlife sanctuaries (WS): Khao Yai NP, Doi Inthanon NP, Nam Nao NP, Khao Sam Roi Yat NP, Khao Sabap NP, Khao Chamao-Khao Wong NP, Khao Kitchakut NP, Erawan NP, Lan Sang NP, Doi Suthep-Pui NP, Salak Phra WS, Phu Khieo WS, Khao Soi Dao WS, Khao Khieo-Khao Chomphu WS, Khao Banthat WS, Phu Miang-Phu Thong WS, Doi Chiang Dao WS, Salawin WS, Mae Tun WS, and Khun Yuam WS (IUCN 1979); and Thaleban NP (Dobias 1982). They may also occur in Huai Kha Khaeng WS (Seidensticker and McNeely 1975) and Maenam Phachi WS (Prakobboon 1979).

Conservation Measures Proposed: The vegetative cover of Thailand's steep limestone hills should be protected from destructive fires. The protection of the animals from hunting should continue. Efforts to educate villagers on the need to preserve serow, such as those under way in Sumatra (West 1979), should be initiated. Such measures should include admonitions that there is no scientific basis for the curative powers ascribed to *Capricornis* flesh. Because these animals are wary and inhabit such inaccessible places, little research has been done on them. Studies on the ecology of the Thai serow would allow the formulation of sound management plans.

Goral
Naemorhedus goral Hardwicke 1885
Mammalia, Artiodactyla, Bovidae

Status: Endangered.
IUCN (1968): Threatened.
CITES (1979): Appendix I.
USFWS (1980a): Endangered.
WARPA (1980): Reserved.

Population Size and Trend: The total number in Thailand has never been estimated (IUCN 1968). Leng-Ee (1978) stated that 20-50 inhabit Mae Tun Wildlife Sanctuary in Chiang Mai Province. Early in this century Evans (1905) thought this form to be rare and local in northern Burma.

Distribution and History of Distribution: This primitive bovid ranges from the Amur River valley in southeastern Siberia south through Mongolia, most of China, and Korea, to Punjab, Kashmir, Nepal, Assam and the northern parts of Burma and Thailand. In Thailand it occurs in the mountains at the headwaters of the Mae Ping (Fig. 105; Kloss and Gairdner 1923, Ellerman and Morrison-Scott 1951, Walker 1975, Lekagul and McNeely 1977a, Schaller 1977). The range map given by Lekagul and McNeely (1977a:721) is in error.

Geographic Status: Thai goral occur at the southern extreme of the species' range and may be relicts.

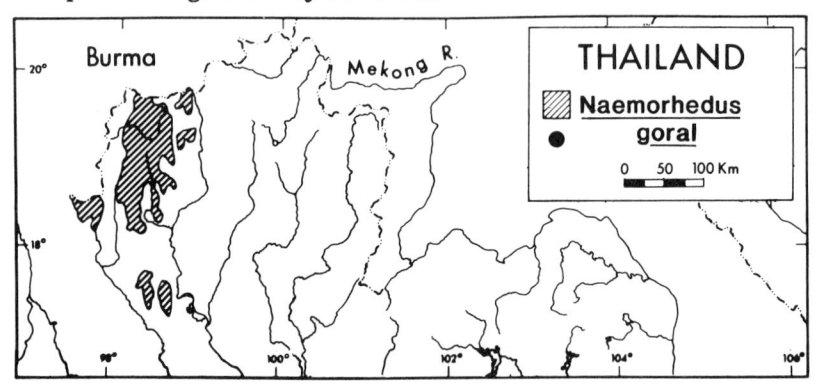

Fig. 105. Distribution of the Goral (*Naemorhedus goral*).

Habitat Requirements and Habitat Trend: Goral range from sea level to as high as 4,000 m in the Himalayas. "Within this altitudinal range, the goral's choice of habitat is liberal as long as the terrain is steep, rocky, and provides some cover" (Schaller 1977:67). The goral is mainly a browser. The diet includes grasses, forbs, low shrubs, and the twigs and leaves of larger trees. (Evans 1905, Lekagul and McNeely 1977a, Schaller 1977).

Vulnerability of Species and Habitat: Their apparent attachment to a small home range makes goral vulnerable to human predation. The rugged terrain these animals prefer is among the last to be affected by human settlement. The flesh is quite palatable, but the animals have good vision, rapid escape responses, and a pelage that disguises them well (Evans 1905, Kloss and Gairdner 1923, Lekagul and McNeely 1977a, Schaller 1977).

Causes of Threat: Although they are locally common where

they occur (B. Lekagul, personal communication), the restricted distribution in Thailand makes them susceptible to extirpation by locally intense hunting pressure and other disruptive forces.

Responses to Habitat Modification: Unknown.

Demographic Characteristics: In the wild, mating takes place in November and December. One or two kids are born after a gestation of approximately 6 months (data on reproduction in captivity are slightly different). Sexual maturity is attained in 2-3 years. Longevity is unknown but probably 8-10 years (Bromlej 1956, Dobroruka 1968, Lekagul and McNeely 1977a).

Key Behaviors: Goral are typically solitary, but pairs form during the rut and groups of 4-12 have been reported. *N. goral* form attachments to a limited home range and habitually deposit dung in certain locations. Territoriality has been predicted. The elaborate courtship displays seen in many members of the Caprinae have not been described for goral. Young goral probably pass through a short hiding phase before beginning to follow their mothers. The animals feed from before dawn to mid-morning and then drink and rest in the rocks or scrub for the day. They graze again from late afternoon to dark. On overcast days more diurnal activity may occur. When startled, goral emit alarm calls that are quickly taken up by others in the area. They are adept climbers and can swim as well (Evans 1905, Kloss and Gairdner 1923, Lekagul and McNeely 1977a, Schaller 1977).

Conservation Measures Taken: Hunting of this species is prohibited in Thailand (WARPA 1980). Goral are rarely kept in zoos. The potential for captive breeding has been demonstrated (Dobroruka 1968), but the paucity of zoo stock available for breeding has led to hybridization of the Thai form, *N. g. griseus*, with the Korean form, *N. g. raddeanus*. In Thailand it has been reported from the following wildlife sanctuaries: Doi Chiang Dao (IUCN 1979), Mae Tun (Leng-Ee 1978), and Salawin (Prakobboon 1979).

Conservation Measures Proposed: Surveys are needed to determine the true range of *N. goral* in northern Thailand, its presence in protected areas, and the effects of hunting on it. Studies on any aspect of its biology would be helpful. Conservation officers on the local level should learn to differentiate goral from the similar but larger serow to reduce spurious reports of goral and to prevent any populations from being overlooked. Because it has not been possible to maintain the genetic integrity of goral in the world's zoos, wildlife officials should consider establishing their own captive breeding herd of Thai *N. g. griseus*.

Literature Cited

Acharjyo, L. N. and Misra. 1973. A note on the birth of a Malayan giant squirrel, *Ratufa bicolor*, in captivity. Journal Bombay Natural History Society 70:375.

Ackery, P. R. 1975. A guide to the genera and species of Parnassiinae (Lepidoptera: Papilionidae). Bulletin British Museum (Natural History), Entomology 31(4):71-105.

Agrawal, V. C. and S. Chakraborty. 1979. Taxonomic notes on some Oriental squirrels. Mammalia 43:161-172.

Alfred, E. R. 1964. The fresh-water food fishes of Malaya. I. *Scleropages formosus* (Mull. and Schl.). Federated Malay States Museums Journal 9:79-83.

Alfred, E. R. 1968. Rare and endangered fresh-water fishes of Malaya and Singapore. Pp. 325-331 *in* L. M. Talbot and M. H. Talbot (eds.), Conservation in tropical South East Asia, IUCN Publications new series No. 10. 550 p.

Alfred, E. R. 1969. Conserving Malayan fresh-water fishes. Malayan Nature Journal 22:69-74.

Ali, R. 1983. Conservation biology: an evolutionary-ecological perspective [book review]. Natural History Bulletin Siam Society 31:99-103.

Ali, S. and S. D. Ripley. 1968. Handbook of the birds of India and Pakistan. Vol. 1. Oxford University Press, Bombay, London, New York. 380 p.

Ali, S. and S. D. Ripley. 1969*a*. Handbook of the birds of India and Pakistan. Vol. 2. Oxford University Press, Bombay, London, New York. 345 p.

Ali, S. and S. D. Ripley. 1969*b*. Handbook of the birds of India and Pakistan. Vol. 3. Oxford University Press, Bombay, London, New York. 380 p.

Ali, S. and S. D. Ripley. 1970. Handbook of the birds of India and Pakistan. Vol. 4. Oxford University Press, Bombay, London, New York. 265 p.

Ali, S. and S. D. Ripley. 1972. Handbook of the birds of India and Pakistan. Vol. 7. Oxford University Press, Bombay, London, New York. 236 p.

Ali, S. and S. D. Ripley. 1973. Handbook of the birds of India and Pakistan. Vol. 8. Oxford University Press, Bombay, London, New York. 277 p.

Allen, G. M. 1940. The mammals of China and Mongolia. American Museum Natural History, New York. 1350 p.

Allen, G. M. and H. J. Coolidge. 1940. Mammal and bird collections of the Asiatic Primate Expedition. Bulletin Museum Comparative Zoology, Harvard 7:131-166.

Anderson, J. 1871. Description of a new genus of newts from western Yunnan. Proceedings Zoological Society London 1871:423-425.

Anonymous. 1976. Otters and their conservation in Thailand. Tigerpaper 3(2):16.

Aquilina, G. D. and R. H. Beyer. 1979. The exhibition and breeding of binturongs, *Arctictis binturong*, as a family group at Buffalo Zoo. International Zoo Yearbook 19:185-188.

Archibald, G. W., S. D. H. Lantis, L. R. Lantis, and I. Munetchika. 1980. Endangered ibises Threskiornithinae: their future in the wild and in captivity. International Zoo Yearbook 20:6-17.

Areeratana, S. 1970. Fishes of the family Clariidae found in Thailand. Inland Fisheries Division, Department of Fisheries, Technical Paper No. 9:1-16.

Asakura, S. 1969. A note on the bear hybrid *Melursus* x *Helarctos* at Tama Zoo, Tokyo. International Zoo Yearbook 9:88.

Asdell, S. A. 1965. Patterns of mammalian reproduction. 2nd edition. Constable, London.

Askins, R. 1977. Sciuridae. Pp. 337-387 *in* B. Lekagul and J.A. McNeely, Mammals of Thailand. Association Conservation Wildlife, Bangkok. 758 p.

Austin, O. L., Jr. 1948. The birds of Korea. Harvard Museum Comparative Zoology Bulletin 101:1-301.

Austin, O. L., Jr. and N. Kuroda. 1953. The birds of Japan: their status and distribution. Museum Comparative Zoology Bulletin 109:279-627.

Auffenberg, W. 1979. Intersexual differences in behavior of captive *Varanus bengalensis* (Reptilia, Lacertilia, Varanidae). Journal Herpetology 13:313-315.

Auffenberg, W. 1981. Combat behavior in *Varanus bengalensis* (Sauria: Varanidae). Journal Bombay Natural History Society 78:54-72.

Badham, M. 1973. Breeding the Indian smooth otter, *Lutrogale perspicillata sindica* x *L. p. perspicillata*, at Twycross Zoo. International Zoo Yearbook 3:145-146.

Bakeev, Y. N. 1978. Changes in range and abundance of the jackal in the north Caucasus. Byulleten Moskovskogo Obschestva Ispytatelei Prirody Otdel Biologicheskii 83:45-57.

Balasingam, E. and M. K. b. M. Khan. 1969. Conservation of the Perak River terrapins (*Batagur baska*). Malayan Nature Journal 23:27-29.

Barker, D. G., J. B. Murphy, and K. W. Smith. 1979. Social behavior in a captive group of Indian pythons, *Python molurus* (Serpentes, Boidae), with formation of a linear social hierarchy. Copeia 1979:466-471.

Barnes, R. G. 1976. Breeding and hand rearing of the marbled cat, *Felis marmorata*, at the Los Angeles Zoo. International Zoo Yearbook 16:205-208.

Bechstein, J. M. 1799. *In* Pennant, Uebers. vierf. Thiese. I:98.

Beebe, W. 1926a. Pheasants--their lives and homes. Vol. I. Doubleday, Page, and Company, Garden City, New York. 257 p.

Beebe, W. 1926b. Pheasants--their lives and homes. Vol. II. Doubleday, Page, and Company, Garden City, New York. 309 p.

Bell *in* Gray. 1830. Illustrations of Indian zoology. Pt. 1, pl. 6; Synopsis reptilium or short description of the species of reptiles.

Benedict, F. G. 1936. The physiology of the elephant. Carnegie Institute Washington, Washington, D.C. 302 p.

Bennet. 1833. Proceedings Zoological Society London 1833:68.

Benveniste, R. E. and G. J. Todaro. 1975. Segregation of RD-114 and FeLV related sequences in crosses between domestic cat and leopard cat. Nature 256(5526):506-508.

Berkson, G., B. A. Ross, and S. Jatinandana. 1971. The social behavior of gibbons in relation to a conservation program. Pp. 225-255 *in* L. A. Rosenblum (ed.), Primate behavior: developments in field and laboratory research. Academic Press, New York.

Bernstein, I. S. 1967. Intertaxa interactions in a Malayan primate community. Folia Primatologica 7:207.

Bernstein, I. S. 1968. The lutong of Kuala Selangor. Behavior 32:1-16.

Bertrand, M. 1969. The behavioral repertoire of the stumptail macaque: a descriptive and comparative study. Bibliotheca Primatologica 11. Krager, Basel.

Blakeslee, C. K., C. G. Rice, and K. Ralls. 1979. Behavior and reproduction of captive brow-antlered deer, *Cervus eldi thamin* (Thomas 1918). Saugetierkundliche Mitteilungen 27(2):114-127.

Blanc, M. and F. d'Aubenton. 1965. Sur la présence de *Scleropages formosus* (Müller et Schlegel 1844), poisson de la famille des Osteoglossidae dans es eaux douces du Cambodge. Bulletin du Muséum National D'Histoire Naturelle 37:397-402.

Blanford, W. T. 1888-1891. Fauna of British India. Mammalia. Taylor and Francis, London. 617 p.

Bhaskar, S. 1979. The status of sea turtles in the eastern Indian Ocean. Unpublished report, photocopy. 19 p.

Bleeker, P. 1851*a*. Bijdrage tot de kennis der ichthyologische fauna van Borneo, met beschrijving van 16 nieuwe soorten van zoetwatervisschen. Natuurkundig Tijdschrift voor Nederlandsch Indie 1:1-16.

Bleeker, P. 1851*b*. Vijfde bijdrage tot de kennis der ichthyologische fauna van Borneo, met beschrijving van eenige nieuwe soorten van zoetwatervisschen. Natuurkundig Tijdschrift voor Nederlandsch Indie 2:415-422.

Bleeker, P. 1853*a*. Nieuwe tientallen diagnostiche beschrijvingen van nieuwe of weinig bekende vischsoorten van Sumatra. Natuurkundig Tijdschrift voor Nederlandsch Indie 5:495-534.

Bleeker, P. 1853*b*. Zevende bijdrage tot de kennis der ichthyologische fauna van Borneo. Zoetwatervisschen van Sambas, Pontianak en Pengaron. Natuurkundig Tijdschrift voor Nederlandsch Indie 5:427-462.
Blyth, E. 1842. Journal Asiatic Society Bengal 11(1):461.
Blyth, E. 1846. Journal Asiatic Society Bengal 14(2):866.
Blyth, E. 1848. Journal Asiatic Society Bengal 17(1):252.
Blyth, E. 1855. Journal Asiatic Society Bengal 24(3):266.
Blyth, E. 1859. Journal Asiatic Society Bengal 28:296.
Blyth, E. 1863. Exhibition of a new deer from Siam. Proceedings Zoological Society London 1863:155-158.
Boddaert. 1783. Table des planches enlumineez d'histoire naturelle, p. 54.
Boelkins, R. C. and A. P. Wilson. 1972. Intergroup social dynamics of the Cayo Santiago rhesus (*Malaca mulatta*) with special reference to changes in group membership by males. Primates 13:125-139.
Boonruang, P. and B. Phasuk. 1975. Species composition and abundance distribution of anomuran sand crabs, and bionomics of *Emerita emeritus* (L.) along the Indian Ocean coast of Thailand (Decapoda: Hippidae). Phuket Marine Biological Center, Research Bulletin No. 8:1-19.
Boswall, J. and S. Kanwanich. 1978. The birds of Phi Phi Le Island, Krabi, Thailand. Natural History Bulletin Siam Society 27:83-92.
Boulenger, G. A. 1885. Catalogue of the lizards in the British Museum (Natural History). Vol. II. 2nd edition. British Museum (Natural History), London.
Boulenger, G. A. 1898. Description of a new genus of cyprinoid fishes from Siam. Annals Magazine Natural History, Series 7, 1:450-451.
Boulenger, G. A. 1912. A vertebrate fauna of the Malay Peninsula from the Isthmus of Kra to Singapore, including the adjacent islands. Reptilia and Batrachia. Taylor and Francis, London. 294 p.
Bowler, J. K. 1977. Longevity of reptiles and amphibians in North American collections. Society for the Study of Amphibians and Reptiles. Miscellaneous Publications. Herpeteological Circular No. 6, 32 p.

Bradley, J. 1876. A narrative of travel in Burma, Siam, and the Malay Peninsula, London.

Brahmachary, R. L. 1979. The scent marking of tigers. Tigerpaper 6(2-3):19-20.

Brain, C. K. 1970. New finds at the Swartkrans Australopithecine site. Nature 225(5238):1112-1119.

Brockelman, W. Y. 1975. Gibbon populations and their conservation in Thailand. Natural History Bulletin Siam Society 26:133-226.

Brockelman, W. Y. 1978. Preliminary report on relations between the gibbons *Hylobates lar* and *H. pileatus* in Thailand. Pp. 315-318 *in* D. J. Chivers and K. A. Joysey (eds.), Recent advances in primatology. Vol. 3. Evolution. Academic Press, New York.

Brockelman, W. Y. 1979. Conservation of the pileated gibbon in Thailand. Final report to the Charles A. Lindbergh Fund, Inc. Mimeo, 58 p.

Brockelman, W. Y. and N. Nadee. 1977. Preliminary survey and biogeographic analysis of the birds of the Surin Islands, Thailand. Natural History Bulletin Siam Society 26(3-4):211-226.

Bromlej, G. F. 1956. Goral (*Naemorhedus caudatus raddeanus* Hende, 1894). Zoologicheskii Zhurnal 35:1395-1405.

Brown, L. and D. Amadon. 1968. Eagles, hawks and falcons of the world. McGraw-Hill Book Co., New York. 945 p.

Bulir, L. 1972. Breeding binturongs, *Arctictis binturong*, at Liberec Zoo. International Zoo Yearbook 12:117-118.

Bunyavejchewin, S. 1983. Analysis of the tropical dry deciduous forest of Thailand. I. Characteristics of the dominance-types. Natural History Bulletin Siam Society 31:109-122.

Burton, R. W. 1940. The Indian wild dog. Journal Bombay Natural History Society 41:691-715.

Bustard, R. 1972. The leathery turtle. Oryx 11:233-239.

Caldecott, J. O. 1985. An ecological, and behavioural study of the pig-tailed macaque. Karger, Basel, Switzerland. 262 p.

Carpenter, C. R. 1940. A field study in Siam of the behavior and social relations of the gibbon (*Hylobates lar*). Comparative Psychology Monograph 16:1-212.

Carr, A. 1986. Rips, FADS, and little loggerheads. BioScience 36:92-100.

Carson, C. 1981. Male midwifery. Zoonooz 44(3):8-9.
Chantalakhana, C. 1975. The buffaloes of Thailand--their potential, utilization and conservation. In H. Fischer (ed.), The Asiatic water buffalo. Proceedings of an international symposium held at Khon Kaen, Thailand, March 31-April 6, 1975. Food and Fertilizer Technology Center, Taipei, Taiwan.
Chapin, J. P. 1954. The African river martin and its migration. Ann. Mus. Congo Zool. 1:9-15.
Chasen, F. N. 1939. The birds of the Malay Peninsula. Volume 4. H. F. and G. Witherby, Ltd., London.
Chasen, F. N. 1940. A handlist of Malaysian mammals. Bulletin Raffles Museum 15:1-209.
Chasen, F. N., and C. B. Kloss. 1927. Spolia Mentawiensia--Mammals. Proceedings Zoological Society London 1927:797-840.
Chavan, S. A. 1980. Status of panther (*Panthera pardus*) in Gir Sanctuary. Tigerpaper 8(4):12-14.
Cheke, A. S. 1973*a*. Marbled cat in Chieng Mai. Journal Siam Society, Natural History 24(3-4):468.
Cheke, A. S. 1973*b*. New locality for *Tylototriton verrucosus*. Natural History Bulletin Siam Society 24(3-4):467.
Cheng, T.-h. 1963. China's economic fauna: birds. Science Publishing Society, Beijing. 694 p.
Chevey, P. 1930. Sur un noveau silure géant du Mékong, *Pangasianodon gigas* nov. g., nov. sp. Bulletin Zoologique Societe France 55:536-542.
Chivers, D. J. 1973. Introduction to the socio-ecology of Malayan forest primates. Pp. 101-146 *in* R. P. Michael and J. H. Crook (eds.), Comparative ecology and behaviour of primates. Academic Press, New York.
Chivers, D. J. 1978. The gibbons of peninsular Malaysia. Malayan Nature Journal 30:565-581.
Choy, P. K. 1980. Breeding the great Indian hornbill *Buceros bicornis* at Jurong bird park. International Zoo Yearbook 20:204-206.
Christiansen, B. 1979. Mangrove forest resources and their management in Asia and the Far East. FAO Regional Office for Asia and the Far East, Bangkok. Mimeo, 97 p.
CITES. 1977. Annual report.

CITES. 1978. Annual report.
CITES. 1979. Convention on International Trade in Endangered Species of Wild Fauna and Flora. Regulations and appendices published by the Federal Wildlife Permit Office, United States Fish and Wildlife Service, Washington, D.C.
Clark, C. W. 1973. The economics of overexploitation. Science 181:630-634.
Cockrill, W. R. (ed.). 1974. The husbandry and health of the domestic buffalo. Food and Agriculture Organization of the United Nations. Rome, Italy.
Cocks, A. H. 1881. Note on the breeding of the otter. Proceedings Zoological Society London 1881:249-250.
Cohen, J. A. 1977. A review of the biology of the dhole or Asiatic wild dog (*Cuon alpinus* Pallas). Animal Regulation Studies 1(1977):141-158.
Cohen, J. A. 1978. *Cuon alpinus*. Mammalian Species 100:1-3.
Cohen, J. A., M. W. Fox, A. J. T. Johnsingh, and B. D. Barnett. 1978. Food habits of the dhole in south India. Journal Wildlife Management 42:933-936.
Coolidge, H. J. 1940. The Indochinese forest ox or kouprey. Memoirs Museum Comparative Zoology, Harvard University 54(6):421-531.
Courtois, F. 1927. Memoires concernant l'histoire naturelle de la Chine. 'Les Oiseaux de Musee de Zikawei 5:124-159.
Cowan, I. McT. and C. W. Holloway. 1978. Geographical location and current conservation status of the threatened deer of the world. Pp. 11-22 *in* Threatened Deer. International Union for Conservation of Nature and Natural Resources, Gland and Morges, Switzerland. 434 p.
Crawford, D. N. 1972. First Australian record of the Asiatic dowitcher. Emu 72(3):112-113.
Crockett, C. M. and W. L. Wilson. 1980. The ecological separation of *Macaca nemestrina* and *M. fascicularis* in Sumatra. Pp. 148-181 *in* D. G. Lindburg (ed.), The macaques: studies in ecology, behavior, and evolution. Van Nostrand Rheinhold Co., New York. 384 p.

Curtin, S. H. and D. J. Chivers. 1978. Leaf-eating primates of peninsular Malaysia: The siamang and the dusky leaf-monkey. Pp. 441-464 *in* G. G. Montgomery (ed.), The ecology of arboreal folivores. Smithsonian Institution Press, Washington, D.C. 574 p.

Cuvier, G. L. C. F. D. 1823. Ossements Foss. 4:325.

Cuvier, G. L. C. F. D. and A. Valenciennes. 1840. Histoire naturelle des poissons. 15:386.

Cuvier, G. L. C. F. D. and A. Valenciennes. 1844. Histoire naturelle des poissons. 17:348.

d'Aubenton, F. 1965. *Notopterus blanci* n. sp., nouvelle espèce de poisson Notopteridae du haut Mékong Cambodgien. Bulletin Muséum National D'Histoire Naturelle 37:261-264.

Dathe, H. 1961. Breeding the Malayan bear (*Helarctos malayanus*). International Zoo Yearbook 3:94.

Dathe, H. 1968. Breeding the Indian leopard cat, *Felis bengalensis*, at East Berlin Zoo. International Zoo Yearbook 8:42-44.

Dathe, H. 1970. A second generation birth of captive sun bears. International Zoo Yearbook 10:70.

Davidar, E. R. C. 1975. Ecology and behavior of the dhole or Indian wild dog, *Cuon alpinus* (Pallas). Pp. 109-119 *in* M. W. Fox (ed.), The wild canids: their systematics, behavioral ecology and evolution. Van Nostrand Reinhold Company, New York. 508 p.

Davidson, A. 1975. Fish and fish dishes of Laos. Imprimerie Nationale Vientiane, 189 p.

Davis, D. D. 1962. Mammals of the lowland rain-forest of North Borneo. Bulletin National Museum, State Singapore 31:1-129.

Davison, G. W. H. 1981. Diet and dispersion of the great argus *Argusianus argus*. Ibis 123:485-494.

de Alwis, W. L. E. 1973. Status of Southeast Asia's small cats. Pp. 198-208 *in* R. L. Eaton, (ed.), The world's cats. Vol. 1. World Wildlife Safari, Winston, Oregon. 349 p.

de Rooij, N. 1915. The reptiles of the Indo-Australian archipelago. Vol. I. E. J. Brill, Ltd., Leiden.

de Rooij, N. 1917. The reptiles of the Indo-Australian archipelago. Vol. II. E. J. Brill, Ltd., Leiden. 334 p.

De Shauensee, R. M. 1984. The birds of China. Smithsonian Institution Press, Washington, D.C. 602 p.

Deignan, H. G. 1945. The birds of northern Thailand. Smithsonian Institution, U. S. National Museum Bulletin 186:1-616.

Deignan, H. G. 1963. Checklist of the birds of Thailand. Smithsonian Institution, U. S. National Museum Bulletin 226:1-263.

Delacour, J. 1947. Birds of Malaysia. MacMillan Company, New York. 382 p.

Delacour, J. 1949a. A new subspecies of *Pavo muticus*. Ibis 91:348-349.

Delacour, J. 1949b. The genus *Lophura* (gallopheasants). Ibis 91:188-220.

Delacour, J. 1951. The pheasants of the world. Country Life Ltd., London, Charles Scribner's Sons, New York. 347 p.

Delacour, J. 1959. The waterfowl of the world. Volume 3. Country Life Ltd., London. 270 p.

Delacour, J., P. Jabouille, and W. P. Lowe. 1928. On the birds collected during the third expedition to French Indo-China. Ibis 4:23-51.

Denis, Armand. 1965. Cats of the world. Constable, London. 119 p.

Deraniyagala, P. E. P. 1939. Tetrapod reptiles of Ceylon. Vol. 1. Testudinates and crocodilians. Ceylon Journal Science. Colombo Museum Natural History Series. Dulau and Company, London. xxxii + 412 p.

Deraniyagala, P. E. P. 1955. Some extinct elephants, their relatives and the two living species. Ceylon National Museum Publication. 161 p.

Deraniyagala, P. E. P. 1957. Reproduction in the monitor lizard *Varanus bengalensis* (Daudin). Spolia Zeylanica, Bulletin National Museum Ceylon 28:161-166.

Deraniyagala, R. Y. 1957. Pseudo-combat of the monitor lizard *Varanus bengalensis* (Daudin). Spolia Zeylanica, Bulletin National Museum Ceylon 28:159.

Desai, J. H. 1974. Observations on the breeding habits of the Indian smooth otter, *Lutrogale perspicillata*, in captivity. International Zoo Yearbook 14:123-124.

Desmarest. 1819. Nouv. Dict. H.N. 32:458.

Desmarest. 1822a. Ency. Meth. Mamm. 2:377.

Desmarest. 1822b. Mammalogie. 2:399.

Dickinson, E. C. 1964. An account of the Doi Inthanon Expedition 1963, including a contribution to the ornithology of that mountain. Natural History Bulletin Siam Society 20:279-292.

Dickinson, E. C. 1966. Notes upon a collection of birds made by Frank Gill Esq. off the west coast of peninsular Thailand. Natural History Bulletin Siam Society 21:243-249.

Dickinson, E. C. 1970. Birds of the Legendre Indochina expedition. American Museum Novitates 2423:1-17.

Dickinson, E. C. and S. Chaiyaphun. 1970. Notes on Thai birds. 2. A first contribution to our knowledge on the birds of Thung Salaeng Luang National Park, Phitsanulok Province. Natural History Bulletin Siam Society 23:(4-5):515-526.

Dickinson, E. C. and S. Chaiyaphun. 1973. Notes on Thai birds. 4. Birds collected in Phu Kradueng National Park, Loei Province. Natural History Bulletin Siam Society 25(1-2):33-39.

Dittus, W. P. 1980. The social regulation of primate populations: a synthesis. Pp. 263-286 in D. G. Lindburg (ed.), The macaques: studies in ecology, behavior, and evolution. Van Nostrand Rheinhold Co., New York. 384 p.

Dobias, R. S. 1981. A search for the white-eyed river martin *Pseudochelidon sirintarae* at Bung Boraphet, central Thailand. Unpublished report in the files at the Faunal Preservation Society.

Dobias, R. S. 1982. Thaleban National Park. Conservation News 3 (Association for the Conservation of Wildlife, Bangkok).

Dobroruka, L. J. 1968a. Breeding group of goral at Prague Zoo. International Zoo Yearbook 8:143-145.

Dobroruka, L. J. 1968b. A note on the gestation period and rearing of young in the leopard, *Panthera pardus*, at Prague Zoo. International Zoo Yearbook. 8:65.

Dobroruka, L. J. 1975. Notes on the behavior of the Malayan giant squirrel, *Ratufa bicolor*. International Zoo Yearbook 15:207-212.

Duplaix, N. and F. W. King. 1975. TRAFFIC report on international wildlife trade in Thailand, 31 March to 6 June 1975. Unpublished report. Photocopy. 24 p.

Duplaix-Hall, N. 1972. Notes on maintaining river otters in captivity. International Zoo Yearbook 12:178-181.

Duplaix-Hall, N. 1975. River otters in captivity: a review. Pp. 315-327 *in* R. D. Martin, (ed.), Breeding endangered species in captivity. Academic Press, New York. 420 p.

Edmond-Blanc, F. 1947. Contribution to the knowledge of Cambodian wild ox or kouproh. Journal Mammalogy 28:245-248.

Ehrenfeld, D. 1979. Conservation problems. World Conference on Sea Turtle Conservation, November 26-30, 1979, Washington, D.C., U.S.A. Natural History Notes new series 1(3):1-12.

Eisenberg, J. F. and M. Lockhart. 1972. An ecological reconnaissance of Wilpattu National Park, Ceylon. Smithsonian Contributions Zoology 101:1-118.

Elgood, J. H., C. H. Fry, and R. J. Dowsett. 1973. African migrants in Nigeria. Ibis 115:1-59.

Ellerman, J. R. and T. C. S. Morrison-Scott. 1951. Checklist of Palearctic and Indian mammals. British Museum (Natural History), London. 810 p.

Elwes, H. J. 1891. On butterflies collected by Mr. W. Doherty in the Naga and Karen Hills and in Perak. Proceedings Zoological Society London 1891:249-289.

Enderlein, P. 1976. Report from the second expedition to the Dongrak Mountain Range in eastern Thailand in search for kouprey (*Bos sauveli*). Food and Agriculture Organization, United Nations, Regional Office for Asia and the Far East, Bangkok. Mimeo, 14 p.

Enderlein, P. and J. F. Maxwell. 1976. A preliminary report from an attempt to find evidence for the presence of kouprey (*Bos sauveli*) in eastern Thailand and a recommendation to the Government of Thailand to set aside the Dongrak Mountain Range for conservation purposes. FAO, UN, ROAFE, Bangkok. Mimeo, 7 p.

Enderson, J. H. 1969. Peregrine and prairie falcon life tables based on band-recovery data. Pp. 505-509 *in* J. J. Hickey (ed.), Peregrine falcon populations: their biology and decline. University Wisconsin Press, Madison (Wisconsin), New York, and London. 596 p.

Erlinge, S. 1967. Home range of the otter, *Lutra lutra* L., in southern Sweden. Oikos 18:186-209.

Erlinge, S. 1968a. Territoriality of the otter, *Lutra lutra* L. Oikos 19:81-98.

Erlinge, S. 1968b. Food studies on captive otters, *Lutra lutra* L. Oikos 19:259-270.
Erlinge, S. 1969. Food habits of the otter, *Lutra lutra* L., and the mink, *Mustela vison* Schreber, in a trout water in southern Sweden. Oikos 20:1-7.
Erlinge, S. 1972. Interspecific relations between otter, *Lutra lutra*, and mink, *Mustela vison*, in Sweden. Oikos 23:327-335.
Eschscholtz. 1829. Zool. atlas, l, p. 3, pl 3.
Estes, R. and J. Goddard. 1967. Prey selection and hunting behaviour of the African wild dog. Journal Wildlife Management 3:52-70.
Eudey, A. A. 1979. Differentiation and dispersal of macaques (*Macaca* spp.) in Asia. Ph.D. Dissertation, University California, Davis. 241 p.
Eudey, A. A. 1980. Pleistocene glacial phenomena and the evolution of Asian macaques. Pp. 52-83 *in* D. G. Lindburg (ed.), The macaques: studies in ecology, behavior, and evolution. Van Nostrand Reinhold Co., New York. 384 p.
Evans, G. D. 1905. Notes on the goral found in Burma. Proceedings Zoological Society London. 1905(2):311-314.
Evans, G. H. 1910. Elephants and their diseases. Government Press, Rangoon. 343 p.
Eve, R. and A.-M. Guigue. 1982. Birds on Ko Libong, southern Thailand. Natural History Bulletin Siam Society 30:91-104.
Ewer, R. F. 1973. The carnivores. Cornell University Press, Ithaca, New York. 494 p.
Fairley, J. S. and S. C. Wilson. 1972a. Autumn food of otters (*Lutra lutra*) on the Agivey River, County Londonderry, Northern Ireland. Journal Zoology (London) 166:468-469.
Fairley, J. S. and S. C. Wilson. 1972b. Food of otters (*Lutra lutra*) from Co. Galway, Ireland, and notes on other aspects of their biology. Journal Zoology (London) 166:469-474.
Fellner, K. 1965. Natural rearing of clouded leopards, *Neofelis nebulosa*, at Frankfurt Zoo. International Zoo Yearbook 5:111-113.
Feng, Z., C. Zhen, and G. Cai. 1980. Mammals from southeastern Xizang (Tibet). Acta Zoologica Sinica 26:91-97.
Fennell, C. M. and B. King. 1964. New occurrences and recent distributional records of Korean birds. Condor 66:239-246.

Ferrier, V. and J. C. Beetschen. 1973. Investigations on the chromosomes of *Tylototriton verrucosus* and of viable hybrids from the cross female *Pleurodeles waltii* and male *Tylototriton verrucosus* (Amphibia: Urodela: Salamandridae). Chromosoma (Berlin) 42(1):57-69.

Ferrier, V., J. C. Beetschen, and A. Jaylet. 1971. The obtaining of a viable inter-generic hybrid between two European and Asiatic urodele amphibians, *Pleurodeles waltii* female x *Tylototriton verrucosus* male (Salamandridae). Comptes Rendus Hedbomadaires des Seances de L'Academie des Sciences, Ser. D. Sci. Nat. 272(24):3079-3082.

Firouz, E. 1976. Environmental and nature conservation in Iran. Environmental Conservation 3:33-42.

Fischer. 1814. Zoogn. 3:301.

Fisher, J., N. Simon, J. Vincent, and the Survival Service Commission of IUCN. 1969. Wildlife in danger. Viking Press, New York. 368 p.

Fittkau, E. J. 1973. Crocodiles and the nutrient metabolism of Amazonian waters. Amazonia 4:103-133.

Fleagle, J. G. 1978. Locomotion, posture, and habitat utilization in two sympatric, Malaysian leaf-monkeys (*Presbytis obscura* and *Presbytis melalophos*). Pp. 243-251 in G. G. Montgomery (ed.), The ecology of arboreal folivores. Smithsonian Institution Press, Washington, D.C. 574 p.

Flower, S. S. 1900. On the mammals of Siam and the Malay Peninsula. Proceedings Zoological Society London 1900:306-379.

Flynn, R. 1978. The Sumatran rhinoceros in the Endau-Rompin National Park of peninsular Malaysia. Malayan Nature Journal 4:5-12.

Flynn, R. and M. T. Abdullah. 1984. Distribution and status of the Sumatran rhinoceros in peninsular Malaysia. Biological Conservation 28:253-273.

Fontaine, P. A. 1965. Breeding clouded leopards, *Neofelis nebulosa*, at Dallas Zoo. International Zoo Yearbook 5:113-114.

Fooden, J. 1971. Report on primates collected in western Thailand, January-April, 1967. Fieldiana (Zoology) 59:1-62.

Fooden, J. 1980. Classification and distribution of living macaques (*Macaca* Lacepede, 1799). Pp. 1-9 *in* D. G. Lindburg (ed.), The macaques: studies in ecology, behavior, and evolution. Van Nostrand Rheinhold Co., New York. 384 p.

Fooden, J. 1982. Taxonomy and evolution of the *Sinica* group of macaques: 3. Species and subspecies accounts of *Macaca assamensis*. Fieldiana Zoology, new series 10:1-52.

Fooden, J. 1986. Taxonomy and evolution of the *Sinica* group of macaques: 5. Overview of natural history. Fieldiana Zoology, new series 29:1-22.

Forbes, W. S. 1881. Observations on the incubation of the Indian python (*Python molurus*) with special regard to the alleged increase of temperature during that process. Proceedings Zoological Society London 1881:960-967.

Forster, J. R. 1781. Indische Zool., 1781, p. 40.

FPS (Fauna and Flora Preservation Society). 1980. Kouprey alive, well and protected. Oryx 16:238.

FPS (Fauna and Flora Preservation Society). 1980. Three Java tigers killed. Oryx 15:444.

Freeland, W. J. and D. H. Janzen. 1974. Strategies in herbivory by mammals: the role of plant secondary compounds. American Naturalist 108:269-289.

Frith, C. B. and V. E. Douglas. 1978. Notes on ten Asian hornbill species (Aves: Bucerotidae) with special reference to growth and behavior. Natural History Bulletin Siam Society 27:35-82.

Furtado, J. I. and D. B. C. Scott. 1971. Notes on *Scleropages formosus* (Muller and Schlegel) (Osteichthyes, Osteoglossidae) in Malaya. Malaysian Agriculture Journal 48:38-43.

Furuya, Y. 1962. The social life of the silvered leaf-monkeys, *Trachypithecus cristatus*. Primates 3:41-60.

Furuya, Y. 1965. Social organization of the crab-eating monkey. Primates 6:285-336.

Furuya, Y. 1976. Otters in Padas Bay, Sabah, Malaysia. Journal Mammalogical Society Japan. 7:39-43.

Gale, U. T. 1974. Burmese timber elephant. Trade Corporation, Rangoon. 162 p.

Gairdner, K. G. 1914. Note on two rare mammals, Berdmore's rat (*Hapalomys longicaudatus*) and Fea's muntjak (*Cervulus feae*). Journal Natural History Society Siam 1:115-116.

Gairdner, K. G. 1915. Additions to the mammalian fauna of Ratburi. Journal Natural History Society Siam 1:252-255.

Geidel, B. and W. Gensch. 1976. The rearing of clouded leopards, *Neofelis nebulosa*, in the presence of the male. International Zoo Yearbook 16:124-126.

Gensch, W. 1963. Successful rearing of the binturong. International Zoo Yearbook 4:75-76.

Geoffroy. 1826. Dict. cl. d'Hist. Nat. IX:519.

Geoffroy, E. St.-H. 1831. Voyage aux Indes-Orientales, par le nord de l'Europe, les provinces du Caucase, la Georgie, l'Armenie et la Perse, suivi de details topographiques, statistiques, et autres sur le Pegou, les Isles de Java, de Maurice et de Bourbon, sur le Cap-de-bonne-Esperance et Sainte-Helene, pendant... 1825-29. Mammiferes. M.C. Belanger, Paris.

Geptner, V. G. 1971. Systematic status of the Amur wild cat and some other east Asian cats referred to as *Felis bengalensis*. (In Russian). Zoologicheskii Zhurnal 50(11):1720-1727.

Gibson-Hill, C. A. 1949. An annotated checklist of the birds of Malaya. Bulletin Raffles Museum, Singapore 20:1-299.

Gibson-Hill, C. A. 1950. Notes on the clouded leopard. Journal Bombay Natural History Society 49(3):543-546.

Giles, F. H. 1937. The riddle of *Cervus schomburgki*. Journal Siam Society, Natural History Supplement 11(1):1-34.

Ginsberg, J. 1981. The status of sea turtles in Tarutao National Park, Satun, Thailand. Tigerpaper 8(2):27-29.

Gittins, S. P. 1977. The species range of the gibbon *Hylobates agilis*. *In* D. J. Chivers and K. A. Joysey (eds.), Recent advances in primatology. Vol. 3. Evolution. Academic Press, New York.

Glenister, A. G. 1955. The birds of the Malay Peninsula, Singapore and Penang. Oxford University Press, London. 282 p.

Gmelin. 1789. Caroli a Linne... Systema naturae. 1(2):571.

Golani, I. 1923. Non-metric analysis of behavioral interaction sequences in captive jackals (*Canis aureus* L.). Behavior 44(1-2):89-112.

Golani, I. and A. Keller. 1975. A longitudinal field study of the behavior of a pair of golden jackals. Pp. 303-335 *in* M. W. Fox (ed.), The wild canids: their systematics, behavioral ecology, and evolution. Van Nostrand Reinhold Company, New York. 508 p.

Golani, I. and H. Mendelssohn. 1971. Sequences of pre-copulatory behavior of the jackal, *Canis aureus*. Behaviour 38(1-2):169-192.
Goodwin, D. 1977. Pigeons and doves of the world. 2nd edition. British Museum (Natural History) Publication 663:1-446.
Gore, M. E. J. and W. Pyong-Oh. 1971. The birds of Korea. Royal Asiatic Society, Seoul. 450 p.
Gray, J. E. 1831*a*. Characters of a new genus of fresh water tortoise from China. Proceedings Zoological Society London 1831:106-107.
Gray, J. E. 1831*b*. Synopsis reptilium or short descriptions of the species of reptiles. Part 1. Cataphracta, tortoises, crocodilians, and enaliosaurians. 24 p.
Gray, J. E. 1837. Charlesworth's Magazine Natural History, new series 1:579.
Gray, J. E. 1842. Annals Magazine Natural History 10:263.
Gray, J. E. 1853. Proceedings Zoological Society London 1853:191.
Gray, J. E. 1865. Proceedings Zoological Society London 1865:123.
Gressitt, J. L. 1970. Biogeography of Laos. Pacific Insect Monographs 24:573-626.
Griffith. 1821. Descr. Anim. (Carn.), p. 37.
Griffith. 1844. Proceedings Linnean Society London 1:217.
Groves, C. P. 1967. On the rhinoceroses of South-East Asia. Saugetierkunde Mitteilungen 15:221-237.
Guehler, U. 1933. Further examples of Schomburgk's deer. Journal Siam Society, Natural History Supplement 9(1):147-149.
Guldenstaedt. 1776. Nov. Com. Acad. Petrop. 20:483.
Günther. 1873. Proceedings Zoological Society London 1873:413.
Gyi, K. M. 1969. The occurrence of *Tylototriton verrucosus* Anderson 1871 (Urodela: Salamandridae) at Taunggyi, Burma. Union Burma Journal Life Sciences 2:23-26.
Gyldenstolpe, N. 1914. Mammals collected or observed by the Swedish zoological expedition to Siam 1911-1912. Arkiv fur Zool. 8(23):1-36.
Gyldenstolpe, N. 1916. Kungl. Svenska Vet.-Akad. Handl. 56(2):134.
Gyldenstolpe, N. 1919. A list of the mammals at present known to inhabit Siam. Journal Natural History Society Siam 3(2):127-175.

Gyldenstolpe, N. 1920. A nominal list of the birds at present known to inhabit Siam. Ibis 2:735-780.
Halbrook, R. S., J. H. Jenkins, and P. B. Bush. 1980. Mercury accumulation in Georgia otters. Pp. 44-57 *in* N. Duplaix (ed.), Proceedings of the second working meeting of the Otter Specialist Group, held at the Florida State Museum, Gainesville, 27-29 March 1980. IUCN, Gland, Switzerland. 243 p.
Halder, U. 1976. Okologie und verhalten des banteng (*Bos javanicus*) in Java: eine feldstudie. Verlag Paul Parey, Hamburg and Berlin. 124 p.
Hall, B. P. 1956. First record of the Chinese lesser crested tern, *Thalasseus zimmermanni*, from Thailand. Bulletin of the British Ornithological Club 76:87.
Halls, J. A. T. 1982. The current status of Craseonycteris thonglongyai. Conservation News 3 (Association for the Conservation of Wildlife, Bangkok).
Hamilton, F. 1822. An account of the fishes found in the River Ganges and its branches.
Hardwicke. 1821. Transactions Linnaean Society London 13:236.
Hardwicke. 1825. Transactions Linnaean Society London 14:518.
Harper, F. 1945. Extinct and vanishing mammals of the Old World. Special Publication 12, American Committee for International Wild Life Protection, New York Zoological Park, New York. 850 p.
Harrison, J. L. 1954. The natural food of some rats and other mammals. Bulletin Raffles Museum 25:157-165.
Harrison, J. L. 1961. The natural food of some Malayan mammals. Bulletin National Museum, State Singapore 30:5-18.
Harrison, J. L. 1962. The distribution of feeding habits among animals in a tropical rain forest. Journal Animal Ecology 31:53-63.
Harrison, J. L. and R. Traub. 1950. Rodents and insectivores from Selangor, Malaya. Journal Mammalogy 31:337-346.
Harrisson, B. 1974. Animal trade, an international issue. International Zoo Yearbook 14:13-21.
Harrisson, T. H. 1951. Humans and hornbills in Borneo. Sarawak Museum Journal 3(new series):400-413.
Harrisson, T. H. and L. C. Yin. 1965. To scale a pangolin. Sarawak Museum Journal 12(25-26):415-418.

Hatt, R. T. 1959. The mammals of Iraq. Misc. Publ. Museum Zoology, University Michigan 106:1-113.

Havmoller, R. 1926. A herd of wild elephants in peninsular Siam. Journal Siam Society Natural History 6:365.

Hayashi, F. and Y. Mori. 1979. Studies on the damage to forest trees by Japanese serows (*Capricornis crispus*) from the standpoint of forestry. 1. Research Bulletin Faculty Agriculture, Gifu University 42:99-108.

Hemmer, H. 1976. Gestation and postnatal development in felids. Pp. 143-165 *in* R. L. Eaton (ed.), The world's cats. Vol. 3, No. 2. Carnivore Research Institute, Seattle, Washington. 179 p.

Hendrickson, J. R. 1958. The green sea turtle, *Chelonia mydas* (Linn.), in Malaya and Sarawak. Proceedings Zoological Society London 130(4):455-535.

Hendrickson, J. R. 1961. Nature conservation in West Malaysia. Malayan Nature Journal (special issue):214-223.

Henry, G. M. 1971. A guide to the birds of Ceylon. 2nd Edition. Oxford University Press, London. 457 p.

Herbert, E. G. 1924. Nests and eggs of birds in central Siam (part 3). Journal Natural History Society Siam 6:293-311.

Herre, V. W. 1979. Remarks on the evolution of languages of mammals: the variability of the intraspecific communication of canids. Zeitschrift Zoologische Systematik Evolutionforschung 17:151-173.

Heude. 1888. Mem. Hist. Nat. Emp. Chinois 2:50.

Hewson, R. 1964. Couchbuilding by otters, *Lutra lutra*. Journal Zoology (London) 159:524-527.

Hewson, R. 1973. Food and feeding habits of otters, *Lutra lutra*, at Loch Park, north-east Scotland. Journal Zoology (London) 170:159-162.

Hickey, J. J. 1969. Peregrine falcon populations: their biology and decline. University Wisconsin Press, Madison (Wisconsin), New York, and London. 596 p.

Hill, C. A. 1964. The cat with the flat head. Zoonooz 37:3-5.

Hill, J. E. 1961. Notes on flying squirrels of the genera *Pteromyscus*, *Hylopetes*, and *Petinomys*. Annals Magazine Natural History, series 13, 4:721-738.

Hill, J. E. 1974. A new family, genus and species of bat (Mammalia: Chiroptera) from Thailand. Bulletin British Museum (Natural History), Zoology 27:301-336.

Hodgson. 1829. Asiatic Researches 18(1):178, 2 pls.

Hodgson. 1842. Calcutta Journal Natural History 2:57

Hoffmann, R. S. 1986. A new locality record for the kouprey from Viet-Nam, and an archaeological record from China. Mammalia 30:391-395.

Hoi-Sen, Y. 1973. Totally protected and protected wild mammals of peninsular Malaysia. Malayan Nature Journal 26:77-80.

Holdridge, L. R. 1967. Life zone ecology. Tropical Science Center, San Jose, Costa Rica. 206 p.

Holdridge, L. R., W. C. Grenke, W. H. Hatheway, T. Liang, and J. A. Tosi, Jr. 1971. Forest environments in tropical life zones. Pergamon Press, New York, Sydney. 747 p.

Holmes, D. A. 1973. Bird notes from southernmost Thailand, 1972. Natural History Bulletin Siam Society 25(1-2):39-66.

Holmes, D. A. 1977. A report on the white-winged wood duck in southern Sumatra. Wildfowl 28:61-64.

Holmes, D. A. and D. R. Wells. 1975. Further observations on the birds of South Thailand. Natural History Bulletin Siam Society 26:61-78.

Honegger, R. E. 1975. The crocodilian situation in European zoos. International Zoo Yearbook 15:277-283.

Hoogerwerf, A. 1950. De witvlengeleend, *Cairina scutulata*, van de Grote Soenda eilanden. Ardea 38:64-69.

Hoogerwerf, A. 1969. On the ornithology of the rhino sanctuary Udjong Kulon in West Java (Indonesia). Natural History Bulletin Siam Society 23(1-2):9-66.

Hoogerwerf, A. 1970. Udjong Kulon: the land of the last Javan rhinoceros. E. J. Brill, Leiden. 512 p.

Hooijer, D. A. 1974. *Manis paleojavanica* from the Pleistocene of Gunung Butak, Java. Proceedings Koninklijke Nederlandse Akademie van Wetwnschappen. Series B. Physical Sciences 77:198-200.

Hopwood, J. C. 1921. The nidification of the masked finfoot (Heliopias personata). Journal Bombay Natural History Society 27:634.

Horsfield. 1821. Transactions Linnaean Society London 13:175.

Hubback, T. R. 1937. The Malayan guar or seledang. Journal Mammalogy 18:267-279.
Hume, A. O. 1875a. Stray Feathers 3(4):296, pl. 3.
Hume, A. O. 1875b. Stray Feathers 3(4):300.
Hume, A. O. and E. W. Oates. 1890. The nests and eggs of Indian birds. Vol. 3. 2nd edition. R. H. Porter, London.
Husain, K. Z. 1977. The white-winged wood duck project. Tigerpaper 4(1):6-8.
Husar, S. 1978. *Dugong dugon*. Mammalian Species 88:1-7.
Hutton, A. F. 1949. Mammals of the High Wavy mountains. Journal Bombay Natural History Society 1(2):113-114.
Ide, G. S. and J. B. Kethley. 1977. *Thewkachlea ratufi* n.g., n. sp., an unusual new cheylitid mite (Cheyletidae: Acariformes) from the giant squirrel, *Ratufa*, (Sciuridae: Rodentia) in Sabah and Thailand. Annals Entomological Society America 70:559-562.
Igarashi, S. 1979. A new papilionid butterfly of the genus *Bhutanitis* from northern Thailand. Tyo to Ga 30(1-2):69-72.
Illiger, A. K. W. 1815. Abh. Ak. Wiss. (Berlin) 1815:90, 99.
Inger, R. F. 1970. A new species of frog of the genus *Rana* from Thailand. Fieldiana Zoology 51(14):169-174.
IPPL (International Primate Protection League). 1978. Laotian-Belgium traffic in mammals. International Primate Protection League Newsletter 5(3):2-5.
IPPL. 1979. A second shipment of "Laotian mammals." International Primate Protection League Newsletter 6(3):4.
Irwin, A. J. 1914. Notes on the races of serow, or goat-antelope, found in Siam. Journal Natural History Society Siam 1:19-26.
Ito, T. 1971. On the estrous cycle and gestation period of the Japanese serow, *Capricornis crispus*. Journal Mammalogical Society Japan 5:104-108.
IUCN Red Data Book: International Union for Conservation of Nature and Natural Resources. (Date varies with dates of separate sheets.) Vol. 1, Mammalia, 1978; Vol. 2, Aves, 1979; Vol. 3, Amphibia and Reptilia, 1979; Vol. 4, Pisces, 1977.

IUCN 1968: Talbot, L. M. and M. H. Talbot (eds.). 1968. Conservation in tropical South East Asia. IUCN Publications new series no. 10, Morges, Switzerland. 550 p. (Contributions by many authors.)
IUCN. 1971a. Crocodiles. IUCN Publications new series, Supplementary Paper No. 32, 191 p. (Contributions by many authors.)
IUCN. 1971b. Marine turtles. IUCN Publications new series, Supplementary Paper No. 12:1-109.
IUCN. 1976. Summary review of projects, status reports and conservation activities associated with the IUCN Threatened Deer Programme June 1975 to December 1976. Deer Specialist Group Newsletter No. 2, December 1976, IUCN, Morges, Switzerland.
IUCN. 1978a. Threatened deer. International Union for Conservation of Nature and Natural Resources, Morges, Switzerland. 434 p.
IUCN. 1978b. Bangkok-Brussels--it's monkey business. IUCN Bulletin 9(9):52.
IUCN. 1979. International Union for Conservation of Nature and Natural Resources. 1979. Conservation for Thailand--Policy Guidelines. Morges, Switzerland. Mimeo, Vol. 1, 144 p.; Vol. 2, 139 p.
Jackson, P. 1979. The World Wildlife Fund and the tiger. Tigerpaper 6(2-3):2-4.
Jayewardene, E. D. W. 1975. Breeding the fishing cat, *Felis viverrina*, in captivity. International Zoo Yearbook 15:150-152.
Jenkins, D. 1980. Ecology of otters in northern Scotland. I. Otter (*Lutra lutra*) breeding and dispersion in mid-Deeside, Aberdeenshire in 1974-1979. Journal Animal Ecology 49:713-735.
Jenkins, D. 1981. Ecology of otters in northern Scotland. IV. A model scheme for otters, *Lutra lutra* L., conservation in a freshwater system in Aberdeenshire. Biological Conservation 20:123-132.
Jenkins, D. and G. O. Burrows. 1980. Ecology of otters in northern Scotland. III. The use of feces as indicators of otter (*Lutra lutra*) density and distribution. Journal Animal Ecology 49:755-774.

Jenkins, D. and R. J. Harper. 1980. Ecology of otters in northern Scotland. II. Analyses of otter (*Lutra lutra*) and mink (*Mustela vison*) feces from Deeside, N.E. Scotland in 1977-78. Journal Animal Ecology 49:737-754.

Jenkins, D., J. G. K. Walker, and D. McCowan. 1979. Analyses of otter (*Lutra lutra*) feces from Deeside, N.E. Scotland. Journal Zoology (London) 187:235-244.

Jintanugool, J., A. A. Eudey, and W. Y. Brockelman. 1982. Species conservation priorities in Thailand. Pp. 41-51 *in* R. A. Mittermeier and W. R. Konstant (eds.), Species conservation priorities in the tropical forests of Southeast Asia. Occasional Papers IUCN Species Survival Commission 1, International Union for the Conservation of Nature and Natural Resources, Gland, Switzerland.

Johns, A. D. 1986. Effects of selective logging on the behavioral ecology of West Malaysian primates. Ecology 67:684-694.

Johnsingh, A. J. T. 1979. Ecology and behaviour of the dhole or Indian wild dog, *Cuon alpinus* Pallas 1811, with special reference to predator-prey relationships at Bandipur. Unpubl. Ph.D. Diss., Madurai University, Madurai, India. 308 p.

Johnstone, S. T. 1972. Slimbridge: curator's report for 1971. Wildfowl 23:135-136.

Jones, M. L. 1968. Longevity of primates in captivity. International Zoo Yearbook 8:183-192.

Jorgensen, A. 1949. Siams vadefugle. Dansk Orn for Tidsskr. 43:60-80, 150-162, 216-237, 261-279.

Jones, G. S. 1975. Notes on the status of *Belomys pearsoni* and *Dremomys pernyi* (Mammalia, Rodentia, Sciuridae) on Taiwan. Quarterly Journal Taiwan Museum 28(3-4):403-406.

Kahl, M. P. 1972. Comparative ethology of the Ciconiidae. Part 4. The "typical" storks (genera *Ciconia*, *Sphenorhynchus*, *Dissoura*, and *Euxenura*). Zeitschrift Tierpsychologie 30:225-252.

Kahl, M. P. 1973. Comparative ethology of the Ciconidae. Part 6. The black-necked, saddlebill, and jabiru storks (genera *Xenorhynchus*, *Phippiorhynchus*, and *Jabiru*). Condor 75:17-27.

Kear, J. and G. Williams. 1978. Waterfowl at risk. Waterfowl 29(1978): 5-21.
Kellert, S. R. 1985. Social and perceptual factors in endangered species management. Journal Wildlife Management 49:528-536.
Kerr. 1792. Animal Kingdom:151.
Keulen-Kromhout, G. van. 1978. Zoo enclosures for bears (Ursidae): their influence on captive behaviour and reproduction. International Zoo Yearbook 18:177-186.
Khan, M. K. b. M. 1964. A note on *Batagur baska* (the river terrapin or tuntong). Malayan Nature Journal 18:184-187.
Khan, M. K. b. M. 1969. Population and distribution studies of Perak elephants. Malayan Nature Journal 23:7-14.
Khan, M. K. b. M. 1973. Studies of the seledang (*Bos gaurus*) in the State of Perak. Malayan Nature Journal 26:163-169.
Khan, M. K. b. M. 1976. Malayan elephant, its management and problems. Nature Malaysiana 1(1):38-43.
King, B. F. and E. C. Dickinson. 1975. A field guide to the birds of South-East Asia. Williams Collins Sons and Company, Ltd., London. 480 p.
King, B. F. and S. Kanwanich. 1978. First wild sighting of the white-eyed river martin, *Pseudochelidon sirintarae*. Biological Conservation 13:183-185.
King, F. W. 1974. Trade in live crocodilians. International Zoo Yearbook 14:52-56.
King, F. W. and P. Brazaitis. 1971. Species identification of commercial crocodile skins. Zoologica 56(2):15-17.
King, F. W. and J. S. Dobbs. 1975. Crocodilian propagation in American zoos and aquaria. International Zoo Yearbook 15:272-277.
King, F. W., H. W. Campbell, H. Messel, and R. Whitaker. 1979. Review of the status of the estuarine or saltwater crocodile, *Crocodylus porosus*. Unpublished report. 33 p.
Kleiman, D. G. 1967. Some aspects of social behavior in the Canidae. American Zoologist 7:365-372.
Kleiman, D. G. 1974*a*. Scent marking in the binturong. Journal Mammalogy 55:224-227.

Kleiman, D. G. 1974b. The estrous cycle in the tiger (*Panthera tigris*). Pp. 60-75 *in* R. L. Eaton (ed.), The world's cats. Vol. II. Feline Research Group, Woodland Park Zoo, Seattle, Washington. 260 p.

Kloss, C. B. 1932. Notes on the Malayan races of *Ratufa affinis*. Bulletin Raffles Museum 7:1-2.

Kloss, C. B. and K. G. Gairdner. 1923. The goral in Siam. Journal Natural History Society Siam. 6(1):135-137.

Koford, C. B. 1965. Population dynamics of rhesus monkeys on Cayo Santiago. Pp. 160-174 *in* I. DeVore (ed.), Primate behavior: field studies of monkeys and apes. Holt, Rinehart and Winston, New York.

Koford, C. B. 1966. Population changes in rhesus monkeys: Cayo Santiago, 1960-1964. Tulane Studies Zoology 13:1-7.

Kowalski, K. 1976. Mammalian fauna of Japan. Przeglad Zoologiczny 20(2):185-194.

Krause, W. J. and C. R. Leeson. 1974. The stomach of the pangolin (*Manis pentadactyla*) with emphasis on the pyloric teeth. Acta Anatomica 88:1-10.

Kruuk, H. 1972. The spotted hyaena: a study of predation and social behavior. University Chicago Press, Chicago. 335 p.

Kruuk, H. and R. Hewson. 1978. Spacing and foraging of otters (*Lutra lutra*) in a marine habitat. Journal Zoology (London) 185:205-212.

Kruuk, H. and M. Turner. 1967. Comparative notes on predation by lion, leopard, and wild dog in the Serengeti area, East Africa. Mammalia 31:1-27.

Kucherenko, S. P. 1976. The common otter (*Lutra lutra*) in the Amur-Ussuri district. Zoologicheskii Zhurnal 45:904-911.

Kurland, J. A. 1973. A natural history of Kra macaques (*Macaca fascicularis* Raffles 1821) at the Kutai Reserve, Kalimantan Timur, Indonesia. Primates 14:245-262.

Kuroda, N. 1936. On a new breeding ground for *Pseudototanus guttifer*. Tori 9:232-238.

Kuschinski, L. 1974. Breeding binturongs, *Arctictis binturong*, at Glasgow Zoo. International Zoo Yearbook 14:124-126.

La Touche, J. D. D. 1931-34. A handbook of the birds of eastern China. Vol. 2. Taylor and Francis, London. 566 p.

Lagler, K. F. 1976a. Field investigations, Appendix Vol. 1. Fisheries and integrated Mekong River Basin development. University Michigan, School Natural Resources.

Lagler, K. F. 1976b. Terminal report, executive volume. Fisheries and integrated Mekong River Basin development. University Michigan, School Natural Resources. Mimeo, 367 p.

Lamprecht, J. 1978. On diet, foraging behavior, and interspecific food competition of jackals in the Serengeti National Park, East Africa. Zeitschrift Saugetierkunde 43:210-223.

Lancaster, W. E. 1975. Exhibiting and breeding the Asian small-clawed otter, *Amblonyx cinerea*, at Adelaide Zoo. International Zoo Yearbook 15:63-65.

Latham. 1790. Index Orn. (India) 2:670.

Latham. 1790. Index Orn. (India) 2:709.

Lauhachinda. 1969. Thesis, Kasetsart University, Bangkok.

Lekagul, B. 1952. On the trail of the kouprey or Indo-chinese forest ox (*Bibos sauveli*). J. Bombay Natural History Society 50:623-628.

Lekagul, B. 1963. Report on Javan and Sumatran rhinos on the Thai-Burmese border. Conservation News, Association Conservation Wildlife, Bangkok 3:23.

Lekagul, B., K. Askins, J. Nabhitabhata, and A. Samruadkit. 1977. Field guide to the butterflies of Thailand. Association Conservation Wildlife, Bangkok. 260 p.

Lekagul, B., and E. W. Cronin, Jr. 1974. Bird guide of Thailand. 2nd edition. Association Conservation Wildlife, Bangkok. 316 p.

Lekagul, B. and J. A. McNeely. 1977a. Mammals of Thailand. Association Conservation Wildlife, Bangkok. 758 p.

Lekagul, B. and J. A. McNeely. 1977b. Elephants in Thailand: importance, status, and conservation. Tigerpaper, 4(3):22-25.

Lekagul, B. and D. Damman. 1977. Sea turtles. Conservation News, Association Conservation Wildlife, Bangkok. 1977:15.

Leng-Ee, P. 1978. The conservation of protected large mammals in Thailand. Photocopy, 13 p.

Leng-Ee, P. 1979a. Status of the tiger in Thailand. Tigerpaper 6(2-3):21.

Leng-Ee, P. 1979*b*. Status of the otters in Thailand. Agenda item CSS 79/52/12/11. Otter Specialist Group, Survival Service Commission, IUCN, Gland, Switzerland.

Lewis, R. E., J. H. Lewis, and S. I. Atallah. 1968. A review of Lebanese mammals: Carnivora, Pinnipedia, Hyracoidea and Artiodactyla. Journal Zoology (London) 154:517-531.

Li, S. 1976. New records of Chinese fish from the Lancang River, Yunnan Province, China. Acta Zoologica Sinica 22:117-118.

Lim, B.-L. 1973. The banded linsang and the banded musang of West Malaysia. Malayan Nature Journal 26(3-4):105-111.

Lim, B.-L. and C. Betterton. 1977. *Paragonimus westermani* in Malaysian Felidae and Viverridae: probable modes of transmission in relation to host feeding habits. Journal Helminthology 51:295-299.

Lim, B.-L. and I. A. R. b. Omar. 1961. Observations on the habits in captivity of two species of wild cats, the leopard cat and flat-headed cat. Malayan Nature Journal 15(1-2):48-51.

Lim, B.-L., I. Muul, and C. K. Shin. 1977. Zoonotic studies of small animals in the canopy transect at Bukit Lanjan Forest Reserve, Selangor, Malaysia. Malayan Nature Journal 31:127-140.

Lindburg, D. G. 1969. Rhesus macaques: mating season mobility of adult males. Science 166:1176-1178.

Lindburg, D. G. 1971. The rhesus in North India: an ecological and behavioral study. Pp. 1-106 *in* L. A. Rosenblum (ed.), Primate behavior: developments in field and laboratory research. Vol. 2. Academic Press, New York.

Lindburg, D. G. 1977. Feeding behavior and diet of rhesus monkeys (*Macaca mulatta*) in a Siwalik forest in North India. Pp. 223-249 *in* T. H. Clutton-Brock (ed.), Primate ecology: studies of feeding and ranging behavior in lemurs, monkeys, and apes. Academic Press, London.

Linnaeus, C. 1758. Systema naturae per regna tri natura, secundum classes, ordines, genera, species cum characteribus, differentias, synonymis, locis. 10th edition. Laurentii Salvii, Stockholm. 824 p.

Linnaeus, C. 1766. Systema naturae. 12th edition, tome 1, p. 268.

Linnaeus, C. 1771. Mantiss. Plant. II. p. 251.

Liu, C.-C. 1950. Amphibians of western China. Fieldiana Zoology Memoirs 2:1-400.

Louwman, J. W. W. 1970. Breeding the banded palm civet and the banded linsang, *Hemigalus derbyanus* and *Prionodon linsang*, at Wassenaar Zoo. International Zoo Yearbook 10:81-82.

Louwman, J. W. W. and W. G. van Oyen. 1968. A note on breeding Temminck's golden cat, *Felis temminckii*, at Wassenaar Zoo. International Zoo Yearbook 8:47-49.

Lubbock, M. 1979. Aviculture, 1978. Wildfowl 30(1979):170-175.

MAB 1979: Library of Congress. 1979. Draft environmental report on Thailand. United States Man and the Biosphere Secretariat, Department of State, Washington, D.C. Photocopy, 83 p.

MacDonald, S. M. and C. F. Mason. 1976. The status of the otter (*Lutra lutra* L.) in Norfolk. Biological Conservation 9:119-124.

MacDonald, S. M., C. F. Mason, and I. S. Coghill. 1978. The otter and its conservation in the River Teme catchment. Journal Applied Ecology 15:373-384.

Mack, D. 1977. Annual report. TRAFFIC, U.S.A., Washington, D.C.

Mack, D., N. Duplaix, and S. Wells. 1979. The international trade in sea turtle products. TRAFFIC report.

MacKenzie, M. J. S. and J. Kear. 1976. The white-winged wood duck. Wildfowl 27:5-17.

MacKinnon, K. S. 1978. Stratification and feeding differences among Malayan squirrels. Malayan Nature Journal 30(3-4):593-608.

Madoc, G. C. 1950. Field notes on some Siamese birds. Bulletin Raffles Museum 23:129.

Madge, S. G. 1969. Notes on the breeding of the bushy-crested hornbill, *Anorrhinus galeritus*. Malayan Nature Journal 43:389-401.

Madsen, K. K. 1980a. Search for the eastern sarus crane on Luzon, Philippines. Report to the International Crane Foundation. Photocopy, 11 p.

Madsen, K. K. 1980b. Comments concerning the reintroduction of the eastern sarus crane on Luzon in the Republic of the Philippines. Report to the International Crane Foundation. Photocopy, 3 p.

Maia, L. C. M. 1970. The present position of the wild water buffalo in Asia. Loris 7(2):86-88.

Marshall, J. T. 1981. The agile gibbon in south Thailand. Natural History Bulletin Siam Society 29:129-136.

Marshall, J. T., Jr. 1977. Muridae. Pp. 397-487 in B. Lekagul and J. A. McNeely (eds.), Mammals of Thailand. Association Conservation Wildlife, Bangkok. 758 p.

Marshall, J. T., Jr. and E. R. Marshall. 1976. Gibbons and their territorial songs. Science 193:235-237.

Marshall, J. T., Jr., B. A. Ross, and S. Changtharojuong. 1972. The species of gibbons in Thailand. Journal Mammalogy 53:479-486.

Marshall, J. T., Jr. and V. Nongngork. 1970. Mammals of Samui Island, Thailand. Natural History Bulletin Siam Society 23(4-5):501-508.

Martin, W. 1836. Proceedings of November 8, 1836. Richard Owen, Esq., in the Chair. Proceedings Zoological Society London 1836:107-108.

Mason, C. W. and H. Maxwell-Lefroy. 1912. The food of birds of India. Mem. Agr. Dept. India, Entomological Series. Vol. 3.

Masui, M. 1967. Birth of a Chinese pangolin at Ueno Zoo, Tokyo. International Zoo Yearbook 7:114-116.

Maxwell, F. D. 1911. Reports on inland and sea fisheries in the Thongwa, Majungnya, and Bassein districts and turtle banks of the Irrwaddy Division. Rangoon Government Printing Office. 57 p.

Mazak, V. 1968. Nouvelle sous-espece de tigre provenant l'Asie du sud-est. Mammalia 32:104-112.

McClelland. 1842. Calcutta Journal Natural History 2:417.

McClure, H. E. 1964. Some observations on primates in climax dipterocarp forests near Kuala Lumpur, Malaya. Primates 5:39-58.

McClure, H. E. 1970. Notes on three Thai birds. Natural History Bulletin Siam Society 23:331-344.

McClure, H. E. 1974a. Some bionomics of the birds of Khao Yai National Park. Natural History Bulletin Siam Society 25(3-4):99-193.

McClure, H. E. 1974b. Migration and survival of the birds of Asia. U. S. Army Component, SEATO Medical Research Laboratory, Bangkok, Thailand. v + 476 p.

McClure, H. E. and S. Chaiyaphun. 1974. The sale of birds at the Bangkok "Sunday Market," Thailand. Natural History Bulletin Siam Society 24:41-78.

Mclure, H. E. and P. Kwanyuen. 1973. The avifaunal complex of an open-billed stork colony (*Anastomus oscitans*) in Thailand. Natural History Bulletin Siam Society 25:133-155.

McClure, H. E. and B. Lekagul. 1961. Some birds of the Mae Ping river in northern Thailand. Natural History Bulletin Siam Society 20:1-8.

McCusker, J. S. 1974. Breeding Malayan sun bears, *Helarctos malayanus*, at Fort Worth Zoo. International Zoo Yearbook 14:118-119.

McGreggor, R. C. 1909. A manual of Philippine birds. Manila Bureau Printing, Manila. 769 p.

McKay, G. M. 1973. Behavior and ecology of the Asiatic elephant in southeastern Ceylon. Smithsonian Contributions Zoology, No. 125:1-113.

McNeely, J. A. 1975. Draft report on wildlife and national parks in the Lower Mekong Basin. Mekong Committee, ECAFE. Mimeo, 119 p.

McNeely, J. A. 1977. Mammals of the Thai mangroves. Tigerpaper 4(1):10-15.

McNeely, J. A. 1979a. The world's smallest mammal. Tigerpaper 6:47-48.

McNeely, J. A. 1979b. Status of tiger in Indonesia. Tigerpaper 6(2-3):21-22.

McNeely, J. A. and E. W. Cronin. 1972. Rhinos in Thailand. Oryx 11:457-460.

McNeely, J. A. and A. Laurie. 1977. Rhinos in Thailand. Oryx 13:486-489.

McNeely, J. A., Jr. and J. Seidensticker. 1974. Huay Kha Khaeng: a preliminary ecological survey, 27 November to 10 December, 1974. Association Conservation Wildlife, Bangkok. Mimeo, 6 p.

Mees, G. F. 1975. Identiteit en status van *Sterna bernsteini* Schlegel. Ardea 63:78-86.

Medway, Lord. 1964. The marmoset rat. Malayan Nature Journal 18:104-110.
Medway, Lord. 1966. Observations on the fauna of Pulau Tioman and Pulau Tulai. 2. The mammals. Bulletin National Museum, Republic Singapore 34:9-32.
Medway, Lord. 1969. The wild mammals of Malaya. Oxford University Press, London. 127 p.
Medway, Lord. 1970. Breeding of silvered leaf-monkey, *Presbytis cristata*, in Malaya. Journal Mammalogy 51:630-632.
Medway, Lord. 1975. Food of a tapir, *Tapirus indicus*. Malayan Nature Journal 28(2):90-93.
Medway, Lord. 1978. The wild mammals of Malaya (peninsular Malaysia) and Singapore. 2nd edition. Oxford University Press, Kuala Lumpur. 128 p.
Medway, Lord and I. C. T. Nisbet. 1966. Bird report: 1964. Malayan Nature Journal 19:160-194.
Medway, Lord and I. C. T. Nisbet. 1967. Bird report: 1965. Malayan Nature Journal 20:59-80.
Medway, Lord and D. R. Wells. 1976. The birds of the Malay Peninsula. Vol. 5. Conclusions, and survey of every species. H.F. and G. Witherby Ltd., London. 448 p.
Melville, D. and P. D. Round. 1982. Further records of the Asian dowitcher *Limnodromus semipalmatus* from Thailand, with notes on its distribution and identification. Natural History Bulletin Siam Society 30:199-204.
Melquist, W. E., and M. G. Hornocker. 1980. Development and use of a telemetry technique for studying river otter. Pp. 66-85 *in* N. Duplaix (ed.), Proceedings of the second working meeting of the Otter Specialist Group, held at the Florida State Museum, Gainesville, 27-29 March 1980. IUCN, Gland, Switzerland. 243 p.
Miller, G. S., Jr. 1900. Mammals from Langkawi and Butang Islands. Proceedings Biological Society Washington 13:187-193.
Miller, R. 1975. Notes on the behaviour of hog deer in an enclosure. Natural History Bulletin Siam Society. 26(1-2):105-131.
Milne-Edwards. 1871. Nouv. Arch. Mus. 7:93.
Mishra, H. R. and J. L. D. Smith. 1979. Dispersal studies. Tigerpaper 6(2-3):9-11.

Mouhout, H. 1964. Travels in the central parts of Indochina. Vol. 1-2. John Murray, London.

Moll, E. O. 1978. Drumming along the Perak. Natural History 87:36-43.

Muckenhirn, N. 1975. Nonhuman primates, usage and availability for biomedical programs. National Academy Sciences, Washington, D.C.

Muckenhirn, N. A. and J. F. Eisenberg. 1973. Home ranges and predation of the Ceylon leopard (*Panthera pardus fusca*). Pp. 142-175 *in* R. L. Eaton, (ed.), The world's cats. Vol. 1. World Wildlife Safari, Winston, Oregon. 349 p.

Müller, P. L. S. 1776. Linne's völlstandigen. Naturyst. Suppl. 21.

Müller, S. 1838. Tijdsch. Nat. Gesch., bol. 5, p. 77.

Müller, S. 1839. In Temminck, Verh. Nat. Ges. Ned. Overz. bezitt. Zool. (Zoogd. 1839):35, 56, 107, 112.

Müller, S. and H. Schlegel. 1844. Beschrijving van een' nieuwen zoetwater-visch van Borneo, *Osteoglossum formosum*. *In* Temminck, Verhandeligen over de natuurhjke geschiedenis der Nederlandsche oberzeesche bezittingen, door de Leden der Natuurkundige commissie in Indie en andere Schrijvers, p. 1-28.

Murphy, E. T. 1976. Breeding the clouded leopard, *Neofelis nebulosa*, at Dublin Zoo. International Zoo Yearbook 16:122-124.

Murton, R. K. 1972. The ecology and status of Swinhoe's egret, with notes on other herons in southeastern China. Biological Conservation 4:89-96.

Murty, V. S. 1976. Studies on growth checks on scales of *Barbus (Puntius) sarana* (Hamilton-Buchanan) from Lake Kolleru, Andhra Pradesh, with comments on growth checks reported on hard parts of some Indian fishes. Proceedings Indian Academy Science 83B:85-102.

Musser, G. G. 1972. The species of *Hapalomys* (Rodentia: Muridae). American Museum Novitates 2503:1-27.

Muul, I. and B.-L. Lim. 1970. Ecological and morphological observations of *Felis laniceps*. Journal Mammalogy 51:806-808.

Muul, I. and B.-L. Lim. 1971. New locality records for some mammals of West Malaysia. Journal Mammalogy 52:430-437.

Muul, I. and B.-L. Lim. 1974. Reproductive frequency in Malaysian flying squirrels, *Hylopetes* and *Pteromyscus*. Journal Mammalogy 55:393-400.

Muul, I. and B.-L. Lim. 1978. Comparative morphology, food habits, and ecology of some Malaysian arboreal rodents. Pp. 361-368 *in* G. G. Montgomery (ed.), The ecology of arboreal folivores. Smithsonian Institution Press, Washington, D.C. 574 p.

Muul, I. and K. Thonglongya. 1971. Taxonomic status of *Petinomys morrisi* (Carter) and its relationship to *Petinomys setosus* (Temminck and Schlegel). Journal Mammalogy 52:362-369.

Myers, N. 1973. The spotted cats and the fur trade. Pp. 276-326 *in* R. L. Eaton (ed.), The world's cats. Vol. 1. World Wildlife Safari, Winston, Oregon. 349 p.

Myers, N. 1975. Wildlife in China. International Wildlife 5(4):4-11.

Myers, N. 1976. Status of the leopard and cheetah in Africa. Pp. 53-69 *in* R. L. Eaton (ed.). The world's cats. Vol. III, No. 1. Department Zoology, University Washington, Seattle. 95 p.

Myers, N. 1980. Conversion of tropical moist forests. National Academy of Sciences, Washington, D.C., 205 p.

Nakamura, A., M. Thant, and T. Sugiyama. 1978. Abnormal limb regeneration in the Burmese newt, *Tylototriton verrucosus*, induced by chemical mutagens as a screening test for teratogenicity. Mutat. Res. 54(2):247.

Nasher, A. D. A. M. and I. A. Nader. 1975. Natural history of the Harrison's gerbil, *Gerbillus dasyurus mesopotaminae*. Bulletin Natural History Research Center, University Baghdad 6:60-63.

National Research Council (U.S.A.). 1981. The water buffalo: new prospects for an underutilized animal. National Academy Press, Washington, D. C. 116 p. (Available from Commission on International Relations (JH-217), National Research Council, 2101 Constitution Avenue, Washington, D.C. 20418, USA)

National Research Council (U.S.A.). 1983a. Crocodiles as a resource for the tropics. National Academy Press, Washington, D. C. 55 p. (Available from Commission on International Relations (JH-217), National Research Council, 2101 Constitution Avenue, Washington, D.C. 20418, USA)

National Research Council (U.S.A.). 1983b. Managing tropical resources: banteng and other little-known Asian animals. National Academy Press, Washington, D.C. (Available from Commission on International Relations (JH-217), National Research Council, 2101 Constitution Avenue, Washington, D. C. 20418, USA)

Nechaev, V. A. 1978. A contribution to the biology and behaviour of *Tringa guttifer* on the Sakhalin Island. Zoologicheskii Zhurnal 57:727-737.

Neese, H. C. 1976. Kouprey clues and rhino news. Wildlife 18(9):410-411.

Neill, W. 1971. The last of the ruling reptiles. Columbia University Press, New York. 486 p.

Nelson, J. B. 1976. The breeding biology of frigatebirds--a comparative review. Living Bird 14:113-156.

Neville, M. K. 1968. Ecology and activity of Himalayan foothill rhesus monkeys. Ecology 49:110-123.

Nieuhoff, J. 1666. Die Gesantschaft der Ost-Indischen Gesellschaft in den vereinigten Niederlandern, an den Tartarischen Cham und nunmehr auch Sinischen Kaiser. J. Mors, Amsterdam. vi + 456 pp.

Nikoloskii, A. A. and A. D. Poyarkov. 1976. The space coordinates of the sound signalization of jackals, *Canis aureus* (Canidae). Vestnik Moskovskogo Universiteta. Seriya VI. Biologiya Postvovedenie 31:3-6.

Nikoloskii, A. A. and A. D. Poyarkov. 1979. Merging of individual characters in the group howling of jackals. Zhurnal Obshchei Biologii 40:785-788.

Noble, G. K. 1954. The biology of the Amphibia. 2nd edition. Dover Publications, Inc., New York.

Northcott, T. H. and D. Slade. 1976. A live trapping technique for river otters. Journal Wildlife Management 40:163-164.

Novikov, G. A. 1956. Fauna of the U.S.S.R., No. 62. Carnivorous mammals. Translated from the Russian and published by the Israel Program for Scientific Translations, Jerusalem, 1962. 284 p.

Nozaki, E., K. Furubayashi, N. Maruyama, K. Tokida, and Y. Totake. 1979. Distribution of Japanese black bear in Kanto District--by the questionnaire and interview method. Journal Mammalogical Society Japan 8:14-32.

NYZS-NZP. 1980. Eld's deer management plan. New York Zoological Society and National Zoological Park, Smithsonian Institution. C. Wemmer, principal author. Photocopy, 9 p.

Oates, E. W. 1883. A handbook to the birds of British Burma, including those found in the adjoining State of Karennee. 2 vols. London.

Ogilvie, C. S. 1958. The binturong or bear-cat. Malayan Nature Journal 13:1-3.

Ogle, D. 1974. A systematic list of birds to be found in a lowland area of Chanthaburi. Natural History Bulletin Siam Society 25(3-4):69-97.

Ogle, D. 1986. The status and seasonality of birds in Nakhon Sawan Province, Thailand. Natural History Bulletin Siam Society 34(2):115-143.

Ognev, S. I. 1931. Mammals of eastern Europe and northern Asia. Translated from the Russian and published by the Israel Program for Scientific Translations, Jerusalem, 1962. 590 p.

Olivier, R. C. D. 1977. IUCN/SSC Asian elephant group news. Tigerpaper 4(4):22-25.

Olivier, R. C. D. 1978a. Present status of the Asian elephant (*Elephas maximus* Linnaeus, 1758). Elephant 2:15-17.

Olivier, R. C. D. 1978b. Distribution and status of the Asian elephant. Oryx 14:379-424.

Olivier, R. C. D. 1978c. On the ecology of the Asian elephant *Elephas maximus* Linn., with particular reference to Malaya and Sri Lanka. Ph.D. Diss., University Cambridge. 454 p.

Olney, P. J. S. (ed.) 1979. International Zoo Yearbook 19:297-428.

Olney, P. J. S. (ed.) 1980. International Zoo Yearbook 20:305-494.

Orians, G. H. and E. W. Pfeiffer. 1970. Ecological effects of the war in Vietnam. Science 168:544-554.

Osbourn, C. F. 1965. The seasonality of calving in water buffalo in Trinidad. Tropical Agriculture (Trinidad) 42:339-344.

Oustalet. 1877. Bull. Soc. Philom. Paris, ser. 7, 1(1):25-27.

Owen. 1853. Catalogue of the osteological series in the College of Surgeons. p. 185.

Paige, J. P. 1965. Field identification and winter range of the Asian dowitcher, *Limnodromus semipalmatus*. Ibis 107:95-97.

Pallas, P. S. 1811. Zoographia Rosso-Asiatica, sistens omnium Animalum in extenso Imperio Rossico et adjacentibus maribus observatorum recensionem, domicilia, mores et descriptiones anatomen atque icones plurimorum. Imperator, Petropolis. 568 p.

Paradiso, J. L. 1972. Status report on cats (Felidae) of the world. U. S. Fish and Wildlife Service, Bureau of Sport Fisheries and Wildlife. Special Scientific Report-Wildlife. No. 157:1-43.

Pauley, J. 1977a. Bangkok Bird Club's December census. Conservation News, Association Conservation Wildlife, Bangkok. June 1977:11-13.

Pauley, J. 1977b. Bangkok Bird Club notes. Conservation News, Association Conservation Wildlife, Bangkok. September 1977: 3 p.

Payne, J. B. 1980. Competitors. Pp. 261-277 in D. J. Chivers (ed.), Malayan forest primates. Plenum Press, New York.

Peakall, D. B. and L. F. Kiff. 1979. Eggshell thinning and DDE residue levels among peregrine falcons *Falco peregrinus*: a global perspective. Ibis 121:200-204.

Pelandok. 1938. Seledang hunting in Pahang. Malayan Forester 7(2):61-71.

Pennant. 1869. Indian zoology. pp. 12-13, pl. 11.

Penyapol, Captain A. 1957. A preliminary study of the sea turtles in the Gulf of Thailand. 9th Pacific Science Congress, p. 1-12.

Pfanner, D. E. 1974. Some additions to the preliminary list of birds of Khao Yai National Park. Natural History Bulletin Siam Society 25(3-4):195-198.

Pfeffer, P., and O. Kim-San. 1967. Le kouprey, *Bos (Bibos) sauveli* Urbain, 1937: discussion systematique et statut actuel. Hypothese sur l'origine du Zebu (*Bos indicus*). Mammalia 31:521-536.

Phasuk, B. and S. Rongmuangsart. 1973. Growth studies on the ridley turtle, *Lepidochelys olivacea olivacea* Eschscholtz, in captivity and the effect of food preference on growth. Phuket Marine Biological Center, Research Bulletin No. 1:1-14.

Pinratana. 1974. Butterflies in Thailand. 1:2.

Pocock, R. I. 1932. The marbled cat (*Pardofelis marmorata*) and some other Oriental species, with the definition of a new genus of the Felidae. Proceedings Zoological Society London 1932:741-766.

Pocock, R. I. 1933. The rarer genera of Oriental Viverridae. Proceedings Zoological Society London 1933:969-1035.

Pocock, R. I. 1939. The fauna of British India, including Ceylon and Burma: Mammalia. Vol. I. 2nd edition. Taylor and Francis, London. 463 p.

Pocock, R. I. 1943. The larger deer of British India. IV. Journal Bombay Natural History Society 44(2):169-178.

Polunin, N. V. C. 1975. Sea turtles: Reports on Thailand, West Malaysia, and Indonesia, with a synopsis of data on the 'conservation status' of sea turtles in the Indo-West Pacific Region. IUCN, Morges. Unpublished report, photocopy. 113 p.

Polunin, N. V. C. 1977. Conservation of sea turtles at Ko Khram. Conservation News, Association Conservation Wildlife, Bangkok. September. 5 p.

Polunin, N. V. C., and N. S. Nuitja. 1979. Sea turtle populations of Indonesia and Thailand (draft). World Conference on Sea Turtle Conservation, November 26-30, 1979, Washington, D.C., U.S.A. 11 p.

Pookaswan, T. 1969. *Pangasianodon gigas* Chevey. Thai Department Fisheries, Inland Fisheries Division, Bangkok, Bulletin No. 7:1-9.

Poonswad, P. 1979. On parasites of the Asian open-billed stork (*Anastomus oscitans*) and their relationships to pila snails and domestic duck. M.S. Thesis, 100 p.

Prakobboon, D. 1979. The management of wildlife sanctuaries in Thailand. Royal Forestry Department. Photocopy, 13 p.

Prater, S. H. 1971. The book of Indian animals. Third revised edition. Bombay Natural History Society. 324 p.

Prynn, D. 1980. Tigers and leopards in Russia's far east. Oryx 15(5):496-503.

Pyle, R. M. and S. A. Hughes. 1978. Conservation and utilization of the insect resources of Papua New Guinea. Report to the Wildlife Branch, Department of Natural Resources, Papua New Guinea. 157 p.

Radhakrishnan-Nair, P. N., and M. Badrudeen. 1975. On the occurrence of the soft-shelled turtle, *Pelochelys bibroni* (Owen), in marine environment. Indian J. Fish. 22(1-2):270-274.

Raemaekers, J. J. and P. M. Raemaekers. 1984. Vocal interaction between two male gibbons, *Hylobates lar*. Natural History Bulletin Siam Society 32:95-106.

Raffles, T. S. 1821. Descriptive catalogue of a zoological collection, made on account of the Honorable East India Company, in the island of Sumatra and its vicinity. Transactions Linnean Society London 13:239-274.

Raffles, T. S. 1822. Transactions Linnaean Society London 13(2):339.

Rainboth, W. J., K. F. Lagler, and S. Sontirat. 1976. Maps of freshwater fish distribution in the Lower Mekong Basin. Working document 31, Mekong basinwide fishery studies. University Michigan, School Natural Resources. Photo offset, 406 p.

Ralls, K., K. Brugger, and J. Ballou. 1979. Inbreeding and juvenile mortality in small populations of ungulates. Science 206(4422):1101-1103.

Ranjitsinh, M. K. 1980. The tiger in the Twenty-first Century. Tigerpaper 7(1):1-3.

Reichenow. 1903. Orn. Monatsber., jahrg. 11, No. 6, June 1903, p. 82.

Reimov, R., and T. Nuratdinov. 1970. Morphological and ecological peculiarities of the jackal (*Canis aureus*) and the jungle cat (*Felis chaus*) in the lower Amudarja flow. Zoologicheskii Zhurnal 49:268-274.

Rickett, C. B. 1903. Additional field notes on the birds of Fohkien. Ibis 3(Ser. 3):215-222.

Ridley. 1899. Journal Straits Branch Royal Asiatic Society. p. 197.

Rijksen, H. D. 1978. A field study on Sumatran orang utans (*Pongo pygmaeus abelii* Lesson 1827), ecology, behaviour and conservation. Wageningen, The Netherlands.

Riley, J. H. 1938. Birds from Siam and the Malay Peninsula in the United States National Museum collected by Drs. Hugh M. Smith and William L. Abbott. Smithsonian Institution, U. S. National Museum Bulletin 172:1-581.

Robinson, H. C. and F. N. Chasen. 1936. The birds of the Malay Peninsula. H. F. and G. Witherby, London.

Robinson, H. C. and C. B. Kloss. 1914. On new mammals, mainly from Bandon and the adjacent islands, east coast of the Malay peninsula. Annals Magazine Natural History 8(13):223-234.

Robinson, H. C. and C. B. Kloss. 1915. Mammals of Koh Samui. Journal Federated Malay States Museum 5(3):130-138.

Robinson, H. C. and C. B. Kloss. 1921. Some birds from Pulo Condore. Journal Natural History Society Siam 5:85-92.

Robson, M. S. and S. R. Humphrey. 1985. Inefficacy of scent-stations for monitoring river otter populations. Wildlife Soc. Bull. 13:558-561.

Rodman, P.S. 1978. Diets, densities, and distributions of Borean primates. Pp. 465-478 in G. G. Montgomery (ed.), The ecology of arboreal folivores. Smithsonian Institution Press, Washington, D.C. 574 p.

Roonwal, M. L., and S. M. Mohnot. 1977. Primates of South Asia. Harvard University Press, Cambridge, Massachusetts, U.S.A. 421 p.

Round, P. D., R. J. Dobias, K. Komolphalin, and S. Duangkhae. 1982. Notes and new distributional information on birds in western peninsular Thailand. Natural History Bulletin Siam Society 30:15-24.

Round, P. D. 1984. The status and conservation of the bird community in Doi Suthep-Pui National Park, north-west Thailand. Natural History Bulletin Siam Society 32:21-46.

Roy, S. D. 1979. Socio-economic aspects of preservation of tigers. Tigerpaper 6(2-3):5-6.

Royal Forestry Department. 1972. Animals exportation from Thailand in 1962-71. Mimeo, 22 p.

Rutgers, A. 1968. Birds of Asia. Taplinger Publishing Company, New York. 321 p.

Sade, D. S. 1965. Some aspects of parent-offspring and sibling relations in a group of rhesus monkeys, with a discussion of grooming. American Journal Physical Anthropology 23:1-18.

Samruadkit, A. and J. Nabhitabhata. Rediscovery of *Stichopthalma godfryi* Rothschild (Rhopalocera: Satyridae; Amathusiinae) in Thailand. Manuscript in preparation.

Sanborn, C. C., and A. R. Watkins. 1950. Notes on the Malay tapir and other game animals in Siam. Journal Mammalogy 31:430-433.

Sauvel, V. 1949. Distribution geographique du kou-prey (*Bibos sauveli* Urb.). Mammalia 13(4):144-148.

Sawat Boonthai, S. About the *Batagur baska* at Pataloong. p. 133-148.

Schaller, G. B. 1967. The deer and the tiger: a study of wildlife in India. University Chicago Press, Chicago. 370 p.

Schaller, G. B. 1972. The Serengeti lion: a study of predator-prey relations. University Chicago Press, Chicago. 480 p.

Schaller, G. B. 1977. Mountain monarchs: wild sheep and wild goats of the Himalaya. University Chicago Press, Chicago. 425 p.

Schenkel, R., and L. Schenkel. 1979. SSC Asian rhino specialist group general report and synopsis. Photocopy, 27 p.

Scheurmann, E. 1975. Observations on the behaviour of the mithan (*Bibos frontalis* Lambert 1837) in captivity. Applied Animal Ethology 1(1975):321-355.

Schlegel, H., and S. Müller. 1844. *In* Temminck, Berh. Nat. Ned. Ind. Rept. 1844, p. 34, pl. iv.

Schmidt, K. P. 1927*a*. The reptiles of Hainan. Bulletin American Museum Natural History 54:395-456.

Schmidt, K. P. 1927*b*. Notes on Chinese amphibians. Bulletin American Museum Natural History 54:553-575.

Schmidt, K. P. 1928. A new crocodile from New Guinea. Publications Field Museum Natural History 12:177-181.

Schneider. 1801. Historiae amphibiorum naturalis et literariae, fasc. 2.

Schreiber, A., R. Wirth, M. Riffel, and H. van Rompaey. 1987. Action plan for global mustelid and viverrid conservation. IUCN/SSC mustelid and viverrid specialist group. Unpublished manuscript, 116 p.

Schreiber, R. W. 1980. The brown pelican: an endangered species? Bioscience 30(11):742-747.

Scopoli. 1786. Deliciae florae et faunae insubricae. 2:93.

Scott, D. B. J., and J. D. Fuller. 1976. The reproductive biology of *Scleropages formosus* (Muller and Schlegel) (Osteoglossomorpha, Osteoglossidae) in Malaya, and the morphology of its pituitary gland. Journal Fish Biology 8:45-53.

Seidenfaden, E. 1923. The "Pla Buk". Journal Natural History Society Siam 6:138-139.
Seidenfaden, E. 1967. The Thai peoples. Siam Society, Bangkok.
Seidensticker, J. 1976. On the ecological separation between tigers and leopards. Biotropica 8:225-234.
Seidensticker, J. 1980. The Javan tiger and the Meru-Betiri Reserve: A plan for management. IUCN and WWF, Gland, Switzerland. 167 p.
Seidensticker, J. 1984. Managing elephant depredation in agricultural and forestry projects. The World Bank, Washington, D.C. 33 p.
Seidensticker, J., and J. A. McNeely. 1975. Observations on the use of natural salt licks by ungulates in Huai Kha Khaeng Wildlife Sanctuary, Thailand. Natural History Bulletin Siam Society 26:24-33.
Seidensticker, J., and M. A. Hai. 1983. The Sundarbans wildlife management plan: conservation in the Bangladesh coastal zone. International Union for Conservation of Nature and Natural Resources and World Wildlife Fund, Gland, Switzerland. 120 p.
Shaw and Nodder. 1797. Nat. Miscl. 9:text to plate 321.
Sidthimunka, A. 1972. The culture of pla duk (*Clarias* spp.). Inland Fisheries Division, Department Fisheries, Technical Paper No. 12:1-17.
Singh, A. 1973. Status and social behavior of the north Indian tiger. Pp. 176-188 *in* R. L. Eaton (ed.), The world's cats. Vol. 1. World Wildlife Safari, Winston, Oregon. 349 p.
Singh, S. D. 1969. Urban monkeys. Scientific American 211(1):108-115.
Sinha, M. 1975. Observations on the biology of *Puntias sarana* (Hamilton) of Loni Reservoir (Madhya Pradesh). Journal Inland Fishery Society India 7:49-57.
Siow, K. T. and E. O. Moll. 1982. Status and conservation of estuarine and sea turtles in West Malaysian waters. Pp. 339-347 *in* K. A. Bjorndahl (ed.), Biology and conservation of sea turtles. Smithsonian Institution Press, Washington, D.C. 538 p.
Smedley, N. 1931. An osteoglossid fish in the Malay Peninsula. Bulletin Raffles Museum 5:67-68.
Smith. 1827. Griffith's Animal Kingdom. 4:399.

Smith, A. P. 1977. Observations of birds in Brunei. Sarawak Museum Journal 25(46):235-259.

Smith, D. 1980. Tiger ecology in Chitawan National Park, Nepal. Paper presented at the Workshop on Conservation and National Parks, United Nations Asia and Pacific Development Institute, Bangkok, 7-12 April 1980.

Smith, H. C. 1931. The monitor lizards of Burma. Journal Bombay Natural History Society 34:367-373.

Smith, H. M. 1931. Descriptions of new genera and species of Siamese fishes. Proceedings United States National Museum 79(7):1-48.

Smith, H. M. 1933. Contributions to the ichthyology of Siam. VII. The featherback fish *Notopterus chitala* in Siam, with notes on its egg-laying and young. Journal Siam Society, Natural History Supplement 9:245-258.

Smith, H. M. 1934. Contributions to the ichthyology of Siam. Journal Siam Society, Natural History Supplement 9:287-325.

Smith, H. M. 1934. Contributions to the ichthyology of Siam. XVII. New cyprinoid fishes. Journal Siam Society, Natural History Supplement 9:305.

Smith, H. M. 1945. The fresh-water fishes of Siam, or Thailand. Smithsonian Institution, United States National Museum Bulletin 188:1-622.

Smith, M. A. 1916. A list of the crocodiles, tortoises, turtles and lizards at present known to inhabit Siam. Journal Natural History Society Siam 2:48-57.

Smith, M. A. 1919. *Crocodilus siamensis*. Journal Natural History Society Siam 3(3):217-221, plates 4-6.

Smith, M. A. 1931. The fauna of British India, including Ceylon and Burma. Reptilia and Amphibia, Vol. 1. Loricata, Testudines. Taylor and Francis Ltd., London. Reprinted 1973 by Ralph Curtis Books, Hollywood, Florida. 185 p.

Smith, M. A. 1932. Some notes on the monitors. Journal Bombay Natural History Society 35:1-5.

Smith, M. A. 1935. The fauna of British India, including Ceylon and Burma. Reptilia and Amphibia, Vol. II. Taylor and Francis, London. 440 p.

Smith, M. A. 1943. The fauna of British India, Ceylon and Burma. Reptilia and Amphibia, Vol. III. Taylor and Francis, London. 583 p.

Smitinand, T. 1966. The vegetation of Doi Chiengdao, a limestone massif in Chiengmai, North Thailand. Natural History Bulletin Siam Society 21:93-128.

Smitinand, T. 1968. Vegetation of Khao Yai National Park. Natural History Bulletin Siam Society 22(3-4):289-305.

Smitinand, T. 1977. Vegetation and ground cover of Thailand. Kasetsart University Department of Forest Biology Technical Paper No. 1. Bangkok. 15 p.

Smitinand, T., T. Shimizu, H. Koyama, and N. Fukuoka. 1970. Contributions to the flora of Southeast Asia. I. Taxonomy and phytogeograpy of some temperate species in Thailand. Southeast Asian Studies 8:171-186.

Smythies, B. E. 1953. The birds of Burma. 2nd edition. Oliver and Boyd, London. 668 p.

Srikosamatara, S. 1980. Ecology and behaviour of the pileated gibbon (*Hylobates pileatus*) in Khao Soi Dao Wildlife Sanctuary, Thailand. M.S. Thesis, Mahidol University, Bangkok. 157 p.

Srivastava, B. P. 1979. Status of tiger in India. Tigerpaper 6(2-3):24-27.

Sobhana, B. and N. B. Nair. 1977. Oogenesis in the olive carp, *Puntius sarana subnasutus*. Zool. Anz. Jena 198:373-379.

Sobhana, B. and N. B. Nair. 1978. Observation on the maturation and spawning of *Puntius sarana subnasutus* (Valenciennes). Indian Journal Fisheries 21(2):357-368.

Soderburg, P. 1967. The newt, *Tylototriton verrucosus* Anderson 1871 in Thailand. Natural History Bulletin Siam Society 22:211-212.

Sontirat, S. and S. Mongkolprasit. 1968. The new featherback fish from Mekong River. Paper presented at the Seventh National Conference in Agricultural Sciences, Kasetsart University, Bangkok. 6 p.

Sontirat, S., S. Mongkolprasit, and P. Wongrat. 1971. Systematic studies of featherback fish in Thailand. Thai Fisheries Gazette 24:383-391.

Sophasan, S. and R. Dobias. 1984. The fate of the "Princess bird," or white-eyed river martin (*Pseudochelidon sirintarae*). Natural History Bulletin Siam Society 32:1-10.

Southern, H. M. 1964. The handbook of British Mammals. Blackwell Scientific Publications, Oxford. 465 p.

Southwick, C. H. 1969. Aggressive behavior of rhesus monkeys in natural and captive groups. Pp. 32-43 *in* S. Garattini and E. B. Sigg (eds.), Aggressive behavior (Proceedings of symposium on biology of aggressive behavior, Milan, 1968). Amsterdam: Exerpta Medica.

Southwick, C. H., M. A. Beg, and M. R. Siddiqi. 1961a. A population survey of rhesus monkeys in villages, towns, and temples of northern India. Ecology 42:538-547.

Southwick, C. H., M. A. Beg, and M. R. Siddiqi. 1961b. A population survey of rhesus monkeys in northern India: II. Transportation routes and forest areas. Ecology 42:698-710.

Southwick, C. H., M. A. Beg, and M. R. Siddiqi. 1965. Rhesus monkeys in North India. Pp. 111-159 *in* I. DeVore (ed.), Primate behavior: field studies of monkeys and apes. Holt, Rinehart and Winston, New York.

Southwick, C. H. and F. L. Cadigan, Jr. 1972. Population studies of Malaysian primates. Primates 13:1-18.

Southwick, C. H. and M. R. Siddiqi. 1970. Primate population trends in Asia, with special reference to the rhesus monkeys in India. Proceedings of the 11th Technical Meeting of the IUCN (New Delhi, November 1969) 1:135-147.

Spain, A. V. and G. E. Heinsohn. 1973. Cyclone associated feeding changes in the dugong (Mammalia: Sirenia). Mammalia 37:678-680.

Sparrman. 1778. Gotheborg. Samhalle Hand. (wet. Afd.) 1:70.

Sprackland, R. G., Jr. 1976. Notes on Dumeril's monitor lizard, *Varanus dumerilii* (Schlegel). Sarawak Museum Journal 24:287-291.

Srikosamatara, S. and S. Doungkhae. 1982. Dry dipterocarp forest as a barrier to gibbon dispersal: a survey in Phu Phan National Park, northeast Thailand. Natural History Bulletin Siam Society 30:25-32.

Stevens, W. E. 1968. The rare large mammals of Malaya. Malayan Nature Journal 22:10-17.

Storer, P. J. 1977. A study of the waterfowl of the Thale Noi waterfowl reserve area. Natural History Bulletin Siam Society 26:317-338.

Storer, P. J. 1978. A biological survey of a lowland evergreen scrub forest and meadowland in southern Thailand. Natural History Bulletin Siam Society 27:93-114.

Storer, P. J. 1979. A survey to identify key elephant areas for elephant conservation efforts in Thailand. IUCN/SSC/WWF Asian Elephant Secretariat, Cambridge, England. Mimeo. 41 p.

Strickland, D. 1967. Ecology of the rhinoceros in Malaya. Malay Nature Journal 20:1-17.

Suckcharoen, S. 1978. Mercury accumulation in *Ipomeoa aquatica* (Forsk) near a caustic soda factory in Thailand. Water, Air, and Soil Pollution 10:451-475.

Suckcharoen, S. 1979. *Ceratophyllum demersum* as an indicator of mercury contamination in Thailand and Finland. Annales Botanici Fennici 16:173-175.

Suckcharoen, S., P. Nuorteva, and E. Hasanen. 1978. Alarming signs of mercury pollution in a freshwater area of Thailand. Ambio 7:113-116.

Sudharma, D. 1976. Beberapa aspek kehidupan buaya juluung (*Tomistoma schlegelii*) dan kemungkinan penbinaan pengamanannya. Institut Pertanian, Bogor.

Sunquist, M. E. 1979. Radio tracking and its application to the study and conservation of tigers. Tigerpaper 6(2-3):7-8.

Swinhoe, R. 1860. The ornithology of Amoy. Ibis 2(Ser. 1):45-68.

Takada, Y. 1979. The food habit of the Japanese black bears in the central mountain area, Nagano prefecture. Journal Mammalogical Society Japan 8(1):40-53.

Tarboton, W. and P. Cardwell. 1968. Breeding observations on the black stork (*Ciconia nigra*). Bokmakierie 20:86-87.

Tariannicov, V. I. 1974. Feeding of *Canis aureus* in the Syrdarja Basin. Zoologicheskii Zhurnal 53:1539-1547.

Taylor, E. H. 1962. The amphibian fauna of Thailand. University Kansas Science Bulletin 43(8):265-599.

Taylor, E. H. 1963. The lizards of Thailand. University Kansas Science Bulletin 44(4):687-1077.

Taylor, E. H. 1965. The serpents of Thailand and adjacent waters. University Kansas Science Bulletin 45:609-1096.

Taylor, E. H. 1966. The lizards of the Philippine Islands. A. Asher and Co., Amsterdam. 269 p.
Taylor, E. H. 1970. The turtles and crocodiles of Thailand and adjacent waters. University Kansas Science Bulletin 49(3):87-179.
Taylor, E. H. and R. E. Elbel. 1958. Contribution to the herpetology of Thailand. University Kansas Science Bulletin 38 pt. II (13):1033-1189.
Temminck, C. J. 1826. Nouveau recueil de planches coloriees d'oiseaux, livr. 66, pl. 389, 1826.
Temminck, C. J. and H. Schlegel. 1845. Fauna Japonica (by P.F. von Siebold). Mammalia, p. 49.
Thailand Institute of Scientific and Technological Research. 1979. Ecological studies for conservation of shore birds in Songkhla Lake. Annual Report 1979. 176 p.
Thomas and Doria. 1889. Ann. Mus. Stor. Nat. Genova 7:92.
Thonglongya, K. 1968. A new martin of the genus *Pseudochelidon* from Thailand. Thai Natural Science Papers, Fauna Series, Number one, Applied Scientific Research Corporation Thailand (now Thailand Institute Scientific Technological Research), Bangkok. 10 p.
Thonglongya, K. 1969. Report on a expedition in northern Thailand to look for breeding sites of *Pseudochelidon sirintarae* (21 May to 27 June 1969). Applied Scientific Research Corporation Thailand, Bangkok Research Report, 17 p.
Timmins, W. H. 1971. Observations on breeding *Aonyx cinerea* at Chester Zoo. International Zoo Yearbook 11:187-189.
Tokura, H., F. Hara, M. Okada, F. Mekata, and W. Ohsawa. 1975. Thermoregulatory responses at various ambient temperatures in some primates. Pp. 171-176 *in* S. Kondo, M. Kawai, and A. Ehara (eds.), Contemporary primatology, 5th International Congress of Primatology, Nagoya 1974. S. Karger, Basel.
TFA 1947. Thai Fisheries Act of B.E. 2490 (1947).
TRAFFIC. 1978. Analysis of international trade in Varanidae 1977. Photocopy. 6 p.
TRAFFIC. 1979. Reptile imports and exports, United Kingdom, 1978. Photocopy. 2 p.
TRAFFIC. 1980a. *Varanus* imports from Thailand (October-December 1980). Photocopy, 2 p.

TRAFFIC. 1980*b*. Reptile imports, Federal Republic of Germany, 1979. Photocopy, 4 p.

TRAFFIC. 1981*a*. TRAFFIC alert--pangolins in peril? Trade Records Analysis of Flora and Fauna in Commerce, Washington, D.C., N. Duplaix, Director. Photocopy, 8 p.

TRAFFIC. 1981*b*. Reptiles imported into the United States in 1980. Draft report.

TRAFFIC. 1984. Lacey Act overview. TRAFFIC (U.S.A.) Newsletter 5(3):11.

Tulloch, D. G. 1978. The water buffalo, *Bubalus bubalis*, in Australia: grouping and home range. Australian Wildlife Research 5:327-354.

Tulloch, D. G. 1979. The water buffalo, *Bubalus bubalis*, in Australia: reproductive and parent-offspring behavior. Australian Wildlife Research 6:265-287.

Tweedie, M. W. F. 1954. The snakes of Malaya. Government Publications Bureau, Singapore. 139 p.

Tytler, H. C. 1912. Notes on butterflies from the Naga Hills. Journal Bombay Natural History Society 21:588-606.

Ulmer, F. A., Jr. 1968. Breeding fishing cats, *Felis viverrina*, at Philadelphia Zoo. International Zoo Yearbook 8:49-55.

Urbain, A. 1937. Le kou-prey ou boeuf gris cambodgien. Bulletin Zoologique Societe France. 62:305-307.

USFWS. 1970. Mammals imported into the United States in 1968. Fish and Wildlife Service, U. S. Department of the Interior, Bureau of Sport Fisheries and Wildlife, Special Scientific Report-Wildlife No. 137. 30 p.

USFWS. 1971. Mammals imported into the United States in 1969. Fish and Wildlife Service, U. S. Department of the Interior, Bureau of Sport Fisheries and Wildlife, Special Scientific Report-Wildlife No. 147. 33 p.

USFWS. 1972. Mammals imported into the United States in 1970. Fish and Wildlife Service, U. S. Department of the Interior, Bureau of Sport Fisheries and Wildlife, Special Scientific Report-Wildlife No. 161. 62 p.

USFWS. 1974*a*. Mammals imported into the United States in 1972. Fish and Wildlife Service, U. S. Department of the Interior, Bureau of Sport Fisheries and Wildlife, Special Scientific Report-Wildlife No. 181.

USFWS. 1974b. Amphibians and reptiles imported into the United States. United States Department of the Interior, Wildlife Leaflet 506.

USFWS. 1980a. Republication of the lists of endangered and threatened species and correction of technical errors in final rules. Federal Register 45(99):33768-33781.

USFWS. 1980b. Two crocodiles endangered. Endangered Species Technical Bulletin 5(1):10-11.

USFWS. 1980c. Reclassification proposed for the leopard. Endangered Species Technical Bulletin 5(4):1, 15-16.

USNM. 1980. (Computer printout of current holdings of primates and carnivores in the collections of the United States National Museum, Smithsonian Institution). Unpublished report. 30 p.

Ukkatawewat, S. 1979. The taxonomic characters and biology of some important freshwater fishes in Thailand. National Inland Fisheries Institute, Technical Paper No. 3.

Ukkatawewat, S. and J. Ratanalhauee. 1978. Checklist of freshwater fauna in the National Inland Fisheries Institute (NIFI) Museum. Bangkok. 30 p.

Valenciennes, A. 1841. Observations faites pendant l'incubation d'une fenelle du Python a deux raies (*Python bivittatus* Kuhl) pendant les mois de mai et juin 1841. Compt. Rend. Acad. Sci. Paris 13:126-133.

van Bemmel, A. C. V. 1967. The banteng, *Bos javanicus*, in captivity. International Zoo Yearbook 7:222-223.

Vancuylenberg, B. W. B. 1977. Feeding behavior of the Asiatic elephant in southeast Sri Lanka in relation to conservation. Biological Conservation 12:33-54.

van der Zon, A. P. M. 1977. Sumatran rhino in Kalimantan (Borneo). Tigerpaper 42:12.

Van Gelder, R. G. 1977. Mammalian hybrids and generic limits. American Museum Natural History, Novitates 2635:1-25.

Van Lawick, H. and J. Van Lawick-Goodall. 1970. Innocent killers. Houghton Mifflin Company, Boston. 222 p.

Van Mierop, L. H. S. and S. M. Barnard. 1976. Observations on the reproduction of *Python molurus bivittatus* (Reptilia, Serpentes, Boidae). Journal Herpetology 10:333-340.

van Nierop, M. M. and J. C. den Hartog. 1984. A study of the gut contents of five juvenile loggerhead turtles, *Caretta caretta* (Linnaeus) (Reptilia, Cheloniidae), from the south-eastern part of the North Atlantic Ocean, with emphasis on coelenterate identification. Zool. Meded. (Leiden) 59:35-54.

Van Peenen, P. F. D., P. F. Ryan, and R. H. Light. 1969. Preliminary identification manual for mammals of South Vietnam. United States National Museum, Washington, D.C. 310 p.

Vaurie, C. 1965. Birds of the Palearctic fauna. Non-Passeriformes. H.F. and G. Witherby, London. 763 p.

Vickers, J. H. 1972. The development of a rhesus breeding colony in India. Pp. 105-108 *in* W. I. B. Beveridge (ed.), Breeding primates. S. Karger, Basel.

Vigors. 1831. Proceedings Zoological Society London 1831:173.

Vigors and Horsfield. 1827. Zool. Journ. 111. 450 p.

Vinegar, A., V. H. Hutchinson, and H. G. Dowling. 1970. Metabolism, energetics, and thermoregulation during brooding of snakes of the genus *Python* (Reptilia, Boidae). Zoologica (New York Zoological Society) 55:19-48.

Volozheninov, N. N. 1972. Feeding of *Canis aureus*, *Vulpes vulpes flavescens*, and *Felis chaus oxianua* in south Uzbekistan. Zoologicheskii Zhurnal 51:1048-1053.

von Nordmann. 1835. P. 17 *in* Erman (ed.), Reise um die Erde durch Nord-Asien. Naturhistorischer Atlas.

Walker, E. P. 1975. Mammals of the world. Third edition. Johns Hopkins University Press, Baltimore. 1,500 p.

Walkinshaw, L. 1973. Cranes of the world. Winchester Press, New York. 370 p.

Wandrey, R. 1975. Contribution to the study of the social behavior of captive golden jackals, *Canis aureus*. Zeitschrift Tierpsychologie 39:365-402.

WARPA. 1972. Wild Animals Reservation and Protection Act of B.E. 2503 (1961) as amended by Announcement of the Revolutionary Party No. 228, B.E. 2515 (1972).

Watanabe, H. and A. Komiyama. 1976. Conservation of wild bears and control of its damage to forest trees. II. Bulletin Kyoto University Forests 48:1-8.

Watanabe, H., N. Taniguchi, and T. Shidei. 1973. Conservation of wild bears and control of its damage to forest trees. I. Bulletin Kyoto University Forests 45:1-8.

Wayre, P. 1976. The river people. Taplinger Publishing Company, New York. 189 p.

Wayre, P. 1979. Otter havens in Norfolk and Suffolk, England. Biological Conservation 16:73-81.

Wayre, P. 1980. The Otter Trust--a progress report. Pp. 196-211 in N. Duplaix (ed.), Proceedings of the second working meeting of the Otter Specialist Group, held at the Florida State Museum, Gainesville, 27-29 March 1980. IUCN, Gland, Switzerland. 243 p.

Webb, J. B. 1975. Food of the otter (*Lutra lutra*) on the Somerset levels. Journal Zoology (London) 177:486-491.

Weber, M. and L. F. de Beaufort. 1965. The fishes of the Indo-Australian Archipelago. Vol. 2. E. J. Brill, Leiden. 404 p.

Webster, M. A. 1976. Endangered species of waders. Tigerpaper 3(2):22.

Wemmer, C. M. 1977. Comparative ethology of the large-spotted civet, *Genetta tigrina* and some related viverrids. Smithsonian Contributions Zoology 239:1-9.

Wemmer, C. and J. Murtaugh. 1981. Copulatory behavior and reproduction in the binturong, *Arctictis binturong*. Journal Mammalogy 62:342-352.

West, J. 1979. Notes on the Sumatran serow, *Capricornis sumatranensis*, at Jakarta Zoo. International Zoo Yearbook 19:252-254.

Wharton, C. H. 1955. A preliminary report on the ecology of the Indo-Chinese forest ox or kouprey, *Novibos sauveli* Urbain. Proceedings 18th Pacific Science Congress 1:445-454.

Wharton, C. H. 1957. An ecological study of the kouprey, *Novibos sauveli*. Institute Science Technology, Manila, Monograph 5:1-111.

Wharton, C. H. 1966. Man, fire, and wild cattle in north Cambodia. Proceedings Annual Tall Timbers Fire Ecology Conference, Tallahassee, Florida 5:23-65.

Wharton, C. H. 1968. Man, fire, and wild cattle in Southeast Asia. Proceedings Annual Tall Timbers Fire Ecology Conference, Tallahassee, Florida 8:107-167.

Wheatley, B. P. 1979. The behavior and ecology of the crab-eating macaque. Tigerpaper 6(2-3):47-48.

Whitaker, R. 1978. Common Indian snakes. MacMillan Company of India, Ltd., New Delhi. 154 p.

Whitaker, R. 1979. A proforma crocodile survey of the Malaysian region. Unpublished report. 6 p.

Whitaker, R. and R. C. Daniel. 1978. The status of Asian crocodiles. Tigerpaper 5(4):12-17.

White, C. M. N. 1975. Migration of Palearctic waders in Wallacea. Emu 75(1):37-39.

Whitehead, G. K. 1972. Deer of the world. Viking Press, New York. 194 p.

Whitmore, T. C. 1975. Tropical rain forests of the Far East. Clarendon Press, Oxford. 282 p.

Wildash, P. 1968. Birds of South Vietnam. Charles E. Tuttle Co., Rutland, Vermont, and Tokyo. 234 p.

Wiles, G. J. 1980. The birds of Salak Phra Wildlife Sanctuary, southwestern Thailand. Natural History Bulletin Siam Society 28:101-120.

Wiles, G. J. 1981. Abundance and habitat preferences of small mammals in southwestern Thailand. Natural History Bulletin Siam Society 29:41-54.

Wirot, N. 1979. The turtles of Thailand. Siamfarm Zoological Garden, Bangkok. 222 p.

Williams, K. D. 1979. Radio-tracking tapirs in the primary rain forest of West Malaysia. Malayan Nature Journal 32(3-4):253-258.

Williams, K. D. and G. S. Petrides. 1980. Browse use, feeding behavior, and management of the Malayan tapir. Journal Wildlife Management 44:489-494.

Williams, L. 1967. Forests of Southeast Asia, Puerto Rico, and Texas. United States Department of Agriculture, Crops Research Division Report CR 12-67, Washington, D.C. 251 p.

Williamson, W. J. F. 1916a. A list of birds not previously recorded from Siam, with notes. Journal Natural History Society Siam 2(1):59-65.

Williamson, W. J. F. 1916b. The giant ibis (*Thaumatibis gigantea*). Journal Natural History Society Siam 2(1):71-72.

Williamson, W. J. F. 1918. New or noteworthy bird-records from Siam. Journal Natural History Society Siam 3(1):15-42.

Williamson, W. J. F. 1921. The giant ibis (*Thaumatibis gigantea*), in Cambodia. Journal Natural History Society Siam 4(3):96.

Willis, R. B. 1980. Breeding the Malayan giant squirrel, *Ratufa bicolor*, at London Zoo. International Zoo Yearbook 20:218-220.

Wilson, V. J. 1976. The leopard in eastern Zambia. Pp. 29-38 *in* R. L. Eaton (ed.), The world's cats. Vol. III, No. 2. Carnivore Research Institute, Seattle, Washington. 179 p.

World Resources Institute. 1985. Tropical forests: a call for action. Three volumes. ($12.50, WRI Publications, PO Box 620, Holmes PA 19043, U.S.A.)

Wong, M. H. 1975. Our disappearing natural environment: the case of Hong Kong. International Journal Ecology Environmental Science 1:133-134.

Wongratana, T. 1984. Range extension of the crocodile salamander, *Tylototriton verrucosus*, to Phu Luang, Thailand. Natural History Bulletin Siam Society 32:107-110.

WWF. 1979. Is it the last kouprey? World Wildlife-India, Newsletter No. 30, reprinted in Tigerpaper 7(2):32. 1980.

Xanten, W. A., H. Kafka, and E. Olds. 1976. Breeding the binturong, *Arctictis binturong* at the National Zoological Park, Washington. International Zoo Yearbook 16:117-119.

Yadav, R. N. 1967. Breeding the smooth-coated Indian otter, *Lutra perspicillata*. International Zoo Yearbook 7:130-131.

Yin, T. 1977. White-winged wood duck in Burma. Journal Bombay Natural History Society 74:171.

Young, G. 1957. Tracks of an intruder. Souvenir Press, London.

Zhang, Y. Z., S. Wang, and G. Q. Quan. 1981. On the geographical distribution of primates in China. Journal Human Evolution 10:215-226.

Zhu-Jin. 1979. The tiger and its conservation in China. Tigerpaper 6(2-3):23.